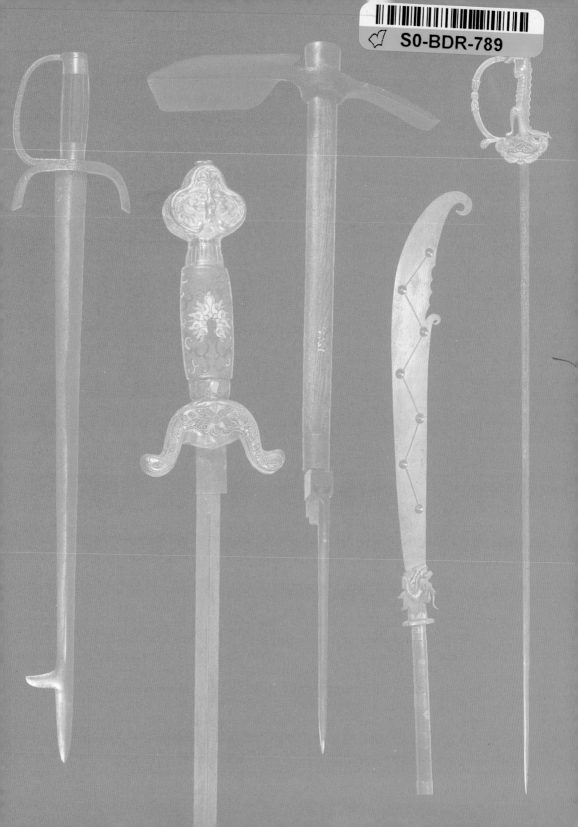

THE COMPLETE WORLD ENCYCLOPEDIA OF

KNIVES, SWORDS
SPEARS & DAGGERS

THE COMPLETE WORLD ENCYCLOPEDIA OF
KNIVES, SWORDS SPEARS & DAGGERS
THROUGH HISTORY IN OVER 1500 PHOTOGRAPHS

HARVEY J.S. WITHERS AND DR TOBIAS CAPWELL

HERMES HOUSE

This edition is published by Hermes House,
an imprint of Anness Publishing Ltd,
Hermes House, 88–89 Blackfriars Road, London SE1 8HA;
tel. 020 7401 2077; fax 020 7633 9499
www.hermeshouse.com; www.annesspublishing.com

Anness Publishing has a new picture agency outlet for images for
publishing, promotions or advertising. Please visit our website
www.practicalpictures.com for more information.

Publisher: Joanna Lorenz
Editorial Director: Helen Sudell
Project Editor: Elizabeth Young
Editors: Sarah Doughty and Hazel Songhurst
Assistant Editor: Cynthia McCollum
Contributing Authors: Jonathan Barrett, Peter Smithurst
and Frederick Stephens
Photography: Gary Ombler (Armouries) and David Cummings (Berman)
Designer: Alistair Plumb
Art Director: Lisa McCormick
Proofreading Manager: Lindsay Zamponi
Production Controller: Bessie Bai

Designed and produced for Anness Publishing by
The Bridgewater Book Company Limited.

Ethical Trading Policy
At Anness Publishing we believe that business should be conducted in
an ethical and ecologically sustainable way, with respect for the
environment and a proper regard to the replacement of the natural
resources we employ.
  As a publisher, we use a lot of wood pulp to make high-quality
paper for printing, and that wood commonly comes from spruce trees.
We are therefore currently growing more than 750,000 trees in three
Scottish forest plantations: Berrymoss (130 hectares/320 acres),
West Touxhill (125 hectares/305 acres) and Deveron Forest (75 hectares/
185 acres). The forests we manage contain more than 3.5 times the
number of trees employed each year in making paper for the books
we manufacture.
  Because of this ongoing ecological investment programme, you, as
our customer, can have the pleasure and reassurance of knowing that a
tree is being cultivated on your behalf to naturally replace the materials
used to make the book you are holding.
  Our forestry programme is run in accordance with the UK Woodland
Assurance Scheme (UKWAS) and will be certified by the internationally
recognized Forest Stewardship Council (FSC). The FSC is a non-
government organization dedicated to promoting responsible
management of the world's forests. Certification ensures forests are
managed in an environmentally sustainable and socially responsible way.
For further information about this scheme, go to
www.annesspublishing.com/trees

Publisher's Note
Although the advice and information in this book are believed to be accurate
and true at the time of going to press, neither the authors nor the publisher
can accept any legal responsibility or liability for any errors or omissions that
may have been made.

With special thanks to the Royal Armouries, Leeds in England and the
Berman Museum of World History, in Anniston, Alabama, USA. Also grateful
thanks for the assistance of Hermann Historica Auctioneers, Munich and
Wallis & Wallis auctioneers, Lewes, England.

Contents

Introduction

Sharp-edged weapons have played a major part in the shaping of human history. They have been used in the hunt for food, in battles of honour and during wars. This comprehensive book provides a fascinating historical insight into the world of knives, daggers, bayonets, swords, sabres, spears and lances, and explores the incredible varieties, histories and origins.

Early daggers, knives and swords

The historical background to the development of the swords, sabres, lances and spears starts with an examination of the simple tools of Stone Age people, including hand-held flint points, sharpened tools and the first axes, which date from 1.4 million years BC. We then move ahead in time to focus on such ancient civilizations as Sumeria and Mesopotamia, where metalworkers began to combine bronze and copper alloys to produce reliable spears, axeheads and swords.

In ancient Egypt, the countless invasions and subsequent assimilations led to the introduction of bronze- and iron-bladed weapons. Iron was being produced in large quantities by Roman times, when soldiers were armed with the feared pugio dagger and gladius sword. Although noted for their reliance on the spear and shield, the Greek infantryman or "hoplite" also carried a straight, double-edged, leaf-shaped short sword known as the "xiphos" and it became the model for the more recognizable Roman "gladius". At this time, Celtic swordsmiths were also producing swords of unique beauty and robustness.

Medieval and Renaissance daggers and swords

The daggers of the first medieval knights were probably similar to small Viking and Saxon handaxes. Like the knight's sword, these handaxes acquired cruciform hilts and often double-edged blades. As armour became more effective, more specialized medieval daggers evolved to defeat it. New hilt types gave a better grip, while blades were narrowed into sharp triangular or square-sectioned spikes.

From before the 11th until after the 16th century, the dagger was an essential battlefield weapon. It was also carried in civilian life for self-defence because, until the 16th century, swords were not worn with everyday dress. When the long, heavy-bladed civilian rapier came into fashion, the dagger became its parrying aid.

ABOVE King Henry VIII (1491–1547) is portrayed in this portrait by Holbein wearing a gilded dagger as part of his courtly dress. The dagger was an essential fashion accessory for medieval and Renaissance men.

RIGHT Soldiers of the Brazilian army, 1830s. Socket bayonets such as the one carried here quickly found their way into all modern armies throughout the world following their introduction in the 18th century.

RIGHT Soldiers of the Brazilian army, 1830s. Socket bayonets such as the one carried here quickly found their way into all modern armies throughout the world following their introduction in the 18th century.

In Europe, the wide-bladed and double-edged Saxon and Viking broadsword would become the inspiration for the early medieval "knightly" sword of the 11th to the 14th century. In both Europe and Asia, polearms (pole-mounted weapons) were used on the battlefield, and in the jousts of the medieval and Renaissance periods, public displays of horsemanship and fighting skills were performed using the lance and the sword.

Sword design changed during the Renaissance and, from around 1400, the emphasis shifted from a sword that had cutting and slashing capabilities to one that could pierce plate armour. Around 1500, the rapier appeared and soon became the sword of choice for a gentleman and the ultimate weapon for trials of honour, such as the duel. German and Swiss mercenaries ("Landsknechte") roamed across Europe, carrying their own huge, two-handed swords and waded into massed rows of enemy infantry, cutting and hacking a passage through for the cavalry.

By the early 1600s sword blades were lighter and could be used rapidly to attack and defend. During the 16th and 17th centuries, more accurate firearms and artillery were developed, and swords were relegated to a secondary role, although they were still regarded as the preferred weapon during close combat.

17th- to 20th-century world bayonets and swords
Just as the dagger was falling out of favour, it found a new role: the dagger became the bayonet.

The earliest Bayonne daggers were probably not bayonets at all but rather ordinary daggers made in southwestern France. In order to transform a musket into a spear for close-quarters combat, soldiers started jamming daggers into the muzzles of weapons. The plug bayonet was born – a short-lived design, since it was impossible to fire the weapon with the bayonet in place. This was replaced by the socket bayonet, which became the standard issue.

Mechanized warfare in the 19th century meant that fighting forces became more diversified. One consequence was more varieties of bayonet, including unwieldy sword bayonets that, though impractical, remained in use through the 1800s. By the 20th century bayonets had begun to revert to their dagger-like origins; most soldiers now carry some form of knife bayonet, which is both an all-purpose tool and a weapon.

The introduction of the smallsword in the late 17th century highlighted the new requirement for both practicality and fashion. On the battlefield, the seasoned soldier knew that a more robust broadsword would always be required, such as the distinctive broadsword of the Scottish Highlander. Wide-bladed and double-edged, this broadsword had an enclosed basket hilt and was devastating when used at close quarters.

During the late 18th and early 19th centuries Europe and the outside world were rocked by countless wars and momentous battles. The swords carried by the major nations at war, particularly the French and

BELOW Ottoman Turkish knife, 17th century. The finest Persian and Turkish daggers were usually forged of watered steel – giving strength and elasticity to the blade – and fitted with jade, ivory or crystal hilts.

Watered steel blade from Persia or India

Jade hilt from Turkey

Butt cap | Spacer | Strong stabbing point

ABOVE Highland dress dirk, Scottish, *c.*1868. The word "dirk" is usually applied to the long fighting knife of the Scottish Highlanders – of which this is a late example – and to certain classes of military dress dagger.

British, are studied, as are the swords that were carried during one of the bloodiest conflicts outside Europe, the American Civil War.

However, by 1914, the sword had become obsolete in battle and, after the First World War, it was relegated to a purely ceremonial role. Indeed, during the rise of Nazi Germany, we see the sword worn simply as a dress accessory.

Asian and African daggers and swords

In Africa fighting knives and daggers assumed exotic, uniquely creative forms. Although important as weapons, many were also status symbols and forms of currency. In the Middle East, the Arab jambiya remains an essential part of formal male dress, and features in celebrations. In Persia, which produced very skilled bladesmiths, known as masters of the art of "watered" or wootz steel. Fine Persian daggers are often superlative jewellery objects, rivalled only by the work of the Mughals from northern India.

In the Far East, the Japanese produced the fabulous tanto and aikuchi, smaller companions of the fabled katana sword of the samurai. The rise of the Samurai warrior class during the 12th century saw the development of the Samurai sword. These swords had a complex and ritualized process of manufacturing. China also has a long history of sword making that

stretches back over 3,000 years and includes such indigenous swords as the famous straight-bladed "jian" and the curved-bladed "dao". In addition, a wide variety of polearms was carried by the Chinese foot-soldier.

The Indian sword was almost totally unaffected by the influences of the West. Even when the British Empire had established virtually complete control over this vast country, Indian swordsmiths continued to produce unique indigenous swords of superb artistry and quality, including the "talwar" and the "khanda". In Africa, there was a dramatic division in sword styles between the Muslim-influenced north of the continent, and the central and southern areas.

In the South Pacific the Indonesian kris, prized by European collectors since the 17th century, is purported to have magical powers and is still felt to embody the spirit of the region.

How to use this book

The book is divided into two main sections, the first, Knives, Daggers and Bayonets, includes the discovery of metalworking and how this improved the ability of early humans to construct edged weapons, the popularity of the ear dagger and knives of the Roman Empire, and how these small weapons evolved into bayonets.

The second second section, Swords and Sabres, describes the Paeolithic origins and the appearance of the first swords in Europe and how the development of these weapons brutally shaped the great civilizations of ancient Egypt, Greece and Rome. The signifcance of the

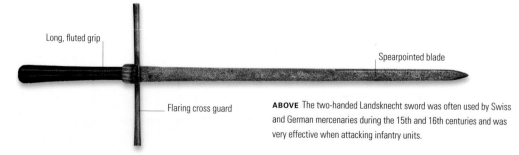

Long, fluted grip

Spearpointed blade

Flaring cross guard

ABOVE The two-handed Landsknecht sword was often used by Swiss and German mercenaries during the 15th and 16th centuries and was very effective when attacking infantry units.

ABOVE The Battle of San Romano in 1432. The medieval battlefield normally comprised a mass of polearms and poleaxes which were used to inflict injuries both from horseback and on foot.

ABOVE A 19th-century Japanese print depicting a Samurai warrior with his sword. Their swords were often given names as a mark of devotion and a belief that their warrior spirit was contained within them.

sword in the artistic and mystical traditons of the Celts is also explored, and there is a look into the world of the medieval knights and crusaders. Each section reveals the fascinating histories of each weapon, from the earliest knives and bronze age weapons to swords of the renaissance and weapons of the modern era.

The directories

Following each history section is a detailed visual catalogue which follows the progression of these sharp-edged weapons from the Stone Age through to the modern-day, and which features hundreds of examples from around the world. From ancient Egyptian flint knives and ballock daggers of medieval Europe to Swords of the Ottoman Empire and the commando knives of World War II, with each entry accompanied by a fabulous photograph of the weapon.

These detailed directories, together with the comprehensive histories, enable enthusiasts to easily identify individual weapons and fully appreciate their unique features, functionality and designs.

The first, A Directory of Knives, Daggers and Bayonets, describes the evolution of these small but deadly weapons from ancient beginnings as sharpened rocks to the very latest blades of hardened steel. It is

intended as a reasonably complete catalogue of all edged weapons shorter than a sword, although this is sometimes a difficult distinction to make.

The second, A Directory of Swords and Sabres features a variety of swords, spears, axes, lances and polearms that were used throughout history. The development of the sword from ancient to modern times includes an enormous variety of styles found within specific time periods and geographical regions which are charted chronologically.

Within each directory, every weapon is described in detail and listed according to country of origin, chronology and type. Each example is discussed and any unusual features are highlighted, and dimensions are included to give an accurate idea of scale. Each entry also has a short description explaining both the function and historical context of the weapon.

Dragon incorporated into handle

ABOVE This British Army officer's sword, *c*.1870, was not used in fighting but carried as a dress sword and only worn on dress occasions. It was a regimental sword of the Border Regiment, based in the north of England.

KNIVES, DAGGERS AND BAYONETS

From the sharp flints with which primitive
humans defended themselves to the
carbon-steel bayonets carried by modern
soldiers, the fighting knife's history is a
complex tale of technical ingenuity, artistic
virtuosity and brutal violence.
This section of the book begins with a look at
the history of knives, daggers and bayonets,
then concludes with a visual directory of the
most significant weapons.

ABOVE An English quillon dagger.
LEFT An artist's depiction of the fighting at the Hotel de Ville,
where bayonets were often used to combat civil disorder, *c.*1900.

This section traces the fascinating history of the fighting blade through to the 21st century.

A history of knives, daggers and bayonets

From the earliest sharpened flints of prehistory to the survival knives and hardened steel bayonets of modern combat, these edged weapons have helped to shape human history. Used by ancient warriors, medieval knights and soldiers of the American Civil War and the two World Wars, they are symbols of power, survival and progress.

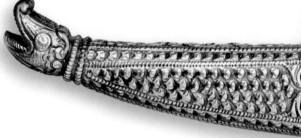

TOP British Elcho sword bayonet, *c.*1872.

MIDDLE TOP American push dagger, *c.*1870.

MIDDLE BOTTOM Balkan Ottoman bichaq, mid-19th century.

BOTTOM Indian chilanum dagger, late 18th century.

The earliest knives

The first weapons invented by humans were made out of the materials that they could pick up off the ground or extract from the bodies of the animals they killed for food. They shaped and sharpened wood, horn and bone for many different uses. They could throw rocks and use them to deal lethal blows. The right sorts of rocks could also be fashioned into extremely sharp cutting tools.

LEFT This late Neolithic flint knife (*c.*2000BC) was found in Jutland, Denmark. Flint flakes have been carefully and skilfully removed to form the sharp blade and tapered grip.

Compared with the most ancient edged implements, the fighting knife and dagger are fairly recent advances. The ancestors of modern humans first began to fashion sharpened objects out of stone about a million years ago. But these early cutting devices were made with a number of utilitarian purposes in mind. Perhaps they could have been used in a fight if the need arose, but there is no evidence to suggest that this was their primary function. Instead, these sharpened stones were mainly used for shaping wooden tools, butchering animals and scraping hides clean before making them into clothes.

The first weapons

The earliest stone tools were not very effective weapons because they were small and did not increase the reach of the user. Neither could they be used to stab, for most had no significant points. The hand axes in use up until around 35,000BC were roughly teardrop-shaped, with a rudimentary point, but these cannot be considered stabbing weapons. As weapons, these axes could have had no more specialist usefulness than any other naturally sharp rock.

For a hand weapon to be considered a fighting knife or dagger, it must increase or alter the user's reach to some advantageous extent, and it must provide the ability to stab. Cutting is in many cases another useful property, but it is secondary in the case of weapons under about 20cm (8in) in length. Stone is a very brittle and weighty material, and could not be used to create weapons with long cutting edges. A stone sword would have been excessively heavy and broken at the first blow. Nonetheless towards the end of the Middle Stone Age (*c.*50,000 years ago), early humans, aided by good stone-working techniques, were able to make short, sharply pointed stabbing knives.

BELOW The design of this Native American antler knife has changed little in 4000 years.

BOTTOM A Bronze Age knife, carved in bone, copies the form of copper knives of the time.

Polished elk antler

Curved bone blade

Wrist thong

ABOVE This group of flint knives of the late Stone Age and Bronze Age shows a degree of variety but also key similarities. The blades must remain short and stout, or they would simply break.

Stone and metal weapons

The use of stone knives did not end suddenly with the discovery of metals around 3500BC. Indeed, most of the finest surviving stone knives and daggers were made as recently as 2000 years into the Bronze Age (c.3500–c.700BC). In some places, metal knives seem to have influenced the form of stone ones; for example, stone daggers found in Scandinavia dating from around 1600BC appear to be direct copies of their metal counterparts. This is probably because early metalworking was well under way around the Mediterranean long before it appeared in northern Europe. Metal daggers from the south may have found their way north, where their forms were copied using local materials. The height of this period of technological crossover, roughly 1800–1500BC, is often referred to as the "Dagger Period" because knives and daggers were clearly enormously popular during this time.

Flint knapping

The process by which a hard stone, such as flint, quartzite or obsidian (a vitreous acid volcanic rock) is reduced to a specific shape for use as a tool or weapon is called flint knapping. Along with the ability to make fire, flint knapping was one of the first great technological advances in human prehistory. The simplest knapping technique is called "direct percussion". The piece of stone is struck with another rock or bit of wood to break smaller pieces off and gradually bring it into the desired shape.

This technique worked well when making simple clubs and hand axes, but it was not precise enough to make something as delicate as a knife blade. In order to avoid breaking the emerging tool itself during the knapping process, early humans developed a more controlled technique called "pressure flaking". The pressure flaker would refine the rough form of the stone by applying careful pressure with a pointed piece of antler. This process could be used to chip tiny fragments of stone away, gradually bringing the object into whatever precise shape was desired. A well-made

pressure-flaked knife is a thing of real beauty. The flaking scars are sometimes arranged with impressive forethought in flowing rows. In other cases the main body of the blade is ground and polished smooth, while the edges retain a contrasting fluted and serrated finish.

Stones suitable for knapping are found in a variety of colours in Europe and the Middle East, and it is clear that many of these appealed to Stone Age toolmakers. Flint occurs in many tints, ranging from a very light yellow through rich amber to dark brown and black. Quartzite appears in black tints, as well as in red, green and white.

RIGHT Striking the piece of flint would quickly break it. Instead, careful pressure is applied to remove one tiny fragment at a time.

The "Dagger Period" 1800–1500BC

Archaeological finds in Scandinavia have given us a
good impression of how the best stone knives and
daggers developed. The earliest examples from the
Dagger Period have long, narrow blades and are
roughly diamond-shaped in profile. One half of the
diamond functioned as the grip or handle but was not
as finely worked as the other end, the blade, which had
precise pressure-flaked edges and a passable point.

ABOVE This detail of a giant statue of a pharaoh, *c.*1260BC, at the Amun
Temple in Luxor, Egypt, shows a decorated dagger thrust into a belt.
The grip is formed by two sculpted heads depicting the sun-god Ra.

The handle end on later examples gradually loses its
taper, becoming more straight-sided, while the
cross-section is rounder for a more comfortable grip.
Finally, the butt of the handle becomes flared to
improve the grip even further. The fully-fledged
dagger of this period, in addition to the well-formed
grip and butt, generally displays a graceful, leaf-shaped
blade that has been cunningly strengthened by
broadening and thickening only where necessary.

Flint knives in ancient Egypt

The ancient Egyptians also continued to make flint
knives well into the Bronze Age. They served as the
Egyptian warrior's sidearms long before any form of
sword was known, and they continued to be used into
the New Kingdom Period (*c.*1567–*c.*1085BC), by which
time metal daggers were well known.

The earliest Egyptian flint knives date from the Early
Dynastic Period (*c.*3100–*c.*2780BC). These weapons are
easily recognizable by their broad, curved blades. On
some examples the flaking pattern has been left over
the whole surface of the blade, while others have been
polished smooth. Grips were made of wood, horn or
bone, and glued firmly in place. On rich examples this
handle was sometimes covered with gold foil or carved
with battle scenes. Shorter versions, at less than 30cm
(12in) in length, were probably serviceable as fighting
weapons, but the longer ones, 38cm (15in) or even
longer, would have been quite fragile and may only
have been used for ritual purposes.

ABOVE Found in Hindsgarl, Denmark, these flint daggers (*c.*1700BC) are
typical of "Dagger Period" flint-work. The grips have imitation stitching
to mimic the leather-bound handles of metal daggers of this period.

Most of the Later Dynastic (*c*.715–*c*.332 BC) and New Kingdom daggers were short, double-edged stabbing weapons, with simple hilts (handles), made of some organic material. New Kingdom daggers tend to be longer and narrower than older forms. Sometimes the grips also have a central rib or swelling.

Flint knives of pre-conquest America

The indigenous cultures of the Americas lived almost universally without metal tools and weapons until the first continuous contacts with Europeans in the 15th and 16th centuries AD. Before then, even in areas where the working of certain metals, primarily gold, was very advanced, tools and weapons remained entirely non-metallic. The ancient tribes inhabiting the present-day West Indies took advantage of the extremely hard woods found in the tropical lowlands to fashion clubs, swords and daggers, while obsidian was a common material used by the Aztecs of Mexico to fashion knives and daggers as well as the blades of their fierce-looking *macuauhuitl* sword-clubs. One chronicler of the Spanish Conquest of Mexico (1519–21) wrote that a native flint knife could cut "like a Toledo knife" – a reference to blades from the Spanish city, renowned for their high quality.

The end of the Stone Age

Stone was the best weapons material to which prehistoric humans had access. It was hard and dense, which meant that it could be given an extremely sharp edge. Even today, obsidian blades are used by optic surgeons because they are much sharper than any steel scalpels. But it was a very difficult material to work with and could only be made to assume a very restricted group of shapes. A stone blade, once broken, could never be repaired or recycled. These limitations led weapon makers to adopt a new material – metal.

ABOVE This striking flint knife blade is one of a number inlaid with stone of a contrasting colour. Found at Tenochtitlan in Mexico, the Aztec capital city, it dates from the Postclassic Period (*c*.AD1325–1521).

BELOW Ritual Egyptian knives of this type were the largest flint weapons ever made. This particular example, now missing its handle, dates from around 3000BC.

Copper, bronze and iron

The discovery of metalworking immeasurably improved the ability of early humans to construct edged weapons. Metal was flexible, much less brittle and more versatile than stone. It could be melted and cast into a huge variety of forms. When broken, it was possible to melt a metal weapon down and reform it. By the Bronze Age (*c.*3500–*c.*700BC), people were constructing more practical metallic fighting knives and daggers.

The first metal to be used for tools and weapons was copper. Small deposits of pure copper, which required no smelting (ore extraction) before working, were found in Mesopotamia, India, Egypt and North America. Copper weapons were being made in the Middle East as early as 6500BC, and in India by perhaps 6000BC. Pure copper weapons may have first been produced in North America by 5500BC, although the best evidence indicates a more recent date.

Between around 3000BC and 500BC, the "Old Copper Complex" people of the Great Lakes region of North America (Michigan and Wisconsin in the United States, and Ontario in Canada) were taking advantage of the pure copper nuggets found in that area to make knives and spearheads. These activities, along with later instances of copper working among native peoples along the northwest coast, remained the only examples of entirely indigenous metalwork practised by North American Indians until the arrival of Europeans in the 15th century AD.

The discovery of smelting

Naturally occurring pure metals were very scarce elsewhere and it was the invention of smelting that advanced the development of metalworking. The vast majority of the Earth's metals are contained within rock in the form of ore. Smelting is the process by which careful heating produces a chemical reaction that separates the metal from the surrounding materials. Once early humans had mastered this

ABOVE This 19th-century illustration is copied from an ancient Egyptian bas-relief depicting a metalworker forging a spear. The knowledge of smelting led the Egyptians and other ancient peoples to discover bronze.

process, their access to metals increased beyond measure. As a result, the rapid evolution of metal-edged weapons began.

Weapons made from copper

Copper is a resilient but very soft metal. Those who made copper weapons had to develop blade shapes that were structurally suited to the material, otherwise

BELOW Certain American Indian tribes have produced copper weapons for thousands of years. This 19th-century dagger, made by the Tlingit of southeastern Alaska and western Canada, has a copper blade.

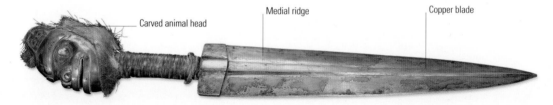

Carved animal head   Medial ridge   Copper blade

Heavy pommel | Ridged grip | Medial ridge

a weapon would simply bend, crumple or collapse when it struck a blow. Daggers were undoubtedly the earliest metal-edged weapons made for fighting, simply because the softness of the material meant that a copper weapon had to be short and very broad. It was also necessary for a copper blade to be quite thick to give it some degree of stiffness. However, an increase in thickness produced an exponential (rather than proportionate) increase in weight, therefore a longer weapon such as a sword was out of the question. The earliest copper daggers had short, stout blades with a triangular outline that to some extent compensated for the softness of the metal. They were either cast in a mould or cut out and hammered into shape.

Early copper daggers were generally composed of a blade and a separate hilt of some hard organic material. Many excavated Mesopotamian graves of the Early Dynastic Period (c.2900–2330BC) have been found to include copper daggers of this type. Hilts were usually riveted to the wide base of the blade, although some surviving examples show no signs of rivets and so were presumably glued in place. A better

ABOVE The form of the latest metal weapons was copied in other materials. This Persian dagger of 1300–1200BC is not bronze but carved wood. The thick medial ridge or spine is designed to stiffen the blade.

BELOW The copper blade of this well-used Bronze Age knife, found in the River Thames in London, has been sharpened many times, grinding it down until only a small stub remains. The grip is a reconstruction.

answer appeared in the form of the tang; the base of the blade was drawn out again into a short, narrow rod, which could then be inserted into the hilt section.

Another key development in the design of early edged weapons was the medial ridge, or rib, cast into both sides of a blade using a two-piece mould. With a thick central spine, the rest of a blade could be made thinner and lighter. Its length and width could be increased, producing a more effective stabbing weapon. Daggers with these stiff medial ridges proliferated throughout the Middle East. The medial ridge was a pivotal development in the evolution of blade forms and remained an essential design element from the Bronze Age to the present day.

BELOW The usual form of bronze daggers was short and wide at the hilt to ensure strength. This example, dating from 2300–1800BC and found in Neuheiligen in Germany, also retains its metal hilt.

Cylindrical grip

Densely ridged blade

The introduction of bronze

Just as copper blades represented a great leap forward from the flint implements of prehistoric times, so too the discovery of bronze drove pure copper weapons into obsolescence. Bronze is an alloy, a mixture of two metals – copper and tin. A recipe for a good weapon was around nine parts bronze and one part tin, although exact proportions were at first hard to achieve. Bronze is harder than copper, resulting in stronger weapons that could take and hold a sharp edge better. Bronze blades could be made narrower and longer than copper ones.

Bronze flowed better than copper into moulds, which increased the possibilities for more elaborate and intricate designs. Hilts began to be cast in one piece with the blade, eliminating the weak point of a riveted joint between hilt and blade. Some of the earliest bronze daggers were

made around 2500BC in the Sumerian city of Ur in Mesopotamia. These weapons have strong, ribbed blades and thick tangs. Early Bronze Age (c.3200–c.2800BC) daggers from Luristan (or Lorestan), an area in the west of modern Iran, were cast in one piece with recesses in the grip to take plates of wood or bone, the earliest known examples of grip "scales". These would later become some of the most common methods of grip construction in knife and dagger making throughout the world.

Mycenaean bronze daggers

Knowledge of bronze and bronze working moved gradually west from the Middle East through the Mediterranean and north into Europe, and by around 1600BC most of the peoples populating central and northern Europe were familiar

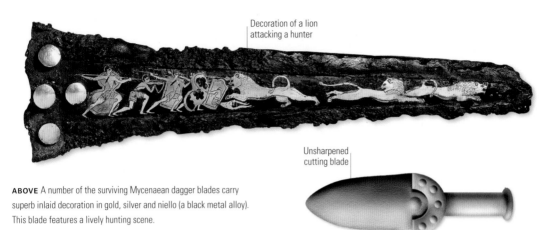

Decoration of a lion
attacking a hunter

Unsharpened
cutting blade

Sharpened
stabbing blade

ABOVE A number of the surviving Mycenaean dagger blades carry
superb inlaid decoration in gold, silver and niello (a black metal alloy).
This blade features a lively hunting scene.

RIGHT After many sharpenings, what was once a wide-bladed,
cutting knife could be transformed into a stout bronze needle, its
sharpness making it an excellent stabbing weapon.

with it. In Greece, the bronze daggers of Mycenae
(c.1600–1100BC) are particularly notable, not only
because of the skill involved in their basic construction
– the fine tapering blades once bearing handles of horn
or ivory held in place with gold-capped rivets – but also
for their exquisite decoration in gold and silver. Some
exhibit well-studied depictions of marine life, while
others bear hunting or battle scenes. These themes
appealed to the warlike, seafaring Mycenaeans, who
dominated the Aegean world by force from around
1400BC, during and after the collapse of the Minoan
civilization (c.3400–c.1100BC). They also may have
destroyed the city of Troy around 1180BC, thus
forming the basis for the later Greek myth.

The knife becomes the dagger
By 1600BC, characteristic northern European bronze
daggers were beginning to appear. One early form,
typical of finds dating from around 1500–1450BC in the
Rhône Valley, Gaul (present-day France), consisted of a
short triangular blade with a rounded base onto which
was riveted a hilt with a semicircular guard (protective
plate), cylindrical grip and flat, circular butt (end).
Metal hilts of this form, cast in one piece, quickly spread
throughout France and across to Italy and other parts
of central Europe.

Before the Middle Bronze Age (c.2800–c.1100BC)
there is little point in discussing the differences between
a dagger and any other sort of knife. But as people
gained mastery over bronze, which allowed them to

diversify the styles and specific uses of weapons, clear
differences began to appear. Simple bronze knives
typical of the Middle Bronze Age in western Europe
(c.1500–c.1100BC) have a wide cutting blade and usually
a rounded tip – an all-purpose tool. But the cutting
edges of a bronze blade had to be continually sharpened.
Although it was harder than copper, bronze still could
only hold an edge for a short period before use dulled it
again. Constant sharpening, during which the edges were
ground down using a whetstone, gradually narrowed the
width of a knife, and after many sharpenings its size was
much reduced and its shape dramatically altered; it
became little more than a sharply tapered spike.

A knife's usefulness as a cutting tool over time
was thus negligible, but undoubtedly humans soon
discovered that such a tool could still be very effective
when used exclusively as a stabbing weapon. It was not
long before new weapons were being purposefully cast
in this acutely pointed shape. During this period in
history, dagger and knife became distinct from each
other. The dagger was being used purely as a killing
tool, almost exclusively for stabbing overarm or
thrusting underarm, while a fighting knife remained
more general in its applications. Of course, distinctions
of this kind gloss over the huge grey areas that always
exist between types, and so the present differentiation
is meant only as a guiding generalization.

Medial ridge

Upward-curving pommel
arms or "antennae"

The Hallstatt culture (*c.*1200–500BC)

Hallstatt is a small lakeside town in Austria, southeast
of Salzburg. In 1846 an enormous ancient cemetery
was discovered there, and excavations carried out
during the second half of the 19th century uncovered
over 1,000 individual graves. The character of the
material possessions found in the graves was very
distinctive, being the earliest appearance of what is
today often termed the "Celtic" style – organic,
flowing forms that expressed the culture's close
affinity with, and religious devotion to, the natural
world. Objects of this style have since been found
throughout Europe, and are collectively referred to
as being part of the Hallstatt culture.

ABOVE This is a typical Hallstatt dagger, which is made of iron
and dates from around 750–450BC. The dagger's blade is well formed
for both cutting and thrusting actions.

The Hallstatt culture dominated most of Europe, in
the east over most of what is now Austria, the Czech
Republic, Slovakia, Slovenia, Croatia, Romania and
Hungary, and in the west across Switzerland and parts
of Italy, France and Germany. Its influence also
extended to Spain and the British Isles. The culture is
especially important because it forms a bridge between
the Late Bronze Age (*c.*1100–800BC) and the earliest
use of iron in Europe from around 800BC.

The dagger as a work of art

Until around 800BC, Hallstatt dagger blades were made
of bronze, and indeed, bronze weapons continued to
be used long after iron was well known throughout
Europe. Hallstatt daggers are often exquisite works of
art as well as weapons, having long, double-edged and
multi-ridged blades. The hilts, usually made of bronze
but sometimes covered in gold, were more intricate in
their design than anything seen previously. The grips,
rather than being just a simple cylinder, were
gracefully tapered above and below a central swelling,
in anticipation of the later Spanish and Roman
versions of this design. Pommels (weights at the end of
the hilt) took distinct forms. Some were of a flattened
oval shape, usually fully pierced with designs. Others
bore two intricate wheel-like structures on either side
of a central block. Perhaps the most famous Hallstatt
hilt was the so-called "antennae" type, the pommel
being constructed of two upward-curving arms.
Hallstatt daggers were also remarkable in that they
were among the first European edged weapons to be
made of a new material introduced from Asia – iron.

LEFT These two dagger hilts from northern Austria are excellent
examples of the best Hallstatt craftsmanship. Their upward-curving
pommel arms are distinguished by complex decorative forms.

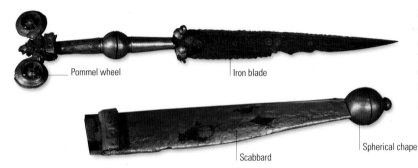

Pommel wheel

Iron blade

Scabbard

Spherical chape

The coming of iron

Grave finds show that the Hallstatt peoples also had contact with Asia Minor – the origin of the earliest discovered iron weapons – from around 1000BC. It is believed that the first iron smelting began in Anatolia, eastern Turkey, about 1500BC. Initially the Hittites, who ruled this region (c.1900–700BC), guarded their discovery because of the great technological advantage that it gave them, but they could not restrict its proliferation for very long. Conquest and seafaring traders brought iron to the Biblical Middle East around 1000BC – the Bible mentions that Goliath carried a dagger of iron into battle – and trade across the Mediterranean brought iron to Greece and Italy by 700BC. The Hallstatt culture, being closely linked to these areas as well as directly to Asia Minor, therefore had multiple sources of iron at its disposal, and it is not at all surprising that the culture's later phases quickly brought the general use of iron to Europe.

The La Tène culture (c.500–0BC)

By around 400BC a different Celtic culture was taking over most of the areas previously dominated by the Hallstatt culture. Named after the area of the eastern end of Lake Neuchâtel in Switzerland where the first group of its objects were found, the La Tène culture represents the bulk of what modern people regard as Celtic. The weapons of this group of peoples usually display fantastic imagination and technical skill, their designs growing out of observations of the natural world that have been elaborated into a realm of wild abstraction, full of curving, twisting forms.

Most La Tène knives and daggers have blades of iron or steel, although the hilts were still often constructed

of bronze. The double-edged daggers of the Hallstatt culture gave way to an increasing preference for broad, single-edged knives. A few double-edged daggers from the La Tène culture are known, and often these exhibit a development of the Hallstatt "antennae" hilt in which the horns of the pommel and guard have been made thicker and given spherical terminals; combined with an added spherical form at the base of the grip between the arms of the pommel, this gives the hilt a distinct anthropomorphic appearance: a small human figure in a spread-eagle position. The figure's head is also sometimes given realistic facial features.

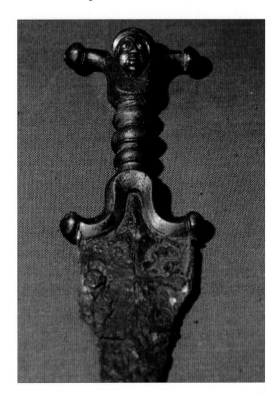

Daggers of the Iron Age

The use of the dagger was not as common in the Iron Age (*c*.1400–*c*.500BC) as it had been throughout the preceding Bronze Age. Unlike their Minoan and Mycenaean ancestors, the warriors of Classical Greece (510–323BC) appear never to have employed the dagger as a military weapon, relying instead on the spear and sword. But in Italy, three vibrant cultures, the Villanovans, the Etruscans and the Romans, each developed forms of the dagger.

Bronze continued to be employed in the making of arms and armour throughout much of the Iron Age. Good-quality bronze was a harder metal than the earliest forms of iron, and it remained the preferred weapons material for a very long time. Iron was more easily sourced and therefore cheaper than the copper used to make bronze, and it had the potential to be forged into sharper- and harder-edged weapons. But the first iron-smelting processes were difficult and not very successful.

Early iron smelting

Metalworkers in the ancient world generally extracted copper metal from ore in furnaces designed to reach temperatures of between 700 and 900 degrees Celsius. It might have been possible to achieve the chemical reactions required to reduce iron from ore at 700 or 800 degrees, but the metal produced remained full of a glass-like substance called slag. This had to be liquefied to separate it from the iron, but this part of the process required a temperature of 1,200 degrees and so was beyond the technology of the time. Iron with a high slag content was brittle and inflexible, and therefore inferior to bronze. Only after metalworkers developed more advanced smelting processes, which could reach the higher temperatures, did they render bronze obsolete and turn to iron as the main raw material used to create weapons.

RIGHT An Etruscan image of the war-god Mars. The Etruscans probably invested symbolic significance in their weapons – this dagger stands for masculinity and military might.

ABOVE A series of bronze Etruscan daggers found at Castione Marchesi in Italy. All display the typical steeply tapered blades, semi-circular guards and cylindrical grips that were common to this culture.

The Villanovans (*c*.1100–*c*.700BC) and Etruscans (*c*.800–*c*.100BC)

These technological difficulties meant that most daggers continued to be made of bronze, even after iron had been introduced. In Italy, the pre-Roman Villanovan and Etruscan cultures both favoured bronze as the material for edged weapons, even though they were both well aware of iron. The Villanovans were the first people on the Italian peninsula to work iron, and from them the technology passed to the Etruscans, who were dominant by the 8th century BC, passing from them to their enemies, the early Romans. However it was only with the rise of Rome as the supreme military power that iron came into widespread use.

Wheel chape

Triple-button pommel

ABOVE This beautiful Villanovan dagger and scabbard, dating from the 6th–3rd century BC, is a good example of how the use of bronze continued well into the Iron Age.

Villanovan and Etruscan daggers are known in three main forms. Most have leaf-shaped blades although some have straight blades that taper sharply in the last third of their length and end in a thickened stabbing point. Others are triangular, with a consistent degree of taper from hilt to point. All three types include multiple ribs down their length.

The blade usually extended into a tang section at its base, onto which fitted a grip of stone, wood or bone. Some grips had "antennae pommels", which are a sign of Celtic influence, while others had simple T-shaped or disk pommels.

By the late 7th century BC the Etruscans had developed into the strongest military power on the Italian peninsula. They moved south over the River Tiber, taking many towns including Rome. The Etruscans retained their hold on southern Italy until 509BC, when the Romans rebelled and declared themselves a republic.

The Romans (800BC–AD410)

For over 1,000 years Rome maintained the fiercest, most disciplined and well-organized war machine in history. It adapted quickly to changes in enemy equipment and tactics, and often embraced them. Foreign innovations that were appropriated by the Romans included mail armour, armoured cavalry, the legendary *gladius*, or short sword, and the *pugio*, or dagger.

RIGHT Most of the earliest evidence for the pugio daggers adopted by the Romans comes from the Iberian Peninsula. This Iberian relief, from the 3rd century BC, shows a man armed with a dagger of pugio form.

FAR RIGHT This classic leaf-bladed Roman pugio blade with raised midrib dates from the 1st century AD. It is a well-designed weapon suitable for both slashing and thrusting attacks.

The Roman dagger appears to have been of Spanish origin. Examples from Numantia (in north-central Spain) dating from the 4th and 3rd centuries BC are virtually identical to daggers in the later years of the Roman Republic (509–27BC). However, it seems that the dagger was not immediately adopted by the Roman Army. It is not mentioned at all by Polybius (*c.*200–*c.*118BC), the Greek historian who described with great attention to detail the army of the Roman Republic. Initially the Romans seem to have thought of the dagger as a sort of trophy – an item of prestige that lent a certain military muscularity to a man's appearance. Perhaps a dagger pointed him out as someone who had fought for the Roman Republic in the wars abroad.

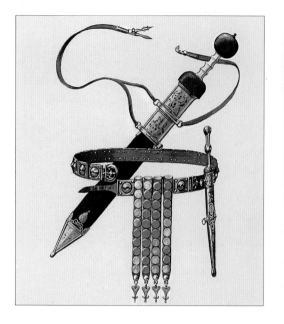

ABOVE The pugio was used in battle, for self-defence and also in the gladiatorial arena. This mosaic of around AD320 shows a gladiator pinning another to the ground while preparing to kill him with the dagger.

LEFT By the 1st century AD the pugio was part of a legionary's basic equipment, worn on the left of a belt that also held the plated *cingulum*.

The legionary pugio

The dagger became a standard part of Roman legionary equipment around the time of Christ. It was taken up as a complement to the sword, worn on the left side of the belt from which also hung the *cingulum*, or girdle. The sword was worn on the right side, suspended from a separate belt. Roman soldiers are frequently depicted armed in this way on tombstones and memorials, as well as in other forms of sculpture.

The pugio had a reasonably wide, waisted blade between 15–35cm (5.9–13.7in) in length. The point was frequently elongated to optimize its use for stabbing, while a strong midrib running down the length of the blade gave it additional strength and rigidity. The hand was protected by a simple guard riveted through the base of the blade, the arms of which sometimes extended a short distance beyond the edges of the blade, although many examples simply sit flush with the base. The pugio handle is very distinctive, having a circular swelling at its mid-point. Early pommels tend to be round, while later types usually have a flattened base or are even crescent-shaped. Generally, the pugio hilt was made in two halves – sometimes in bone or ivory but usually in bronze or iron – that sandwiched either side of the tang and were held in place by rivets through the guard, grip swelling and pommel. Although most pugio hilts were plain, high-status pieces were sometimes inlaid with precious metals.

The decline of the pugio

The legionary pugio dagger seems to have disappeared from use by Roman legionaries around AD200 or possibly earlier. Trajan's Column in Rome – completed AD113 to commemorate the Dacian campaigns of AD101–2 and AD104–6 – one of our most important sources for the appearance of Roman legionaries in the early 2nd century AD, does not include even one dagger.

For whatever reason, the legionary pugio was discarded. A cruder form of this dagger continued to be used by auxiliary troops, soldiers from the Roman Empire's various outer territories. One spectacular find at Künzing, Bavaria, of the stock of a military workshop buried in the 3rd century AD, included 59 dagger blades and 29 sheaths. This indicates that the legionary pugio continued to be used as a military weapon long after it had been abandoned by the legions.

LEFT This Roman pugio, from southern Europe and made in the 1st century AD, retains its iron grip scales decorated with incised grooves and riveted to the blade tang.

The assassination of Julius Caesar, 44BC

In 44BC, Gaius Julius Caesar was the most powerful man in Rome. A great general, he had just been appointed dictator, although Rome was not yet an empire. The granting of absolute power to Julius Caesar was a key step in Rome's transition from a republican to an imperial state. Some members of the Roman senate opposed the slide into dictatorship, and a plot formed to assassinate Caesar.

On 15 March 44BC, Caesar went to a meeting at the request of the Senate to read a petition they wished to put to him. But the petition was a trick, conceived by the assassins, who called themselves "Liberators", to draw him into their trap. As he read the document one of the assassins drew his dagger and struck at Caesar's neck, but managed only to wound him slightly. The rest of the group (some accounts say up to 60 assailants) then attacked, stabbing their victim over and over, in the face, chest, shoulders and sides. Caesar tried to escape, but he stumbled and went down. The attackers continued their frenzied assault, which became so frantic that they accidentally stabbed each other as well as their victim. Caesar eventually died, his body covered in up to 35 stab wounds.

Roman coins commemorating the murder show the head of Brutus on one face and the assassins' daggers on the other: the pugio soon became the Roman legionary's constant companion.

LEFT Caesar's murder was commemorated on Roman coins of *c.*42BC that feature the profile head of Marcus Junius Brutus, leader of the conspiracy, on one side and pugios on the reverse.

BELOW The assassination in the Senate is here recreated by the German historical artist Heinrich Füger (1751-1818).

The Saxon fighting knife

The disintegration of the Roman Empire in the 5th century AD did not at first result in changes in weapons design and manufacture. The Empire's fragments initially tried to retain the trappings of imperial power, but it could not last. The old military structures gave way to much more variegated, clannish warrior cultures founded on personal loyalty and individual prowess. This social change was reflected in the design of weapons.

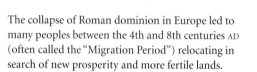

The collapse of Roman dominion in Europe led to many peoples between the 4th and 8th centuries AD (often called the "Migration Period") relocating in search of new prosperity and more fertile lands. Germanic tribes moved north from central Europe, while Scandinavian peoples struck west into Britain, Iceland, Greenland and North America.

ABOVE Found in the River Thames, this fine sax blade bears a unique inscription of the complete Anglo-Saxon runic alphabet and also the name of its maker or owner, Beagnoth.

The sax

Many Germanic tribes took advantage of the Romans' departure from Britain. While raids into Britain had begun before Roman withdrawal in AD410, they

increased dramatically afterwards. These invaders were generically referred to as "Saxons" even though their origins were diverse. Some seized parts of eastern Britain by force, while others allied themselves with the resident Romano-British peoples. Saxon warriors prized the sword above all weapons, but they also became known for a very distinctive fighting knife – the scramasax, seax or sax.

It has long been thought that the term "Saxon" expressed a characteristic preference for the "sax" as a weapon. Its use was not, however, limited to Britain. The earliest known Scandinavian sax dates from about 300BC, and its shape is much the same as those found in a bog at Vimose, on the Danish island of Funen, over six centuries later. In the Early Medieval Period (c.AD500–c.AD1100) the sax was the commonest sidearm of Saxons, Franks and Vikings, later examples having been found in Norway, Sweden, Denmark and mainland Europe.

Types of sax and their uses

The sax was a broad-bladed, single-edged fighting knife, the blade having a strong back and a wedge-shaped cross-section. Its length varied enormously. Smaller examples, almost "pen-knife" types, have blades as short as 7.5cm (3in) long, while the biggest sword versions are

LEFT Among the weapons found in France in a Merovingian grave of the third quarter of the 5th century AD was this early example of a sax, made of iron and with a finely decorated hilt.

Decorated blade

Wooden handle
(now lost)

upwards of 76cm (30in) long. This very large form was called a langseax by the Viking spearmen who favoured it, while the average size, usually with a blade around 15cm (6in) long, was called a handseax. The blade was tapered sharply down its last third, and on the back only the cutting edge remained straight or slightly curved. There was no hand guard and only a simple grip of wood or bone. Sax blades could be very ornate, inlaid with copper, bronze and silver. Sometimes the name of the owner or maker was also inlaid, highlighting how important the sax was both as a prized weapon and as a signed work of art.

Although the sax may look more like a utilitarian, all-purpose knife, it was mainly a weapon for close-quarters combat. While the sword is the weapon most celebrated in early medieval literature, the sax makes several notable appearances. *The Tale of Thorstein Rod-Stroke* describes two men dying from fatal stab wounds dealt with a sax, while one of the most dramatic battlefield episodes occurred at the Battle of Bravoll around AD700, a contest for the Swedish throne between old King Harald War-Tooth and his nephew Sigurd. With most of his royal guard and champions dead or dying, King Harald charged his enemies with a sax in each hand, slaying many men before his skull was smashed by an axe-wielding foe.

Despite the sax's prominence in early medieval culture, the respect accorded fighting knives was minimal compared to the sword and spear. Even the Vikings could belittle the smaller forms of sax. In the Icelandic *Saga of Weapon's Fjord*, the warrior Geitir observes that "he with a little sax must try and try again".

ABOVE Found at Sittingbourne in England, this sax blade is ornately decorated with copper alloy and silver. One side carries the inscription "Sigebereht owns me", while the other reads "Biorhtelm made me".

Links between the sax and dagger

However popular the fighting knife was with individual warriors during the Migration Period and Early Middle Ages, its use was entirely a matter of personal preference. The dagger had not been a mandatory military requirement since it had ceased to be standard issue in the Roman Army. But the Franks under Charlemagne brought back many Roman ideas and regulations, including strict discipline and the use of armoured cavalry. In AD805, five years after being crowned with the title of "Emperor of the Romans", Charlemagne issued an edict that required all of his cavalry to be armed with a mail coat, sword, spear, shield and dagger.

Little is known about the transition from the later saxes of the 11th century to the "knightly" daggers of the 13th and 14th centuries. Many Anglo-Saxons at the Battle of Hastings in 1066 probably carried long saxes, while their Norman enemies, themselves descended from the Vikings, may have been armed with smaller sax-like knives in addition to their swords and spears. Indeed, the sax may not have fallen out of fashion at all; knives looking very much like the sax were still being made in England during the 1400s.

BELOW These two excavated sax blades give a good impression of the more typical proportions of these famous weapons. Found in central Europe, they probably date from the 6th–8th centuries AD.

Medieval daggers

The Medieval Period (*c.*1100–*c.*1450) was the age of the knight and of chivalry. The culture of the mounted warrior changed how combat was conducted and led to a reconsideration of how weapons were used. Knights initially thought the dagger to be unimportant, but by the 14th century it had become an essential part of their equipment. Dagger types evolved and multiplied. Their new significance applied on the battlefield as well as in civilian life.

The use of the dagger had remained a matter of personal preference since its requirement by the Roman legions had been dropped in the 2nd century AD. All manner of knives were no doubt carried by fighting men, but there were no specific regulations or accepted practice. The AD805 edict of the Holy Roman Emperor Charlemagne that all imperial cavalrymen should carry the dagger was significant, but several hundred years would pass before Charlemagne's lead was followed.

The unworthy dagger

During the 12th and 13th centuries, daggers do not seem to have been thought worthy of much notice. Since Roman times, the respected weapons of the elite warrior were the spear and the sword. Daggers rarely appear on the funerary monuments of knights of this period, nor do we find dagger combat depicted in art until around 1250. Perhaps because it was advocated only as a last resort when all other weapons were broken or lost, the dagger does not seem to have interested artists until the middle of the 13th century.

The dagger in the 12th century sometimes carried derogatory associations. Usually called a cultellus or coustel, it was commonly connected with criminals; *coustiller* and *cultellarius* were both terms used to refer to thieves, thugs and bandits. A statute of 1152 issued by the Count of Toulouse in France refers to "evil men, called coustillers, who cause havoc with their daggers after nightfall".

BELOW This detail from a 13th-century manuscript version of the Old Testament shows men armed in the style of the time. One of the central figures can be seen stabbing his enemy with a short dagger.

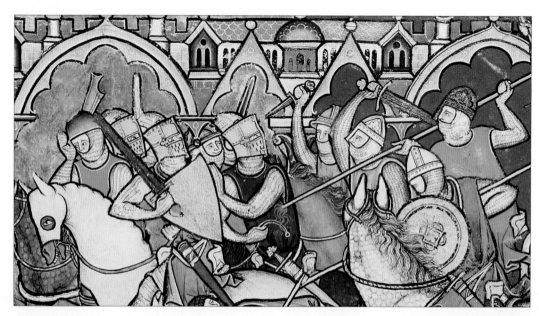

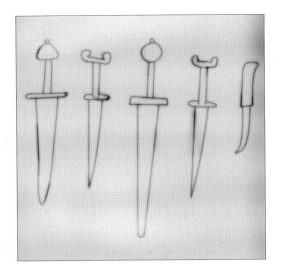

LEFT This illustration, after an 11th-century Italian manuscript, shows the medieval distinction between the two main dagger types: the wide-bladed cutting daggers and the narrow stabbing daggers.

Cutting daggers and stabbing daggers

Despite its wicked reputation, the dagger evolved quickly during the 13th and 14th centuries. By 1300 it was a standard part of the knight's armament, along with the lance, sword and axe or mace. Some daggers remained closely related to knives intended for general use. But others became removed from anything resembling an all-purpose blade, being instead dedicated exclusively to killing people.

Distinctions were clearly being made by the beginning of the 14th century. An inventory of the weapons belonging to Raoul de Nesle, Constable of France, taken after he was killed in 1302, employs specific terminology for two sorts of dagger. The broader-bladed daggers, those resembling utilitarian knives, are called coutiaus à tailler, or cutting daggers. These are distinguished from the coutiaus à pointe, or stabbing daggers.

A number of daggers from this period survive, and they clearly illustrate both types. The cutting daggers are frequently single-edged, with a strong back, the point tapering on the sharp side only, much like a kitchen knife. Stabbing daggers are much longer, narrower and very sharply tapered. By 1375, some forms of stabbing dagger could hardly be considered edged weapons at all; their blades, having no cutting edges, are little more than reinforced spikes of hardened steel for punching through muscle and bone. With enough force behind them, these blades, like giant awls, could probably also pierce the padded textile, mail and light plate armour of the time.

Miséricorde

The word *miséricorde*, meaning mercy or pity, began to be used in the mid-13th century to refer to the dagger wielded by knights. It is commonly thought that the word association comes from the use of the dagger for the mercy killing of wounded men on the battlefield. In fact, it's more likely that it derives from the dagger's effectiveness in compelling an overthrown knight to surrender – with a request for mercy – to avoid being slain in single combat.

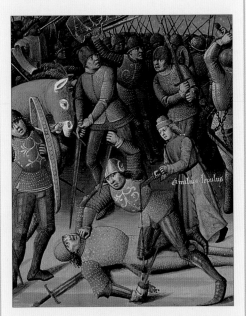

ABOVE This 15th-century manuscript detail shows an armoured warrior preparing to either accept his enemy's surrender or finish the fight with a deadly downward dagger blow.

As blade forms multiplied, so did the forms of dagger hilt. Grouped according to the hilt form, there were four primary types of dagger in common use during the Medieval Period.

Fluted wheel pommel — Cross guard — Single-edged blade

"Antennae" — Down-curved guard — Double-edged blade

Cross-hilt daggers

The first daggers to be generally adopted in the 12th and 13th centuries had simple cross hilts, like diminutive swords. These are often called "quillon" daggers, although this is a post-medieval term (referring to the arms of the cross guard, the bar across the hilt).

Most early cross-hilt daggers have a short cross guard, drooping downwards towards the blade, and a crescent-shaped pommel. Some pommels are in fact more suggestive of a pair of horns, very like the Bronze Age "antennae" and "anthropomorphic" daggers of the Hallstatt and La Tène cultures described earlier.

While medieval cross-hilt daggers with "antennae" pommels seem to have gone out of fashion around 1350, versions with the crescent-shaped pommel continued to be popular into the 15th century; a related group of daggers also exhibit pommels wherein the crescent horns have been brought together to form a fully enclosed ring. Cross-hilt daggers also appear after 1350 with pommels shaped like stars, shields or mushrooms. Polygonal and wheel-type pommels were also common. Richer examples were sometimes decorated with the heraldic arms of the owner, in paint, enamel, gold and silver.

Cross-hilt daggers in art are shown being used both overarm, held with the blade projecting downwards from the base of the fist, and underarm with the blade projecting upwards. But as the 14th century progressed, the exclusive practice of overarm, blade-downwards fighting techniques dominated, and this was reflected in the development of dagger hilts. Some daggers are difficult to hold in any position other than blade-downwards. Well-made weapons often express how

TOP Although their cross guard construction was simple, many medieval daggers have sculpted pommels and guards. This 15th-century cross-hilt dagger has a pommel and guard of copper alloy cast into ornate forms.

ABOVE Certain medieval daggers such as this 14th-century English cross-hilt example bear some resemblance to the earlier Hallstatt types, having comparable "antennae" pommels.

they "wish" to be used when handled, and it is certainly the case that many medieval daggers feel natural and comfortable when held with the blade downwards, but become remarkably awkward when reversed.

The baselard

This dagger was developed in the late 13th century for civilian as well as military use. Especially popular in Italy, but also found in English art of the 14th century, the baselard may have originated in Switzerland, in the city of Basel. An English song dating from the early 15th century neatly expresses how widespread the baselard had become by that time:

There is no man worth a leak,
Be he sturdy, be he meek
But he bear a baselard.

The baselard is recognized by its distinctive hilt, which is again reminiscent of the Hallstatt culture. Baselard hilts are usually shaped like a capital "I" or an upended "H", the bottom cross piece often being wider than the one that forms the guard. The tang is cut to the shape of the whole hilt and sandwiched between plates usually of wood, and the whole assembly is then riveted together. Baselard blades could be either single-

The overarm blow

Humans and many of the great apes instinctively employ the overarm blow struck with the base of the fist. In humans this in-built attack pattern is commonly observed in young children who, when sufficiently annoyed, almost always employ what is sometimes called "the beating movement", striking their source of frustration with elbow bent and arm raised at the shoulder, the fist or open hand then being brought down with great force.

Overarm stabbing blows with a downward-pointing blade can be much more powerful than an underarm thrust. Medieval dagger fighting adopted this instinctive defensive movement and combined it with a weapon well suited to that mode of attack. When used correctly by an expert martial artist such as a knight, who learned his fighting skills as a child and perfected them over many years of constant practice, such a technique became horrifyingly effective. Fought at close range, dagger combat would almost without question lead to serious or fatal injury. As one 15th-century German fight master wrote in his manual on martial arts: "Now we come to the dagger; God help us all!"

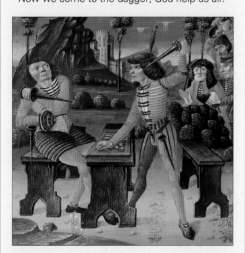

ABOVE This French medieval illustration of a disagreement shows daggers drawn in *The Argument*, from a late 15th-century copy of *The Book of Good Morals* by Jacques le Grant.

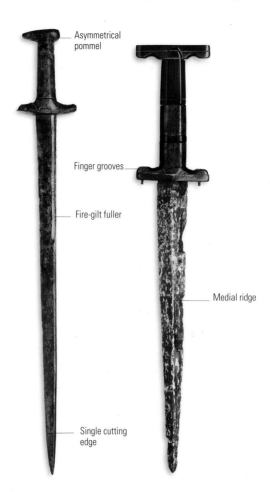

Asymmetrical pommel

Finger grooves

Fire-gilt fuller

Medial ridge

Single cutting edge

ABOVE The I-shaped baselard hilt is seen clearly in these examples. The English type on the left has a long cut-and-thrust blade. The broad-bladed European dagger is an earlier design.

or double-edged, and were generally quite broad. They could also be quite long, more like short swords. The longer forms, however, were not as common as the shorter ones, tending to be more exclusively Swiss.

When worn by warriors, baselards were slung on the right hip, but in civilian life they were usually worn centrally below the waist. From this position the dagger could be swiftly drawn. This method of wearing the dagger could never have avoided the inevitable associations with the erect male genitalia, and from the fashion of wearing the dagger over the groin developed one of the most famous of all European dagger types.

"Trumpet" grip   Single-edged blade

Rondel guard   Tapered thrusting point

The ballock dagger

Medieval culture was full of phallic imagery and it was flaunted rather than hidden. The ballock dagger, which appeared around 1300, was the logical development of the fashion for centrally slung weapons. The hilt was carved out of a single piece of wood and shaped to resemble an erect penis and testicles, with a bulbous pommel and a rounded lobe on either side of the blade in place of the guard. Some examples are very lifelike while others are more stylized.

Despite the apparently unavoidable inspiration for this dagger's distinctive form, the selective

TOP This English ballock dagger, dating from the 15th century, is an early example of the slightly less phallic "trumpet" type, which remained common in the early 16th century.

ABOVE Earlier rondel daggers such as this 14th-century English weapon often have rondels that are reasonably thick; they are frequently made of wood sandwiched between metal disks.

interpretation of the Middle Ages propagated in the 19th century casts a long shadow. The Victorians prudishly renamed these weapons "kidney" daggers, a ridiculous denial of the obvious but one that has survived in usage until very recently.

An important variation of the classic ballock hilt appeared in the 15th century. Here, rather than being surmounted by a bulbous head, the grip flared out almost like a trumpet. The flat-top surface of this flared end was usually capped with a metal disk-shaped plate, often engraved with geometric or vegetal designs. This form never replaced the earlier type, but rather they coexisted well into the 16th century.

The form of blades attached to these hilts varied enormously. The most usual form is triangular in cross-section and tapers consistently from base to point. By the late 14th century, other versions had evolved with square-sectioned tips, to strengthen them for stabbing. Double-edged blades were also fitted to the hilts, although these could never be as wide at the base as those found on baselards, for example; the ballock hilt always required a comparatively narrow blade.

LEFT This detail from *The National Law Codes of Magnus Eriksson* (c.1450) shows the enactment of a violent crime. The distinctive hilt of a ballock dagger can be seen protruding from the victim's chest.

The rondel dagger

It is difficult to be sure when the fourth medieval form of dagger, the rondel dagger, first appeared but it was common by 1350; it may have been known since about 1300. The hilt comprised a grip situated between two disk-shaped "rondels". These gave good protection to the hand while also acting as stops to prevent the hand slipping when a downward stabbing blow was struck. Its use spread over an exceptionally large area, including all of western, central and northern Europe, and even stretching into Poland, and lasted until the mid-16th century.

At first only the guard of rondel-type daggers was disk-shaped, the pommel being polygonal or rounded. But the pommel was soon replaced by another rondel, and the true rondel dagger rapidly assumed an almost universal status as the favourite dagger of knights and men-at-arms. Usually the rondels were strictly circular, although some were faceted, fluted or cusped. The blades tended to be double-edged at first, of flattened diamond section, sometimes even having a central fuller (shallow weight-reducing groove).

After 1400 the rondel dagger evolved considerably. The rondels were made in a number of different ways. Sometimes they were made of wood faced with metal, although more often they were made solely of steel, iron or copper alloy. By the middle of the 15th century, some of the more ornate daggers had rondels built up of multiple disks of different materials – white and yellow metal, but also horn, wood and bone. When smoothed and polished, the edges of these rondels displayed very attractive, multicoloured strata. Sometimes the layering was enhanced with octagonal or hexagonal rather than circular layers.

Rondel dagger grips were constructed in both of the usual ways. Either the tang was made narrow so that it could pass down the centre of the length of the grip to be hammered over on top of the pommel, or it was kept wide and filed into the desired grip shape, with the grip made in two halves, then being riveted onto it on either side.

The basic shape was cylindrical, often widening slightly in the middle and tapering down at either end. Many grip shapes were never more ornate than this simple form. The grip could also be decorated. The more elaborate examples, in particular, tend to be carved or embellished in some way.

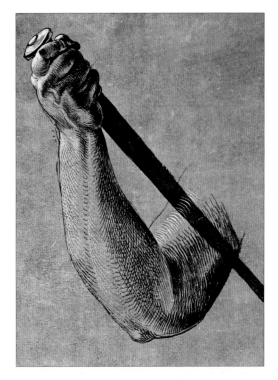

ABOVE This sketch by the German artist Albrecht Dürer is a study of a hand grasping a rondel dagger in the action of plunging it into the chest. It was made in preparation for his painting *The Suicide of Lucretia*, 1518.

Spiral carving was particularly fashionable. The finest examples were made entirely of metal, engraved with intricate designs. Only fragments of these more ornate, knightly rondel daggers survive, although they are depicted frequently on funerary effigies, complete with their exquisitely tooled scabbards. Such elaborate decorated weapons were obvious status symbols.

BELOW Some rondel daggers were extremely ornate. This fragment is all that remains of a once stunning English 15th-century weapon, probably that of a knight. The hilt was entirely fire-gilt (gilded with a heated mix of gold and mercury) and incised with geometric patterns.

Daggers of the Renaissance

Each of the medieval dagger types remained in use throughout the 16th and into the 17th century. Some remained largely unchanged, while others evolved according to more restricted regional fashions. Although in the 16th century the Renaissance dagger was still an important military weapon, it was becoming more common in everyday life and was just as likely to be drawn in a royal palace or urban back alley as on the battlefield.

The 1500s were the golden age of the dagger in Europe. During this century aristocratic fashions in clothes and behaviour became more decadent and extravagant. Nobles dripped with jewels and precious stones, their clothing intricately constructed using many different materials. Individuality had become

LEFT Renaissance daggers were often glamorous fashion accessories, as shown by this south German cross-hilt dagger with a curved blade and hilt with gold, gemstones and cameos.

much more important than it ever had been before, and rich people were anxious to express themselves as individuals through material display. With fine clothes went fine weapons, and the dagger was ever-present, not just as a tool and a weapon but now also as an indispensable fashion accessory.

The assassin's choice

The dagger had been a weapon favoured by assassins since ancient times because its small size made it easy to hide. If discovered its presence could be easily explained, since a knife was routinely carried by most people. During the Renaissance, assassination became more common, particularly in the ruthless political environment of the time. Many rulers and statesmen fell under plunging dagger blades.

One case, which occurred in 1537, was that of Alessandro de' Medici, Duke of Florence, who was lured away from his bodyguards by the temptation of a sexual encounter with the beautiful sister of Lorenzino de' Medici ("Bad Lorenzino"), a distant cousin. Once alone, Alessandro was ambushed and stabbed to death by Lorenzino, who later claimed that he had killed Alessandro for the sake of the Florentine Republic, comparing his deed to Brutus' murder of Julius Caesar. Lorenzino was himself stabbed to death in Venice a year later.

ABOVE The dagger was the constant companion of the Renaissance nobleman. Hans Holbein's 1534 portrait of Charles de Solier, the French envoy at the court of Henry VIII, shows the lord with a fine gilded dagger.

RIGHT A number of Renaissance rulers met a grisly end on the point of an assassin's dagger. In 1589 King Henry III of France was stabbed to death by a Dominican friar, who was then killed by the royal guard.

The landsknecht daggers

The modern term "landsknecht" dagger actually refers to three quite different forms, and is somewhat misleading in any case. The Landsknechts were predominantly German, Swiss and Flemish mercenaries who took part in almost every military campaign of the 16th century and were famous for their flamboyant "puffed and slashed" clothing.

Only the first type of so-called landsknecht dagger can be directly associated with these fierce professional soldiers. Both the two-handed great sword and smaller arming sword, or katzbalger, of the Landsknecht have a characteristic form of guard – the long arms are bent into a nearly circular S-shape. This first class of landsknecht dagger has a guard similarly formed, and its pommel also takes the same flaring form found on surviving katzbalgers. The blade is usually double-edged and tapered evenly from guard to point.

Unlike the first type, there is no stylistic similarity between the second type and the other characteristic landsknecht weapons familiar from pictorial representations. It may be an offshoot of the rondel dagger. One of its defining features is a grip that flares, trumpet-like, towards the pommel, the end of which is covered either with a flat metal disk or a domed plate. The guard is usually formed of a small plate cut into three lobes (rounded projections), which bend down towards the blade like drooping leaves. The length of the scabbard is divided by groups of two or three rings,

wider than the scabbard itself. On finer examples, some or all of the rings are repeatedly sawn vertically, giving the scabbard an appearance in keeping with the elaborate puffed and slashed clothing of the time.

The third type of dagger in this group is essentially a type of cross-hilt dagger. It is also one of the earliest forms to carry a side ring, placed centrally on the outside of the guard to give added protection to the knuckles. This type is also called a Saxon dagger, as many of them were made in eastern parts of the German Empire. The pommels of these Saxon daggers are usually pear-shaped or conical and often capped with a silver plate. Both this plate and the guard are frequently engraved with floral designs, and the grip is wrapped with fine twisted wire. Saxon dagger scabbards often have silver mounts engraved to match the pommel cap (decorative covering) and guard.

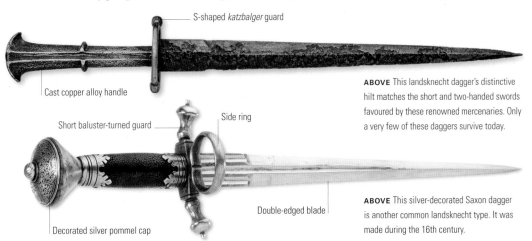

S-shaped *katzbalger* guard

Cast copper alloy handle

ABOVE This landsknecht dagger's distinctive hilt matches the short and two-handed swords favoured by these renowned mercenaries. Only a very few of these daggers survive today.

Short baluster-turned guard

Side ring

Double-edged blade

Decorated silver pommel cap

ABOVE This silver-decorated Saxon dagger is another common landsknecht type. It was made during the 16th century.

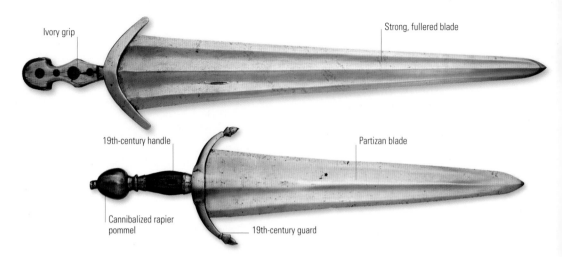

Ivory grip

Strong, fullered blade

19th-century handle

Partizan blade

Cannibalized rapier pommel

19th-century guard

TOP Small cinquedeas are easily classified as daggers, but many have blade lengths closer to short swords. They make effective concussive cut-and-thrust weapons, unlike practically all forms of dagger.

ABOVE Because of their close associations with the Renaissance, cinquedeas were often copied in the 19th century. This fake was built using a staff weapon blade and various other sword hilt parts.

The cinquedea

This type of large Italian dagger is often thought to have gained its name because its extreme width at the guard is about as wide as a man's hand. Since the Italian for "five fingers" is *cinque diti*, this is not an entirely unreasonable assumption. But it is probably not correct. An early 17th-century definition of a cinquedea refers to a Venetian dagger that was five fingers long, not five fingers wide, and the term itself appears not to have been in use earlier than the late 16th century, some time after the supposed cinquedea fell out of fashion. Despite the fact that the use of the term is probably not consistent with the weapon's original historical context, roughly 1450–1520, its present meaning is now universally understood.

The cinquedea was a weapon of high status. The double-edged blade, very wide at the guard, tapered steeply to the point, took the form of a long isosceles triangle and was forged with a series of ridges running down the length of the blade. Two parallel ridges were normally located near the point, these increasing to three in the middle of the blade, with a final set of four at

RIGHT The cinquedea may have been based on weapons of the ancient world such as this Bronze Age Etruscan dagger. Renaissance artists drew much inspiration from ancient Greek and Roman art.

the base. By 1500, cinquedea blades were being elaborately decorated with etched Neo-classical designs or scenes from ancient Greco-Roman myths, as well as with fire gilding and even heat blueing (the application of controlled heat).

The cinquedea hilt was just as distinctive as its blade. The guard was formed into a graceful arch, the arms curving downwards towards the blade, and was often drawn to a point in the centre. Because of the extreme width of the base of the blade, only the tips of the arms extended beyond its edges. The guard was also often etched with twisting vines or foliated scrolls. The ergonomic grip, usually plated with bone or ivory, was scooped out on either side to produce recesses for the fingers on both sides of a central swelling. The tubular rivets holding the ivory or bone plates to the tang were generally filled in with inserts beautifully pierced with geometric designs. The rounded pommel, made in one piece with the grip, was usually covered with a piece of gilded metal.

It is tempting to suggest that the cinquedea was just one of the many products of the infatuation with classical art and culture that characterized the Renaissance Period. The cinquedea certainly resembles some types of wide-bladed Bronze Age dagger. Perhaps the Italian dagger is a direct emulation by Renaissance smiths of an ancient design.

RIGHT Ear daggers appear in several Renaissance portraits, including this one of King Edward VI of England (1537–1553).

The ear dagger

Daggers of eared form may have appeared as early as the 14th century, but their greatest period of popularity occurred during the first half of the 16th century. The ear dagger probably originated in Spain, a result of the influence of Islamic design on the tastes of the Iberian nobility. Eared daggers were being made in Persia during the Bronze Age, and the design remained popular for both sword and dagger hilts throughout the Middle East, or "Levant" as the region was called by Renaissance Europeans. Indeed, the ear dagger was referred to in Italy as *alla Levantina*, a term that clearly demonstrates the perceived origin of the design.

The ears of the hilt are usually formed as extensions of the very thick tang, which have been hammered out to create the disk-shaped "ears" diverging at sharp angles from the bottom of the grip. The ears were generally faced with plates of ivory, horn or bone. The grip is generally quite narrow, with a slight central swelling. While the earliest ear daggers appear to have had guards not unlike those on rondel daggers, by the 16th century the guard had shrunk to little more than a small anvil or block-shaped spacer, which was plated with the same organic material as the grip and ears.

Ear-dagger blades are invariably double-edged, one edge often beginning lower on the ricasso (the flattened square of blade near the guard) than the other, producing an odd but pleasing offset effect. Some also have specially thickened stabbing points.

RIGHT Ear daggers appear in several Renaissance portraits, including this one of King Edward VI of England (1537–1553).

The ricasso, exposed sides of the tang and area between the ears are sometimes damascened (woven) in gold. One of the most famous makers of ear daggers was Diego de Çaias, a Spanish maker of high-quality weapons in the 1530s and 1540s who was patronized by Francis I of France and Henry VIII of England.

BELOW Ear daggers are like no other form of European dagger, displaying a distinct Middle Eastern inspiration. This early 16th-century example is Italian, although many others were made in Spain.

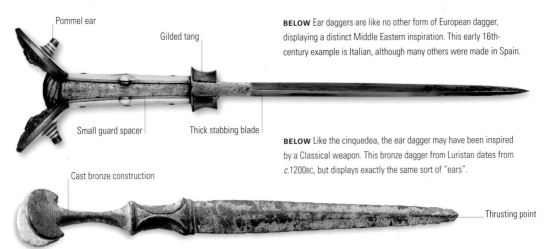

Pommel ear

Gilded tang

Small guard spacer

Thick stabbing blade

Cast bronze construction

BELOW Like the cinquedea, the ear dagger may have been inspired by a Classical weapon. This bronze dagger from Luristan dates from c.1200BC, but displays exactly the same sort of "ears".

Thrusting point

Metal pommel-plate

Wooden rondel guard

Medieval daggers of the 16th century

In addition to the ear dagger, other forms of dagger that had developed during the Middle Ages continued to be made throughout the 16th century. The most common types, prevalent throughout Europe, were cross-hilt daggers. Smaller versions continued to be

ABOVE Despite the fact that the production of rondel daggers seems to have declined quickly after 1500, older weapons such as this late-medieval example, would have remained in use for much longer.

carried for general last-ditch self-defence by both armoured warriors and by civilians, while larger forms had begun to be incorporated into the latest fencing styles by the middle of the century. Ballock daggers also continued to be made in both of their distinctive forms. The grips were still made primarily in wood, although ivory and even agate examples are known. Later ballock dagger blades tend to be very narrow and double-edged, although in some cases they are little more than four-sided spikes.

Rondel daggers, so ubiquitous during the 14th and 15th centuries, seem to have quickly fallen out of favour in the 16th century, either evolving into new forms such as certain of the landsknecht dagger types, or disappearing altogether.

"Swiss" and "Holbein" daggers

Another medieval dagger that developed into a new and distinct form was the baselard. The essential form of what became the 16th-century "Swiss" dagger appeared in the last 20 years or so of the 15th century, when the I-shaped hilt of the baselard developed inward-curving arms, strengthened with metal sleeves, at either end of the grip. The blade of the short-sword type of "Swiss" baselard was shortened to dagger length, but unusually retained its greater width and displayed a slight leaf shape. Apart from a single fuller, "Swiss" dagger blades were left entirely plain. Unlike the earlier baselard, on which the arms of the hilt were formed by the tang over which were laid plates of wood, the hilt of the 16th-century "Swiss" dagger was carved from a single

LEFT The "wound man" figure illustrated common injuries in Renaissance surgical texts. This German version from 1528 includes rondel dagger and knife stab wounds to the abdomen, face and head.

RIGHT In addition to the T-shaped hilt and ornate scabbard, the typical "Swiss" dagger also included a byknife and awl. Decorated to match the scabbard, these fitted into special sleeves in the outer side.

piece of hardwood, the sides of the grip were faceted and the centre was drilled out for the insertion of the narrow tang.

"Swiss" daggers are perhaps most famous for their very elaborate scabbards. The earliest examples were made of wood covered in leather, with a simple metal locket (fitting at the mouth of the scabbard) and chape (fitting at the tip of the scabbard). But after 1510, the metal mounts developed rapidly until the whole front of the scabbard was covered in silver or gilt. This decorative metal sleeve was cast with elaborate, pierced designs in relief, which were often engraved as well to add an additional level of detail.

A number of famous Swiss artists created designs for the decoration of these dagger sleeves, including Urs Graf, Heinrich Aldegrever and Hans Holbein the Younger. These designs usually involved Biblical or mythological scenes. One of Holbein's designs, for which the original drawings survive, depicted the Dance of Death, a popular allegory that expressed the universal nature of death. Death is portrayed as a re-animated skeleton, which dances with people from all levels of society. This design became so common that these weapons are often called "Holbein" daggers.

RIGHT In addition to the T-shaped hilt and ornate scabbard, the typical "Swiss" dagger also included a byknife and awl. Decorated to match the scabbard, these fitted into special sleeves in the outer side.

Byknives

Wooden grip

Foliate scabbard chape

Double-edged blade

ABOVE AND BELOW A number of Renaissance artists drew designs for fine weapons. These illustrations from a book on historical dress and decorations, published in 1843, show 16th-century ornamental weapon designs by Hans Holbein.

Daggers for the Renaissance duel

The dagger forms had diversified in the 14th and 15th centuries, but the fighting methods that employed them had not changed very much by the 1500s – these same basic rondel, ballock and cross-hilted weapons continued to be drawn as a last resort on the battlefield and in daily life. But the new Renaissance fashion for civilian swordmanship also led to new more specialized daggers, intended to be used exclusively as "defencing" weapons.

Renaissance society was strongly influenced by the rise of a new non-noble class who, despite their lack of aristocratic status, were often wealthy and upwardly mobile. Now it was not just the nobility who could afford luxuries such as fine clothes and weapons. The middle class was just as likely as the aristocracy (if not more so) to want to follow the latest fashions and to have the means to do so. They quickly appropriated a number of the traditional status symbols that in the past had always been exclusive to the nobility.

ABOVE Once the art of fighting with the rapier and dagger had become fashionable, weapons makers began producing fine sets with matching decoration. This exceptional Italian set, made in *c*.1600, features sumptuous inlaid and relief ornament.

LEFT The expensively decorated rapier and dagger set was an integral part of a gentleman's rich attire, as can be seen in Nicolas Neufchatel's portrait of Hieronimus Koler (1528–1573).

The sword enters civilian life

One of the most important new symbols of social status adopted by the *nouveau riche* was the sword. In the Medieval Period the sword had been a knightly weapon; it was expensive and its use required many years of dedicated practice. More importantly, the use of the sword in dealing with personal grievances – through trial by combat – was a right restricted to the nobility. By the mid-16th century, most non-noble gentlemen had adopted the sword as a sign of their own economic "nobility". More importantly, they began to wear it at all times. This was a new development; before the 16th century the sword

was never worn with civilian dress except when travelling. This change in the acceptance of weapons in society was observed by the 16th-century chronicler Claude Haton, leading him to write, of the year 1555: "There is no mother's son at this time who did not carry a sword or a dagger."

The duel

These new civilian swords brought with them a perceived right to address personal grievances and disagreements through violence; with weapons close to hand they were more easily drawn in anger, and quickly became a first reaction rather than a last resort. But the autonomous right to settle personal disputes with violence was a right restricted to the aristocracy. This made it a luxury that the middle class wanted. The ancient practice of judicial combat was seized upon by fashionable society and twisted into the private duel, fought anywhere and at any time, often for the most trivial reasons.

Duelling quickly became a craze. Hundreds and then thousands of men were killed each year during the second half of the 16th century, all in supposed "affairs of honour". These disputes could be caused by a verbal slight, physical altercation or even an insulting glance. Sir Walter Raleigh – the famous Elizabethan explorer who established one of the earliest American colonies at Roanoke Island in what is today North Carolina – wrote earnestly that "to give the lie deserves no less than stabbin". It was this brutal subculture that led to a number of key innovations in the design and use of edged weapons.

ABOVE The weapons in legal judicial duels were often the sword and shield, as in this trial by combat fought in Paris in 1547. For impromptu, illegal combats the inconvenient shield was supplanted by the dagger.

BELOW Sometimes there is more to a rapier and dagger set than meets the eye. This unique set, by Tobias Reichel of Dresden, c.1610, includes tiny timepieces hidden in the pommels.

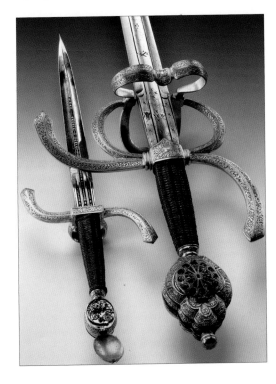

Combat with rapier and dagger

Once the sword was introduced into this new civilian fighting environment, it began to change. Plate armour was not worn in daily life, and so swords began to be designed especially to take on vulnerable but quicker opponents. The use of the thrust became much more important, and sword blades became longer and longer, as the control of distance and the ability to kill an enemy without getting too close became central to civilian fighting styles. By the second half of the 16th century, the civilian sword had evolved into something entirely unlike its military counterpart. The blade was much longer, narrower and thickened down its spine so that it was as ridged as possible, and the hilt – which now had to protect the unarmoured hand – had a number of additional sweeping bars and ring guards added to it. This non-military sword was called *espada ropera* in Spanish, "sword of the robe", or a sword to be worn with civilian clothing. The French called it *épée rapière*, which in turn became the English "rapier".

We tend these days to think of the rapier as a feather-light weapon, the "flashing blade" of the swashbuckling heroes of the silver screen. But this is not really true. Because of their very great length – which often exceeded 1m (3.3ft) or more – and their thickened spines, most rapiers were actually very blade-heavy and somewhat ungainly in the hand.

ABOVE Key targets in rapier and dagger combat were the face and throat. A skilled swordsman could parry and attack at the same time, as shown in this early 17th-century manual by Jacques Callot (*c.*1592–1635).

BELOW Some fencing daggers had special features, such as the long down-curving guards of this Saxon dagger dating to about 1610.

The rapier was an excellent attacking weapon, but a duellist had difficulty bringing it back quickly to defend his body with a parry or blocking move. In order to attack and defend as rapidly as possible, the civilian duellist required a companion weapon. The most common was the shield, which allowed the fighter to defend himself with his left arm while attacking with his right. But shields were not convenient to carry around in daily life. An alternative was found in a weapon that people were already carrying around with them – the dagger.

By the middle of the 16th century, the dagger had become an indispensable self-defence, or "fencing", tool. The art of rapier and dagger fighting was born. The dagger was held in the left hand and used to ward off incoming attacks, leaving the rapier free to deliver lethal thrusts to the opponent's face, throat and body. The most skilled swordsman could defend himself with the dagger and attack with the rapier in a single movement. The dagger could also be used to stab the opponent if he came too close.

The *Duel des Mignons*: the advantages of a dagger

One very famous duel was fought in Paris on 27 April 1578, during the reign of Henry III (*r.*1574–89). The *mignons* (French for "favourites") were a group of obsequious young noblemen with whom the French king surrounded himself. They were known for their effeminate manners and dress, long hair and decadent, shallow lifestyle, and they became deeply unpopular with the French people. At the time of the duel, the French Court had become polarized into factions, one side supporting the king and the other side supporting his bitter rival, the Duc de Guise, a lord who enjoyed widespread popularity. The disagreement that formed the basis for the duel was said to have involved certain courtly ladies, although this may have only been a pretext.

The duel was fought between the courtiers Jacques de Quélus, who supported the king, and Charles de Balzac, Baron d'Entragues, a close ally of the Duc de Guise. Each man brought with him two companions, or seconds, and a bloody three-on-three encounter followed. One second on each side was killed outright. D'Entragues' other second died of his wounds the next day, while Quélus' other second survived with a serious head injury. The main combatants were both severely wounded. D'Entragues perhaps could be considered the victor, since he survived. Quélus suffered 19 wounds and took 33 days to die in terrible agony.

Before he died Quélus complained that the duel had been unfair, for while he had fought only with his rapier, d'Entragues had been armed with a dagger as well as his rapier. D'Entragues is said to have responded: "So much the worse for him; he ought not to have been such a fool as to have left his dagger at home."

BELOW The famous *Duel des Mignons* which was fought in Paris on 27 April 1578 during the reign of Henry III, as imagined by the 19th-century historical artist Cesare-Auguste Detti, *c.*1847.

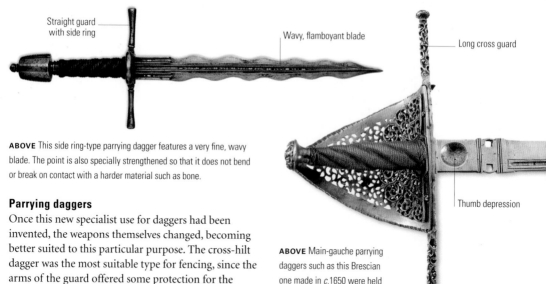

Straight guard with side ring

Wavy, flamboyant blade

Long cross guard

Thumb depression

ABOVE This side ring-type parrying dagger features a very fine, wavy blade. The point is also specially strengthened so that it does not bend or break on contact with a harder material such as bone.

Parrying daggers

Once this new specialist use for daggers had been invented, the weapons themselves changed, becoming better suited to this particular purpose. The cross-hilt dagger was the most suitable type for fencing, since the arms of the guard offered some protection for the hand. To provide even more protection, a simple ring of metal was added to the outside of the guard. The arms of the guard were also lengthened and were often curved down towards the blade. This provided the duellist with the opportunity to ensnare his opponent's blade. If a duellist parried an attack with the lower part of his dagger blade and gave a swift twist of his wrist, his opponent's blade might become trapped between his own blade and one of the arms of the guard. His opponent's weapon might remain ensnared only for a moment, but that moment could afford the duellist the opening he required to strike a killing blow.

ABOVE Main-gauche parrying daggers such as this Brescian one made in c.1650 were held in the left hand with the thumb placed on the base of the blade.

Because of the way in which parrying daggers were used in conjunction with the rapier, they are today often called "left-hand daggers". Finer examples were made in sets with matching rapiers; sometimes the mounts and fittings of the sword belt were also decorated in the same way.

The blade of the parrying dagger tended to be somewhat longer than that of most other daggers of the time, generally being 30–45cm (12–18in) long. It was double-edged with a specially thickened ricasso that helped it resist the shock of repeated blows struck against enemy swords. It usually had a strong diamond-shaped cross-section and an even taper from guard to point. The rear side of the ricasso usually had an oval depression shaped into it. When the duellist held his dagger so that the knuckles were protected by the side ring, he would usually place his thumb on the ricasso to strengthen his parrying grip; this depression gave him better purchase on the weapon. Towards the end of the 16th century the blades of parrying daggers became more ornate and more flamboyant. They were often filed with very deep ridges and grooves running down their whole lengths. The troughs between the

LEFT *To the Death: A Sword and Dagger Fight Wherein One Hand Beats Cold Death Aside While The Other Sends It Back.* The full title of this 19th-century imagining of a rapier and dagger combat sums up the style.

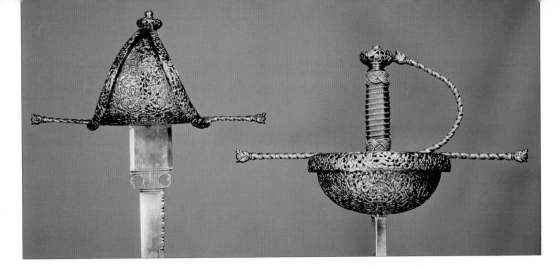

ridges were frequently pierced with groups of minuscule round, square or diamond-shaped holes. Cutting deep grooves into the blade, as well as punching large numbers of tiny holes into it, reduced its weight very significantly, and it was a useful way of fine-tuning the balance of the weapon without compromising its strength or rigidity. Some blades were also given wavy edges, producing an impressive and perhaps intimidating visual effect.

Main-gauche daggers

The name of these daggers translates from the French as "left hand". Since the 19th century, English-speaking collectors have, however, used the term to refer specifically to a type of 17th-century parrying dagger that appeared in Spain and Spanish-held parts of the Low Countries and Italy. This weapon is most easily recognized by the curved, usually triangular knuckle guard extending over the hilt, the wide end of which attaches to the guard while the narrow point is affixed to the pommel. The arms of the guard are almost always very long, much longer than those found on any other form of dagger, and usually carry knob-like terminals. Main-gauche dagger pommels normally take the form of a flattened sphere, although some pommels are pear-shaped.

The blades are just as distinctive as the hilts. Some are long, narrow and double-edged, while others are single-edged and wider. The most common blade form, however, is made up of a very wide ricasso, usually pierced with a pair of large holes or sword-catching slots at the top, which then modulates into a narrow, sharply tapered section that forms the main body of the blade. In most cases these upper sections

are single-edged along the lower half of their lengths, and double-edged on the top half to the point. The back of the lower section is very often decorated with file-work along the back; similar decoration is also very often found on both edges of the ricasso section.

Cut-out ricasso

Knuckle guard

ABOVE The most distinctive feature of the typical main-gauche dagger is the triangular knuckle guard, which is generally decorated with chiselling as illustrated on this Brescian example, c.1650.

17th- and 18th-century daggers

Despite the continuing popularity of combat with both rapier and parrying dagger in Spain and Italy after 1600, the practice suffered a general decline elsewhere in Europe. Swords became lighter, smaller and quicker to deploy, and as methods of fighting with the sword alone became dominant, the dagger quickly fell out of use. Consequently, the wearing of the dagger as a fashion statement also disappeared in most places.

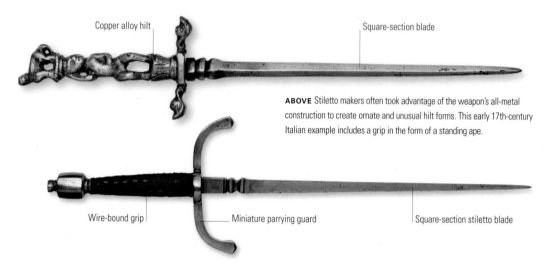

Copper alloy hilt

Square-section blade

ABOVE Stiletto makers often took advantage of the weapon's all-metal construction to create ornate and unusual hilt forms. This early 17th-century Italian example includes a grip in the form of a standing ape.

Wire-bound grip

Miniature parrying guard

Square-section stiletto blade

The elegant small sword was adopted throughout Europe almost as soon as it appeared. As well as being a brutally effective duelling weapon, its small size made it easy to carry, and its form was perfectly in tune with the mannered extravagance of the contemporary trends in art, clothing and behaviour. The carrying of daggers began to be seen as conservative or even uncivilized. By the late 17th century, daggers were distinctly out of date, surviving only as a form of localized traditionalism.

The stiletto

In the early 1600s a diminutive form of the ring-hilted parrying dagger appeared. Although it was designed in the same way as its larger cousin, with a straight or dropping cross guard and a side ring, this little weapon was too small to be used for fencing. The blade had been reduced to little more than a three- or four-sided needle of steel, and the stiletto was the result. The typical stiletto, or "stylet", of the 17th century was a very small, all-metal weapon usually measuring

ABOVE The stiletto finds its earliest origins in miniaturized parrying daggers such as this example. They were made as elegant fashion items but never meant to be used in sword fights.

20–23cm (8–9in) long. The rectangular- or triangular-section blade was very narrow, had no cutting edges and tapered to an extremely sharp point. Most of the best surviving examples are Italian and are usually exquisite demonstrations of steel cutting and chiselling. The hilt echoed the pervading fashions in architecture; the arms of the guard, grip and pommel were usually baluster-turned into undulating vase-like or bulbous shapes, and terminated in or incorporated rounded buttons, spheres and ovoid forms; the spaces between them were sometimes faceted, tapered or decorated with foliate designs in relief. Occasionally the grip and/or pommel were sculpted into the shapes of human or animal figures.

One variation was the larger gunner's stiletto. These military weapons had much longer blades, generally measuring 30–50cm (12–20in). The grip was usually

made of horn, while the steel guard and pommel were often blued or blackened. The most characteristic aspect of the gunner's stiletto was the numbering on the blade. The incremental sequence varies but is most commonly 1, 3, 6, 9, 12, 14, 16, 20, 30, 40, 50, 60, 90, 100, 120. Between each number was engraved a line, which made the blade look something like a ruler.

The numbers represent the most widely used Italian artillery calibres of the time. It is therefore reasonable to assume that these daggers might originally have been designed as tools that artillerymen could use to measure the bore of a cannon, or the diameter of a cannon ball; the number corresponding to the closest line then indicated the correct weight of the ball. However, most of the surviving examples differ in the arrangement of the lines in relation to the numbering, so most would never have worked as instruments for weight calculation. They are therefore purely conventional, probably made for artillerymen as some kind of badge or status symbol. They had an impressive scientific appearance, and that was evidently more highly valued than any genuine functionality.

English cross-hilt daggers

Another of the very few distinctively 17th-century daggers appeared in England during the very early 1600s and remained popular there until at least 1675. The cross hilt of this form was comprised of a rectangular block supporting baluster-turned arms, or quillons, and usually displaying the typical English taste for foliate ornamentation in relief, which on finer examples was sometimes also encrusted in silver. Daggers of this form had no pommel. The hardwood, generally fluted grip simply swelled at the end, echoing the form of earlier ballock daggers.

The narrow blade of the 17th-century English dagger was split into three areas: a short, unsharpened ricasso of rectangular section; a middle cutting area of triangular section having a single sharpened edge, the back being characteristically serrated like a saw; and a reinforced stabbing point of diamond section. The ricasso and mid-section are often etched with heads in profile, scrolling vegetation and mottos, and many examples are also dated.

BELOW English daggers of the 17th century are easily recognized by their characteristic hilts and heavily etched blades, many of which are dated like this example, which is marked 1628.

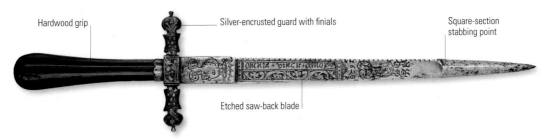

Hardwood grip | Silver-encrusted guard with finials | Square-section stabbing point

Etched saw-back blade

RIGHT Typical "Mediterranean" dirks such as this one made in the second half of the 18th century in Liguria, northwestern Italy, have very wide bases waisting into narrow tangs.

Locket

Chape

Grooved handle

Ricasso decorated with rooster

Double fuller

"Mediterranean" dirks

A third important group of daggers appeared along the north coast of the Mediterranean in the mid-1600s. The weapons, collectively referred to as "Mediterranean" dirks, were actually made in a wide range of sizes and display an extraordinary variety of ornament.

The one-piece handle, made of wood, ivory or horn, is always bored through its centre to accept the narrow tang of the blade; the end is capped with metal, often silver, and the end of the tang peened (hammered) over to secure the blade. The handle in most cases also swells slightly away from the blade. "Mediterranean" dirks almost never have any form of guard. The top of the handle is generally covered with a metal sleeve or protective band at the bottom of the hilt called a

ferrule, which modulates upwards into the blade via a short post, called the root of the blade. This is usually turned or faceted in a similar manner to, although stouter than, the balustered forms found on stilettos of the same period.

"Mediterranean" dirks carry either single- or double-edged blades. The single-edged types usually have a deep, unsharpened section called a choil dropping down from the handle in the manner of most kitchen knives. Usually the choil is straight, although in some cases it takes a graceful recurved line. The double-edged Mediterranean blade resembles a broad spearhead, with rounded shoulders at the base. Generally the edges of both types do not taper in straight lines but rather bulge slightly like a very

Braided leather sheath

Claw handle

Sheath fringe

ABOVE This Native American fighting knife incorporates a European "butcher" knife blade of the 18th or early 19th century, having a straight unsharpened back and curved cutting edge.

Scalping

One practice closely associated with the darker aspects of the frontier experience in North America during the 17th, 18th and 19th centuries was scalping. This brutal exercise in mutilation involved the victim being pinned down to the ground on his or her chest, with one of the attacker's knees or feet placed between the shoulder blades. The head was yanked up by the hair and a deep incision cut all the way around the hairline with a long fighting knife. A swift tug on the handful of hair tore the skin from the skull like a bloody rag.

The scalping of dead enemies was a rare form of trophy-taking in battle among certain Native American tribes before the arrival of Europeans. It had also been practised intermittently in Europe for thousands of years. But it was encouraged on an unprecedented scale in North America after the arrival of European colonists, and was practised by white men as well as native peoples, on living as well as dead victims. In the late 17th century, scalping was endorsed by both sides during the Anglo-French conflicts that played out for nearly 100 years across what is now the United States

and Canada. The French began paying for British scalps in the 1680s, and the British reciprocated by offering as much as £100 (about £8,000 today) for French and Indian scalps in the 1690s.

RIGHT This French 18th-century lithograph depicts an Iroquois warrior scalping a bound captive. He is in the process of pulling the scalp off while applying pressure with his right foot.

---

shallow arch. Most single-edged varieties are also sharpened on the top a few centimetres off the back. Most good examples are decorated at the base of the blade with relief ornament, engraving and piercings.

American "butcher" and "scalping" knives

The fighting knives carried on the North American frontier were quite different from the ornate daggers made in Europe, being plainer, cruder and designed to work well for a much wider range of uses – fighting men and wild animals but also undertaking the daily tasks associated with living in the forests and mountains of the frontier. The large size of these knives can be inferred from descriptions of soldiers joining the American Army in 1775, who, we are told, carried "butcher" or "scalping" knives. Because they were

simply made by local craftsmen according to individual preference, they are almost impossible to date precisely, and very little else can be said about them for certain.

Despite these difficulties, it is possible to identify two basic knife forms typically carried by Americans in the 18th century. One was essentially a cross-hilt dagger with a stout double-edged blade, short guard and wooden grip that was simply tapped in place around the tang. The second was single-edged, usually with a slight curve to the back and a shallow choil above the grip. As with contemporary "Mediterranean" dirks, these American weapons looked very much like utilitarian knives, and undoubtedly this similarity led to them being described as "butcher" knives. Given the brutal use to which these knives were put, by all sides in the North American wars, it is an apt description.

Scottish dirks

The 17th century brought with it a rapid decline in the evolution and use of traditional daggers in most parts of Europe. But in a few more isolated areas, the practice of wearing and fighting with the dagger continued unabated. In northern Europe the persistent development of the essentially medieval weapon is most noticeable in Scotland, where, sometime in the 17th century, one of the most iconic daggers of all time appeared.

The four important members of the medieval family of daggers experienced quite divergent later histories. The basic cross-hilted dagger multiplied into a number of more specialized forms in the 16th and 17th centuries, including the assorted forms of parrying dagger, stiletto and English dagger of the 1600s. The baselard was transformed into the classic "Swiss" dagger before disappearing by 1600. The rondel dagger, which had been such an essential part of the armoured warrior's arsenal, became scarcer as warfare became modernized and hand-to-hand combat between men-at-arms declined. The last of the great medieval dagger forms, the ballock, died out everywhere in Europe except in Scotland, where it evolved into two important new forms.

The dudgeon dagger

In the first quarter of the 17th century the earlier of the two Scottish derivatives of the medieval ballock dagger appeared in Lowland Scotland. It was generally called a "dagger of dudgeon" or simply "dudgeon

ABOVE This early 17th-century dudgeon dagger shows clearly its descent from earlier ballock daggers of the 15th and 16th centuries. It retains its cutting edges, but the thick spine makes it primarily a stabbing weapon.

dagger". The 17th-century term "dudgeon" referred to the hardwood that was used to fashion the hilt. A single piece of hardwood, most commonly boxwood but also ebony, ivy root and others, was carved into a particular interpretation of the distinctive ballock hilt design. The lobes below the base of the blade were generally quite small and much less bulbous than their medieval forebears, and were often decorated with little copper-alloy or silver rosettes on the top of each lobe. These rosettes were actually washers supporting rivets that held in place a crescent-shaped iron or steel spacer seated on the base of the blade between it and the top of the hilt. The grip swelled towards its top end, but again not in so obvious a

BELOW Dudgeon daggers display very fine etched decoration on their blades, frequently involving scrolling foliage as seen here.

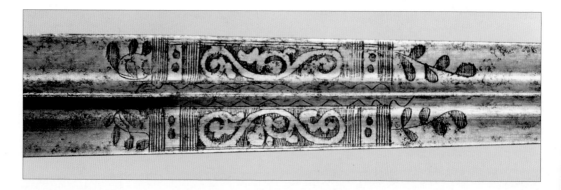

Etched and
gilt blade

Dudgeon handle

Metal chape

Open-work
locket

ABOVE This very fine dudgeon dagger in a private collection may have belonged to François Ravaillac, murderer of King Henry IV of France. It is undoubtedly Scottish; the scabbard appears to be later European work.

way as earlier forms of ballock dagger. The grip was usually faceted and bored out for the tang of the blade; the end of the tang, where it protruded from the top of the grip, was generally covered with a metal button.

The long, narrow blade is the most instantly recognizable part of the dudgeon dagger, for despite

LEFT This portrait of François Ravaillac commemorates him as the royal assassin of Henry IV. The artist has chosen to depict him grasping a dudgeon dagger with a wavy, flamboyant blade.

each of the surviving examples being unique, the blades are all obviously of a type. They taper evenly from base to point and are almost always of a strong diamond (almost square) section, the sides being deeply hollow-ground. Occasionally this shaping is taken to an extreme degree, producing a blade that is essentially flat but which carries a very thick medial ridge. Sometimes the section is varied within zones along the length of the blade; one of these multi-section blades might begin with a typical rectangular-section ricasso, modulating to a hollow-ground diamond-section zone a few centimetres or so up the blade, then giving way to a single-edged area and finally ending with a square-section stabbing point.

Dudgeon dagger blades are always etched with scrolling vines and leafy patterns. Some also carry mottos or invocations. Some are dated, the dates always falling between 1600 and 1625, although it is certain that they were fashionable for a longer period. In 1635 the soldier, politician and writer Sir William Brereton wrote that on a visit to Edinburgh he bought "a dudgeon-hafted dagger … gilt". All known dudgeon dagger blades are (or were) fire-gilt over their entire surfaces, the gold combining with the etching to give the weapons a very rich appearance.

Several other notable figures in the 17th century owned dudgeon daggers. One is said to have belonged to François Ravaillac (1578–1610), the Catholic zealot who stabbed to death King Henry IV of France (1553–1610). Another was confiscated from Colonel Thomas Blood (1618–1680) after his failed attempt to steal the Crown Jewels of England in 1671.

Ivory hilt Cut-down sword blade Double-fullered blade

The Highland dirk

The success of the dudgeon dagger kept the ballock dagger alive in Scotland after it had vanished everywhere else in Europe. While the dudgeon dagger was primarily carried in the Lowlands, as well as finding its way to a limited degree to England and the Continent, it may also have made an impression on the Gaelic-speaking Highlanders in the northwest of Scotland. The Highlanders still fought in an essentially medieval way, with swords, round shields and staff weapons. It may not have been long before a few dudgeon daggers fell into the hands of some of the richer clan warriors. Copies were made bigger and longer, better suited to use on the battlefield. By 1650 the Highland dirk had been created.

A number of features connect the Highland dirk and the earlier dudgeon dagger. Highland craftsmen generally used their own type of "dudgeon", namely bogwood, for the construction of the hilt. Bogwood was taken from ancient trees that had been submerged in the local peat bogs for thousands of years. The wood that was used to make dirk hilts, usually oak, was partially fossilized and consequently very hard – perfect for the purpose and easily accessible.

Dirk hilts were also cast in solid brass or, more rarely, carved in bone. They also generally displayed the spacers between blade and hilt observed on the earlier

TOP The bogwood hilts of Highland dirks like this one from around 1740 were often decorated with brass plaques or plates. Sometimes the whole hilt would be made of solid brass.

ABOVE This 18th-century dirk is fitted with a less common type of hilt, carved in ivory. Bone was also occasionally used. Here a single piece of ivory has been cut and filed to create a very attractive spiralled grip.

dudgeon daggers, along with a more stylized version of the ballock hilt. The lobes were much subtler, sometimes becoming flattened against the sides of the grip. Only an echo, if anything, of their original inspiration was suggested in the carving of the hilt, which was now covered in intricate knotwork designs. The pommel was flattened and widened into a disk shape, undoubtedly to provide a better grip in battle, and usually covered with a metal cap.

Highland dirk blades could be either single- or double-edged. Single-edged examples tended to be very broad at the ricasso and tapered evenly to a sharp point. The thick back of the single-edged dirk blade was often decorated with file marks or serrations and emphasized

BELOW Decorated dress dirks were produced in large numbers from the 19th century. This silver-mounted example made in Edinburgh in *c.*1900 has a small byknife and fork contained in special scabbard sleeves.

Fork

Byknife

Silver locket

Basket-weave carving

by a fuller running parallel just inside of it. Frequently, the back only extended two thirds of the way towards the point, the last third being double-edged. Other blades were entirely double-edged; indeed it was not uncommon for them to be fashioned out of old or broken sword blades.

Dirk blades were generally very long, some measuring 46cm (18in) or more. Like their medieval ancestors, they were used to stab overarm, with the blade below the fist. When the Highland warrior was fully armed, with his sword in his right hand and his *targe* (shield) in his left, the dirk was sometimes also grasped in the left hand. If enough of the blade extended below the edge of the shield, the dirk could be used offensively in that position, or passed to the right hand if the sword was lost.

After 1750 the Highland dirk began to change, shifting from a traditional weapon used by people living an ancient lifestyle into a somewhat gaudy showpiece. It became a signature badge of the Highland regiments of the British Army and the essential features became exaggerated. The grip began to be studded with small round-headed nails and bulged much more drastically in its midst, taking on an exaggerated thistle shape. In the 19th century the craze for all things Scottish turned the Highland dirk into a parody of itself, the carving of the hilt degenerating into second-rate basketwork, the scabbards set with hulking silver or gilt mounts, and the whole object finished off with large yellow crystals called cairngorms (or more often, glass imitations). This modern version, much removed from the original form, remains a standard part of formal Highland dress.

The sgian dubh (skean dhu)

Another small Scottish knife that should be mentioned at this point, although it is really a 19th-century creation, is the *sgian dubh* (*skean dhu*), or "black knife". Like the later Highland dirk, this very small knife is still worn as part of Highland dress. While this weapon may be a descendant of knives carried by Highland warriors, there are no surviving examples that date from earlier than the 19th century. It is therefore generally thought, probably correctly, that the sgian dubh was a product of the Romantic revival of Highland dress in the 1800s.

RIGHT The famous sgian dubh may be descended from small knives hidden up the sleeve, but in their well-known form they are entirely modern and cosmetic, as is this early 20th-century Edinburgh-made example.

Silver spacer

Silver scabbard chape

LEFT The *c.*1870 portrait of John Chisholm of the Clan Chisholm (factions of which fought on both sides at the Battle of Culloden) shows Highland dress complete with the long dirk worn on the right side and the sgian dubh down the right stocking.

17th- and 18th-century bayonets

Early long-guns were one-shot weapons. After firing, they took time to reload. In that time an enemy could rush the shooter to attack him at close-quarters. The shooter could defend himself with an empty musket by swinging it like a club, but this required space to move – an uncommon luxury in pitched battle. The invention of the bayonet made it possible to transform the musket into a short spear, perfect for close combat.

Bone/ivory handle

Decorative cross-guard finials

Dagger-type blade

It is remarkable that so soon after the enormous technological breakthrough that was the hand-held firearm, men were searching for a way to turn it back into one of humanity's most ancient weapons – a spear. Until the mid-17th century, the spear and the firearm worked together – an army's musketeers were protected by ranks of soldiers armed with long spears called pikes. The pikemen formed a hedge-like defence, which kept the enemy from rushing the musketeers while they reloaded. But this meant that any man with a pike was restricted to an entirely defensive role. This was wasteful and military theorists worked hard to find a way to give the musketeer defensive as well as offensive capabilities. Initial efforts were not very successful. One idea was for the musketeer to unscrew the head of his musket-rest and then insert the long staff into the barrel of his musket, turning it into a spear. But this process was quickly found to be slow and troublesome.

The birth of the bayonet

It is not known when and from whom the inspiration of wedding a knife to the end of a musket first came, but it is likely to have happened in or near Eibar in the Basque province of Guipúzcoa, northwestern Spain. Eibar was an important centre for the production of weapons during the late 16th century, an industry that was also the economic mainstay of many surrounding towns. It is possible that daggers designed for wedging into the muzzles of long-guns

ABOVE This English plug bayonet of the late 17th century shows a very fine inlaid handle. It is fitted with a decorated pommel cap and an ornately wrought cross guard.

were being produced here as early as the 1580s, probably for hunters. Like the soldiers of the time, hunters were armed with single-shot firearms and were in danger of being charged by their wounded prey; they thus had to be protected by another man with a spear. A knife jammed quickly into the barrel of the long-gun allowed a man to hunt alone. It would not be long before the military potential of this invention was realized.

The daggers of Bayonne

This specialized dagger, which would later become universally known as the "bayonet", initially referred to any dagger made in Bayonne in the southwestern corner of France, not far from Eibar. It may have been first employed in battle during the French Wars of Religion (1562–1629). At the Battle of Ivry in 1590, King Henry IV of France is said to have armed his troops with bayonets. Henry himself came from the Basque region where the bayonet was probably developed and at the time of the battle he did not have enough pikemen. The musket-dagger from his native land would have been an excellent solution to this problem. Voltaire (1694–1778), the great French dramatist and satirist, certainly believed that King Henry's men had bayonets at Ivry. In reference to

what turned out to be Henry's great victory, Voltaire in 1723 wrote one of the most evocative descriptions of this new weapon:

United with the musket, the bloody knife
Already for both sides posed a double death.
This weapon which once, to depopulate the earth,
In Bayonne was invented by the demon of war
Mustered simultaneously, those worthy fruits of Hell,
Which are most terrible, the fire and the steel.

The city of Bayonne had also produced edged weapons during the 16th century. The earliest known use of the term "bayonet" describes "a gilded dagger which was given the name Bayonnet". A French-English dictionary of 1611 defines the word as "a kind of small flat pocket dagger… or a great knife to hang at the girdle". Other sources mention daggers "of Bayonne". It seems that these weapons did not differ very greatly from other common types of daggers. Yet once the idea of the bayonet (as it is now understood) had taken off, Bayonne could have become the first manufacturer of the weapon on a large scale. It would not therefore be surprising if such a precise term as "bayonet", a word that lacked an equally unambiguous meaning, were to have gained a more exact use in the application to this newly specialized weapon.

ABOVE *The Battle of Ivry*, by Peter Paul Rubens, *c.*1628–1630. Henry IV's famous victory on 14 March 1590 over the Catholic League is said to have been the first time the bayonet was deployed as a battlefield weapon.

BELOW Musketeers had to be protected when reloading. Here they are marching alongside halberdiers, although pikemen were commonly used to guard them on the battlefield until the introduction of the bayonet.

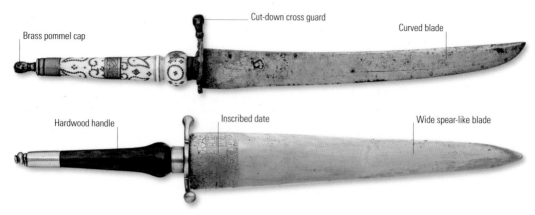

Brass pommel cap — Cut-down cross guard — Curved blade

Hardwood handle — Inscribed date — Wide spear-like blade

Plug bayonets

An important early reference to the military bayonet was made by Jacques de Chastenet (1600–1682), a French commander and native of Bayonne. In a description of the soldiers under his command in 1647, he wrote:

…they had bayonets with handles one foot long, and the blades of the bayonets were as long as the handles, the ends of which were adapted for putting in the barrels of the muskets to defend themselves, when attacked after they had fired.

This passage is not only the first reliable source that places the bayonet in a military context, it is also the first definite use of the term "bayonet" in reference to an edged weapon designed to be inserted into the barrel of a firearm. De Chastenet is discussing what we now call a "plug bayonet", essentially a dagger with a tapered grip that can be jammed firmly into the firing end or muzzle of a musket.

Although undoubtedly an important innovation, the plug bayonet was not without its drawbacks. Once embedded in an enemy, it could be hard to withdraw without it popping out of the barrel, making repeated attacks very difficult. More crucially, the musket could not be fired with the bayonet in place. This weakness of the design had serious consequences. At the Battle of Killiecrankie (1689) the British Army was defeated by the Jacobites, mostly Highland Scots, because their musketeers had to pause to fix bayonets. The Jacobites therefore wisely employed the famous "Highland Charge". After firing the few firearms that they had, the Jacobites rushed downhill into the British line armed with swords and shields. While this tactic meant that the Jacobites received a full barrage of musket fire

TOP English bladesmiths initially experimented with curved bayonet blades, such as this one dated 1680, but they were soon abandoned.

ABOVE This slightly later example of an English bayonet, dated 1686, is more typical in form, having a blade that is not dissimilar to the wide spearheads of previous centuries.

BELOW French military scientist Sébastien Le Prestre, Seigneur de Vauban, developed the socket bayonet as a response to the plug bayonet's debilitating drawback of preventing fire while being fixed. His work revolutionized early modern warfare.

LE MARÉCHAL
DE VAUBAN.

as they raced in, those that survived were suddenly amongst their enemies before bayonets could be fixed. At such close range, the swords and shields of the Jacobites outclassed those redcoats who had managed to put their bayonets to use. The British forces were cut to pieces, suffering over 2000 casualties.

The socket bayonet

A number of plug bayonet modifications were considered as ways of getting around the essential firing problem. The "ring bayonet" is often thought to have been one of these modifications, wherein a pair of rings was used to fix the bayonet to the side of the musket barrel. There is, however, no evidence that ring bayonets actually existed beyond the drawing board. Another short-lived idea was the "folding bayonet"– a thin, spear-like projection permanently attached to the barrel, which hinged into place.

The plug bayonet was made obsolete by the invention of the socket bayonet. This new form was composed of a tubular sleeve that fitted over the end of the musket's barrel, to the side of which was welded a bayonet blade. The famous military scientist Sébastien Le Prestre, Seigneur de Vauban (1633–1707), was the most active early developer of the socket bayonet, if not its inventor. In 1687 he wrote that as a result of the adoption of the socket bayonet:

…a soldier with a single weapon would have two of the best in the world in his hand… he could fire and reload very quickly without removing the bayonet. By doing this, there is no doubt that a batallion armed in this way…would be worth at least two of any existing batallions and would be in a position to scorn the pikes and the cavalry of any country…

De Vauban advocated a bayonet blade that was triangular in section, with one flat side facing against the barrel. The earliest socket bayonets had blades

ABOVE King Frederick II of Prussia (1712–1786), called "the Great", was one of the greatest military leaders of all time. This 19th-century lithograph shows him at the head of his army, which bristles with bayonets.

welded directly to the socket, but this was not ideal as slightly bent blades could project into the bullet's path. They also made muzzle loading difficult; a musketeer might accidentally stab himself in the hand while ramming down a charge. To improve the design, the blade was placed on the end of a short arm, or shank, which projected out and away from the line of fire, placing the blade along its own parallel path.

Although a great many slight adjustments to this bayonet concept were to come, the essential idea proved so successful that this remained the standard bayonet form for nearly 200 years. Thus what was really a late 17th-century piece of technology was still in use during World War I, and was even reintroduced by the British Army during World War II.

BELOW Some early socket bayonets such as this 18th-century example had wide blades like the earlier plug versions, but were supported by an L-shaped bracket and socket.

Shell-guard

Mortise

19th-century edged weapons

The Industrial Revolution ushered in the mass production of weapons. Knives and daggers continued to be made by hand but traditional bladesmiths were less essential. The use of fighting knives for personal defence declined dramatically in Europe, but less so in the United States. Mass production made it possible to standardize bayonet manufacture, and millions of duplicates of pattern types were produced for every major world army.

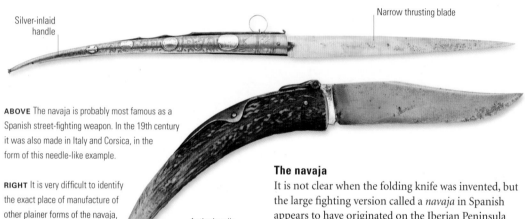

Silver-inlaid handle

Narrow thrusting blade

ABOVE The navaja is probably most famous as a Spanish street-fighting weapon. In the 19th century it was also made in Italy and Corsica, in the form of this needle-like example.

RIGHT It is very difficult to identify the exact place of manufacture of other plainer forms of the navaja, like, for example, this simple antler-handled weapon.

Antler handle

In the first half of the 19th century, most European countries were establishing professional police forces charged with keeping the public peace. Law and order became an expected part of everyday civilian life, and personal violence became increasingly unacceptable. The fashion for men to carry knives and daggers as a matter of routine fell away rapidly as the sense of a need for public decorum and civility prevailed in the minds of law-abiding people. An important exception to this general social trend was the recently formed United States of America.

Knives in the United States

In the first half of the 19th century most American men wore knives. The seemingly marked increase in the practice during the 1820s and 1830s, in direct contrast to European developments, was perhaps due to the increasing social discord that later culminated in the American Civil War (1861–65). During these turbulent decades, several key knife-types stood out.

The navaja

It is not clear when the folding knife was invented, but the large fighting version called a *navaja* in Spanish appears to have originated on the Iberian Peninsula in the 18th century. It was a single-bladed weapon (as distinct from later multi-bladed utility knives), the blade having a clipped point and usually being 15–20cm (6–8in) long, although some extended to 30cm (1ft) or even more. The blade was locked open by means of a spring catch. To release it, one usually pulled up on a ring or chain to free the catch and release the blade, which could then be closed again. The narrow grip, which could be straight although most were curved, was usually made up of an iron lining decorated with stag or cow horn. More expensive examples were ornamented with ivory and sometimes even gold.

The navaja was known as the weapon of workers, criminals and sailors. It was made in France, Italy and Corsica as well as Spain. In 1849, a manual on navaja fighting techniques was published in Madrid; it also contained instruction on how to fight with other knives and with scissors.

In North America the navaja is also considered a classic fighting knife, especially in California where no doubt this particular weapon was one of the many legacies of former Spanish rule. The navaja must have been common in the streets of old San Francisco,

which appears to have been an especially violent place in the mid-19th century. One account describes a lawman being stabbed by a judge, although whether or not he used a navaja is not mentioned.

The push dagger

Another classic American weapon of the early 19th century was the push dagger. This deadly little weapon was composed of a stout double-edged blade with a short, round-section tang that terminated in a transverse grip – of bone, horn or wood – giving the dagger an overall T-shape. A man would grip a push dagger in his fist with the blade protruding between the middle and ring fingers, the base of the blade sitting a little less than 2.5cm (1in) above the knuckles. He would strike a blow with a swift punching movement; bystanders might not even be aware that a knife attack had occurred, nor even the victim until he caught sight of his own blood.

The push dagger scabbard was often made to be worn upside-down inside a coat or jacket, having a spring clip to retain the weapon and a hook on the end of the chape for suspension. In this way a man could easily secrete a push dagger about his person and draw it quickly when the need arose. Almost all surviving examples (before their re-emergence in the 20th century) seem to date from before around 1860.

ABOVE This portrait of James Bowie (1793–1836) was probably completed in the late 1820s, around the time he and his brother Rezin were perfecting their famous knife.

ABOVE The 1836 storming of the Alamo mission by Mexican troops. James Bowie died during the battle, purportedly defending himself from his sickbed with firearms and his knife.

The Bowie knife

In 1827 an Arkansas plantation owner named Rezin Pleasant Bowie was attacked by a bull. Rezin tried to stab the bull in the head, but his knife could not pierce the bull's skull. Rezin managed to survive nonetheless, and in his quest for a more reliable knife he had an old file ground down to create a large single-edged knife. The blade was over 23cm (9in) long and 4cm (1.5in) wide, and it was fitted with a cross guard and simple wooden grip. Rezin gave a knife of this form to his brother James, who later that same year was involved in the famous "sandbar fight" at Vidalia, Louisiana, on the Mississippi River. James was shot and stabbed, but still managed to use his brother's knife to disembowel one assailant, wound another and chase off a third. The local press reported the fight, along with details of James Bowie's unusually large knife, and a legend began.

"Jim" Bowie's fame increased in 1829 when he wounded and then spared a man in a knife fight. That episode in itself would perhaps not have proved newsworthy but for the fact that shortly thereafter

Bowie was attacked by three associates of his defeated opponent. He apparently decapitated one and disembowelled another. The third fled.

The knife that Jim Bowie used in 1829 was a new version that he had commissioned himself, a modification of his brother Rezin's original idea. The weapon had a longer blade with a clipped point sharpened on both sides. This design became the basis for the traditional Bowie knife, as it is known today.

In 1830 Jim Bowie moved to Texas and became involved in the local rebellion against Mexican rule. After numerous battles, he ended up at the siege of the Alamo in 1836. One hundred and eighty-eight Texans defended this small mission complex against an overwhelming Mexican force. When the Mexicans stormed the mission, the Texans killed at least 200 and wounded another 400 before being wiped out. Bowie was ill in bed during the final assault; nevertheless, he is said to have defended himself with his pistols, a broken rifle and his famous knife before being killed.

After this last battle, it seemed that everyone wanted a Bowie knife, even if nobody could agree on what it was supposed to look like. Clearly it needed to have a

BELOW The English manufacturer James Rodgers & Co produced a number of different types of Bowie knife for the American market in the years immediately before the American Civil War. This Rodgers "medium" includes an antler grip.

Spherical guard terminal

Clipped point

Antler grip

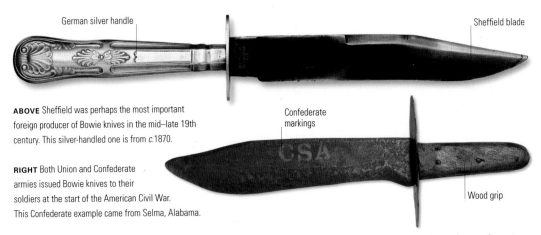

German silver handle

Sheffield blade

ABOVE Sheffield was perhaps the most important foreign producer of Bowie knives in the mid–late 19th century. This silver-handled one is from *c.*1870.

RIGHT Both Union and Confederate armies issued Bowie knives to their soldiers at the start of the American Civil War. This Confederate example came from Selma, Alabama.

Confederate markings

Wood grip

big blade and there was a general consensus that it should be single-edged. Soon the name "Bowie knife" was used to refer to any large single-edged knife. They began to be manufactured in Mississippi, Louisiana, Arkansas, Texas, Tennessee and Missouri. The blades were 23–38cm (9–15in) long and generally 4–5cm (1.5–2in) wide. The guards were straight or S-shaped, while grips were usually made of wood or antler. Many Bowie knives were also customized and personalized by their owners in some way.

English cutlery manufacturers quickly realized the potential of this product and began exporting it in large numbers for sale to hunters, trappers, soldiers and others in the harsh environment of the American frontier. As more Bowie knives became available, firms began to compete by producing more elaborate and expensive versions. Mother-of-pearl and turtle-shell grips were mounted on silver hilts, while blades were acid-etched and even blued and gilt. English makers also emblazoned them with jingoistic slogans conceived to appeal to Americans at the time, such as "Death to Traitors" (hinting at rising pre-Civil War tensions), "Death to Abolition" (appealing to the predominant southern demand for the continuation of slavery), and "Equal Rights and Justice for All" (representing the northern stance against slavery).

At the beginning of the American Civil War, the Bowie knife was popular on both sides, the Confederates favouring a version fitted with a D-shaped knuckle guard. This initial popularity in a way mirrored the original passion for the war in both the Union and Confederate States, and just like that enthusiasm, it died out as the conflict became longer and bloodier. By the end of the war both North and South had discarded their fighting knives, and after peace was declared the wearing of knives became distinctly unfashionable. By 1880, the true Bowie knife had disappeared.

LEFT Bowie knives were popular with trappers, mountain men and cowboys. Here the famous gunfighter James Butler "Wild Bill" Hickok (1837–1876) is photgraphed with two revolvers and a long Bowie knife.

"Zigzag" slot

The socket bayonet

This bayonet remained the primary type issued to the rank-and-file soldier throughout most of the 19th century. While blade forms varied to some extent, the main area of improvement in the 1800s was the method of attachment. In the 18th century the most common method had been a "zigzag" slot in the socket, which engaged with the forward sight and locked with a half turn. This method was not entirely satisfactory. At the battle of Meeanee, during the Indian Sind campaign of 1843, British soldiers encountered problems when their enemies started pulling the bayonets off in combat, requiring them to be tied on more securely with string. British arms manufacturers were meanwhile experimenting with new spring mechanisms to lock the bayonet down more securely.

The spring bayonet

The Hanoverian spring catch came into service in the same year as Meeanee. This little S-shaped catch, fitted to the barrel, engaged a collar on the bayonet and made it more difficult to be dislodged. The locking ring was an even better idea, and was quickly taken up by France and other European countries. The locking ring allowed the sight to seat down into the socket slot through a notch at its join, but then was rotated to lock behind the sight. Britain adopted the locking ring in 1853, when it was fitted to the Enfield rifle bayonet.

The sword bayonet

Late in the 18th century, in Denmark, attempts were made to create two weapons in one when the 1791 cavalry sword was converted into a bayonet by shortening the blade and fitting an attachment mechanism to the side of the weapon. The British married similar long "sword" bayonets to the 1800 Baker and 1837 Brunswick rifles. The French introduced perhaps the most popular sword

Spring catch

Hollow-ground blade

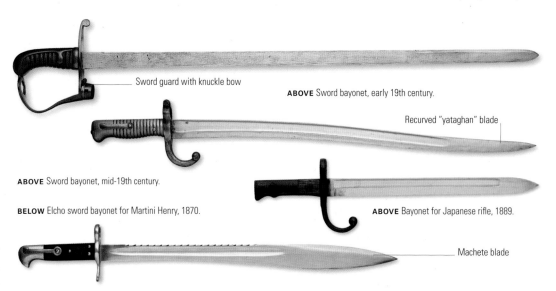

Sword guard with knuckle bow

ABOVE Sword bayonet, early 19th century.

Recurved "yataghan" blade

ABOVE Sword bayonet, mid-19th century.

BELOW Elcho sword bayonet for Martini Henry, 1870.

ABOVE Bayonet for Japanese rifle, 1889.

Machete blade

RIGHT Francis Richard Charteris, Lord Elcho, 10th Earl of Wemyss, was a prominent Whig politician, commander of the London Scottish Regiment, and inventor of the Elcho bayonet. He died at the age of 96 in 1914.

bayonet pattern in 1842. It had a brass hilt, simple cross guard, and a beaked pommel. The recurved "yataghan" blade-shape was taken from the famous Turkish sword. It was enormously successful and adopted in Scandinavia, Austria, Britain, the United States and many other countries. The British 1853 and 1856 artillery bayonets were carbon-copies of the French 1842, while in the United States various yataghan-bladed bayonets appeared; these included the 1855 and 1861 (Navy) patterns.

The sword bayonet remained popular until the late 19th century despite being heavy and impractical, and a large number of sword designs proliferated after 1850. Britain took the lead, developing many versions in the ultimately futile search for a multi-use weapon. Cutlass bayonets were issued to the Navy and knuckle-guard types developed for artillerymen. One of the oddest was Lord Elcho's "1870 experimental sword bayonet", which was also a sword, saw and machete. The Elcho suffered from the flaw inherent in all combination weapons – any attempt to design for multiple uses always compromises each of those uses. It was very expensive to manufacture and its heaviness made shooting difficult. Initially rejected, the Elcho was revived in 1895 and saw limited use in the Ashanti campaign of 1895–6.

The long and complicated exercise of developing the sword bayonet was proved to be ultimately futile, being the wrong weapon for a rapidly modernizing battlefield. Artillery and overall firepower superiority were the keys to modern war, and the bayonet was essentially a defensive weapon of last resort. Sword versions were consequently discarded in favour of smaller knife types. In 200 years the bayonet, which had begun its history as a knife jammed into the muzzle, had returned to its roots.

20th-century edged weapons

Advances in firearms technology, and the soldier's increased individual firepower created by the widespread adoption of bolt-action magazine rifles by the early years of the 20th century, reduced the chances of close contact with the enemy. However, bayonets and fighting knives still maintained their place in the soldier's armoury, whether as weapons on the battlefield or ceremonial items on the parade ground.

During the early years of the 20th century, warfare underwent its most dramatic changes since the appearance of the firearm. At sea vast increases in naval firepower meant that battleships now engaged at ranges of miles rather than yards. Boarding parties wielding cutlasses and axes were becoming a distant memory and submarines added a new dimension as stalking assassins. Warfare took to the air, at first tentatively and then in earnest, allowing death to be dealt from above and taking conflict beyond the battlefield to the towns and cities of the enemy. Land warfare also underwent dramatic change. New types of artillery meant that it outranked every other weapon on the battlefield. When joined by the machine gun both had a devastating impact on the way battles were fought. The days of stalemate entrenchment dawned with World War I (1914–18). When the idea emerged of placing artillery and machine guns in armour-plated, fast-moving vehicles, entrenchment gave way to "Blitzkrieg" – lightning war – in World War II (1939–45).

But technology tends to advance faster than the abilities of soldiers to integrate it into new tactics and strategies effectively, especially if they have been tutored in the "old ways". Although long sword bayonets and battlefield derring-do such as cavalry and bayonet charges had been rendered ineffective by the late 19th century, a surprisingly long time had to pass before this equipment and such practices were finally discarded in favour of equipment and tactics more suited to the needs of the tasks in hand.

Bayonets of World War I

Despite the fact that in the late 19th century long sword bayonets had been found to be too cumbersome and awkward to be really effective, most nations retained them as they entered World War I. The old idea of "reach" – the ability to outreach the enemy's rifle with a bayonet attached – persisted. Austro-Hungarian infantrymen were issued with the 1895 Mannlicher 8mm rifle which was fitted with a long sword bayonet. The Turks, carrying the Mauser Gewehr 98 7.65mm rifle, also preferred a very long-bladed bayonet with a cross guard, which had a hook-shaped quillon. Whether used to allow rifles to be stacked together neatly in a tripod arrangement or, as some would believe, to ensnare the enemy's bayonet blade and either break it or deflect the thrust, these bayonets were still far more likely to become snagged on something inconsequential

RIGHT An illustration of a French bayonet charge at Valmy featured on the front page of this French newspaper in 1915.

BELOW The optimistic French bayonet charges of the first half of World War I employed the long needle-bladed Lebel bayonet like this pre-1916 example.

Narrow hollow-ground blade

All-metal grip

at a crucial moment. The Italian bayonets for the Mannlicher-Carcano and Vetterli-Carcano rifles of the late 19th century which saw service in World War I resembled the British 1907 Pattern.

The British, who had discarded their various long sword bayonets in favour of the shorter knife patterns of 1888 and 1903, returned before World War I to a long-bladed sword bayonet design, the 1907 Pattern, which replaced the 1903 Pattern on their SMLE (Short, Magazine, Lee-Enfield) rifles. The 1907 Pattern, which was equipped with a 43cm (17in) blade, was produced initially with a cross guard featuring a "hook" quillon, reflecting widespread 19th-century fashion. The design was very successful; basically copied from the Japanese Model 1897 Arisaka bayonet, more than 2.5 million were produced in Britain. However, as soldiers found the hooked quillon of this bayonet to be a nuisance, the decision was made to abandon the hook design in 1913 before it had even been used in earnest. The United States of America's Model 1917 was a copy of

the British 1914 Pattern bayonet design, itself a modification of the 1907 Pattern but with a longer, straight cross guard.

Another inconvenience of a long bayonet is its weight. Some countries tried to retain the length of the sword bayonet while also avoiding the weight problem. The French developed the long epee bayonet for their 1886 Pattern Lebel rifle, the very narrow blade of which was given a cruciform cross-section to reduce weight even further while at the same time retaining strength. The Russians – perhaps the most poorly equipped major army of the war – went one step further and removed even more weight by abandoning a conventional hilt and using a socket bayonet with a cruciform-sectioned blade on the 1891 Moisin Nagant 7.62mm rifle. This in itself was simply a continuation of tradition, an almost identical form of bayonet being used on the Russian Model 1871 Berdan rifle. In Britain, the contemporary long Model 1895 socket bayonet was designed for the new Lee-Enfield rifle.

BELOW An early British 1907 Pattern complete with hooked quillon. Although the hook was officially declared obsolete in 1913, some still entered World War I in their unmodified state.

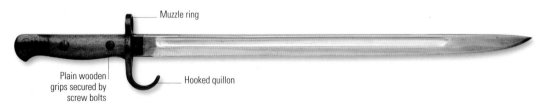

Muzzle ring

Plain wooden grips secured by screw bolts

Hooked quillon

Grooved metal handle

World War I German bayonet forms

Germany had adopted a short "knife" bayonet for the Model 1884 Mauser rifle, and this bayonet continued in use on the Mauser Gewehr Model 1898. The Germans therefore entered the war with a shorter bayonet than those of most of the other protagonists. Even so, the *seitengewehr* (sidearm) bayonet originally designed for the Gewehr 1898 rifle had a blade that was even longer than that of the British 1907 Pattern, and it also saw service. In 1905, Germany found a middle ground in bayonet design with the introduction of the so-called "butcher knife" or "butcher blade" bayonet. The terminology was probably invented by the Allies as part of a propaganda campaign, but the blade certainly had an unusual

ABOVE This ersatz bayonet of around 1916 was modified to fit the German M88/98 Mauser rifle.

shape with its increasing width towards the point, reminiscent of the British Elcho of 1871. In various forms this new German bayonet was probably the most widely used during the war. By 1916 Germany was suffering from an increasingly stressed economy and a shortage of raw materials as a result of an Allied naval blockade. In an effort to keep its troops supplied, Germany developed simplified designs and manufacturing techniques. Even old sword blades were cut down and fitted with mounts for Mauser rifles. The Germans also began to recycle captured weapons, and many Belgian, French and Russian bayonets were converted to fit German rifles. These two types of weapon were generally referred to as *ersatz*, or "emergency", bayonets and exist in huge variety.

Bayonets of World War II

After World War I, the relevance of the bayonet in modern warfare was frequently questioned. The number of bayonet wounds inflicted in World War I appears to have been minimal. For example, one study showed that of a sample of 200,000 wounds suffered by British soldiers, only 600 were caused by bayonets, while the American forces estimated that only .024 per cent of their injuries were bayonet-related. Even so, bayonets remained a standard part of the infantryman's equipment on both sides during World War II. Some of the types common in World War I remained in use during World War II, the Japanese Arisaka bayonet being one example. But the general trend was towards shorter versions.

The British began to replace their 1907 Pattern with a series of short knife bayonets. Some, like the No 5 bayonet for the Jungle Carbine, had a more or less conventional hilt similar to that of the 1907 Pattern.

LEFT British troops, equipped with standard-issue bayonets fitted to their rifles, make fun of Mussolini's characteristic arrogant posture in this portrait of *Il Duce* after the capture of Cyrenaica, Libya, in 1941.

Its blade was very different, not only in being much shorter but also in being more akin to that of the fabled Bowie knife. But most of this new series utilized what was in effect a return to the principle of the socket bayonet. The No 4 bayonet for the new No 4 rifle had a cruciform-section blade very similar to that of the French 1886 Lebel but only 20cm (9in) in length. It was fitted to a relatively simple block with a locking device for attachment to the muzzle of the rifle. The rifle muzzle itself had two lugs which engaged with internal slots in the "socket" or muzzle ring of the bayonet. This more or less experimental Mk I bayonet was quickly replaced in 1940 by the Mk II, which had a plain round "spike" or "pig-sticker" blade and was easier and cheaper to manufacture.

This trend continued with the No 7 bayonet. This again had the Bowie-type blade and a complex hilt, which allowed it in one mode to be gripped and used as a knife. The pommel could also be swivelled through 180 degrees, allowing it to act as a socket for fitting to the rifle. Both the No 5 and No 7 bayonets are also characterized by their very large muzzle rings. In the case of the No 5, this allowed the bayonet to accommodate the mouth of the flash hider (the device that masked the firing flash). In the case of the No 7, the "muzzle ring" did not function in that capacity at all. Finally, the No 9 bayonet was produced for the Royal Navy and was a cross between the No 5 and No 4 series in that it had a Bowie blade fitted to a socket.

When the United States entered the war in 1941, most American infantrymen were armed with the pre-World War I 41cm (16in) M1905 Pattern bayonet (later renamed the M1942). But like most other nations, the United States soon recognized the necessity of utilizing a shorter knife pattern, which could also be used as a fighting knife. The M1 bayonet, which had a much shorter 25cm (10in) blade, was introduced in 1943.

Muzzle ring

ABOVE The popular Japanese 1897 Pattern Arisaka bayonet was copied for the British 1907 design, which was used until the end of World War II.

BELOW The majority of modern bayonet designs focused on multi-use weapons. The 1940 British "pig-sticker" reverted to the other extreme previously inhabited by socket types – it was exclusively a bayonet.

Muzzle ring

Spike

The bayonet in conflict

The effectiveness of the bayonet not only as a hand-to-hand combat weapon but as a psychological weapon was clearly demonstrated during the Battle of the Reichswald Forest in February 1945. At one stage, groups of British and German soldiers were engaged in a bitter firefight as they hid in ditches and holes. With no more than 200m (650ft) between them, the British decided to rush the German line. They fixed bayonets and ran forward. As soon as the British charge began, the Germans ceased fire and raised their hands in surrender. For these modern soldiers, trained to kill from afar and demoralized by many months of continual combat, the threat of "cold steel" was clearly too much. This was the last bayonet charge of the war.

The fighting knives of World Wars I and II

Above all, World War I was characterized by trench warfare. After an initial advance into Belgium and northern France, the German army was halted by the Allied forces. Both sides "dug in" and fortified their positions with trench systems that extended for hundreds of miles. This stalemate situation led to hand-to-hand fighting on a limited scale. If one side mounted a full-scale assault, rushing en masse across the landmines and barbed wire of "no man's land", any troops who were fortunate enough to get past the enemy machine guns had to be prepared to fight at close quarters in the confined environment of the enemy trench. Here the long-bladed bayonet was of little use, since there was no space to wield it. Trench combat thus necessitated the military reinstatement of the dagger, or fighting knife.

Some early trench knives were simply fashioned from cut-down bayonets, although they were also made from many other objects, including the metal posts that were used to support the barbed-wire

ABOVE Bayonets line the trenches along the Western Front where German soldiers keep guard during World War I.

defences. As well as their role as close-range combat weapons, trench knives were also useful to small raiding parties sent into enemy territory to take prisoners or gather intelligence, when the ability to kill silently was all-important.

World War I brought the fighting knife officially back to the battlefield after a 200-year absence. Its modern relevance having been acknowledged, the development of the military fighting knife continued throughout the period between the wars.

The Mark I trench knife

During the last five months of World War I, the United States made an extensive study of all the diverse forms of trench knife then in use. It rated them on several points, including the blade's weight, length and shape, suitability to be carried while crawling and the probability of the knife being knocked from the hand. The results of these tests led to the development of the Mark I trench knife, which was intended to combine all of the best aspects of the weapons included in the study. The Mark I was composed of a 17cm (7in)

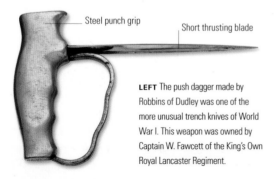

Steel punch grip

Short thrusting blade

LEFT The push dagger made by Robbins of Dudley was one of the more unusual trench knives of World War I. This weapon was owned by Captain W. Fawcett of the King's Own Royal Lancaster Regiment.

Cast-brass hilt

Short double-edged blade

U.S. 1918
L.F&C-1918

ABOVE The brass-hilted 1918 Mark I trench knife gave the user a choice of several carefully balanced modes of attack – stabbing, slashing, punching and pummelling.

Partially sharpened back edge

Steel pommel cap

ABOVE The more functional design of the 1942 Mark 3 knife did away with the "knuckleduster" feature, although the solid steel pommel cap could still strike concussive blows.

double-edged blade designed for both cutting and thrusting, and a cast-bronze hilt that incorporated individual loops for the fingers, forming a knuckleduster. It even had a pointed nut on the pommel to secure the hilt and blade together, but which was also able to fracture the skull if used with sufficient force. Although none were manufactured after the 120,000 produced in the United States and France in 1918, this weapon remained in use alongside later knives until it was declared obsolete in January 1945.

The Mark 3 trench knife

When the United States entered the war in 1941, the only fighting knife in the US Army's inventory was the Mark I. A new production run of this model was proposed but then ruled out; the bronze required for the cast hilt was a critical strategic metal, and it was felt that a better design could be found. After several studies, the new knife was designated Mark 3, and was described in the US Army's Catalog of Standard Ordnance Items as "developed to fill the need in modern warfare for hand-to-hand fighting … designed for such shock units as parachute troops and rangers." The knife had a short, straight blade 17cm (7in) long, with a 7cm (3in) "false" edge, and a corrugated grip constructed of compressed leather washers. Some 590,247 Mark 3s were manufactured before production was cancelled in August 1942.

CACCIALI VIA!
SOTTOSCRIVETE AL PRESTITO

ABOVE A typical patriotic poster of World War I, this one Italian, showing a brave soldier defending his home and loved ones.

Cross-hatched grip

Flattened diamond-section blade

The FS "commando" knife

In 1940 the British Army formed its first Special Forces unit, the "Commandos", to strike key targets along the Normandy coast of France. The training of this small, elite force was entrusted to Captain William Fairbairn and Captain Eric Sykes. Both had been members of the Shanghai police force, where they had studied martial arts and learned their special skills of armed and unarmed combat, including the ability to use anything at hand, however unlikely, as an effective weapon. They also learnt how to kill silently.

When they took up their new duties, Fairbairn and Sykes discovered the Commandos were armed with a

ABOVE A Fairbairn-Sykes "commando" knife, *c.*1942. The design of the weapon is remarkably medieval, with a long grip, short cross guard, and diamond-section cut-and-thrust blade.

knuckleduster-type knife, the BC41. But Fairbairn and Sykes had their own views on knives and approached the Wilkinson Sword Company, Britain's best-known manufacturer of edged weapons, with an original design. The first shipment of Fairbairn-Sykes (FS) fighting knives arrived in January 1941. The FS knife had a tapering 18cm (7in) double-edged blade, a simple oval cross guard, and a long, slightly bulbous, metal handle. The first pattern of knives had fine cross-hatching to provide a firm grip when the hands were wet, whether with rainwater, seawater or blood. Later models had grips encircled by a series of ribs or grooves. The blades were honed to an edge that would cut paper, and the cross guard was not to prevent an opponent's knife sliding down the blade but to prevent the user's hand from doing the same and suffering serious injury when thrusting with the knife. The knife was made so that the point of balance was on the hilt just behind the cross guard.

The preferred method of carrying the knife was in a sheath sewn to the inside of the left trouser pocket – a pistol was to be carried in the right-hand pocket. But the knife could be worn in many places – on the belt, down the boot or up the sleeve. It could also be sewn to the uniform in any other way that the individual soldier preferred. Many versions of the FS knife were produced, and its design was copied by the Special Forces of other countries; 3,420 were delivered to the US Army in 1943, this version being designated V-42. More British-made FS knives were sold to American soldiers stationed in England before they were deployed to continental Europe or North Africa. The US Marine Corps also adopted the knife for a short period.

LEFT The Fairbairn-Sykes knife could be worn in many different ways. This photograph of a British Commando involved in the raid on Dieppe, taken on 20 August 1942, shows one strapped to the ankle.

The US Navy Mark 2 and the USMC "KA-BAR"

During World War II, the US Navy developed its own fighting knives, primarily for shore personnel near the front line and combat swimmers, or "frogmen". The US Navy Mark 2 Utility Knife was a relation of the Army Mark 3; like it, the Navy Mark 2 had a handle composed of compressed leather washers. The blade was more like that of a small Bowie knife, being nearly 18cm (7in) long with a clipped point. The first combat knife made specifically for the US Marine Corps was identical to the Navy Mark 2 apart from the marks on the blade. Officially called the "fighting-utility knife", it soon became known among Marines as the "KA-BAR", after the trademark of the Union Cutlery Company, which manufactured the earliest versions. By 1943 these knives were in general use, and they remained the US Marine's trusted companion in many subsequent campaigns.

20th-century ceremonial knives

Swords, in both past civilian life and within military forces up to the present day, have been the primary symbol of rank and still have their place on the parade ground and at other ceremonial occasions. In some instances, knives of one form or another have also served a similar function.

The naval dirk worn by the midshipman originally marked him out as a junior officer, and awards of this classic weapon have continued to be made. Similarly, the elaborately adorned dirk of the Scots Guards once served them on the field of conflict and now serves them on parade. The dirk is not only an ongoing part of a military tradition, but also an important part of Highland dress and is still seen on "civilian" occasions such as weddings and other celebrations. The unusual but famous traditional kukri was often worn as part of

ABOVE A Boy Scout in uniform with an unusual sheath knife, with wooden slab grips instead of grips of imitation stag or compressed leather washers.

ceremonial dress by the British Army's Gurkha regiment. The sight of these knives in those same hands created a legendary and formidable combination, sufficient to instil fear in the heart of anyone who might face them in battle.

On a completely different level, the traditional parade uniform of the Boy Scouts' would have been incomplete at one time without the sheath knife. It wasn't, of course, carried as a weapon but as a tool for use in field craft.

BELOW Along with the Fairbairn-Sykes commando knife, the US Navy Mark 2, perhaps most famous as the US Marine Corps' KA-BAR, is one of the world's most successful modern combat knives.

Compressed leather grip | Clipped point

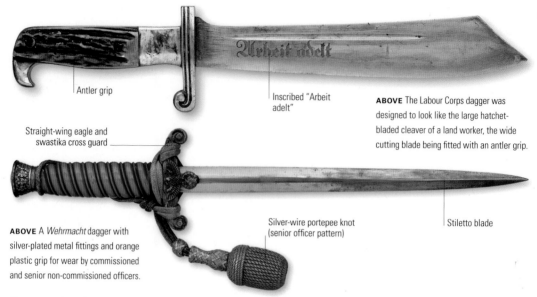

Antler grip

Inscribed "Arbeit adelt"

ABOVE The Labour Corps dagger was designed to look like the large hatchet-bladed cleaver of a land worker, the wide cutting blade being fitted with an antler grip.

Straight-wing eagle and swastika cross guard

Silver-wire portepee knot (senior officer pattern)

Stiletto blade

ABOVE A *Wehrmacht* dagger with silver-plated metal fittings and orange plastic grip for wear by commissioned and senior non-commissioned officers.

Daggers of the Third Reich

The concept of the "dress" dagger flourished during the German Third Reich, and an almost boundless variety were created for every branch of the military, quasi-military and even many non-military state organizations. In 1933 a delegation from the sword-making city of Solingen approached Germany's new leader Adolf Hitler with a proposal. It was suggested that the Nazi Party adopt various types of sword and dagger as status and distinguishing symbols for its members. Solingen had been a world-famous centre for the production of fine-edged weapons since the Middle Ages, but defeat in World War I had hit its industry very badly and many of its craftsmen were out of work. Hitler and some of his close associates had embraced and almost resurrected certain aspects of German medieval culture as part of Nazi ideology, and they enthusiastically approved the idea.

The first member of what would become the huge family of Nazi daggers was introduced in 1934 for the *Sturm Abteilung* ("Stormtroopers"), or SA, the Nazi Party's private police force. Solingen craftsmen took as their model the characteristically Germanic "Swiss" or "Holbein" dagger of the 16th century. The design was simplified but the overall form of the I-shaped hilt, with brown grips made of walnut or similar wood, remained unchanged. The broad, spear-pointed blade was etched with the motto *Alles für Deutschland* ("Everything for Germany"). Shortly thereafter, a very

BELOW An off-duty German officer in Paris in 1941, his uniform complete with standard dress dagger.

RIGHT This 1937 photo taken in Nuremberg of Josef Goebbels (left) and Hermann Göring, two of Hitler's closest aides, shows Göring with one of the many forms of Nazi "Holbein"-type dress dagger.

RIGHT This 1937 photo taken in Nuremberg of Josef Goebbels (left) and Hermann Göring, two of Hitler's closest aides, shows Göring with one of the many forms of Nazi "Holbein"-type dress dagger.

similar dagger was commissioned for the *Schutzstaffel* ("Protective Squadron"), or SS, the Nazis' elite guard. This weapon was almost identical to the SA version, apart from its black hilt and the motto on the blade: *Meine Ehre heißt Treue* ("My Honour is Named Loyalty"). The Army, Airforce and Navy each had their own distinctive daggers, the most distinctive of all, perhaps, being the 1st Pattern *Luftwaffe* ("Airforce") dagger produced in classical "Holbein" style and with a large circular pommel and winged cross guard.

Gradually, nearly every organization of the Nazi Party acquired its own ceremonial knife. They included the Motor Transport Corps, the National Political Education Institute and the Hitler *Jugend* ("Hitler Youth"), an equivalent of the Boy Scout movement but with its main focus on training young minds in Nazi ideology. Dress daggers were also produced for the Postal Protection Service, Waterways Protection Police, Diplomatic Service, the Red Cross and National Forestry Service. Even the Fire Service had parade axes for firemen and daggers for officers.

One of the most distinctive civil service daggers was awarded to the *Reicharbeitsdienst* ("Labour Corps"). Designed to look suitably rustic, the workman-like Labour Corps dagger, often referred to as a "hewer", had a broad chopping blade, staghorn grip and appropriate motto: *Arbeit adelt* ("Labour ennobles"). Special versions of many daggers were also produced for officers and for presentation purposes.

Perhaps one of the rarest presentation daggers is the naval dress dagger awarded by Grand Admiral Erich Raeder, of which only six are thought to exist. It has an elaborately decorated scabbard, a Damascus blade and a 17-diamond swastika in the pommel.

This almost obsessive trend in dagger design by the Third Reich was never copied by other countries. However, many of them adopted ceremonial daggers on a far more limited scale. Until the 1950s, Soviet Russia and many countries under Soviet influence issued such daggers to their army, air force and naval officers. Some South American countries also used them. The Japanese also adopted dress daggers within their military circles. But on the whole this trend has now largely disappeared, and these daggers are preserved only by collectors.

BELOW The SA dagger, manufactured between 1934 and 1945, was perhaps the most common of the many Nazi daggers of "Holbein" form.

SA badge rondel

Inscribed "Alles für Deutschland"

Nazi eagle insignia

African knives and daggers

As is true of tribal cultures everywhere in the world, the common traditional weapons in Africa were the bow and arrow and the spear. But the native peoples of the African continent also created a profusion of other weapons, including a bewildering multitude of daggers and knives. Despite a generally simple level of technology, the work of African bladesmiths is exceptional in terms of its quality, originality, functionality and design.

Although copper and bronze were commonly worked throughout Africa, iron had been the predominant metal for making weapons since ancient times. Iron ore is found in most parts of Africa – mined but also found close to the surface near rivers or deposited in dry river beds. By the 4th or 3rd century BC, iron was being worked in what is now northwestern Tanzania, northern Nigeria and the Sudan. Excavations of the ancient Nubian city of Meroe, on the east bank of the Nile, north of Khartoum, revealed, along with over 200 pyramids, gigantic slag

heaps which testify to very considerable ironworking activities. The context of the excavation site demonstrates that iron was being worked there on an industrial scale by at least the 1st century AD.

In theory, the design of an African edged weapon should be characteristic of, or relate to the specific tribe that created it. However, a well-made weapon was always valuable, a useful trade item or literal form of currency, and so it should not be surprising that the weapons forged by a particular tribe were found in the possession of many of their neighbours. Migration and displacement due to environmental or territorial factors also disseminated distinctive weapons forms over much larger areas.

It is very difficult, therefore, to date particular African weapons precisely or to identify their exact place of origin positively. Weapons studied by early explorers from Europe were usually named after the area where they were found. But this may not have been the land of the tribe who made them. Also, tribal names could be derived from many different things, features in the landscape for example, and one tribe might have more than one name. Yet it is possible to discuss in a general way the areas or cultures that are most closely associated with distinctive knife forms.

Baule knives and daggers

The Baule tribe of the Ivory Coast are famous not only for their wooden figurines and masks but also for their skill in working iron, brass, bronze and gold, and the Baule smith was a skilled weapons maker. The blades of Baule knives and daggers vary considerably in form. Some are long and very wide, being either steeply

LEFT Knives and other edged weapons were collected in Africa by many 19th-century travellers. In this illustration a group of objects collected by Professor Friedrich Ratzel in the Upper Congo, 1898, is shown. The group appears largely to be made up of Ngala, Ngombe and Kuba weapons.

ABOVE This rare 19th-century drawing shows the traditional metalworking processes practised in Africa for hundreds of years, including smelting iron ore in a bloomery and beating a lump of iron, or "bloom".

tapered down the top half or tightly waisted and leaf-shaped. Others are shorter, having a simple, straight shape with a clipped point, not unlike a Japanese dagger or tanto. Another Baule knife form, specifically for ceremonial or ritual purposes, is very wide, curved and sickle-like. Hilts are usually carved of wood, while scabbards are often made of leather exquisitely tooled with geometric patterns or covered with brightly coloured shells.

The knives and daggers of the Azande tribe

Perhaps one of the most martial of all African tribes, the Azande inhabited parts of what is now the Democratic Republic of Congo, southwestern Sudan, and the southeastern end of the Central African Republic. Although technically very militant by traditional standards, the Azande took careful measures to prevent excessive violence in war, which for them was to a great extent symbolic. A battle could be decided by the death or even wounding of an individual opponent, while surrounded and trapped enemies would be allowed to escape, their symbolic defeat having been achieved.

The knives and daggers of the Azande are well made and finely decorated. Ceremonial weapons sometimes have blades of copper, while most practical examples

are of iron. Their long leaf blades are designed both for cutting and thrusting, and are generally decorated with tight groups of file-lines or grooves. Sometimes the blades are pierced with large holes or slots. The hilts are often covered with narrow ribbons of copper or bronze, which are either wrapped or plaited around them. Especially valuable knives are sometimes fitted with hilts of elephant ivory, carved with geometric designs.

The Azande traditionally used knives as a form of currency. An Azande dowry, or bridewealth, for example, might be given in the form of a number (usually 40) of dagger blades.

ABOVE Knives and other edged weapons often have purposes other than combat. These elaborate Congolese throwing knives, made of copper, are intended as tributes for Azande leaders from their vassals.

Knives and daggers of the Fang tribe

Living in southern Cameroon, the Gabonese Republic and Equatorial Guinea, the Fang are the creators not only of the remarkable *bieri*, reliquary sculptures that probably had a strong influence on the early development of cubism, but also of the so-called "bird's-head" knife. The concept of this strange, other-worldly weapon may have been inspired by the African horn raven (*Bucorvus caver*). The bird's-head knife is often thought to be a throwing knife, although this is debatable.

The Fang are also known for a long dagger, which is somewhat reminiscent of the Roman gladius, or short sword, having a straight, wide blade. These practical fighting daggers were combined, like the gladius, with a large, square shield, which protected most of the warrior's body while he closed with his enemy and stabbed him with the knife.

ABOVE The Fang *bieri* or "bird's-head" knife is one of the most striking of all African weapons. The triangular blade cut-out contrasts with its gentle curves, a quality that appealed to Cubist artists, such as Picasso.

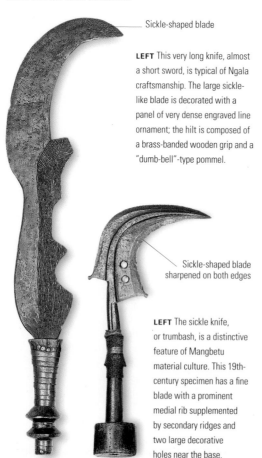

Sickle-shaped blade

LEFT This very long knife, almost a short sword, is typical of Ngala craftsmanship. The large sickle-like blade is decorated with a panel of very dense engraved line ornament; the hilt is composed of a brass-banded wooden grip and a "dumb-bell"-type pommel.

Sickle-shaped blade sharpened on both edges

LEFT The sickle knife, or trumbash, is a distinctive feature of Mangbetu material culture. This 19th-century specimen has a fine blade with a prominent medial rib supplemented by secondary ridges and two large decorative holes near the base.

The Mangbetu hooked sickle knife

The trumbash, of the Mangbetu in the northwestern corner of the Democratic Republic of Congo is a hooked sickle knife, and easily recognized. The wide blade is formed with a graceful if abrupt right-angle change about halfway along its length. The edges of the blade trace various paths in relation to the centre line, some examples being more angular while others are more rounded and uniformly curved.

Whatever the exact shape, these weapons always possess a singular boldness. The blades are usually ridged in all sorts of highly individual ways, with some ridges being very sharp and narrow, others being wider and flat-topped. Some blades are pierced with pairs of large, round holes, and are sometimes forged with short, knob-like projections at the base of both edges. All of these aspects contribute to a sense of the Mangbetu sickle knife being a piece of abstract art as well as a weapon. The handle is usually carved out of wood or ivory. Many have pommels in the form of a

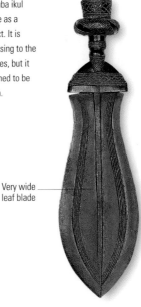

RIGHT The form of the Kuba ikul attests to this object's role as a peaceful ceremonial object. It is beautifully made and pleasing to the eye, with fluid, flowing lines, but it has been purposely designed to be inconvenient as a weapon.

Very wide leaf blade

LEFT This intricately decorated Kuba mask displays the rich artistic culture of this Central African people. The weapons they produce are equally ornate and complex in their design.

large, cylindrical block, sometimes studded with brass nails. The heavy pommel of the trumbash even led to a nonsensical myth that they were dropped on the heads of enemies by warriors hiding in trees. Other grips are carved in the form of a human head and upper body. These, like many Mangbetu figures, are immediately identifiable because of the elongated skulls that they depict; traditionally, Mangbetu babies' heads were bound to induce them to grow into a stretched form that was considered to be eminently attractive.

Knives and daggers of the Kuba

The Kuba kingdom, a pre-colonial state centred near the land south of the Kasai River in Central Africa, was actually a conglomeration of many smaller tribes conquered by the original Kuba or Buschoog ("people of the throwing knife"). Famous as artists obsessed with glorious surface ornament, the Kuba produced extraordinary helmet-like masks, richly patterned textiles and beautiful weapons, the most idiosyncratic of which is the ikul. This very wide, leaf-bladed knife is said to have been introduced by King Shyaam aMbul aNgoong, the founder of the Kuba kingdom, in around 1600. The ikul was an emblem of peace. It is often

depicted on Kuba king figures, or *ndop*, which portray the monarch with an ikul in his left hand and an ilwoon, or sword of war, in his right, symbolizing the ruler's dual role as war-leader and peacemaker.

Ikuls are made with blades of iron or copper fitted with grips of wood, often inlaid with brass or copper; to further accentuate their role as symbols of peace, some ikuls are made entirely of carved wood.

Knives of the Ngala and the Ndjembo people

Congolese Ngala knives appear in three main forms. The first is very long, double-edged and curved in a shallow, graceful arc. The second is shorter and wider, the blade often tear-shaped with one or two ridges. The third is almost a form of machete – wide-bladed and long, decorated with ridges, profuse file-lines and cross-hatching. The leading edge is recurved and the trailing edge cut into a series of cuspings, the point forming a stout hook. These knives were often taken to be decapitation implements, but are more likely to have had ceremonial significance. Closely related to the Ngala knife is that of the neighbouring Ndjembo. This is of a similar length but straight until it divides into two long points that curve inwards in a crescent shape.

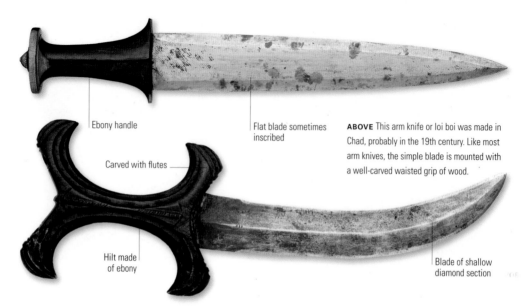

Ebony handle

Flat blade sometimes inscribed

ABOVE This arm knife or loi boi was made in Chad, probably in the 19th century. Like most arm knives, the simple blade is mounted with a well-carved waisted grip of wood.

Carved with flutes

Hilt made of ebony

Blade of shallow diamond section

African arm daggers

The dagger worn on the arm, or loi boi, is a uniquely African weapon popular among various tribes in many different regions of the continent. Generally it is worn in a scabbard attached by means of leather loops or thongs to the inner side of the left forearm, with the blade pointing up towards the elbow and the handle sitting close to the inside of the wrist. From here the arm dagger can be swiftly drawn when needed. Occasionally, it is instead worn on the outside of the upper arm with the blade facing downwards.

Arm daggers are associated with a number of the peoples inhabiting the Sahara and the Sahel – the border country of the Sudan between the northern desert regions and the central tropics. Northern examples are very often fitted with European knife or bayonet blades, or cut-down sword blades.

In northwest Africa the tribe most famous for their use of the arm dagger, or telek, is the Tuareg. Tribes in northern Nigeria, particularly the Nube and the Berom, also make arm daggers in the Tuareg style.

Arm daggers are also very popular among the Hausa of Cameroon. As in most traditional societies, a high-quality dagger for the Hausa reflects the owner's wealth and social status. Hausa daggers are not unlike Swiss daggers of the 15th and 16th centuries – with vaguely I-shaped hilts and wide, straight-sided blades that taper rapidly down the last third of their length to a very sharp stabbing point.

ABOVE This Sudanese dagger, which was made around 1900, has a less common curved blade and displays an ergonomic hilt not unlike the European baselard or Indian chilanum.

BELOW The Tuareg warriors of northwest Africa carry a variety of weapons but their most distinctive side arm is the telek or arm dagger.

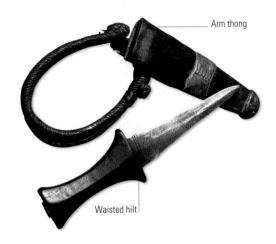

Arm thong

Waisted hilt

ABOVE The arm dagger is a common traditional weapon in many parts of North Africa. This Sudanese example is reasonably typical, with a simple waisted hilt and arm-thonged scabbard.

African throwing knives

The vast group of African multi-bladed weapons that ethnographers have commonly awarded the term "throwing knives" are unlike any other weapons found anywhere else in the world. Many types do not in fact appear to have been intended for throwing, while others, like the Fang "bird's-head" knife, could be thrown on occasion, though this was probably not its main method of use.

However, some types are without question carefully engineered as lethal aerial blades, which spin through the air like multi-bladed, razor-sharp boomerangs. Indeed, the earliest versions of these unusual weapons

may have developed from the very ancient idea of the throwing stick. Emil Torday, an early 20th-century traveller, collector and museum curator, wrote poetically about the use of throwing knives by Kuba warriors:

> *… then all of a sudden, some objects, glittering in the sun as if they were thunderbolts, come whirling with a weird hum through the air. The enemy warriors raise their shields; the shining mystery strikes it, rebounds into the air and continues to the attack; it smites the warrior behind his defence with its cruel blades. A weapon which is capable of killing behind a shield cannot fail to cause a panic …*

African throwing knives are usually classified into two very general groups: the circular type and the F-type. The former have blades that extend away from the centre of gravity, usually in three directions, while the latter are, to a greater or lesser degree, shaped in the form of the letter "F".

In addition to the Kuba, a great many tribes claim throwing knives as their traditional weapons, including the Azande, Ingessana (Tabi Hills, Sudan), Hutu (Rwanda, Burundi), Bwaka (Central African Republic), Ngbaka (northwest Congo), Masalit (Darfur, Sudan), Sara (Chad) and Nsakara (northeast Congo). The throwing knives of this last tribe are said to be some of the best, with their centre of gravity perfectly placed to produce a good spin. The flight characteristics of Nsakara throwing knives are considered excellent, the slight angling of the blade relative to its plane converting rotational motion into lift, essentially creating a somewhat stable propeller effect which increases the weapon's range and accuracy.

BELOW This Somali throwing knife appears to have been used a number of times, whether it was intended for fighting or not. Three of the blades appear to have been broken off and welded back in place.

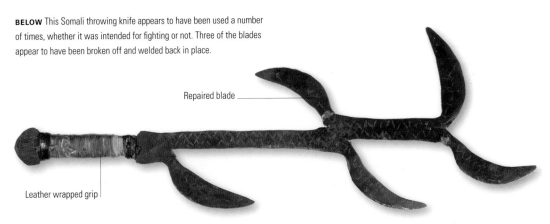

Repaired blade

Leather wrapped grip

Persian and Middle Eastern daggers

Persian daggers from before the 15th century are difficult to identify, as very few of them remain. But from the mid-1400s onwards, a greater number of spectacular pieces have survived. The best 15th-, 16th- and 17th-century examples are signed or have key features that allow them to be more accurately dated and attributed. Some embody distinctive Persian styles, while others represent general fashions throughout the Middle East.

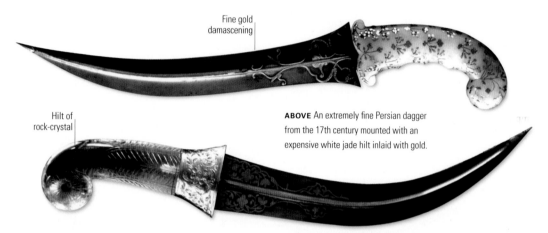

Fine gold damascening

Hilt of rock-crystal

ABOVE An extremely fine Persian dagger from the 17th century mounted with an expensive white jade hilt inlaid with gold.

ABOVE The hilt of this dagger, like the example above, was made in the 1600s in Persia. It is carved from a single piece of almost flawless rock-crystal, a rare material requiring very skilled carving.

For centuries Persia was at the heart of the Islamic world, situated between Turkey and Arabia to the west and Muslim Afghanistan and India to the east. It was a geographical, cultural and military crossroads. The Seljuk Turks ruled Persia from 1037 until the early 13th century, when they lost it to the Khwarezmids, another Turkic people of Mamluk origin. The Shahs of the Khwarezmid Empire in turn had to defend Persia against Genghis Khan, who in 1219 seized key locations along the Silk Road including Samarkand (in modern Uzbekistan) and Otar (a city in what is today Kazakhstan). Subsequently most of Persia became a part of the vast Mongol Empire. Not until 1292 did it return to Muslim rule with the conversion of Ghazan Khan (1271–1304) Persia's Mongol overlord.

Years of conquest and reconquest followed Ghazan's secession from the Chino-Mongol Empire, the borders being continually redrawn by successive invaders, most notably the Turco-Mongol warlord Timur the Lame (1336–1405), who conquered Persia and established the Muslim Timurid Dynasty at the end of the 14th century. The Timurid Emirs ruled Persia for nearly 100 years until the establishment of the Safavid Dynasty in 1500. Under the Safavids, Persia entered its greatest cultural period since the first Islamic conquest in the 7th century.

Weapons production in Persia

Persian weapons were famous throughout the Middle East from ancient times. Samarkand and Isfahan were especially renowned as centres for the production of the finest swords and daggers. Persia was wealthy in the natural resources required for the production of high-quality weapons – iron, silver and gold. A long tradition of the scientific study of metals in the Islamic world led to the development of "watered" steel, fusions of high- and medium-carbon steels that displayed in good measure the two key properties of an excellent blade – hardness and elasticity. The extraordinary silk-like patterns that formed on the surfaces of these blades when etched with acid were a sure sign of their quality.

The problems of identification

Today it is often very difficult to identify daggers, and blades in general, as specifically Persian, partly because so few have survived from earlier times, but mainly because the arms trade operated on a scale far larger and more expansive than Persia itself. Indian blades were imported into Persia, where they might be decorated and assembled into complete weapons by the local craftsmen, while Persian work was also exported, not only back to India but also west into Arabia and Turkey.

Our modern understanding is further hampered by the fact that specialist researchers did not begin the scholarly study of Persian weapons dating from the 15th to 19th centuries until the 1970s. Thus a great deal of basic research is still lacking, and ways of dating daggers in particular, though now much improved, are still very generalized. Indeed, many daggers that bear dated inscriptions remained unread until the late 20th century.

ABOVE Daggers have been made throughout the Islamic world for hundreds of years. This scene of a Yemeni daggersmith's workshop is undoubtedly a sight that has remained largely unchanged in centuries.

The kylin clue

Depictions of the mythical beasts known as kylins appear in art throughout the Middle and Far East. Although exact portrayals vary, the kylin is usually shown as a hooved, dragon-like creature with a scaly body and antlers similar to those of a stag. It is often depicted with its body bathed in fire. It is invariably believed to be a creature sent to punish the sinful, or to protect the good from evil. It is also sometimes considered the pet of divine beings.

Kylins appear on certain early Persian daggers of the 15th century. The specific nature of these appearances, along with dragons and birds, is closely comparable to the decoration on the exquisite leather bindings on Persian manuscripts of the 1400s. Although precise dating of manuscripts of this period is difficult, there seems to be no suggestion that any of them could be later than 1500. It seems likely, therefore, that the presence of such beasts on the hilt of a fine Persian dagger is a good indicator of an early date.

RIGHT The kylin is as iconic in Eastern culture as dragons are in Western medieval and Renaissance art. The horned heads, scales and fiery tails of these Chinese figures are very similar to dragons.

Decoration and inscriptions

The best daggers produced in Persia and Turkey were usually fitted with hilts carved out of rock-crystal, jade or ivory, or forged of watered steel. Expensive dagger hilts and scabbards were also studded with gems, cabochons often being preferred, perhaps because they resembled drops of blood or water. One poem found on several surviving daggers, in Persian *ruba'i* rhyme, includes a vivid reference to this form of decoration:

Every time that thy dagger talked of vengeance,
It brought the times into confusion by its shedding
* of blood!*
By the elegance and purity of the stones which are on it,
It recalled a willow-leaf covered with dew!

Persian blade inscriptions were usually evocative of, or at least appropriate to the function or character of the dagger, both as a weapon and as a symbol:

I wanted so much to have a gleaming dagger,
That each of my ribs became a dagger.

Stab my breast several times with a dagger,
Open in my heart several doors of delight!

Dating Persian daggers

Although curved blades have been traditionally preferred throughout the Middle East, many of the best Persian daggers carry straight double-edged blades. Fine Persian blades of the 15th, 16th and 17th centuries are usually decorated with poetic inscriptions. The weapons can be dated through careful examination of the language and type of script used in the inscriptions. Verses in Turkic might lead one to assume that a particular dagger was of Turkish origin. But Turkic was also used by the Safavid Court. In such cases the script itself, rather than the language, might be the most vital clue. Turkic verses sometimes appear on daggers written in fluid *nasta 'liq* script, a style of writing that originated in Persia.

Another important indicator of the date of a fine Persian dagger is the exact character of the background against which the script is set. For example, 15th-century blades tend to have inscriptions set against a plain background, while in the 16th and 17th centuries the backgrounds were usually filled in with flowers, leaves and coiling vines, the density of which seems to increase along with the date of the work.

ABOVE Persian noblemen's daggers, though decorative, were also used to settle feuds. This detail from the 14th-century *Jami al-tawarikh*, a history of 13th-century Persia, shows the murder of a nobleman.

Others equate daggers and the wounds they can inflict with women and love:

> That oppressive mocker holds in her hand the
>   dagger of vengeance,
> In order to shed men's blood, what more does
>   she hold in her hand?
> Draw the dagger and pull the heart from our breast,
> So that thou mayest see our heart among the lovers.

Finally, many inscriptions are much simpler and more straightforward:

> Be happy.

The Arabian jambiya

By far the most ubiquitous form of dagger found throughout the Arab world was the jambiya. The name of the weapon is derived from the Persian world *jamb*,

ABOVE The jambiya is still commonly worn in many parts of the Arab world. This young Yemeni man wears his dagger at the waist, tucked into a wide belt as is the usual way in this part of the world.

Wooden grip

Matching scabbard locket

Silver-hilted sheath

Decorative edging

meaning side. It is often very difficult to distinguish a khanjar from a jambiya and vice versa; indeed, since both terms were used very generally, and meant different things in different parts of the Middle East, as well as in North Africa, India and elsewhere, distinction may be an impossible task. Despite this, writers in English are often tempted to apply general foreign terms to very specific types of weapon, for which they were never intended. The terms *khanjar* and *jambiya* simply mean "dagger". Nevertheless, for the purposes of this book, khanjar is used to refer to the narrower-bladed Indo-Persian daggers which are favoured in the eastern parts of the Muslim world, while jambiya refers in the most generalized terms to the classic "Arabian" dagger that is easily recognized by its wide, steeply curved blade encased in an often highly decorated scabbard that exaggerates the curved form.

LEFT This good-quality Yemeni jambiya was made in around 1900. It retains its original scabbard and belt, with mounts that have been decorated to match the hilt sheath of the dagger.

The jambiya blade

The arc of the jambiya blade often begins gradually, just forward of the hilt, but increases rapidly in its sweep closer to the point. The blades are often very wide and stiffened by a very proud medial rib. Scabbards usually exaggerate the curved form even further, the scabbard chape often being brought to a full right angle or even turning back up towards the grip.

While both edges of the jambiya blade were sharpened, the inner edge, much like an amputation knife, was kept especially honed. The blades were said to cut easily through the thickest clothes to the bone. The inner edge was used to slash the throat of an enemy, while the curved design made it possible to stab around the opponent's body to strike his back or kidneys. In 1877 an Englishman named John Fryer Keane visited Mecca and described the jambiya as being excellent for cutting through skin and hair, and also stated that it would cut through a rolled-up sheepskin with a single slash.

The hilt is usually a simple waisted affair, having a flat-topped pommel and similarly formed forward section – without any arms or guard – shaped to fit flush with the locket of the scabbard. Hilts are made of wood, bone, ivory or rhinoceros horn. The jambiya remains an important part of traditional male formal dress in the Middle East, especially in Yemen, Oman and Saudi Arabia. Worn centrally at the waist, the dagger was a prominent fashion statement but was also very quick to draw if the need arose. As jewellery items, jambiya hilts may also be further decorated with gold or silver filagree, amber, coins, coral or semi-precious stones.

Later Persian daggers

Many of the antique Persian daggers on the market today are khanjars dating from the Qajar Period (1781–1925). Most of these are composed of a hilt shaped like a capital "I", carved from either walrus or elephant ivory, joined to a blade having a graceful curve and either a prominent medial rib or central fuller. Normally the blades are made of watered steel. The hilts are usually carved with scenes from Persian history and mythology. A rarer type of khanjar from the Qajar Period features a hilt and scabbard flamboyantly decorated with multicoloured enamel. The cities of Shiraz and Isfahan were both famous centres of fine enamelling: indeed, Isfahani enamellers are still renowned in modern Iran.

Sharp ridged point

The kard

In addition to the curved jambiya and khanjar designs, straight-bladed daggers were also common throughout Persia, Turkey and the wider Middle East. The two most universal forms were the kard and the peshkabz.

Kard simply means "knife" and this term is still used today to refer to an ordinary kitchen knife. The historical weapon does indeed strongly resemble a cooking knife, having a long, usually single-edged, straight blade and a simple grip. Such a weapon, though primarily intended for fighting, would inevitably be used for other purposes. Timurid miniatures show men cutting dough and slitting the throats of sheep with kards.

Some kards make their primary role as a combat weapon more explicit; the points are sometimes specially thickened and shaped like a modern armour-piercing bullet to strengthen them for

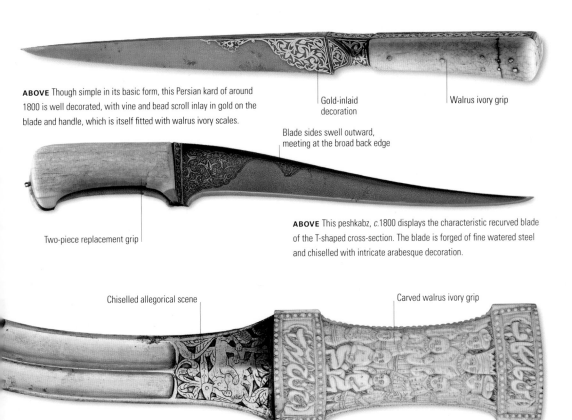

ABOVE Though simple in its basic form, this Persian kard of around 1800 is well decorated, with vine and bead scroll inlay in gold on the blade and handle, which is itself fitted with walrus ivory scales.

Gold-inlaid decoration

Walrus ivory grip

Blade sides swell outward, meeting at the broad back edge

Two-piece replacement grip

ABOVE This peshkabz, *c.*1800 displays the characteristic recurved blade of the T-shaped cross-section. The blade is forged of fine watered steel and chiselled with intricate arabesque decoration.

Chiselled allegorical scene

Carved walrus ivory grip

stabbing. These reinforced points were common enough to warrant their own term; in Persian they are fittingly described as *noke makhruti*, a term meaning "cone-point".

Kard grips were frequently made of walrus ivory, although elephant ivory examples are known. Khan Alam, Persian ambassador to the Mughal Court in India during the early 17th century, gave the Emperor Jahangir a dagger with a handle of a special type of walrus ivory speckled with black crystals ("piebald" ivory). The Great Mughal was very impressed and compared the dagger handle to the swirling pattern of watered steel. Horn was another material commonly used for kard grips, as was steel enamelled or decorated with gold overlay.

The peshkabz

The term *peshkabz* originally described the front of a girdle that Persian men wore while wrestling. The use of the same term to describe a dagger then seems

ABOVE The carved ivory hilts of Persian khanjars of the Qajar Period are very distinctive. The handles feature very fine carved relief work, and are usually fitted with blades of a high quality.

to indicate that a peshkabz was worn centrally, as opposed to the khanjar and the kard, which were tucked to the right and left sides respectively. Of course, multiple knives of these various types were often carried together at the same time

The blade of a peshkabz is easily recognized by its steeply tapered straight or recurved blade, the characteristic feature being its especially thick back. To achieve this thickness while keeping the weight down, the smith would grind down the sides of the blade immediately below the back, so that the back itself could remain 1.5–2mm (.0059–.0078in) wide; the result of this grinding was to give the blade a T-shaped cross-section, rather than the much heavier wedge shape that would otherwise have been the result of the thickening of the back to this extent.

Indian daggers

Daggers from India take many strange and unusual forms. Their variety is a testament to the importance of the elite warrior class for both the Islamic and Hindu traditions. Weapons from the Muslim Mughal Empire, which expanded into northern India in the 16th century, are similar to the Persian weapons from which they are descended, while others, originating in the southern Hindu kingdoms, are unlike anything anywhere else.

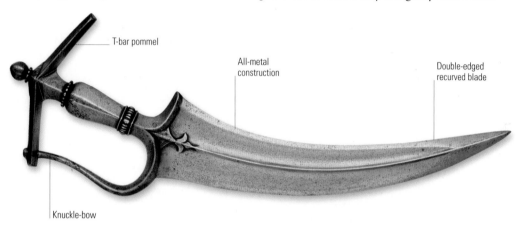

T-bar pommel

All-metal construction

Double-edged recurved blade

Knuckle-bow

India is a vast subcontinent, a place of bewildering variety in art, language and belief. For thousands of years it has been a cultural crossing point, where vast invading empires collided while diverse localized tribes struggled to maintain their lands and unique customs. But even as India's many peoples struggled against each other for territorial and economic supremacy, their many distinctive cultures could not help but influence each other to varying degrees. Thus, for example, did the Muslim Mughals, who were of Persian origin, adopt much from the Hindu and tribal peoples that they conquered in the northern parts of the Indian subcontinent.

The chilanum

One uniquely Indian dagger form is the chilanum. It is characterized by its double-edged recurving blade, usually having a strong central spine and two or more fullers, and by its unusual hilt – the pommel drawn out into a drooping "T", or sometimes curving, frond-like arms. The guard is similarly shaped but with shorter arms, the forward arm often being drawn out to form a knuckle guard. While it has been suggested that the

ABOVE This fine all-steel *chilanum*, made in the south of India in the late 18th century, displays all of the usual features of its type – the drooping T-shaped pommel, knuckle-bow and gently curved blade.

chilanum is Nepalese in origin, it seems to have evolved in the south of India, where it was clearly very common from the 16th century. Sometimes chilanum hilts are carved from hard stone, although most are metal, usually made of steel in one piece with the blade.

Mughal princes were renowned throughout the world for their love of gems and jewels. The finest Mughal chilanums had hilts of pure gold embellished with inlaid precious stones. The chilanum was supposedly introduced to the Mughals by the Rajputs, by way of Emperor Akbar's marriages to Rajput princesses, which brought with them military alliances and a complex intermingling of the Islamic and Hindu cultures. Chilanum blades were invariably of the finest watered steel, and the arms of the guard were worked into plant or animal forms. A famous portrait of Shah Jahan (1592–1666), painted in 1617, shows the Mughal emperor and builder of the Taj Mahal wearing just such a chilanum in his qamarband (waist band).

Wootz steel blades

Some Indian and Persian dagger blades display a beautiful wavy, flowing pattern. This pattern indicates that the blade is made of a high-quality steel generally known today as "wootz". The term perhaps is a derivation or corruption of *ukku*, an old south Indian word for steel.

Possibly as early as the 3rd century BC, centres in south India and Sri Lanka were producing this very high-carbon steel in crucibles; iron and wood charcoal were placed in the crucible, which was heated in a furnace. This produced an iron and carbon alloy – steel. The crucible process causes iron carbide particles to scatter throughout the crystalline structure of the steel. When the steel is tempered through heating and quenching, these particles form into bands. When the steel is lightly etched, by applying a mild acid such as vinegar to its surface, these bands react differently from the steel around them and discolour, producing

the extraordinary "watered" pattern. This pattern not only gives the blade an almost magical appearance, it is also a useful indicator of technical quality. This is because patterned blades, having a high carbon content, are very strong and can hold a razor-sharp edge.

RIGHT The mesmerizing patterns of a wootz blade are brought out only when the blade is lightly etched with a weak acid. Over-polishing can easily eradicate the visible pattern.

The khanjarli

An 18th-century variation of the chilanum is the khanjarli. This dagger may be recognized by its wide, mushroom-like pommel, which supplants the chilanum's T-bar but performs very much the same function: to brace the hand against slippage while dealing overarm blows. Khanjarli pommels and grips are usually made of bone or ivory, two pieces sandwiching the tang and riveted in place. The khanjarli is thought to be Maratha in origin, and is usually associated with Vizianagaram in Orissa, a

region famous for its elephants and ivory work. This has led to the suggestion that the distinctive ivory-handled khanjarlis come mainly from this part of India. The Marathas conquered Orissa in the 18th century, and undoubtedly the khanjarli design spread outside of its area of origin in subsequent campaigns.

BELOW Both the chilanum and its cousin the khanjarli were sometimes fitted with recurved blades like this fine example forged in wootz.

Multi-ribbed blade

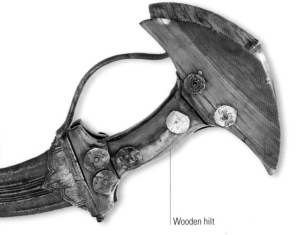

Wooden hilt

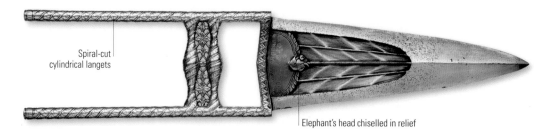

Spiral-cut
cylindrical langets

Elephant's head chiselled in relief

The katar

The most famous Indian dagger is without doubt the katar, or jamdhar. The basic katar is composed of a short, wide blade from the base of which emanate two long, metal langets spaced apart from each other by the width of the user's hand. Between the langets is placed a pair of bars that form the grip of the weapon. So unlike most conventional daggers, which when held project their blades along a line approximately 90 degrees to that of the user's forearm, the katar places the blade in line with the arm, so that the striking action is essentially the same as a punch. Therefore, when striking correctly the user is able to put the whole weight of his body behind his dagger blows. Because the force of katar strikes could be so great, many examples have specially thickened points, to help prevent them bending or breaking. These points may also have improved the katar as an armour-piercing weapon, with which the user could literally punch through the textile, mail and perhaps even plate armour of his opponents on the battlefield.

One Indian fighting style, in evidence from the 16th century onwards, involved two katars, one held in each hand. With each fist armed with a lethal 1ft (30cm) or more of razor-sharp steel, the Indian warrior must have adopted a technique not unlike that of the pugilist, punching at the head and body of his opponent with sudden, lightning-fast attacks.

The katar seems to be of south Indian origin, earliest forms being closely associated with the Vijayanagara Kingdom, a south Indian empire in the Deccan founded in the 14th century. One of the most famous groups of these daggers came from the armoury at Thanjavur, which, with the armoury's

ABOVE This Rajasthani katar of about 1850 carries a typically heavy blade, thickened at the point and ideally suited to stabbing through the light armour typically worn in northwestern India.

dissipation in the late 19th century, has today come to be spread throughout many different museum collections. These early katars generally include a leaf or shell-like plate that protects the back of the hand, usually elaborately decorated with piercing and file-work.

Towards the end of the 16th and into the 17th century, European blades began to be imported into India in very large numbers and many katars dating from the late 1500s and early 1600s are fitted with such blades, which are often broken sword blades. By the second half of the 17th century the more enveloping hand guard was beginning to be discarded in favour of the simpler hilt that is now familiar as the classic katar form.

Stout, straight katar blades are common, but they are by no means the only type. Regional tastes led to a profusion of flamboyant katar designs. While the straight-bladed versions tended to be fashionable in the north of India, wavy or curved blades seemed more popular in the south. Multi-bladed weapons with two or even three blades were not uncommon. Other katars, sometimes referred to as "scissors" katars, were cleverly constructed so that when the grips were squeezed together, the blade split into three, rather like the European sword-catching parrying daggers of the late 16th and 17th centuries. Perhaps the most novel variation

LEFT Like most combination weapons, the effectiveness of pistol katars like this c.1850 weapon is uncertain. The 9.5mm calibre pistols were fired by triggers pulled by the index and little fingers.

on the katar theme was a Rajasthani type that was fitted with two very small flintlock or percussion pistols, one flanking each edge of the blade. The triggers were fitted inwards over the grip, which meant that they could be pulled by the index and little fingers, one at a time or simultaneously. Multiple katars are also known in which one or two smaller katars fit inside a larger one constructed as a sort of sleeve.

Katars were also important status symbols and many survive with extraordinarily varied forms of decoration. Hilts covered in enamel, gems and gold koftgari, blades chiselled with complex figures, scenes and abstract ornament, and sheaths covered in rich silk or velvet were the prize possessions of, for example, the famous Rajput warriors of northwest India. Many Rajput and Mughal princes and noblemen were portrayed with their katars tucked away safely at their waists, ready at all times if needed for self-defence but also an obvious sign of wealth and position. Katars were even used by the Mughal nobility to hunt tigers. Employed in pairs, one katar in each hand, this was without doubt the most impressive but also most hazardous of hunting practices.

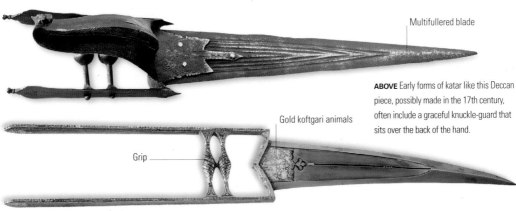

Multifullered blade

ABOVE Early forms of katar like this Deccan piece, possibly made in the 17th century, often include a graceful knuckle-guard that sits over the back of the hand.

Gold koftgari animals

Grip

ABOVE Katar design varies greatly. Here the arms of the hilt are extended, and the blade has a gentle curve.

RIGHT When the forward grip-bar of the "scissors" katar is squeezed, the blade spreads apart into three.

Grip-bars in the squeezed position

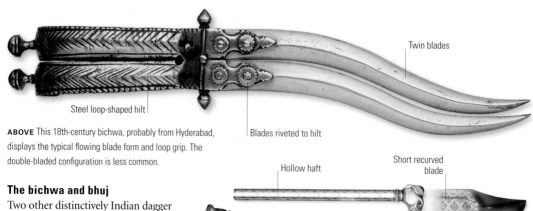

ABOVE This 18th-century bichwa, probably from Hyderabad, displays the typical flowing blade form and loop grip. The double-bladed configuration is less common.

Twin blades

Steel loop-shaped hilt

Blades riveted to hilt

The bichwa and bhuj

Two other distinctively Indian dagger types are the *bichwa*, or "scorpion" dagger, and the *bhuj*, or "elephant" dagger. The bichwa usually has a simple all-metal hilt, having a knuckle guard but no other distinctive features, and a recurved blade, but one much narrower than that found on most chilanums and khanjarlis. Like the latter, the bichwa is probably a Maratha design. This small dagger was easily hidden up a sleeve or in the qamarband, and was especially useful as a weapon for clandestine attack. It is perhaps most famous as the concealed weapon of the famous Maratha war-leader Shivaji (1630–1680), whose Robin Hood-like adventures are still told in the form of stories, poems and films. Shivaji is said to have had a bichwa named *Bhavani* ("giver of life"), which he used (although some accounts insist he used a *bagh-nakh*, or "tiger-claw") to disembowel Afzal Khan, a general in the service of the Mughal Emperor Aurangzeb (1618–1707), who tried to assassinate him during a supposedly friendly meeting.

BELOW This Mughal khanjar is mounted with a classic horsehead grip of jade inlaid with gold. The blade is probably Persian, indicated by the palmette ornament at the ricasso and the recessed panels of the blade.

Hollow haft

Short recurved blade

Stiletto hidden in haft

Scabbard

ABOVE The bhuj represents one of the most unorthodox dagger designs. The elegant dagger blade is mounted at a right angle to a short metal haft. The haft is usually hollow, inside which is often hidden another dagger of more conventional form, a short spike mounted onto the underside of the screw-threaded pommel.

The bhuj takes its name from the city in the Kachchh district of Gujarat (in the extreme west of India) where it was supposedly invented. It is sometimes also referred to as a *gandasa*, or "axe-knife", and is made up of a short, very heavy dagger blade that surmounts a short, axe-like haft (handle). The head of an elephant in profile is very often worked into the metal forming the base of the blade, hence the further nickname "elephant" dagger. Sometimes a small stiletto-like dagger is hidden in the haft of the bhuj, the butt cap of which unscrews to release it.

Recurved blade

Inlaid jade hilt

Koftgari decoration

One of the most popular techniques used for the decoration of fine daggers in India was koftgari, a particular type of gold inlay. The origin of the term is a brilliant evocation of the process; the Persian word *koft* means "interwoven", while a *gar* was a goldsmith or gold-beater.

The koftgari process starts with a piece of steel being cross-hatched with hundreds of tiny scratches, made with a special stout knife. Minute strands of gold wire are then worked into the surface, and are held there because the soft gold is pushed down into the scratches, becoming in a way interwoven with the steel.

This process was used to create all sorts of intricate designs, from simple plant forms and geometric patterns to complex scenes including gardens, buildings, trees and animals.

ABOVE The very elegant koftgari work on this Indian katar, which dates from the early 19th century, includes representations of cheetahs, water buffalo and lions.

LEFT Fine weapons made in Lucknow in northern India, such as this 19th-century peshkabz, usually include silver hilts embellished with brightly coloured enamelling.

The Persian influence

While the katar and chilanum originated in the south, the bhuj from the far west, and the khanjarli from the east, other dagger types were introduced from the north. The khanjar was perhaps one of the commonest forms throughout Indo-Persia, popular in Mughal India and Afghanistan but also within the rest of the Islamic world. It is probably of Persian origin, brought to India in the 15th century with the conquest of the first Mughal Emperor. The khanjar's most recognizable attribute is its supremely graceful recurved blade, often with a thickened reinforced stabbing point. Indian khanjar hilts, like those of the Middle East, lack a guard and are usually carved from a single piece of ivory, jade, agate or similar hard stone. Some especially fine examples are made of clear rock-crystal. The handles are often inlaid with precious and semi-precious stones and gold, and commonly carved into horses', rams' and tigers' heads. In depictions of Mughal noblemen these distinctive handles are often seen protruding from their sashes.

Some dagger forms were popular throughout India, but others were only found close to their areas of introduction. The peshkabz and the kard were Persian in origin, introduced by the Mughals. The peshkabz was never adopted with any regularity beyond the north. The kard caught on to some extent in central India, but remained perhaps less common as a fighting weapon. It was common throughout Rajasthan and down into central India, carried along, undoubtedly, by the progress of the Mughal Empire's incursions from the north.

The kris of South-east Asia

Most weapons are something more than a killing tool. They are symbols of status, signifiers of wealth and prestige, or badges of allegiance. But rarely are they believed to possess genuine supernatural powers and seldom is their physical appearance so conducive to such beliefs. The other-worldly appearance of the kris, and the mystical belief system that surrounds it, has promoted a unique relationship between the weapon and its world.

From the 1st century AD onwards, trade routes expanded east from India into Assam, Burma, Indonesia and Malaysia. With the accompanying migrations came also cultural and religious transmission. Hinduism became the dominant faith in some areas of the Malay Peninsula and Archipelago, while Islam and Buddhism prevailed in others. The major faiths intermingled with a bewildering variety of indigenous belief systems practised by many diverse ethnic groups, and so it is not surprising that the weapons found in this vast area are equally multifarious. Indian, Chinese and European influences combined with unique local styles and designs, creating a vast range of edged weapons.

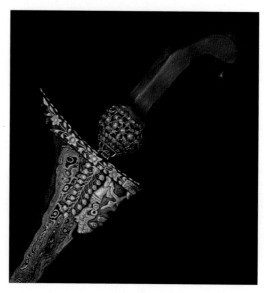

ABOVE A fine kris blade must be mounted with a hilt of equal quality. This example has been intricately carved in a highly individual and complex manner using very diverse materials.

The origins of the kris

This vibrant set of ethnic communities – where many belief systems existed side by side – might not seem like the most obvious environment for a single iconic weapon to evolve. After all, as we have seen, cultural diversity in India generated a great variety of weapons forms and designs. Yet one form of dagger did indeed rise above the many other types of knife and sword in use throughout the Malay Archipelago. The kris, or keris, achieved a cultural status unique in the world history of daggers. It was this weapon, thought to have originated in Java, that later spread throughout southeast Asia – perhaps the only weapon whose use was shared by the many peoples of that region.

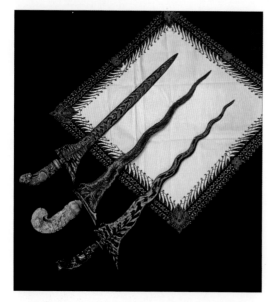

ABOVE The belief in the magical power of the kris is not difficult to understand when one sees a kris blade of exceptional quality, such as these Javanese examples, rippling with swirling colour.

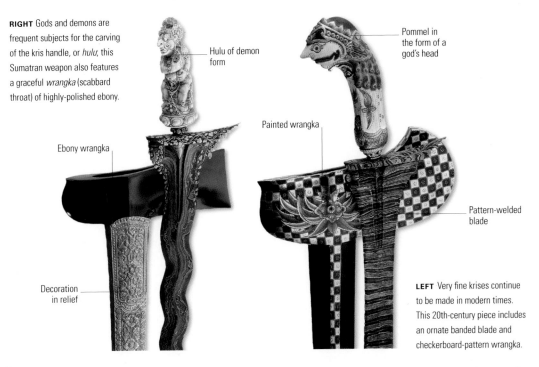

RIGHT Gods and demons are frequent subjects for the carving of the kris handle, or *hulu,* this Sumatran weapon also features a graceful *wrangka* (scabbard throat) of highly-polished ebony.

Hulu of demon form

Ebony wrangka

Decoration in relief

Painted wrangka

Pommel in the form of a god's head

Pattern-welded blade

LEFT Very fine krises continue to be made in modern times. This 20th-century piece includes an ornate banded blade and checkerboard-pattern wrangka.

It has been suggested that the kris was inspired by the stingray's stinger, while other theories relate it to the ancient Chinese ko, or dagger-axe, which, like the kris, projects its blade at a right angle to the user's grip. Whatever the origin, it seems clear that the kris had defined itself as a distinctive Malay weapon by the 14th century. A carving at the mid-14th-century Hindu temple of Candi Sukuh in Java depicts a god forging a kris, while one of the earliest known examples bears a date corresponding to AD1342.

The kris blade

This knife is characterized by its long, narrow blade, which can be either straight or, more famously, wavy. Kris blades are pattern-welded works of art, made of up to seven types of iron (meteoric iron being highly prized) and steel braided and forged together. After being formed, the kris blade was carefully ground, polished, boiled in a potion of water, sulphur and salt, and rubbed with lime juice. These processes brought out the blade's welded pattern; not only did the different metals darken and discolour to different degrees, the citric acid also ate into them in varying amounts. Thus the pattern, or *pamor*, of the blade took on a striking, three-dimensional quality, like tiny

meandering canyons and rivers. Malay smiths created around 150 different pamors, each being given a poetically evocative name, such as "tender coconut leaf", "spray of jasmine", "venerable serpent", "flowering of nutmeg", "snakeskin" and "rind of the watermelon".

Although kris forms vary enormously, most blades flare out at the base to form a pointed projection sometimes called the "elephant's trunk". They are fitted with a narrow metal band forming the *ganja*, or guard. A thin tang is forged out of the ganja and inserted into the *ukiran*, or handle, and secured with a gummy paste. The ukiran of the kris is usually a work of art in itself. Beautifully sculpted in ivory (elephant, walrus or even mammoth), horn, wood, bone, brass, silver or gold, kris handles take many forms. Hindu gods and demons, animals, scrollwork, phallic symbols and a number of basic ergonomic forms are all common.

In combat the kris was predominantly a thrusting weapon. The position and shape of the grip, not unlike that of a pistol, allowed the blade to project along the same line as the forearm. Like the Indian katar, it was not uncommon for two krises to be used in combat, one in each hand. The distinctive sheath could also be used to block an opponent's blows.

Foreign interest

Since westerners first became aware of the kris, it has been a source of fascination and curiosity. Sir Francis Drake (*c.*1540–1596) brought krises back to England from Java in 1580, while another was sent to King James I (1566–1625) as a gift in 1612. They also became popular with European artists in the 16th and 17th centuries. Rembrandt (1606–1669), for example, included krises in several of his works. He grasps one in an engraved and etched self-portrait (mistakenly titled *Self-Portrait with Raised Sabre*), while a soldier plunges another into Samson's eye in *The Blinding of Samson*.

A magical relationship

A kris was, for its owner, an intensely personal object. It was washed and anointed during annual rituals, during which offerings were also made to it, in similar fashion to the sword worship practised by some Indian Hindus. A kris was considered one of a man's basic possessions, along with a house, a wife and a horse. It asserted a man's identity and associations, both within his family and in society in general. A kris passed down through a family was a tangible bond between a man and his ancestors, a link between the living and the dead. In Java the relationship between a kris and its owner was so strong that the weapon could actually stand in for a bridegroom at his wedding if for some reason he was unable to be present himself.

The kris was also believed to possess many mystical properties. Some have been said to fly out of their sheaths at night to kill unsuspecting victims. Others were thought to have healing powers. One of the most widely held ideas was that a kris could kill someone just by being pointed at them; great care was therefore taken in the handling of a kris to prevent accidental harm caused by someone inadvertently coming in line with the point. In Bali, specially designed kris stands in the form of animals or demons held the weapon vertically to minimize the danger from its projected magical energy. It is also said that the very best krises can kill simply by being driven into the footprint, shadow or a photo of the intended victim.

An ancient weapon in a modern world

Krises featured in Indonesian warfare into the 20th century. During the Philippines Campaign (1899–1905), local kris-wielding warriors mounted many ambushes and nocturnal attacks against the American military. In 1903, the US Army fought a group of Moros near Jolo that included 4000 men armed with krises.

Their leader was later captured, but the American force guarding him was in turn ambushed by men with krises; he was rescued and a number of the Americans killed or injured, including the commander, whose hand was so badly slashed that several of his fingers had to be amputated.

Since the 1960s, the kris has begun to lose much of its cultural and religious influence in Indonesian society. Although a small number of master smiths practising the traditional art form can still be found, they are now very few. Transmission of the skill of kris making has also been made difficult as the younger generation becomes increasingly westernized.

Efforts from the 1990s onwards have, however, revived the craft of kris making to some extent, and in 2005 UNESCO heralded the kris a Masterpiece of the Oral and Intangible Heritage of Humanity (Third Proclamation).

RIGHT This drawing made in 1864 gives some idea of what an Indonesian (Javanese) warband might have looked like. The leading warrior holds his kris, signifying his elite status, high in the air.

ABOVE Another kris appears in Rembrandt's *The Blinding of Samson* (1636); here a soldier plunges one into Samson's eye. It was undoubtedly thought to be suitably exotic and thus appropriate to the Biblical theme.

The Japanese tanto

Unlike the many different dagger forms that evolved elsewhere in Asia, those of Japan remained remarkably consistent in design throughout their long history. A short, single-edged, thick-backed blade, ground to a steep wedge shape in cross-section, remained the sidearm of samurai warriors for several hundred years. In that time the design changed very little, remaining essentially a miniature version of the swords with which it was partnered.

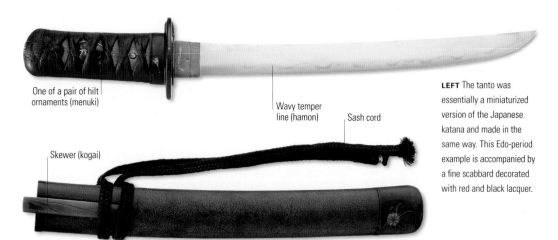

One of a pair of hilt ornaments (menuki)

Wavy temper line (hamon)

Sash cord

Skewer (kogai)

LEFT The tanto was essentially a miniaturized version of the Japanese katana and made in the same way. This Edo-period example is accompanied by a fine scabbard decorated with red and black lacquer.

The distinctive Japanese dagger, the tanto, is thought to have first appeared in the pre-medieval Heian Period (AD794–1185). Early tantos seem to have been very basic utilitarian implements, unworthy of note. It was not until the very end of that era that the tanto distinguished itself, as a work of art as well as a weapon, during the bloody Gempei War (1180–85) fought between the rival Minamoto and Taira clans.

By this time the warrior culture of the samurai had fully developed, and along with it, codified systems of combat. Warriors of the late Heian Period carried the bow, a long-bladed staff weapon called a naginata and the long sword, or tachi, as their primary weapons, along with the tanto as a weapon of last resort. These weapons, and the sequence of their use, are vividly described in an account of the first Battle of Uji (1180), the opening battle of the Gempei War. One passage from the epic *Tale of the Heike* (1371), as follows, relates how the warrior Tsutsui Jomyo Meishu fought the Taira samurai on the Uji bridge itself, in an attempt to prevent them crossing and destroying the fleeing Minamoto forces:

And loosing off twenty arrows like lightning flashes he slew twelve of the Taira samurai and wounded eleven more … throwing away his bow … With his naginata he cut down five of the enemy but with the sixth the blade snapped ... he drew his tachi … and cut down eight men. But as he brought down the ninth with an exceedingly mighty blow on the helmet, the blade broke at the hilt .... Then seizing his dagger, which was the only weapon he had left, he plied it as one in a death fury.

The tanto and ritual suicide

This dagger was not only the samurai's final option in hand-to-hand combat. It was also the weapon with which he killed himself when defeated in battle or dishonoured. After the destruction of his forces by the Taira at Uji, the Minamoto commander Yorimasa quickly wrote a death poem on the back of his war fan before using his tanto to cut two long slashes into his abdomen. This is the earliest known instance of a samurai committing *seppuku*, or ritual suicide after a battlefield defeat.

A lethal work of art

Following the Gempei War and throughout the subsequent Kamakura Period (1186–1333), which marks the beginning of the Middle Ages in Japan, the tanto developed into a weapon pleasing to the eye and worthy of respect, as skilfully made and as beautifully decorated as any sword. The blade was constructed in the same way as that of the sword; it was single-edged and strong-backed, 15–30cm (6–12in) long, with an asymmetric point tapering diagonally to the back.

Early forms of the dagger were also termed *koshi-gatana*, or "loin-sword" and were worn tucked into the armoured samurai's sash, or *uwa-obi*. While the

ABOVE This dramatic detail from an early 17th-century version of the Kamakura/Muromachi *gunki-mono* ("war-tales") shows the monk Mongaku attacking a samurai with a *tanto*.

earliest forms had curved blades, by the Muromachi Period (1334–1572) nearly straight blades became more common. The dagger's companion, the sword, was also changing; the long tachi was increasingly being replaced by the shorter, handier katana. The katana was not slung like the tachi but thrust through the girdle along with the dagger. The mounts of these early sword and dagger sets often did not match, although later they would be decorated as a pair.

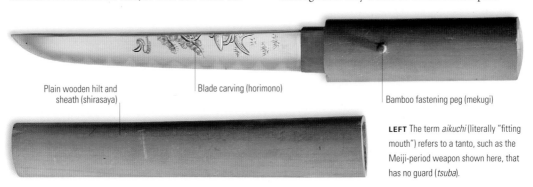

Plain wooden hilt and
sheath (shirasaya)

Blade carving (horimono)

Bamboo fastening peg (mekugi)

LEFT The term *aikuchi* (literally "fitting mouth") refers to a tanto, such as the Meiji-period weapon shown here, that has no guard (*tsuba*).

desperate sacrifice was later held up as a powerful example of samurai honour and loyalty; the bloodstained floorboards from the room where the women and children died were later built into the ceiling of a nearby temple.

The decline of the tanto

The tanto was gradually being replaced as the companion weapon of the sword during the violent Momayama Period (1573–1603). The Edo (or Tokugawa) Period (1603–1867) that followed began with the unification of Japan under Tokugawa Ieyasu (1543–1616) and ushered in over 250 years of cultural development and relative peace. The tanto fell quickly out of use as the symbolism of weapons became as important as their application. Although the production of the more symbolic elements of the samurai's dress, namely his armour and sword, continued, the making of the tanto fell dramatically, and most of those made were imitations of the daggers of previous eras.

In 1868 the Medieval Period in Japan officially came to an end with the Meiji Restoration, which ended the rule of the Tokugawa shoguns and established a new line of imperial rulers. Members of the Imperial Court adopted ancient, pre-shogunate fashions, including the wearing of the tachi and tanto. Many daggers were produced before World War II, but Japan's defeat in 1945 and subsequent weapons ban meant that they ceased being made once again.

The kaiken

Noblewomen used a smaller version of the tanto called a kaiken to commit suicide with a swift thrust to the throat, especially in cases where the castle of their lord was taken by storm. In the Siege of Fushimi in 1596, the entire family of the castle's lord, Torii Mototada, killed themselves to avoid capture when this great fortress – near Kyoto – fell after a great battle. This

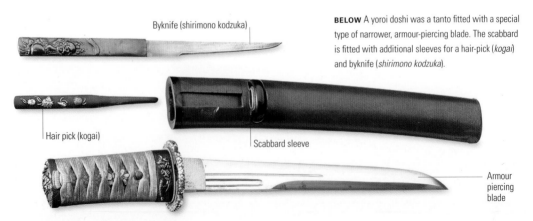

Byknife (shirimono kodzuka)

Hair pick (kogai)

Scabbard sleeve

BELOW A yoroi doshi was a tanto fitted with a special type of narrower, armour-piercing blade. The scabbard is fitted with additional sleeves for a hair-pick (kogai) and byknife (shirimono kodzuka).

Armour piercing blade

Seppuku

As *bushido* – the Japanese warrior code – developed in the 12th and 13th centuries, seppuku quickly became one of its central elements. Unlike the European code of chivalry, which required defeated and captured knights to be compassionately treated, bushido advocated contempt for one's defeated enemies; if taken prisoner, a samurai was tortured and killed. Seppuku initially evolved as an honourable way for warriors to avoid capture after defeat in battle, but later became a way to salvage and even increase one's honour in recompense for some disreputable or disgraceful act. It was also adopted as a more respectable alternative to execution granted to condemned samurai.

Seppuku provided perhaps the most iconic role for the dagger in Japan. It involved the seated samurai taking up his tanto and plunging it into the left side of his own abdomen. He then calmly cut a long slash across his stomach. The bravest samurai would sometimes attempt a second cut, either another horizontal slash or an even more excruciating vertical cut, before expiring in agony.

As late as the 1860s, Algernon Bertram Freeman-Mitford, the British ambassador to Japan, described in his book *Tales of Old Japan* a seppuku ritual witnessed by a colleague:

The case of a young fellow, only twenty years old, of the Choshiu clan, which was told me the other day by an eye-witness, deserves mention as a marvellous instance of determination. Not content with giving himself the one necessary cut, he slashed himself thrice horizontally and twice vertically. Then he stabbed himself in the throat until the dirk protruded on the other side, with its sharp edge to the front; setting his teeth in one supreme effort, he drove the knife forward with both hands through his throat, and fell dead.

BELOW This fabricated seppuku ritual was staged in about 1875. Two samurai act as witnesses while another acts as headsman.

The modern era

Today, knives, daggers and bayonets are found all over the world. Although the role of a separate fighting knife has diminished, the bayonet remains standard issue to every infantryman serving in a professional army. At the same time, fine-quality edged weapons have gained respect as an art form. Created by modern smiths drawing on 6000 years of experience, these art-object weapons are at once traditional and highly contemporary.

Outside the military world, specialist fighting knives are still produced for the purposes of self-defence, and the demand for survival knives and multi-use "sportsmen's" knives is as strong as ever. Additionally, many people around the world collect historic edged weapons, as much for their craftsmanship as their history. This concept of knives as objects of creative design as well as utility is a growing trend among many modern bladesmiths, especially in the United States.

The art of the knife

Craftsmen today have the huge advantage in their work not only of exact temperature and time control but also the knowledge of precisely why different metals behave the way they do, and exactly how their properties may be manipulated to produce a very wide range of forms and varying effects. Heat and chemical processes, for example, can now be used to create an extraordinary range of colours in steel, giving visual qualities to modern knives that were never possible before. A seemingly endless array of materials are at the disposal of the modern craftsman,

ABOVE Dated 2005, the etched, heat-tinted blade, crucible steel bolsters and handle made of blackwood burl and fossilized mammoth tooth of this fine specimen demonstrate the creativity of modern smiths, such as P.J. Ernest.

BELOW Richard Furrer's "Palm-leaf Bowie" combines a Javanese *Blarka Ngirdi* ("Palm-Leaf") pamor, typical Bowie "Spanish notch" and a Japanese-style *mokume-gane* wood-grain metal guard. The handle is a 30,000-year-old Walrus tusk.

Polished wood scabbard

Walrus-ivory handle

Bowie-style Spanish notch

"Palm leaf" pamor blade pattern

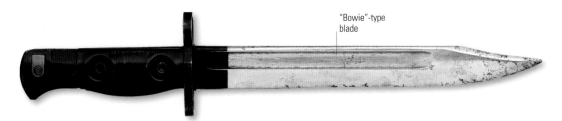

"Bowie"-type blade

ABOVE The L1A3 knife bayonet for the British 7.62mm SLR was introduced in 1959 and remained in use for nearly 30 years. It was used with legendary effectiveness in the Falklands War.

not only modern or rare metals such as titanium, meteoric iron, and many forms of exotic watered steels, but also more unusual organic materials and minerals such as fossilized mammoth and mastodon ivory, hematite and tanzanite.

The modern bayonet

With advances in automatic weapons, one could easily assume that the bayonet would quickly become obsolete. However, bayonets are still issued to infantrymen in most modern armies. How could such an apparently outdated weapon as the bayonet, devised more than 400 years ago, continue to demand a special place in the soldier's arsenal?

The bayonet's functions in present-day war zones are diverse. Despite the increasing effectiveness of firearms in close combat, the bayonet remains an important alternative. In the Vietnam War, US Marines and the North Vietnamese Army fought each other with fixed bayonets at the Siege of Khe Sanh (30 March 1968). At the Battle of Mount Tumbledown (13–14 June 1982) during the Falklands War, British troops stormed Argentinean positions with fixed bayonets in a famous night attack. More recently, in the Second Gulf (Iraq) War (2003–), soldiers from the Argyll and Sutherland Highlanders regiment of the British Army executed a bayonet charge against members of a Shi'ite militia who had ambushed them near the city of Amara (reported 15 May 2004).

The bayonet was not an uncommon sight during both Iraq wars. In the unpredictable environment of urban warfare, especially when clearing buildings or bunkers, an attack at close quarters is always a danger and a fixed bayonet a

Wire-cutting tool

Scabbard

ABOVE The old desire to design a bayonet that serves more than one function continues today; this knife bayonet for the British SA-80 assault rifle is also intended to convert for use as a wire-cutter.

sensible precaution. The bayonet obviously becomes more important to a soldier who runs out of ammunition, but it can also prove a decisive weapon in the face of a surprise attack during reloading, or similar circumstances. Yet perhaps just as important as its practical fighting applications are the psychological advantages: the inexperienced soldier may feel more confident entering battle at close quarters with his bayonet in place; the fierce aspect of the edged weapon is just as strong today as it ever was. It serves to embolden the wielder and often terrifies the enemy. It also gives the modern soldier the sense that he is a part of a martial tradition and in possession of an ancient warrior skill that makes him better than his ill-disciplined opponent. These are advantages that cannot be overcome by technological change. At least, not yet.

Knives, daggers and bayonets come in an incredible variety of forms, depending on their historical period and origin.

A directory of knives, daggers and bayonets

In this informative catalogue, you will find details of some of the most important weapons from around the world and throughout history, along with information about their manufacture and use. Arranged chronologically as well as by geographical area, each of the weapons has a description and a specification that lists its country of origin, date and length.

TOP A Japanese Arisaka bayonet, 1939, with a heavily blued hilt.

MIDDLE TOP German Luftwafte Flying Officer's dagger, 1934.

MIDDLE BOTTOM Indian Coorg Tamil knife, mid-19th century.

BOTTOM A British bayonet for sappers and miners, 1st Pattern 1842, with sword-type guard.

Design of knives, daggers and bayonets

The creation of an aesthetically pleasing and successful fighting knife, dagger or bayonet involves a number of considerations. Foremost of these is the intended method of use of the weapon. The size and shape of the blade are of primary importance here –

for example, stabbing daggers require a slender blade, while daggers intended to be used in rapier combat need to be strong – although the balance and proportions of the weapon also contribute to its effectiveness for a particular use.

Types of knives and daggers

Stabbing

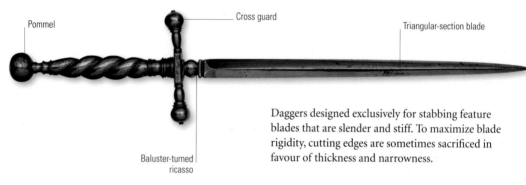

Pommel

Cross guard

Triangular-section blade

Baluster-turned ricasso

Daggers designed exclusively for stabbing feature blades that are slender and stiff. To maximize blade rigidity, cutting edges are sometimes sacrificed in favour of thickness and narrowness.

Cut and thrust

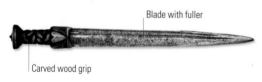

Blade with fuller

Carved wood grip

Most fighting knives and daggers are designed for both stabbing and slashing. These functions must be carefully balanced – a knife cannot do both perfectly.

Parrying

Wavy edge

Daggers designed to be used in rapier combat have to be large and strongly built, so that they can stand up to blows from opposing sword blades.

Folding

Clipped point blade

Brass hilt fitting with inlay

Fighting knives which have blades folding down into the handle are easy to carry about one's person. They usually have single-edged blades.

Push

Wide double-edged blade

Stag-horn grip

Push daggers are more unusual, perhaps because their method of use – a punching action with the blade projecting in front of the fist – is so specific.

African sickle blade

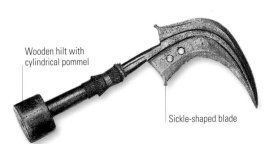

Wooden hilt with cylindrical pommel

Sickle-shaped blade

Large fighting knives with C-shaped blades are rare but not unknown; the cutting edge is on the concave side. These knives are often used to strike hammer-like blows with the point.

African throwing knife

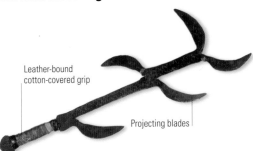

Leather-bound cotton-covered grip

Projecting blades

Single-blade throwing knives rely on the thrower accurately judging distance and rotation in the throw. Multi-bladed versions are designed to produce a blade-strike, whatever the point of impact.

Parts of a dagger and scabbard

The precise ways in which edged weapons are constructed varies tremendously. Likewise, the exact parts that make up a knife or dagger, and the names of those parts, depends on how and where the weapon has been built. Shown below are some of the basic elements that make up most forms of dagger and fighting knife.

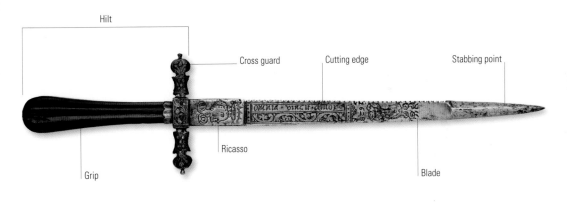

Hilt

Cross guard

Cutting edge

Stabbing point

Ricasso

Grip

Blade

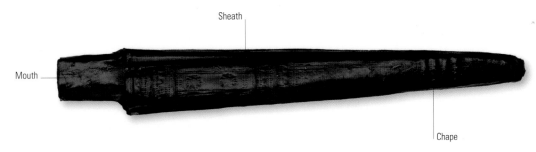

Sheath

Mouth

Chape

Types of bayonets

Plug

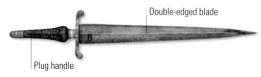

Double-edged blade

Plug handle

The earliest bayonet was simply a cross-hilt dagger with the handle tapered down so that it could be jammed into the end of the musket.

Socket

Socket

Narrow stabbing blade

The socket bayonet fitted around the muzzle, with the blade slung underneath to the side, allowing the musket to be fired with the bayonet fixed.

Sword

Deep fuller

Single edge

Sword bayonets were the result of an effort to combine the reach of a long blade with a hilt, allowing use as an independent weapon.

Knife

Short, double-edged blade

Assymetric guard

The knife bayonet was introduced in the late 19th century. Here the bayonet returned to its origins, coming to resemble a small all-purpose dagger again.

Parts of a bayonet

Bayonet terminology varies depending on the type of bayonet as, unlike most other small-edged weapons, different types of bayonet feature specific mechanical components – for example the devices for attachment to the firearm. Some of the most essential 19th- and 20th-century terms are given below.

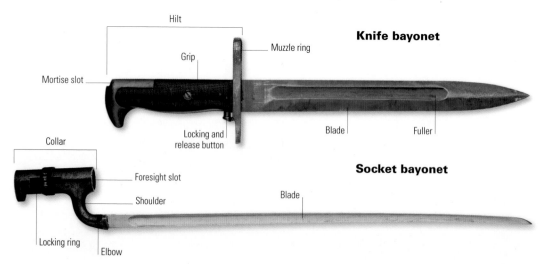

Hilt

Grip

Muzzle ring

Knife bayonet

Mortise slot

Locking and release button

Blade

Fuller

Collar

Socket bayonet

Foresight slot

Shoulder

Blade

Locking ring

Elbow

Types of blades

The form of the blade of an edged weapon determines everything about it – its method of use as well as the effects it can produce. The blade shape also gives the weapon its particular identity or "personality", bringing aesthetic attractiveness as well as deadly functionality.

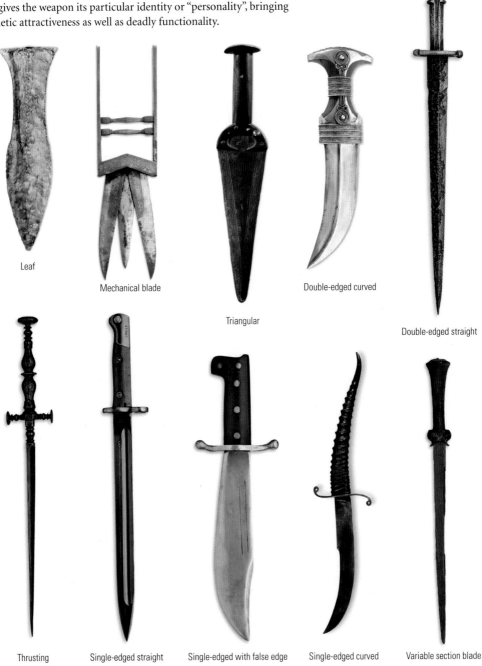

Leaf

Mechanical blade

Triangular

Double-edged curved

Double-edged straight

Thrusting

Single-edged straight

Single-edged with false edge

Single-edged curved

Variable section blade

Blade cross-sections

The cross-section shape of the blade of any edged weapon plays an essential role in determining the way in which that weapon performs. It determines whether the weapon is dedicated to one use, being better suited either to cutting or thrusting, or conversely, whether it is intended to provide a decent level of general effectiveness in both forms of attack. Cross-section shapes vary enormously; there are a small set of basic shapes, each of which has formed the basis for the development of more complex designs.

Basic blade sections

Flattened oval or lenticuler

This is one of the most ancient blade sections, found on flint knives of *c.*2000BC and earlier. The middle of the blade is kept thick to retain strength, while each side is smoothly tapered down to the two cutting edges.

Spined flat section

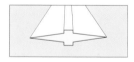

Blades with a simple flat section, though straightforward in design and easy to make, are very weak and therefore very rare. Most flat-sectioned blades of the Bronze Age, for example, have a specially thickened, straight-sided medial spine, to prevent the blade from simply collapsing on impact.

Wedge section

All single-edged or "backed" blades are of wedge section, with the thick unsharpened back providing the blade's strength and rigidity. The design is typically found on the early medieval scramasax, as well as on many medieval "cutting" daggers.

Diamond section

This is an excellent shape for daggers and knives intended primarily for stabbing because it provides very high rigidity at the cost of the cutting edges. Cutting edges can be retained with the flattened diamond section, but the decreased taper sacrifices some of the spine thickness.

Square section

A more extreme move towards an exclusively thrusting capability, with no edges of any sort. It's ideal for stabbing but the lack of a cutting edge is somewhat limiting.

Triangular section

Another dedicated thrusting design, the triangular section is conceived to perform like the square section blade but with a reduced overall weight. For this reason it is commonly found on socket bayonets of the 18th and 19th centuries.

T-section

The T-section is an unusual variation of the wedge-section concept. The thickness of the back has been ground almost entirely away, leaving only a narrow shelf. This is a design unique to certain types of Indo-Persian peshkabz.

More complex sections

By the Medieval Period, blades started to develop with more than one cross-section. For example, the base of the blade might be made in a rectangular section to provide maximum strength at the guard; the middle of the blade could be shaped into a wedge section to give a long cutting edge; while the forward part might use a flattened diamond section to create a sharper point and better thrusting capability. These blades made up of more than one cross-section also reflect light in an interesting way.

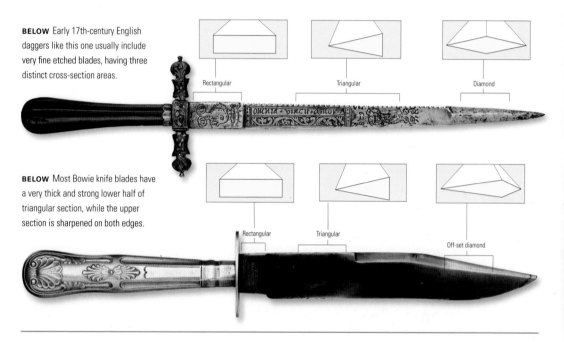

BELOW Early 17th-century English daggers like this one usually include very fine etched blades, having three distinct cross-section areas.

Rectangular   Triangular   Diamond

BELOW Most Bowie knife blades have a very thick and strong lower half of triangular section, while the upper section is sharpened on both edges.

Rectangular   Triangular   Off-set diamond

The fuller

Maintaining strength while reducing weight is important in blade design. The fuller is key to this. A shallow groove down a blade's length reduces its weight but does not weaken it. By the Medieval Period most blades had fullers, either down the middle or offset. The fuller was never a "blood-groove", nor did it make the weapon easier to pull out of an enemy's body. It was simply a way of optimizing weight. Some blades have multiple fullers – some very shallow and wide, others very narrow and quite deep.

Single-fullered flattened diamond section

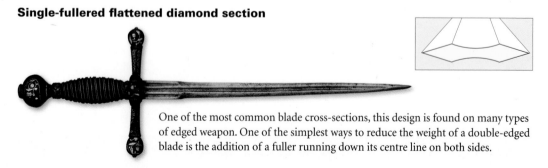

One of the most common blade cross-sections, this design is found on many types of edged weapon. One of the simplest ways to reduce the weight of a double-edged blade is the addition of a fuller running down its centre line on both sides.

Offset fullered wedge section

This is another very common design, one that takes some of the weight out of the thick back of the blade while retaining overall strength.

Multi-fullered wedge section

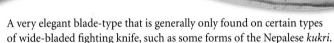

A very elegant blade-type that is generally only found on certain types of wide-bladed fighting knife, such as some forms of the Nepalese *kukri*.

Multi-fullered flattened diamond section

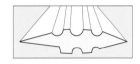

This very large group appears in many diverse variations. Some display only two or three shallow broad fullers, while others involve up to five very narrow and deep grooves, to the point where the overall cross-section before fullering is lost.

Hollow-ground triangular section

A hollow-ground blade involves one or more fullers that have been widened to take up the whole width of the blades' surface. Hollow-ground triangular sections are found on many socket bayonet patterns.

Cruciform section

Found on several 19th-century bayonet types, this design is almost never used on any other sort of edged weapon; blades of this type are comparatively difficult to make and the benefits are minimal.

Decorations

Many decorative techniques were available to the makers of edged weapons, some spread by the export of the weapons themselves, others by the migration of their creators. The type and extent of the decoration was determined by the financial means of the person commissioning it, meaning that weapons were generally viewed as important indicators of social status. Most decorative processes were practised by specialists; decoration was almost never carried out by the weaponsmith himself. The finest and most beautiful weapons are often those that have been decorated by means of more than one process.

Engraving

Decorative silver finish

Engraved swastika on chape

A sharp graving tool is used to trace a design by cutting channels or furrows directly into a metal surface. In Europe this process was used throughout the Medieval and Renaissance Periods, although by the 15th century it had been largely superseded by etching, which was less difficult and time-consuming.

Etching

Fluted dudgeon wood grip

Long double-edged blade

Etched decoration to blade

This is a process of producing a design on metal by "biting" it away with acid. The surface to be etched is covered with an acid-resistant coating (the "resist"), usually a wax or varnish. The design is then scraped out in the resist with a graving tool. When the object is washed in acid, the exposed design becomes permanently etched into the metal. In "raised" etching the design is painted on to the metal surface in the resist substance, leaving the background exposed. This produces a very bold three-dimensional effect.

Steel-chiselling

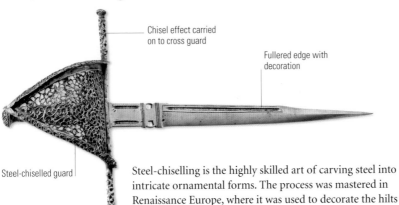

Chisel effect carried on to cross guard

Fullered edge with decoration

Steel-chiselled guard

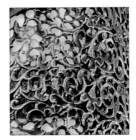

Intricate steel-chiselling

Steel-chiselling is the highly skilled art of carving steel into intricate ornamental forms. The process was mastered in Renaissance Europe, where it was used to decorate the hilts of fine swords and daggers, as well as the locks of firearms.

Punchwork

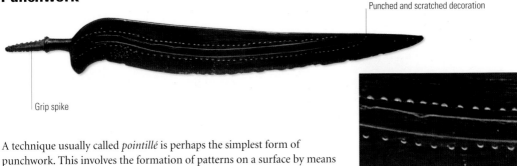

Punched and scratched decoration

Grip spike

A technique usually called *pointillé* is perhaps the simplest form of punchwork. This involves the formation of patterns on a surface by means of lightly punched dots, sometimes of varying sizes and depths. More complex effects were produced through the use of shaped punches.

Punched decoration along the blade

Enamelling

Not to be confused with paint that is sometimes called enamel, true enamel is a brilliantly coloured vitreous substance applied in the form of a powder and heated until it begins to melt, coalescing into a smooth, glassy surface. Enamel is obviously very delicate and easily broken and is therefore usually found only on weapons intended purely for decorative or ceremonial use.

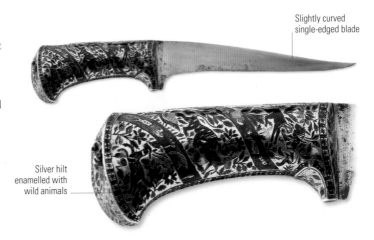

Slightly curved single-edged blade

Silver hilt enamelled with wild animals

Blueing

When highly polished steel is heated, it changes colour, passing through darkening shades of blue, until it reaches purple and black. If a particular temperature can be maintained for a certain period of time, the colour produced will remain after the steel cools. The rich tints produced with heat processes – "blueing" – were often used to decorate the hilts of edged weapons.

Wood grip covered with ray skin

Fire- or mercury-gilding

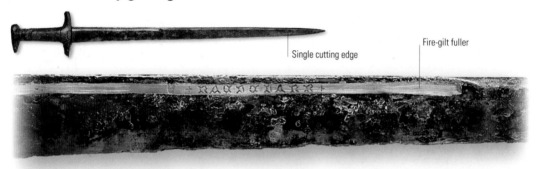

Single cutting edge

Fire-gilt fuller

This is perhaps the most common traditional way of applying gold to steel. An amount of gold dust was first mixed with mercury. The gold dissolved in the mercury forming an amalgam or paste-like mixture. This substance was then applied to the steel surface. The piece was then heated to boil or "fume" off the mercury, leaving the gold permanently bonded to the steel. The same technique could also be used to apply silver to steel.

Encrustation

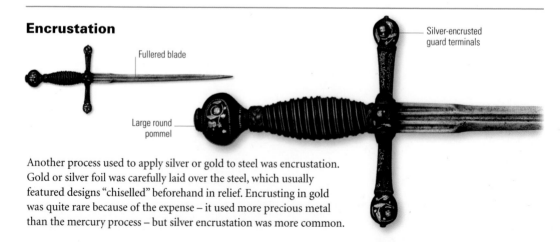

Fullered blade

Silver-encrusted guard terminals

Large round pommel

Another process used to apply silver or gold to steel was encrustation. Gold or silver foil was carefully laid over the steel, which usually featured designs "chiselled" beforehand in relief. Encrusting in gold was quite rare because of the expense – it used more precious metal than the mercury process – but silver encrustation was more common.

Inlay

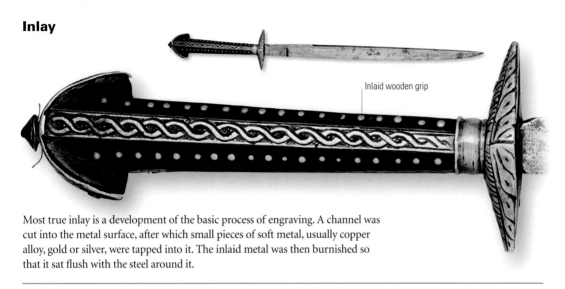

Inlaid wooden grip

Most true inlay is a development of the basic process of engraving. A channel was cut into the metal surface, after which small pieces of soft metal, usually copper alloy, gold or silver, were tapped into it. The inlaid metal was then burnished so that it sat flush with the steel around it.

Damascening

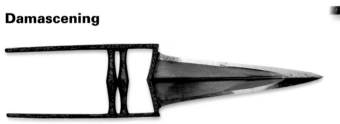

Damascening inlay

The use of the term "damascening" in English dates to at least the 16th century. True damascening is a form of inlay, wherein the precious metal, usually gold, is laid into a channel having a cross-section shaped like an upside down "Y". This technique was much rarer than "false" damascening with which it is often confused.

False or Counterfeit Damascening

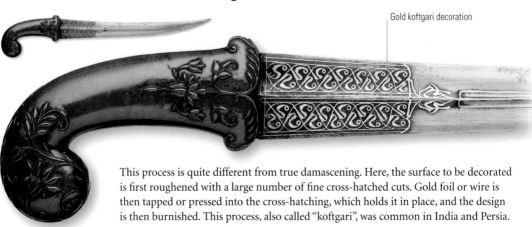

Gold koftgari decoration

This process is quite different from true damascening. Here, the surface to be decorated is first roughened with a large number of fine cross-hatched cuts. Gold foil or wire is then tapped or pressed into the cross-hatching, which holds it in place, and the design is then burnished. This process, also called "koftgari", was common in India and Persia.

Stone Age blades

For thousands of years the only edged weapons available to prehistoric peoples were simple stone hand axes. These were grasped in the palm and used to strike overarm cutting blows. Over 2000 centuries, these tools slowly began to take on a more recognizable blade shape. Some of the finest flint knives were made as recently as 1500BC, after which point they were rendered obsolete by bronze weapons.

Palaeolithic hand axe, 300,000BC

This quartzite hand axe is a rare example of the precision knapping skills of Palaeolithic humans. The cutting edge is placed at a right angle to the line of direct force, and the butt has been shaped with a few perfect knap-strikes to sit comfortably in the palm.

Cutting edge

DATE	300,000BC
ORIGIN	PALAEOLITHIC
LENGTH	17.8cm (7in)

Palaeolithic hand axe, 100,000–60,000BC

This flint core axe shows a very important development, for the maker's intention seems to have been to create a weapon or tool with a more prominent point. It is not in any sense a true stabbing blade, but the fact that a point will more effectively focus the force of a blow into a small area seems here to be well understood. The point and cutting edge have been skillfully pressure-flaked. Their patterns combined with the smooth white cortex produce a very beautiful sculptural effect.

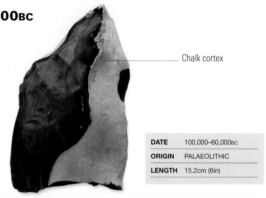

Chalk cortex

DATE	100,000–60,000BC
ORIGIN	PALAEOLITHIC
LENGTH	15.2cm (6in)

Neolithic chisel, 6000–3000BC

Tip

Long, narrow shape

As the skills of the flint-knapper became more advanced, tools could be shaped into more specialized forms. This Neolithic mottled flint chisel has taken on a form that is much more blade-like, being much longer and narrower in comparison to earlier tools.

DATE	6000–3000BC
ORIGIN	NEOLITHIC
LENGTH	17cm (6.75in)

Dagger of the Iceman

This small dagger was among a number of perfectly preserved objects found with "Ötzi the Iceman", an extraordinarily well-preserved natural mummy of a Chalcolithic (Copper Age) man who died c.3300BC in the Ötztal Alps on the Italo-Austrian border. When he died, possibly of an arrow wound in his shoulder or a blow to his skull, the Iceman's body froze in glacial ice and was there preserved until its discovery in 1991.

The dagger is made of a short flint blade and a handle of ash wood. The scabbard is woven from fibrous plant bark. This is the fighting weapon of a man whose death was a direct result of violence; the blade still bears traces of the blood of one of the Iceman's enemies.

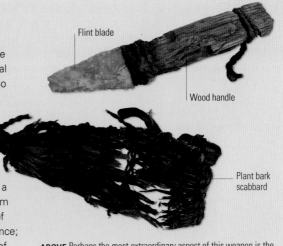

Flint blade

Wood handle

Plant bark scabbard

ABOVE Perhaps the most extraordinary aspect of this weapon is the fact that it survives with all of its organic material elements intact.

Bronze Age dagger, c.1800–1500BC

Cutting edge

DATE	c.1800–1500BC
ORIGIN	BRONZE AGE
LENGTH	11.4cm (4.5in)

This late flint dagger, made as the use of metal was becoming more widespread, is a good example of a fully-fledged bladed weapon. Two pressure-flaking techniques have been used; larger flakes have been removed to form the grip, while much finer, tiny pieces have been taken away to create the edges of the razor-sharp blade.

Bronze Age dagger, 1600BC

Imitation stitching

DATE	1600BC
ORIGIN	BRONZE AGE
LENGTH	18cm (7.1in)

This beautiful weapon, typical of the best "Dagger Age" pieces, is a direct copy of a bronze knife. An impressive detail is the zigzag ridge that runs down the grip – an imitation of the stitching on the leather grip of this weapon's bronze counterpart.

Ancient Egyptian knives and daggers

The dagger had become a common weapon among ancient Egyptians long before the Early Dynastic Period (*c.*3150–2686BC). Fine flint daggers were produced, the best-known being cleaver-like ceremonial knives. Few Old Kingdom (2686–2134BC) daggers are known. More survive from the Middle (2040–1640BC) and New (1570–1070BC) Kingdoms, usually fitted with copper, bronze, or in a few cases, gold blades.

Egyptian ceremonial knife blade, *c.*3000BC

Pressure-flaked pattern

Handle was positioned here

This object is one of several ceremonial knife blades dating from the Predynastic Period in Egypt (*c.*5000–*c.*3100BC). It is now less recognizable as a knife because of the loss of its handle. Weapons of this type are in fact very beautiful works of art, the wavy patterns on the blade created with great skill by a master flint-knapper.

DATE	*c.*3000BC
ORIGIN	EGYPTIAN
LENGTH	18cm (7.1in)

Egyptian dagger, New Kingdom, *c.*1570–1085BC

Multifullered blade

Grip scales lost

This bronze dagger from the 18th, 19th or 20th Dynasty is comparable to weapons from Bronze Age Europe and Asia. The blade is quite wide for its length, the hilt ergonomically shaped and stepped on its outer edge to hold the missing grip scales. In these ways it is similar to bronze daggers from ancient Persia.

DATE	*c.*1570–1085BC
ORIGIN	EGYPTIAN
LENGTH	unknown

Egyptian knife, New Kingdom, *c.*1570–1085BC

Rounded point

Wooden grip

The wooden grip of this New Kingdom dagger may be original. It is fitted to a short blade of bronze, the profile of which shows it to be a serviceable cut-and-thrust weapon. The point may have become rounded due to wear, although it could have been made so. A rounded but razor-sharp tip would still slash flesh and split bone.

DATE	*c.*1570–1085BC
ORIGIN	EGYPTIAN
LENGTH	unknown

Egyptian thrusting dagger, New Kingdom, *c.*1570–1085BC

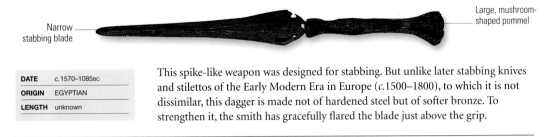

Narrow stabbing blade

Large, mushroom-shaped pommel

DATE	c.1570–1085BC
ORIGIN	EGYPTIAN
LENGTH	unknown

This spike-like weapon was designed for stabbing. But unlike later stabbing knives and stilettos of the Early Modern Era in Europe (*c.*1500–1800), to which it is not dissimilar, this dagger is made not of hardened steel but of softer bronze. To strengthen it, the smith has gracefully flared the blade just above the grip.

Egyptian funerary dagger, New Kingdom, *c.*1370–1352BC

Hunting scenes in relief

Enamel decoration

Solid gold blade

DATE	c.1370–1352BC
ORIGIN	EGYPTIAN
LENGTH	31.8cm (12.5in)

Only Egyptian royalty could afford daggers with blades of pure gold. This ornately decorated solid gold weapon armed the boy-king, Tutankhamun, for the afterlife. A dagger and sheath of solid gold were also found among the tomb effects of Queen Ahhotpe, mother of Ahmosis I, founder of the 18th Dynasty of the New Kingdom during which Tutankhamun reigned.

Egyptian funerary dagger, New Kingdom, *c.*1370–1352BC

Iron blade

Enamelled bands

Palmette ornamentation

DATE	c.1370–1352BC
ORIGIN	EGYPTIAN
LENGTH	34.3cm (13.5in)

The iron blade of Tutankhamun's second dagger may seem plain compared to the gold of its companion, but it is even more precious. Its composition is 97 per cent iron and three per cent nickel. This means it is meteoric iron, very rare and more valuable than gold. The pommel is rock-crystal and the hilt is decorated with enamel.

Bronze Age edged weapons

For 2,000 years bronze was the most advanced metal available. Despite the fact that bronze work hardens, weapons made out of this alloy still had to be designed to take account of its softness and propensity to deform during use. Most bronze daggers are relatively short with a sharp taper to help maintain rigidity, a requirement often enhanced by a strong medial ridge running down the blade.

French Bronze Age dagger, 1800–1500BC

Cylindrical grip

Densely ridged blade

This fine bronze dagger was found at Mirabel in France, and dates from the French Early Bronze Age, 1800–1500BC. The triangular blade, the edges of which are decorated with a number of ridges and grooves, is riveted to a separate hilt. Daggers of this type may have inspired the cinquedea of Renaissance Italy.

DATE	1800–1500BC
ORIGIN	FRENCH BRONZE AGE
LENGTH	27cm (11in)

Luristan dagger, 1200BC

Hilt block

Grip scale recess

This beautiful dagger is one of many found at Luristan. It is elegantly designed to make the best use of the material while minimizing the effects of its limitations. The sharply tapered blade is strengthened with quite a wide medial ridge, whilst the thick, crescent-shaped hilt block strengthens the top of the grip against breakage.

DATE	1200BC
ORIGIN	LURISTAN (IRANIAN)
LENGTH	41.5cm (16.3in)

European knife blade, 1200–1000BC

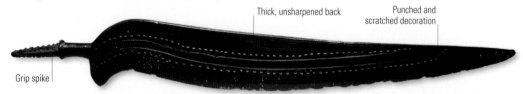

Thick, unsharpened back

Punched and scratched decoration

Grip spike

This long blade demonstrates a different approach to the problem of how to build a sound edged weapon out of bronze. The strength and rigidity derive not from a steep taper and thick medial ridge, but from the overall thickness of much of the blade and its wedge-shaped section, with a thick back and single cutting edge.

DATE	1200–1000BC
ORIGIN	EUROPEAN
LENGTH	30cm (11.8in)

Luristan dagger, 1200–800BC

Finger grooves   Narrow blade

DATE	1200–800BC
ORIGIN	LURISTAN (IRANIAN)
LENGTH	27cm (11in)

This fine bronze dagger is another Luristan find. Dating from 1200–800BC, it falls within the Ancient Persian Iron Age. The finely shaped handle is designed to fit perfectly into the hand, with finger grooves for a comfortable grip. It was also originally fitted with grip scales of wood or some other organic material.

Weapons from Luristan

Some of the largest groups of Bronze Age objects ever found come from sites in Luristan (also Lorestan), in what is now northwestern Iran. Excavations in the 20th century uncovered tools, ornamental objects and very large numbers of weapons made by the ancient semi-nomadic people who lived in this mountainous part of the Middle East. Along with many swords, axes and spearheads, the weapons included a great many daggers, cast in bronze and usually fitted with grip scales of wood, horn or bone. Some of the best bronze daggers from Luristan in fact probably date from the Iranian Iron Age, c.1200–650BC, although many others have been found that belong to the Iranian Bronze Age, c.3500–1250BC.

BELOW Many ruined settlements like this one are preserved all over northwestern Iran, and have been extensively excavated yielding a large number of weapons, tools and other objects.

Daggers of the Classical World

We often imagine Greek and Roman warriors armed with shining bronze arms and armour. It is, however, important to remember that iron was well known by this time. Bronze and iron coexisted as weapons materials for centuries. Bronze was harder than early iron, but iron was cheaper. Almost all Roman weapons had iron blades. Roman smiths also made use of a new alloy of iron and carbon: steel.

Hallstatt "antennae" dagger, *c.*750–450BC

"Antennae" pommel

Damaged "antennae" guard

DATE	c.750–450BC
ORIGIN	HALLSTATT CULTURE
LENGTH	unknown

This classic Hallstatt "antennae" dagger is an excellent example of its type, not only because of the distinctive form of the hilt but also because it is made of iron. The Hallstatt were the first Bronze Age Europeans to master this metal.

Villanovan dagger and scabbard, 600–300BC

Wheel chape

Triple-button pommel

This exquisite Villanovan dagger, from tomb 11 at the Necropolis at Villanueva de Teba, is a beautiful example of the best ornamented bronze-work. The aesthetic influence on later Roman pugios is also apparent in the banded construction of the scabbard and in the overall proportions of the weapon.

DATE	600–300BC
ORIGIN	VILLANOVAN
LENGTH	unknown

English or German dagger and scabbard, 600–300BC

Bronze-banded scabbard

The design of this iron-bladed dagger is associated with southern Germany. It closely resembles the Roman pugio and may be one of its precursors. It was found in the River Thames, but was most likely imported into Britain rather than made there. The bronze-banded scabbard is probably the work of a local metalworker.

DATE	600–300BC
ORIGIN	ENGLISH/GERMAN
LENGTH	35.6cm (14in)

Roman pugio and scabbard, AD100

Strong thrusting point

All-iron construction

Iron scabbard frame

DATE	AD100
ORIGIN	ROMAN
LENGTH	unknown

By the 1st century AD the Roman pugio had assumed a very consistent form and construction. Both hilt and blade were usually made of iron, the hilt being decorated according to the particular owner's status and either left plain or tinned, silvered or gilded.

Roman pugio, AD100

Medial ridge

Wheel pommel

DATE	AD100
ORIGIN	ROMAN
LENGTH	26.5cm (10.4in)

This worn, bent example has a less pronounced point than many other examples, but otherwise it is fairly typical, having a narrow medial ridge running down the whole length of the blade. The grip displays the usual central swelling and wheel pommel, while the guard is decorated with incised lines and beading.

Roman officer's pugio, c.AD100–300

Silvered hilt

Wide, tapering leaf blade

DATE	c.AD100–300
ORIGIN	ROMAN
LENGTH	unknown

Pugios of this type remained in use until the middle of the 2nd century AD. With its silvered and finely worked hilt, it is clear this weapon belonged to a Roman officer, a centurion or perhaps a navarch. The decorative rope motif on the grip may indicate an association with a commander in the Roman Navy. This dagger survives in exceptional condition, one of the finest remaining Roman examples.

Daggers of the Medieval Period

The dating of the Medieval Period is very difficult. Working exclusively in the context of weapons history, it is possible to consider the Medieval Period, or "Middle Ages", as beginning with the collapse of the western Roman Empire in the 5th century (the Early Medieval Period, often wrongly called the "Dark Ages"), continuing through the early 14th century (the "High" Middle Ages), and ending sometime in the 15th century (the "Late" Middle Ages). Daggers developed a great deal during these ten centuries.

Central European scramasax blades, 500–600

Wide, unsharpened back

Tang

Asymmetric, stabbing point

Cutting edge

Although they are now in a heavily corroded "excavated" condition, these two Early Medieval sax blades still give a very good impression of their original shape. The wide, thick-backed form, ideal for cutting and slashing, angles sharply down in the upper third to form a very long stabbing point. It is not surprising that this impressive, multifunctional design remained popular throughout central, northern and western Europe for nearly 1,000 years.

DATE	500–600
ORIGIN	CENTRAL EUROPEAN
LENGTH	26cm (10.2in)

English cross-hilt dagger, c.1200–1300

Up-curving pommel arms

Down-curving guard

Double-edged blade

This classic High Medieval dagger carries a distinctive type of pommel, made essentially as a mirror of the cross guard. Medieval daggers of this type recall the "anthropomorphic" designs of the Hallstatt and La Tène Celts. A number of these daggers survive, many of which have been found in London. The type is probably not exclusively English and was undoubtedly also popular on the Continent.

DATE	c.1200–1300
ORIGIN	ENGLISH
LENGTH	30.5cm (12in)

English cross-hilt dagger, 1400

Square-section point

Copper-alloy hilt

DATE	1400
ORIGIN	ENGLISH
LENGTH	29cm (11.4in)

The guard and pommel of this fine dagger are made of a copper alloy instead of iron or steel. The missing grip may have been covered with a colourful textile. The blade is purely for stabbing, although the bladesmith has gone to some trouble to shape it into a more elegant form than a simple square-section spike. The blade's deeply fullered lower half transitions gracefully into the square-section upper half.

English or Scottish cross-hilt dagger, *c.*1300–1400

Drooping guard

Wheel pommel

Sharply tapered blade

DATE	c.1300–1400
ORIGIN	ENGLISH/SCOTTISH
LENGTH	33.8cm (13.3in)

Although its blade is relatively short, its narrowness and very sharp taper indicate that this dagger is undoubtedly what medieval people would recognize as a *couteau à pointe*, or "stabbing knife". The guard is of an interesting type, the arms drooping diagonally down towards the blade and swelling towards the ends. The guard block also extends down to sit flush with the wooden grip, which like those of most other surviving medieval daggers is not lost. Guards very similar to this are one of the characteristic features of Scottish medieval swords, of which this may be a diminutive.

German cross-hilt dagger, late 15th century

Variable-section blade

Pierced guard

DATE	late 15th century
ORIGIN	GERMAN
LENGTH	44cm (17.3in)

This very ornate dagger probably dates from the very end of the Medieval Period and may be of German origin. The pommel and guard are of copper alloy. The blade is especially interesting in that along its length the cross-section changes four times, beginning with a double-edged section at the guard to single-edged a few centimetres above the guard, and alternating back and forth to the point.

Rondel daggers

By the middle of the 14th century the rondel dagger was becoming the most fashionable type worn by all classes, both in war and for self-defence in daily life. Some have single-edged blades, while others are stabbing tools, the blades being merely long steel spikes. The disks or rondels were constructed of diverse materials – wood, horn, copper alloy, iron or steel – and can vary greatly in diameter. Nevertheless, they always grip the user's hand tightly, giving a solid seat for a powerful downward thrust.

English rondel dagger, *c.*14th century

Small rondel guard

"Teacosy" pommel

This weapon was found in the River Thames in London. It shows one of the characteristic features of the earliest forms of rondel dagger: while the guard is composed of a metal disk, the pommel is not, but is instead a heavy half-round "tea cosy" form found on many 12th- and 13th-century swords.

DATE	c.14th century
ORIGIN	ENGLISH
LENGTH	unknown

The suicide of Lucretia

Since weapons rarely survive in pristine, undamaged condition, it is vital to look at depictions of weapons in art. Most artists attempted to represent weapons as faithfully as possible. They can be seen as the artist himself saw them – bright, polished, with all decoration intact. Some artistic themes are very useful to weapons researchers. In the study of daggers, the tragic subject of Lucretia, a semi-mythical Roman noblewoman, is especially relevant. Her rape and subsequent suicide by stabbing was thought to have led to the foundation of the Roman Republic. Botticelli, Raphael and many other artists painted pictures of her, and these works usually include excellent renderings of daggers from the artist's time, usually of a very high quality to emphasize Lucretia's noble status.

RIGHT Lucretia supposedly stabbed herself to death after being dishonoured by the son of the last king of Rome. The popular outrage that followed brought the overthrow of the ancient Roman monarchy.

English (?) rondel dagger fragment, *c.*1400

Engraved geometric decoration

Fire-gilt surface

DATE	c.1400
ORIGIN	POSSIBLY ENGLISH
LENGTH	9.6cm (3.8in)

This broken piece of gilt metal is the grip and pommel of a once extremely fine rondel dagger, undoubtedly the weapon of a knight. The ornate geometric decoration is typical of knights' daggers as depicted on English funerary effigies of the late 14th and early 15th centuries. The squared, four-petal flower motif on the pommel is especially common in late medieval English metalwork; the same pattern was used to decorate copper-alloy boxes, candlesticks and armour.

English or Scottish rondel dagger, 15th century

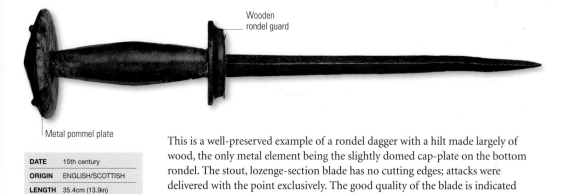

Wooden rondel guard

Metal pommel plate

DATE	15th century
ORIGIN	ENGLISH/SCOTTISH
LENGTH	35.4cm (13.9in)

This is a well-preserved example of a rondel dagger with a hilt made largely of wood, the only metal element being the slightly domed cap-plate on the bottom rondel. The stout, lozenge-section blade has no cutting edges; attacks were delivered with the point exclusively. The good quality of the blade is indicated by its mark – a letter "I" standing on a letter "O", inlaid in copper alloy.

English (?) rondel dagger, 15th century

Long, single-edged blade

Original wooden grip

DATE	15th century
ORIGIN	POSSIBLY ENGLISH
LENGTH	51.6cm (20.3in)

Its considerable length indicates that this dagger is undoubtedly a weapon of war, made long to pierce with lethal effect the multilayered armour of plate, mail and textile worn at the time. The metal rondels are quite thick and of a comparatively small diameter. Also unusual is the original wooden grip – the grips of most medieval daggers have long since rotted away, leaving only the exposed tang.

English rondel dagger, 15th century

Wooden grip

Forward-curving back

This small dagger is interesting because the original wooden grip survives, as do the wooden rondels which are capped with metal washers. Also, the single-edged wedge-section blade is unusual in that the back curves gently forward towards the cutting edge as it tapers to the point. This specimen was found in the River Thames in London under Southwark Bridge.

DATE	15th century
ORIGIN	ENGLISH
LENGTH	unknown

German rondel dagger, *c.*1500

Thick spike blade

Triple-lobed guard

The copper-alloy hilt of this weapon is unusual in that the guard, rather than being a simple disk – like that fitted to the end of the tang – is formed into three knobs, or lobes. This form is very similar to certain types of German, so-called "landsknecht" daggers fashionable in the early to mid-16th century. The thick, heavy blade is triangular in section and entirely suited to such common medieval fighting techniques as stabbing blows to the opponent's skull.

DATE	c.1500
ORIGIN	GERMAN
LENGTH	34cm (13.4in)

English rondel dagger, *c.*1510

Small rondel guard

Heavy fluted pommel

Strong medial rib

This late rondel dagger was found in the River Thames near Southwark in London. The heavy iron pommel is unusual and recalls the earliest forms of rondel dagger which had similar rounded pommels instead of the wide disk. The dagger was discovered along with the remains of its leather scabbard, and two small byknives for eating and other utilitarian purposes.

DATE	c.1510
ORIGIN	ENGLISH
LENGTH	unknown

Baselards

There was considerable variation in the size of baselards, some being small daggers, others short swords. The hilt always displays the distinctive I-shape, being two plates of wood sandwiching the tang, which is forged to the same shape. The small dagger baselards were most common in Italy during the late 14th and early 15th centuries. The longer sword baselards were closely associated with Germany and Switzerland.

European baselard dagger, c.1400

Medial ridge

Finger grooves

DATE	c.1400
ORIGIN	EUROPEAN
LENGTH	33.3cm (13.1in)

The smaller dagger version of the baselard seems to have appeared first, the longer versions appearing later. This example is for the most part representative of late 14th- and early 15th-century baselards, apart from the ergonomic finger grooves carved into the guard and pommel cross pieces, which are perhaps more atypical.

English long baselard, c.1490–1520

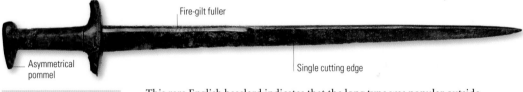

Fire-gilt fuller

Asymmetrical pommel

Single cutting edge

DATE	c.1490–1520
ORIGIN	ENGLISH
LENGTH	68.2cm (26.9in)

This rare English baselard indicates that the long type was popular outside Switzerland and Germany. It is an excellent cut-and-thrust blade. The hilt includes an asymmetrical pommel with an extended forward section; this allowed the user to make deadly whipping cuts, using his little finger as a fulcrum.

Swiss or German long baselard, 1520

Double-edged blade

Symmetrical wooden hilt

This standard early 16th-century baselard features the more usual symmetrical hilt, the cross guard being slightly wider than the pommel, which in this case has been widened into a roughly lenticular form. Unlike the English example above, this weapon is fitted with a plain, double-edged blade of flattened diamond section.

DATE	1520
ORIGIN	SWISS/GERMAN
LENGTH	unknown

Ballock daggers

Often referred to as "kidney" daggers even today, the form of these uniquely recognizable knives makes their true inspiration fairly obvious. While ballock knives shocked Victorian scholars of weapons into renaming them, to the medieval mind the open and public display of a phallic icon was not necessarily erotic at all. Rather it may have been an apotropaic defence intended to ward off evil.

English or Scottish ballock dagger, 14th century

Lobe rivet

Copper-alloy spacer

This ballock dagger clearly foreshadows the dudgeon daggers of the 17th century. It is a very early example of the placement of a metal spacer between the top of the lobes and the base of the blade. The spacer is secured by means of two rivets, one passing through each lobe, a method found on most surviving dudgeon daggers.

DATE	14th century
ORIGIN	ENGLISH/SCOTTISH
LENGTH	25.1cm (9.9in)

English ballock dagger, 15th century

Metal pommel button

This very long 15th-century example already looks something like its late 17th-century descendant, the Scottish Highland dirk. The hilt appears to be carved out of some very hard root or bogwood, while the thickly backed, single-edged blade is similar to the later Highland dirk blades in terms of its size and proportions.

DATE	15th century
ORIGIN	ENGLISH
LENGTH	29.2cm (11.5in)

English or Scottish ballock dagger, 15th century

Copper-alloy base plate

Shaped to scabbard

Like many examples of its type, this flared-base ballock dagger is fitted with a copper-alloy base plate. This plate is not only a convenient opportunity for incised decoration; it also provides a secure seat for the end of the tang, which passes down the centre of the wooden grip and out through a hole in the base plate, to be peened over, thus holding hilt and blade together.

DATE	15th century
ORIGIN	ENGLISH/SCOTTISH
LENGTH	39cm (15.4in)

English or Scottish ballock dagger, 15th century

Flaring grip

Toothed spacer

DATE	15th century
ORIGIN	ENGLISH/SCOTTISH
LENGTH	36.5cm (14.4in)

The lobes of ballock daggers with flared, trumpet-like grips are generally smaller in proportion to the blade than those of daggers with bulbous ends, the lobes of which are usually significantly wider than the base of the blade. This example also has a metal spacer between lobes and blade, with teeth above and below the blade to ensure a snug fit in the scabbard. The flared trumpet hilt appeared in the 15th century and remained popular into the 16th century. It may have been intended to provide a platform similar to that of the rondel dagger, allowing a firmer grip.

English or Scottish ballock dagger, 15th century

Carved testicular lobes

DATE	15th century
ORIGIN	ENGLISH/SCOTTISH
LENGTH	unknown

This fairly standard ballock hilt, carved in the usual way from a single piece of wood, is fitted to a noteworthy single-edged blade. In its form and especially its point, the blade closely resembles the earlier medieval dagger of the type called in textual sources *couteau à tailler*, or "cutting knife", the single sharpened edge of which curves gently upward towards the straight, unsharpened back to form an asymmetric point, not unlike that of a typical kitchen knife.

English (?) ballock dagger, 15th century

Hollow-ground diamond section

Triangular section

DATE	15th century
ORIGIN	POSSIBLY ENGLISH
LENGTH	34.7cm (13.7in)

This purposefully lifelike ballock hilt, the grip slightly curved, is fitted to a remarkable blade. The lower third of the blade is of a standard triangular construction, but it changes quite suddenly, and the upper two-thirds of the blade consists of a skilfully hollow-ground diamond section. This produces a blade that is extremely strong at the base but still narrow enough at the point to slide with ease between the ribs of an enemy. Elaborate blades like this are rare on ballock daggers, being perhaps more commonly found with rondel hilts.

Daggers of the Renaissance

The 16th century was an important turning point in the history of weapons. While traditional fighting methods, with swords, daggers and staff weapons, were still essential, new gunpowder-weapon technology was evolving rapidly. As the 1500s progressed, edged weapons started to become less important on the battlefield. But in civilian life they became much more significant. Duelling became common, and the dagger formed an integral part of most self-defence, or "fencing", systems of the time.

Italian ear dagger, *c.*1500

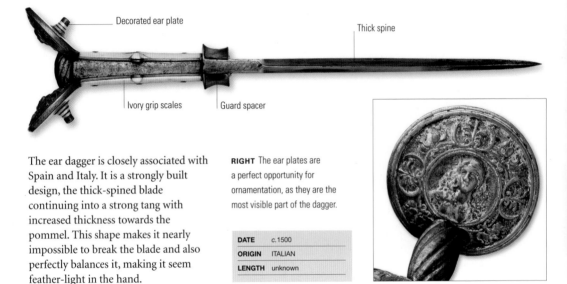

Decorated ear plate

Thick spine

Ivory grip scales

Guard spacer

The ear dagger is closely associated with Spain and Italy. It is a strongly built design, the thick-spined blade continuing into a strong tang with increased thickness towards the pommel. This shape makes it nearly impossible to break the blade and also perfectly balances it, making it seem feather-light in the hand.

RIGHT The ear plates are a perfect opportunity for ornamentation, as they are the most visible part of the dagger.

DATE	c.1500
ORIGIN	ITALIAN
LENGTH	unknown

German rondel dagger, early 16th century

Offset blade

Beaded rondel guard

This weapon is a good example of a late rondel dagger, the final form that this type assumed before falling out of use around the middle of the 16th century. It displays two key improvements that were made to the rondel dagger design around 1500: the rondel guard has been folded down at a 90-degree angle on the side, allowing it to rest against the body during routine wear. In addition, the blade is not located centrally in the guard but is offset towards its folded section; this also helps the weapon to rest flat against the hip.

DATE	early 16th century
ORIGIN	GERMAN
LENGTH	36cm (14.2in)

German "Landsknecht" dagger, 16th century

Copper alloy hilt

Circular katzbalger S-guard

Strong, double-edged blade

DATE	16th century
ORIGIN	GERMAN
LENGTH	unknown

This exquisite and typologically important dagger is a very rare example of one made in the same style as the legendary *katzbalger* ("cat-fighter") short swords of the feared German and Swiss mercenaries known as Landsknechts. Hilts of this type were made not only for Landsknecht daggers and short swords, but also for their famous giant two-handed swords. The key features are the circular guard composed of a single bar forged into a tight S-shape, the slightly tapered grip flaring towards the pommel area and the small beaks on either side of the pommel.

Saxon side-ring dagger, *c.*1570

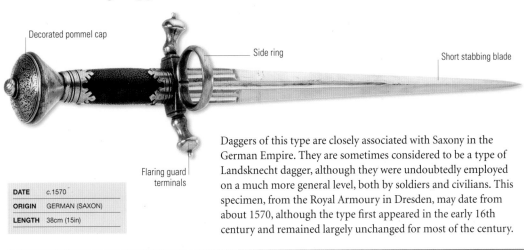

Decorated pommel cap

Side ring

Short stabbing blade

Flaring guard terminals

DATE	*c.*1570
ORIGIN	GERMAN (SAXON)
LENGTH	38cm (15in)

Daggers of this type are closely associated with Saxony in the German Empire. They are sometimes considered to be a type of Landsknecht dagger, although they were undoubtedly employed on a much more general level, both by soldiers and civilians. This specimen, from the Royal Armoury in Dresden, may date from about 1570, although the type first appeared in the early 16th century and remained largely unchanged for most of the century.

Italian cross-hilt dagger, late 16th century

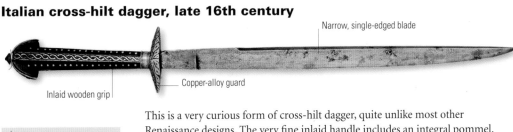

Narrow, single-edged blade

Inlaid wooden grip

Copper-alloy guard

DATE	late 16th century
ORIGIN	ITALIAN
LENGTH	37.2cm (14.6in)

This is a very curious form of cross-hilt dagger, quite unlike most other Renaissance designs. The very fine inlaid handle includes an integral pommel. The guard is very narrow in proportion to the length of the blade, which is quite extreme. The profile of the blade seems to be a forerunner to later types of Mediterranean fighting knife, especially the navaja.

Cinquedeas

Because their blades tend to be short and narrow, almost all forms of dagger are stabbing and slashing weapons. They cannot be used to deliver cutting blows, as their smallness rules out any sort of concussive potential. A unique exception to this rule, the cinquedea, appeared in the mid-15th century in Italy. Many cinquedeas could be described either as a dagger or short sword. They were designed primarily for dealing blows with their sharp edges rather than the point. Therefore the blade was usually very wide.

Italian short cinquedea, c.1500

Filigree handle inserts

Thick spine

Short dagger blade

The range of sizes in which cinquedeas were made was very wide. Although many are quite long and very effective as short cut-and-thrust swords, others, like this one, are quite small. The broad, sharply tapered blade, with its thick central spine, is ideally suited to thrusting. Here an ancient Bronze Age idea has been improved upon through its rendering in hardened steel.

DATE	c.1500
ORIGIN	ITALIAN
LENGTH	42cm (16.5in)

Italian short cinquedea, c.1500

Full-size hilt

Boomerang-shaped guard

Copper-alloy pommel cap

Short, sharply tapered blade

Although it is in an excavated condition, this elegant little weapon is an excellent example of the smaller form of cinquedea. The hilt is designed in the usual way for this style, being the same size as most of the larger forms, and has a copper-alloy pommel cap. The small but fearsome blade displays a needlelike reinforced point. This weapon was once in the collection of the British arms and armour scholar Charles Alexander, Baron de Cosson (1843–1929).

DATE	c.1500
ORIGIN	ITALY
LENGTH	37cm (14.5in)

Italian cinquedea, early 16th century

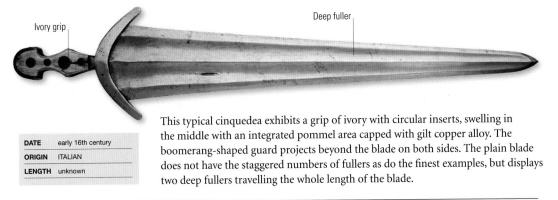

Ivory grip

Deep fuller

DATE	early 16th century
ORIGIN	ITALIAN
LENGTH	unknown

This typical cinquedea exhibits a grip of ivory with circular inserts, swelling in the middle with an integrated pommel area capped with gilt copper alloy. The boomerang-shaped guard projects beyond the blade on both sides. The plain blade does not have the staggered numbers of fullers as do the finest examples, but displays two deep fullers travelling the whole length of the blade.

North Italian cinquedea, early 16th century

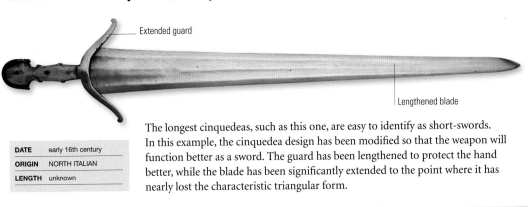

Extended guard

Lengthened blade

DATE	early 16th century
ORIGIN	NORTH ITALIAN
LENGTH	unknown

The longest cinquedeas, such as this one, are easy to identify as short-swords. In this example, the cinquedea design has been modified so that the weapon will function better as a sword. The guard has been lengthened to protect the hand better, while the blade has been significantly extended to the point where it has nearly lost the characteristic triangular form.

Replica cinquedea, 19th century

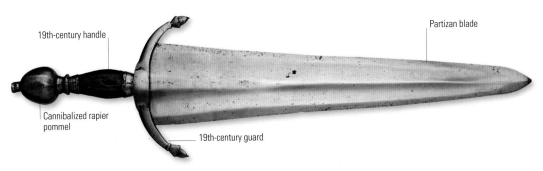

Partizan blade

19th-century handle

Cannibalized rapier pommel

19th-century guard

DATE	19th century
ORIGIN	UNKNOWN
LENGTH	unknown

Cinquedeas were very popular with 19th-century collectors. Their desirability led to a flood of fakes. Some were complete fabrications, others made up of original parts. This one has been constructed using a 16th-century rapier pommel, a 19th-century grip and guard, and the blade of a 16th- or 17th-century staff weapon.

"Side ring" parrying daggers

By the second half of the 16th century, rapier fencing almost always required a parrying dagger held in the left hand. Until the mid-17th century, parrying daggers were almost always of the "side ring" type, having a simple cross guard onto which was attached a metal ring that protected the outside of the hand. Parrying daggers were often decorated to match their rapiers, although very few matching sets survive.

German parrying dagger, late 16th century

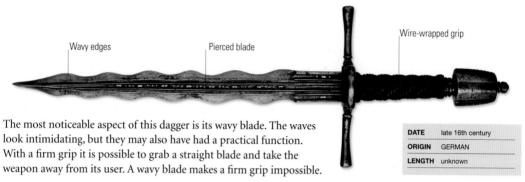

Wire-wrapped grip

Wavy edges

Pierced blade

The most noticeable aspect of this dagger is its wavy blade. The waves look intimidating, but they may also have had a practical function. With a firm grip it is possible to grab a straight blade and take the weapon away from its user. A wavy blade makes a firm grip impossible.

DATE	late 16th century
ORIGIN	GERMAN
LENGTH	unknown

English parrying dagger, late 16th century

Heavily pitted surface

Very worn blade

Fluted pommel

This rare English parrying dagger was found in the River Thames in London. After several hundred years underwater, the surface is now heavily pitted, but the fluted pommel and guard are still recognizable. This was a weapon of quality, although unusually it lacks a side ring.

DATE	late 16th century
ORIGIN	ENGLISH
LENGTH	unknown

German parrying dagger, c.1600

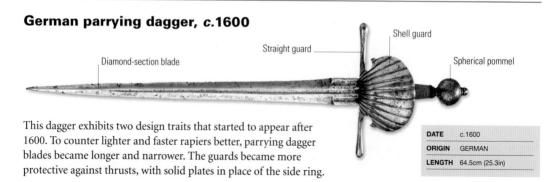

Shell guard

Straight guard

Spherical pommel

Diamond-section blade

This dagger exhibits two design traits that started to appear after 1600. To counter lighter and faster rapiers better, parrying dagger blades became longer and narrower. The guards became more protective against thrusts, with solid plates in place of the side ring.

DATE	c.1600
ORIGIN	GERMAN
LENGTH	64.5cm (25.3in)

German parrying dagger, *c.*1600

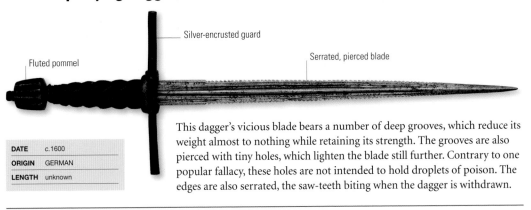

Fluted pommel

Silver-encrusted guard

Serrated, pierced blade

DATE	c.1600
ORIGIN	GERMAN
LENGTH	unknown

This dagger's vicious blade bears a number of deep grooves, which reduce its weight almost to nothing while retaining its strength. The grooves are also pierced with tiny holes, which lighten the blade still further. Contrary to one popular fallacy, these holes are not intended to hold droplets of poison. The edges are also serrated, the saw-teeth biting when the dagger is withdrawn.

German parrying dagger, *c.*1600

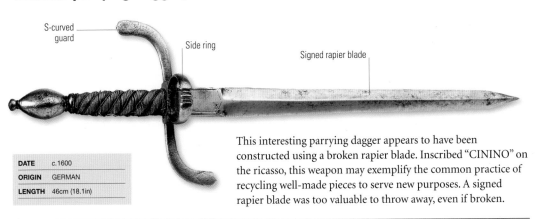

S-curved guard

Side ring

Signed rapier blade

DATE	c.1600
ORIGIN	GERMAN
LENGTH	46cm (18.1in)

This interesting parrying dagger appears to have been constructed using a broken rapier blade. Inscribed "CININO" on the ricasso, this weapon may exemplify the common practice of recycling well-made pieces to serve new purposes. A signed rapier blade was too valuable to throw away, even if broken.

Italian left-handed dagger, *c.*1600

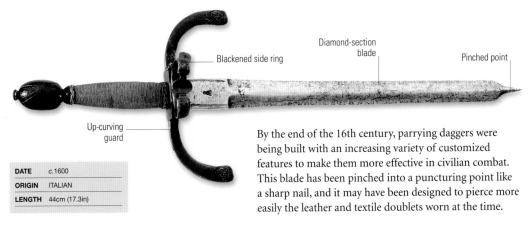

Blackened side ring

Diamond-section blade

Pinched point

Up-curving guard

DATE	c.1600
ORIGIN	ITALIAN
LENGTH	44cm (17.3in)

By the end of the 16th century, parrying daggers were being built with an increasing variety of customized features to make them more effective in civilian combat. This blade has been pinched into a puncturing point like a sharp nail, and it may have been designed to pierce more easily the leather and textile doublets worn at the time.

Spanish sword-catcher, *c.*1600

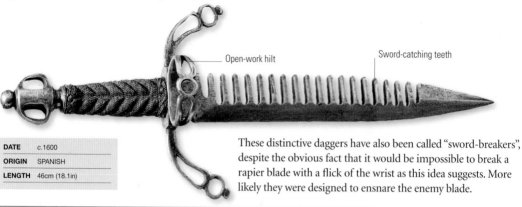

Open-work hilt

Sword-catching teeth

DATE	c.1600
ORIGIN	SPANISH
LENGTH	46cm (18.1in)

These distinctive daggers have also been called "sword-breakers", despite the obvious fact that it would be impossible to break a rapier blade with a flick of the wrist as this idea suggests. More likely they were designed to ensnare the enemy blade.

English parrying dagger, blade dated 1608

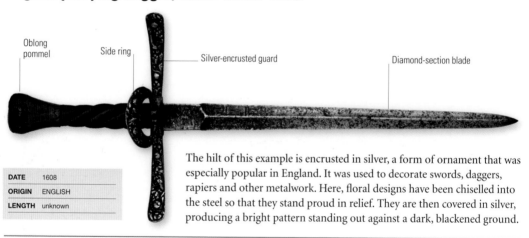

Oblong pommel

Side ring

Silver-encrusted guard

Diamond-section blade

DATE	1608
ORIGIN	ENGLISH
LENGTH	unknown

The hilt of this example is encrusted in silver, a form of ornament that was especially popular in England. It was used to decorate swords, daggers, rapiers and other metalwork. Here, floral designs have been chiselled into the steel so that they stand proud in relief. They are then covered in silver, producing a bright pattern standing out against a dark, blackened ground.

German parrying dagger, *c.*1610

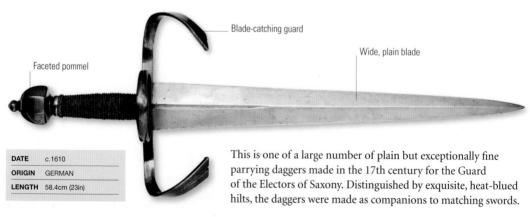

Blade-catching guard

Wide, plain blade

Faceted pommel

DATE	c.1610
ORIGIN	GERMAN
LENGTH	58.4cm (23in)

This is one of a large number of plain but exceptionally fine parrying daggers made in the 17th century for the Guard of the Electors of Saxony. Distinguished by exquisite, heat-blued hilts, the daggers were made as companions to matching swords.

English parrying dagger, early 17th century

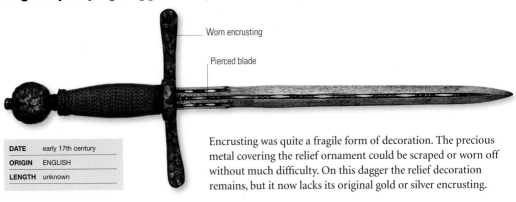

Worn encrusting

Pierced blade

DATE	early 17th century
ORIGIN	ENGLISH
LENGTH	unknown

Encrusting was quite a fragile form of decoration. The precious metal covering the relief ornament could be scraped or worn off without much difficulty. On this dagger the relief decoration remains, but it now lacks its original gold or silver encrusting.

German (?) parrying dagger, c.1600–20

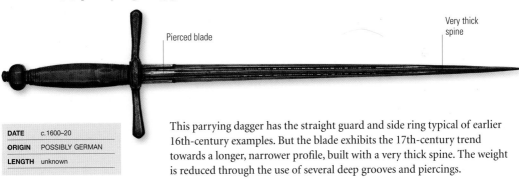

Pierced blade

Very thick spine

DATE	c.1600–20
ORIGIN	POSSIBLY GERMAN
LENGTH	unknown

This parrying dagger has the straight guard and side ring typical of earlier 16th-century examples. But the blade exhibits the 17th-century trend towards a longer, narrower profile, built with a very thick spine. The weight is reduced through the use of several deep grooves and piercings.

English dagger, c.1610–25

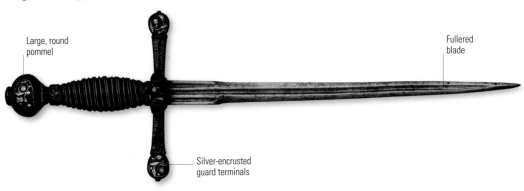

Large, round pommel

Fullered blade

Silver-encrusted guard terminals

DATE	c.1610–25
ORIGIN	ENGLISH
LENGTH	unknown

The style of the English hilt of this dagger is typical of the Jacobean period (1603–1625). The large, rounded pommel and straight cross guard with large, knob-like terminals, as well as the encrusting in silver, is typical of English taste of the early 17th century. The same design features are also found on contemporary dress swords.

17th-century main-gauche daggers

Main gauche simply means "left hand", and is therefore no more specific a term than "parrying dagger". It originally denoted a dagger that was meant for rapier and dagger fencing, as opposed to more general uses, as well as self-defence. However, over time it has come to be applied more specifically in English. Today it is used, rightly or wrongly, to refer to this quite late class of Italo-Spanish fencing dagger.

Spanish main-gauche dagger, *c.*1640

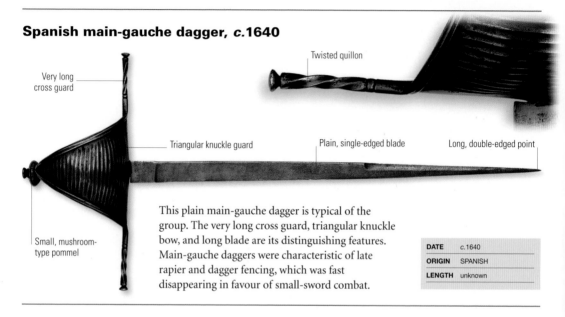

Very long cross guard

Twisted quillon

Triangular knuckle guard

Plain, single-edged blade

Long, double-edged point

Small, mushroom-type pommel

This plain main-gauche dagger is typical of the group. The very long cross guard, triangular knuckle bow, and long blade are its distinguishing features. Main-gauche daggers were characteristic of late rapier and dagger fencing, which was fast disappearing in favour of small-sword combat.

DATE	c.1640
ORIGIN	SPANISH
LENGTH	unknown

Southern Italian main-gauche dagger, *c.*1650

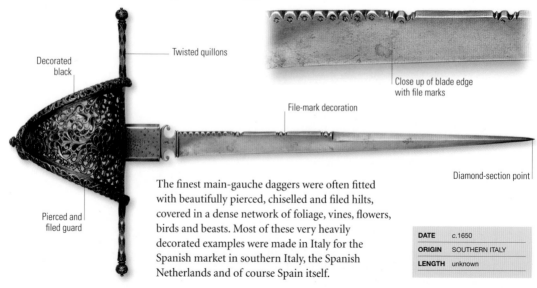

Decorated black

Twisted quillons

Close up of blade edge with file marks

File-mark decoration

Diamond-section point

Pierced and filed guard

The finest main-gauche daggers were often fitted with beautifully pierced, chiselled and filed hilts, covered in a dense network of foliage, vines, flowers, birds and beasts. Most of these very heavily decorated examples were made in Italy for the Spanish market in southern Italy, the Spanish Netherlands and of course Spain itself.

DATE	c.1650
ORIGIN	SOUTHERN ITALY
LENGTH	unknown

Italian main-gauche dagger, *c*.1650

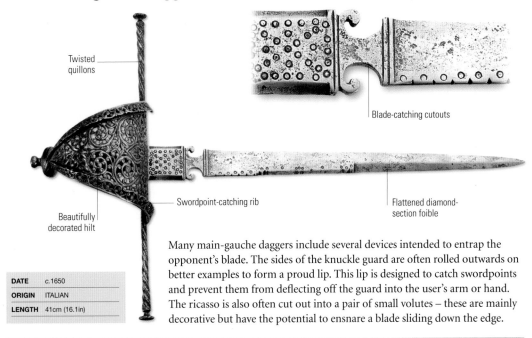

Twisted quillons

Blade-catching cutouts

Beautifully decorated hilt

Swordpoint-catching rib

Flattened diamond-section foible

DATE	c.1650
ORIGIN	ITALIAN
LENGTH	41cm (16.1in)

Many main-gauche daggers include several devices intended to entrap the opponent's blade. The sides of the knuckle guard are often rolled outwards on better examples to form a proud lip. This lip is designed to catch swordpoints and prevent them from deflecting off the guard into the user's arm or hand. The ricasso is also often cut out into a pair of small volutes – these are mainly decorative but have the potential to ensnare a blade sliding down the edge.

German main-gauche dagger, *c*.1660

This is an interesting German variation on the main-gauche theme. Rather than the usual triangular knuckle guard, this weapon is fitted with a rounded dish guard, acid-etched in the typical German manner, with additional bars at the edges. This piece was undoubtedly made as an en suite mate to a cup-hilt rapier with a guard having similar specific features, now lost. The blade is also typically German: very narrow with a deep central fuller along the lower half, in the trough of which is the maker's signature.

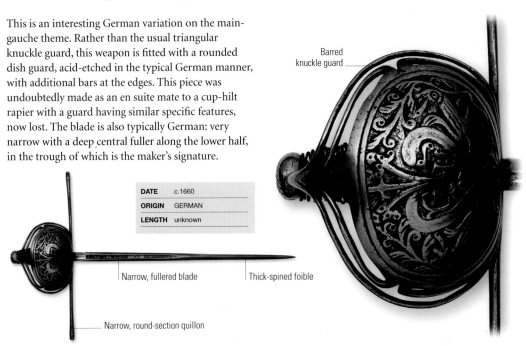

Barred knuckle guard

DATE	c.1660
ORIGIN	GERMAN
LENGTH	unknown

Narrow, fullered blade

Thick-spined foible

Narrow, round-section quillon

17th-century stilettos

The stiletto or stylet appeared late in the 16th century. Its development probably began with the production of miniature side-ring daggers. One of these little daggers would have been too small for fencing, but it nevertheless adhered to the fashion of the time.

Since it was useless as a fencing implement, this new form of dagger quickly lost its resemblance to the larger parrying dagger. At the height of its popularity in the mid-17th century, the all-metal stiletto was a weapon purely of last resort and of assassination.

Spanish stiletto, late 16th century

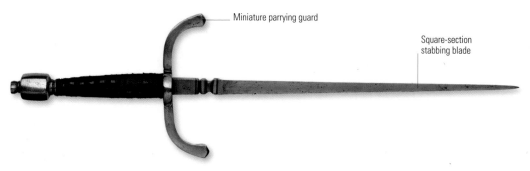

Miniature parrying guard

Square-section stabbing blade

This weapon could easily be mistaken for a typical late 16th-century parrying dagger, if not for its size and blade-type. It is perhaps three-quarters the size of a full-size parrying dagger, and thus is too small and delicate for sword-fighting. Its blade also has no sharp edges, being square in cross-section. The base or ricasso of the blade also exhibits a new decorative feature, a turned area just forward of the guard that emphasizes the delicate refinement of the weapon's lines. This "baluster-turning" quickly became a standard feature of 17th-century stilettos.

DATE	late 16th century
ORIGIN	SPANISH
LENGTH	unknown

Italian stiletto, late 16th century

Discoidal pommel

Long, triangular blade

Tapering baluster grip

Turned ricasso

This weapon is a superb demonstration of steel cutting, the hilt turned into a beautifully proportioned piece of architecture in miniature. The grip mutates skillfully from discoidal knobs into flowing tulip-like forms and continues seamlessly on to the strong needle-like blade. These all-metal weapons were accompanied by equally elegant scabbards, made entirely of steel or wood; three or four narrow lengths glued together to house the either triangular- or square-section blade and covered in paper-thin leather.

DATE	late 16th century
ORIGIN	ITALIAN
LENGTH	unknown

Italian stiletto, early 17th century

Cast copper-alloy hilt

Short, square-section blade

DATE	early 17th century
ORIGIN	ITALIAN
LENGTH	20cm (7.9in)

The hilt of this stiletto is quite different from the baluster-turned types. Instead of being cut out of a single piece of steel, the hilt of this weapon has been modelled in wax and then cast in copper alloy. The grip takes the form of an ape standing on its hind legs, and on its head stands a small animal, probably a dog.

Italian stiletto, *c.*1600

Baluster-turned hilt

Short blade

DATE	c.1600
ORIGIN	ITALIAN
LENGTH	unknown

Despite their overall smallness, most stilettos have a blade that makes up around three-quarters of their total length. This example is somewhat unusual in that its total length is divided nearly equally between blade and hilt. Such a small weapon would be especially easy to hide about one's person.

Italian stiletto, *c.*1600

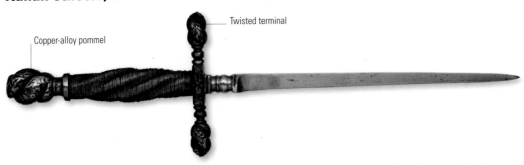

Twisted terminal

Copper-alloy pommel

DATE	c.1600
ORIGIN	POSSIBLY ITALIAN
LENGTH	unknown

This weapon shows a different construction to many other stilettos of the time. Here the pommel and guard are made in copper alloy, while the grip is wrapped in fine wire. The hilt seems out of proportion to the blade; it may be that the blade and hilt did not originally belong together.

Italian stiletto, *c.*1600

Baluster-turned ricasso

Triangular-section blade

While the blades of some stilettos are entirely plain, many of the finer examples display baluster-turnings on the base of the blade as well as the hilt. This produces an attractive unity between hilt and blade, a detail seen on very few forms of edged weapon. The grip of this example has been cut into a fluid, twisting form.

DATE	*c.*1600
ORIGIN	ITALIAN
LENGTH	unknown

Italian stiletto, *c.*1600

Spherical pommel

Swelling grip

Single cutting edge

Most all-metal stilettos with baluster-turned hilts have a spherical, discoidal or ovoid pommel, the size of which is carefully designed to balance the blade in the hand. When the perfect balance is achieved, the weapon seems almost weightless in the hand. The shape of the guard terminals usually matches that of the pommel, while the grip is usually twisted into graceful architectural forms.

DATE	*c.*1600
ORIGIN	ITALIAN
LENGTH	unknown

Italian gunner's stiletto, 1600

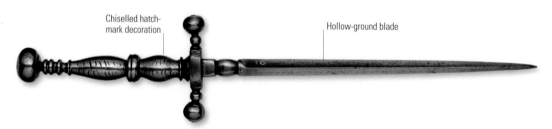

Chiselled hatch-mark decoration

Hollow-ground blade

Although the plainly smooth-surfaced stilettos are the most common, a number of examples show chiselled or punched decoration as well, such as the hatch-marks on the grip of this piece. The back of this blade is numbered, supposedly to enable the owner to determine the weight of a cannon ball so that he could range a shot effectively. However, the numbering is non-functional, and the blade is too short to be used as a measuring device.

DATE	1600
ORIGIN	ITALIAN
LENGTH	unknown

Italian stiletto, early to mid-17th century

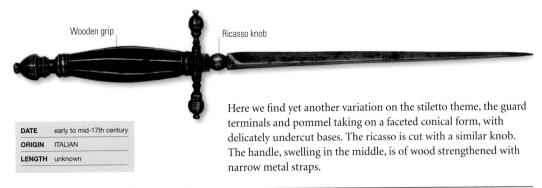

Wooden grip

Ricasso knob

DATE	early to mid-17th century
ORIGIN	ITALIAN
LENGTH	unknown

Here we find yet another variation on the stiletto theme, the guard terminals and pommel taking on a faceted conical form, with delicately undercut bases. The ricasso is cut with a similar knob. The handle, swelling in the middle, is of wood strengthened with narrow metal straps.

Spanish stiletto, late 17th century

Etched ricasso

Disk guard

Ribbed handle

DATE	late 17th century
ORIGIN	SPANISH
LENGTH	45.2cm (17.8in)

This later stiletto takes a very unusual form. While the grip flares towards the pommel, in a manner not unlike some earlier 16th-century daggers, the guard is really that of a small-sword in miniature; it is, however, too small to be an actual sword that has been broken and cut down.

Spanish stiletto dividers, *c.*1700–50

Splitting blade

Pivoting joint

Etched and gilt decoration

DATE	c.1700–50
ORIGIN	SPANISH
LENGTH	unknown

It was very popular in the Renaissance to draw parallels between the fighting arts and the sciences. Fight masters often saw themselves as scientists as well as martial artists, and they strove to communicate their skills in a learned, scientific way. This led to a fashionable association between weapons and scientific instruments, and thus noblemen often liked to collect both. The idea of combining the two into a single object, the stiletto that split apart to form a pair of architect's dividers, first occurred in the 16th century and was repeated many times.

17th-century plug bayonets

At some early date someone had the idea of whittling down the wooden haft of a knife and plugging it into the muzzle of a gun, turning it into a thrusting spear. This probably happened in Europe, and some believe the term "bayonet" is derived from the name of the French cutlery town, Bayonne. The gun was of course disabled, but if a spear was needed then the enemy were too close for the lack of a gun to be a problem.

British officer's or sporting bayonet, c.1660

Bone/ivory hilt

Decorative cross-guard finials (one missing)

Unusual curved blade

The elaborate and decorated bone or ivory hilt suggests this bayonet was for an officer or for sporting use. With such hard material, it is doubtful whether the hilt could have been secured in the muzzle and there are no marks to indicate its use in this way. The weapon was probably used merely as a knife.

DATE	c.1660
ORIGIN	BRITISH
LENGTH	41cm (16.1in)

British officer's or sporting bayonet, c.1660

Bone/ivory hilt

Dagger-type blade

Decorative cross-guard finials

This is another example of a decorated bone or ivory hilt but slightly less elaborate than the one above. While this weapon has a more conventional blade, both have a number of features that are almost identical, such as the tang buttons on the pommels and the cross guards, suggesting that they may be by the same maker.

DATE	c.1660
ORIGIN	BRITISH
LENGTH	45.1cm (17.8in)

British military bayonet, c.1680

Round hilt with pommel cap and cross guard (damaged)

Wide, thin, single-edged blade with false edge

Common to all plug bayonets is a slender, round, tapering handle with a bulbous swelling near where it joins the blade. The handle has to be resilient enough to allow it to be pushed into the muzzle and stay there, but not so tightly that it can't be removed. Most handles are therefore wooden as this material is slightly elastic.

DATE	c.1680
ORIGIN	BRITISH
LENGTH	45.8cm (18in)

British officer's bayonet, 1686

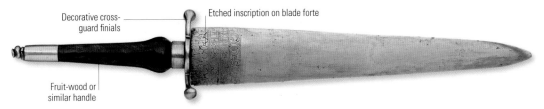

Decorative cross-guard finials

Etched inscription on blade forte

Fruit-wood or similar handle

DATE	1686
ORIGIN	BRITISH
LENGTH	46cm (18.1in)

This plug bayonet conforms more to the general type of serviceable military bayonet with its wooden handle, but it is of better quality than usual, suggesting that the weapon may have belonged to an officer. This is supported by the fact that the blade is inscribed "GOD SAVE KING JAMES THE 2 1686", which is an unusual feature on any type of bayonet and is useful for dating this general style.

British officer's bayonet, 1686

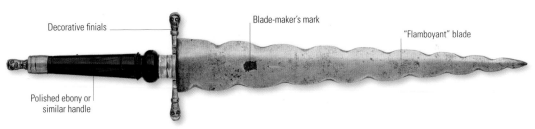

Decorative finials

Blade-maker's mark

"Flamboyant" blade

Polished ebony or similar handle

DATE	1686
ORIGIN	BRITISH
LENGTH	45.4cm (17.9in)

A bayonet as distinctive and of such quality as this one, with its highly polished grip of either ebony or other exotic wood and its gilded brass fittings, was undoubtedly used by an officer. The pommel, tang button and cross guard show close similarity to those of the two officer's bayonets on the previous page. The most distinctive feature is obviously the blade with its sinuous wavy edges, often referred to as "flamboyant" because of its likeness to a flickering flame.

Scandinavian officer's bayonet, 1700

Bulbous finials

Flattened diamond-section blade

Hilt with decorated gilt brass fittings

Blade-maker's mark

DATE	1700
ORIGIN	POSS. SCANDINAVIAN
LENGTH	48.7cm (19.1in)

A good-quality, possibly Scandinavian, bayonet. It has a wooden grip, painted possibly in imitation of tortoiseshell or an exotic wood, and gilded decorated brass hilt fittings. The cross guard with its downturned finials is more reminiscent of many 19th-century sword bayonets than of the typical English plug bayonet. Like others of this class, it shows few if any signs of having been thrust into a muzzle.

17th- and 18th-century civilian daggers

Walking-out and dress-type swords and daggers became a prominent feature among the rising classes in the period following the Reformation. Although such weapons were still very expensive, there was a larger class of people who could now afford them.

Daggers and knives that were primarily intended for functional use were often completed to a level of decoration that suggested the object might also be worn as an item of jewellery or statement of rank, as well as having a more practical day-to-day use.

English dagger, 1628

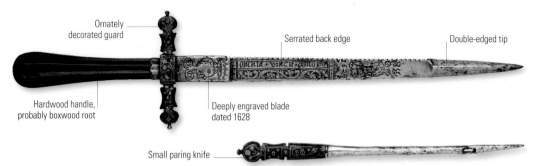

Ornately decorated guard

Serrated back edge

Double-edged tip

Hardwood handle, probably boxwood root

Deeply engraved blade dated 1628

Small paring knife

This very fine, high-quality combination set comprises a main dagger and matching paring knife, both of which fit together in the same scabbard. The blade of the main knife is beautifully decorated with deep engraving. The serrated edge had a practical application in that when cutting a joint of meat it could sever through the toughest parts; the paring knife was used to secure the treated item in position.

DATE	1628
ORIGIN	ENGLISH
LENGTH	32.7cm (12.9in)

The cutler's trade

In 17th- and 18th-century Europe, improved trade routes meant that raw materials such as iron were transported more easily to the main commercial towns and cities. Aided too by advances in industrial power, Solingen in Germany and Sheffield in England became important centres of blade production.

It took many craftsmen to produce a good-quality edged weapon. The manufacture of the blade was a highly skilled art and there were also specialist cross-guard and pommel makers, scalers (grip makers) and scabbard and sheath makers.

RIGHT A German bladesmith in his workshop. Many of Europe's best cutlers worked in Solingen, Germany and Sheffield, England.

English dagger, 1631

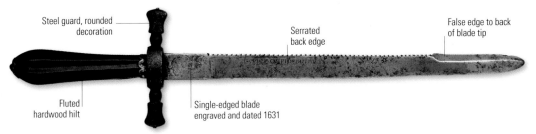

Steel guard, rounded decoration

Serrated back edge

False edge to back of blade tip

Fluted hardwood hilt

Single-edged blade engraved and dated 1631

DATE	1631
ORIGIN	ENGLISH
LENGTH	26.3cm (10.4in)

This is a fine example of a gentleman's utility knife, having a fluted wooden grip, and a steel ferrule and cross guard. The latter is simplistically decorated with rounded finials. The blade is flat and single-edged, yet has a sharpened false edge at the tip. The back edge of the blade is serrated. Engraved decoration on the blade indicates that it dates from 1631.

English dagger, mid-17th century

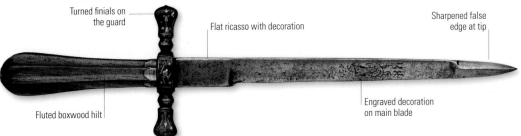

Turned finials on the guard

Flat ricasso with decoration

Sharpened false edge at tip

Fluted boxwood hilt

Engraved decoration on main blade

DATE	mid-17th century
ORIGIN	ENGLISH
LENGTH	31.4cm (12.4in)

This dagger has an interesting blade construction. The flat ricasso extends the back flat of the blade along almost the full length, effectively making this a single-edged knife with a double-edged tip. The steel guard is nicely formed with domed terminals and decoration on the quillon block. The fluted boxwood hilt is typical.

English quillon dagger, 1678

Slender quillons with rounded finials

Sharpened edge

Wooden haft, with wire-wrapped grip

Broad ricasso with dedication

DATE	1678
ORIGIN	ENGLISH
LENGTH	31.4cm (12.4in)

This English quillon dagger is inscribed on the blade "Memento Godfrey...1678". The long blade is single-edged for most of the length, and the ricasso area is broad and flat with the inscribed decoration. The tang of the blade is concealed by an ovoid-section wooden grip, which is covered with a twisted-wire wrapping.

Dutch or German quillon-form hunting dagger, *c.*1700

S-shaped guard with lion's-head finials

Single-edged blade, double-edged at tip

Carved wood grip

Inscribed decoration on blade

DATE	c.1700
ORIGIN	DUTCH/GERMAN
LENGTH	40.8cm (16.1in)

The structure and style of the grip on this weapon suggests that it is a hunting knife, and most probably Dutch or perhaps German in origin. It dates from the latter part of the 1600s or possibly the early 1700s. The ornate cross guard is brass, S-shaped and decorated with miniature lion's-head finials. The long, narrow, tapered blade has an inscribed decoration and is single-edged along most of its length, narrowing to a double-edged tip.

French or German stiletto, early to mid-18th century

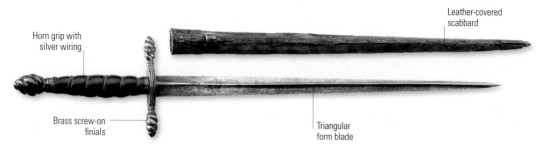

Leather-covered scabbard

Horn grip with silver wiring

Brass screw-on finials

Triangular form blade

This stiletto is French or possibly German. The triangular-section blade has a forte with remnants of decorative etching and gilding and the point has been lightly resharpened. Grooved finials are screwed onto quillons, the grip covered with silver-wire winding. The front of the brass scabbard has a leather cover; the rear is engraved with scrolling vine patterns.

DATE	early to mid-18th century
ORIGIN	FRENCH/GERMAN
LENGTH	48cm (18.9in)

Spanish or Italian short stiletto, mid-18th century

Blade double-edged towards tip

Horn grip

Decorated ricasso

This short thrusting stiletto is possibly the accompanying knife to a larger hunting weapon. It has an interesting horn, or narwhal, grip with decoration and wiring. The steel pommel cap has engraved decoration, and the steel ricasso of the blade a chiselled decoration. The blade has a long fore edge and a short false edge.

DATE	mid-18th century
ORIGIN	SPANISH/ITALIAN
LENGTH	24.9cm (9.8in)

Italian or Dalmatian Schiovona dagger, 1790

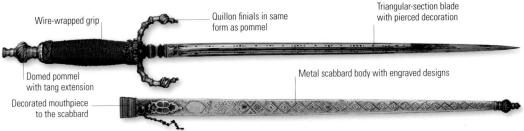

Wire-wrapped grip

Quillon finials in same form as pommel

Triangular-section blade with pierced decoration

Domed pommel with tang extension

Metal scabbard body with engraved designs

Decorated mouthpiece to the scabbard

The slender blade of this dagger is triangular in section with pierced decoration on the facings. The ricasso of the blade is decoratively segmented and may disguise a join where a new tang has been added. The pommel and cross-guard terminals are of matching design and the centre section of the guard is decorated with coloured, semi-precious stones. The grip is of wood with wire wrapping.

DATE	1790
ORIGIN	ITALIAN/DALMATIAN
LENGTH	45cm (17.8in)

Italian dagger, late 18th century

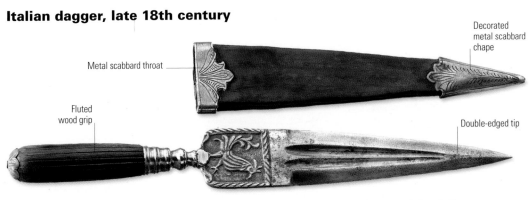

Decorated metal scabbard chape

Metal scabbard throat

Fluted wood grip

Double-edged tip

DATE	late 18th century
ORIGIN	ITALIAN
LENGTH	35cm (13.8in)

This late 18th-century knife is of a pattern popular around the Mediterranean. It has a distinctive blade with a double fuller, which converges towards the blade tip, and the ricasso features a relief-engraved emblem of a cockerel. The fluted wood grip has polished steel mounts, and the leather scabbard has steel mounts.

Italian utility knife, late 18th century

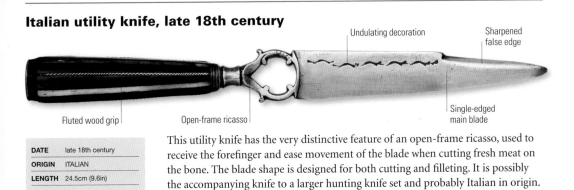

Undulating decoration

Sharpened false edge

Fluted wood grip

Open-frame ricasso

Single-edged main blade

DATE	late 18th century
ORIGIN	ITALIAN
LENGTH	24.5cm (9.6in)

This utility knife has the very distinctive feature of an open-frame ricasso, used to receive the forefinger and ease movement of the blade when cutting fresh meat on the bone. The blade shape is designed for both cutting and filleting. It is possibly the accompanying knife to a larger hunting knife set and probably Italian in origin.

18th- and 19th-century naval dirks

It was in the latter half of the 18th century that some short swords and dirks started to be carried by midshipmen and officers of the English Navy, and often these were conversions from other, broken weapons.

Such damaged weapons were far too valuable to be discarded, but instead could be resurrected as short swords, and the evolution into short dirks appears to have been influenced by this trend.

French long-bladed dirk (conversion), late 18th century

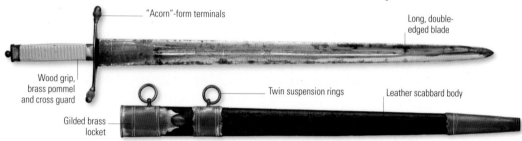

"Acorn"-form terminals

Long, double-edged blade

Wood grip, brass pommel and cross guard

Twin suspension rings

Leather scabbard body

Gilded brass locket

The blade of this conversion dirk appears to be from a hunting sword and it is engraved with scrolling designs. The grip's square form could be French and the leather scabbard appears to have gilded brass fittings. The "acorn" decoration on the cross guard doesn't seem to fit "naval traditions".

DATE	late 18th century
ORIGIN	FRENCH
LENGTH	58cm (23in)

British (?) long-bladed naval dirk (conversion), late 18th century

Shortened blade from a different sword

Bone hilt housing tang of blade

Unusual double guard

This interesting dirk is composed partially from a short sword, possibly a spadroon. The assembly of the blade, cross guard, grip and pommel is secured by drawing the tang of the blade through the pommel cap and peening (hammering) it into place.

DATE	late 18th century
ORIGIN	POSSIBLY BRITISH
LENGTH	61cm (24in)

British naval dirk (conversion), early 19th century

Downturned quillons with bulbous terminal

Blade from sword or bayonet

Fluted bone grip

This is quite a substantial item, and appears to be more similar to a short sword than a dirk. The blade is not dissimilar to some of the variations found on the bayonet for the English Baker rifle, although it is by no means certain that this is what this weapon has been converted from.

DATE	early 19th century
ORIGIN	BRITISH
LENGTH	58cm (23in)

American naval dirk, early 19th century

Short cross guard with eagle decoration

Twin suspension rings

Ivory grip

Brass scabbard body

DATE	early 19th century
ORIGIN	AMERICAN
LENGTH	19cm (7.5in)

This American Naval dirk has a brightly polished, slender, double-edged blade with a flattened diamond section. There are gilt-copper hilt fittings and a lion's-mask pommel, and an embossed cross guard with an eagle head holding a ball in its beak. The grip is turned ivory. The gilded brass scabbard has twin suspension rings.

Spanish naval officer's hanger sword, early 19th century

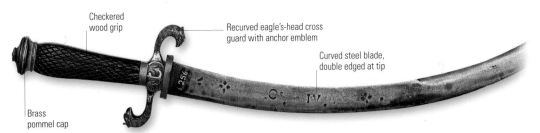

Checkered wood grip

Recurved eagle's-head cross guard with anchor emblem

Curved steel blade, double edged at tip

Brass pommel cap

DATE	early 19th century
ORIGIN	SPANISH
LENGTH	44.5cm (17.5in)

The curved blade of this Spanish naval officer's hanger sword from the early 1800s is single-edged with a double-edged tip. Stampings on the blade indicate "Cs IV" (Carlos IV, who died in 1819). The hilt fittings are brass, the pommel is in the form of a flattened urn, and the cross guard is decorated with eagle's-head terminals and an anchor emblem on the quillon block.

British long-bladed naval dirk, early 19th century

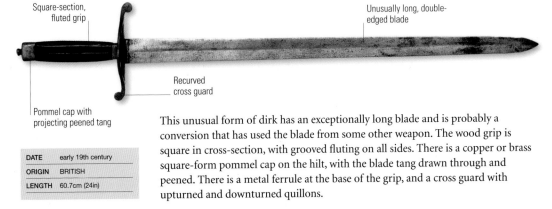

Square-section, fluted grip

Unusually long, double-edged blade

Recurved cross guard

Pommel cap with projecting peened tang

DATE	early 19th century
ORIGIN	BRITISH
LENGTH	60.7cm (24in)

This unusual form of dirk has an exceptionally long blade and is probably a conversion that has used the blade from some other weapon. The wood grip is square in cross-section, with grooved fluting on all sides. There is a copper or brass square-form pommel cap on the hilt, with the blade tang drawn through and peened. There is a metal ferrule at the base of the grip, and a cross guard with upturned and downturned quillons.

French boarding dagger, mid-19th century

Steel lanyard ring

Steel cross guard

Turned wood hilt

Although commonly called a "boarding dagger", this is actually an "on-board" utility knife. Whereas knives were not normally carried on deck (for safety reasons), they were often required for work on the rigging. The lanyard ring was secured to a cord tied to the belt, as a prevention against loss if dropped.

DATE	mid-19th century
ORIGIN	FRENCH
LENGTH	35.6cm (14in)

British naval hanger, *c.*1850

Carved bone grip

Recurved brass cross guard

Curved "cut-and-thrust" blade

Brass pommel in the form of lion's head

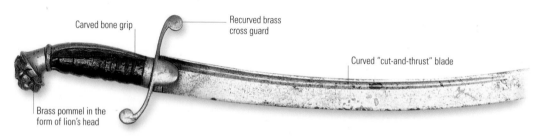

This naval hanger has a long, curved blade of the "cut-and-thrust" form, being mostly single-edged with a flat back and long fuller. The last third of the blade is double-edged. The pommel, backstrap, ferrule and cross guard are made of brass, the pommel decoration being that of a lion's head. There is no record of this pattern of hanger being issued to the English Navy; it is probable that they were sold to privateers, or even as export items to foreign naval powers.

DATE	*c.*1850
ORIGIN	BRITISH
LENGTH	45.7cm (18in)

Spanish naval dirk, 19th century

Double-edged blade with central spine

Plain steel cross guard

Turned steel hilt fittings

This is not strictly a naval dirk but more of a maritime knife used by sailors. The blade has a long, flat ricasso which tapers to a point to form the central spine of the blade. The cross guard is plain, flat and tapered, and the hilt is composed of an elongated ferrule and pommel cap connected by the central grip made of bone. The fluted grooves are not simply decoration but intended to improve the grip.

DATE	19th century
ORIGIN	SPANISH
LENGTH	32cm (12.6in)

Georgian dirks

The term "Georgian dirk" really embraces weapons from the mid-1700s to the start of Queen Victoria's reign. The Industrial Revolution had evolved, and more efficient means for the production of metal wares had come into being, as well as a growing middle class of people who could afford expensive items. The Georgian dirk offered a form of weapon that was also ornate enough to be considered a form of male jewellery.

British Georgian naval dirk, early 19th century

Cross guard with "bud" finials

Engraved copper scabbard

Suspension rings

Pistol-form grip with four sections of grooved banding

DATE	early 19th century
ORIGIN	BRITISH
LENGTH	22.8cm (9in)

The scabbard carrying the slender, curved, single-edged blade is engraved copper, with gilding featuring scrolling and checkering designs. Metal portions of the hilt are made of copper with gilding. The cross guard features "bud"-type finials and a double-crescent langet at the centre of the guard.

British Georgian dirk, early 19th century

Cross guard with shell emblems

Single-edged blade with flat back and fuller

Carved ivory grip

DATE	early 19th century
ORIGIN	BRITISH
LENGTH	27.4cm (10.8in)

This broad, single-edged blade has etched, blued and gilt decoration. The blade has a flat back, with a single fuller running along most of the back edge. Metal portions of the hilt are gilded copper, comprising a pommel with lion's-mask motif, ferrule and a cross guard with shell emblem finials.

British Georgian naval dirk, early 19th century

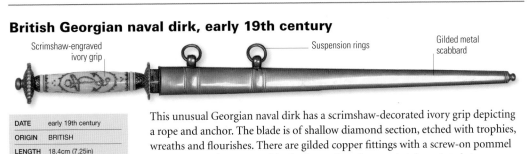

Scrimshaw-engraved ivory grip

Suspension rings

Gilded metal scabbard

DATE	early 19th century
ORIGIN	BRITISH
LENGTH	18.4cm (7.25in)

This unusual Georgian naval dirk has a scrimshaw-decorated ivory grip depicting a rope and anchor. The blade is of shallow diamond section, etched with trophies, wreaths and flourishes. There are gilded copper fittings with a screw-on pommel and an unusual cross guard in the form of an elongated eight-pointed star.

British Georgian naval dirk, *c.*1820

Silver-decorated pommel

Suspension rings

Decorated brass scabbard

The blade of this unusual Georgian naval dirk has a plain, flattened diamond section. The turned ivory grip has a silver pique-work design of a fouled anchor in an oval, and the initials "RC" in scrolls. The small, rounded rectangular brass guard has a matching pommel embossed with tiny scales within a studded border. The brass scabbard is ornately engraved with a button chape and two suspension rings.

DATE	c.1820
ORIGIN	BRITISH
LENGTH	21.6cm (8.5in)

British Georgian naval dirk, *c.*1820

Turned ivory grip

Coiled snake-design pommel

Ornate buckles for former handling straps

Gilded metal scabbard, fully engraved

This Georgian naval dirk has a blade of shallow diamond section. The blade is etched with a crown, anchor and foliage designs. The grip is turned ivory, topped with a metal pommel bearing the unusual design of a coiled snake. The cross guard is formed as a small oval disc, engraved with the legend *Palmam Qui Meruit Feriat* ("Let him who merits bear the palm").

DATE	c.1820
ORIGIN	BRITISH
LENGTH	17.8cm (7in)

British Georgian dirk hanger, *c.*1820

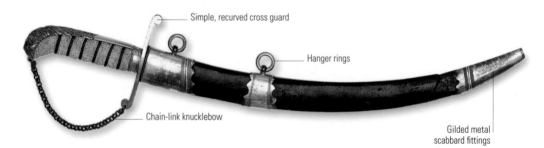

Simple, recurved cross guard

Hanger rings

Chain-link knucklebow

Gilded metal scabbard fittings

This dirk is like a small-sized hanger featuring a curved, single-edged blade etched with a decoration consisting of scrolled foliage, and a panel with the engraved initials "CLP" – presumably those of the former owner. The hilt comprises a brass backstrap in the form of a lion's head, with a segmented bone grip and gold wiring. The chain-link knucklebow appears to be a contemporary addition. The scabbard is made of black leather, with gilded metal fittings.

DATE	c.1820
ORIGIN	BRITISH
LENGTH	30.5cm (12in)

British Georgian naval officer's dirk, *c.*1820

Turned ivory grip

Leather scabbard body
with metal fittings

Foliage-form
quillons

DATE	c.1820
ORIGIN	BRITISH
LENGTH	27.4cm (10.8in)

This extremely handsome naval dirk is reputed to have belonged to a member of the Suckling family. The blade is etched with the manufacturer's details: "Drury, sword cutler, 32 Strand, London". The blade is also etched with designs of a rope and fouled anchor, military trophies and scrolling foliage. There are gilded metal fittings to the hilt and to the black leather scabbard.

The Georgian Era

The period of British history known as the Georgian era spanned 1714–1830 and is named after its four monarchs, George I, George II, George III and George IV. It also included the nine-year Regency period presided over by the Prince Regent (later George IV). A time of huge social, political and economic change in Britain, it was an era that saw the agricultural revolution and the birth of the industrial age. Overseas, the battle for the American colonies was lost but the acquisition of foreign lands heralded an expanding empire.

The British throne had passed to the Hanoverian George I (1714–27) on the death of Queen Anne. His disinterest in ruling led to the appointment of the first Prime Minister. George II's reign (1727–60) saw territorial gains in America and Africa during the Seven Years War with France. Bouts of insanity rendered George III (1760–1820) unstable and in 1810 his son George became Prince Regent. A flamboyant figure famous for his extravagant lifestyle, his reign marked the start of social, legal and electoral reforms. His brother William IV succeeded him to the throne in 1830.

RIGHT A portrait of King George I painted by Sir Godfrey Kneller (1646–1723). The German-speaking king never learned English and preferred ministers to rule on his behalf.

Highland daggers and dirks

The distinctive Scottish dirk evolved from the early style "kidney dagger", which in turn had been developed from the "ballock knife". Two bulbous kidney-shaped lobes in the place where the quillons of the guard might exist were a characteristic feature. The knife was originally intended as an all-round survival and utility item, and some early examples had a serrated back edge. In later years, this feature became a symbolic series of indentations on the back of the blade, rather than being a serviceable sawtooth.

English or Scottish dudgeon-hilted dirk, 1603

Fluted dudgeon wood grip

Long, double-edged blade

This is a fine example of an early English, or probably Scottish, dirk having the characteristic "kidney-shaped" lobes covering the shoulders of the blade. The hilt is made of dudgeon, or boxwood root, with the tang of the blade drawn through and peened over. The blade is long, with a strong central spine running the entire length.

DATE	1603
ORIGIN	ENGLISH/SCOTTISH
LENGTH	46cm (18.1in)

Scottish dirk, c.1740

Carved wood grip

Heart-shaped escutcheon

Long, single-edged blade with flat back

This dirk, from the time of the Scottish Uprisings, has a long, single-edged blade, double-edged at the tip, and with a flat back and long fuller. The tang of the blade is drawn through the hilt and secured through a metal disc that protects the top of the wood grip. The grip itself is carved in a Celtic form of entwined design. The guard of the hilt forms an elliptical sleeve covering the shoulders of the blade.

DATE	c.1740
ORIGIN	SCOTTISH
LENGTH	41.5cm (16.3in)

Scottish dirk with ivory grip, mid-18th century

Carved bone or ivory hilt

Long, single-edged blade with flat back

This fine dirk has an ivory, or walrus tusk, hilt comprised of three sections. The pommel portion features a protective metal plate on the top, through which the tang of the blade has been drawn and secured. The grip is carved with a curved fluting, and the guard comprises an oval sleeve fitting over the shoulders of the blade.

DATE	mid-18th century
ORIGIN	SCOTTISH
LENGTH	50.3cm (19.8in)

Scottish military dress dirk, 1879

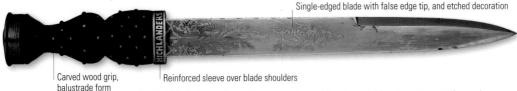

Single-edged blade with false edge tip, and etched decoration

Carved wood grip, balustrade form

Reinforced sleeve over blade shoulders

DATE	1879
ORIGIN	SCOTTISH
LENGTH	37cm (14.6in)

This dirk is the military form as adopted by the Highland regiments from the mid-1800s and is intended for parade and dress wear. The carved wood grip mimics the design of woven straps secured in place with steel pins. The base of the grip features a metal ferrule with the words "GORDON HIGHLANDERS".

Scottish full dress Highlander dirk, c.1900

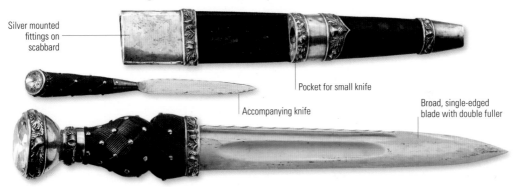

Silver mounted fittings on scabbard

Pocket for small knife

Accompanying knife

Broad, single-edged blade with double fuller

DATE	c.1900
ORIGIN	SCOTTISH
LENGTH	40cm (15.7in)

A full dress dirk with Cairngorm stones set in the pommel of both the dirk and the small knife. An interesting feature of the blade is the flat back with implied serration, and the two fullers – one thin and long close to the back, the other broader and shorter on the main body. Metal fittings are of finely chiselled silver.

Scottish Highland dirk with Cairngorm, c.1900

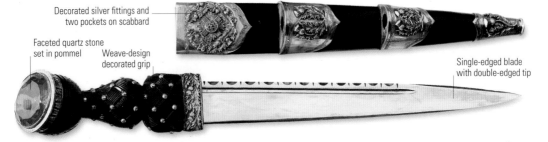

Decorated silver fittings and two pockets on scabbard

Faceted quartz stone set in pommel

Weave-design decorated grip

Single-edged blade with double-edged tip

DATE	c.1900
ORIGIN	SCOTTISH
LENGTH	47cm (18.5in)

This is a full dress Highland dirk. The carved wood grip has silver mounts, the pommel mount featuring a faceted quartz stone (Cairngorm), and a basket-weave design to the grip with silver pins. The single-edged blade bears a scalloped design on the back (symbolic of a serrated edge). The scabbard pockets are for a knife and fork.

19th-century hunting and Bowie knives

The period from the end of the Napoleonic Wars in 1815 until the early 20th century heralded a boom period for European knife-makers. New markets were being established, primarily in the newly formed United States of America. In the aftermath of the American Civil War, economic development was fast expanding and the demand for commercial products was higher than could be supplied by the domestic economy. Europe took advantage of the new American market and exports of cutlery soared.

British knife by Wostenholm, Sheffield, mid-19th century

Metal escutcheon for engraving owner's name

Decorated cross guard with silver finish

Stag-horn grip scales

Single-edged blade with double-edged tip

A deluxe-quality British knife, manufactured by the firm of George Wostenholm – at one time the second-largest knife manufacturer in Sheffield. The blade and tang are constructed of a single piece of steel, the tang area (hilt) being faced with stag-horn scales secured by three rivets. The middle rivet is covered by a metal escutcheon (which could be engraved with an owner's name or initials). The steel guard is decorated with a scalloped design and is polished and nickel-plated. The straight, double-edged blade features an elongated ricasso which tapers into a central spine.

DATE	mid-19th century
ORIGIN	BRITISH
LENGTH	34cm (13.4in)

American CSA fighting knife, 19th century

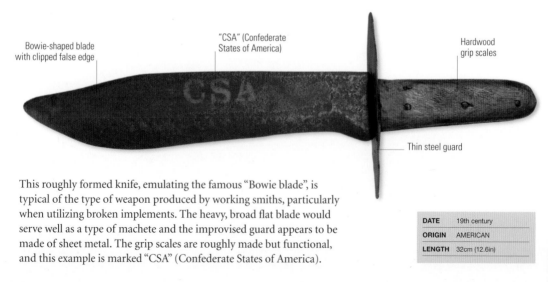

Bowie-shaped blade with clipped false edge

"CSA" (Confederate States of America)

Hardwood grip scales

Thin steel guard

This roughly formed knife, emulating the famous "Bowie blade", is typical of the type of weapon produced by working smiths, particularly when utilizing broken implements. The heavy, broad flat blade would serve well as a type of machete and the improvised guard appears to be made of sheet metal. The grip scales are roughly made but functional, and this example is marked "CSA" (Confederate States of America).

DATE	19th century
ORIGIN	AMERICAN
LENGTH	32cm (12.6in)

British coffin-handled hunting knife, mid-19th century

Stamped or etched brand name and trademark, and emblem of pyramids

Carved horn grip scales

Silver- or nickel-finished escutcheon

DATE	mid-19th century
ORIGIN	BRITISH
LENGTH	unknown

The "coffin-handle" knife was so named because of its superficial resemblance in shape to wooden coffins of the time. The design of this knife was particularly popular in the mid-19th century, and the British concern of George Nixon, etched on the blade, was an established knife-maker in this style. The Nixon name later changed to Nixon & Winterbottom.

British Bowie knife by Rodgers, mid- to late 19th century

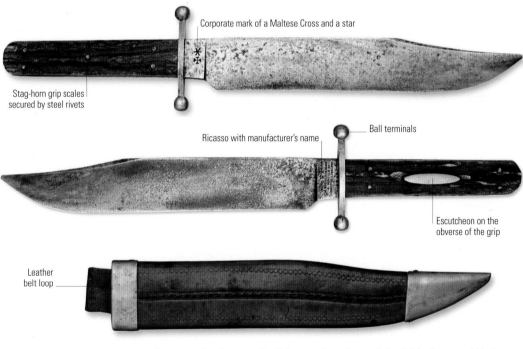

Corporate mark of a Maltese Cross and a star

Stag-horn grip scales secured by steel rivets

Ricasso with manufacturer's name

Ball terminals

Escutcheon on the obverse of the grip

Leather belt loop

DATE	mid- to late 19th century
ORIGIN	BRITISH
LENGTH	31.1cm (12.2in)

A fine example of a Bowie knife by Joseph Rodgers of Sheffield. The typical blade broadens slightly towards the tip, where the flattened back edge forms a sharpened false edge. The body of the blade is sharpened for the entire length, except at the ricasso where it narrows and thickens. The simple straight hilt has stag-horn grip scales. The cross guard is steel and nickel-plated with ball-end finials. The leather scabbard has a belt loop, and nickel-plated fittings to the locket and the chape.

British Sheffield-made Bowie knife, mid-19th century

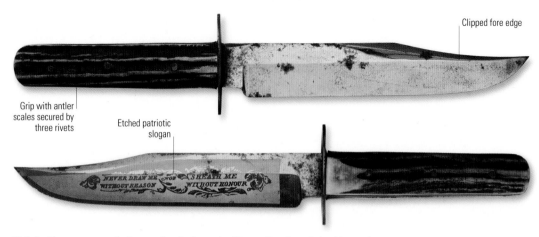

Clipped fore edge

Grip with antler scales secured by three rivets

Etched patriotic slogan

NEVER DRAW ME NOR SHEATH ME WITHOUT REASON WITHOUT HONOUR

This knife pattern, made famous by the legend of James Bowie and the Alamo, is typical of the many pieces produced in Sheffield in the mid-19th century, and mainly intended for the American market. This specimen, manufactured by Edward Pierce and Co., is etched with the somewhat pious legend: "Never draw me without reason nor sheath me without honour".

DATE	mid-19th century
ORIGIN	BRITISH
LENGTH	32cm (12.6in)

British Raj personalized hunting knife, late 19th century

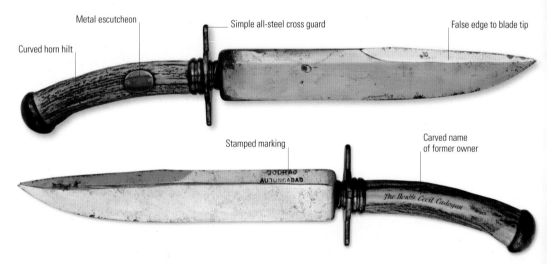

Metal escutcheon

Simple all-steel cross guard

False edge to blade tip

Curved horn hilt

Stamped marking

Carved name of former owner

BODRAU AURUNGABAD

The Honble Cecil Cadogan

This is a well-made hunting knife, but seemingly of a type produced in British India during the days of the Raj. The tang of the blade has been curved to fit the stag-horn grip, and secured firmly with a large metal cap at the pommel. The blade bears the stamped legend "Bodrau Aurungabad", presumably the arsenal in India where it was manufactured. The side face of the grip has been smoothed, and then engraved with the name: "The Honble [Honourable] Cecil Cadogan".

DATE	late 19th century
ORIGIN	BRITISH RAJ
LENGTH	30cm (11.8in)

British Raj double-edged hunting knife, late 19th century

Simple steel cross guard

Antler-horn grip secured with a steel end cap

Double-edged blade with broad central fuller

Stamped name "BOPUT"

DATE	late 19th century
ORIGIN	BRITISH RAJ
LENGTH	32cm (12.6in)

A stylishly manufactured hunting knife, apparently made under British rule in India. A wide fuller runs for most of the length of the substantial double-edged blade. The grip is made of horn and has a sturdy steel cross guard. The steel cap forming the pommel has the tang drawn through and peened over.

German single-edged hunting knife, late 19th century

Stag-horn grip scales secured by three rivets

Plain steel quillon

Single-edged blade with double-edged tip

DATE	late 19th century
ORIGIN	GERMAN
LENGTH	31cm (12.2in)

A typically styled hunting knife by Friedrich Neeff and Son, Solingen. The underside of the grip is contoured for the fingers, the steel cross guard is nickel-plated and the single-edged blade is double-edged at the tip. It was a form made in similar style by many of the German arms companies in the Ruhr Valley.

British Bowie-bladed knife, late 19th century

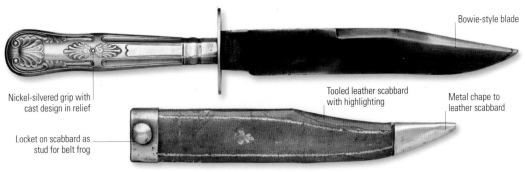

Bowie-style blade

Nickel-silvered grip with cast design in relief

Locket on scabbard as stud for belt frog

Tooled leather scabbard with highlighting

Metal chape to leather scabbard

DATE	late 19th century
ORIGIN	BRITISH
LENGTH	32cm (12.6in)

This is an unnamed example of a Bowie-bladed knife – not a true Bowie in the sense of being a workable hunting knife, but an example of a weapon designed as an ornament. The hilt style, with the classical decoration in relief, is reminiscent of the cutlery styles popular during the closing years of the 19th century.

19th-century folding knives

Folding knives, or clasp-knives, were one of the great innovations of the 19th century, for now it was possible to carry a knife where the blade was safely contained out of harm's way when not in use. Folding knives were very popular among the northern Mediterranean countries where they were known as navaja knives, the word *navaja* being Spanish for "clasp-knife". The usefulness of this design ultimately manifested itself in its most prolific form – the "pocket knife" or "penknife" as we know it today.

Italian or Corsican navaja knife, 19th century

Decorated metal hilt

Narrow, pointed single-edged blade

When opened, the blade of this 19th-century navaja knife is locked into position via a long spring on the back edge of the hilt. The clip of the spring can be released by pulling on a ring, which frees the blade for folding into the hilt. The above example has a metal hilt inset with silver inlay that features engraved decoration.

DATE	19th century
ORIGIN	ITALIAN/CORSICAN
LENGTH	35cm (13.8in)

Spanish (?) navaja folding knife, 19th century

Decorated metal hilt

Ring and spring locking mechanism

Knife blade closed

Narrow, pointed, single-edged blade

This navaja, possibly of Spanish origin, is shown with the blade both open and closed, and demonstrates that even a folding knife can have a blade as long as the hilt. Some examples of this knife pattern had a sliding tube at the top end of the hilt, which could be passed over the tip of the blade to firmly lock it in the closed position.

DATE	19th century
ORIGIN	POSSIBLY SPANISH
LENGTH	35cm (13.8in)

Spanish navaja knife, late 19th century

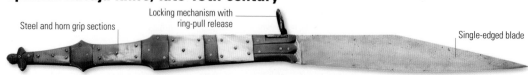

Steel and horn grip sections

Locking mechanism with ring-pull release

Single-edged blade

This mass-produced navaja knife bears the stamped marking "Navajas de Toledo", the city of Toledo being the main producer (and exporter) for the Spanish cutlery industry. The hilt portions are made of steel with horn scales pinned into recesses. The exposed blade, when opened, is just under 25.4cm (10in) in length.

DATE	late 19th century
ORIGIN	SPANISH
LENGTH	54.5cm (21.5in)

German large folding knife, late 19th century

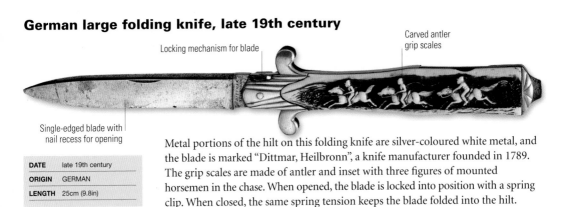

Locking mechanism for blade

Carved antler grip scales

Single-edged blade with nail recess for opening

DATE	late 19th century
ORIGIN	GERMAN
LENGTH	25cm (9.8in)

Metal portions of the hilt on this folding knife are silver-coloured white metal, and the blade is marked "Dittmar, Heilbronn", a knife manufacturer founded in 1789. The grip scales are made of antler and inset with three figures of mounted horsemen in the chase. When opened, the blade is locked into position with a spring clip. When closed, the same spring tension keeps the blade folded into the hilt.

Corsican navajas, late 19th century

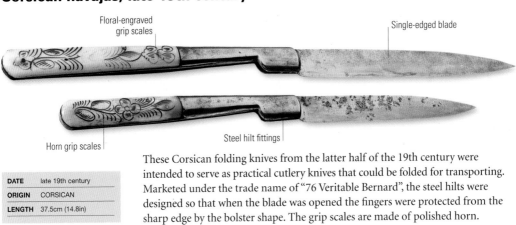

Floral-engraved grip scales

Single-edged blade

Horn grip scales

Steel hilt fittings

DATE	late 19th century
ORIGIN	CORSICAN
LENGTH	37.5cm (14.8in)

These Corsican folding knives from the latter half of the 19th century were intended to serve as practical cutlery knives that could be folded for transporting. Marketed under the trade name of "76 Veritable Bernard", the steel hilts were designed so that when the blade was opened the fingers were protected from the sharp edge by the bolster shape. The grip scales are made of polished horn.

Indian folding clasp-knife, 1875–1930

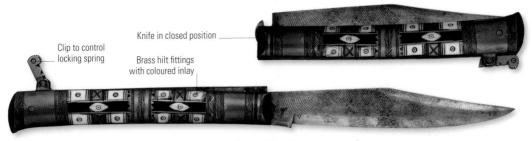

Clip to control locking spring

Knife in closed position

Brass hilt fittings with coloured inlay

This clasp-knife was one of many patterns mass-produced for the export markets of the British Raj during the late 19th and early 20th centuries. The short steel blade, with clipped point, folds out and is locked into position by a spring and clip that form the back section of the hilt. At the top end of the hilt is a hinged lever, which when raised depresses the spring and unlocks the blade, in readiness for closing.

DATE	1875–1930
ORIGIN	INDIAN
LENGTH	25cm (9.8in)

19th-century civilian fighting knives

The knife in its various forms has always found favour as a weapon of offence by the criminal and been used for self-defence by the citizen. Unlike a firearm, especially in the era of muzzle loading, a knife did not require special skills for loading, cleaning and maintenance. A knife was cheaper than a firearm. There was no ammunition supply to worry about. Except in the case of the switchblade, there was no risk of mechanical malfunction at a crucial moment. And, for those who might benefit, it was silent in use.

British daggerstick, *c.*1800

Ivory handle carved with dog's mask

Stiletto blade

Malacca cane body

Disguising a weapon always gave its user an advantage and the practice was not confined to the underworld. Most gentlemen in Georgian and Victorian England carried walking canes and were always at risk from attack on the badly lit streets. When not wearing a weapon, it made sense to carry one in the shaft of a cane.

DATE	c.1800
ORIGIN	BRITISH
LENGTH	25cm (9.8in)

African flywhisk dagger, 1870

The nature of this dagger suggests that it could have been used by a plantation owner, government official or military officer somewhere in the African colonies. Alternatively, it could have been used by a tribal chieftain, both to keep away flies and as a symbol of rank. In either case, one can imagine the need to have a weapon to hand.

DATE	1870
ORIGIN	AFRICAN
LENGTH	22cm (8.7in)

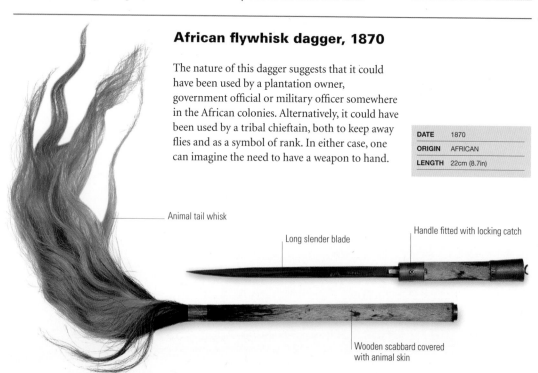

Animal tail whisk

Long slender blade

Handle fitted with locking catch

Wooden scabbard covered with animal skin

Spanish fighting knives, 19th century

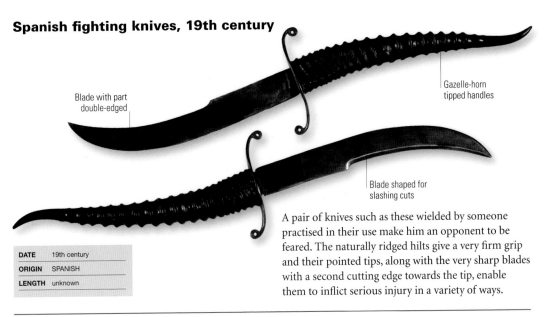

Blade with part double-edged

Gazelle-horn tipped handles

Blade shaped for slashing cuts

DATE	19th century
ORIGIN	SPANISH
LENGTH	unknown

A pair of knives such as these wielded by someone practised in their use make him an opponent to be feared. The naturally ridged hilts give a very firm grip and their pointed tips, along with the very sharp blades with a second cutting edge towards the tip, enable them to inflict serious injury in a variety of ways.

Italian knife with ivory grip, 19th century

Ivory hilt with pommel carved as Turk's head

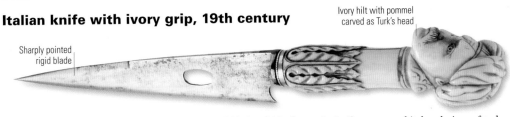

Sharply pointed rigid blade

DATE	19th century
ORIGIN	ITALIAN
LENGTH	28cm (11in)

The broad pointed blade of this dagger is similar to many kitchen knives of today but it leaves little doubt as to what its real purpose was. The plain functionality of the blade is made up for by a silver inlaid ivory hilt elaborately carved to represent acanthus leaves and with a pommel in the form of a Turk's head.

American push dagger, *c.*1870

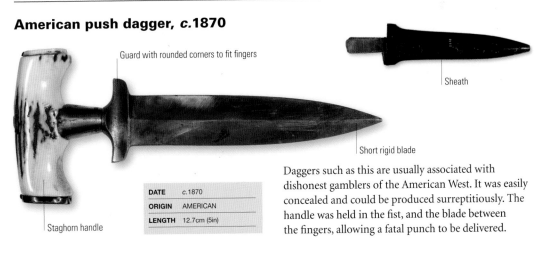

Guard with rounded corners to fit fingers

Sheath

Short rigid blade

Staghorn handle

DATE	c.1870
ORIGIN	AMERICAN
LENGTH	12.7cm (5in)

Daggers such as this are usually associated with dishonest gamblers of the American West. It was easily concealed and could be produced surreptitiously. The handle was held in the fist, and the blade between the fingers, allowing a fatal punch to be delivered.

19th-century combination knives

The combination of a gun with a knife was not a new concept. Military guns with bayonets, or civilian pocket pistols with folding bayonets, were commonplace to give an added degree of protection.

With the advances in gun technology during the 19th century, and the development of the self-contained cartridge, a new type of weapon with multi-shot capability evolved alongside traditional knife pistols.

French knife pistol, 19th century

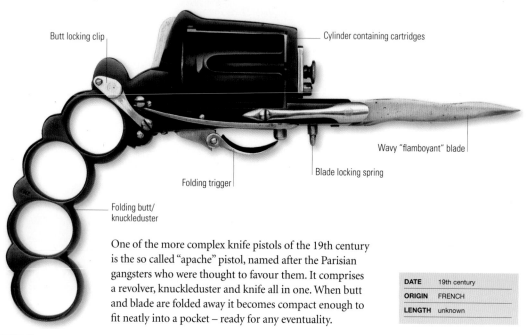

Butt locking clip

Cylinder containing cartridges

Wavy "flamboyant" blade

Blade locking spring

Folding trigger

Folding butt/ knuckleduster

One of the more complex knife pistols of the 19th century is the so called "apache" pistol, named after the Parisian gangsters who were thought to favour them. It comprises a revolver, knuckleduster and knife all in one. When butt and blade are folded away it becomes compact enough to fit neatly into a pocket – ready for any eventuality.

DATE	19th century
ORIGIN	FRENCH
LENGTH	unknown

Belgian pin-fire dirk pistol, *c.*1870

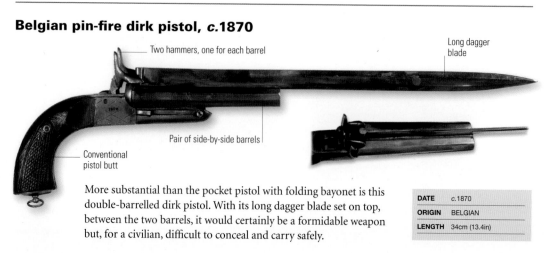

Two hammers, one for each barrel

Long dagger blade

Pair of side-by-side barrels

Conventional pistol butt

More substantial than the pocket pistol with folding bayonet is this double-barrelled dirk pistol. With its long dagger blade set on top, between the two barrels, it would certainly be a formidable weapon but, for a civilian, difficult to conceal and carry safely.

DATE	c.1870
ORIGIN	BELGIAN
LENGTH	34cm (13.4in)

Belgian knife pistol, *c*.1870

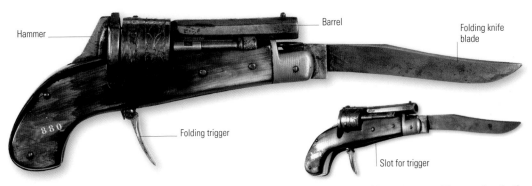

Hammer

Barrel

Folding knife blade

Folding trigger

Slot for trigger

DATE	c.1870
ORIGIN	BELGIAN
LENGTH	unknown

This combination weapon features a six-shot double-action cartridge revolver built in the form of a large pocket knife. Weapons like this do not offer a comfortable or secure grip for use as a revolver and are much less common than their single-shot counterparts. But perhaps it was sufficient to scare a victim or would-be attacker.

European knife-pistol-club, late 19th century

Long wooden-hafted club

Trigger and trigger guard

Spiked steel studs

Stiletto blade

DATE	late 19th century
ORIGIN	EUROPEAN
LENGTH	unknown

This multipurpose European weapon is almost medieval in concept. As a club, with spiked steel studs, it would be lethal in itself, but add a stiletto-like blade and a single-shot pistol and it becomes a formidable close-quarter weapon for either offence or defence. Similar devices without the pistol component were resurrected in the trenches of World War I.

The "apaches" of Paris

Every major city had its underworld members, whether engaged in petty theft or major crime. Victorian London had its "Bill Sykes" characters as portrayed by Dickens, the early 1900s United States had its immigrant Mafia and Paris was terrorised by gangs of "apaches", many wielding their unique revolver-knuckleduster-knives. Often lampooned for what is perceived as their characteristic dress of hooped shirt and black beret, these gangsters were notorious for their ruthlessness.

RIGHT The "apaches" were famous for their disregard of law and order as this illustration from a 1907 edition of *Le Petit Journal* clearly shows.

18th- and 19th-century socket bayonets

The problem with plug bayonets was that they literally plugged the muzzle, rendering the gun incapable of being fired. Nor were they really secure; a good wrench could pull them out of the muzzle, leaving the soldier at a disadvantage. The breakthrough was the socket bayonet – a blade fitted to a tube that slid over the muzzle and could be secured in place, allowing the gun to be fired.

British socket bayonet, *c.*1690

Dog-mask ornamentation

Clipped point

DATE	c.1690
ORIGIN	BRITISH
LENGTH	unknown

This unusual bayonet is an early example of a socket bayonet. With its elaborate design and decoration, however, it was more likely a sporting accessory than a battlefield weapon. A spring catch allows the pommel cap to be removed, opening up the tubular hilt and enabling it to fit on the muzzle of a gun.

British socket bayonet, *c.*1700

Split socket with reinforcing collar at each end

Shell guard

Heavy blade with spear point

Zigzag slot to engage with stud on barrel

At the time the socket bayonet was introduced, manufacture of gun barrels was not a precise art. To overcome this, sockets had reinforcing collars at each end and were split along their length so their diameters could be adjusted to fit the musket. This socket bayonet with its dagger-like shell guard is typical of its period.

DATE	c.1700
ORIGIN	BRITISH
LENGTH	44.3cm (17.4in)

British socket bayonet, East India Company, 1797

Socket with L-shaped slot

Wide, flat, triangular-section blade tapering to point

Spring retaining catch fitted

With a plain zigzag slot, the bayonet was not locked in place, and could easily be removed accidentally during use by pulling and twisting. The East India Company introduced this simple spring, possibly the design of Ezekiel Baker, which latches against the fixing stud once the bayonet is in place.

DATE	1797
ORIGIN	BRITISH
LENGTH	51.5cm (20.3in)

British bayonet for India Pattern musket, 1800

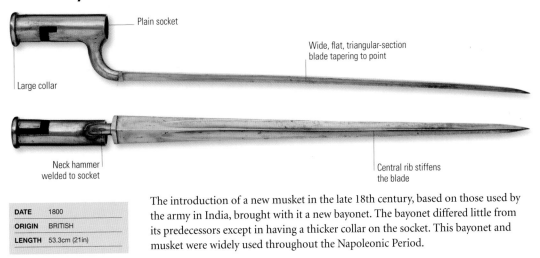

Plain socket

Wide, flat, triangular-section blade tapering to point

Large collar

Neck hammer welded to socket

Central rib stiffens the blade

DATE	1800
ORIGIN	BRITISH
LENGTH	53.3cm (21in)

The introduction of a new musket in the late 18th century, based on those used by the army in India, brought with it a new bayonet. The bayonet differed little from its predecessors except in having a thicker collar on the socket. This bayonet and musket were widely used throughout the Napoleonic Period.

British bayonet with Gill's experimental locking system, *c.*1800

Tubular socket

Wide, shallow, triangular-section blade

Pivoted lever

DATE	c.1800
ORIGIN	BRITISH
LENGTH	50.5cm (19.9in)

This standard service bayonet was modified by having a spring-loaded lever fitted to the socket collar. The nose of the lever is held in place behind the front sight when the bayonet is fitted, preventing its accidental removal. The old zigzag slot has been filled and a new one cut, bringing the bayonet below the barrel.

British bayonet for sea service musket, *c.*1805

Tubular socket

Flat, vertical blade with short false edge

Zigzag slot placed bayonet on the right when fixed

This bayonet is unusual in having a flat blade as opposed to the more usual flattened, triangular section. Although dated to the Napoleonic Period, the weapon may derive from the 18th century. Surviving records show that at that time the only bayonets that could fit this description were a number commissioned for naval use.

DATE	c.1805
ORIGIN	BRITISH
LENGTH	54cm (21.2in)

German or Swedish (?) bayonet, Model 1811, *c.*1811

Socket with
locking ring

Hollow-ground,
triangular-section blade

This bayonet is of unusual proportions and uncertain origin, though it closely
resembles the Model 1811 for the Swedish infantry musket. The long, slender neck
connects to an unusually long blade, offset much further from the socket than
most other bayonets of this type. Its most interesting feature is the beautifully
made locking ring, hinged at the bottom to facilitate assembly and replacement,
and which is guided in its movement by a pin riding in a slot.

DATE	c.1811
ORIGIN	GERMAN/SWEDISH(?)
LENGTH	70cm (27.6in)

French bayonet, Model 1822, 1822

Socket with zigzag
slot on left

Hollow-ground,
T- section blade

Locking
ring

This bayonet is based on the model of 1777, introduced under General Gribeuval
(1715–1789) as part of his programme to standardize French military equipment. It
was the first to employ a locking ring placed in the centre of the socket to secure the
bayonet. The Model 1822 bayonet differs only in being slightly longer and by having
a slightly different pattern of locking ring which provides a more secure attachment.

DATE	1822
ORIGIN	FRENCH
LENGTH	53.1cm (21in)

Austrian bayonet, System Augustin rifle, Model 1842, 1842

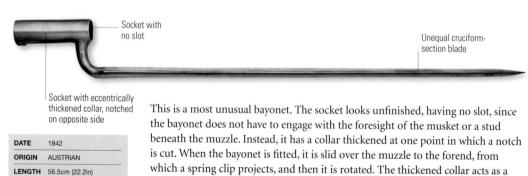

Socket with
no slot

Unequal cruciform-
section blade

Socket with eccentrically
thickened collar, notched
on opposite side

DATE	1842
ORIGIN	AUSTRIAN
LENGTH	56.5cm (22.2in)

This is a most unusual bayonet. The socket looks unfinished, having no slot, since
the bayonet does not have to engage with the foresight of the musket or a stud
beneath the muzzle. Instead, it has a collar thickened at one point in which a notch
is cut. When the bayonet is fitted, it is slid over the muzzle to the forend, from
which a spring clip projects, and then it is rotated. The thickened collar acts as a
cam, lifting the spring catch which falls into the notch and secures the bayonet.

British bayonet for sappers and miners, 1st Pattern 1842, 1842

Sword-type guard

Saw-back blade

DATE	1842
ORIGIN	BRITISH
LENGTH	77.9cm (30.7in)

As can be seen, this bayonet has a very elaborate hilt, similar in style to many swords of the period, and a tubular socket which acted as the grip. It is equipped with a heavy blade, having a double row of saw-teeth along its wide back edge. This feature was intended to be used for cutting wood, though if used on anything other than shrubbery it must have been hard and exhausting work. These weapons never actually went into production and this one, probably the sample pattern, is thought to be the only one ever made.

British bayonet for sappers and miners carbine, 2nd Pattern 1842, 1842

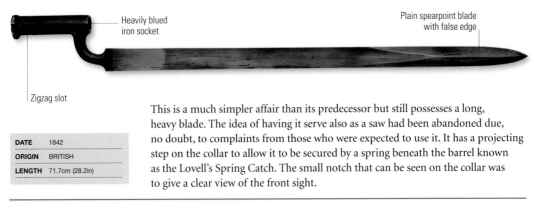

Heavily blued iron socket

Plain spearpoint blade with false edge

Zigzag slot

DATE	1842
ORIGIN	BRITISH
LENGTH	71.7cm (28.2in)

This is a much simpler affair than its predecessor but still possesses a long, heavy blade. The idea of having it serve also as a saw had been abandoned due, no doubt, to complaints from those who were expected to use it. It has a projecting step on the collar to allow it to be secured by a spring beneath the barrel known as the Lovell's Spring Catch. The small notch that can be seen on the collar was to give a clear view of the front sight.

British bayonet for Enfield rifle, Pattern 1853, 1853

Blued iron socket

Equilateral triangular-section blade cants outwards when fitted

Slot engages with front sight and locking ring closes behind it

A good wrought-iron socket fitted with a locking ring and a narrow, sharply pointed, triangular-section blade of the best Sheffield steel gave the Pattern 1853 bayonet a superb quality and singularity of purpose. It was by far the finest bayonet ever to enter British military service up to that time.

DATE	1853
ORIGIN	BRITISH
LENGTH	51.5cm (20.3in)

American bayonet, Winchester Model 1873 musket, 1873

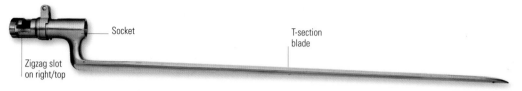

Socket

T-section blade

Zigzag slot on right/top

Unusually, these bayonets lack any markings. However, they are distinguished by being arranged to sit beneath the barrel when fitted, are finished bright all over, and have a long taper between the blade and the neck. They were not used in the US armed forces but were supplied with muskets to many South American countries.

DATE	1873
ORIGIN	AMERICAN
LENGTH	54.5cm (21.5in)

American bayonet, Springfield Model 1873 rifle, 1873

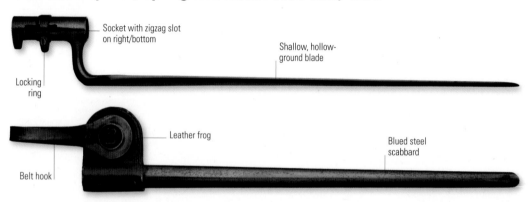

Socket with zigzag slot on right/bottom

Shallow, hollow-ground blade

Locking ring

Leather frog

Blued steel scabbard

Belt hook

The bayonet for the new Model 1873 Springfield "trapdoor" rifle so closely resembled the models of 1855 and 1870 that these were often converted by having the sockets resized to fit the smaller-diameter barrel of the 1873 rifle. It was the first American bayonet to be blued all over.

DATE	1873
ORIGIN	AMERICAN
LENGTH	54.1cm (21.3in)

British bayonet for Martini-Henry, Pattern 1876, 1876

Blued iron socket

Equilateral triangular-section blade

Zigzag slot to engage with front sight

The new Pattern 1876 bayonet was modelled on the Pattern 1853 but with some adjustments. The smaller-diameter barrel of the Martini-Henry rifle required a smaller diameter socket and, to compensate for it being a shorter rifle, the blade was made longer to maintain the "reach".

DATE	1876
ORIGIN	BRITISH
LENGTH	65.8cm (25.9in)

Dutch bayonet, Beaumont-Vitali rifle, Model 1871/88, 1888

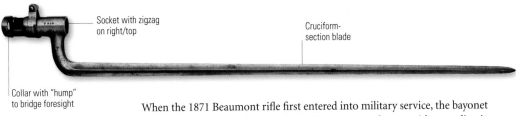

Socket with zigzag
on right/top

Cruciform-
section blade

Collar with "hump"
to bridge foresight

DATE	1888
ORIGIN	DUTCH
LENGTH	57.1cm (22.5in)

When the 1871 Beaumont rifle first entered into military service, the bayonet designed for it included a complex locking ring attachment with two adjusting screws. With the transition in 1888 from the single-shot rifle to magazine loading on the Vitali principle, the locking ring design was amended to a more conventional form with a single adjusting screw.

The 54th Massachusetts Volunteer Infantry

The Pattern 1853 Enfield rifle and bayonet was created for the British soldier using technology largely developed and perfected in the United States. Ironically, it played a significant role in the bloodiest war of the mid-19th century, the American Civil War. This was perhaps the first and last conflict in which this fine weapon was used in such large numbers – over 1 million were supplied in roughly equal numbers to both sides by British arms manufacturers. The 54th Massachusetts Volunteer Infantry was one of the more famous

regiments to carry the rifles. It was the first military unit composed of African-American soldiers and it led one of the most legendary exploits of the Civil War, the assault on Fort Wagner. The heroism of one soldier, Sergeant William Carney, led to his becoming the first African-American to be awarded the Congressional Medal of Honor.

BELOW This lithograph by Currer & Ives, *The Gallant Charge of the 54th Regiment from Massachusetts*, depicts the assault by Union African-American troops on the Confederate-held Fort Wagner.

19th-century sword bayonets

The 19th century was a time of great innovation. It witnessed a complete transformation of the firearm, from the single-shot, muzzle-loading flintlock at its outset to the self-contained metallic cartridge and magazine-loading multi-shot rifles at its end. This innovation and diversity was not limited to the firearm itself but also found expression in a great diversity of bayonet designs.

British volunteer sword bayonet, c.1810

Iron "stirrup" hilt

Single-edged spearpoint blade

Muzzle ring with locking collar

The style of hilt on this bayonet is similar to the 1796 Pattern light cavalry sword, and was perhaps modelled on that since these bayonets were for use by mounted volunteers. They were not official issue and several varieties exist, some having brass hilts. They were generally used with rifles similar to the Baker rifle.

DATE	c.1810
ORIGIN	BRITISH
LENGTH	77.7cm (30.6in)

British Baker rifle sword bayonet, c.1815

Blade with fuller running the entire length

Pronounced S-shaped quillons

The S-shaped cross guard differs from any of the official military-issue varieties and suggests this might be a prototype or experimental bayonet, or even one for volunteers. Its blade with a fuller that runs to the tip is also an unusual feature since most Baker sword bayonets had plain blades.

DATE	c.1815
ORIGIN	BRITISH
LENGTH	75.2cm (29.6in)

British Baker rifle "hand" bayonet, c.1825

Catch release button

Thin sheet cross guard

Triangular-section blade

In 1825 the Rifle Brigade complained their "hand" or knife bayonets were too heavy. Their colonel submitted an alternative with a buckhorn handle which was much lighter. It was rejected by the Ordnance Board as being too fragile, and this one, with a smaller brass hilt, may have been created in its place for trial.

DATE	c.1825
ORIGIN	BRITISH
LENGTH	54.4cm (21.4in)

British Baker rifle sword bayonet with saw-back, *c.*1850

Cast-brass hilt

Blade with saw-back

Knuckle guard

In 1815 a sawback bayonet for the Baker rifle was suggested but seems not to have been developed. The one illustrated is probably a Second Pattern sword bayonet from around 1805 modified at a much later date, since it carries the royal monogram of Queen Victoria stamped on the pommel.

DATE	c.1850
ORIGIN	BRITISH
LENGTH	75.2cm (29.6in)

French Sabre-lance du Mosqueton des Cent Gardes, 1854

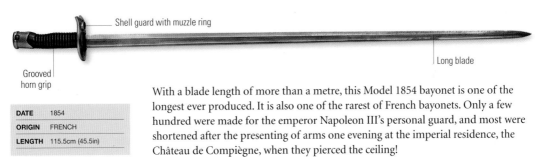

Shell guard with muzzle ring

Long blade

Grooved horn grip

DATE	1854
ORIGIN	FRENCH
LENGTH	115.5cm (45.5in)

With a blade length of more than a metre, this Model 1854 bayonet is one of the longest ever produced. It is also one of the rarest of French bayonets. Only a few hundred were made for the emperor Napoleon III's personal guard, and most were shortened after the presenting of arms one evening at the imperial residence, the Château de Compiègne, when they pierced the ceiling!

British Lancaster bayonet, Pattern 1855, 1855

Muzzle ring

Pipe-back extending across to point

Black leather scabbard with brass furniture

Knurled leather grips

DATE	1855
ORIGIN	BRITISH
LENGTH	73.2cm (28.8in)

In 1855 the Corps of Sappers and Miners adopted Lancaster's oval-bored carbine and with it this very distinctive bayonet. Unlike most other British bayonets it has a brass pommel and cross guard, reminiscent of continental practice, and a so-called "pipe-back" blade. In this type of blade, the rounded back extends as a rib across the centre of the tip, creating a second or "false" edge. The bayonet was later adopted by the Royal Army Medical Corps as a sidearm.

American bayonet for Harper's Ferry rifle, 1855

One-piece cast-brass hilt

Straight cross guard with muzzle ring

Straight, single-edged blade turned upwards at point

This new service rifle with a calibre of .58 inches closely followed the British .577 inch Enfield Pattern 1853 rifle. The bayonet, representative of the early stages in the adoption of sword bayonets by the US military, also exhibits European influence with a brass hilt. It has a curious upturn at the point of the blade, rarely seen on bayonets of any nationality.

DATE	1855
ORIGIN	AMERICAN
LENGTH	67.3cm (26.5in)

British bayonet for Jacob's double-barrelled rifle, c.1859

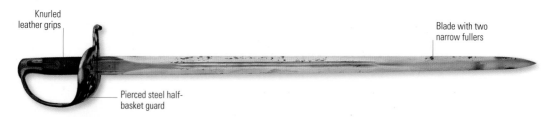

Knurled leather grips

Blade with two narrow fullers

Pierced steel half-basket guard

These bayonets were not official British military issue. They were designed by John Jacob for use with his double-barrelled rifle by the Indian Scinde Irregular Horse, which he commanded. Both rifle and bayonet were made by Swinburn and Son of Birmingham. With twin fullers and spear point, the blade resembles Scottish broadswords, and it has a heavy-gauge "half-basket" type of guard, making it weigh more. It would have made an ungainly weapon when fitted to the heavy rifle.

DATE	c.1859
ORIGIN	BRITISH
LENGTH	90.7cm (35.7in)

British naval cutlass bayonet, 1859

Knurled leather grips

Sheet-steel bowl guard

Plain blade with additional false edge

This is the second type of cutlass bayonet designed for use with the Pattern 1858 Naval Rifle. The first bayonet had ribbed wooden grips whereas this model has the more conventional checkered or "knurled" leather variety. It may have been successful as a cutlass but, as with the Jacob bayonet, when fitted to a rifle it must also have created a very unwieldy combination.

DATE	1859
ORIGIN	BRITISH
LENGTH	81.9cm (32.3in)

American sword bayonet for Navy rifle, Model 1861, 1861

Muzzle ring

Blade with slight double curve

Cast-brass hilt

Downturned quillon

Black leather scabbard

Chape

Locket

This bayonet was designed by Admiral John A. Dahlgren for use with the Plymouth/Whitneyville naval rifle. It was manufactured by the Collins Company of Hartford, Connecticut, who had a reputation for the great variety and high quality of axes they produced. With its heavy muzzle ring and cross guard with a slightly downturned quillon, it closely resembles the bayonets for the Spencer, Merrill and Zouave rifles. With their ribbed cast-brass grips and varying degrees of double curvature in their blades, these all reflect the trend in Europe, especially France, for "yataghan"-bladed sword bayonets. This bayonet was equipped with a heavy black leather scabbard fitted with a brass "top locket", or mouthpiece, a stud for securing it in a carrying "frog" and a brass tip or "chape".

DATE	1861
ORIGIN	AMERICAN
LENGTH	71cm (28in)

French sword bayonet for Chassepot rifle, 1866

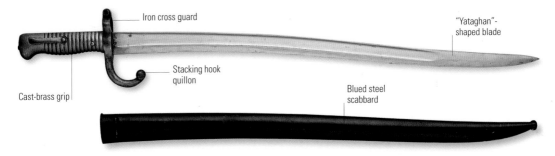

Iron cross guard

"Yataghan"-shaped blade

Stacking hook quillon

Cast-brass grip

Blued steel scabbard

Following the example set by Prussia in adopting Nicholas von Dreyse's new breech-loading needle-fire rifle with self-contained cartridge, the French responded by developing what was to become known as the Chassepot rifle. This rifle brought with it one of the world's most familiar bayonets. Their decorative hilts with cast-brass grips and polished-steel cross guard with a large hook quillon, combined with a stylish "yataghan" blade, heralded a new fashion in bayonet design which was copied almost worldwide. Add to that the allure of the name of the maker and date of manufacture engraved in script on the wide back edge of the blade, and it is easy to understand why they have adorned innumerable walls. But their true value lies in their representing the beginnings of a new era in firearms evolution.

DATE	1866
ORIGIN	FRENCH
LENGTH	70cm (27.6in)

British naval cutlass bayonet, 1872

Knurled leather grips

Reduced-diameter muzzle ring

Sheet-steel bowl guard

Straight, plain blade with additional false edge

The Pattern 1872 was the third and final cutlass bayonet to be put into service, differing from its predecessors with its narrower, straight blade. This certainly made it lighter but still created an unwieldy combination when fitted to a rifle. Few were newly manufactured, most being converted from the Pattern 1859 cutlass bayonet.

DATE	1872
ORIGIN	BRITISH
LENGTH	79.5cm (31.3in)

British Elcho bayonet for Martini-Henry, *c.*1872

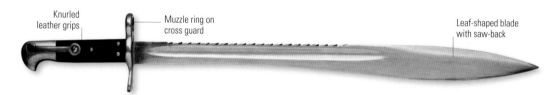

Knurled leather grips

Muzzle ring on cross guard

Leaf-shaped blade with saw-back

One of the most distinctive and unusual of British bayonets, designed by Lord Elcho, this seems to place greater emphasis on its effectiveness as a tool for sawing wood or hacking shrubbery than as a weapon. The leaf or spear shape of the blade perhaps inspired the German bayonet at the end of the century. This weapon was only partially successful as a tool and its function as a bayonet was questionable. Few were made and issued, and more conventional bayonets were used instead.

DATE	c.1872
ORIGIN	BRITISH
LENGTH	64.1cm (25.2in)

Austrian sword bayonet, Werndl rifle, 1873

Muzzle ring

"Yataghan"-shaped blade

Hooked quillon

Knurled leather grip

Frog stud

Blued steel scabbard

Mouthpiece

This bayonet was used with various models of the Austrian Werndl military rifle and was basically a modification of its forerunner, the model of 1867. It used a coil spring in place of the leaf spring to operate the locking catch. Like the Chassepot of 1866, it has a distinctive "yataghan"-shaped blade.

DATE	1873
ORIGIN	AUSTRIAN
LENGTH	60.6cm (23.9in)

French bayonet, Gras rifle, Model 1874, 1874

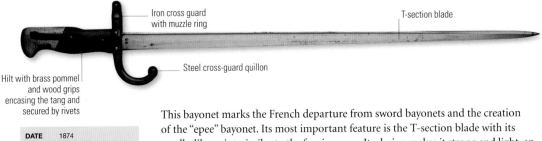

Iron cross guard
with muzzle ring

T-section blade

Steel cross-guard quillon

Hilt with brass pommel
and wood grips
encasing the tang and
secured by rivets

DATE	1874
ORIGIN	FRENCH
LENGTH	64.3cm (25.3in)

This bayonet marks the French departure from sword bayonets and the creation of the "epee" bayonet. Its most important feature is the T-section blade with its needle-like point, similar to the fencing epee. Its design makes it strong and light, an ideal combination for a bayonet. It was copied in the last of the British cavalry swords, the 1908 Pattern, and was the forerunner of the later Lebel bayonet.

British artillery sword bayonet, 1879 Pattern, 1879

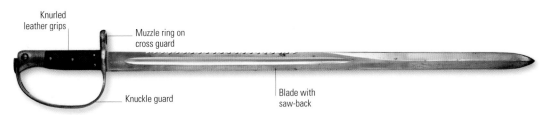

Knurled
leather grips

Muzzle ring on
cross guard

Knuckle guard

Blade with
saw-back

DATE	1879
ORIGIN	BRITISH
LENGTH	75.6cm (29.8in)

This was produced as one alternative to the Elcho bayonet. In view of its length and the nature of its hilt, the term "sword bayonet" is very apt. The knuckle guard made it easier to grip for use as a saw, and its longer blade made it more effective as a sword or as a bayonet when fitted to the short artillery carbine. However, its double row of teeth made its use as a saw very hard work, and like many dual-purpose bayonets it was never completely successful in either role.

Portuguese sword bayonet, Guedes rifle, Model 1885, 1885

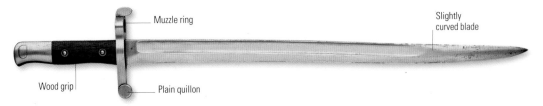

Muzzle ring

Slightly
curved blade

Wood grip

Plain quillon

DATE	1885
ORIGIN	PORTUGUESE
LENGTH	60.8cm (23.9in)

The "yataghan" shape of this bayonet is less pronounced, as the trend was now towards straight blades. Although for Portuguese use, these bayonets and their rifles were manufactured at the Steyr factory in Austria. The bayonets are usually marked with the place and date of manufacture on the back edge. The decorative hilt of an earlier era has been replaced with a more functional but finely engineered hilt.

British Lee-Metford bayonet Mk I, 1888

Muzzle ring

Double-edged blade
with spear point and
central rib

Locking catch
release button

This Model 1888 was the second pattern bayonet adopted for the Lee-Metford rifle,
the first having the grips secured by three rivets. This rifle was fitted with a cleaning
rod which projected from the bayonet mounting stud beneath the barrel. As a
consequence, the hilt had a cavity within it to accommodate the end of the rod, and a
drain hole at the bottom of this cavity was provided, adjacent to the upper grip rivet.

DATE	1888
ORIGIN	BRITISH
LENGTH	42.2cm (16.6in)

British sword bayonet Mk IV, 1887 Pattern, 1891

Straight quillon
with small finial

Stepped muzzle ring

Knurled
leather grips

Spearpoint blade
with fullers

The last of a series of bayonets developed for the Martini-Henry rifle, it evolved
from experimental bayonets developed in 1886 for a proposed smaller-bore
Martini-Henry rifle. This rifle was abandoned following the adoption of the Lee
series of small-bore, bolt-action, magazine-loading rifles in 1888. The days of the
Martini as a mainline weapon were numbered, but the experimental rifles were
modified to standard Martini calibre, these 1887 Pattern bayonets being adapted to
fit. As secondary arms, many of these rifles and bayonets were issued to the Navy.

DATE	1891
ORIGIN	BRITISH
LENGTH	60.3cm (23.7in)

German Mauser bayonet, 1884–1945

Fuller

Hilt with plain wood grips and flash guards

Blued spear
point blade

This bayonet, the third model, became the prototype for most bayonets used on
Gewehr 98 and Kar 98 rifles until 1945. While following the same basic design,
numerous variations occur. This example has plain wood grips secured by screw
bolts, and on the back of the hilt a flash guard to protect the wood grips.

DATE	1884–1945
ORIGIN	GERMAN
LENGTH	39cm (15.4in)

19th-century knife bayonets

Many soldiers throughout the 19th century carried their own personal knives for use in a difficult situation, since none were officially issued. But the idea of combining the function of a bayonet with that of a knife is always a compromise. To make it handy enough to be used as a knife means the weapon has to be short. By making it short enough, the important element of "reach" is lost, which puts a soldier at a disadvantage when confronted by an enemy with a long bayonet fixed to his rifle.

Japanese bayonet for Murata rifle, Type 20, 1887

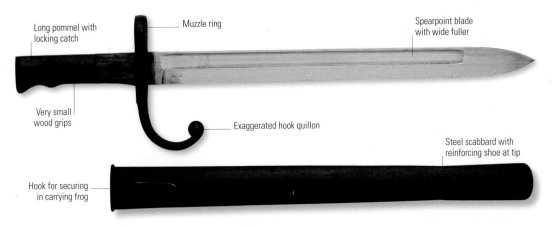

Long pommel with locking catch

Muzzle ring

Spearpoint blade with wide fuller

Very small wood grips

Exaggerated hook quillon

Steel scabbard with reinforcing shoe at tip

Hook for securing in carrying frog

DATE	1887
ORIGIN	JAPANESE
LENGTH	37cm (14.6in)

This bayonet was developed for the Murata Type 20 rifle and carbine, although it could also fit the Type 22 rifle. The whole hilt is very short, barely 90mm (3.5in), making it difficult to grasp despite the supposed shaping to fit the fingers, and giving the impression of an overly large hooked quillon.

Dutch Mannlicher carbine bayonet, 2nd type, 1895

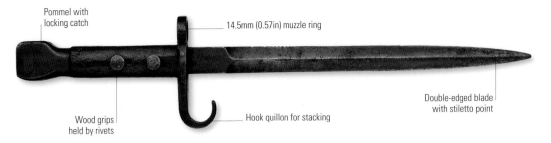

Pommel with locking catch

14.5mm (0.57in) muzzle ring

Wood grips held by rivets

Hook quillon for stacking

Double-edged blade with stiletto point

DATE	1895
ORIGIN	DUTCH
LENGTH	37.5cm (14.8in)

This bayonet was produced in two models for the Mannlicher cavalry carbine. The first had a short straight quillon, while this one, the Model 1895, has the stacking hook. Without the hook it is loosely reminiscent of the British 1888 Patterns. Its size and slender double-edged blade made it a useful fighting knife.

Presentation knives and daggers

Compared with the presentation of swords as marks of military achievement or personal respect, the presentation of knives of any form is a far more unusual occurrence. In the Third Reich in Germany, however, the reverse was true, and presentation of daggers based around the standard service patterns was widely practised. Even rarer are those knives presented to civilians to mark various occasions.

German presentation hunting hanger, mid-19th century

Decoration blade with inscription

Cross guard with "hoof" finials

Decorative brass pommel cap

An unusual German presentation hunting hanger with a polished blade, finely frost-etched to depict huntsman, deer and game birds. It also carries the inscription: *Urerm Vorstandsmitglied Jon, Gefken fur 25 Jahrige treue Dienste gewidmetvon Schutzen-verein worpedorf*, which means it was presented to a founder or first director, Jon Gefken, of the Worpedorf Rifle Club, for 25 years' faithful service.

DATE	mid-19th century
ORIGIN	GERMAN
LENGTH	35.6cm (14in)

South African presentation Bowie knife, 1885

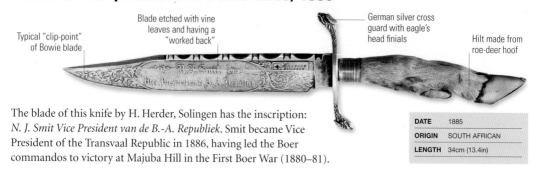

Blade etched with vine leaves and having a "worked back"

Typical "clip-point" of Bowie blade

German silver cross guard with eagle's head finials

Hilt made from roe-deer hoof

The blade of this knife by H. Herder, Solingen has the inscription: *N. J. Smit Vice President van de B.-A. Republiek*. Smit became Vice President of the Transvaal Republic in 1886, having led the Boer commandos to victory at Majuba Hill in the First Boer War (1880–81).

DATE	1885
ORIGIN	SOUTH AFRICAN
LENGTH	34cm (13.4in)

German Imperial dagger, 1900

Finials with lapis lazuli button at the tip

Blued and gilt blade with etched decoration

DATE	1900
ORIGIN	GERMAN
LENGTH	47cm (18.5in)

This dagger is of standard form with its gilt brass scabbard and hilt with open crown pommel. What distinguishes it are the buttons of lapis lazuli set into the quillons and the richly decorated blade, with anchor and sailing ship, inscribed with the Frisian sailor's motto: *Rüm Hart – Klaar Kimming* or "Bold Heart – Clear Horizon".

British RN midshipman's presentation dirk, 1897 pattern, 1905

Lion's-head pommel

Suspension rings

Swept quillons with acorn finials

Royal Navy emblem

Wood grip covered with ray skin

DATE	1905
ORIGIN	BRITISH
LENGTH	37cm (14.6in)

This Royal Navy midshipman's presentation dirk, with blued and gilt blade, carries the inscription: "Chief Captain's Prize Awarded to R. C. R. Peploe HMS Britannia, December 1905". Although of standard overall pattern, such presentation dirks, especially from such a notable ship, are very rare. Supplied by J. R. Gaunt and Sons.

Saudi Arabian presentation jambiya, 20th century

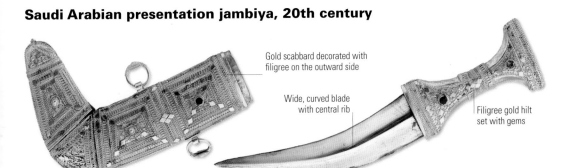

Gold scabbard decorated with filigree on the outward side

Wide, curved blade with central rib

Filigree gold hilt set with gems

DATE	20th century
ORIGIN	SAUDI ARABIAN
LENGTH	25.4cm (10in)

In style, this is a typical jambiya of Saudi Arabia with its boot-shaped scabbard and wide, curved and sharply pointed blade. What makes it unusual are its hilt and scabbard, each elaborately decorated with gold wire filigree. A jambiya such as this would only be worn by the highest-ranking members of society.

German Third Reich naval officer's dirk, 1933–45

Ivory grip with decorative wire binding

Blue and gilt blade with etched decoration

Elaborate globular finials

Eagle pommel with swastika

DATE	1933–45
ORIGIN	GERMAN
LENGTH	24.9cm (9.8in)

This is a rare presentation dagger to a Third Reich *Kriegsmarine* (Navy) officer. It differs from the standard-issue dagger in having blued and gilt panels of etched decoration on the blade depicting a warship and the eagle and swastika. Unfortunately, it has no presentation inscription so the recipient is unknown. Supplied by a well-known maker, E W Holler of Solingen.

Unusual bayonets

Most bayonets, though they may differ in details such as the shape and material of the hilt, the method of locking on to the gun, or the shape and length of the blade, still conform to a more or less conventional overall pattern. There are those, however, that differ widely from the conventions of their time. For example, some bayonets may have been developed for special purposes; some may be the first tentative steps into a new form ahead of their time; while others are just simply bizarre with no obvious explanation.

British socket bayonet, 1680

Plain split tube with zigzag slot to engage with stud on barrel

Semicircular hollow blade welded to socket

This is probably one of the simplest, though most likely experimental, bayonets developed at a time when the socket bayonet was first coming into existence. It consists of an iron-tube socket split along its full length, and locking slots that could fit over the muzzle and lock onto a rectangular stud. Attached to the socket is a tapered, hollow, pointed blade. The design was resurrected, again experimentally, by BSA in 1948 for use on submachine guns.

DATE	1680
ORIGIN	BRITISH
LENGTH	50.6cm (19.7in)

British plug bayonet, 1686

Flat blade thickened in the centre

Maker's mark

This is a most unusual plug bayonet by any standards and the reason behind its design can only be guessed at. With a blade 65mm (25.6in) wide, it could even function as a trowel, but entrenchment was not a feature of 17th-century warfare. The Rose and Crown mark suggests it was made by William Hoy about 1686.

DATE	1686
ORIGIN	BRITISH
LENGTH	29.4cm (11.6in)

British spear bayonet for Egg's carbine, 1784

Conventional socket
with zigzag slot

Spear point

DATE	1784
ORIGIN	BRITISH
LENGTH	84.5cm (33.3in)

One of the most unusual bayonets produced for British military service was this spear bayonet. It was designed for use with a new breech-loading flintlock cavalry carbine produced in 1784 by Durs Egg at the request of the Duke of Richmond, Master General of Ordnance. The bayonet's length made it impossible to carry it in the normal way of a scabbard attached to the belt. So it was designed to be reversed on the muzzle when not in use and, as a further refinement, the trigger guard had a shaped pocket at its forward end into which the tip of the spearhead could be lodged. It was not widely issued and was more experimental in nature.

American trowel bayonet, 1873

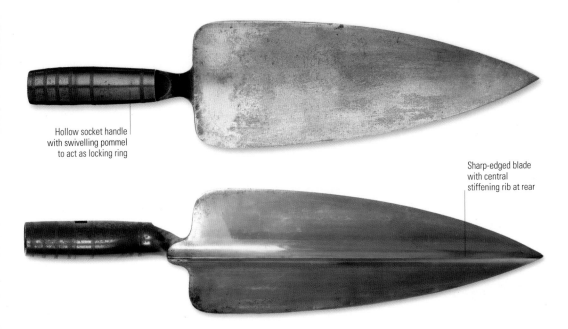

Hollow socket handle
with swivelling pommel
to act as locking ring

Sharp-edged blade
with central
stiffening rib at rear

DATE	1873
ORIGIN	AMERICAN
LENGTH	35.7cm (14.1in)

Viewed as a weapon, this Model 1873 bayonet could be considered barbaric. However, it was not a weapon. It was designed as a spade, or for use in the hand as a trowel. It was the third of its type used in American service, and it has the elegance of simplicity and good design.

18th- to 20th-century integral bayonets

The idea of a bayonet permanently attached to a firearm has been explored with varying success over two centuries. It is only practical if the bayonet can be stowed away when not in use but easily deployed as needed. It was used in the 18th and 19th centuries on civilian weapons like blunderbusses and pistols, where the blade was folded away and held against a spring, and could be opened by a trigger. It was tried on some military firearms but never extensively. It has regained popularity in some military circles more recently.

British flintlock blunderbuss by Grice with spring bayonet, *c.*1780

Muzzle fitted with retaining catch for bayonet on underside

Triangular hollow-ground blade

Ramrod pipes offset to allow bayonet to lie beneath barrel

Pivot for bayonet mounted on barrel

The blunderbuss, a muzzle-loading firearm, was a popular means of self-defence in the homes of the gentry. Being a single-shot weapon, the fitting of a spring-loaded bayonet that could be brought into use simply by moving a catch gave the user a second line of defence if a shot failed to achieve its purpose.

DATE	c.1780
ORIGIN	BRITISH
LENGTH	24.9cm (9.8in)

British Elliott's carbine with folding bayonet, 1785

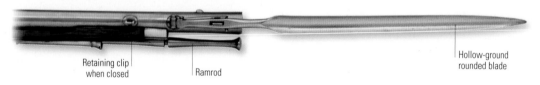

Retaining clip when closed

Ramrod

Hollow-ground rounded blade

The folding bayonet was also experimented with by the military authorities in Britain for use by cavalry, but it was never adopted. In comparison with a socket bayonet mounted on the muzzle, the mountings of a folding bayonet were flimsy and would hardly stand up to the rigours of extended use in battle.

DATE	1785
ORIGIN	BRITISH
LENGTH	39.9cm (15.5in)

American ramrod bayonet, Springfield rifle, Model 1884, 1884

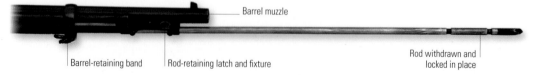

Barrel muzzle

Barrel-retaining band

Rod-retaining latch and fixture

Rod withdrawn and locked in place

A clearing rod that could double as a bayonet had been used on the North-Hall musket in 1833 but was resurrected for use on this Springfield rifle. A notch cut in the sharpened rod, combined with a catch beneath the barrel of the gun, allowed the bayonet to be pulled forward and locked firmly in position.

DATE	1884
ORIGIN	AMERICAN
LENGTH	59.2cm (23.3in)

Japanese military carbine, Arisaka Type 44, 1911

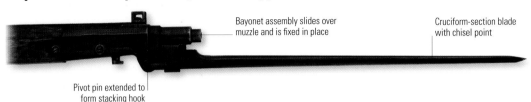

Bayonet assembly slides over muzzle and is fixed in place

Cruciform-section blade with chisel point

Pivot pin extended to form stacking hook

DATE	1911
ORIGIN	JAPANESE
LENGTH	43.9cm (17.2in)

This Japanese bayonet was developed for the Arisaka Type 44 carbine used by mounted troops. It could be locked in the open or closed position by a simple catch, and when not in use was folded away beneath the barrel. Carbines with these bayonets saw service until the end of World War II.

Chinese AK47 assault rifle, Type 56, 1980

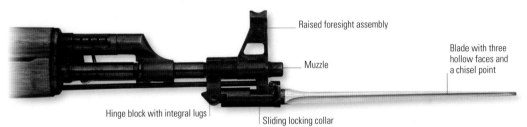

Raised foresight assembly

Blade with three hollow faces and a chisel point

Muzzle

Hinge block with integral lugs

Sliding locking collar

DATE	1980
ORIGIN	CHINESE
LENGTH	36.2cm (14.3in)

The simple, reliable and rugged AK47 has become ubiquitous, continuing to find many adherents more than 60 years after it was developed by Mikhail Kalashnikov in 1947. This one, made in China, was used by Iraqi forces during the Gulf War of 1990–91. It is fitted with a short folding bayonet.

Italian Fascist Youth (*Balilla*) Carbine with folding bayonet

The Italian Fascist Youth organization was created shortly after the rise to power of Benito Mussolini. It replaced the traditional boy scout movement for boys between the ages of 8 and 14 years. The age range was later extended up to 18 years. Like the later Hitler Youth movement, its main objective was to indoctrinate young Italians in the principles of fascism. But it was also intended to provide basic military training and to this end, the older boys were issued with rifles. Only 750mm (29.5in) long and complete with a 250mm (9.8in) folding bayonet, blunted at the tip to avoid accident, these rifles were fully functional miniature versions of the Mannlicher Carcano cavalry carbines.

ABOVE The Italian Fascist Youth organization shared many of the same ideals as the later Hitler Youth movement. During military exercises, older boys were armed with bayonet rifles.

Fighting knives of World War I

When Europe went to war in 1914, it was not foreseen that a new form of combat would emerge – trench warfare. The dilemma experienced by all sides when overrunning an enemy position was that the long length of a rifle with fixed bayonet quickly became a dangerous hindrance. To fight and survive in a narrow trench, a soldier needed a more compact fighting knife: the trench dagger was about to evolve.

German fighting knife, 1914

Strong, single-edged blade with double-edged tip

Hardwood grip scales, grooved for easy grip

Short steel cross guard

Known by the Germans as the *Nahkampfmesser* ("Close-combat knife"), a wide range of patterns was created for the German war effort. This example is a style that was widely reproduced by many companies, such as Gottlieb Hammesfahr and Erfurt Gewehrfabrik, although many examples are unmarked.

DATE	1914
ORIGIN	GERMAN
LENGTH	28cm (11in)

German fighting knife, 1914

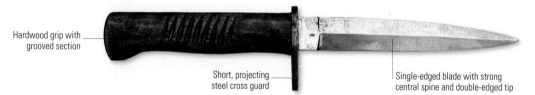

Hardwood grip with grooved section

Short, projecting steel cross guard

Single-edged blade with strong central spine and double-edged tip

A variation pattern of the close-combat knife, with a wooden grip. This specimen was possibly made by the company of Ernst Busch, Solingen, which is known to have manufactured an identical specimen with a solid-steel hilt. Both patterns are considered to be quite uncommon variations.

DATE	1914
ORIGIN	GERMAN
LENGTH	28.6cm (11.3in)

British push dagger, by Robbins of Dudley, 1916

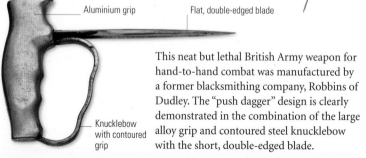

Aluminium grip

Flat, double-edged blade

Leather sheath with securing strap and loop

Knucklebow with contoured grip

This neat but lethal British Army weapon for hand-to-hand combat was manufactured by a former blacksmithing company, Robbins of Dudley. The "push dagger" design is clearly demonstrated in the combination of the large alloy grip and contoured steel knucklebow with the short, double-edged blade.

DATE	1916
ORIGIN	BRITISH
LENGTH	17.5cm (6.8in)

French fighting knife, 1916

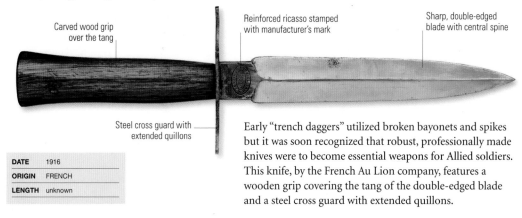

Carved wood grip over the tang

Reinforced ricasso stamped with manufacturer's mark

Sharp, double-edged blade with central spine

Steel cross guard with extended quillons

DATE	1916
ORIGIN	FRENCH
LENGTH	unknown

Early "trench daggers" utilized broken bayonets and spikes but it was soon recognized that robust, professionally made knives were to become essential weapons for Allied soldiers. This knife, by the French Au Lion company, features a wooden grip covering the tang of the double-edged blade and a steel cross guard with extended quillons.

American Model 1917 knucklebow knife, 1917

Leather scabbard body with steel mounts

Hardwood grip

Triangular-section blade

Steel knucklebow with pyramidal projections

DATE	1917
ORIGIN	AMERICAN
LENGTH	37cm (14.6in)

This close-quarter fighting knife was issued to US troops when they joined the European campaign. It is distinguished by a bayonet-style blade and knucklebow guard.

American knuckle knife, Model 1918, 1918

Spiked steel stud, securing the hilt to the tang

Solid brass grip with date and manufacturer's initials (Landers, Frary & Clark)

Brass quillon

Strong, double-edged blade

Brass studded knuckleduster grip

DATE	1918
ORIGIN	AMERICAN
LENGTH	29.6cm (11.6in)

This US-manufactured knuckle knife was originally completed with a black finish to the blade, hilt and metal parts of the scabbard. The French Au Lion company produced supplies in Europe, which were distinguished by their bright polish (with the Au Lion stamp on the ricasso). The hilts were marked only with the U.S. 1918 mark.

Bayonets of World War I

At the outbreak of World War I, military thinking had changed little since the mid-19th century, despite the advent of vastly improved firepower. It was still thought that troops could be deployed in massed ranks and engage in bayonet charges. But this was a war of entrenchment and little mobility, and the fields of Flanders showed the deadly futility of the fixed-bayonet charge across No Man's Land against a barely visible dug-in enemy defended by barbed wire, machine guns, mortars and artillery.

French Lebel epee bayonet, 1886

Muzzle ring

Hook quillon

Cupro-nickel or brass grip

Long, slender and sharply pointed blade

The Lebel bayonet with its long, slender, cruciform blade, resembling the fencing sword, or epee, is probably one of the most distinctive bayonets from its era. It was first introduced in 1886 for use with the new Lebel rifle, the world's first small-calibre, high-velocity rifle utilizing a smokeless propellant.

DATE	1886
ORIGIN	FRENCH
LENGTH	64cm (25.2in)

American Springfield bayonet, 1905

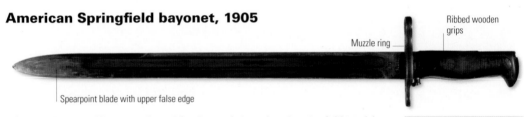

Ribbed wooden grips

Muzzle ring

Spearpoint blade with upper false edge

This was the second bayonet adopted for the newly introduced Springfield Model 1903 rifle, which initially used the bayonet of its predecessor, the Krag. However, President Theodore Roosevelt insisted a new bayonet with a longer blade be designed to compensate for the shorter length of the rifle.

DATE	1905
ORIGIN	AMERICAN
LENGTH	52.6cm (20.7in)

British SMLE bayonet, Pattern 1907, 1907

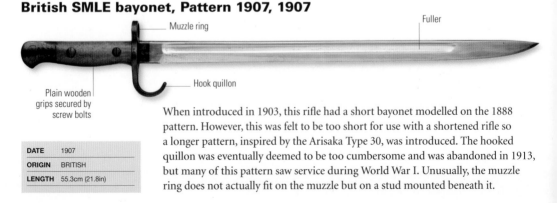

Muzzle ring

Fuller

Hook quillon

Plain wooden grips secured by screw bolts

DATE	1907
ORIGIN	BRITISH
LENGTH	55.3cm (21.8in)

When introduced in 1903, this rifle had a short bayonet modelled on the 1888 pattern. However, this was felt to be too short for use with a shortened rifle so a longer pattern, inspired by the Arisaka Type 30, was introduced. The hooked quillon was eventually deemed to be too cumbersome and was abandoned in 1913, but many of this pattern saw service during World War I. Unusually, the muzzle ring does not actually fit on the muzzle but on a stud mounted beneath it.

British bayonet Pattern 1913, 1914

Muzzle ring on extended cross guard

Blade identical to the Pattern 1907

Wooden grips with a distinctive pair of grooves

DATE	1914
ORIGIN	BRITISH
LENGTH	55.6cm (21.9in)

This Pattern 1913 bayonet, whilst very similar to the Pattern 1907, was designed to fit the Pattern 1914 rifle, a rapid adaptation of the Pattern 1913 experimental rifle discontinued at the outbreak of war and modified to .303in calibre. Unlike the SMLE, this rifle had a muzzle projecting beyond the end of the stock, and so this bayonet was designed so that the muzzle ring actually fits on the muzzle. It therefore has an extended cross guard to enable it to do that.

American bayonet for American Enfield rifle Model 1917, 1914

Wooden grips with distinctive pair of grooves

Muzzle ring on extended cross guard

Blade identical to Patterns 1907 and 1913

Drain hole

The British Pattern 1914 rifle and bayonet were already being manufactured under contract in America when it entered the war. Adapted to .30-06 calibre, the Pattern 1914 rifle became the Model 1917. Both rifle bayonets are identical, except for the US ownership marks and date on the American blade.

DATE	1914
ORIGIN	AMERICAN
LENGTH	54.4cm (21.4in)

German Mauser bayonet Model 98/05, 1915

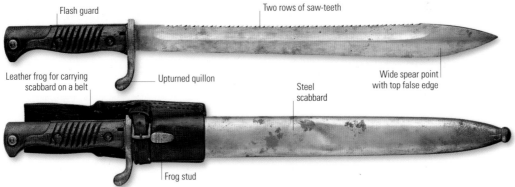

Flash guard

Two rows of saw-teeth

Leather frog for carrying scabbard on a belt

Upturned quillon

Steel scabbard

Wide spear point with top false edge

Frog stud

Numerous bayonets exist for the German Gewehr 98 rifle of 1898. This model with saw-teeth originated in 1905 for issue to infantry NCOs. The more durable scabbard dates from 1914. Saw-teeth were provided for cutting brushwood, not for inflicting more severe wounds, a popular misconception at the time.

DATE	1915
ORIGIN	GERMAN
LENGTH	50.8cm (20in)

American Model 1915 bayonet, 1915

Stub quillon

Plain wooden grips

Metal sheath with leather frog

Spearpoint blade with upper false edge

Muzzle ring

A Russian contract for 300,000 Model 1895 rifles and bayonets was placed with the Winchester company in 1915, and in Russia this bayonet is referred to as the Model 1915. The steel parts are polished bright and the Winchester name appears on the blade side of the cross guard.

DATE	1915
ORIGIN	AMERICAN
LENGTH	51.7cm (20.4in)

Canadian Ross rifle bayonet, 1915

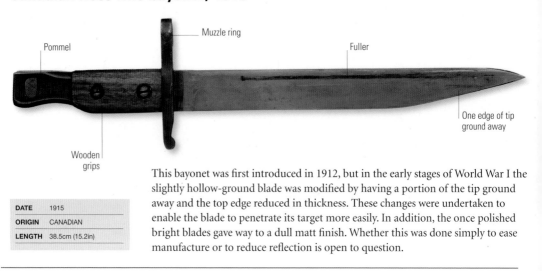

Muzzle ring

Pommel

Fuller

One edge of tip ground away

Wooden grips

DATE	1915
ORIGIN	CANADIAN
LENGTH	38.5cm (15.2in)

This bayonet was first introduced in 1912, but in the early stages of World War I the slightly hollow-ground blade was modified by having a portion of the tip ground away and the top edge reduced in thickness. These changes were undertaken to enable the blade to penetrate its target more easily. In addition, the once polished bright blades gave way to a dull matt finish. Whether this was done simply to ease manufacture or to reduce reflection is open to question.

German Mauser ersatz bayonet, 1916

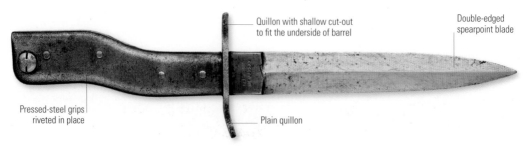

Quillon with shallow cut-out to fit the underside of barrel

Double-edged spearpoint blade

Pressed-steel grips riveted in place

Plain quillon

The term "ersatz" means a substitute or makeshift, in this case indicating that it was constructed using metal grips riveted together, on the grounds of speed and convenience. The hilt was usually painted field grey and the blade polished bright. This bayonet also functioned as a convenient trench knife.

DATE	1916
ORIGIN	GERMAN
LENGTH	26.1cm (10.3in)

German Mauser ersatz bayonet, 1916

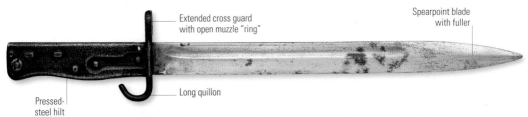

Extended cross guard
with open muzzle "ring"

Spearpoint blade
with fuller

Pressed-
steel hilt

Long quillon

DATE	1916
ORIGIN	GERMAN
LENGTH	43cm (17in)

This is another example of the many ersatz bayonets produced, again for use with the Model 88 and 98 Gewehr rifles or captured French Lebel and Russian Mosin-Nagant rifles. The pressed-steel hilt is a little more elaborately formed, although on this example the quillon has been bent further backwards subsequent to manufacture. Like the other bayonets, this would have had a hilt and scabbard painted field grey, and a polished blade.

British mountable revolver bayonet for Webley Mk VI, 1916

Locking latch each side to
engage behind foresight

Cast-bronze one-
piece hilt

T-section blade
from Gras bayonet

Thumb button for
operating locking latch

Profile to fit the hinge
of a revolver blade

DATE	1916
ORIGIN	BRITISH
LENGTH	32.4cm (12.8in)

This bayonet was the brainchild of Lieutenant Arthur Pritchard. Made by Greener of Birmingham, it used a Gras bayonet blade and was only for private purchase. The pommel sits tightly up against the revolver frame. The muzzle ring slides over the foresight and is locked in place by two sprung levers on the cross guard.

German Mauser ersatz bayonet, 1917

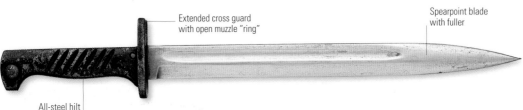

Extended cross guard
with open muzzle "ring"

Spearpoint blade
with fuller

All-steel hilt

DATE	1917
ORIGIN	GERMAN
LENGTH	43.9cm (17.3in)

These ersatz versions of the Model 88/98 bayonets were designed to fit the Model 88 and 98 rifles and, by using adapters, captured Russian Mosin-Nagant and French Lebel rifles too. The all-steel hilt reflects the grooved wooden grips of the standard bayonet and was originally painted field grey. It has the open muzzle "ring" common on many ersatz bayonets.

Survival weapons of World War II and after

As the world went to war in 1939, fighting knives and other survival weapons were redesigned to fill a variety of purposes, depending upon the conditions under which they would be used. Some pieces were designed solely as assassination items, while others were intended to double as working tools for building shelter or finding food. Part of the early training for British Commandos was for each man to take his turn locating food – namely, to find an animal or bird, kill it, butcher it, cook it and supply it to his colleagues.

American Carlson's Raiders machete (Collins Pattern No 18), 1934 onward

Black/green horn grip secured by five rivets

Steel cross guard, upturned on both sides

Broad falchion-shaped blade, with prominent false edge

Scabbard decorated with leather tooling and the Collins' company logo

Brown leather scabbard with belt loop

Issued to the 2nd Marine Raider Battalion during the Guadalcanal Campaign in the Pacific, this knife's "machete-style" hilt is common to a number of Collins' weapons; its distinctive "beaked" pommel ensures a firm grip. The single-edged blade, with false edge tip, makes it an excellent all-round tool as well as a weapon.

DATE	1934 onward
ORIGIN	AMERICAN
LENGTH	36cm (14.2in)

German flight utility knife, 1936 onward

Folding "Marlin" spike

Wooden grip scales secured by steel rivets

Folding trigger-release

Single-edged rust-free steel blade

DATE	1936 onward
ORIGIN	GERMAN
LENGTH	35.2cm (13.9in)

Originally introduced for the army parachute units, the knife was subsequently adopted by all Luftwaffe parachute units. The knife blade was normally retracted, to keep it out of the way and prevent accidental injury to the wearer; it could be released by one hand. By holding the knife down and pushing the trigger, the blade drops into position, useful if a parachutist is trapped in a tree.

Soviet fighting knife, Armenian pattern, 1940 onward

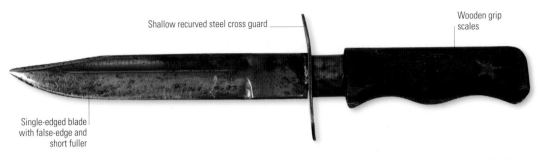

Shallow recurved steel cross guard

Wooden grip scales

Single-edged blade with false-edge and short fuller

DATE	1940 onward
ORIGIN	ARMENIAN
LENGTH	26cm (10.2in)

Manufactured in Armenia for the Soviet Armenian troops fighting alongside the Red Army, this weapon was intended as a general service knife, although its usefulness as a close-combat weapon was not overlooked. The blade is single-edged, with a double-edged tip and a fuller close to the back of the blade. This specimen has a ferrule between the main grip and the guard. In post-war years, the Armenian contingents continued to equip their troops with a similar dagger, although the main Russian troops preferred to have dual-purpose knife-bayonets.

English Fairbairn-Sykes commando knife, 2nd pattern, 1941 onward

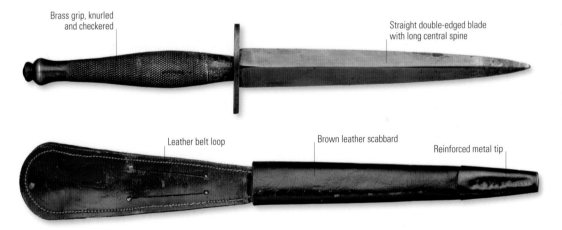

Brass grip, knurled and checkered

Straight double-edged blade with long central spine

Leather belt loop

Brown leather scabbard

Reinforced metal tip

DATE	1941 onward
ORIGIN	ENGLISH
LENGTH	30cm (11.8in)

The classic fighting knife of the Commando, the Fairbairn-Sykes knife is perhaps the most identifiable commando knife in the world, and its design features were copied by many other nations for their own special troops. The blade is a straight stiletto form, double-edged with a central spine, and the tang of the blade projects through the hilt and is secured at the other end with a locking button. The finely checkered grip is made of turned brass, while the guard is made of steel and rounded at the end of the quillons. This specimen is an example of the Fairbairn-Sykes 2nd pattern (the 1st pattern had a recurved cross guard and a more acutely pointed blade with flat ricasso). It appears to be a private purchase example, as the scabbard is shown without the usual leather side tags.

American USMC KA-BAR (USN Mk 2) fighting-utility knife, 1941 onward

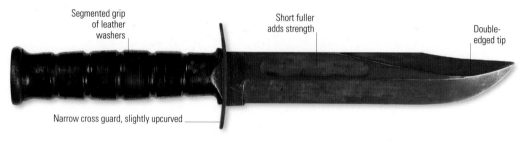

Segmented grip of leather washers

Short fuller adds strength

Double-edged tip

Narrow cross guard, slightly upcurved

One of the most successful fighting-utility knives ever made, the KA-BAR was created by the Union Cutlery Company of Olean, New York State. Designed as an all-purpose survival tool, it is equally effective as a hammer, can opener or defensive weapon. Initial manufacture was exclusive to Government Order, and the knife was adopted by the US Marine Corps and the Navy.

DATE	1941 onward
ORIGIN	AMERICAN
LENGTH	32cm (12.6in)

British and American OSS/SOE dart and wrist dagger, 1942 onward

Triangle-section blade with deep fuller

Cylindrical dart, fired from small crossbow

Smooth rounded hilt and pommel

Specially manufactured out of surgical steel, these weapons were designed for dispatching an opponent quietly. The dart could be fired from a folding, pistol-sized crossbow, while the wrist dagger was carried in a leather sheath with arm or leg straps for concealment. The weapons were mainly deployed behind enemy lines.

DATE	1942 onward
ORIGIN	BRITISH & AMERICAN
LENGTH	17.5cm (6.8in)

English Fairbairn-Sykes commando knife, 3rd pattern, 1942 onward

Turned and ribbed grip

Straight double-edged blade

The 3rd pattern Fairbairn-Sykes knife was the version that was most widely manufactured, both during World War II and well into the postwar years. Following the production of the original pattern by Wilkinson Sword, the design was modified and improved in the following models, and then contracted out to other manufacturers. The ringed grip is the distinguishing feature of the the 3rd pattern dagger, more than 1 million of which are thought to have been produced.

DATE	1942 onward
ORIGIN	ENGLISH
LENGTH	29.6cm (11.7in)

American Mk 3 trench knife with M8 scabbard, 1943 onward

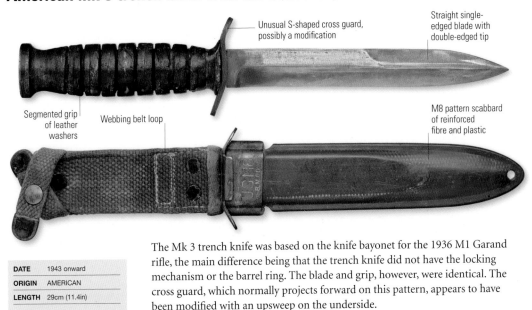

Unusual S-shaped cross guard, possibly a modification

Straight single-edged blade with double-edged tip

Segmented grip of leather washers

Webbing belt loop

M8 pattern scabbard of reinforced fibre and plastic

DATE	1943 onward
ORIGIN	AMERICAN
LENGTH	29cm (11.4in)

The Mk 3 trench knife was based on the knife bayonet for the 1936 M1 Garand rifle, the main difference being that the trench knife did not have the locking mechanism or the barrel ring. The blade and grip, however, were identical. The cross guard, which normally projects forward on this pattern, appears to have been modified with an upsweep on the underside.

German utility-fighting knife for the Bundeswehr, c.1970s

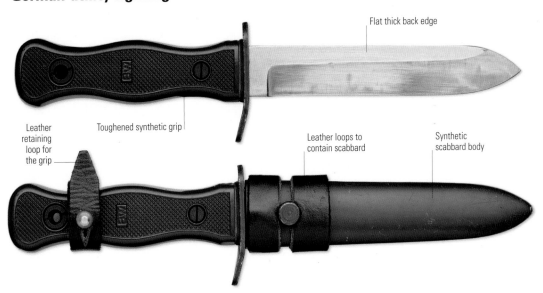

Flat thick back edge

Leather retaining loop for the grip

Toughened synthetic grip

Leather loops to contain scabbard

Synthetic scabbard body

DATE	c.1970s
ORIGIN	GERMAN
LENGTH	26cm (10.2in)

Although the role of the fighting knife in modern armies has diminished, military thinking still holds that a neat general-purpose knife is a useful tool. Advances in materials now mean that non-rusting and non-degrading components can be used to assemble knives capable of lasting for years without any visible deterioration.

German Third Reich edged weapons

The city of Solingen, in the Ruhr Valley, has been recognized as a centre of excellence in the production of edged weapons for over 700 years. Following the German surrender and disarmament after World War I, its edged-weapons industry experienced a period of steep decline. Swords and daggers, which had been prevalent in the Imperial Period, had always been viewed as symbols of authority and officialdom, particularly in Prussian culture. The emergence of the National Socialist Government (NSDAP) in 1933 created an opportunity to develop weapons of a new design to reflect the culture of the Third Reich.

German Hitler Youth knife, *c.*1933

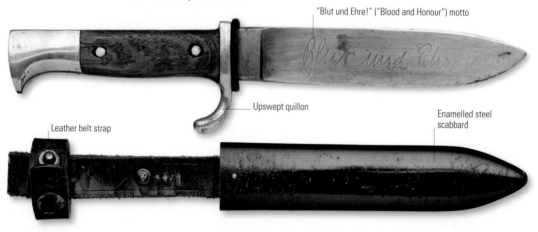

"Blut und Ehre!" ("Blood and Honour") motto

Upswept quillon

Enamelled steel scabbard

Leather belt strap

The Hitler Youth knife (HJ Fahrtenmesser, "Hiking Knife") was put into production in 1933. The blade is short and single-edged (examples made before 1938 featured the *Blut und Ehre!* motto) and the hilt is steel with a nickel plate finish. The knife would usually feature the Hitler Youth swastika emblem.

DATE	c.1933
ORIGIN	GERMAN
LENGTH	24.8cm (9.8in)

German SA service dagger, *c.*1933

"Alles für Deutschland" ("Everything for Germany") motto

National Socialist emblem

Steel blade

SA emblem

The SA, or *Sturm Abteilung* ("Storm Detachment"), were the militia who kept order at Nazi Party meetings. This service dagger was introduced in 1933 and based on a south German medieval design. The wood-and-steel hilt is emblazoned with National Socialist and SA emblems. The accompanying brown metal scabbard would have been ornamented with nickel trimmings.

DATE	c.1933
ORIGIN	GERMAN
LENGTH	35.4cm (14in)

German SS officer's dagger, 1936

"Meine Ehre heißt Treue" ("My Honour is named Loyalty") motto

Silver eagle and swastika emblem

Steel blade, unsharpened

SS runic badge in grip

DATE	1936
ORIGIN	GERMAN
LENGTH	37cm (14.6in)

Introduced in December 1933, the SS dagger was based on the same design as the SA dagger, but with minor differences. The grip is made of hardwood which is stained black and has silver finish insignia, including the SS runic symbol at the top of the grip. The cross guards are finished in a nickel silver plating.

German RAD hewer, *c.*1934

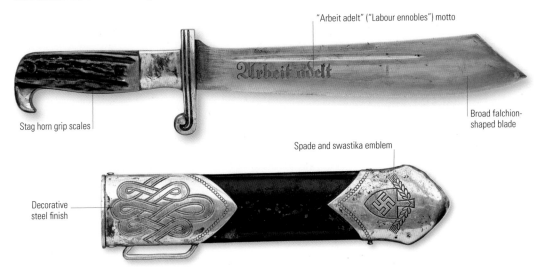

"Arbeit adelt" ("Labour ennobles") motto

Broad falchion-shaped blade

Stag horn grip scales

Spade and swastika emblem

Decorative steel finish

DATE	c.1934
ORIGIN	GERMAN
LENGTH	37.7cm (14.8in)

The RAD (*Reichs Arbeit Dienst*, "Reich's Labour Service") aimed to give young people experience of manual labour in the community. The design of this heavy-duty hewer, which was carried by full-time personnel only, was based on a traditional German hatchet. A heavily ornamented black metal scabbard carried the broad steel blade, which was falchion shaped with a short fuller close to the back edge. The organizational motto, *Arbeit adelt*, is etched on the blade. The hilt is made of iron, with nickel plating and stag horn grip scales. The steel scabbard has decorated steel fittings: the upper one bears a scroll design, while the lower one features a version of the national emblem of the RAD service – a spade head with swastika and corn stalks.

German Luftwaffe Flying Officer's dagger, 1934

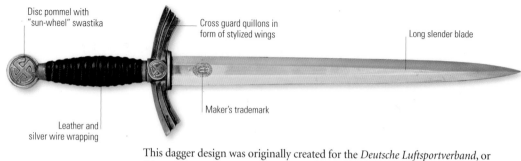

Disc pommel with "sun-wheel" swastika

Cross guard quillons in form of stylized wings

Long slender blade

Maker's trademark

Leather and silver wire wrapping

DATE	1934
ORIGIN	GERMAN
LENGTH	50.5cm (20in)

This dagger design was originally created for the *Deutsche Luftsportverband*, or "German Airsports Organization", which was a secret means of training air personnel while Germany was forbidden to operate a military air force under the terms of the Treaty of Versailles of 1919. In March 1935, the Luftwaffe came into existence and Germany declared its intention to begin rapid military expansion. This dagger would have been carried in a blue leather-wrapped scabbard with chain suspension.

The restoration of German pride

Uniforms and edged weapons had long been regarded as symbols of rank and status in Germany. The German love of order and discipline seemed to have come to the fore at around the time of Bismarck and the creation of the Second Reich (1871–1918). In this period of industrial growth and new prosperity, virtually every organization and service within Germany wore a uniform and carried a sword or dagger. This kind of adornment extended beyond the navy and army to hunters, postal workers, railway officials and so on.

In the years following World War I, most of this was swept away with the austerity of the new Weimar Republic and the heavy reparations imposed upon the defeated Germany. One of the key promises made by Hitler, sensing the people's resentment at the outcome of the war, was that he would restore German pride. The adoption of dress weapons for the Nazis' militarist formations was one aspect of this. New Nazi-inspired uniforms and daggers were created for other services, too, such as the German Red Cross and the Civil Service. The psychological effect was palpable. People started to feel important again; they were being given recognition and status.

ABOVE Adolf Hitler taking the salute at the 1938 Party Rally in Nuremberg. In the foreground is Reichs Labour Service leader Konstantin Hierl, wearing his own special RAD hewer. Another officer wears the 1937 Pattern RAD officers' hewer.

German army officer's dagger, 1935

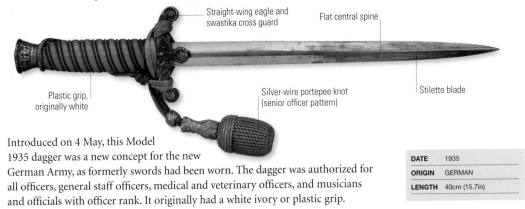

Straight-wing eagle and swastika cross guard

Flat central spine

Plastic grip, originally white

Silver-wire portepee knot (senior officer pattern)

Stiletto blade

Introduced on 4 May, this Model 1935 dagger was a new concept for the new German Army, as formerly swords had been worn. The dagger was authorized for all officers, general staff officers, medical and veterinary officers, and musicians and officials with officer rank. It originally had a white ivory or plastic grip.

DATE	1935
ORIGIN	GERMAN
LENGTH	40cm (15.7in)

German Luftwaffe dagger, 1937

White, plastic grip over wood base, with silver-wire wrap

Stiletto blade with flat central spine

Globe-form pommel

Cross guard in the form of an eagle clutching the swastika

DATE	1937
ORIGIN	GERMAN
LENGTH	40cm (15.7in)

Introduced in 1937 for Luftwaffe officers, this stylish new dagger features a cross guard in the form of the Luftwaffe eagle. The thin stiletto blade is unsharpened and is secured to the hilt with the tang passing through the grip and screw-locked with a globe pommel. The pommel is decorated with oak leaf motifs and a swastika. Some deluxe examples of this dagger had an ivory grip with a Damascus steel blade.

German state official dagger, 1938

White mother-of-pearl grip scales

Unsharpened stiletto blade

Silver-plated hilt in the form of a stylized eagle head

Cross guard in the form of a political pattern eagle and swastika

DATE	1938
ORIGIN	GERMAN
LENGTH	40cm (15.7in)

Introduced in March 1938 for all State and Civil Service Leaders, this dagger is very stylish, having an elegant hilt in the form of an eagle's head, with mother-of-pearl grip scales. All the hilt metal parts are made of brass, with a silver plate finish. The cross guard is very distinctive, featuring a political form spread-wing eagle, with upturned tips to the wings and a wreath with a swastika emblem clutched at the talons.

Bayonets of World War II

By the time World War II erupted, warfare had become much more mechanized. Soldiers were also more mobile and the widespread adoption of the submachine gun and automatic rifle meant that troops had greater individual firepower. But the need for close-quarter engagement still arose, in street fighting or commando operations, where the bayonet, especially the shorter versions, came into its own.

German or Belgian Mauser export bayonet, 1920s–30s

Plain wooden grip — Full muzzle ring — Single-edged blade with fullers

This is a typical Mauser "export" bayonet, manufactured in vast quantities in both Germany and Belgium and exported around the world during the interwar years. Unlike the majority of German service bayonets at this time, the export bayonets often had a complete muzzle ring and were either deeply blued or polished all over.

DATE	1920s–30s
ORIGIN	GERMAN/BELGIAN
LENGTH	38.5cm (15.2in)

Japanese Arisaka bayonet, 1939

— Muzzle ring — Fuller

Plain wooden grips encasing the tang and secured by rivets — Hook quillon

This bayonet was created to fit the Type 99 Arisaka rifle introduced in 1939. It is almost identical to the original Arisaka bayonet, the Type 30 of 1897, and at the time of production had a heavily blued hilt and either a bright or blued blade.

DATE	1939
ORIGIN	JAPANESE
LENGTH	73.5cm (28.9in)

British entrenching tool/bayonet, 1939–45

This was not designed as a weapon. As a wartime expedient, the helve of the entrenching tool was adapted to accept the No. 4 bayonet so it could be used as a probe for detecting landmines. The spade portion could easily be removed for this type of work and to simplify carrying.

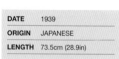

DATE	1939–45
ORIGIN	BRITISH
LENGTH	unknown

No. 4 spike bayonet — Wooden haft — Spade

British bayonet for the No 4 rifle, No 4, Mk II, c.1940

Hollow socket

Plain spike blade

The No 4 rifle and bayonet were urgently introduced at the start of the war. This rifle was a simplified version of the SMLE (Short, Magazine, Lee-Enfield).

DATE	c.1940
ORIGIN	BRITISH
LENGTH	25.4cm (10in)

British Sten machine carbine bayonet, Mk I, 1942

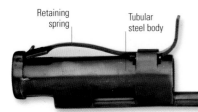

Retaining spring

Tubular steel body

Originating with Captain White of the Glasgow Home Guard, it reappeared in 1942 as the redesigned Mk I. The 20cm (8in) steel spike is welded to a steel body and uses a leaf spring clip attachment.

DATE	1942
ORIGIN	BRITISH
LENGTH	30cm (11.8in)

American bayonet for Garand M1 rifle, Model M1, 1943

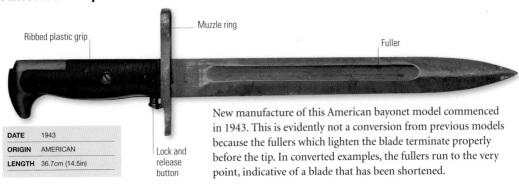

Ribbed plastic grip

Muzzle ring

Fuller

Lock and release button

DATE	1943
ORIGIN	AMERICAN
LENGTH	36.7cm (14.5in)

New manufacture of this American bayonet model commenced in 1943. This is evidently not a conversion from previous models because the fullers which lighten the blade terminate properly before the tip. In converted examples, the fullers run to the very point, indicative of a blade that has been shortened.

American bayonet for M1 carbine, Model M4, 1944

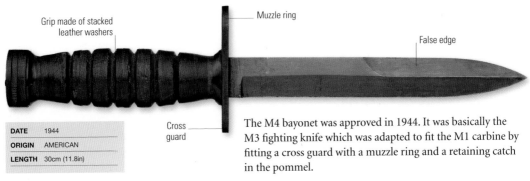

Grip made of stacked leather washers

Muzzle ring

False edge

Cross guard

DATE	1944
ORIGIN	AMERICAN
LENGTH	30cm (11.8in)

The M4 bayonet was approved in 1944. It was basically the M3 fighting knife which was adapted to fit the M1 carbine by fitting a cross guard with a muzzle ring and a retaining catch in the pommel.

Bayonets up to the present day

Despite the increasingly hi-tech nature of warfare, reliance still has to be ultimately placed on the soldier at the battlefront. When all else fails, the bayonet, used in its traditional role on the rifle, or used with stealth as a fighting knife, or used as a combination tool, is probably more an essential piece of equipment than it was in the past. Even now, a soldier on parade would be incomplete without one.

Czech VZ/24 knife bayonet, c.1926

Full muzzle ring   Spearpoint blade

Introduced around 1926 for the VZ/24 rifle, this is a shortened version of the VZ/23, and several variants exist. Unusually, the cutting edge of the blade is on the upper side. It was widely exported to Europe, the Middle East and South America.

DATE	c.1926
ORIGIN	CZECH
LENGTH	43.3cm (17in)

British knife bayonet, No 7, Mk I, 1945

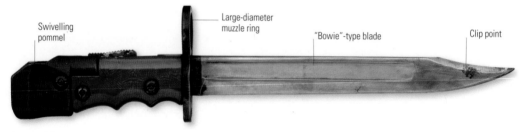

Swivelling pommel   Large-diameter muzzle ring   "Bowie"-type blade   Clip point

Designed for the No 4 rifle, this knife bayonet was first used on the Sten gun Mk V. After limited use, around 1947 the Guards began to use it for parade duty and this continued until the 1970s. The unusual swivelling pommel allowed the weapon to be used as a bayonet or, in the position shown, as a fighting knife.

DATE	1945
ORIGIN	BRITISH
LENGTH	32.3cm (12.7in)

Russian knife bayonet for AK47 assault rifle, 1947

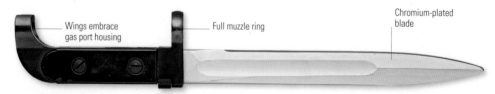

Wings embrace gas port housing   Full muzzle ring   Chromium-plated blade

DATE	1947
ORIGIN	RUSSIAN
LENGTH	32.6cm (12.8in)

This is a bayonet of very distinctive appearance. The pommel has two projections that partially wrap around the barrel, and slide along it when fitted, to give extra support. The cross guard has a traditional muzzle ring; immediately to the rear of this are the two locking catches that engage in recesses on the barrel.

British L1A3 bayonet for L1A1 SLR, 1957

Pressed-steel grips

"Bowie"-type blade with false edge

One of a series of bayonets for this rifle, all with minor differences and all evolving from the No 5 bayonet. This one has a recessed lock-release button on the other side of the pommel and a fuller which terminates close to the hilt. All have blackened hilts.

DATE	1957
ORIGIN	BRITISH
LENGTH	30.5cm (12in)

South African pattern No 9 socket bayonet, c.1960

DATE	c.1960
ORIGIN	SOUTH AFRICAN
LENGTH	17cm (6.7in)

This hybrid, consisting of the No 4 rifle type of socket and the blade of the S1 (Uzi) submachine gun bayonet, was issued to local defence groups.

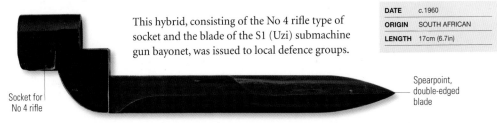

Socket for No 4 rifle

Spearpoint, double-edged blade

British knife bayonet L3A1 for SA80 (L85A1) rifle, 1985

Slot for stud on scabbard

Tubular handle

Clip point and part-serrated edge

DATE	1985
ORIGIN	BRITISH
LENGTH	28.6cm (11.3in)

This bayonet, a stainless-steel investment casting with tubular hilt, departs widely from earlier concepts. The blade is serrated like a kitchen knife and has a hole to engage with a stud on the scabbard, for use as a wire-cutter. Later, a bottle-opener was built into the hilt.

French knife bayonet for SIG 540/542 rifle, 1985

Plano-convex blade

DATE	1985
ORIGIN	FRENCH
LENGTH	unknown

Plastic-sheathed steel hilt

This is an elegantly simple but purposeful bayonet of Swiss design for the SIG rifle used by the Foreign Legion. It has a tubular steel hilt, partly encased in plastic with a catch built into the pommel, and a slender blade that is flat on one face and convex on the other.

209

Civilian knives to the present day

From the 19th century to the 21st century, the development of the modern knife has seen many novel interpretations. Revised and modified variations of some ancient knife styles came into being, together with "automatic" knives which flick open mechanically. Today, the classic Bowie knife endures in numerous updated forms alongside expressive, free-flowing styles that make the most of modern technology, such as the extravagant designs of Spanish knife-maker Martinez Albainox.

British bichwa double-bladed parrying knife, late 20th century

Wood grip scales mounted on central tang, secured by rivets

Short, double-edged blade either side of main grip

Short, double-edged blade either side of main grip

Smooth knucklebow

The bichwa (sometimes spelled bich'hwa) originated in India and usually had slightly curved, or wavy, blades. Some examples had two blades either side of the central grip. It was designed as a parrying knife, used in the left hand to thwart an opponent's blade, while the right hand retained a longer offensive weapon (sword or long dagger). This example appears to be a privately manufactured item, European and of modern construction.

DATE	late 20th century
ORIGIN	BRITISH
LENGTH	36.4cm (14.3in)

German flick knife, late 20th century

Release spring for locking clip

Locking clip under cross guard

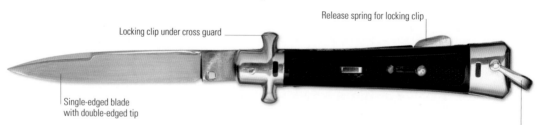

Single-edged blade with double-edged tip

Lanyard ring

The flick-knife is, in reality, a spring-operated lock-back knife. The design has been known since the latter part of the 19th century, although its widespread popularity (and notoriety) seems to be encapsulated in the "Teddy boy" era of the early 1950s. The blade is folded into a hilt like a regular clasp-knife, and locked into position – under spring tension – with a clip. Depression of the button on the face of the grip releases the blade which swings out and into the open position, locked there by a spring clip inside the cross guard. Depressing a release spring on the side of the grip allows the blade to be folded back into a safe, closed position.

DATE	late 20th century
ORIGIN	GERMAN
LENGTH	24cm (9.4in)

West German Bundeswehr gravity knife, 1970s onward

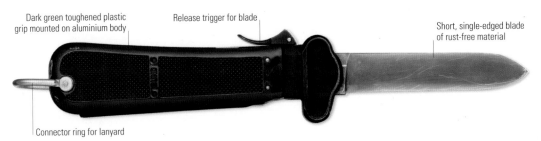

Dark green toughened plastic grip mounted on aluminium body

Release trigger for blade

Short, single-edged blade of rust-free material

Connector ring for lanyard

DATE	1970s onward
ORIGIN	WEST GERMAN
LENGTH	25.7cm (10.1in)

The design of this item has been clearly influenced by the World War II flight utility knife for the *Fallschirmjäger* (Paratroopers). Construction features have been improved, and the knife is lighter than the original wartime version. It is also designed to be stripped down for easy maintenance and repair work. The original examples were not designed to strip down, and were prone to fracturing on the spring.

West German spring-operated switchblade knife, 1970s onward

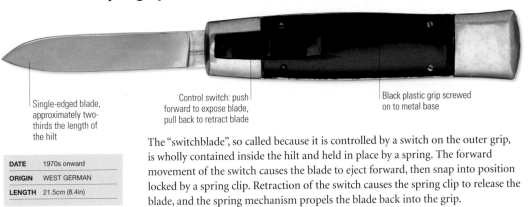

Single-edged blade, approximately two-thirds the length of the hilt

Control switch: push forward to expose blade, pull back to retract blade

Black plastic grip screwed on to metal base

DATE	1970s onward
ORIGIN	WEST GERMAN
LENGTH	21.5cm (8.4in)

The "switchblade", so called because it is controlled by a switch on the outer grip, is wholly contained inside the hilt and held in place by a spring. The forward movement of the switch causes the blade to eject forward, then snap into position locked by a spring clip. Retraction of the switch causes the spring clip to release the blade, and the spring mechanism propels the blade back into the grip.

American Applegate-Fairbairn knife, 1980s

Short double-edged blade with engraved facsimile signatures

Steel cross guard with short, downswept quillons

Grooved grip scale of tough synthetic secured to the tang with a single screw

DATE	1980s
ORIGIN	AMERICAN
LENGTH	28cm (11in)

This knife was a joint venture by Rex Applegate, America's leading exponent of military close-combat knife-fighting, and W. Fairbairn, of the famous Fairbairn and Sykes design team. It appears that only commemorative copies were produced, for collectors interested in the historical association.

American keyring punch dagger and sheath, late 20th century

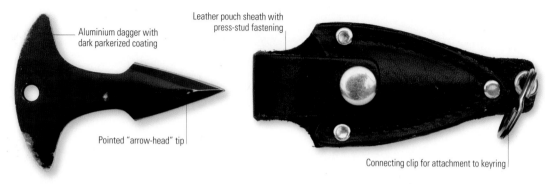

Aluminium dagger with dark parkerized coating

Leather pouch sheath with press-stud fastening

Pointed "arrow-head" tip

Connecting clip for attachment to keyring

Intended as a personal self-defence item, this punch dagger is an evolutionary development of the punch daggers designed in the United States in the mid-1800s. Although not designed to create a knife-like slash wound, it is a formidable item when held in the clenched fist – capable of breaking a bone with a direct hit.

DATE	late 20th century
ORIGIN	AMERICAN
LENGTH	7.2cm (2.8in)

Taiwanese butterfly knife, late 20th century

Two-part hilt in stainless steel

Short single-edged blade with double-edged tip

This folding knife does not have a tang. The blade is riveted to the two halves of the grip, each rivet acting as a hinge. Separating the halves of the grip at the base causes one half and the blade to swing around so that the blade faces down and insets into the grip. The second part of the grip follows round and covers the rest of the blade – now totally enclosed within the two halves of the grip.

DATE	late 20th century
ORIGIN	TAIWANESE
LENGTH	23.4cm (9.2in)

American Damascus steel knife, present day

Handle scales made from mammoth tooth

Curved Damascus steel blade

This vibrantly coloured fixed-blade knife, by the California knife-maker P. J. Ernest, is made from Damascus steel in the ladder pattern. Both the knife and bolsters were heat-coloured to bring out the intricate pattern of the steel. The handle scales are made from Siberian mammoth tooth.

DATE	present day
ORIGIN	AMERICAN
LENGTH	17.5cm (6.8in)

American bodyguard knuckleduster knife, present day

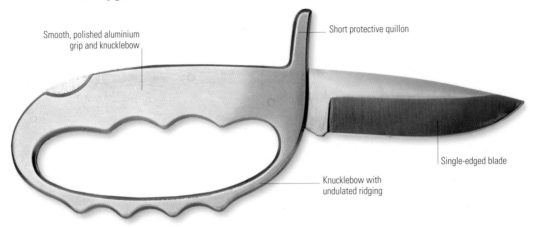

Smooth, polished aluminium grip and knucklebow

Short protective quillon

Single-edged blade

Knucklebow with undulated ridging

DATE	present day
ORIGIN	AMERICAN
LENGTH	23cm (9.1in)

The interpretation of what is permissible to carry as an item of self-defence is quite different in the United States compared to Europe. The above item is clearly of very modern manufacture, and is a very clean, 20th-century style. Designed as a "bodyguard" item, the intended market is unclear. Trained personnel, licensed as bodyguards, would be permitted to carry such a defensive weapon. If carried by an unlicensed person it carries the risk of being presumed to be a weapon of assault rather than defence.

Spanish Martinez Albainox knife, present day

Curved grip

Sharply curved blade

Notched lower edge

Pommel

Secondary blade

DATE	present day
ORIGIN	SPANISH
LENGTH	28.5cm (11.2in)

There is a school of modern knife-making that promotes the concept of knives of somewhat fantastical form – seemingly more rooted in the world of science-fiction than practical knife design. The above specimen by the Spanish company Martinez Albainox is clearly an impressive example. Intended purely as a collector's piece, the artistic sweep of the blade and the flow of the metal present a surreal appearance when compared to the utter simplicity of design of the Applegate-Fairbairn knife, for example. There are so many exposed points and edges on the item that any bearer might be advised to wear a suit of chain mail before unsheathing this weapon!

African knives and daggers

It is not surprising that the forms of knives and daggers found in Africa are almost infinitely diverse, given the size of the continent, the tribal nature of the people, and pervasive influences from the ancient Egyptians, Romans and other invader/trader nations.

Although the workmanship cannot compare with that of other continents, the artistic style with which African smiths have designed their weapons is unsurpassed. The abstract nature of African art, its originality and vitality, attract worldwide admiration.

Yakoma or Ngbandi knife, mid-19th century

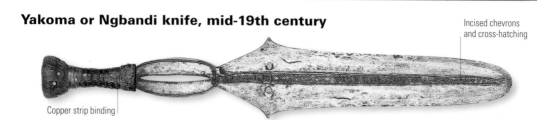

Incised chevrons and cross-hatching

Copper strip binding

The tribal knives of the Yakoma and Ngbandi are similar and difficult to tell apart. In addition to their formal function, they were also used as currency, in particular to pay a "bride price". This blade has some nicely incised decoration; the hilt is bound with copper and it is made with a leather-covered pommel.

DATE	mid-19th century
ORIGIN	ZAIREAN
LENGTH	48.3cm (19in)

Mangbetu knife, mid-19th century

The Mangbetu of northeastern Zaire called this weapon a "trumbash", and its very particular shape is said to derive from ancient Egypt. In fact, a contemporary illustration of Rameses III (king of Egypt 1184–1156BC) shows him using a very similar "sickle-sword" when in the act of executing his enemies.

Sickle-shaped blade sharpened on both edges

Wooden hilt with cylindrical pommel

DATE	mid-19th century
ORIGIN	ZAIREAN
LENGTH	22.9cm (9in)

Konda shortsword, mid-19th century

Wooden sheath covered with brass nail heads

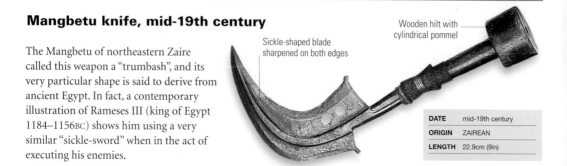

Disc pommel in a "sun hat" shape

This handsome knife was produced by the Konda of Haute-Zaire. Although its general shape commends it to close fighting, there is no doubt that in peaceful times it would have doubled as a particularly useful general-purpose knife. The wooden hilt and sheath are studded with brass nail heads forming a dense covering.

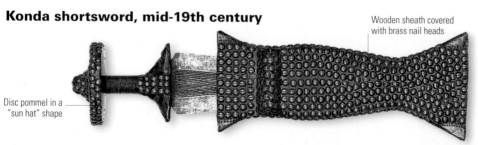

DATE	mid-19th century
ORIGIN	ZAIREAN
LENGTH	31.2cm (12.25in)

Ngala knife, late 19th century

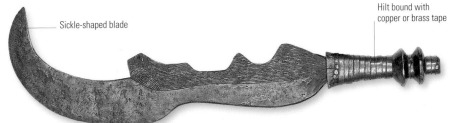

Sickle-shaped blade

Hilt bound with copper or brass tape

DATE	late 19th century
ORIGIN	ZAIREAN
LENGTH	43.2cm (17in)

These Ngala swords from Zaire, with their unique form of sickle-shaped blade, were sometimes used for a particularly gruesome form of execution. The victim was secured to the ground with his head tied to a supple tree bent over for the purpose. At the moment of decapitation the head was catapulted into the distance.

Sudanese dagger, late 19th century

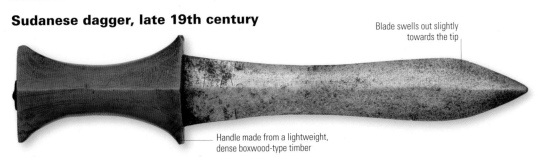

Blade swells out slightly towards the tip

Handle made from a lightweight, dense boxwood-type timber

DATE	late 19th century
ORIGIN	SUDANESE
LENGTH	26.7cm (10.5in)

This dagger from Sudan is typical of those carried by followers of the Mahdi during the last quarter of the 19th century. It was intended primarily for stabbing, and the blade swells out towards the tip, which is slightly thickened in section. The blade is sharp on both edges and is contained in a leather sheath lined with cotton.

Sudanese double dagger, late 19th century

Blades etched with inscriptions in Thuluth script

Coloured-glass beadwork

DATE	late 19th century
ORIGIN	SUDANESE
LENGTH	56cm (22in)

This double dagger comes from Sudan and is associated with followers of the Mahdi during the 1880s. The blades are etched with inscriptions in Thuluth script, which derives from that used by the Mamluks for monumental inscriptions. The wooden grip and sheaths are covered with multicoloured beadwork.

Hadendoa dagger, late 19th century

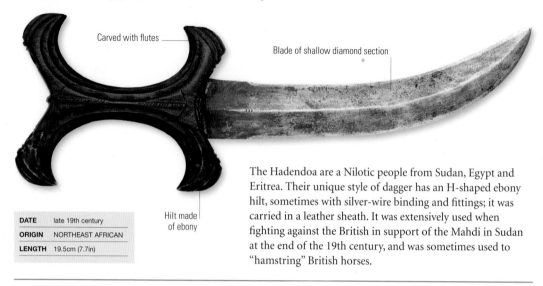

Carved with flutes

Blade of shallow diamond section

Hilt made of ebony

DATE	late 19th century
ORIGIN	NORTHEAST AFRICAN
LENGTH	19.5cm (7.7in)

The Hadendoa are a Nilotic people from Sudan, Egypt and Eritrea. Their unique style of dagger has an H-shaped ebony hilt, sometimes with silver-wire binding and fittings; it was carried in a leather sheath. It was extensively used when fighting against the British in support of the Mahdi in Sudan at the end of the 19th century, and was sometimes used to "hamstring" British horses.

Nubian arm dagger, *c*.1900

Flat blade sometimes inscribed

Ebony hilt

Nubia is a region of Sudan close to the River Nile. These daggers are found in leather sheaths which have woven leather straps to bind them to the wearer's arm. The circular pommel is lathe-turned and looks very similar to the counter used in the game of draughts. Often the dagger hilts have a pommel made of ivory.

DATE	*c*.1900
ORIGIN	NUBIAN
LENGTH	27.4cm (10.8in)

Somali "Billa" knife, *c*.1900

Silver pommel

Ivory hilt

Thin, broad blade

This Somali knife was produced by Arab cutlers who imported the skills of silversmithing from Oman. Arab interaction with Africa's east coast occurred through trade and traders; indeed, Zanzibar was ruled by Oman and Muscat during the 18th and 19th centuries. Only the finest of these knives have hilts of ivory and silver; others are made from horn or wood.

DATE	*c*.1900
ORIGIN	SOMALI
LENGTH	43.4cm (17.1in)

Sudanese throwing knife, *c.*1900

Leather-bound cotton-covered grip

Projecting blades

These multi-bladed throwing knives do not seem to have been produced for use, and may have had a ceremonial function or even have been made purely for the souvenir market. Sometimes stamped with geometric ornament, they have grips often bound with leather over cotton cloth.

DATE	c.1900
ORIGIN	SUDANESE
LENGTH	unknown

Moroccan jambya or koummya, early 20th century

Wooden grip

Sharp inside cutting edge

Metal pommel

These daggers are among the most numerous ever to have been produced in Africa, and their design conforms very closely. However, the grips can be made from wood, bone or ivory, while the mounts are of brass, silver and even gold. The blades are mostly plain or undecorated.

DATE	early 20th century
ORIGIN	MOROCCAN
LENGTH	31cm (12.2in)

Central African arm knife, 20th century

Very shallow diamond-section blade

Iron pommel integral with the blade

These parts are made from woven leather

This type of arm dagger is commonly encountered all over Central and North Africa, from Nigeria to Sudan, and from the Sahara Desert to Cameroon. They are distinguished by the woven leather bindings to the hilt and by the protruding flattened iron pommel. They were and still are made by a large variety of tribes and craftsmen, perhaps the finest being Mandingo leatherworkers.

DATE	20th century
ORIGIN	CENTRAL AFRICAN
LENGTH	unknown

Persia, Middle East and Turkey

This geographic area has been home to a multitude of peoples and dynasties possessing fabulous wealth and artistry, and this is reflected in their weapons. The best knives and daggers came from the court workshops set up to reflect the majesty, wealth and reputation of their patrons. The quality of production would tend to diminish with distance from court, where function and cost were critical considerations.

Venetian or Turkish khanjar dagger, *c.*1520

Brightly gilt

Ivory grip with incised design filled with black substance

This most unusual dagger was made in Venice for the Turkish market. The blade shape is found on daggers from the Mediterranean to Scotland. Venetian craftsmen specialized in the manufacture of weapons and armour for export to Turkey, and they were very accomplished at interpreting Turkish ornament.

DATE	*c.*1520
ORIGIN	VENETIAN/TURKISH
LENGTH	38.6cm (15.2in)

Ottoman Turkish knife, 17th century

Blade made from watered steel

Jade hilt inlaid with gold and stones

The blade of this dagger comes from Persia or India, and is made from watered steel. The jade hilt is only inlaid with gold at the top and the rest of the hilt is plain to enable the dagger to slide down deep into its sheath, with only the decorated pommel showing. The hilt is Turkish and dates from the 17th century.

DATE	17th century
ORIGIN	OTTOMAN TURKISH
LENGTH	19cm (7.5in)

Persian khanjar, *c.*1800

This fine Persian khanjar has a walrus-ivory hilt of the best quality. It is beautifully carved with a naked couple standing between two trees; at their feet are three naked children. It was made during the Qajar Dynasty, *c.*1800. The depiction of naked human figures is unusual in Persian art, but other daggers with similar subjects are known. It is possible they were made for the prurient, or for non-Muslims. The blade is made from finely watered steel.

DATE	*c.*1800
ORIGIN	PERSIAN
LENGTH	39cm (15.4in)

Central reinforcing rib

Finely carved walrus-ivory hilt

Ottoman Turkish khanjar with nephrite grips, early 18th century

Jade grip inlaid with gold

Twin fullers lined with brass

Three garnets on pommel

DATE	early 18th century
ORIGIN	OTTOMAN TURKISH
LENGTH	34cm (13.4in)

The two-piece grips are made of jade. There are two different types of jade called nephrite and jadeite respectively; the former is slightly harder than the latter. This classic Ottoman dagger dates from the early 18th century, although the shape of the hilt is more commonly found on daggers of the 17th century.

Ottoman Turkish silver-mounted khanjar dagger, *c.*1740

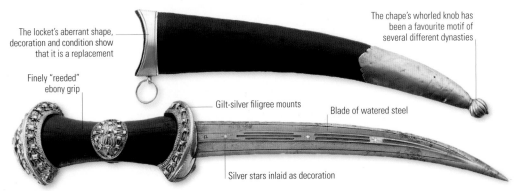

The locket's aberrant shape, decoration and condition show that it is a replacement

The chape's whorled knob has been a favourite motif of several different dynasties

Finely "reeded" ebony grip

Gilt-silver filigree mounts

Blade of watered steel

Silver stars inlaid as decoration

DATE	c.1740
ORIGIN	OTTOMAN TURKISH
LENGTH	42cm (16.5in)

Silver stars are found inlaid into Turkish blades from the 17th to the 19th centuries. This dagger, dating from *c.*1740, has a "reeded" ebony grip and is fitted with fine-quality filigree mounts made from gilt silver. This is a large dagger, and the original owner would have worn it in a prominent position.

Ottoman Turkish bichaq knife with agate grip, early 19th century

Agate hilt

Silver sheath mounts

DATE	early 19th century
ORIGIN	OTTOMAN TURKISH
LENGTH	33cm (13in)

The bichaq serves principally as a knife, although it could be called into service as a dagger. This Ottoman example has an agate hilt with a gold-set jewel inlaid into the pommel. The blade has a false-damascened inscription, and it retains its original silver-mounted sheath. It dates from the early 19th century.

Ottoman Turkish khanjar, early 19th century

Brass hilt

Chiselled, raised central rib

The shape of this dagger was found across Ottoman Turkey during the 18th and 19th centuries, but it is particularly associated with the Kurds. The grip is made from brass, and the double-edged blade is carved with a central rib and forms two shallow "fullers" between it and the slightly raised edges.

DATE	early 19th century
ORIGIN	OTTOMAN TURKISH
LENGTH	40.5cm (15.9in)

Uzbek kard, early 19th century

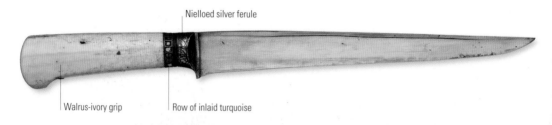

Nielloed silver ferule

Walrus-ivory grip

Row of inlaid turquoise

This dagger comes from Bukhara in Uzbekistan (formerly Turkestan), which was an important city on the Silk Road. Their weapons production famously employed the use of turquoise, either cut or polished, or as polished chips. The silver ferrule is decorated with niello (a shiny black alloy) and the grip is made from walrus tusk.

DATE	early 19th century
ORIGIN	UZBEK
LENGTH	unknown

Ottoman Turkish stiletto, early to mid-19th century

Gilt brass mounts

Blade as slender as possible, yet sufficiently strong so as not to bend or break

This unusual dagger dates from the period during the 19th century when Turkey was intensely influenced by Western Europe (especially France). It is Turkish-made, but this particular type of dagger is known as a stiletto in Europe. The hilt and sheath mounts are made from gilt brass, whilst the blade is a simple, slender but strong spike designed for maximum penetration.

DATE	early to mid-19th century
ORIGIN	OTTOMAN TURKISH
LENGTH	33.5cm (13.1in)

Persian khanjar, early to mid-19th-century

An attractive Qajar khanjar built to create an impression, this dagger is fitted with a dark-coloured watered blade that has been chiselled and false damascened with an allegorical scene of a lion attacking an antelope. The hilt features two cabochon turquoises in gold mounts; the use of gold on the black blade combines with the light-coloured walrus-ivory hilt to produce a rich effect.

Walrus-ivory hilt

Dark watered blade
(Qara Khorasan)

Allegorical scene of
strength victorious

DATE	early to mid-19th century
ORIGIN	PERSIAN
LENGTH	37cm (14.6in)

Lawrence of Arabia

T.E. Lawrence ("Lawrence of Arabia") famously led an army of Arab tribes to victory against the Turks during World War I. Many depictions of Lawrence, such as this portrait, show him wearing Arab dress and a dagger. One particular dagger owned by Lawrence has an interesting history. In 1917, he was in Jidda for talks with Sharif Husain – head of the Arab nationalists – when he made his way illegally to Mecca. There he ordered a dagger with a gold hilt and sheath, probably supplying his own gold sovereigns to be melted down. "I did it because I wanted to choose my own gold dagger ... (it was made) ... in the third little turning to the left off the main bazaar, by an old Najd goldsmith." Lawrence sold the dagger in 1923 for £125 to his friend Lionel Curtis, who presented it to All Souls College, Oxford, where it remains. He used the money to refurbish Clouds Hill, his Dorset home close to where he was killed riding his motorcycle on 19 May 1935.

RIGHT Portrait of T.E. Lawrence wearing the silver-gilt Meccan dagger presented to him by Sharif Nasir in 1917.

Balkan Ottoman bichaq, mid-19th century

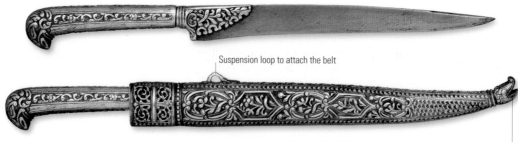

Suspension loop to attach the belt

Zoomorphic finial with a hole in the mouth to allow for drainage

A silver-mounted Ottoman knife, or bichaq, from the Balkans. The scrolling foliate ornament covers the hilt as well as the sheath, whilst the pommel is in the form of a stylized animal's head, as is the finial of the sheath. The blade of the knife is thin and probably intended to function mostly as a utility knife.

DATE	mid-19th century
ORIGIN	TURKISH (BALKANS)
LENGTH	27cm (10.6in)

Saudi Arabian janbiyya/khanjar, mid-19th century

This silver-mounted Arabian janbiyya is from the Hijaz-Asir region. The double-edged blade is almost flat and has a simple chiselled device. The hilt and sheath are covered with silver, which is decorated with engraved decoration, granulation and filigree. Colloidal hard soldering is the process whereby tiny silver balls (granulation) or decorative silver wire (filigree) are applied decoratively to a silver ground with an organic compound. The work is then covered with silver salt and heated until the organic compound is driven off, and the salt turns to metal and fuses the decoration to the ground.

DATE	mid-19th century
ORIGIN	SAUDI ARABIAN
LENGTH	56cm (22in)

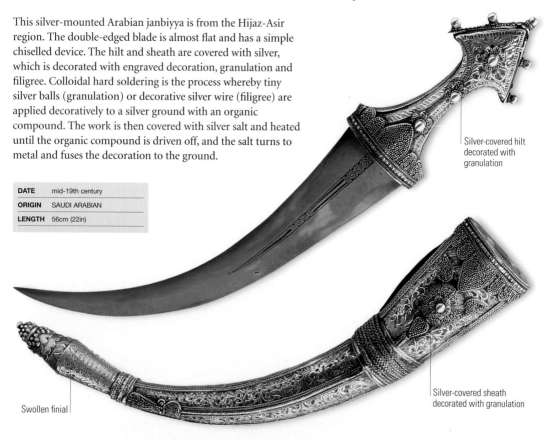

Silver-covered hilt decorated with granulation

Silver-covered sheath decorated with granulation

Swollen finial

Omani janbiyya/khanjar, mid-19th century

The hilt of this Omani janbiyya, or dagger, is made from horn, probably from a rhinoceros, and was presumably believed to possess magical properties or to confer virility to its owner. Subsequent to the decline in the supply of rhinoceros horn, the giraffe horn and hoof became a popular material for use on grips. Now that conservation has become of great concern, the grips are usually made from plastic.

Granulation and filigree decoration

Hilt made from rhinoceros horn

DATE	mid-19th century
ORIGIN	OMANI
LENGTH	unknown

Saudi Arabian janbiyya/khanjar, late 19th century

These janbiyyas with their distinctive long, curved blades are particularly associated with the conservative Wahabi sect of Sunni Muslims. The grip is made from horn, and reinforced with steel, copper and brass; the front has extensive silver ornamentation. The blade is noticeably thin and flat. The sheath, from a later date, is covered with multicoloured leatherwork.

DATE	late 19th century
ORIGIN	SAUDI ARABIAN
LENGTH	63cm (24.8in)

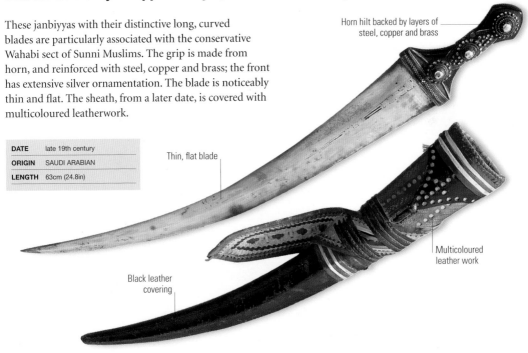

Horn hilt backed by layers of steel, copper and brass

Thin, flat blade

Multicoloured leather work

Black leather covering

Yemeni khanjar and sheath, late 19th century

This is the classic form of Arabian khanjar and probably comes from Yemen. The horn is decorated with gold-foil imitations of the Venetian ducat (coin).The gold ducat was clearly held in esteem long after the Venetians ceased to be actively involved in trade in the area. The blades are burnished bright and the Indian-made sheath is fitted with a pierced silver chape.

DATE	late 19th century
ORIGIN	YEMENI
LENGTH	28cm (11in)

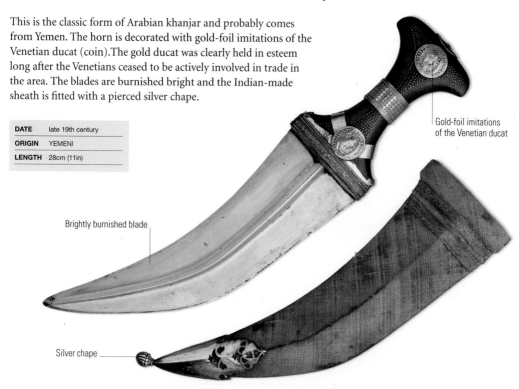

Gold-foil imitations of the Venetian ducat

Brightly burnished blade

Silver chape

Saudi Arabian janbiyya/khanjar, late 19th century

This massive dagger from Hijaz or Asir, western Saudi Arabia, is easily amongst the longest ever produced. The polished blade is stoutly reinforced by the raised central rib, and the hilt is secured by large and prominent silver-headed rivets. It seems likely that this weapon would also have been employed for various everyday purposes.

Large silver-headed rivets secure the grips

Stout reinforcing rib

Sheath covered in brown leather

DATE	late 19th century
ORIGIN	SAUDI ARABIAN
LENGTH	65cm (25.6in)

Persian khanjar, 19th century

Etched arabesque decoration

Two cutting edges
at this point

Carved walrus-tusk hilt

DATE	19th century
ORIGIN	PERSIAN
LENGTH	41cm (16.1in)

The hilt of this 19th-century Persian khanjar is carved from a single section of walrus tusk and depicts a fashionably dressed couple carved in relief. The curved blade is T-section for half the length of the back edge, and is etched at the forte with an arabesque design. The blade is also etched with a pattern intended to imitate the watering of "Damascus" steel.

Omani janbiyya/khanjar, *c.*1900

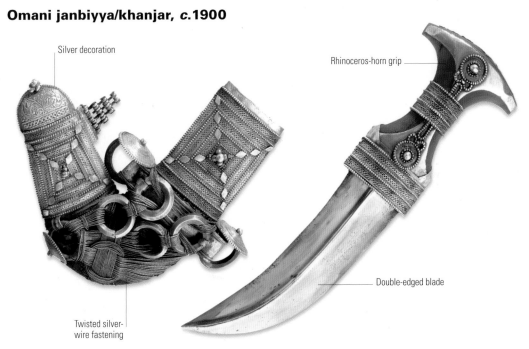

Silver decoration

Rhinoceros-horn grip

Double-edged blade

Twisted silver-
wire fastening

DATE	c.1900
ORIGIN	OMANI
LENGTH	32cm (12.6in)

The silversmiths of Oman are renowned for their skills, particularly in the use of granulation. The back of the chape is embossed by the maker ʾamal Abdullah Al-Beham ("the work of Abdullah Al-Beham"), and the front of the sheath sports seven thick rings of silver. These are secured with twisted-silver wire, and the largest outside rings are used to fasten the sheath to a broad belt.

Saudi Arabian (probably Meccan) janbiyya/khanjar, *c.*1900

Both the hilt and the sheath are entirely covered with sheet silver on this dagger which probably comes from Mecca. The decorative silver ornaments applied to the hilt help provide a decent grip, whilst the sheath has engraved borders and an upturned finial, or *thum* (literally, "garlic bulb" in Arabic).

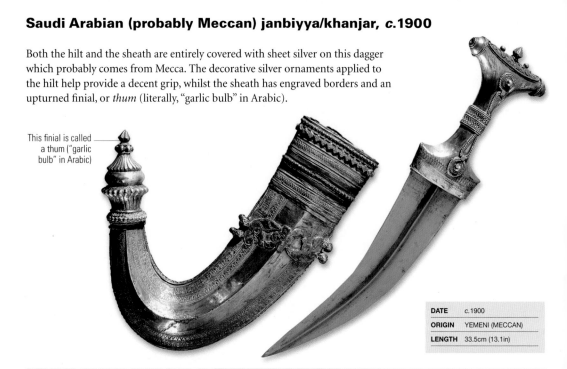

This finial is called a thum ("garlic bulb" in Arabic)

DATE	c.1900
ORIGIN	YEMENI (MECCAN)
LENGTH	33.5cm (13.1in)

Saudi Arabian janbiyya/khanjar, early 20th century

Few Arabian daggers are quite so distinctive as this example from Asir or Tehama in Saudi Arabia. The silver hilt and sheath display granulation as a decorative technique that also helps provide a firm grip. These elaborate daggers are still produced by Arab silversmiths for the tourist market today.

DATE	early 20th century
ORIGIN	SAUDI ARABIAN
LENGTH	46.5cm (18.3in)

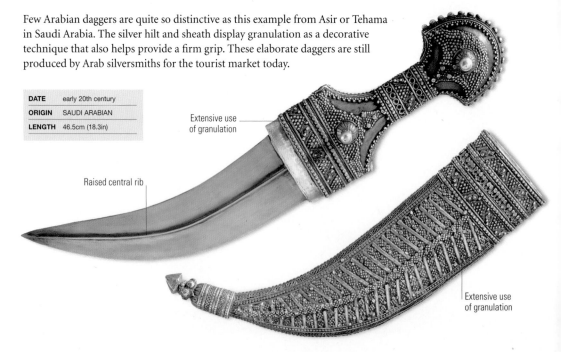

Extensive use of granulation

Raised central rib

Extensive use of granulation

Omani janbiyya/khanjar, mid-20th century

Perhaps the most common dagger from the Arabian Peninsula, this example comes from Oman. The wooden hilt is faced with an undecorated sheet of silver, whilst the silver band at the bottom is embossed with foliage, and is designed to fit over the top of the sheath to prevent the ingress of sand and water.

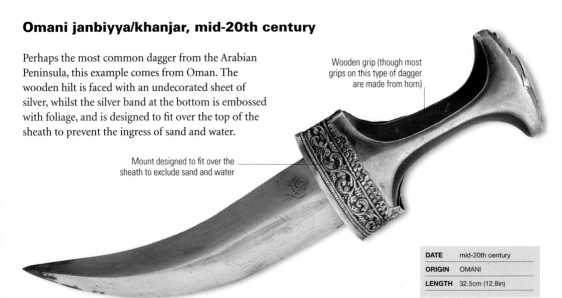

Wooden grip (though most grips on this type of dagger are made from horn)

Mount designed to fit over the sheath to exclude sand and water

DATE	mid-20th century
ORIGIN	OMANI
LENGTH	32.5cm (12.8in)

Omani janbiyya/khanjar, c.1975

This late 20th-century Omani janbiyya is of poor quality. These types of daggers were produced not only for the tourist industry but also to fulfil a domestic Omani convention that the janbiyya (or khanjar) is an integral part of the national dress. It is unlikely that such a weapon would ever be required to see service.

DATE	c.1975
ORIGIN	OMANI
LENGTH	99cm (39in)

Silver sheet

Top of chape fits within hilt mount

Embossed silver mount

Raised medial rib

227

Indo-Persian khanjars

The expression "Indo-Persian" covers both the vast subcontinent of India itself and the lands occupied or ruled over by Persia when its empire was at its apogee. *Khanjar* is the general Arabic word for dagger.

Often, however, the term is used by collectors to describe a body of daggers with curved, double-edged blades from India, mostly with jade hilts, and from Persia, frequently with walrus-ivory or steel hilts.

Indian khanjar with Mughal hilt, late 17th century

Gold koftgari decoration

Shallow fullers

Carved jade hilt

The hilt is made from dark green nephrite (jade), the supply of which is supposed to have been exhausted before the end of the 17th century. The classic Mughal "pistol"-shaped hilt is carved with flowers and foliage in relief. The blade, which is probably of later date, is decorated with a repeated interlaced geometric pattern in gold koftgari.

DATE	late 17th century
ORIGIN	INDIAN
LENGTH	unknown

Indian khanjar, *c.*1700

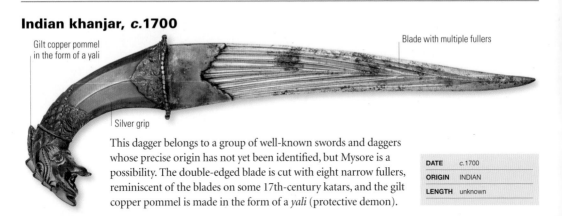

Gilt copper pommel in the form of a yali

Blade with multiple fullers

Silver grip

This dagger belongs to a group of well-known swords and daggers whose precise origin has not yet been identified, but Mysore is a possibility. The double-edged blade is cut with eight narrow fullers, reminiscent of the blades on some 17th-century katars, and the gilt copper pommel is made in the form of a *yali* (protective demon).

DATE	c.1700
ORIGIN	INDIAN
LENGTH	unknown

Indo-Persian khanjar and scabbard, early 19th century

A good-quality Persian dagger, the blade is of watered steel and is chiselled with the image of a lion attacking a gazelle (an allegorical scene). The ivory hilt is carved from a single piece of walrus tusk with figures and an inscription meaning "The shining blade of this amazing khanjar is so sharp it can split a thorn".

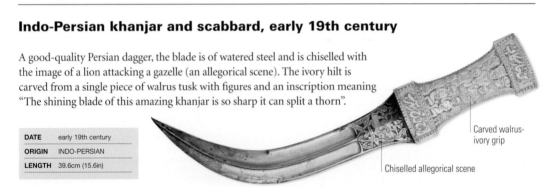

DATE	early 19th century
ORIGIN	INDO-PERSIAN
LENGTH	39.6cm (15.6in)

Carved walrus-ivory grip

Chiselled allegorical scene

Indian khanjar, *c.*1900

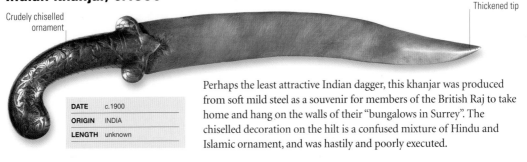

Crudely chiselled ornament

Thickened tip

DATE	c.1900
ORIGIN	INDIA
LENGTH	unknown

Perhaps the least attractive Indian dagger, this khanjar was produced from soft mild steel as a souvenir for members of the British Raj to take home and hang on the walls of their "bungalows in Surrey". The chiselled decoration on the hilt is a confused mixture of Hindu and Islamic ornament, and was hastily and poorly executed.

Indo-Persian five-bladed khanjar, mid-19th century

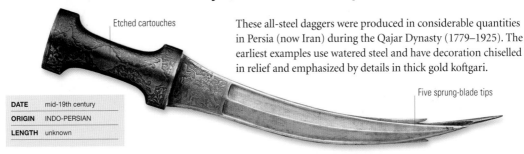

Etched cartouches

These all-steel daggers were produced in considerable quantities in Persia (now Iran) during the Qajar Dynasty (1779–1925). The earliest examples use watered steel and have decoration chiselled in relief and emphasized by details in thick gold koftgari.

Five sprung-blade tips

DATE	mid-19th century
ORIGIN	INDO-PERSIAN
LENGTH	unknown

Indo-Persian five-bladed khanjar, mid-19th century

Chiselled decoration

The three all-steel Persian daggers on this page each have blades with multiple points which spring apart once the dagger is unsheathed. The cutler requires considerable forging and tempering skills to produce these blades.

Etched Islamic inscriptions

Five sprung-blade tips

DATE	mid-19th century
ORIGIN	INDO-PERSIAN
LENGTH	45.5cm (17.9in)

Indo-Persian triple-bladed khanjar, late 19th century

Three sprung-blade tips

DATE	late 19th century
ORIGIN	INDO-PERSIAN
LENGTH	49cm (19.3in)

The steel grip of this triple-bladed dagger is filled with a plaster-like substance which swells when moisture is absorbed. When this happens, the braised seam will begin to split open, as is the case here. Cartouches filled with Islamic inscriptions can clearly be seen decorating the hilt.

Indo-Persian kards

Kard is Farsi (the most widely spoken Persian language) and refers to a dagger with a straight, single-edged blade where the hilt is without a guard. Collectors apply the term to similar daggers from India and the Middle East. They may be fitted with delicately worked hilts of exotic materials, with blades of fine watered steel, but each will be of the same form as those made from more common materials.

Persian gold-inlaid kard, *c.*1800

Single-edged blade | Gold-inlaid decoration | Walrus-ivory grip

A classical Persian dagger of *c.*1800, this kard has a fine watered-steel single-edged blade which is decorated with gold-inlaid foliage in relief at the forte. This decoration continues around the grip strap. The grips are made from two pieces of walrus ivory. It seems ironic that these beautiful daggers were intended to be entirely covered by their sheath, with the exception of the last inch of the hilt.

DATE	c.1800
ORIGIN	PERSIAN
LENGTH	37.5cm (14.7in)

Uzbek kard with lapis lazuli hilt, *c.*1800

Lapis lazuli hilt | Ring of turquoise

Lapis lazuli from Afghanistan is one of the most attractive stones with an intense blue colour. The ring at the base of the grip is decorated with polished turquoise, and this is almost a signature of production from Bukhara in Uzbekistan (formerly Turkestan). The small metal ferrule at the forte of the blade is also a feature of edged weapons from the Balkans.

DATE	c.1800
ORIGIN	UZBEK
LENGTH	34.7cm (13.6in)

Indian kard with stone handle, *c.*1800

Thickened tip | Finely chiselled detail | Hilt made from "the stone of Jaissalmer"

This high-quality Indian kard has a watered steel blade and is chiselled with foliage at the forte, while the tip is thickened to add strength at the point of impact. The hilt is made from "the stone of Jaissalmer", a yellow- and orange-coloured conglomerate which is highly attractive due to its clearly visible constituent parts.

DATE	c.1800
ORIGIN	INDIAN
LENGTH	44cm (17.3in)

Persian chiselled kard, *c.*1800

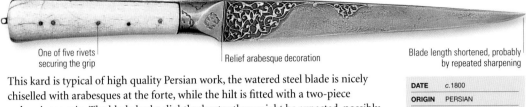

One of five rivets
securing the grip

Relief arabesque decoration

Blade length shortened, probably
by repeated sharpening

This kard is typical of high quality Persian work, the watered steel blade is nicely chiselled with arabesques at the forte, while the hilt is fitted with a two-piece walrus ivory grip. The blade looks slightly shorter than might be expected, possibly reduce in length by repeated sharpening during its working lifetime.

DATE	c.1800
ORIGIN	PERSIAN
LENGTH	38.5cm (15.2in)

Afghan "Khyber knife", early 19th century

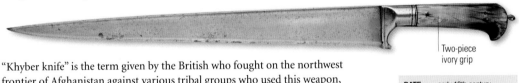

Two-piece
ivory grip

"Khyber knife" is the term given by the British who fought on the northwest frontier of Afghanistan against various tribal groups who used this weapon, including the Mahsud, Pathans, Afridis and Waziris. The term is a slight misnomer because these weapons were used more as short swords than knives. Apart from the general shape, the defining feature is the very strong T-section blade.

DATE	early 19th century
ORIGIN	AFGHAN
LENGTH	58.6cm (23.1in)

Persian/Turkestan kard, early 19th century

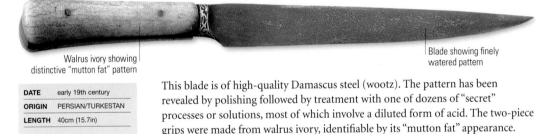

Walrus ivory showing
distinctive "mutton fat" pattern

Blade showing finely
watered pattern

DATE	early 19th century
ORIGIN	PERSIAN/TURKESTAN
LENGTH	40cm (15.7in)

This blade is of high-quality Damascus steel (wootz). The pattern has been revealed by polishing followed by treatment with one of dozens of "secret" processes or solutions, most of which involve a diluted form of acid. The two-piece grips were made from walrus ivory, identifiable by its "mutton fat" appearance.

Indo-Persian kard with green jade hilt, 18th century

Finely watered blade

Jade hilt

DATE	18th century
ORIGIN	INDO-PERSIAN
LENGTH	37cm (14.6in)

The back edges of kard blades are slightly convex. This blade is made of crucible steel and shows a "watered" pattern which is an intrinsic property of the metal. The blade could have been made in either India or Persia, whilst the tapered jade hilt was probably made within the Ottoman Empire or in India.

Indian kard, early 19th century

Spiral-carved
jade hilt

Gilt copper ferrule

Lahore is situated in the middle of the Punjab, and was an important centre of
weapons production, particularly for the Sikhs. The unifying feature of Lahori
arms production is the gold koftgari in geometric patterns, or a repeated
foliate and floral motif often incorporating arabesques.

DATE	early 19th century
ORIGIN	INDIAN
LENGTH	unknown

Indian kard, early to mid-19th century

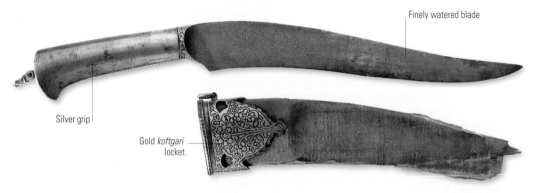

Finely watered blade

Silver grip

Gold *koftgari*
locket

The shape of this fine-quality dagger from Rajasthan is testament to the care
and skill of its maker. The recurved blade is made from finely watered wootz
(crucible steel) and the grips are silver. The remaining mount (locket) of the
sheath is decorated with gold koftgari. Rajasthan has a number of cities famed
for the excellence of their swordsmiths and edged-weapons production.

DATE	early to mid-19th century
ORIGIN	INDIAN
LENGTH	31cm (12.2in)

Indian silver-mounted kard, early to mid-19th century

Lion's-head pommel

Fairly crude blade

This silver-mounted Indian kard was probably made for a departing member of the
Raj, and is quite an appropriate metaphor for the British who were soon to leave
India. The lion looks both comic and bedraggled, a spent and forlorn force whose
time has come. The blade is the work of a smith rather than a cutler, whilst the
silver hilt and sheath have both been hastily fabricated.

DATE	early to mid-19th century
ORIGIN	INDIAN
LENGTH	unknown

Turkish kard, early to mid-19th century

Faceted jade grip | Gold false-damascened inscription | Watered wootz steel blade

DATE	early to mid-19th century
ORIGIN	TURKISH
LENGTH	26cm (10.2in)

This Turkish kard has been made with a jade hilt and the blade is of oriental Damascus steel (wootz). At the forte, next to the silver ferrule, it has been false-damascened with a gold inscription, typical of many kards and bichaqs produced in considerable quantities within the Ottoman Empire during the 19th century.

Afghan "Khyber knife", mid-19th century

Horn grips

DATE	mid-19th century
ORIGIN	AFGHAN
LENGTH	71cm (27.9in)

These short swords are always found with meticulously sharpened blades. Enormous strength was given to the blades by their T-section. The bolsters and grip straps were manufactured from steel or brass, and the grips, though normally of horn, were sometimes made from ivory or wood.

Afghan "Khyber knife", mid-19th century

Horn pommel

T-section blade with flat back edge | Brass ferrules | Bone grips

DATE	mid-19th century
ORIGIN	AFGHAN
LENGTH	72cm (28.3in)

The hilt of this "Khyber knife" is quite distinctive; there exists a matching smaller dagger which was probably carried through the same belt or sash. The grips are made from horn, though occasionally ivory was used, and the black buffalo-horn pommel is decorated with fine nail holes into which zinc foil has been pushed.

Turkish kard, c.1870

Gold false-damascened inscription | Gold-inlaid floral decoration | Pear-shaped pommel

DATE	c.1870
ORIGIN	TURKISH
LENGTH	35cm (13.7in)

The hilt of this Ottoman Turkish dagger is made from polished sections of hard stone which have been inlaid with gold in a floral pattern. Frequently daggers with this type of hilt are found to incorporate cylindrical sections of the *munal* (mouthpiece) from a discarded *nargil* (water pipe), often with undecorated pommels.

Indo-Persian peshkabz

These daggers are common to Persia and northern India. They have single-edged blades which can be straight, curved or recurved. They are normally encountered with a T-section blade which imparts considerable strength. These daggers are found in a multitude of different qualities, from the refined and exotic court workshop productions to those produced by the Pathan tribal smiths in Afghanistan.

Indian peshkabz, mid-18th century

Ivory grips · Gold koftgari ornament · Reinforced cutting edge

This Indian peshkabz is fitted with a blade of wootz steel which has been decorated with gold koftgari at the forte. The two-piece ivory grips show signs of cracking due to age. The slightly thickened cutting edge further reinforcing the strength of the blade can be clearly seen.

DATE	mid-18th century
ORIGIN	INDIAN
LENGTH	48cm (18.9in)

Persian peshkabz, c.1800

Blade sides swell outward to meet the back edge

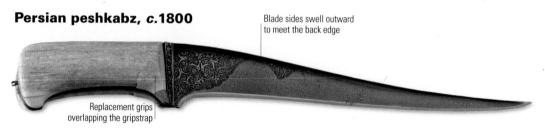

Replacement grips overlapping the gripstrap

The recurve-shaped blade is made from finely watered steel, and the sides swell sharply outward before meeting the broad back edge. Chiselled arabesque decoration adorns the forte. The replacement two-piece walrus ivory grip overlaps the gripstrap; the original grip would have only reached the edge of the gripstrap.

DATE	c.1800
ORIGIN	PERSIAN
LENGTH	42cm (16.5in)

Indian peshkabz, early 19th century

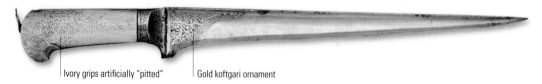

Ivory grips artificially "pitted" · Gold koftgari ornament

The blade of this peshkabz is probably the most lethally efficient of any stabbing dagger ever devised. It derives its strength from the T-section which extends almost to the point. Such a blade would be perfect for penetrating the riveted links of a mail shirt. The ivory grips have been typically "pitted" to provide a firm hold.

DATE	early 19th century
ORIGIN	INDIAN
LENGTH	43cm (16.9in)

Rajasthani gold-inlaid peshkabz, early 19th century

Button unscrews to reveal a hollow grip

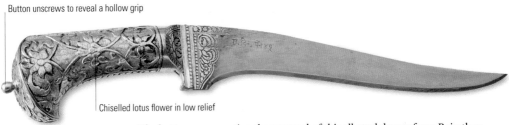

Chiselled lotus flower in low relief

DATE	early 19th century
ORIGIN	INDIAN (RAJASTHANI)
LENGTH	34.5cm (13.5in)

The button surmounting the pommel of this all-steel dagger from Rajasthan unscrews and the pommel hinges to reveal a hollow grip which could be used as a container. Similar but more elaborate examples contain small instruments, while legend has it that the space was used for more sinister purposes by would-be poisoners. The hilt is well chiselled in low relief with a repeated lotus flower pattern.

Indian peshkabz, early 19th century

The chape is missing and has been replaced with a piece of leather

Silver hilt and locket enamelled with wild animals

DATE	early 19th century
ORIGIN	INDIAN
LENGTH	31.5cm (12.4in)

During the 18th and 19th centuries, Lucknow was famous for, amongst other crafts, its enamel work. The silver hilt and locket of this peshkabz are decorated with diagonal bands inhabited by assorted wild animals in multicoloured enamel. The predominant colours associated with Lucknow are blue and green.

Indian peshkabz with gilt copper hilt, c.1850

Foiled glass, or pastes

Gilt copper mounts (not gold)

DATE	c.1850
ORIGIN	INDIAN
LENGTH	35.6cm (14.1in)

The hilt of this dagger is its most impressive part. It is made from gilt copper and is set with pastes of various colours. The overall effect is one of great richness, which has been achieved at limited expense. Such daggers were produced with matching sheaths and were made to satisfy the demand from well-off foreign buyers.

Indian knives, daggers and bayonets

The diversity of weapons found on the Indian subcontinent reflects the influences this area has absorbed from invading peoples throughout history. They include Persians, Greeks, Hindus and Muslims, with European influences later on. Apart from the excellence of their manufacture, it should be remembered that many weapons were invested with a spiritual or religious dimension by their owners.

Mysore bichwa, 18th century

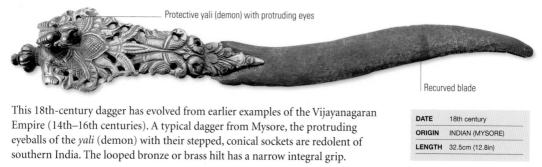

Protective yali (demon) with protruding eyes

Recurved blade

This 18th-century dagger has evolved from earlier examples of the Vijayanagaran Empire (14th–16th centuries). A typical dagger from Mysore, the protruding eyeballs of the *yali* (demon) with their stepped, conical sockets are redolent of southern India. The looped bronze or brass hilt has a narrow integral grip.

DATE	18th century
ORIGIN	INDIAN (MYSORE)
LENGTH	32.5cm (12.8in)

Mysore socket bayonet (sangin) of Tipu Sultan, late 18th century

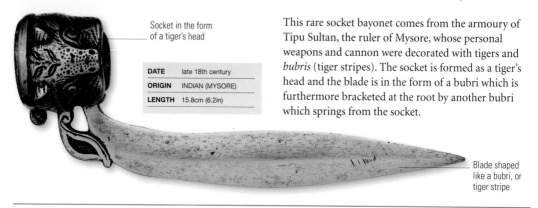

Socket in the form of a tiger's head

DATE	late 18th century
ORIGIN	INDIAN (MYSORE)
LENGTH	15.8cm (6.2in)

This rare socket bayonet comes from the armoury of Tipu Sultan, the ruler of Mysore, whose personal weapons and cannon were decorated with tigers and *bubris* (tiger stripes). The socket is formed as a tiger's head and the blade is in the form of a bubri which is furthermore bracketed at the root by another bubri which springs from the socket.

Blade shaped like a bubri, or tiger stripe

Indian plug bayonet signed by Anvar, late 18th century

Silver koftgari decoration

Ivory grip

Short cross piece

The European plug bayonet design was later used as a model for hunting knives in France and Spain in the second half of the 18th century. This example is a southern Indian interpretation of one such hunting knife. The blade and cross piece are decorated with silver koftgari and signed '*amal Anvar* ("the work of Anvar").

DATE	late 18th century
ORIGIN	INDIAN
LENGTH	57cm (22.4in)

Indian bichwa with double blade, *c.*1800

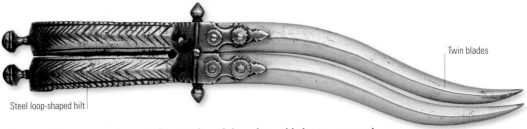

Twin blades

Steel loop-shaped hilt

The word *bichwa* means "scorpion" in Hindi, and these dagger blades are supposed to have gained their name from their likeness to the tail of a scorpion or from their ability to "sting". The steel hilt is loop-shaped and the knuckle guards are cut with chevrons. There are bud-shaped finials to the pommel, and two buds protrude laterally as short quillons, or guards. This example is quite uncommon in having two blades and probably comes from Hyderabad. Being relatively easy to make, the bichwa has persisted into the 20th century as a decorative dagger.

DATE	c.1800
ORIGIN	INDIAN
LENGTH	32.8cm (12.9in)

Nepalese kukri, mid-19th century

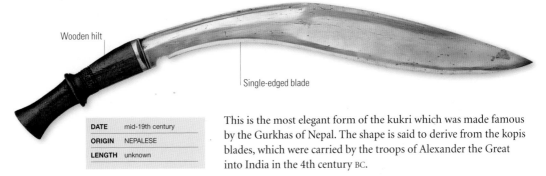

Wooden hilt

Single-edged blade

DATE	mid-19th century
ORIGIN	NEPALESE
LENGTH	unknown

This is the most elegant form of the kukri which was made famous by the Gurkhas of Nepal. The shape is said to derive from the kopis blades, which were carried by the troops of Alexander the Great into India in the 4th century BC.

Nepalese kukri, mid-19th century

The cho (or kauri), a feature of unknown purpose which has provoked endless speculation

Ivory lion's head

DATE	mid-19th century
ORIGIN	NEPALESE
LENGTH	40.6cm (16in)

The carving of a lion's-head pommel on the ivory grip of this kukri is a very unusual feature and denotes a high-status client. The blade too is a little unusual, and carving the channels and ridges into it in such a symmetrical and aesthetically pleasing manner requires a considerable degree of skill as well as artistry. The Gurkhas have earned a formidable reputation using this weapon for their fearlessness and bravery.

Mysore "knuckleduster" knife, early 19th century

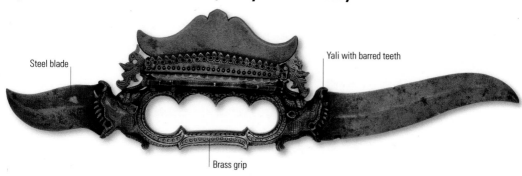

Steel blade

Yali with barred teeth

Brass grip

This very exotic-looking Indian weapon from Mysore is a "knuckleduster" with two blades. The grip is made from brass and the steel blades protrude from yali heads. The manufacture is particularly well executed. Similar weapons, without blades, are used for a type of fighting during Dasara festivities and are called vajramustis.

DATE	early 19th century
ORIGIN	INDIAN (MYSORE)
LENGTH	32cm (12.6in)

Indian "tiger-claw" dagger, early 19th century

Integral steel blade

Finger ring

Steel claws

The all-steel *bagh nakh*, or "tiger's claw", is a uniquely Indian weapon and is designed for slashing. One was famously used in 1659 by Shivaji when he killed Afzal Khan; it had been concealed until the last moment within the palm of Shivaji's hand. The two rings are for the outside fingers, and the other fingers would lie on top of the steel claws.

DATE	early 19th century
ORIGIN	INDIAN
LENGTH	unknown

Coorg Tamil knife (pichangatti), mid-19th century

"Clip back" tip

Silver hilt

Heavy blade with single edge

The *pichangatti* (the word means "hand knife") is a Tamil knife from Coorg. It has a broad, heavy, single-edged blade which turns up slightly at the tip. The hilts are often to be found made from silver, although brass and wood are also common. Most were made in the late 19th century and seem to have been used as utility knives or for chopping.

DATE	mid-19th century
ORIGIN	INDIAN (COORG)
LENGTH	unknown

Coorg Tamil knife (pichangatti), mid-19th century

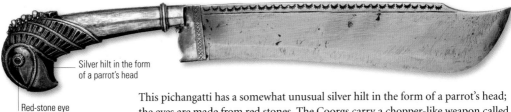

Silver hilt in the form
of a parrot's head

Red-stone eye

DATE	mid-19th century
ORIGIN	INDIAN (COORG)
LENGTH	25.5cm (10in)

This pichangatti has a somewhat unusual silver hilt in the form of a parrot's head; the eyes are made from red stones. The Coorgs carry a chopper-like weapon called an ayda katti in a metal carrier called a todunga, and this is held in place by a belt. The correct position for the pichangatti is in the front of this belt. The sheath of this knife is bound with silver and from it, suspended from a chain, is a small kit of personal grooming tools for cleaning nails and ears.

Assam dagger (dha) with carved horn hilt, mid-19th century

Single-edged blade

Carved horn handle
incorporating a demonic figure

DATE	mid-19th century
ORIGIN	INDIAN (ASSAM)
LENGTH	23.6cm (9.3in)

This type of dagger, called a dha, is the classic Burmese form and is often found with a carved ivory hilt. The blades are slightly curved and single edged. This particular example has an unusual, carved buffalo-horn hilt, and is said to have come from Assam, close to Burma but sufficiently distant to have developed a somewhat unusual hilt. Formal Burmese dha hilts are carved with an assortment of demonic figures, sometimes in contorted poses.

Mysore bichwa, mid-19th century

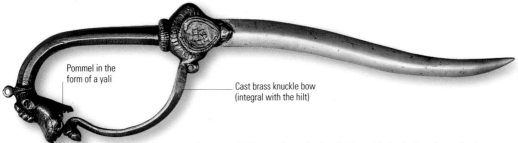

Pommel in the
form of a yali

Cast brass knuckle bow
(integral with the hilt)

DATE	mid-19th century
ORIGIN	INDIAN (MYSORE)
LENGTH	unknown

The recurved shape of this southern Indian bichwa blade derives from the horn daggers made by the Dravidians (aboriginal inhabitants of India), who made their daggers from lengths of animal horns. The brass hilt has been cast in one piece and the pommel is in the form of a yali. The root of the hilt, however, is of such confused and debased design that it is likely to be of quite a late date.

Indian katars

The Indian katar is a punching dagger and, as such, the design is unique. It is an ancient Hindu weapon which was adopted by the Muslims. Usually made of all-steel construction, the hilt commonly consists of a pair of handlebars at right angles to the sides which extend upwards parallel with the user's arm. The triangular-shaped blade is normally cut with a number of fullers, although in the 16th and 17th centuries it became fashionable to fit katars with European blades which have parallel sides.

Indian katar, 17th century

Yali head (protective demon)

Sail-shaped guard

Multifullered blade

This form of katar, with its sail-shaped guard and multifullered blade, comes from the Vijayanagara Empire, which lasted until 1646 but whose power declined after a defeat in 1565. The twin-ball shapes inbetween the handlebars are hollow, and the sail-shaped guard that protects the back of the hand has a finial in the form of a yali.

DATE	17th century
ORIGIN	INDIAN
LENGTH	56.5cm (22.2in)

Northern Indian katar, late 18th century

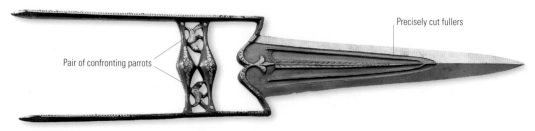

Precisely cut fullers

Pair of confronting parrots

The thickened tips of katar blades are often referred to as being "armour piercing". It is likely that only slender blades like this would stand a chance of performing that function. The twin handlebars are separated by a pair of confronting birds and the hilt retains traces of gold koftgari decoration. The fullers on the blade have been well cut.

DATE	late 18th century
ORIGIN	NORTHERN INDIAN
LENGTH	42.5cm (16.7in)

Rajasthani katar, 1800

Thickened point

Gold koftgari decoration

DATE	1800
ORIGIN	INDIAN (RAJASTHANI)
LENGTH	30.5cm (12in)

This is a classic Rajasthani katar which has seen much use. The thickened point is clearly visible, and the irregular and "waisted" outline of the cutting edges are testament to the vigorous and persistent sharpening that it has undergone. The hilt is thickly covered with a conventional design of gold koftgari decoration.

Indian katar with scabbard, early 19th century

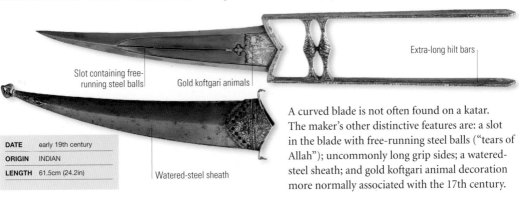

Extra-long hilt bars

Slot containing free-running steel balls

Gold koftgari animals

Watered-steel sheath

DATE	early 19th century
ORIGIN	INDIAN
LENGTH	61.5cm (24.2in)

A curved blade is not often found on a katar. The maker's other distinctive features are: a slot in the blade with free-running steel balls ("tears of Allah"); uncommonly long grip sides; a watered-steel sheath; and gold koftgari animal decoration more normally associated with the 17th century.

Rajasthani katar with elephant's head, dated 1849

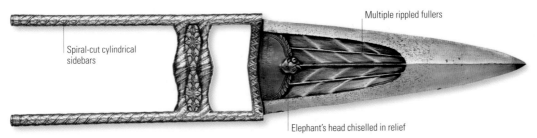

Multiple rippled fullers

Spiral-cut cylindrical sidebars

Elephant's head chiselled in relief

DATE	1849
ORIGIN	INDIAN (RAJASTHANI)
LENGTH	40.4cm (15.9in)

This katar belongs to a distinctive group of katars produced at Bundi in Rajasthan during the 18th and 19th centuries. This example is dated 1907, Vikrama era (AD1849), and belonged to the Maharajah of Bundi. Hand-forged, beautifully finished and with a hilt covered with gold foil, it was exhibited at the Great Exhibition of 1851 in Crystal Palace, London.

Indian katar, mid-19th century

Produced well into an era when such weapons had
almost become redundant, this katar is nevertheless
of reasonable quality. The hilt is decorated with gold
koftgari, and the steel sheath is pierced with a pattern
including pairs of confronting parrots within foliage,
all of which is enhanced by further gold koftgari
decoration. The extremes of both heat and moisture
encountered in India would have rendered steel a most
unsuitable material for a dagger sheath.

DATE	mid-19th century
ORIGIN	INDIAN
LENGTH	40.5cm (15.9in)

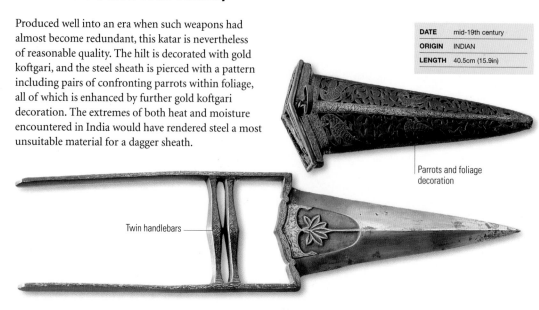

Parrots and foliage
decoration

Twin handlebars

Indian katar with two percussion pistols, 18th to mid-19th century

In order to embrace "modern technology",
a good-quality 18th-century Indian katar
has been refurbished during the middle of
the 19th century. A pair of percussion
pistols has been added to the hilt sides,
and the whole hilt has been covered with
silver-gilt koftgari. The resulting ungainly
weapon provides a strange foil for the
beautifully carved Mughal iris flowers at
the root of the blade.

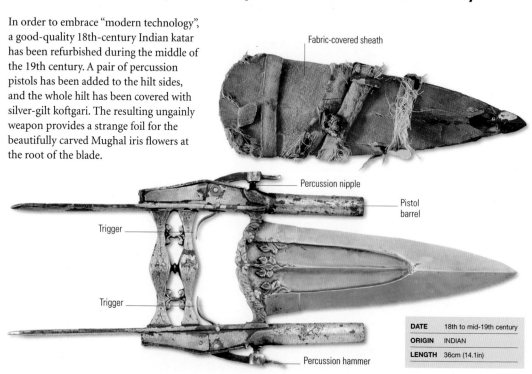

Fabric-covered sheath

Percussion nipple

Pistol
barrel

Trigger

Trigger

Percussion hammer

DATE	18th to mid-19th century
ORIGIN	INDIAN
LENGTH	36cm (14.1in)

Indian scissors katar, late 19th century

Silver koftgari decoration
of the poorest quality

DATE	late 19th century
ORIGIN	INDIAN
LENGTH	41cm (16.1in)

The scissors katar is mechanical and when the twin handlebars are squeezed tightly, the main hollow blades hinge open to reveal a shorter blade within. These were contrived for a European market, and however impractical, they appealed to the same sentiments as those invoked by Q's special weapons for James Bond.

Indian scissors katar, late 19th century

Two hollow blades hinge open to
reveal another blade within

Handlebars, when squeezed,
cause the blade to open

DATE	late 19th century
ORIGIN	INDIAN
LENGTH	36cm (14.2in)

This is another example of the scissors katar. A very similar example was given to the Prince of Wales during his tour of India in 1875–76 by the Raja of Mandi (in the Punjab). They are normally decorated with silver koftgari and their survival rate in the west, and in Britain in particular, seems to have been quite high.

Indian scissors katar, late 19th century

Hollow blades in
the open position

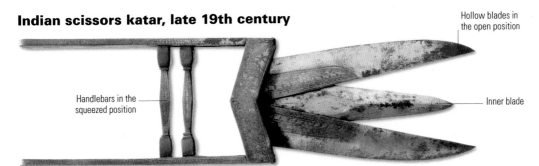

Handlebars in the
squeezed position

Inner blade

DATE	late 19th century
ORIGIN	INDIAN
LENGTH	40cm (15.7in)

Evidence that the design is fatally flawed is provided by the fact that the blades cannot be made to open once the katar has been thrust into a body, and if the katar were to be used with the blades in the open position the force on the outer blades would have to be absorbed by the hinge pins at the root of the blades.

Indian chilanums and khanjarlis

The chilanum is an all-steel dagger with a recurved double-edged blade. The blade shape probably developed from the Dravidian horn dagger which was made from a longitudinal section along an animal horn. Examples occur from the early 16th century in Vijayanagara, and were used by Hindus (Marathan) and Muslims (Deccani) alike. The dagger evolves in easily recognizable stages into the khanjarli, whose defining characteristic is the large, lunette-shaped pommel normally made of ivory.

Vijayanagaran chilanum, *c.*1600

This all-steel dagger represents the earliest form of chilanum in this group and the design can be seen in miniature paintings dating from the 16th century. It is made from a single piece of steel, and the grip and pommel button are both lathe-turned. Miniature paintings from the various Indian courts are an invaluable source of information for the student of Indian weapons. Although the artistic conventions result in images quite different from their European counterparts, details have been rendered with astonishing fidelity.

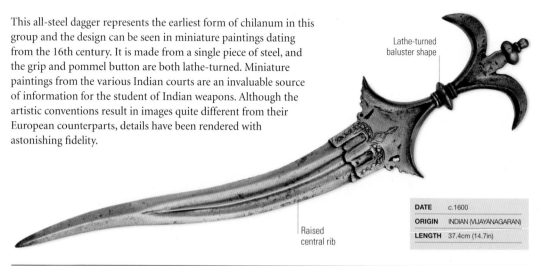

Lathe-turned
baluster shape

Raised
central rib

DATE	c.1600
ORIGIN	INDIAN (VIJAYANAGARAN)
LENGTH	37.4cm (14.7in)

Deccani chilanum with spiral decoration, early 17th century

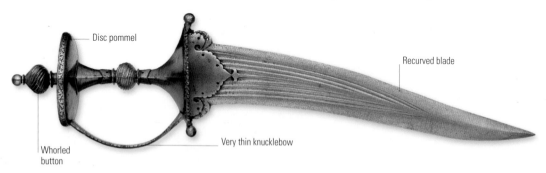

Disc pommel

Recurved blade

Whorled
button

Very thin knucklebow

A group of chilanums of identical design made of polished steel exist in Bikaner in Rajasthan. Probably originating in the Deccan, they are distinguished by their circular pommels, whorled buttons, and by their slender knucklebows which appear to be almost an afterthought. This example is unusual in having gold-damascened (koftgari) ornament; those in Bikaner are perfectly plain. It is not certain whether the decoration is contemporary or from a later period.

DATE	early 17th century
ORIGIN	INDIAN (DECCANI)
LENGTH	42cm (16.5in)

Indian Mughal dagger with knucklebow, *c.*1625

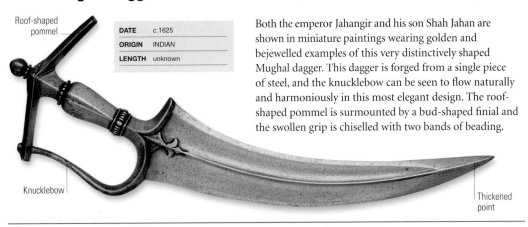

Roof-shaped pommel

Knucklebow

Thickened point

DATE	c.1625
ORIGIN	INDIAN
LENGTH	unknown

Both the emperor Jahangir and his son Shah Jahan are shown in miniature paintings wearing golden and bejewelled examples of this very distinctively shaped Mughal dagger. This dagger is forged from a single piece of steel, and the knucklebow can be seen to flow naturally and harmoniously in this most elegant design. The roof-shaped pommel is surmounted by a bud-shaped finial and the swollen grip is chiselled with two bands of beading.

Deccani chilanum, mid-17th century

Multifullered blade

Silhouette of a protective force

DATE	mid-17th century
ORIGIN	INDIAN (DECCANI)
LENGTH	39cm (15.4in)

Representing a classic and fully accomplished all-steel chilanum, the hilt of this dagger sits easily on the blade. The multifullered blade is reminiscent of katar blades from the same period. The pierced silhouette at the base of the hilt is a representation of a protective force.

Indian khanjarli, *c.*1700

Traditionally associated with Orissa and the Hindus of Vizianagram, khanjarli daggers probably come from a much wider area. Their defining design feature is the large lunette-shaped ivory pommel, the ivory grips, and the recurved blade which betrays their common ancestry with the chilanum. This example has a slender knucklebow.

Slender knucklebow

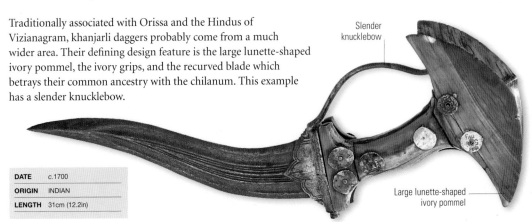

DATE	c.1700
ORIGIN	INDIAN
LENGTH	31cm (12.2in)

Large lunette-shaped ivory pommel

The Indonesian kris

The pre-eminent Hindu dagger from Indonesia is the kris. Examples from the 14th-century Majepahit Empire are not uncommon, and their lineage probably goes back to the Bronze Age Dong-Son era.

The smith would use iron from more than one source, one of which traditionally came from meteoric ore which had a high nickel content. The resulting blade patterns and carved hilts are highly regarded.

Sumatran kris, *c.*1800

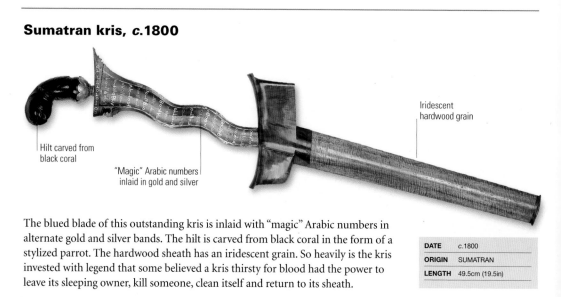

Iridescent hardwood grain

Hilt carved from black coral

"Magic" Arabic numbers inlaid in gold and silver

The blued blade of this outstanding kris is inlaid with "magic" Arabic numbers in alternate gold and silver bands. The hilt is carved from black coral in the form of a stylized parrot. The hardwood sheath has an iridescent grain. So heavily is the kris invested with legend that some believed a kris thirsty for blood had the power to leave its sleeping owner, kill someone, clean itself and return to its sheath.

DATE	c.1800
ORIGIN	SUMATRAN
LENGTH	49.5cm (19.5in)

Javanese kris, mid-19th century

The carved wooden hilt of this kris is intended to represent the god Raksha (or Raksasa), who is usually depicted with a long flowing coiffure. He is enveloped in foliage and his presence wards off evil spirits. The *pendok* (metal sheath covering) is made from nickel and chased with foliage. The armorial device engraved on the pendok was most likely introduced into Indonesia by the Dutch colonial power.

Wooden hilt carved with the god Raksha

Nickel pendok with engraved decoration

DATE	mid-19th century
ORIGIN	JAVANESE
LENGTH	35cm (13.8in)

Malayan kris, mid-19th century

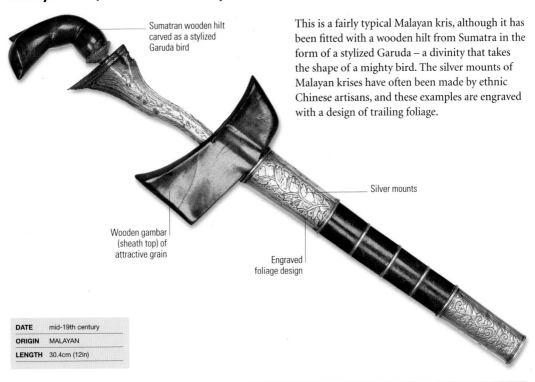

Sumatran wooden hilt carved as a stylized Garuda bird

This is a fairly typical Malayan kris, although it has been fitted with a wooden hilt from Sumatra in the form of a stylized Garuda – a divinity that takes the shape of a mighty bird. The silver mounts of Malayan krises have often been made by ethnic Chinese artisans, and these examples are engraved with a design of trailing foliage.

Silver mounts

Wooden gambar (sheath top) of attractive grain

Engraved foliage design

DATE	mid-19th century
ORIGIN	MALAYAN
LENGTH	30.4cm (12in)

Maduran kris, mid-19th century

Pamor (watering), revealed by etching

The ivory hilt of this kris is typical of those carved on the island of Madura. The top of the blade exhibits the *pamor*, or watered pattern, created by the smith who forged iron of differing composition. The silver *pendok* (stem cover) is elaborately embossed with a Bonaspatti mask, the face of a popular Hindu divinity.

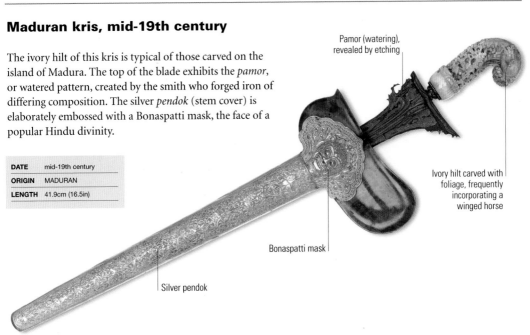

DATE	mid-19th century
ORIGIN	MADURAN
LENGTH	41.9cm (16.5in)

Ivory hilt carved with foliage, frequently incorporating a winged horse

Bonaspatti mask

Silver pendok

Malayan bade-bade, mid-19th century

Ferrule of gold

Hardwood sheath stem

Hilt carved from a sperm whale's tooth

The bade-bade is the classic Malayan knife. It has a slightly curved, slender blade sharpened on the inside edge. The hilt is carved from a whale's tooth, the sheath from hard wood and the top from ivory. Although mainly a cutting implement, the bade-bade could be used as a dagger.

DATE	mid-19th century
ORIGIN	MALAYAN
LENGTH	22.8cm (9in)

Malayan kris, mid-19th century

Malaya is rich in exotic timber, and very fine-grained woods have been chosen to manufacture this kris. The blades of such krises are often cleaned with lime juice, which relies on its citric acid content to etch the blade. They are then wiped with sandalwood oil for protection.

Blade cleaned with lime juice, then oiled with sandalwood oil.

Fine grain hilt

Fine "iridescent" grain

DATE	mid-19th century
ORIGIN	MALAYAN
LENGTH	33cm (13in)

Malayan kris, 19th to 20th century

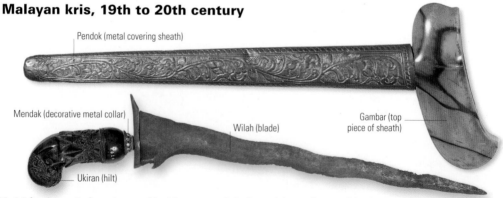

Pendok (metal covering sheath)

Mendak (decorative metal collar)

Wilah (blade)

Gambar (top piece of sheath)

Ukiran (hilt)

No Malaysian or Indonesian would wish to own a kris that might not be propitious for good health, good fortune, wealth or good luck. Consequently, the *lok* (waves) of the blade are each counted by a would-be purchaser. An odd number is considered auspicious to some, an even number to others. The blade of this Malay kris is 19th-century in origin but the hilt and sheath are 20th-century.

DATE	19th to 20th century
ORIGIN	MALAYAN
LENGTH	unknown

Javanese kris, *c.*1900

Classic Yogyakarta (Java) hilt

This is an example of the classic Javanese kris. The *pamor* (or pattern) of the blade is created by a smith working with two different steels, one of which usually contains nickel. When the blade has been polished, it is covered with an acidic coating (often lime juice) which etches the steels differentially, thus producing the visible colours. The *gambar* (top of the sheath) is carved from an exotic wood with the random patterns of "doreng" grain. The hilt is the classic Yogyakarta (Java) form, possibly the most commonly encountered.

DATE	*c.*1900
ORIGIN	JAVANESE
LENGTH	47cm (18.5in)

Pamor (pattern)

The kris stand

Traditionally, the kris was kept on a wooden board, which was often carved and sometimes painted. Only a very few antique sculptural kris stands of the type shown here are known. However, when Bali became popular as a tourist destination in the 1960s, a market developed for these extraordinary objects and production was revived. Skilfully carved from a single piece of wood, they are mostly in the form of brightly painted Hindu divinities. Typical figures include Ganesh (the elephant god), Hanuman (the monkey god) and Wayang figures (shadow puppets). Each figure is ostensibly designed for a kris to be held in the hand. The degree of skill used in the manufacture of some of the stands is very great indeed. The krises which the stands support also continue to be made and some are highly sought-after; the most exquisite specimens are very valuable.

RIGHT The stand on the right holds an "executioner's kris". The victim was tied to a chair and the long, slender blade thrust downwards into the heart.

Japanese daggers

The Japanese blade and its fittings represent the highest artistic achievement of the bladesmith anywhere in the world. They are regarded with the same reverence others hold for a great painting and its frame. Blades may be recognized as productions by different schools or individual smiths, and each will vary slightly in detail. Any comprehensive approach requires some understanding of Japanese and the swords and daggers themselves. To fully appreciate a blade's qualities, it must be held in the hand.

Japanese yoroi toshi, *c.*1400

Peg hole (mekugi-ana)

The blade of this yoroi toshi dagger is intended to pierce armour so is quite thin in width, broad across the back edge and almost straight. The tang (*nakago*) is pierced with a hole (*mekugi-ana*) to receive a bamboo peg which secures the hilt. The remains of an earlier such hole shows the blade was originally longer.

DATE	c.1400
ORIGIN	JAPANESE
LENGTH	30.6cm (12in)

Japanese aikuchi, 1625 and later

Hoshi mon (family badge) representing three stars

European signature (part), "Mefecit Solingen 1625"

The aikuchi is simply a Japanese dagger mounted without a guard (*tsuba*) to protect the hand. This dagger is almost certainly unique: the blade was made in Solingen (Germany) and is dated 1625. The rest was made later. It has been re-used by a Japanese smith and mounted for the Sanga family who used the *hoshi mon*.

DATE	1625 and later
ORIGIN	JAPANESE
LENGTH	48.7cm (19.2in)

Japanese tanto, late Edo, *c.*1840

Guard (tsub)

Pommel cap (kashira)

Grip ferrule (fuchi)

The attractive copper-alloy (*shakudo*) mounts of this tanto are decorated in relief with gold and are typical of the late Goto School. Warriors form a perennially favourite motif, and those here are worked in high relief against a granular ground (*nanako*) made with a punch that produces a tiny hemisphere.

DATE	late Edo, c.1840
ORIGIN	JAPANESE
LENGTH	39cm (15.3in)

Japanese ken, late Edo, *c.*1850

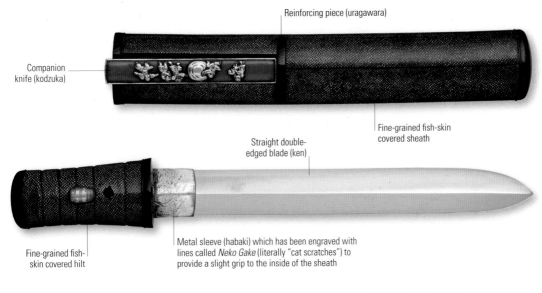

Reinforcing piece (uragawara)

Companion knife (kodzuka)

Fine-grained fish-skin covered sheath

Straight double-edged blade (ken)

Fine-grained fish-skin covered hilt

Metal sleeve (habaki) which has been engraved with lines called *Neko Gake* (literally "cat scratches") to provide a slight grip to the inside of the sheath

DATE	late Edo, c.1850
ORIGIN	JAPANESE
LENGTH	30.8cm (12.1in)

The straight double-edged sword or dagger is called a ken, and is the weapon carried by some Buddhist divinities. It originated in China from whence the sword (and Buddhism) was introduced into Japan during the 7th and 8th centuries. Consequently many such ken were made for temple presentation.

Japanese tanto, late Edo, *c.*1860

Wavy temper line (hamon)

One of a pair of hilt ornaments (menuki)

Skewer (kogai)

End mount (kojiri)

DATE	late Edo, c.1860
ORIGIN	JAPANESE
LENGTH	43.3cm (17in)

The hilt (*tsuka*) of this tanto is bound with silk tape, although sometimes string, leather or even baleen was used. The grip is covered with ray skin (*same*) and fitted with two small ornaments (*menuki*) before being bound. The menuki provide a more secure grip. The sheath is fitted with an end mount (*kojiri*) intended to protect the sheath, but in practice it is merely a vehicle for further ornamentation.

Japanese aikuchi, late Edo, *c.*1860

Silk strap (sageo), used to tie the sheath to a belt

Brass skewer (kogai)

Mouthpiece (koi guchi, meaning "carp mouth")

Lacquered hilt with brass mount

In this example of a Japanese aikuchi, the mounts (*koshirae*) are made from brass (*sentoku*), while the hilt (*tsuka*) and sheath (*saya*) are beautifully lacquered. This particular dagger was made in the second half of the 19th century during the late Edo period. The *kogai* (skewer) was carried in a slot in the scabbard.

DATE	late Edo, c.1860
ORIGIN	JAPANESE
LENGTH	33.5cm (13.1in)

Japanese tanto, Meiji, *c.*1870

Plain wooden hilt and sheath (shirasaya)

Bamboo fastening peg (mekugi)

Blade carving (horimono)

This blade is contained within a plain wooden hilt and sheath, usually made of magnolia wood, known as a *shirasaya*. It is entirely devoid of any fittings, and even the *habaki* has been replaced by a wooden equivalent made as an integral part of the hilt. The shirasaya is intended to protect the blade and to provide a suitable method of storage; it is not intended to be used. This blade has a carved decoration called *horimono*.

DATE	Meiji, c.1870
ORIGIN	JAPANESE
LENGTH	32cm (12.6in)

Japanese tanto, Meiji, blade date 1877

Utility knife (kodzuka)

Metal sleeve (habaki)

DATE	Meiji, blade date 1877
ORIGIN	JAPANESE
LENGTH	41cm (16.1in)

The beautifully lacquered, curved and segmented sheath of this tanto dagger probably betrays the maker's intention to sell it to a foreign (*namban*) buyer. The blade is dated 1877, and although some very fine blades were produced at this time the majority were intended for foreign consumption. The European "aesthetic movement" of the late 19th century was partly informed by Japanese art, and both Europe and the United States evinced a seemingly boundless appetite for Japanese art and artefacts.

Japanese dagger, early 19th century

Sheath lacquered for durability

Ray-skin (same)-
covered grip

Narrow grooves (hi)

DATE	early 19th century
ORIGIN	JAPANESE
LENGTH	43cm (16.9in)

A blade which has been formed with no ridges on either side has a shape called *hira zukuri*. This particular example has been cut with a pair of short shallow grooves called *hi*. The mounting is tasteful and of good quality. The sheath is covered with lacquer which provides a very durable finish; it is made from the ground-up wing cases of various beetles.

SWORDS
AND SABRES

From the primitive edged weapons used by
early humans through to those of the modern
world, the history of the sword is a
fascinating one. It has been used as a fighting
weapon, a symbol of authority, a mark of
social rank and as a ceremonial object.
This section features the history of swords
and sabres, followed by a visual directory of
the most significant swords and sabres, from
Ancient Egyptian and Saxon weapons to
Cavalry lances and presentation swords.

ABOVE A German cavalry officer's dress sword.
LEFT Depiction of the charge of the Scot Greys supported by the
Highlanders at the Battle of Waterloo by Richard Caton Woodville.

This section traces the fascinating history of swords, sabres, spears and lances through to the 20th century.

A history of swords and sabres

Since the first flint spearheads emerged at the dawn of humanity around 600,000 years ago, edged weapons have played an incredible role in the shaping of human history. Used by people as diverse as the ancient Egyptians, medieval knights and American civil war soldiers, these weapons have become some of history's most powerful status symbols.

TOP French dragoon officer's sword, Model 1854.

TOP RIGHT German Luftwaffe sword, *c.*1941.

MIDDLE Spanish swept-hilt rapier *c.*1650.

BOTTOM RIGHT French cavalry officer's sword *c.*1780.

The origins of edged weapons

Around 2.5 million years ago, the first recognized edged tools were developed when so-called "Stone Age" peoples began to fashion simple hunting tools from flint and obsidian. The impact of prolonged droughts and the constant territorial battle for a reliable source of food inevitably led to conflict between neighbouring tribes. The weapons of hunting, including the axe and spear, were soon readily transformed into weapons of combat.

LEFT The Neolithic period is known as the New Stone Age. This ancient cave painting depicts a hunting scene in Libya.

antler horn. Finely crafted examples of these laurel-leaf points were unearthed in the 1860s at the prehistoric site of La Solutré, near Mâcon in Burgundy. Sources of good flint were highly prized; it is thought that some communities would travel up to 160km (100 miles) in order to obtain suitable working materials for tools and weapons. Such advanced tools were first used by Neanderthal man, and then *Homo sapiens*, around 35,000BC. *Homo sapiens* and later sub-groups (such as

Early use of tools

The first widespread use of tools occurred during the Palaeolithic Age (the Old Stone Age), between *c.*2.5 million and 8500BC. The hand axe was the most important tool of this period and would have been designed to provide both a cutting edge and a sharp point. It is impossible to assign to these axes a purely combative role as their primary function would have been either to attack animals or to remove their flesh and hide, but the axes would no doubt have been effective as both slashing and thrusting weapons. Flint and stone were shaped and tied to a wooden handle, and then bound with animal sinew and tendons. Later, in the Neolithic period (the New Stone Age), 13,000–8500BC, an opening was developed in the axehead to accept a handle.

The Stone Age spear was one of the earliest weapons used for hunting animals. Like the hand axe, the spearhead would have been secured by tying it with sinew or leather strips to a longer handle.

Hand-held flint and stone tools were gradually replaced by finely sharpened flint blades. The process of manufacturing such blades involved a technique known as pressure flaking, which involved skilfully knapping the flint with a pointed piece of hard wood or

The Clovis Spear point

Clovis flint points are the oldest known flint projectile points found in North America. They date to around 13,500 years ago and were used by the ancient peoples of the Americas, the Paleo-Indians. The first Clovis flint point was excavated in Clovis, New Mexico, in 1931. Many points were excavated alongside the remains of hunted Ice Age animals, particularly mammoths. The points are thin, fluted in shape and created from pressure flaking. Due to their small size, they were easily carried and became one of the first highly mobile edged tools, or possibly weapons, in human history. Inhabitants of the Americas in the Archaic period (8000–1000BC) are believed to be direct descendants of Paleo-Indians.

ABOVE This is an Archaic period Clovis spear point from the Americas. The Archaic period preceded the adoption of farming.

Cro-Magnon man) began to create semi-permanent agricultural settlements in the Old World between 35,000BC and 10,000BC.

From hunting to farming (7000–6000BC)

Following the end of the Ice Age (10,000BC), humans began to make the transition from semi-nomadic hunters to creators of established farming communities. The practice of agriculture began in the then fertile plains of Mesopotamia (comprising present-day Iraq, Turkey, Syria and Jordan). The natural requirement for defence of these settled areas also coincided with the development of more robust, edged weapons. One of the earliest excavated farming settlements can be found in the village of Çatal Hüyük (c.6700–5650BC) in central Anatolia (present-day Turkey). Numerous pressure-flaked projectile points and simple flint

daggers were found during excavations, and indicate that the use of tools, whether for domestic or defensive purposes, had become an important part of daily life.

The Americas (8000BC–AD1000)

Paleo-Indians are believed to be the first people to have inhabited a large number of areas in the Americas about 11,000 years ago. It is thought that they were nomadic hunter-gatherers. Paleo-Indians are understood to have hunted with both fluted, stone-pointed wooden spears and the atlatl (a leveraged weapon that fired short spears). In addition, they probably foraged for edible plants. The Archaic period (8000–1000BC) is characterized by subsistence economies supported through the exploitation of nuts, seeds and shellfish. Between 1000BC and AD1000 Woodland Indians hunted small game and foraged in the forests.

The atlatl – Stone Age machine gun

Archaeologists believe that during the Palaeolithic Age, points or darts were attached to short wooden shafts and then mounted into sockets on heavier spear shafts. This created a form of reloadable, hand-held spear, or *atlatl* (taken from the Aztec language, Nahuatl).

The back end of the spear was fitted into the atlatl. The thrower would hold the atlatl and its flint dart in place, with the elbow bent and the hand resting beside the ear. A forward motion with the shoulder straightened the elbow and the wrist flicked the atlatl forward, creating the necessary momentum to propel the dart at great speed – an action which has been compared to that of a fly fisherman casting his line. Atlatl weights, commonly called "banner stones", are wide and flat shaped, with a

large hole drilled into the centre. This may have been a clever improvement to the design as it made the atlatl quieter when swung, so it was less likely to alert prey or other hunters. However, another theory suggests that the banner stone was carried primarily by hunters as a spindle weight to produce string from natural fibres gathered while hunting.

Atlatls are thought to have originated in North Africa over 25,000 years ago. These weapons have been recreated in modern times and shown to have the potential to kill animals at 40m (131ft). Despite their obvious capability to kill humans, they are more likely to have been used for hunting and bringing down big game. Great skill would have been required to wield such a weapon although its accuracy tends to decrease when used over larger distances.

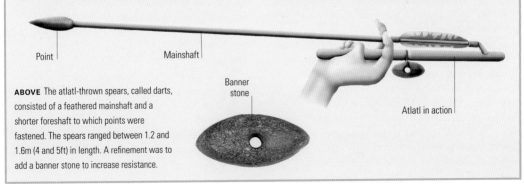

Point | Mainshaft | Banner stone | Atlatl in action

ABOVE The atlatl-thrown spears, called darts, consisted of a feathered mainshaft and a shorter foreshaft to which points were fastened. The spears ranged between 1.2 and 1.6m (4 and 5ft) in length. A refinement was to add a banner stone to increase resistance.

Bronze Age weapons

New technologies to refine, smelt and cast metal ores were first used during the Bronze Age (*c.*3500–700BC). Early civilizations in the Middle East began to combine bronze or copper alloys to produce spears, daggers, swords and axes. Later, swordsmiths started producing finely detailed swords with stronger iron blades. These techniques spread to China, India, South-east Asia and Europe, where they would have a profound influence on future warfare.

Pommel | Hilt | Raised strengthening ridge

Early metal weapons

With the introduction of copper alloys (90 per cent copper and 10 per cent tin), the bronzesmith was able to produce a much harder metal. Its hardness and consequent durability were wholly dependent on the temperature that could be achieved during smelting. The higher the temperature, the harder the metal would become. Iron ore was also discovered and soon became the material of choice for the production of bladed weapons. Iron ore was abundant and, like copper alloys, it could be heated to high temperatures by using charcoal. Immersion of the blade in water and continuous hammering to form a well-tempered blade developed a consistent surface that was less prone to fracture and breakage than bronze or copper. Most blades would have been cast in stone, metal or clay moulds.

The sword in Europe from *c.*2000BC

Although it is difficult to date precisely when the sword was first introduced into Europe, there is general agreement that long-bladed swords were being manufactured around 2000BC. Their appearance in Europe was probably independent of earlier developments in metalworking seen in the Near East and the Aegean. Distinctive flint swords have been found from this date in Denmark and northern Europe, including riveted bronze swords with triangular blades from the early Bronze Age.

In the later Bronze Age, swords were cast in one piece, including the grip and pommel (the knob at the top of the handle or hilt). Many differing pommel

ABOVE This short sword was made between 3200 and 1150BC. The decorated hilt and round pommel were later replacements.

shapes also emerged. One of the most common swords is the antenna (or voluted) sword. This had a two-pronged or scrolled, inwardly curving pommel, said to represent the outstretched hands of a human figure. Sword shapes also varied, from broad-leaf shapes to straight forms that featured grooves, sometimes erroneously described as "blood channels", but more likely to have been designed to provide a lighter and more easily wielded sword.

The carp's tongue sword

Common in western and eastern Europe around 1000BC were a group of bronze swords known as "carp's tongue" swords. A significant number of this distinct sword type were discovered at excavations in the Thames Valley and Kent during the mid-20th century. The most notable find was at the Isleham Hoard, in Cambridgeshire, England. It comprised more than 6,500 objects made of bronze, including many swords of carp's tongue design. They had wide, tapering blades which were useful for slashing, with a thinner, elongated end suitable for stabbing. This style of sword is thought to have originated in north-western France.

The socketed axe

Another important military innovation of the Bronze Age Mesopotamian armies in the Middle East, and one that would have an enormous impact on future

Hilt and blade cast in one piece

Leaf-shaped blade

BELOW These Bronze Age socketed axes were used as both domestic tools and close-quarter combat weapons.

ABOVE A complete Bronze Age sword (top) with hilt and leaf-shaped blade (c.1100BC) and a large bronze spearhead (bottom) from 700BC.

battlefield warfare, was the introduction of the socketed axe. Previously, ancient axe makers had struggled to keep the axehead firmly attached to the haft (the handle), especially when handling the axe with considerable force. The Sumerians devised a cast bronze socket that slipped over the haft and was secured with rivets. Its development was probably a consequence of the introduction of primitive forms of body armour and the need to penetrate this armour with sufficient force. Later axes would have narrower points that could be used to penetrate bronze plate armour. The axe would remain an integral battle weapon for the next 2,000 years.

The sickle sword of Mesopotamia

One of the earliest societies in which organized warfare was waged was the Sumerian culture of southern Mesopotamia (c.3000BC). Even at this early stage of human civilization, professional standing armies were being used to defend communities. Although the most common weapons used by the Sumerians, and later the Assyrians (c.1100–600BC), included the spear and bow, warriors also carried a sharply curved sickle sword.

Introduced around 2500BC, this all-metal sword had a single-handed grip and a blade of around three grip lengths. A stunning example in the British Museum,

London, England, has the following inscription on the blade: *Palace of Adad-nirari, king of the universe, son of Arik-den-ili, king of Assyria, son of Enlil-nirari, king of Assyria.* It is believed that this sword was owned by the Assyrian king Adad-nirari I, who conquered northern Mesopotamia (c.1307–1275BC). Mesopotamian art frequently depicts the sickle sword as a symbol of authority, and it is often seen placed in the hands of gods and kings.

BELOW An illustration of a sickle sword, 1307–1275BC, from the Middle Assyrian period (the reign of Adad-nirari I).

Single-edged blade

Ancient Egyptian weapons

The Egyptian armies of the Old Kingdom (c.2649–2134BC) and Middle Kingdom (c.2040–1640BC) fought primarily on foot and in massed ranks. Their soldiers were lightly equipped with shield, bow, spear and axe. The constant wars and invasions of the later dynasties brought with them the assimilation and transference of diverse military technologies. This greatly expanded their range of weapons, which diversified to include plate armour, chariots and, more importantly, the sword.

Introduction of the sword

Following the collapse of central government in Egypt due to internal rebellion, the Hyksos peoples of Palestine took advantage of this instability and invaded Egypt around 1640BC. They ruled Egypt for over 200 years and brought with them striking advances in weapon making, particularly the use of metal in the manufacture of swords and edged weapons.

The adoption of the sword in ancient Egypt was a direct consequence of the introduction of metal. Prior to this, axes and spears were fashioned from flint, and swords were simply not available. Copper had already been utilized for some time, but bronze was the first material consistently used for sword blades, as it was much harder and easier to work. Sickle-shaped swords (originally inherited from the Sumerians) were gradually replaced by swords with slightly curving blades. The "Sea Peoples", invaders from the Aegean and Asia Minor who first attacked Egypt during the reign of Merenptah (1213–1202BC), also introduced straight, two-edged blades with sharp, stabbing points. Contemporary depictions of battles show massed infantry using both jabbing and slashing swords.

The influence of iron

Throughout the Mediterranean during the New Kingdom period of Rameses III (c.1186–1155BC), the smelting of iron ore had a direct impact on Egypt, enabling swords to be produced with much longer and sturdier blades. Examples of swords with blade lengths of up to 75cm (30in) have been unearthed from royal tombs.

RIGHT This ancient Egyptian warrior is depicted carrying a long, double-edged and broad-bladed sword. It is probably a one-piece construction.

The spear

Primarily a weapon used for hunting, the Egyptian spear never surpassed the bow and arrow, which remained the standard weapon of the Egyptian Army. During the Old Kingdom (c.2649–2134BC) and Middle Kingdom (c.2040–1640BC), simple pointed spearheads were constructed from either flint or copper and attached to long wooden shafts by means of a tang (the hidden portion or "tongue" of a blade running through the handle). In the later New Kingdom (c.1550–1070BC), stronger bronze blades were secured by a more reliable socket.

Spears were made for either throwing or thrusting, and were especially useful when chasing fleeing enemies and stabbing opponents in the back. They were regarded primarily as auxiliary weapons and called upon by charioteers when they had spent all their arrows and needed some form of close protection. The following description of Amenhotep II's victory at the Battle of Shemesh-Edom c.1448BC (in Upper Galilee, now modern-day

LEFT Carved by an unknown Egyptian artist during the 18th Dynasty, c.1567–1320BC, this relief depicts two soldiers, one carrying a spear.

The khepesh – sword of the Pharaoh

Originally a throwing weapon of sickle-sword shape, the khepesh could also be used as a conventional slashing or cutting sword. It appears to have been a favoured weapon of the Pharaoh, as he is often depicted wielding it against enemies or during a hunt. The discovery of the tomb of Tutankhamun (r. c.1361–1352BC) by Howard Carter in 1922 revealed remarkable insights into the lives of ancient Egyptians. One of the numerous objects found in the tomb included a ceremonial shield, which depicted the young Pharaoh "smiting a lion" with a khepesh.

ABOVE The Tomb of Tutankhamun. The king is depicted in a number of battle scenes, although it is not known whether he actually took part in any campaigns.

Inside edge

Ivory handle

ABOVE An Egyptian bronze khepesh sword with a handle inlaid with ivory. The sword comes from El-Rabata and dates to the New Kingdom, c.1250BC.

Israel) is recorded at the Temple of Karnak (built over a period of some 1,600 years from around 1500BC), near Luxor in Egypt:

Behold His Majesty was armed with his weapons and His Majesty fought like Set in his hour. They gave way when His Majesty looked at one of them, and they fled. His Majesty took all their goods himself, with his spear…

Karnak Stele of Amenhotep II
from W.M. Flanders Petrie, *A History of Egypt, Part Two.*

The battle-axe

There were two distinct types of battle-axe used by the Egyptian soldier: the cutting axe and the piercing axe. The cutting axe, used during the early kingdoms, had a head attached to a long handle and would have been used at arm's length. The blade head was attached to the handle through a groove and then tightly bound with leather or sinew. This axe was especially effective against opponents who wore little body armour, particularly Egypt's African enemies, like the Nubians. It was usually deployed after the enemy had been routed (often by the archers), rather than as a weapon against massed ranks.

The cutting axe was later superseded by the piercing axe that was designed to penetrate armour. Unlike contemporary Asiatic societies (especially the Sumerians and the Assyrians), who used a blade cast with a hole through which the handle was inserted and firmly attached by rivets, the Egyptians continued to use the antiquated method of a mortise-and-tenon joint (a tenon is a tongue that slots into a hole called the mortise) to fix the blade to the handle. This made the battle-axe inherently weaker. During the invasion by the Hyksos around 1640BC, this obsolete weaponry, coupled with the invaders' use of horse-drawn chariots, long swords and stronger bows, proved fatal for the lightly armed Egyptians.

ABOVE A painted relief of light infantry with standards, battle-axes and palm fronds, from the temple of Hatshepsut in Thebes, Egypt, c.1480BC.

Ancient Greek weapons

The ancient Greeks (*c.*750–146BC) regarded the sword as strictly an auxiliary weapon, one that would never supplant their battle-proven reliance on the spear. The spear enabled the heavily armoured hoplites, or infantrymen, to stand together and protect each other within the close formation of their phalanx wall of shields and spears. This allowed them to repeatedly fight and win battles against far superior opposition.

The hoplites

Infantry foot-soldiers, the ancient Greek hoplites (from the Greek word *hoplon*, or armour) formed the military backbone of the Greek city states. Hoplites were recruited mainly from the wealthier and fitter middle classes, and bore the financial responsibility to arm themselves. Bronze armour, sword, spear and shield all had to be provided from solely private means. Hoplites were not full-time professional soldiers whose only life was war. They had volunteered to serve their state only in times of war (usually in the summer), and, if they survived, would return afterwards to their civilian roles. The hoplite was a true manifestation of the classical Greek ideal of shared civic responsibility.

ABOVE Mosaic showing Alexander the Great, leader of the Macedonians, hunting a lion with a doru (spear) in the 3rd century BC.

The spear

A Greek infantryman's main battle weapon was the spear, or doru. Measuring around 2.7m (8.8ft) in length, it would have been held in one hand, while the shield (aspis) was grasped in the other. The spearhead was leaf-shaped, socketed and made of iron. At the butt of the shaft was a sharp bronze spike, or sauroter ("lizard killer"), which could be thrust into the ground for added stability. In extremis, when the spearhead was broken, the sharp spike could be flipped around and used as a weapon of last resort.

The Macedonians, under the leadership of Alexander the Great (356–323BC), also developed their own spear or pike, the sarissa. Little is known about it, but it is thought to have been up to twice the length (around 4–5m/13–16.4ft) of the doru and had to be wielded underarm with two hands. This meant that the usual protection of the shield-and-spear phalanx could not be utilized, and so a small shield, or pelte, was strapped to the left forearm. The sarissa's great length meant that it could keep the opposing troops at a distance, enabling the Macedonian cavalry to wheel around the flanks of an enemy and strike with devastating effect.

ABOVE Spartan hoplites, *c.*500BC, wearing Corinthian helmets. In addition to the shield and spear, hoplites would have also carried a sword.

The phalanx – ancient armoured fist

Derived from the Greek word *phalangos* (meaning "finger"), the hoplite phalanx was made up of a tight formation of spearmen, armed with large, concave shields that rested on the soldier's left shoulder and protected the man next to him, thus forming an all-enveloping, locked curtain of defence. The phalanx was typically about eight men deep, with the front ranks projecting their spears forwards. The key to the success of the phalanx was the ability of the soldiers to keep together and not break the formation. This was not always easy, especially for the first few ranks, who were the main combatants, as the rear ranks' main purpose was to continually push their phalanx forward and maintain its shape.

There has been much debate as to how the spear was used while in the phalanx: was it held aloft or under the arm? Some authorities believe that it had to be held aloft, as it would have been impractical for a hoplite to hold his spear underarm, in case the sharp butt spike injured the man behind him. The use of the sword by the hoplites in the phalanx would have been regarded as a highly dangerous manoeuvre, because it necessitated breaking up the shape and, consequently, the defensive cohesion of the phalanx.

LEFT A stone depiction of Greek hoplites standing in phalanx formation, from *c.*400BC.

The sword

There is great irony in noting that the most successful sword design of the Ancient World was developed by the Greeks, who were ostensibly spearmen. The sword was never regarded as a main battle weapon and played a purely secondary role. Once the spears had been thrown or lost in battle, swords were then engaged to finish the conflict in a decisive manner.

The main battle sword of the ancient Greek military was the xiphos. Introduced around 800–400BC, it comprised a straight, double-edged, leaf-shaped blade of around 65cm (25.6in), and was particularly effective at slashing and stabbing. The Spartans carried a slightly shorter sword of the same design as the xiphos. This design probably influenced the later Roman gladius, or short sword.

Mounted Greek cavalry used a curved sword, or makhaira (meaning "to fight"). It had a large, slightly curved falchion-type blade and was designed to deliver a heavy slashing blow at speed.

The use of a curved blade for mounted horsemen would remain a constant feature of cavalry swords for the next 2,500 years.

ABOVE A frieze from the Mausoleum of Halicarnassus, *c.*350BC, depicting a mythical battle between the Greeks and the Amazons.

Ancient Celtic weapons

The warrior Celts (*c.*600BC–AD50) were famed for their ferociousness and tenacity in battle, and even received grudging respect from their Roman adversaries. The early Celts fought mainly on foot (later in chariots and on horseback), and relied heavily on the awesome psychological and physical impact of a massed charge of their warriors. Armed with either sword or spear and protected with little more than a shield or helmet, they defeated the mighty Roman legions and, in 390BC, even sacked Rome itself.

Symbolism of the Celtic sword

The Celtic sword symbolized to its owner power, strength, honour and ultimate glory in battle. The fine quality and extraordinary skills required to produce these swords meant that they were extremely expensive and normally reserved for nobles and chieftains. The sword was often buried with its owner amongst his many other possessions, or symbolically thrown into water as a gift to the gods or spirits.

The falcata

With a large inwardly curving, single-edged blade rather like a kukri (heavy, curved Nepalese knife), the falcata was an extremely devastating weapon. Hilts were iron, hook-shaped and sometimes decorated with stylized horse or bird-head pommels. The origin of the

falcata was pre-Roman and it is likely to have been a development of the ancient Greek sickle-shaped sword, or kopis. The sword could deliver a very powerful blow, something akin to an axe strike but with the slashing capabilities of a conventional sword. Contemporary Roman writers often describe how the falcata had the capacity to split both shield and helmet. The Celts of Hispania (Spain) were said to be the most feared exponents of this sword and it was a common weapon encountered by Roman forces during the early years of the Roman Republic (509–124BC).

The manufacture of the falcata

During this possibly unique process of manufacture, various forged steel plates were buried in the ground, usually for more than three years, and allowed to corrode. They would then be dug up and any weak or spurious metal would be separated and discarded. Any remaining good steel was reforged again through the traditional Celtic method of pattern welding – the practice of forming a blade from several metal pieces of differing composition. The blades were then forge-welded together and manipulated to form a pattern, making it considerably harder. In response to these much tougher blades, the Roman legions redesigned their shields and armour to give them more protection. The introduction of the Roman gladius, or short sword, was said to be a direct reaction to the Roman soldiers' battlefield experience of the falcata.

Longer Celtic swords

The growing use of cavalry and, later, the war chariot meant that Celtic warriors needed a longer sword to effectively reach down and strike at an opponent.

LEFT Relief plaque, made from copper with silver and gold plating, of a warrior wielding a long-bladed Celtic sword from the 1st century AD.

These long swords, with an average blade length of around 70cm (27.5in), had wood, bone or horn hilts, with blades manufactured in iron or steel. Scabbards were normally constructed from plates of iron and suspended from a belt of iron links.

The Celts were one of the first European peoples to discover how to smelt iron, and by the time they made contact with the Romans they had developed consistent methods of producing better balanced swords that were more resilient and longer. It is therefore curious that the Roman writer Polybius (c.203–120BC) reported that, at the Battle of Telamon (225BC), the Gauls had carried inferior iron swords which bent at the first stroke and had to be straightened with the foot against the ground. This is also mentioned by Plutarch (c. AD46–127), but it seems more likely that this was Roman propaganda, as subsequent archaeological testing of excavated Celtic sword blades indicates that the quality of the iron and steel was quite exceptional.

The spear

A standard battlefield weapon for the Celtic warrior, the Celtic spear or javelin normally comprised an ash wood pole around 2m (6.5ft) in length, fitted with a large iron, leaf-shaped and socketed spearhead.

ABOVE Three Celtic spearheads from the La Tène period, each with a leaf-shaped, finely ridged, slightly bent blade. Two of the examples have holes in the socket for attaching the head to the shaft.

Following military experience gained after initial contact with the Roman armies from the 1st century AD, the Celts changed the design of their spearheads so that they possessed a narrower profile. This was a reaction to the Roman use of protective body armour and the need to find a spear that could effectively puncture their plate. Spears and javelins were also carried in bunches by young warriors, or "gaesatae". These were paid mercenaries who had gained a fearsome reputation for their bravery. Once they had thrown all the spears at the enemy, they would retrieve them from the ground or their opponents' bodies.

The swords of the La Tène culture

Archaeological finds from the La Tène settlement on the north edge of Lake Neuchâtel in Switzerland, dating to around 500–1BC, highlight the Celtic genius for creating swords with complex abstract and organic decoration on both the hilt and the scabbard. Blades were double-edged and straight, and made from pattern-welded iron or steel. They are found in both long and short versions. Many finely worked hilts also feature human heads and other anthropomorphic and zoomorphic motifs.

RIGHT A 1st or 2nd century BC sword and scabbard from La Tène in Switzerland.

Ancient Roman weapons

The army of ancient Rome (800BC–AD476) was a formidable fighting force – well disciplined, organized and supplied with an array of effective and battle-proven weapons. The sword and spear were the infantryman's main weapons, and the spectacular military successes of the Roman legions throughout Europe and the Near East lay in the disciplined battlefield application and relentless training in the use of these weapons.

The gladius

A short stabbing weapon with a blade length of around 50–60cm (19.6–23.6in), the gladius was the primary fighting sword of the Roman soldier. Its origins are somewhat uncertain, simply because very few examples have been unearthed by archaeologists and the only identifiable gladii have come not from Italy but from Germany. This sword was described by the ancient Romans as the "gladius hispaniensis", in recognition of a similar type of Celtic design encountered by the Romans during their conquest of Hispania (modern-day Spain) during the Second Punic War (218–201BC). Before this, Roman soldiers would have used swords of Greek origin.

The hilt, or capulus, of the gladius featured a rounded grip, moulded with four finger ridges to allow a comfortable and firm hold upon the sword. Pommels were bulbous and normally of plain form. The scabbard was made of wood, covered with leather and strengthened by a rigid frame of brass or iron.

Wearing the gladius

Although in later centuries most swords would be worn traditionally on the left side, the gladius was worn on the right side. This allowed the wearer to draw with the right hand and at the same time carry a heavy shield in the left hand. This can be confirmed from the depictions of Roman soldiers on tombstones, wall paintings and friezes. The tombstone of Annaius Daverzius, an auxiliary infantryman who served with the Cohors III Delmatarum, a Roman garrison stationed in Britain during the 1st century AD, shows his sword attached on the right side of his belt by four suspension rings. As an acknowledgement of his status, a centurion was allowed to wear his sword on the left.

RIGHT Legionaries, carrying gladius swords, are depicted during battle in a relief carving from the base of a column found at Magonza, Italy.

The gladius in battle

If used with enough force and directed at the most vulnerable parts of the body, particularly the stomach, the stab of a gladius blade into the flesh of an opponent was nearly always fatal.

Roman soldiers fought as a single fighting unit within an organized and massed formation. This fighting block comprised hundreds of men standing

ABOVE A battle between Roman and Germanic armies, depicted as a relief on a marble sarcophagus, *c.* AD180–190.

shoulder to shoulder. They had to keep this formation solid and it was crucial, therefore, that all soldiers fought with the gladius placed in their right hand. Any left-handed recruit would have this hand strapped behind his back during training, and it would be kept tied until he learned to fight with the right hand as well as he would have done with the left. Wearing the gladius on the right also meant that the drawing of the sword would not interfere with soldiers on either side, and would also not restrict the use of the Roman scutum (the shield).

The Roman line would wait for the enemy to come right up to it and then await the order to advance. Upon receiving this order, all soldiers would take one step forward and thrust their shields, or scuta, into the bodies and faces of the enemy, causing them to lose their balance and so render them temporarily vulnerable. The shield was then quickly withdrawn and the gladius thrust into the body of the opponent. The Roman soldier was taught to deploy the gladius horizontally, so piercing the enemy's ribs and penetrating to his vital organs.

BELOW A gladius and scabbard, which belonged to an officer of Tiberius (42BC–AD37), the second Emperor of Rome.

Etched gold decoration

Traces of wood from scabbard

Steel blade, badly rusted and corroded

The spatha

By the middle of the 1st century AD, the gladius had been replaced by the spatha (*spada* is the modern-day Italian word for sword). It had a much longer blade (60–80 cm/23.6–31.5in) and shorter point. The sword was Celtic in origin and it is probable that Gallic cavalry (from Gaul, in modern-day France), in the employ of Rome, introduced the sword to the Roman Army during the time of Julius Caesar (100–44BC) and Augustus (63BC–AD14). It was a slashing weapon and designed to be used by both the Roman cavalry and infantry.

The manufacture of swords

By the time of the Roman Republic (*c.*509–44BC), the use of steel in the manufacture of swords was well advanced and Roman swordsmiths smelted iron ore and carbon in a bloomery furnace (the predecessor of the blast furnace). The temperatures in these furnaces could not achieve the high levels required to fully melt the iron ore, so the swordsmith had to work with pieces of slag (residue left after smelting) or bloom (mass consisting mostly of iron), which were then forged into the required blade shape. These pieces or strips of cooling metal were welded together for increased blade strength. During this process the owner's initials or full name were sometimes engraved onto the blade.

The pilum

Around 2m (6.5ft) in length, the main heavy spear or javelin used by the Roman Army was the pilum. It consisted of a socketed iron shank with a triangular head. The pilum weighed in at around 3–4kg (6.6–8.8lb); later versions produced during the Empire (27BC–AD476) were lighter. The pilum would have been thrown by charging legionaries and could easily penetrate shield and armour from a range of around 15m (49.2ft). A lighter, thrusting spear, the hasta, was also used for close-combat situations.

The narrow, spiked shape of the spearhead meant that when it became stuck in the wood of an opponent's shield it was extremely difficult to dislodge, so disrupting the opponent at a critical moment of battle. He might have to relinquish his shield, leaving himself extremely vulnerable to the oncoming Roman infantry. Even if he was able to remove the spear, he couldn't throw it back at the Romans because the soft iron of the spear shank meant that it bent on impact and so became useless as a weapon. In the aftermath of a Roman victory, used pila were gathered from the battlefield and sent back to the Roman Army blacksmiths for straightening. The Roman military strategist Vegetius (*c.* AD450) comments on the effectiveness of the pilum:

As to the missile weapons of the infantry, they were javelins headed with a triangular sharp iron, eleven inches or a foot long, and were called piles. When once fixed in the shield it was impossible to draw them out, and when thrown with force and skill, they penetrated the cuirass without difficulty.

from *De Re Militari* (*c.* AD430)

Later, a further development of the pilum was introduced: the spiculum. Vegetius notes its power:

They had likewise two other javelins, the largest of which was composed of a staff five feet and a half long and a triangular head of iron nine inches long. This was formerly called the pilum, but now it is known by the name of spiculum. The soldiers were particularly exercised in the use of this weapon, because when thrown with force and skill it often penetrated the shields of the foot and the cuirasses of the horse.

from *De Re Militari* (*c.* AD430)

The contos

A long, wooden cavalry lance which was 4–5m (13.1–16.4ft) in length, the contos derived its name from the Greek word *kontos*, or "oar", which probably gives some indication as to the length of the lance. It took two hands to wield, so the horseman had to grip his mount by the knees. To be able to do this effectively would have taken considerable strength and training.

ABOVE Made in the Roman provincial style, this contos lance head dates from the 2nd century AD.

LEFT Roman soldiers carrying light spears (lancea) and shields. Detail of a relief from the Antonine Column, Rome, erected *c.* AD180–196 in recognition of the Roman victory in battle over a Germanic tribe.

BELOW Dating from AD70, this inscribed Roman commemorative stone depicts a horseman (Vonatorix) wielding a spear.

Saxon weapons

Around AD400, the Saxons came to England with a reputation for warlike ferocity and a strong reverence for the sword as a potent symbol of both strength and martial spirit. The mass of Anglo-Saxon warriors normally carried a shield and dagger (seax) and fought with spears and axes. More sophisticated members of the nobility and professional soldiers carried spears (similar to the Roman pilum) and swords.

The Saxon sword

Through excavating numerous graves in England, archaeologists have learnt that the Anglo-Saxons often chose to bury their dead with a full array of weapons and armour. These grave weapons are normally of great beauty and artistry, highlighting the belief that a warrior needed to take with him into the afterlife (or in later Christianized Anglo-Saxon society – heaven), material proof of the great status afforded to its owner while alive.

Ownership of both sword and spear defined the Anglo-Saxon warrior as a free man, compared with slaves (oeows) who were forbidden from carrying any arms. The great cost of acquiring a serviceable sword would also have shown the owner to be a man of means and rank. A typical Anglo-Saxon sword had a long, straight, double-edged blade with an average length of around 90cm (35.4in).

The Saxon spear

In Anglo-Saxon burial grounds, the spear is by far the most common type of weapon unearthed and is regarded as the primary armament of the Anglo-Saxon warrior. All ranks of society carried the spear, from king and eorl (earl), to the lowly ceorl (free man of the

Double wings

Long spearhead for deeper penetration

ABOVE A winged Saxon spearhead (top) with double wings to prevent an opponent's blade travelling down the spear. A slim spearhead (bottom) to allow penetration through armour.

lowest rank) or conscripted peasant. Comprising a leaf-shaped iron spearhead and wooden shaft, traditionally made of ash, a typical spear measured around 1.5–2.5m (4.9–8.2ft) in length.

The spear would have been held in one hand while a shield was grasped in the other. It was extremely effective when used in a mass formation, most notably the famous Anglo-Saxon "shieldwall" or shildburh. It was this shildburh that faced William the Conqueror at the Battle of Hastings. It was only compromised when

BELOW In a detail from the Bayeux Tapestry, 1082, the English soldiers, who are all on foot, protect themselves with a shield wall while the Normans mount a cavalry attack.

The Saxon battle-axe

Anglo-Saxon warriors inherited the two-handed "bearded" battle-axe from earlier generations of Danish Viking invaders who had employed it with great effect to board enemy ships. The Anglo-Saxons soon became extremely proficient at using the battle-axe. With its 1.2m (3.9ft) haft and large honed axehead of around 30cm (11.8in), it had the capacity to shatter shields and inflict grievous wounds. Swung from side to side, it could cut down a mounted soldier and his horse in a single blow.

These long axes were wielded by the huscarls (King Harold's personal bodyguards) and described as cleaving "both man and horse in two". One of the drawbacks of using the two-handed axe is that while raised above the head it momentarily left the user dangerously exposed at the front to sword or lance

thrusts. Despite this, the sight of a mass of axe-wielding Anglo-Saxon warriors approaching the enemy's ranks normally had the desired psychological effect, with many contemporary accounts noting that the opposition simply fled from the battlefield.

RIGHT A later depiction of the felling of King Harold II (c.1022–1066) by a Norman arrow at the Battle of Hastings (1066).

the Normans feigned a cavalry retreat, deliberately allowing themselves to be chased, whereupon they suddenly wheeled back and charged the openly exposed Anglo-Saxons. This was a fatal error by the pursuers and dictated the eventual outcome of the battle.

In contemporary descriptions of the Battle of Maldon in AD991 (situated on the modern-day Essex coast in England), the Anglo-Saxon Eorl Byrhtnoth is depicted as throwing two types of spear or javelin, both long and short. It is interesting that it was only when injured by a Viking spear, and finally exhausting his supplies of spears, that he eventually resorts to using his sword.

Anglo-Saxon women warriors

It was not only men who fought and became respected heroes during the Anglo-Saxon period. Recent archaeological discoveries have raised the possibility that women also took part in warfare.

In the village of Heslerton, in North Yorkshire, England, two female burials were unearthed in 2000. Dated to around AD450–650, both women had been buried with spears and knives. Just outside Lincoln, a town in eastern England, the skeleton of another Anglo-Saxon woman warrior (c. AD500) was found with a dagger and shield.

Procopius (c. AD500–565), the late Roman Byzantine scholar, notes in his history of the Gothic Wars (AD535–552) that an unnamed Anglo-Saxon princess, from the tribe of Angilori and described as "the Island Girl", led an invasion of Jutland (western Denmark) and captured the German King Radigis of the Varni.

Aethelflaed, eldest daughter of Alfred the Great of England (c. AD849–899), was known as the Lady of Mercia and was at the forefront of many battles against the invading Vikings. Aethelflaed was also responsible for the construction of a number of Anglo-Saxon fortifications.

The Sutton Hoo sword

The sword is part of a magnificent hoard of royal Anglo-Saxon treasures found in a huge ship grave, in Suffolk, England, in 1939; its design is based on the earlier Roman spatha, or cavalry sword. Its decoration includes a hilt comprising a beautiful gold and cloisonné garnet pommel and gold cross guard. The iron blade is heavily corroded but the original pattern welding is still identifiable and includes eight bundles of thin iron rods hammered together to form the pattern. This would have given the sword exceptional strength, although it is more likely that it was produced solely as a sumptuous grave gift.

Viking weapons

The Vikings were Scandinavians who colonized parts of Europe from the 9th to the 11th century. Vikings revered the sword above all weapons. The passing of a family sword from father to son was considered a major event. Even better was the knowledge that a sword had been wielded in battle or in a feud by a great warrior or nobleman. This gave the sword added status and was thought to imbue the blade with special powers. The Viking armoury also included the spear and battle-axe, the first-line weapons launched against an enemy.

Double-edged blade

Viking weapons

The main Viking battlefield weapons employed during first contact with the enemy were the spear and battle-axe. One of the reasons why the sword usually took a secondary role in the initial phase of a battle was that the continual striking of one sword

ABOVE A Viking sword from the 10th century with lobed pommel. The wide, double-edged blade would have made it a very powerful weapon.

edge against another would have inflicted large nicks to the blade and eventually removed the consistency and effectiveness of its finely sharpened edge.

Because of this, once the spear or axe had done its work, the Viking warrior would then draw his sword and look for exposed and softer areas of the body to attack. Skeletons of Viking battlefield victims unearthed by archaeologists consistently exhibit more spear wounds than sword cuts, highlighting the selective use of Viking swords in battle.

The Viking spear

A Viking warrior's most common battlefield weapon, the spear, comprised a simple iron, broad-leafed or spiked point on a wooden (normally ash) shaft, with a total length of around 1–2m (3.2–6.5ft). Spearheads with wings were called barbed spears. The spear was extremely effective and used for both thrusting and throwing, with larger-headed spears being used for cutting. There is evidence that the spears used to cut through chainmail were used one-handed as well as two-handed. A skilled Viking spearman was reputed to be able to throw two spears at once, using both hands, and also to catch a spear in flight and hurl it back at the opposition. A sword was then used in close-combat fighting.

LEFT A 9th-century Viking-decorated stone carving from Gotland, Sweden, depicts two soldiers fighting with swords.

Pommels and scabbards

The Viking sword pommel (located at the end of the hilt) is one of the most distinctive characteristics of a Viking sword. Most pommels were cast in solid iron (its weight providing a counterbalance to the weight of the blade), but there are also fine examples in bronze and also of iron inlaid with sheets of silver. Pommels ranged from the early pyramidal shapes of c. AD800 to the later, more complex pommels that were formed from triangular segments.

The great artistry and imagination of the Viking metalworker is clearly evident in these pommels and cross guards, with complex interlaced and geometric patterns worked in both silver and bronze gilt.

A scabbard (sheath or case) was made of two carved pieces of wood, glued at the sides and sometimes covered in leather or fur. The mouth and chape (the metal plate at the point) of the scabbard

ABOVE A Viking sword hilt with a cocked hat or lobed pommel. The decoration includes stamped abstract cartouches.

were sometimes mounted with decorated silver or bronze gilt. The sword would have been carried using a baldric (waist or shoulder belt).

The Viking battle-axe

When wielded with appropriate force, the Danish long-handled or "bearded" battle-axe was a devastating weapon. Its design was based on domestic Viking wood-splitting axes found throughout Scandinavia during the Viking period and evolved for use in battle. The battle-axe had a much larger head of either crescent or convex shape, which favoured downward blows, with a long wooden haft measuring 1–2m (3.2–6.5ft) in length. Sometimes blades were forged with an especially hardened double edge. They could also be forged quite thinly to give the user a lighter, more easily handled weapon.

The Viking sword

About 70–80cm (27.5–31.5in) long, the wide, double-edged blade of a Viking sword had shallow fullers, or so-called "blood grooves". The grooves were not actually designed to allow the blood to run down easily but rather to reduce the weight of the blade and give it added flexibility. The Vikings had a very close relationship with their swords, borne out by the personalized names they gave them, including Gramr ("Fierce"), Fotbitr ("Leg-biter") and Meofainn ("Decorated down the middle"). Swords were not common or inexpensive weapons and it is likely that they were mainly carried by persons of rank and wealth.

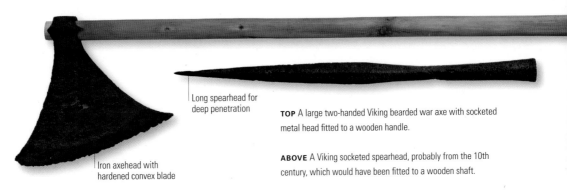

Long spearhead for deep penetration

Iron axehead with hardened convex blade

TOP A large two-handed Viking bearded war axe with socketed metal head fitted to a wooden handle.

ABOVE A Viking socketed spearhead, probably from the 10th century, which would have been fitted to a wooden shaft.

Viking sword manufacture

The smelting of iron ore with carbon to produce fine steel was well known to the Vikings and contributed to their reputation for producing blades of superb quality. They are best known for the complex process of pattern welding employed in their manufacture.

Modern X-ray technology of surviving blades now enables us to see how Viking smiths produced patterned blades by welding long strips of iron and steel together, forging them into square rods then finally twisting or folding these rods into small bunches, so creating the hard inner core of the blade. The outer cutting edge of the blade was welded to this inner core, using the best steel. Finally, the blade was carefully ground and polished with acid to reveal the extensive patterning.

Smiths worked hard to produce their own distinctive patterns. Their pride in such skilled work resulted in many blades being engraved with their makers' names, notably "Ulbehrt", "Lunvelit" and "Ingelri".

RIGHT A 12th-century carving from a wood panel in a church in Setesdal, Norway, depicts a scene from the Norse legend of Sigurd (Siegfried). Here, the dwarf Regin and his helper are shown forging a sword on an anvil.

Viking sword duels

The Vikings engaged in formal duels, or holmganga, to settle feuds. Holmganga roughly translates as "island going" and indicates that most duels took place on small islands where limitations of space (and, consequently, options for retreat), could be strictly enforced. The area of combat was determined by the laying out of a square cloth. Furrows were marked out around the cloth and the space was enclosed by a rope. Each of the combatants was allowed a second whose role was to hold the warrior's shield. Swords were the weapon of choice.

The duel did not commence with both warriors rushing at each other. Instead, each man took his turn at making one strike against his opponent. If a combatant chose this opportunity to back off and in so doing placed his foot outside the cloth, he was deemed to have run away and the fight would be stopped. If a strike was effective and incapacitating, the wounded party was allowed to stop the fight but was then obliged to forfeit a sum of money to his winning opponent.

RIGHT Two swords that display the distinctive punched and geometric decoration that was common on Viking sword pommels.

Orkneyinga Saga

Settling a feud by single combat with swords is a common theme in Viking sagas. One of the most famous accounts of the bloody use of a sword in such a feud is retold in the *Orkneyinga Saga* (c.1200), a unique historical narrative of the Orkney Islands that covers the period from its capture by Norwegians in the 9th century until the early 1200s.

The saga recounts how Rognvald, a Norwegian chieftain who ruled Orkney in c. AD860, was burnt to death in his own home by two of Harald Fairhair's sons. Bent on revenge, Rognvald's son Einar struck down and killed one of Harald Fairhair's sons, Halfdan Halegga. The victim's body was found the next day on the side of a hill, and the shape of an eagle had been cut into his back with a sword. More gruesomely, the ribs had been removed from the backbone and his lungs splayed out to represent the eagle's wings. Einar believed this display a worthy sacrifice to the Norse war god, Odin.

RIGHT The Norse god Odin with his sword and two ravens. He was the god of war and battle and the bringer of victory.

The sword in Viking sagas

The Vikings were great storytellers and believed that recounting tales was a gift, handed to them by the all-powerful war god, Odin. Without any means of writing them down, the Viking storytellers or skalds prided themselves on recalling epic stories and passing them on to others. Through these tales, the Vikings ensured that details of their religious beliefs and adventures were passed on from one generation to the next. Skalds were often employed by kings who wanted to be revered throughout their kingdoms. Although the stories were likely to have been exaggerated by the skalds, there is probably some truth in their telling of the events that occurred.

The ancient sagas of both the Vikings and the Anglo-Saxons frequently refer to the great strength of a sword blade and its apparent capability to hew a man in two. Sword strokes were aimed primarily at the head and neck, and were calculated to be killing blows. The following description from a later Icelandic text, describing events in the 10th and 11th centuries, underlines the devastating effect of a single sword blow:

ABOVE A detail from a stone carving from Gotland representing Valhalla, the great hall of the god Odin. Here warriors enjoyed a glorious afterlife awaiting the final battle against the forces of evil.

Then Thorbjorn rushed upon Grettir and struck at him, but he parried it with the buckler in his left hand and struck with his sword a blow which severed Thorbjorn's shield in two and went into his head, reaching the brain.

from *Grettir's Saga* (c.1400)

Medieval weapons

Feudal armies in Europe from the 11th to the 14th century produced a core group of premium fighting men – the mounted knights. Over time, they became more heavily armoured and reliant upon the shattering force of horse, lance and wide-bladed sword. In their wake, massed ranks of foot-soldiers engaged the enemy with long polearms (essentially weapons mounted on the end of a long pole), hoping to dismount and finish off any enemy knight. The fighting was brutal and bloody, conducted in a crush of jabbing, thrusting weapons.

1066 – the battlefield

The Battle of Hastings (1066) saw William of Normandy (*c.*1028–1087) unleash the devastating power of his heavily armoured knights for the first time on British soil. During many hours of hard fighting, King Harold II (*c.*1022–1066) and his fellow Anglo-Saxon defenders were constantly harried by repeated Norman cavalry charges. This type of mounted and mobile warfare was unknown to the Anglo-Saxons, who were predominantly foot soldiers, and it was only their fortunate selection of superior and defensible terrain prior to the battle that stopped them from being immediately overwhelmed.

The Norman war sword

A double-edged, razor-sharp broadsword with an average length of around 75cm (29.5in), was the main battle weapon of the Norman knight of the medieval period. It was ideal for swinging at speed and downward slashing. It would be used one-handed and in conjunction with a large, kite-shaped shield.

LEFT In this detail from the Bayeux Tapestry, Harold II's Anglo-Saxon troops, led by an armoured standard bearer and a warrior with an axe, confront a Norman cavalryman armed with a lance.

BELOW This sword is a "transitional" piece between the Viking and medieval period. It has a distinctive "brazil nut" pommel that was common in the early medieval period and the cross guard has increased considerably in width, while the blade is also more finely tapered.

Straight, squared cross guard

Fuller (bevelled groove) extends to almost complete length of tapered blade

LEFT A 13th-century French soldier. He carries a double-edged broadsword with brazil nut pommel and down-sloping cross guard.

BELOW RIGHT William the Conqueror, accompanied by knights and soldiers, from a page of illustrated Latin text from the 14th century.

The Norman lance

Although it is called a lance, Norman knights used what could more accurately be described as a long, wooden spear with a simple, spiked end. It would be held firmly under the arm in order that the maximum force of both man and horse could be transmitted into the charge. Once the enemy had been engaged, the lance could also be transformed into an effective close-combat thrusting weapon, or simply thrown.

The "knightly" or "arming" sword

During a period when there was a practical need for a substantial and sturdy fighting weapon on the battlefield, the medieval "knightly" or "arming" sword was carried. Most battles in Europe took the form of two heavily armed and armoured scrums locked in a frenetic life-or-death struggle to push the enemy back, coupled with the added difficulty of trying to kill or maim as many enemies as possible in a very limited amount of space. It was quite common for soldiers to be literally crushed to death by their own side as the battle moved along.

Sword manufacture

Before the 9th century good sources of quality iron ore were not always available and many swords were often forge-welded from a selection of smaller iron pieces, thus reducing the inherent strength of the blade. Conversely, swordsmiths also forged high-quality swords using a process known as pattern welding, using rods of superior iron. The process required that the rods be tightly twisted together, so creating a much stronger and more durable blade with great qualities of tempering. The interlocking of these rods under great heat, and their sudden cooling and hammering, created distinctive forging patterns on the blade's surface. This diversity of swirling patterns was highly prized by an owner.

By the 9th century in Europe, the blast furnace became widespread and the need for pattern welding diminished. During the centuries that followed, the technique was slowly lost, and by 1300 there are few examples of its use. The technique survived, however, in Scandinavia, where good-quality iron ores and charcoal were widely available.

The typical style of the "knightly" or "arming" sword was firmly established by the 12th and 13th centuries. In general terms, it comprised a long, broad-bladed cutting and thrusting sword with double fullers (bevelled grooves); a plain crossbar hilt; and a wheel, brazil nut, ovoid or mushroom-shaped pommel. This sword design had remained virtually unchanged since the Viking invasions (AD793–*c*.1066), and over the next three centuries there was to be little innovation. Most blades and hilts were plain, although some surviving blades are found with inlaid decoration, mostly in the form of large, punched lettering or symbols, normally of a religious or mystical nature. Pommels of this period can also be found with inset heraldic devices, denoting particular royal or noble families. Rare specimens have pommels of agate, inlaid gold or rock crystal.

Swords would have been pattern forged or "braided" in the manner of earlier Viking swords, making them excellent fighting weapons – very strong and not prone to breakage. Swords were normally combined with either a large shield or buckler (small shield), although there are many contemporary images and written descriptions that describe the use of the knightly sword without a shield. This was thought to enable the free hand to grab or grapple with opponents. A knight would have worn this large sword whether in armour or not. He would have been considered "undressed" without his sword.

Medieval ceremonial swords

Swords produced specifically for use at royal coronations and similar ceremonies began to appear from the 11th century onwards. They were not designed for battle and were kept safely in churches, palaces and state arsenals. Decoration was profuse and the scale was deliberately large and impressive. One of the swords of Charlemagne (or Charles the Great), King of the Franks (r. AD742–814), is preserved in the Schatzkammer (Treasury) in Vienna. The blade is single-edged, slightly curved and overlaid with copper decoration, including dragon motifs. Hilt and scabbard are covered in silver gilt. The grip is wrapped in fishskin, set at an angle and very reminiscent of Near Eastern swords of the period. The second sword sometimes attributed to Charlemagne is found in the Louvre, Paris. The ornamentation on the hilt suggests it was carried by him, but it was also known to have been used as a ceremonial sword when Philip the Bold was crowned in 1270.

RIGHT A line drawing of one of two swords attributed to Charlemagne or Charles the Great (r. AD742–814). The sword is kept in the Louvre Museum in Paris.

Large, rounded pommel with flattened sides

Blade graduating to spear point

Cruciform-shaped cross guard

LEFT A knight's sword, *c*.1250–1300, with a narrow blade, light enough to use on foot. This sword has a spear-point blade and impressive cutting and thrusting capabilities.

A longsword with a highly tapered blade which could be used to penetrate armour.

Downward-curving quillons

Blade with strong needlepoint for penetration

The medieval sword in battle

A contemporary Florentine description of the Battle of Kosovo, between the Serbs and the Ottoman Empire in 1389, highlights the "knightly" aspect of the use of the sword and its perceived retributory power.

Fortunate, most fortunate are those hands of the twelve loyal lords who, having opened their way with the sword and having penetrated the enemy lines and the circle of chained camels, heroically reached the tent of Amurat himself…Fortunate above all is that one who so forcefully killed such a strong vojvoda by stabbing him with a sword in the throat and belly. And blessed are all those who gave their lives and blood through the glorious manner of martyrdom…

Response from the Florentine Senate (1389)

The medieval longsword

A natural progression from the two-handed "arming" or "knightly" swords of the early to mid-medieval period was the first longswords, with the main difference being an increase in blade length. The double-edged blade was 80–95cm (31–37in) long and weighed in at approximately 1–2kg (2.2–4.4lb). This was very much a sword of the late medieval period and was used from around 1350 to 1550. The length of the grip was also extended to allow a more powerful and directed use of two hands, but the traditional cruciform hilt was still retained.

The longsword was a new departure in sword design and this innovation was soon witnessed in its battlefield application. It had the usual cutting

ABOVE A 14th-century French battle scene. The chaotic nature of a medieval battle is very evident.

functions expected of a broadsword but the blade profile had become thinner and was now designed (through stiffening of the blade tip) to thrust and penetrate plate armour. The longsword would come to prominence during the Renaissance, when the battlefield became a testing ground for new forms of penetrative edged weapons. The terms "hand-and-a-half sword", "greatsword" and "bastard sword" are different classifications of swords of this period.

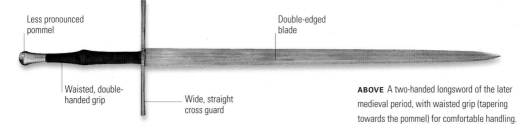

Less pronounced pommel

Waisted, double-handed grip

Wide, straight cross guard

Double-edged blade

ABOVE A two-handed longsword of the later medieval period, with waisted grip (tapering towards the pommel) for comfortable handling.

Medieval polearms

Massed formations of infantry soldiers carrying polearms was a common sight on the battlefields of Europe from the medieval period right through to the early 1700s. The fighting part of the polearm was placed on the end of a long shaft and they were specially designed to disable and inflict crushing injuries upon knights. Cheap to produce in large numbers and versatile on the battlefield, these weapons became the mainstay of the European medieval foot-soldier when engaged in close combat.

The bardiche

A particularly brutal polearm used extensively in medieval and Renaissance Europe, the bardiche found particular favour in eastern Europe and Russia. Blade design varied considerably from country to country, but the main characteristic was a substantial cleaver-type blade and attachment to the pole by means of two widely spaced sockets. Blade length was around 60cm (23.6in), although the haft was unusually short at approximately 1.5m (4.9ft). This weapon appeared top-heavy and impractical, but the bardiche was regarded more as a heavy axe and wielded accordingly.

The bill

With a tradition going back to the Viking Age, the bill is commonly regarded as the national weapon of the English both during and beyond the medieval period, although it was used elsewhere in Europe, particularly Italy. As with many polearms, the bill developed from an agricultural tool, the billhook, and displayed a hooked chopping blade with several protruding spikes, including a pronounced spike at the top of the haft, resembling a spearhead. The bill also had a strong hook for dismounting cavalry. Used skilfully, it could snag onto any loose clothing or armour and wrench

Poleaxe   Bardiche   Bill   Glaive   Partizan   Halberd   Pike

the target from his horse and throw him to the ground. English bills tended to be shorter with the emphasis more on the chopping action of the blade, while Italian bills had a very long spiked end, resulting in its use as a thrusting weapon.

The glaive

Similar in design to the Japanese naginata, the glaive originated in France, and its single-edged blade was attached to the haft by means of a socket shaft. Blade length was typically around 55cm (21.6in), with a wooden pole 1.8–2.1m (5.9–6.8ft) long. Medieval Swedish infantry adapted the glaive by fixing a double-edged sword blade to the haft. Glaives with small hooks are known as "glaive-guisarmes".

The halberd

The halberd is a crude, rectangular blade, shaped to a point at the top; the earliest known use of the halberd comes from an excavated example from the battlefield at Morgarten (1315) in Switzerland. The word "halberd" originated from the German halm (staff) and barte (axe). Over time, the halberd's spear point was improved to allow it to be used to repel oncoming horsemen. The haft of the halberd was also reinforced with thick metal rims, making it more effective and durable when blocking blows from an enemy sword or axe.

The partizan

Smaller than normal polearms at 1.8–2m (5.9–6.6ft), the partizan was constructed from a spearhead or lancehead, with an added double axehead at the bottom of the blade. It proved not to be as effective as other polearms and it was gradually withdrawn from frontline use. It remained as a ceremonial weapon and many have elaborately decorated blades. Partizans were carried right through to the Napoleonic Wars (1804–15).

The pike

A ubiquitous battlefield weapon during the medieval period, the pike was simply a very long, thrusting spear employed by infantry as both a static defensive weapon against cavalry attacks and as an attacking polearm, when used in massed ranks and close formation. The combined length of both haft and head rose over time to a staggering 3–4m (9.8–13.1ft), sometimes even 6m (19.6ft), and it was this very length that was both its strength and also its inherent weakness. The pikeman could stand at a relatively safe distance from close combat, but the weapon's unwieldiness could also prove dangerous for him. A pikeman was armed with sword, mace or dagger in case his pike was lost in battle.

Medieval and Renaissance jousts

Jousts and tournaments took the form of individual combat between armoured knights, mounted or on foot, using lances, swords, axes and maces. Jousting was first practised in the early Middle Ages. During these colourful public events, two knights fought to enhance their martial reputation. The melée, a tournament (or tourney), provided the audience with the spectacle of many knights involved in mass trials by combat. Compared with warfare proper, this form of organized "entertainment" was only one step away from the real thing.

Origins of the tournament

The first written record of a formulated set of tournament rules is usually credited to a Frenchman, Geoffroi de Purelli, in 1066. Unfortunately, his guidelines were of limited use to him as he was killed at the very tournament for which he had composed the rules. Despite this early setback, the popularity of jousting was firmly established in western Europe by the 13th century and it continued as a public sport well into the 1600s.

Military service in the medieval period

Medieval knights were obliged to provide military service to their king, lord or liege on a regular basis. Warfare during this period, although perhaps exciting to a young knight on his first campaign, was, for most of those involved, extremely unpleasant. Living conditions were usually poor and, if the knight was not killed or badly wounded in battle, the combination of disease or hunger would normally carry him away. But there could be an opportunity for redemption amidst this state of wretchedness. By showing valour and courage on the battlefield, he had the opportunity to establish a martial reputation with the consequent possibility of great financial and social rewards from his master, or even the king.

On the other hand, equivalent fame and fortune, combined with regular practice in the use of weapons, could also be gained in peacetime and without embarking on a long and possibly fatal campaign of war. This alternative avenue was to be found in the joust and tournament.

RIGHT A knight is unhorsed with a jousting lance. The illustration is taken from the *Codex Manesse* by Walther von Klingen, Zurich, *c.*1310–40.

The individual joust

A joust was a horseback encounter between two knights with lances. The object was to unhorse the opponent. If a combatant struck either rider or horse with his lance, he was automatically disqualified. This was known as "tilting". If the opponent was not unhorsed but a clean hit was made to the centre or "boss" of his shield, points would be awarded.

LEFT A knight with jousting lance, *c.*1500. His plate armour includes an extra protective layer near his vulnerable left side.

The melée or tourney

Taking the form of massed trials by arms in a public arena, the melée or tourney was a popular part of the tournament in the 12th and 13th centuries (jousting became popular later on). It was a savage and brutal fixture, with many lives lost and serious injuries sustained. Upon hearing the call to charge, rival knights rode or ran onto the tournament field and proceeded to unhorse or attack their designated opponents with a selection of weapons, including broadsword, war axe, club or mace.

In some competitions, the melée was more organized, with combat restricted to a series of three strokes per weapon: for example, three tilts of the lance or three strokes of the sword, and the same for both battle-axe and mace. To actually kill an opponent during a tournament was considered morally wrong, although the ferocity of the combat sometimes inevitably led to fatalities.

RIGHT In this French 14th-century illumination the knight Lancelot is depicted in single combat, watched by King Arthur and Guinevere.

The jousting lance

Jousting lances were made of solid oak and it would have required considerable strength, force and accuracy to unseat an opponent. It would certainly have taken a significant strike to shatter a lance. Knights practised their technique against a specially constructed target, or quintain, a life-sized re-creation of an opponent's lance, helmet and shield. In modern-day re-creations of the joust, a lightweight, wooden lance is used in order that it can break more easily and so lessen the impact on an opponent.

Two types of horses were used during the joust. Warmblood chargers were selected for their stamina and quickness in the charge, whereas heavy warhorses or coldblood destriers were chosen for their large bulk, which made them deliberately slower but able to pack a heavier punch upon contact. Horses were trained to canter at an ambling pace to give their riders stability and enable them to focus and aim better with their lances.

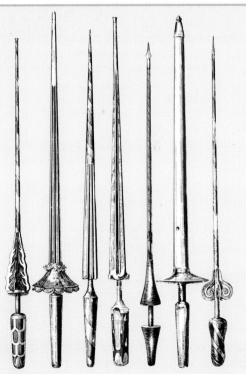

RIGHT A selection of jousting lances. At the end of each lance was a coronal (crown-shaped metal cap) consisting of three or more metal prongs, designed to catch onto the opponent's shield.

Swords of the Renaissance

The soldier of the mid-1500s witnessed dramatic advances in military technology. Swords, bows and pikes were now being challenged by early artillery, hand-held guns and complex siege weapons. In response, combatants became more heavily armoured. The sword evolved from being a purely slashing weapon to one that could pierce and break through plate armour. New sword types also appeared, from the huge two-handed broadsword of the Landsknecht to the handy short-bladed falchion of the ordinary infantryman.

ABOVE A Polish estoc, which would have been used by the cavalry. The needle-like blade was ideal for penetrating armour.

The estoc or tuck sword

Stiff, lozenge or diamond-shaped thrusting blades were now replacing the wide-bladed and cruciform-hilted swords typical of the medieval period. This new type of sword was known to the French as an estoc and to the English as a tuck.

The estoc featured a long, two-handed grip, enabling the bearer to achieve maximum effect as he thrust the sword downwards into armour. This sword was particularly effective at splitting chainmail and piercing gaps in armour. Due to the narrowness of the blade, it had no discernible cutting edge but a very strong point. Opponents who had lost the protection of their armour during the heat of battle were still dispatched by the traditional double-edged cutting sword, held in reserve for just such an eventuality. Versatility and a range of weapons to hand was still an important and practical factor.

The "hand-and-a-half" sword

Common throughout Europe from the beginning of the 15th century, the "hand-and-a-half sword" is also referred to as a "longsword". The contemporary term "bastard sword" derives from it being regarded as neither a one-handed nor a two-handed sword. Despite these perceived drawbacks, it possessed a reasonably long grip and shorter blade, which allowed one hand to hold the narrow grip firmly, while a couple of fingers placed strategically on the forte gave the soldier extra leverage and manoeuvrability when wielding. The length of these swords was around 115–145cm (45.3–57in).

The falchion

Although the falchion's design had originated in ancient Greece, the sword experienced a widespread revival during the Renaissance, particularly in Italy, France and Germany. This short-bladed sword had a straight or slightly curved blade, with cross guards either absent or very simple.

BELOW The "hand-and-a-half" sword has a short grip that accommodates one hand, while the fingers of the second hand are placed on the blade forte to allow extra leverage and control when swinging the blade.

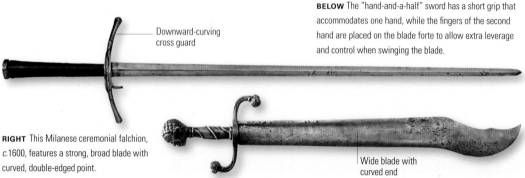

Downward-curving cross guard

RIGHT This Milanese ceremonial falchion, *c.*1600, features a strong, broad blade with curved, double-edged point.

Wide blade with curved end

Two-handed (Zweihänder) swords

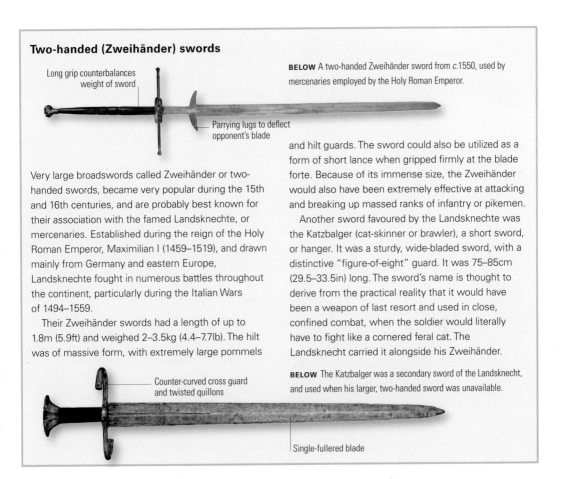

Long grip counterbalances weight of sword

BELOW A two-handed Zweihänder sword from c.1550, used by mercenaries employed by the Holy Roman Emperor.

Parrying lugs to deflect opponent's blade

Very large broadswords called Zweihänder or two-handed swords, became very popular during the 15th and 16th centuries, and are probably best known for their association with the famed Landsknechte, or mercenaries. Established during the reign of the Holy Roman Emperor, Maximilian I (1459–1519), and drawn mainly from Germany and eastern Europe, Landsknechte fought in numerous battles throughout the continent, particularly during the Italian Wars of 1494–1559.

Their Zweihänder swords had a length of up to 1.8m (5.9ft) and weighed 2–3.5kg (4.4–7.7lb). The hilt was of massive form, with extremely large pommels

and hilt guards. The sword could also be utilized as a form of short lance when gripped firmly at the blade forte. Because of its immense size, the Zweihänder would also have been extremely effective at attacking and breaking up massed ranks of infantry or pikemen.

Another sword favoured by the Landsknechte was the Katzbalger (cat-skinner or brawler), a short sword, or hanger. It was a sturdy, wide-bladed sword, with a distinctive "figure-of-eight" guard. It was 75–85cm (29.5–33.5in) long. The sword's name is thought to derive from the practical reality that it would have been a weapon of last resort and used in close, confined combat, when the soldier would literally have to fight like a cornered feral cat. The Landsknecht carried it alongside his Zweihänder.

Counter-curved cross guard and twisted quillons

BELOW The Katzbalger was a secondary sword of the Landsknecht, and used when his larger, two-handed sword was unavailable.

Single-fullered blade

The falchion was primarily a side-weapon and was usually carried by the infantry. Because of its short blade and ease of manoeuvrability, the falchion became the precursor to the hunting sword.

The cinquedea, or "five-fingered" sword

Another distinctive short sword that developed in Italy during the Renaissance was the cinquedea. The shape and form of the cinquedea typifies the Renaissance belief in the importance of artistry, combined with a newly rediscovered passion for the classical world. It was worn mainly with civilian dress and comprised a very wide blade of five-fingered

span. The hilt was normally of simple form, with a severely waisted grip. Because of its wide blade, many swordsmiths took the opportunity to embellish the swords with exquisite engraving and gilding. The sword would have been worn in the small of the back in order that it could be drawn laterally.

There is some debate as to whether the cinquedea was actually a dagger rather than a sword. The average length is noted at 40–50cm/16–19in (and there are even two-handed versions known), so this probably indicates that the cinquedea fits more comfortably within the broad family of swords rather than dagger types.

RIGHT A cinqueda sword, with typical pronounced medium ridge, or spine, running down the centre of the blade.

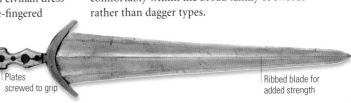

Plates screwed to grip

Ribbed blade for added strength

ABOVE Sword and scroll of Anne de Montmorency, 1493–1567, from the *Hours of Constable Anne de Montmorency*.

Ceremonial swords

The increasing power and wealth of the European monarchies and city states during the Renaissance meant that the sword did not only serve a purely military function. It also became a manifestation of the rank and status of the privileged, and its most notable appearances were at royal coronation ceremonies. Although the medieval cruciform-hilted sword had fallen out of favour on the Renaissance battlefield, being superseded by more complex and enclosed-hilt forms, it was still retained for ceremonial purposes – perhaps recalling a more "knightly" time – when a gentleman or courtier swore allegiance to his king by the kiss of a knightly sword. These "bearing" swords were carried before kings, queens and senior clergy. The sword of Frederick I of Saxony, presented to him by Emperor Sigismund I of Germany in 1425, has a

cruciform hilt inset with rock crystal and heavily gilded in gold and silver. There is also a massive 15th-century bearing sword, supposedly made for either Henry V of England or Edward, Prince of Wales, which has a total length of over 228cm (88.6in). Ceremonial swords were also presented as symbols of state office. From the 14th century onwards, English mayors were granted the right (usually by the monarch) to carry a great civic sword on ceremonial occasions. This tradition was upheld for centuries and many historic towns in the United Kingdom still retain these swords. The earliest recorded civic sword still in existence is to be found in Bristol and is thought to date from around 1373. Constables of France, including such notables as Bertrand du Guesclin and Anne de Montmorency, carried bearing swords.

In terms of sheer brilliance of decoration and craftsmanship, the ceremonial swords presented by the Renaissance popes must rank as the apogee of 16th-century sword decoration. Given with a richly embroidered belt and cap by the pope each year on Christmas Day, invariably to members of the European Catholic nobility, these great two-handed swords were fabulously ornate and featured a profusion of precious stones and extensive gold and silver metalwork.

The development of hunting swords

Hunting had always been the favoured and exclusive pursuit of the nobility since the early medieval period and Renaissance hunters continued this pastime with vigour. The depiction of the royal hunt was a popular subject for artists and many painters and weavers of tapestry found the drama of the chase and final kill with sword and spear irresistible.

The falchion sword, or short hanger, was well known to the infantry as a side-weapon. It was first adopted during the 14th century, specifically as a dedicated hunting weapon. In later years, a saw-back blade was also incorporated for ease of cutting up the kill, followed by the development of a specialist set of tools for pairing. This combination of sword and skinning tools was known as a garniture, or trousse. As the owners of these hunting swords invariably had great financial means, decoration of the swords became ever more elaborate.

LEFT An illustration of a hunting sword with pommel and crossbar decorated by birds' heads. It has a saw-back blade for cutting the kill.

Swords of justice, swords of execution

Inscription

Great swords were also employed as both symbols and facilitators of judicial law. Many local courts of justice placed a large bearing or executioner's sword on the courtroom wall. The presence of the executioner's sword was not purely symbolic for it had a practical application in the actual beheading of prisoners. It was often highly decorated and engraved with prayers for the condemned, warnings against transgressions and vivid images of beheadings, hangings and torture.

Executioners' swords were more common in continental Europe from the 1400s, particularly Germany, with England still preferring the axe. The sword hilt was normally of conventional cruciform shape with a large counter-balancing pommel. It was very well constructed, with high-quality steel used for the manufacture of the blade. The blade edge was extremely sharp and it was a requirement of the executioner to keep it well honed so that the head of the victim could be severed in one mighty blow. Blades were broad and flat backed, with a rounded tip. The sword was designed for cutting rather than thrusting, so a pointed tip (as in the case of military blades) was unnecessary.

ABOVE This German executioner's sword has a double-edged blade with a blunt, lightly rounded point. Many surviving "execution swords" are actually swords of justice which would be carried before the judge to indicate his power over life and death.

ABOVE In this detail from the above sword, an etched inscription can be seen. In German it reads *"Ich Muß straffen daß verbrechen – Als wie Recht und Richter sprechen"*. Translated, this means "I have to punish crime as the law and judge tell me".

An executioner's sword in the British Museum, London, has the following words engraved on the blade in Latin. It translates as: "When I raise this sword I wish the sinner eternal life / The Sires punish mischief: I execute their judgement." When no longer used for executions, swords became ceremonial.

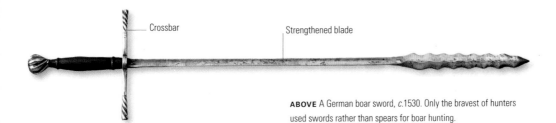

Crossbar

Strengthened blade

ABOVE A German boar sword, *c.*1530. Only the bravest of hunters used swords rather than spears for boar hunting.

Another sword designed solely for the hunt was the boar sword. Based on the triangular-bladed estoc or tuck, its greatly stiffened blade was designed to withstand the power of a charging boar or other large animal. The boar sword was introduced during the 14th century and by around 1500 it had developed a faceted or leaf-shaped spear point. A crossbar was later added near the end of the blade to prevent an animal running up the length of the blade and so making it difficult to retrieve.

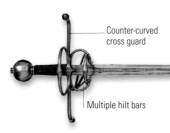

Counter-curved
cross guard

Multiple hilt bars

BELOW A German rapier dating from *c*.1560–70. It has a large
spherical pommel that counterbalances the weight of the blade.

The rapier

Spain is normally cited as the first country to have
introduced the rapier, or *espada ropera* (sword of
the robe), during the late 1400s. This designation
highlighted the new-found ability for a gentleman to
wear these swords with ordinary civilian dress, rather
than needing to don his armour. Italy, Germany and
England adopted the rapier soon afterwards.

In its most complete and recognizable form, the
rapier came into full prominence during the early
16th century. In the mid-1400s, precursors of the
rapier (including the standard cruciform-hilted sword)
had begun to develop a primitive knuckle guard and
forefinger ring or loop. By 1500, a series of simple bars
were joined to the knuckle guard to form a protective
hilt. At this time, the blade was still a wide, cutting
type, and it is only well into the 16th century that the

slender rapier blade was fully developed. This typically
thin blade was deemed impractical for use during
heavy combat on the battlefield so the rapier was
viewed primarily as a "civilian" duelling sword. The
new rapier hilt, however, was adopted by the military
but with the retention of a wider, more traditional
broadsword fighting blade.

The blade

Sword blades were manufactured in Toledo and
Valencia (Spain), Solingen and Passau (Germany),
and Milan and Brescia (Italy). They were sold as
unhilted blades and then hilted locally at their eventual
destinations throughout Europe. Some blades are
marked by their maker, although many are plain.
Notable bladesmiths' names include Piccinino, Caino,
Sacchi and Ferrara from Italy, Johannes, Wundes and
Tesche (Germany) and Hernandez (Spain). Respected
names were often stamped on blades by lesser-known
rivals to enhance the value of an inferior sword.

BELOW Italian rapier,
c.1610. Of true swept-hilt
form, it has deep chiselling
to the knuckle guard.

BELOW A North European
duelling rapier, *c*.1635,
with a distinctive elongated
and fluted pommel.

BELOW A Spanish cup-hilt
rapier, *c*.1660. The cup and
hilt are extensively pierced.
It has very long, straight,
slender quillons with finials
to each end.

BELOW An English rapier
with a finely chiselled cup
hilt, *c*.1650. The blade is
stamped "*Sahagum*".

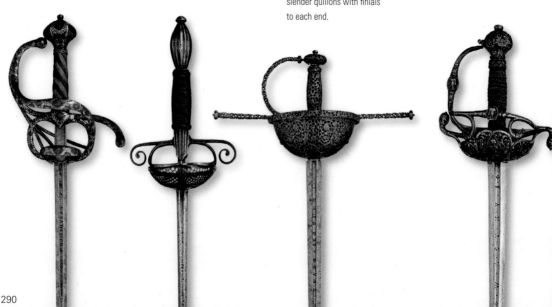

The hilt

Renaissance swordsmen were presented with many differing styles of rapier, which had developed over time and in different areas. This difference was normally displayed in the sword hilt rather than the blade. To make identification clearer, historians have divided the hilt into a series of distinct evolutions from primary, basic, quarter, half, to three-quarter and then full hilts. Some examples have just a simple loop and knuckle guard, while later rapiers exhibit multiple ring guards and S-shaped upswept and downswept quillons (cross pieces at right angles to the blade and hilt). These later, more extravagant rapiers are commonly described as being of "swept-hilt" form. Large ovoid or octagonal pommels were necessary to counterbalance the weight of the long blade.

The development of the rapier

In the 16th century, the first 50 years could truly be called the age of the rapier. This century witnessed the rapier being worn as the ultimate fashion accessory and signifier of rank. Great competition was placed at Court to be the nobleman with the most grandly ornate sword, and contemporary paintings vividly show the wide range of rapiers available to those willing to pay the vast sums needed to purchase such a "trophy" piece.

By the end of the 16th century, blade lengths had reduced, making the rapier more manageable in the hand. Hilt design had now become significantly complex and, with increased blade-to-blade action, more emphasis was laid on protecting the hand. In the 1600s we see the addition of more side plates and shell guards for this purpose.

The rapier and fencing

Modern fencing emerged during the latter half of the 15th century and is directly attributable to the development of the rapier as a weapon of choice for a gentleman. The first fencing manuals were published in Spain in 1471 and 1474. In Germany, the Marxbruder and Federfechter fencing guilds were given a letter of privilege by Emperor Friedrich III in 1478, enabling them to recruit members and teach the art of fencing.

In Italy and central Europe a left-handed dagger (main gauche) was developed and used in conjunction with the rapier, and sometimes also a small shield, or "buckler", would be used to parry the sword blows. More noblemen died during the 16th century from duelling than conventional warfare.

RIGHT A sword fight with rapiers. This illustration was taken from a woodcut, c.1656.

17th- and 18th-century swords

A dramatic change in sword design appeared in the 17th and 18th centuries. The long-bladed rapier of the Renaissance and the great two-handed sword of the Landsknechte had become obsolete as the changing nature of war relegated the sword to a more secondary role, being steadily overtaken by more reliable and destructive firearms. Despite this, the military sword was still regarded as an effective weapon. Civilian gentlemen now carried smaller, lightweight, ornamented swords, as dictated by the changing fashion of the day.

ABOVE A French smallsword, from *c*.1770. The blade is decorated with scrolling foliage, highlighted in blue and gilt.

The smallsword

Towards the end of the 17th century, the need to carry a substantial sword in civilian life diminished and gentlemen began to adopt a sword of smaller proportions. It was described as a "town", "walking" or "court" sword and would later develop into the smallsword proper. In England, this change coincided with a period of relative social stability after the English Civil War (1642–51), and a growing belief that there was less need to be heavily armed when going about one's business.

These early "transitional" or part-rapier smallswords were more practical when used in close order combat (particularly the now-popular duel), and were also considered more comfortable to wear alongside the civilian dress that had now superseded the wearing of armour in public.

The traditional rapier hilt was also replaced by new hilt styles from the 1700s, including a stylized shell guard and smaller quillons, thinner knuckle guards and a wider range of pommel styles. Extra *pas-d'âne* rings (the inwardly curving quillons that reached the base of the shell guard) were added to the hilt. *Pas d'âne* literally means "a donkey's steps".

LEFT In *Portrait of a Gentleman, c.*1640 (oil on canvas), the subject carries an early form of basket hilt, combined with a backsword blade.

BELOW An ornate French smallsword hilt, *c*.1760. The pommel, knuckle guard and shell guard are deeply embossed. The blade is engraved with numerous decorative motifs.

ABOVE Probably French with a Spanish blade. It is likely that this duelling rapier, *c.*1670, would have been used in conjunction with a gauntlet and cloak in the left hand, acting as a distraction to the opponent.

The function of the sword also changed. It had now become not just a weapon of defence or attack but also a distinctive signifier of rank and very much influenced by the vagaries of fashion. The smallswords worn at European courts were soon copied within society's more fashionable circles. During the late 17th and early 18th century, the dominant decorative influence in European society was French design and this became a powerful stimulus in smallsword design and decoration. The Rococo movement was at its height and the incorporation of shell-like curves, foliage and classical imagery is very evident in hilt design. Advances in technology and metalworking meant that smallswords were more easily manufactured in

combinations of iron, steel, brass, silver and, occasionally, gold. The craftsmen who produced these smallswords were only limited by the depth of the client's purse and their own imagination. Consequently, the swords displayed a stunning range of quality, ornamentation and sheer creative elegance.

Military influence

As the 18th century progressed, the smallsword entered the military arena and was adopted by officers. Ordinarily, they tended to purchase more than one sword, and the smallsword, with its less robust, yet elegant proportions, was deemed more suitable for formal or "walking out" occasions, particularly parades and balls where it was seen as a status symbol. A more practical fighting sword of larger dimensions and wider blade was still carried into battle although some hilts were of smallsword design.

The colichemarde blade

In the late 1600s the normally flat rapier blade of the late Renaissance was superseded by an important technological breakthrough, when a group of German sword makers developed the colichemarde blade. This radical new blade shape was of trefoil, or three-sided, form and "hollow ground" with a hexagonal or diamond-shaped profile. The forte was also purposely wider and longer, giving the blade more strength. This new-found manoeuvrability allowed the weight of the sword to be concentrated in the hand, so providing more control and precision when thrusting.

The technical knowledge needed to produce these hollow-ground blades was jealously guarded by the German sword makers, despite attempts by the English government to bring over German workers. A rival sword factory was eventually established at Shotley Bridge in County Durham, in 1690. Its attempts at producing hollow-ground

blades were not successful and it reverted to manufacturing swords of a more traditional and flat-backed design.

The popularity of colichemarde blades was quite short-lived and by the mid-1700s, blade shape was already changing again. The demise of the colichemarde blade was due partly to its greater suitability for duelling over everyday or military use.

RIGHT Duelling in the 17th century. The antagonist on the right has adopted a typical duelling pose.

thought to be either Eurasian or Arabic. The Ottoman Turks had carried curved "mameluke" swords for many years. It is likely that the spread of the Ottoman Empire into eastern Europe by the late 1600s created an opportunity for western sword makers to examine captured examples of this new form of sword, eventually interpreting and converting them into more "western" sword styles.

Emergence of heavy and light cavalry

By the mid-1600s, European nations began to establish permanent standing armies, dividing them into designated infantry and cavalry regiments. Cavalry regiments took this transformation a stage further by making a distinction between light and heavy cavalry. The swords issued to these different branches of the army also changed, with the heavy cavalry carrying a long, straight, thrusting blade, and the light cavalry a slightly shorter, slashing, curved blade (although the widespread adoption of a curved blade would appear much later, in the early 1700s).

The backsword

Like most European nations, English cavalry troopers of the 17th century favoured a heavy backsword. Common hilt styles included an enclosed, multi-bar iron basket hilt with a large apple-shaped pommel. This design originated in Germany and northern Europe, and was later taken to a new level of sophistication by the work of Scottish basket hilt makers. The basket hilt, in many different forms, was carried by cavalry

BELOW A French cavalry backsword, dating from *c.*1690. The hilt is made up of a complex series of intertwined bars.

BOTTOM The blade of this English mortuary sword, *c.*1645, is double-edged and multi-fullered (a number of grooves).

Cavalry swords

The cavalry sword was still a horseman's most effective weapon of defence and attack up to the 18th century. Unlike the infantry soldier, who began to rely more on musket and pistol, the cavalry soldier carried a firearm only as his secondary weapon of defence. It was therefore crucial that he had a sword capable of producing a devastating effect when combined with his horse's speed and his own strength and skill. The sword needed to be heavy and robust, with a long cut-and-thrust blade, fixed to a large hilt, affording good protection to the sword hand.

The use of a straight-bladed and single-edged cavalry "backsword" had been well established by the 1600s. These swords were carried throughout Europe and became the mainstay for cavalry formations. The early 18th century also witnessed the growing influence of cavalry sabres with curved blades. Their origins are

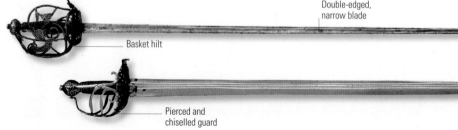

Double-edged, narrow blade

Basket hilt

Pierced and chiselled guard

Thrusting blade

regiments well into the 18th century. Parallel to this was the development of a more robust "military" version of the newly adopted smallsword (normally for officers). It had a bilobate (two-branched) counter-guard, large ovoid pommel and broadsword blade.

The "mortuary sword" of the English Civil War

During the English Civil War (1642–51) the so-called "mortuary" sword was another peculiarly English sword type carried extensively. It was given the erroneous title "mortuary" by Victorian sword collectors because of the application of decorative work to the hilt that featured a series of engraved human faces, supposedly in memory of the beheaded Charles I (executed in 1649) and his wife, Henrietta Maria. Although there is a mortuary sword in the collection of HM The Queen at Windsor that bears a likeness to Charles I and his queen, mortuary swords with human faces were being carried as early as 1635. Not all of them display human faces as the primary decorative motif. Alternative hilt decoration comprises armed figures, coats of arms and extensive engraving, including both fanciful and geometric designs.

ABOVE A mid-17th century English backsword with a mortuary-type hilt. It was reputed to have been used by Oliver Cromwell during the siege of Drogheda in 1649.

The main features of the mortuary sword are a dish- or boat-shaped guard with a wide wrist guard and two branched knuckle bows screwed to the pommel. Shield-shaped langets (to guard the shaft) are found at the top of the blade forte and probably acted to keep the hilt solid into the blade. Blades were normally of backsword type and single or double-edged towards the end of the blade to enable a thrusting capability.

The mortuary sword, which fell out of use around 1670, was carried by both Royalist and Parliamentarian cavalry throughout the English Civil War. Oliver Cromwell was believed to have carried a mortuary sword during the Battle of Drogheda, in 1649, and an example attributed to him still exists in England.

BELOW Oliver Cromwell at the siege of Drogheda, 1649. Instead of starving the Royalist garrison into submission, Cromwell ordered an assault. This was eventually successful and led to a terrible massacre of both the military and civilians.

Brass "cat's-head" pommel

BELOW A schiavona sword of a type carried by Slavonian soldiers who acted as guards to the Doge of Venice up until the late 18th century.

Steel hilt decorated with studs

The schiavona

Slavonic mercenaries from eastern Europe, particularly the Balkan or Dalmatian region, carried distinctive broadswords and are thought to be the originators of the schiavona sword. These mercenaries were vicariously employed by both Spain and the Republic of Venice during the 16th and 17th centuries, but the schiavona is probably best known for its Venetian association. The Council of Ten, or Consiglio dei Dieci, under which the Doge (head of state) administered the Venetian state during the 1600s, hired many of these Dalmatian mercenaries to protect and promote Venetian interests. A large store of schiavona swords is still present in the Armoury of the Doge's Palace, in Venice. Most are stamped with the "CX" mark for the Consiglio dei Dieci.

The schiavona sword has a most distinctive hilt design. Hilt styles differ but they all exhibit the common feature of having a multi-leaf-shaped guard and "cat's-head", or katzenkopfknauf, pommel in either brass, bronze or iron. Early examples are simpler in form with less complex basket hilts, whereas later schiavonas are usually of higher quality, with the hilt bars cast in one piece.

This particular sword proved popular with central and north European cavalry during the 17th and 18th centuries. Its long and wide blade was very effective as a slashing weapon, allowing the horseman both to cut and to thrust.

Hunting swords

The dedicated European hunting sword came into prominence during the mid-1600s. Its rise was attributed to the increasing use of firearms and the changing nature of the hunt. Now the hunting sword was used to dispatch wounded or exhausted game brought to bay by the hounds, rather than being the

BELOW The Council of Ten at the Doge's Palace, Venice, painted in the 18th century. The council hired mercenaries during the 17th and 18th centuries to fight for Spain and the Republic of Venice.

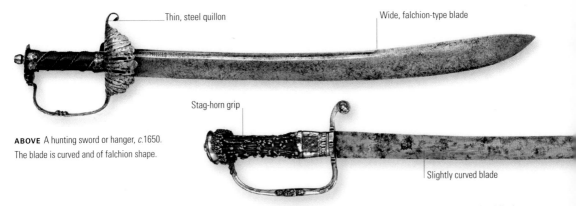

Thin, steel quillon

Wide, falchion-type blade

Stag-horn grip

Slightly curved blade

ABOVE A hunting sword or hanger, *c*.1650. The blade is curved and of falchion shape.

ABOVE The hilt of this hunting sword, 1650–75, is English, while the blade is German. The hilt is cast in hallmarked silver.

primary weapon of choice for the outright kill. Later, this sword would become more of an ornament than a functional weapon.

From around 1650, the most common form of hunting sword style was a short, lightweight hanger with a broad, single-edged, straight or sometimes slightly curved blade, typically no more than 64cm (25in) long. Some earlier blades had serrated back edges that could be used for sawing through bone.

Although hunting swords were used throughout western Europe, they were most popular in the German-speaking countries and France. Hunting swords were also referred to as hangers because they hung vertically from a sword belt, or baldric. German hunting swords are more commonly known as hirschfangers, which translates as "deer catchers".

Hunting sword hilts

Many different materials were incorporated into the construction of the hunting sword hilt, with a combination of two or three being quite common. Silver, brass, bronze, steel and later, silver was widely used. In England, silver was a popular metal for the manufacture of hunting sword hilts. The hilt would be cast in silver and then designs worked onto it, with prominent hallmarks stamped on the hilt, enabling identification of the maker and the place of manufacture.

Blade decoration

Although the hilts were furnished from many sources, the blade was normally obtained from Solingen, north-western Germany, which had a virtual monopoly on hunting sword blades from the 17th to the 19th century. Decoration of the blade usually took the form of an

etched or engraved design, including scenes of the hunt and related animal motifs. A gold wash or gilt finish would sometimes be applied over these designs. Towards the middle of the 18th century, both blue and gilt were commonly applied to the blades.

Sword scabbards and sword styles

The hunting sword scabbard was in itself a very skilled piece of work. Each scabbard was individually constructed and fitted to its own sword. Scabbards of the 17th century were normally made from thin, shaped pieces of wood, glued together to form a rigid base that would receive an external covering of parchment, calfskin or Morocco leather. Scabbard mounts included a metal locket at the upper end and a chape at the tip. A stud was also fixed to the locket that would be placed in the eye of a belt frog worn around the waist or over the shoulder.

Occasionally, a pocket was constructed in the locket mount, containing either a small knife or a fork. The handles on these tools were matched with the sword hilt and designed to complement the rest of the outfit to form a set, or trousse.

Through the 17th and into the first half of the 18th century, hunting swords became even more ornamental and were decorated in the Baroque style. Based on classical ideals, this was ebullient in spirit and characterized by rich decorative effects, including the use of prolific foliage, rounded contours and heavy symmetrical volutes. By the mid-18th century, the Rococo style had taken over and motifs based on shell and rock forms, foliage, flowers, "C" scrolls and tortuous curves were now in vogue.

Scottish Highlander swords

For centuries the Scottish Highlander fought with a distinctively Scottish range of weapons. Most notable were the broadsword, targe (small shield), dirk (dagger) and polearm. Over time the Highland broadsword eclipsed the others, both in its unique design and in the associated romance that has captured the imagination of many. It took many forms: from the massive two-handed claymore of the 16th century to the agile basket hilt, wielded at the Battle of Culloden in 1746.

Langet

Quatrefoils

16th- and 17th-century Highland swords

Before the introduction of a recognized basket hilt, the Scottish Highlander already carried at least three distinct sword types. The first comprised the claidheamh mor (claymore), which was a double-edged broadsword. Introduced during the 1500s, it was of hand-and-a-half length, with a long, broad blade of diamond section, with a cross guard angled towards the blade. The end of the cross guard was also decorated with brazed iron quatrefoils (four-leafed flower petals).

ABOVE A claymore, *c.*1600. This large sword was the mainstay of the Highlander until the late 17th century.

In the late 16th and early 17th centuries, Highlanders also carried the claidheamh da laimh, a two-handed sword. It was similar to contemporary German or Swiss two-handed (Zweihänder) swords used by Landsknechte, or mercenaries. The few surviving Scottish examples have Scottish hilts fitted with German blades. The hilt includes an oval shell guard and long, flattened, downswept quillons. The third sword type is referred to as the "lowland sword". It had a very long blade with a characteristic side ring to the hilt, globular pommel and quillons set at right angles to the blade, terminating in knobs. These great lowland swords were used for many years, and even as late as 1746, after the Battle of Culloden, many examples were subsequently found on the battlefield.

Origins of the Scottish basket hilt

The geographical origin of the distinctly "Scottish" basket-hilted sword was not actually Scotland. Swords with basket hilts are thought to have originated in Germany, Scandinavia and even England, where basket hilts of simple form were already known by the early 1500s. The development of an enclosed hilt was a natural consequence of the need for more protection to the hand at a time when the wearing of armour,

LEFT A Scottish Highlander with basket hilt and targe (shield) at the Battle of Culloden, 16 April 1746.

RIGHT In this 17th-century oil painting of Mungo Murray (1668–1700), the fifth son of the Marquis of Athol, the subject is depicted as dressed for hunting in a costume of highland tartan. The sword he carries under his left arm is an early ribbon-hilted broadsword.

RIGHT In this 17th-century oil painting of Mungo Murray (1668–1700), the fifth son of the Marquis of Athol, the subject is depicted as dressed for hunting in a costume of highland tartan. The sword he carries under his left arm is an early ribbon-hilted broadsword.

and particularly the metal gauntlet, had become less common. Why the sword became associated with Highland use is not clear, although it is known that numbers of Scottish mercenaries fought for the English in Ireland during the 16th century, and it is probable that basket-hilted swords were brought back to Scotland and their design copied by local sword makers. They were then known as "Irish" hilts by their English contemporaries.

The first true Scottish basket hilts

There are very few written or visual sources to enable us to determine exactly when the basket hilt began to be carried in the Highlands. The earliest known painting showing a Scottish clansman carrying this type of sword is recorded c.1690. The painting is of a Highland Chieftain by John Michael Wright (1617–94), and shows the subject carrying a broadsword with "beaknose" or ribbon hilt. This comprised a series of welded ribbon-like strips of metal drawn together to form a beak at the front of the basket. The "beaknose" hilt was a uniquely Highland style and differed from English basket hilts in that the pommel was of "coned form" as opposed to the English "apple" shape. Pommel shape is an important indicator of whether a basket hilt is either Scottish or English. A number of characteristic differences between the hilt styles of Scottish and English swords also began to emerge in the 1600s. English hilts tended to have thinner, more spaced, bars, whereas Scottish hilts adopted wider, rectangular plates to either side of the hilt, coupled with decorative heart-shaped piercing.

Highland feuds

The idea of Highland clansmen being compelled to fight each other to the death during a duel is not historically accurate. There were many feuds between rival clans and broadswords were normally employed to settle these quarrels. But they did not always result in the death of one opponent. It was enough for a swordsman to have drawn first blood. Rob Roy MacGregor (1671–1734), the famous Scottish patriot and folk hero, fought a duel with sword and targe just before his death. His opponent, Alasdair Steward of Invernahyle, won the duel with a cut to Rob Roy's arm.

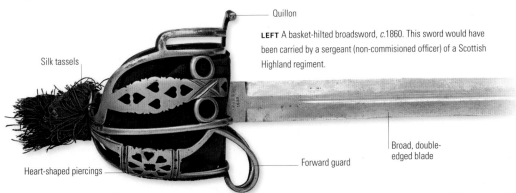

Quillon

LEFT A basket-hilted broadsword, c.1860. This sword would have been carried by a sergeant (non-commisioned officer) of a Scottish Highland regiment.

Silk tassels

Heart-shaped piercings

Forward guard

Broad, double-edged blade

prestigious title of King's Armourer in Scotland (1715), an honour carried on by his eldest son. This family of sword makers produced some very fine basket hilts, noted for their restrained elegance and fine detail.

The wide variety and breadth of quality that we see in Scottish basket hilts indicates that many were produced as part of a "cottage" industry. Most blades were actually imported from the continent, principally Germany and Italy, with the hilts then manufactured and decorated in Scotland. Small workshops in Glasgow, Stirling, Edinburgh and other Highland locations produced the swords with a workforce comprising little more than one or two people.

Post-Culloden and the banning of swords

After the failure of the Highland Scots to restore James Stuart (the Young Pretender) to the English throne at the Battle of Culloden in 1746, the Scottish Highlander lost his right to bear arms, and the carrying of swords was outlawed by the English Government. Most swords were not handed over to the English but hidden. The ban also had a devastating effect on Scottish sword makers, and the production of basket hilts went into steep decline. The subsequent raising of regiments for the newly established British Army in Scotland created a requirement for basic military broadswords. Ironically, most of these were actually

Scottish sword makers

We know of specific Highland makers only in instances where the maker has signed the hilt. Most Scottish-made basket hilts are unsigned, adding to the confusion of identification. Scottish sword makers are normally described as falling into two notable schools of basket-hilted sword making – that of either the "Stirling" or "Glasgow" schools. Edinburgh did manufacture basket hilts but not to the extent of Glasgow and Stirling. Swords of these schools are now acknowledged as representing the apogee of Scottish basket hilt sword making during the 18th century. The superb craftsmanship and detailing to the hilts identify them as being of truly historic form. Two sword-making families, the Simpsons and the Allans, predominated during this period.

During the first quarter of the 18th century, father and son hilt-makers (or "Hammermen") John Allan Sr and Walter Allan Jnr from Stirling produced hilts of rare artistry and freedom of style, many with intricately inlaid brass circles, wavy lines and cross hatching.

The Simpson family of Glasgow included a father and two sons, all confusingly named John. In 1683 the father was admitted as a Freeman of the Incorporation of Hammermen of Glasgow and was later conferred the

BELOW A basket-hilted Scottish sword from *c.*1720 by John Allan, of Stirling.

BELOW A basket-hilted Scottish sword with liner to protect the swordsman's hand from chafing against the hilt bars, *c.*1720.

The Highland charge

This account was written by Major General Hawley (c.1679–1759) before the Battle of Culloden and was meant to give the English soldiers a taste of what it would be like to face a mass charge of Highlanders.

They commonly form their Front rank of what they call their best men or True Highlanders, the number of which being always but few, when they form in Batallions they commonly form four deep...When these Battalions come within a large musket shott or three score yards this front rank gives their fire, and immediately throw down their firelocks and come down in a cluster with their swords and targets, making a noise and endeavouring to pierce the body or battalion before them – becoming 12 or 14 deep by the time they come up to the people they attack.

Records show that in most cases the enemy would have already fled the battlefield before the Highlanders reached them, but in the case of the Battle of Culloden the English forces had established complete military

ABOVE The Battle of Culloden, 16 April 1746. The army of Charles Edward Stuart (the Young Pretender) was swiftly crushed by William, Duke of Cumberland.

superiority, and could rely on the combined forces of the cavalry, infantry squares (armed with musket and fixed bayonet) and strategically placed artillery pieces.

No amount of heroic brute force could withstand this new form of military warfare. The Highlanders were unsurprisingly cut down in swathes.

produced in England. A basket-hilted sword for infantry privates in Highland regiments was issued c.1750–70. It was of relatively poor manufacture, with a thin sheet-metal guard and crude cut-outs in the junction plates. The grip was leather on wood. Blades were manufactured in London or Birmingham and marked with a royal "GR" crown, and the maker's name of either "Iefries" (Jeffries, London) or "Drury" (Birmingham). Most Scottish-made basket-hilted swords after 1746 are likely to have been made for officers in the newly formed Highland regiments.

In 1798, a regulation pattern of Highland Infantry Officer's basket-hilted broadsword was introduced. Its gilt brass basket hilt mirrored previous Highland designs. This pattern was replaced in 1828 by a basket hilt that is still worn by officers of Highland regiments in the British Army.

The Lochaber axe
First noted in the 1600s, the main polearm of the Highlander was the Lochaber axe. Its name derives from the Lochaber area of the Scottish Western Highlands. Agricultural in origin, it was similar to cropping tools such as the scythe. The pronounced

hook at the back of the axe could also have been used to pick up tied bundles. The axes ranged in height from 1.8–2m (5.9–6.5ft), including the haft.

This was a weapon carried extensively by Highland infantry and used primarily against massed cavalry. The axe hook allowed the Highlander to pull the cavalryman off his horse from where he could be swiftly dispatched with the thrusting, spiked end or axe blade.

ABOVE Re-enactors fighting with Lochaber axes and spears. The axes were heavy weapons, used by foot-soldiers for defence against cavalry and as a pike against infantry. The axe consisted of a wooden handle (haft) and a blade.

Napoleonic swords

Sword fighting during the Napoleonic Wars was primitive and brutish, typified by the thundering clash of opposing cavalry regiments and the hacking melee that followed. Unlike modern warfare, where military technology can quickly locate and kill at a distance, the Napoleonic swordsman was alongside his opponent and victim. Ironically, despite this battlefield butchery, the Napoleonic soldier lived in an age of Neo-classical and Romantic revival, in which elegant sword styles were matched by equally opulent uniforms.

British cavalry swords before 1796

Until the introduction of a universal sword for both light and heavy cavalry in 1788, the British Army had left the decision of which swords should be carried to individual colonels of regiments. Unsurprisingly, this led to a chaotic situation, with a plethora of sword types, many varying in both quality and effectiveness. Some unscrupulous colonels purchased cheap, substandard swords in the expectation of pocketing a profit from the deal and some regiments adopted swords that invariably broke on first contact with the enemy. This continual failing of blades during combat forced the authorities to establish a system of official government "proving", or testing, of blades. Eventually, a new series of officially approved cavalry sword patterns was introduced.

At this time, heavy cavalry regiments were issued a large iron or steel basket-hilted broadsword with a long, straight, broad-fullered blade. Military experience soon indicated that it was not a good design, with both officer and trooper versions badly balanced and

cumbersome. The official system of blade inspection was still in its infancy and not all the blades were vigorously tested, so poor blade quality was still a major problem. The light cavalry version comprised a slightly curved blade and stirrup-shaped hilt. It was better received by troopers in the field as the curved blade proved effective at slashing on horseback.

The argument of whether a "cut" or "thrust" blade was most effective in battle would be continually debated within the British Army for the next 100 years, and many sword tests undertaken to establish the truth. This conundrum would not be properly resolved until 1908 when, with the introduction of the 1908 Pattern Cavalry Trooper's Sword, the British Army chose a thrusting rather than a cutting sword.

In 1796, two new sword designs were issued to officers and men. Blades were now subject to a more rigid official testing regime. A punched stamp with a crown and inspector's number was placed on the ricasso (the flat of the blade near the hilt) to indicate that a blade had been passed as suitable for use in combat.

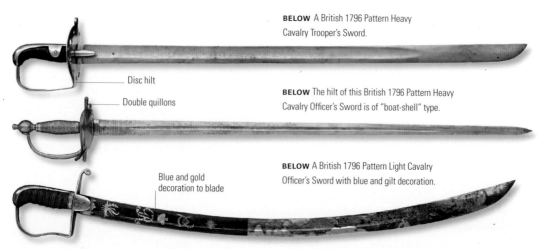

BELOW A British 1796 Pattern Heavy Cavalry Trooper's Sword.

Disc hilt

Double quillons

BELOW The hilt of this British 1796 Pattern Heavy Cavalry Officer's Sword is of "boat-shell" type.

Blue and gold decoration to blade

BELOW A British 1796 Pattern Light Cavalry Officer's Sword with blue and gilt decoration.

British cavalry swords after 1796

The 1796 Pattern Heavy Cavalry Trooper's Sword has found modern-day recognition as the sword favoured by Captain Richard Sharpe of the green-jacketed 95th Rifles Brigade, a colourful and dashing fictional character in the novels by Bernard Cornwell. The practical necessity for an infantry officer to carry such a long sword is a little far-fetched as the weapon

ABOVE The painting *Scotland for Ever*, by Lady Butler, shows the charge of the Royal Scots Greys at Waterloo in 1815. They are depicted carrying the 1796 Pattern Heavy Cavalry Trooper's Sword.

actually measured around 110cm (43.3in) from blade tip to top of the hilt, which would have made it quite a burden to drag around while on foot. The reality is that most rifle officers carried a stirrup-hilted and curved sabre of much smaller proportions.

One of the most famous real-life exponents of this pattern sword was Sergeant Charles Ewart of the 2nd Dragoons (Scots Greys), who captured the French Eagle at the Battle of Waterloo (1815). His later retelling of the act highlights the effectiveness of a large sabre when used in the right hands.

It was in the charge I took the eagle off the enemy; he and I had a hard contest for it; he made a thrust at my groin I parried it off and cut him down through the head. After this a lancer came at me; I threw the lance off my right side, and cut him through the chin upwards through the teeth. Next, a foot soldier fired at me, then charged me with his bayonet, which I also had the good luck to parry, and I cut him down through the head; thus ended the contest.

Sgt. Charles Ewart, 2nd Dragoons
(Scots Greys), Waterloo, 1815
from Edward Cotton, *A Voice from Waterloo* (1862)

The 1804 Birmingham sword trials

Driven by a heady mixture of technological pride and simple xenophobia, two Birmingham-based sword cutlers, James Woolley and Henry Osborn, were so certain of the superiority of their British-made sword blades that they agreed to a series of tests vying their blades against a number of imported German blades from Solingen that were currently being supplied to the British Army. On 7 November 1804, the tests were conducted under the supervision of a Major Cunningham. Predictably (and no doubt foreknown by Woolley and Osborn), the Solingen blades failed in droves, with many of them snapping immediately upon being struck against iron plates or when bent with any force. Both Woolley and Osborn went on to become major suppliers of military swords to the British Army throughout the Napoleonic Wars.

French cavalry swords

The rise of Napoleon Bonaparte coincided with a great revival and interest in the ancient classical world, particularly its architecture and decoration. This creative mood was not lost on French sword makers and Napoleon, who also understood the morale-boosting effect of appearance in his army. This resulted in many new cavalry sword designs being introduced during this period. One of the most influential designs was the AN XIII Heavy Cuirassier Trooper's Sword. It was a very heavy sword, with a four-bar brass hilt and a long, straight, single-edged blade measuring around 95cm (37.4in). It was a fearsome sword when used as a thrusting weapon (almost like a small spear) causing more fatal injuries than the hatchet-bladed and slashing swords of the British cavalry regiments. A French eyewitness recounts the effectiveness of these spear pointed blades but also acknowledges that when a British blade found its mark it could be equally devastating:

We always thrust with the point of our sabres, whereas they always cut with their blade which was three inches wide. Consequently, out of every twenty blows aimed by them, nineteen missed. If, however, the edge of the blade found its mark only once, it was a terrible blow, and it was not unusual to see an arm cut clean from the body.

Captain Charles Parquin, "*Chasseurs à Cheval of the Imperial Guard*"
from Charles Parquin, *Military Memoirs*, ed. (1969)

The French light cavalry trooper carried an elegant three-bar, brass-hilted sword with slightly curved blade, with hussar regiments favouring a stirrup-hilted sword. Elite regiments such as the Imperial Guard Dragoons carried a fine broadsword with brass basket hilt, cap pommel and a hilt with an inset oval plate and a silver or brass flaming grenade badge. The Mousquetaires de la Garde du Roi, who served as the mounted bodyguard to Louis XVIII

(*r*.1814–24) after Napoleon abdicated his throne in 1814, used an equally elegant sword. It was similar to the Imperial Guard Dragoon's sword, but with a cross, fleur-de-lys and sun ray inset within the hilt.

The manufacture of French swords

Swords issued by the government to French cavalry troopers were normally marked on the spine of the blade with the year, month and place of manufacture. From the 1700s, the town of Klingenthal, in Alsace, eastern France, became the official government location for the manufacture of French military

ABOVE In this illustration, *c.*1790, entitled *Officier de Cuirassiers de la Garde Royale*, you can see the sword knot hanging from the sword hilt. It prevented the sword from slipping out of the hand.

Four-bar hilt

ABOVE French Heavy Cuirassier Trooper's Sword, *c.*1810. It was used primarily as a thrusting weapon.

Flattened diamond section
with narrow fuller

ABOVE Small officer's sword, dated 1780, presented to Napoleon
by a friend and comrade who attended military school with him.

swords. It produced an enormous quantity of swords, both before and after the French Revolution. Blades produced during the period of Louis XVIII's monarchy are marked to the spine with a designation of "Rle" (Royal). Those manufactured during the reign of Napoleon are marked with the designation "Imple" (Imperial). After the Napoleonic Wars (1799–1815), French sword hilts and blades were constantly re-used and many Napoleonic era blades were fitted on new hilts well into the 19th century.

Clam or fan-shaped
hilt guard

ABOVE Note the fan-shaped hilt guard
on this French Napoleonic Heavy
Cavalry Officer's Sword from *c*.1800.

The mameluke sword

During the Egyptian campaigns of 1798–1801, the French army was greatly influenced by its military contact with the opposing Mamluk slave troops of the Ottoman (Turkish) Empire. Dressed in colourful robes and armed with pistol, daggers and distinctively curved scimitars, the Mamluks soon caught the attention of many French officers, who quickly adopted their scimitars, now renamed mamelukes, as part of their military uniform.

Evidence of the vogue for mameluke swords amongst French officers is found in the famous painting of *The Battle of the Pyramids* (1810) by Antoine-Jean Gros (1771–1835), in which he depicts *all* of the French officers carrying mameluke swords. Napoleon was so impressed with the fighting spirit of the Mamluks that he went on to purchase 2,000 troops from Syrian merchants, raising a regiment of "Mamelukes", who eventually served in his Imperial Guard. Napoleon also chose a Mamluk (Roustam Raza) to be his personal bodyguard. The mameluke sword was also adopted by British officers, and its influence even spread to the burgeoning United States, where

Marine Lieutenant Francis O'Bannion was presented with a scimitar for his capture of Derne (modern-day Tripoli) in 1804, the first recorded land battle of the US Army on foreign soil.

ABOVE The victorious French officers at the battle of the Pyramids,
21 July 1798, are all carrying mameluke swords.

RIGHT The mameluke sword presented
to Marine Lieutenant Francis O'Bannion,
in recognition of his leadership and success
during the capture of Tripoli, 1804.

British infantry swords

Officers did not carry an officially approved
regulation sword until 1786. Before this, an officer
chose his own sword and most opted for variations of
the popular narrow-bladed smallsword. Some also
opted for short hangers with flat-backed blades.

1786 Pattern Infantry Officer's Sword

Following an Order issued by George III (1738–1820),
the 1786 Pattern Infantry Officer's Sword was
introduced. The Order stipulated that this new sword
pattern must be:

*...strong cut and thrust weapon with blade 32in long
and 1in wide at the shoulder, the hilt to be steel, gilt or
silver according to the buttons of the uniform.*

Grips were composed of either ribbed ivory, ebony
or dark horn, with some swords having a metal
"cigar band" placed around the centre of the grip.
This normally bore an engraved royal crown, the
"GR" cypher of George III, or even a regimental badge.
Hilts had a cushion-shaped pommel and forward
knuckle bow with five decorative balls, or "beads".
These beads are sometimes found on the side guard.

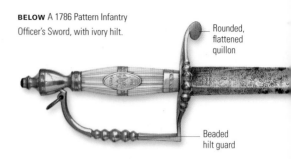

BELOW A 1786 Pattern Infantry
Officer's Sword, with ivory hilt.

Rounded,
flattened
quillon

Beaded
hilt guard

Later versions featured a fixed double-shell guard
and "Adam style" urn pommel (from the Neo-classical
architect Robert Adam, 1728–1792). Both pommel and
quillon were decorated with acanthus leaves.

1796 Pattern Infantry Officer's Sword

The disparate hilt variations were finally standardized
in the 1796 Pattern Infantry Officer's Sword, a weapon
that epitomized the British Napoleonic Infantry
Officer's sword. The original inspiration for the design
came from Prussian military smallswords of the 1750s.
Upon close inspection, it is clear that this rather flimsy
bladed sword would not have stood up to a charging
horseman's broadsword or sabre, but these were times

Sword wounds

Ironically, a clean sword cut received during battle
probably gave you more chance of survival than a
wound caused by a musket ball or artillery. This is
because the steel blade was less likely to contain
deadly infected matter that could be driven into the

body by the discharge of a firearm. Surgeons also
found sword wounds easier to treat through
cauterization, and consequently patients were less
likely to suffer the effects of gangrene and post-
operative infection. Although a cut from a sword
could undoubtedly inflict dreadful wounds,
there are many tales of soldiers receiving
multiple sword wounds and still surviving.
At the Battle of Waterloo (1815), the French
divisional commander, General Pierre-
François Durette, of the Fourth Corps, lost
his hand to a sword cut and also received
life-threatening cuts to the face and head,
leading to blindness in one eye. Remarkably,
he survived these awful injuries and lived on
until 1862.

LEFT The Battle of Waterloo, 18 June 1815. Napoleon is
depicted with sword aloft rallying his men, including the
Imperial Guard (on the right of the image).

The hussars of eastern Europe

A common image in both British and French art of this period, and also found engraved on many sword blades, is the sight of a dashing hussar, sword held aloft. The word *hussar* is Hungarian in origin and loosely translated means "highwayman" or "brigand", but was later used to describe a lightly armed horseman. Hungarian and Polish-Lithuanian hussars of the 17th and 18th centuries were utilized as shock troops during constant wars with the Ottoman Empire in eastern Europe and the Balkans. They carried both curved and straight-bladed swords. Importantly, Polish hussars also retained the lance and were largely responsible for its re-introduction during the Napoleonic Wars. Napoleon formed his own Imperial Guard regiment of lancers in 1810, known as the Red Lancers. They fought with distinction in the Russian campaign of 1812 and the Battle of Waterloo in 1815. Their lances were around 2.74m (9ft) long with a fluted steel point, mounted on a wooden shaft.

LEFT The swords carried by hussars inspired the curved sabres adopted by British light cavalry regiments of the early 19th century.

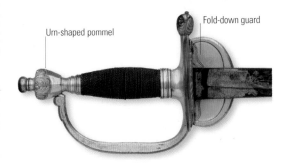

Urn-shaped pommel

Fold-down guard

LEFT A 1796 Pattern Infantry Officer's Sword, with folding shell guard.

1803 Pattern Infantry Officer's Sword

The colourful image of the gallant and dashing light cavalryman or hussar had created a strong impetus within British light cavalry regiments to carry a curved or "hussar" sabre that reflected this new *esprit de corps*. Not to be outdone, the infantry regiments introduced a new pattern of sword based on contemporary light cavalry swords.

The 1803 Pattern Infantry Officer's Sword had a single-edged, curved blade with a lion's-head pommel and a gilt brass knuckle bow. A "GR" royal cypher and crown were affixed within the knuckle bow, and above that was a representation of either a strung bugle, denoting use by a rifle company officer, or a flaming grenade, symbolizing a grenadier company officer. The blade was usually decorated in blue and gilt.

when elegant appearance sometimes took precedence over practicality. Protection for the hand was minimal, with just a single knuckle guard and double shell guard. One of the shell guards was hinged in order that it could be folded and so prevent chafing by the uniform. The grip was bound in either silver wire or applied sheet silver. Blades were lavishly decorated with blue-and-gilt highlighted engraving.

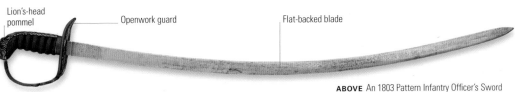

Lion's-head pommel

Openwork guard

Flat-backed blade

ABOVE An 1803 Pattern Infantry Officer's Sword with a lion's-head pommel.

ABOVE Napoleon bids farewell to the Imperial Guard at Fontainebleau in April 1814, after his first abdication and prior to his exile in Elba. The following year he was to lose the Battle of Waterloo.

French infantry swords

Napoleon Bonaparte's armies displayed a far greater range of infantry swords than most of their European counterparts. The perceived importance of rank and regiment was highly regarded within the French Army and we find that an infantry private, sergeant, captain and general officer all carried their own specific model of sword. The early years after the French Revolution (1789–99) saw the development of many distinctive infantry swords, including those carried by prestigious regiments such as the Garde Nationale and Garde Nationale Chasseur. These unique swords featured

Neo-classical helmet pommels and half-basket brass guards with republican emblems (such as the Phrygian cap) placed within the hilt cartouche.

A common type of sword carried by French infantry privates during the Napoleonic Wars was the sabre briquet, which was a short, brass-hilted hanger. It comprised a slightly curved, single-edged, flat-backed blade with brass and leather mounted scabbard. This sword was widely copied throughout Europe and adopted by many countries during the early to mid-1800s. Napoleon also understood the importance of rewarding his favoured regiments with honours or special uniform and equipment privileges. This beneficence also applied to swords. An example of this is the distinctive sword of the Imperial Sappers (Pioneers) of the Old Guard. They were awarded a newly designed uniform including bearskin, felling axe, apron and, more importantly, a striking, cockerel-hilted sword. They were also granted the unique right to grow a beard.

French infantry smallswords and curved sabres

Throughout the 18th century, French infantry officers had always carried a straight-bladed sword. It usually took the form of a traditional smallsword, with pommel styles ranging from plain ovoid to Neo-classical helmet. Shell guards were also classically inspired, with some featuring extensive embossed decoration including victory wreaths, stands of trophies and figures in classical poses.

This style continued throughout the Napoleonic Wars and blades were also frequently finished in blue and gilt. The vogue for Neo-classical hilts and corresponding decoration to the blade influenced the design of other infantry swords, including a wide range of curved infantry sabres, similar to their light cavalry counterparts but with shorter and lighter blades. There was little official pressure formally to regulate these swords and French officers were allowed a great deal of freedom to choose whatever style of sword they wished to carry.

Blue and gilt
decoration

ABOVE A French infantry officer's sabre, Model 1821, decorated with blue and gilt. This form of decoration was beginning to lose favour and later examples have plain blades.

Russian infantry swords

From the mid-1700s, Russia embarked on a sustained period of contact and rapprochement with the West. These new influences hastened changes in civil administration, architectural styles, dress and, most importantly, military organization. The czars had looked with envy at the disciplined troops of Frederick the Great of Prussia (1712–1786) and wanted the same attitude to be instilled within their own ranks. To do this the czars needed to change the whole appearance of the Russian army which, it was hoped, would then improve the military effectiveness of both the officers and rank and file. One of the methods of achieving this goal was to adopt Western military dress and weapons.

By 1800, the Russian infantry officer was carrying a smallsword of European style. The Model 1786 Infantry Officer's Sword had a slightly curved, double-edged blade with a brass, heart-shaped guard and ovoid pommel. It was contained within a leather and brass mounted scabbard. Subsequent patterns (Model 1796 and Model 1798) had straight, single-edged blades with typical Napoleonic double shell guards and pronounced upward quillons.

Lower ranks in the infantry carried simple brass-hilted short swords with shell guards. As the century progressed, the Russian infantry adopted the same style of brass-hilted hanger as that carried by Prussian and English troops.

German infantry swords

The German states of the 18th and 19th centuries normally followed the sword patterns and styles prevalent throughout Europe. In keeping with French and English infantry privates of the mid- to late-1700s, a short, brass-hilted infantry hanger was carried throughout the Napoleonic Wars, particularly by Prussian infantrymen.

By 1800, German officers were already wearing a sword similar in design to the British 1796 Pattern Infantry Officer's Sword (the British had actually copied the pattern from a Prussian design of the 1750s). Hilt design was also heavily influenced by French infantry swords of the period. Sword blades featured engraved decoration, including the coats of arms and royal cyphers of individual states. Blue and gilt were also used extensively. There was no real attempt at uniformity of pattern, and different German states adopted and jealously guarded their own styles of infantry sword.

Austro-Hungarian infantry swords

The Austro-Hungarian infantry officer of the 1800s followed the same path as his British and German counterparts in favouring a smallsword. It included a gilt brass hilt with double boat shell guard and rounded pommel. The blade was straight and double-edged. Blades were normally engraved with the royal cypher and double-headed eagle of the Habsburg monarchy. Austrian infantry officers also carried a wide range of unofficial swords, including wide-bladed and curved "hussar"-type sabres. This type of sword was popular with infantry regiments throughout Europe during the 19th century.

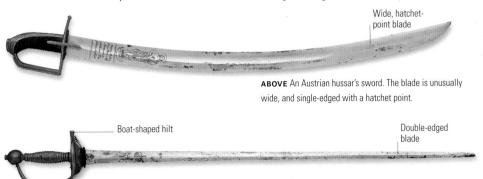

Wide, hatchet-point blade

ABOVE An Austrian hussar's sword. The blade is unusually wide, and single-edged with a hatchet point.

Boat-shaped hilt

Double-edged blade

ABOVE An Austro-Hungarian infantry officer's sword from c.1800. It has a double-edged blade with a double boat shell guard and rounded pommel.

The American sword

At the start of the American War of Independence (1775–83) the opposing armies carried a very similar range of weapons. This was inevitable because the Continental Army of General George Washington (1732–99) included many former British-trained local militias, armed with both British government and their own privately purchased weapons. As the war progressed and the British blockade of ports such as Boston (1775) began to bite, American forces had difficulty sourcing weapons from overseas. This forced them to rely on simple, locally manufactured swords, leading to the adoption of a distinctly "American" sword style.

Colonists' swords in the 16th and 17th centuries

The early settlers of the 16th and 17th centuries, living in newly established colonies such as Virginia and New England, were predominantly of British stock and brought with them significant quantities of edged weapons, particularly swords. Contemporary records of the period and subsequently excavated examples indicate that rapiers, short hangers and long-bladed horsemen's sabres were the most common sword types of this period. Apart from swords brought

directly from England or purchased from passing trading ships, a number of simple, locally forged swords were also manufactured in the colonies.

The American colonies were a crucial part of the expanding empires of both Great Britain and France, so a regular military presence was required to maintain order and promote national interests. During the early 18th century, soldiers from these nations carried the same swords in the colonies as they would have done in their home countries, including short, brass-hilted hangers for infantry troops and short hangers or smallswords for the officers.

The American War of Independence

During the early years of the American War of Independence the colonists fighting against the British and her allies would have carried virtually identical swords to their enemies. Later in the war, when replacements became more difficult to source from overseas, the colonists turned towards domestically manufactured weapons to fill the shortfall. Local American blacksmiths forged simple military blades that were attached to improvised hilts.

Although these blades were never produced to impress (tending to be flat, unfullered and undecorated), they proved quite effective on the battlefield. In the absence of any official style or designated sword patterns for the new Continental Army, American sword makers merely copied or interpreted the British or French patterns available at that time. The main priority of the Continental Army was to produce swords and edged weapons as quickly as possible.

LEFT The surrender of the British General Cornwallis, Yorktown, 1781. It was a tradition that the defeated commanding officer handed over his sword to the victor.

Cavalry swords in the 18th century

American cavalry troops of the 1770s carried an assortment of swords, including long, straight-bladed, basket-hilted broadswords and light cavalry sabres. Many would have been captured from the British. Their armoury also included home-made "D-guard", slotted-hilt, and flat-bladed backswords with simple, turned wooden grips. Typical pommel shapes such as ball, urn, cap, ovoid, high domed, flat or lion's head were also used. Scabbards were manufactured in leather and wood, with crude iron mounts.

Infantry swords in the 18th century

The ordinary American infantry soldier and officer of the 1770s had an extensive range of weapons, many of them captured from the British and some home-produced. The short hanger or hunting sword was favoured by the infantry officer, especially when fighting in the dense forests of North America, where a long-bladed sword was sometimes impractical. Smallswords were also carried by American officers but it is unlikely they would have been the first weapon of choice for combat.

Sword types after the War of Independence

During the War of Independence, the Eagle Pommel Sword became one of the defining "American" sword types of this period. It remained popular after the war.

In the 1800s, many of these swords were supplied to American officers by British-based sword makers, most notably William Ketland and Henry Osborn of Birmingham. In America, Frederick W. Widmann, a German-born sword maker, made distinctive and high-quality Eagle Pommel Swords in Philadelphia during the 1830s and 1840s. Indian-head and Neo-classical helmet pommels were also very popular during this period. Blade decoration began to incorporate specifically nationalistic American themes.

The new cavalry sword of 1798

After independence, the new American government began to form its fledgling army into established regiments, and with this reorganization there was the requirement to arm troops with new swords. The American Congress did not want to rely solely on overseas countries for their swords and so a domestic manufacturer was actively sought for a new model of cavalry sword. Nathan Starr, of Middleton, Connecticut, initially produced 2,000 Model 1798 Cavalry Trooper's Swords.

The sword had a simple stirrup guard with a leather and wood-covered grip, and a single-edged, slightly curved blade. The blade was marked "N Starr & Co." on one side and "US – 1799" on the other. Starr produced updated versions of this sword between 1814 and 1818.

The "Eagle Pommel Sword"

A common weapon of the post-Revolutionary War period was the American "Eagle Pommel Sword". During the war, other animal forms were also used for the pommel, including horses', dogs' and lions' heads. The variety of hilt and pommel types produced by American sword makers is numerous, and they were manufactured in silver, brass and iron, with grips of ivory, horn, wood and leather. They also differed widely in terms of quality and construction, reflecting the challenging conditions and the scarcity of basic materials. The sword makers were usually imitating British and continental sword styles of the period, but the relative naivety of design and crude construction of some types can be differentiated as typically "American". Conversely, there were also many American-made swords of this period that exhibited excellent workmanship.

ABOVE The American Eagle Pommel Sword was used by American officers. Early swords were normally produced in England.

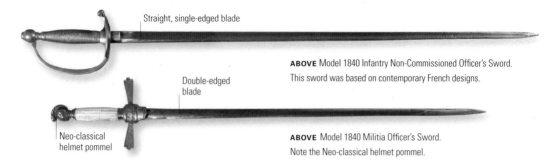

Straight, single-edged blade

Double-edged blade

Neo-classical helmet pommel

ABOVE Model 1840 Infantry Non-Commissioned Officer's Sword. This sword was based on contemporary French designs.

ABOVE Model 1840 Militia Officer's Sword. Note the Neo-classical helmet pommel.

By 1833, the N.P. Ames Sword Company of Springfield, Massachusetts, was manufacturing a robust brass, three-bar hilted cavalry sword with slightly curved blade. It was not well received by soldiers and, in 1840, the company introduced a cavalry trooper's sword of French style. This had a heavy, three-bar, brass hilt and a slightly curved blade with steel scabbard. It was grudgingly known by its users as the "wristbreaker".

This sword was replaced again in 1860 by a much lighter version, which became the standard issue cavalry trooper's sword for Union troops throughout the American Civil War (1861–65). The sword was updated in 1872 and 1906. Officers carried more elaborate versions with etched blades and embossed and gilt-covered hilts.

Infantry swords after 1830
Regulation infantry swords for the US Army began to appear from the 1830s. In 1832, a rather impractical smallsword of English style, with a gilt-brass boat-shell hilt, ovoid pommel and straight blade was introduced for officers of the Infantry, Artillery and Ordnance. There followed a number of other regulation infantry swords including the Model 1840 Foot Officer's Sword, similar to the Non-Commissioned Officer's version. The blade was straight, single-edged, with a double fuller. Decoration included drums, cannons, floral sprays, "US", eagles and crossed military pikes.

During the 1840s, states raised their own militias, and officers were required to provide their own uniform and sword. This gave them the opportunity

to choose from a wide variety of swords from private manufacturers. Differences of design normally centred on the pommel type and blade decoration. Some have Neo-classical helmet pommels in the style of contemporary French infantry swords, and other examples feature diverse interpretations of the American eagle-head pommel.

Militia regiments were also keen to present swords to fellow officers, and some presentation-grade swords are truly spectacular, with grips of engraved brass, silver or even gold, with heavy embossed decoration to the hilt and scabbard mounts. A number of swords were decorated over the entire length of the blade. The regular US Army also carried sword patterns specific to individual departments or branches of service. These included the Model 1834 Revenue Cutter Service Sword; the Model 1840 Engineer's Sword; the Model 1840 Commissary Officer's Sword; and the Model 1832 and Model 1840 Medical Staff Officer's Sword.

Infantry swords after 1850
In the mid-19th century and in keeping with the vogue for French-inspired designs, the US Army introduced a completely new sword for infantry officers. The Model 1850 Foot Officer's Sword is an almost exact copy of the French Model 1845 Infantry Officer's Sword. The blade is slightly curved and single edged, with double fullers. Decoration took the form of an outstretched American Eagle, floral and military motifs, "US" and the US government motto

Curved, slashing blade

ABOVE US Model 1860 Cavalry Trooper's Sword. It was made by Mansfield and Lamb of Forestdale, Rhode Island.

Confederate swords in the American Civil War (1861–65)

Prior to the American Civil War, the US Army was composed of officers and men from both the Southern and Northern states. In general, they carried the same sword models and this continued until war between the Union and Confederacy was declared on 12 April 1861.

During the early days of the war, many Confederate officers still carried their original Union swords but, as the war dragged on and the Union undertook a successful blockade of southern ports, overseas sword imports to the South began to dry up. Some imports still got through and Confederate agents were constantly busy in Europe, sourcing swords from both Britain and Germany, but this was still not enough to furnish a growing Confederate army and to replace the loss of existing swords due to combat. Confederate officers also wanted to differentiate themselves from the enemy and carry swords that reflected their national aspirations. This meant that the Confederate government was forced to turn to local manufacturers to make up the shortfall.

Southern sword makers usually copied the Union sword patterns, but there were subtle changes. These included the replacement of the standard "US" lettering on sword hilts with a "CS" or "CSA", representing the Confederate States or Confederate

ABOVE William Tecumseh Sherman (1820–91) left, Union general, meeting General Joseph E. Johnston (Confederate) to discuss terms of surrender of Confederate forces in North Carolina, 24 April 1865.

States of America. Blade etching also included specifically Southern motifs, including the five-pointed star of the Confederacy or a circle of 11 stars, which represented the 11 Confederate states.

However, most Southern sword makers, working with basic machinery and lacking essential raw materials, were forced to produce rather crudely manufactured swords. The quality deteriorated even further as a number of established Southern sword-making factories were overrun by Union forces towards the end of the war.

BELOW Confederate Cavalry Officer's Sword, c.1864. Standards of manufacture in the north were invariably superior.

_____ Crudely cast hilt

E Pluribus Unum (Out of Many, One). A large number of these swords were imported from Europe at the beginning of the American Civil War to make up for a shortfall in home production.

The Model 1850 Staff and Field Officer's Sword is similar to the Model 1850 Foot Officer except that it has an additional branch to the hilt, with a "US" set between the hilt bars. This was one of the most popular officer's swords carried by line officers and staff officers between 1850 and 1872.

Cavalry swords in the 20th century

The Model 1913 "Patton" hilt Cavalry Trooper's Sword was based on a design presented by the young Lieutenant George S. Patton (1885–1945) of the US Army, later to become a famous American general during World War II. This sword owes more than a passing nod to the popular British 1908 Pattern Cavalry Trooper's Sword but it differs in having a dove-head pommel, slightly lower basket guard and a wider, double-fullered blade.

Post-Napoleonic swords

The massed cavalry charges of the Napoleonic Wars had been a vital shock tactic, however, as the 19th century progressed, their effectiveness began to be questioned, especially in light of the huge advances being made in military technology. The contest between bullet and blade had now become one-sided. In the American Civil War, only 2 per cent of wounds received were from edged weapons. Nonetheless, the sword was still regarded as an essential combat weapon, and efforts were redoubled to design the perfect sword.

Pipe-back blade

ABOVE British 1821 Pattern Heavy Cavalry Officer's Sword with pipe-back (tubular) blade.

British light and heavy cavalry swords

Following the Napoleonic Wars, the British Army introduced a series of cavalry swords with both cut and thrust capabilities. These included the 1821 Pattern Light and Heavy Cavalry Trooper and Officer's swords. The light cavalry version comprised a steel, three-bar hilt and slightly curved, spear-point blade. Heavy cavalry officers also carried a spear-point blade, etched for most of its length, with a pierced bowl guard of acanthus-leafed decoration. Heavy cavalry troopers had a plain, solid bowl guard. The initial reception of these swords by troops in the field was poor, with frequent complaints that blades were too thin and liable to snap in combat. Soldiers also encountered difficulties when attempting to pierce enemy uniforms with their sword points, especially during the Crimean War (1853–56), when the Russian infantryman's thick greatcoat, combined with a rolled blanket worn on his back, made penetration by the blade extremely difficult.

The British universal pattern of 1853

In 1853, the next major change in British sword design occurred, when the differentiation between heavy and light cavalry troopers' swords was finally dropped in favour of a universal pattern. This was the 1853 Pattern Cavalry Trooper's Sword. It had the same three-bar hilt and blade as the previous 1821 pattern but employed a new "patent" grip, designed by the sword maker Charles Reeves, in partnership with fellow sword maker Henry Wilkinson. It was a revolutionary hilt design as it enabled the full width of the tang to be driven the length of the grip, rather than the previously tapered and potentially weaker tangs. Chequered leather grips were then riveted through this full-length tang, adding more strength and durability.

Thrusting versus cutting swords

From the mid-19th century, British cavalry swords went through a further series of changes. The historic argument concerning the use of either a thrusting or a cutting sword continued, with many official army committees established to consider the question. The eventual result of this "decision by committee" process was a predictably unsuitable compromise, with blades being neither fully straight to enable proper thrusting

Riveted grip

Spear-point blade

ABOVE British 1899 Pattern Cavalry Trooper's Sword with a slightly curved, spear-point blade.

The charge of the 21st Lancers, Battle of Omdurman, 1898

During the Second Sudan War, the Battle of Omdurman in 1898 was one of the last occasions when massed British cavalry carrying lances charged in force at the enemy. The future British prime minister, Winston Churchill, was present at the battle as a young cavalry officer attached to the 21st Lancers and he later graphically described his first-hand experiences on 2 September 1898. The sight of the 21st Lancers just before the famous charge was caught by Churchill in typically realistic terms:

...a great square block of ungainly figures and little horses, hung all over with water-bottles, saddle bags, picketing gear, tins of bully beef, all jolting and jangling together; the polish of peace gone; soldiers without glitter; horsemen without grace; but still a regiment of light cavalry in active service against the enemy...

from Winston Spencer Churchill, *The River War: An Historical Account of the Reconquest of the Soudan*, 2 Vols., ed. Col. F. Rhodes (Longmans, Green, London, 1899).

Colonel R.M. Martin, commanding officer of the 21st Lancers, initially engaged his 300 lancers with what appeared to be a few hundred Dervishes from the army of Abdullah al-Taashi (successor to the so-called "Mad Mahdi" Muhammad Ahmed, responsible for the death of General Gordon at Khartoum in 1885). But within seconds, over 2,000 spearmen and swordsmen crouching in a nearby shallow depression had risen to meet the advancing lancers. Having committed the regiment to the charge and too close to wheel around, Martin and his lancers crashed into the waiting Dervishes. Later accounts highlight the sheer brutality and bloodshed experienced during these colonial encounters. For their gallant action against impossible odds and driving back the Dervishes, three Victoria Crosses (the highest award for gallantry in the British Army) were subsequently awarded to members of the 21st Lancers. Their losses were five officers, 65 men, and 120 horses.

RIGHT Charge of the 21st Lancers at Omdurman, 2 September 1898. The battle was seen as Britain's revenge for the death of General Gordon at Khartoum, 1885. The charge of the 21st Lancers was regarded as the last full cavalry charge of a British regiment equipped with lances.

nor sufficiently curved for effective cutting. The patterns of 1864, 1882, 1885, 1890 and 1899 highlight the constant changes made to cavalry swords during this period in order to achieve this requirement.

British infantry swords
The Napoleonic 1796 and 1803 Pattern Infantry Officers' swords had a relatively long service life, and it was not until 1822 that a new pattern replaced them. This was very different in design to its predecessors and featured a "pipe-back" blade with a tubular sectioned back, or spine, to provide extra strength, combined with a "Gothic" gilt brass, half-basket hilt. The term "Gothic" refers to the similarity of the hilt profile to medieval Gothic church windows, the design of which heavily influenced the Gothic Revival in

Britain during the first half of the 19th century. Within the hilt there was placed a "cartouche", or inset panel, featuring a cut-out royal cypher of the reigning monarch: for example, "VR" for "Victoria Regina".

British infantry swords in the late 19th century
The blue and gilt blade decoration favoured by a previous generation of British infantry officers had now become unfashionable, and blades were acid etched (rather than engraved) on a plain background.

Scabbards were leather and gilt brass mounted (for dress), brass or plain steel. The updated 1845 Pattern removed the folding guard, and the original pipe-back blade was replaced in the 1850s by a single-fullered "Wilkinson", spear-point blade that proved less prone to breaking.

Ribbed horn grip

Quillon

ABOVE French Model 1845 Pattern Infantry Officer's Sword. This pattern would have been carried during the Crimean War (1853–56).

In 1892, the blade changed to a "dumb-bell" profile and became a purely thrusting weapon. There was also a complete redesign of the hilt which now took the form of a solid sheet steel, half-basket guard impressed or pierced with the Victorian royal crown and cypher. In 1895 and 1897, there were minor modifications to the hilt, including the addition of a turned-down inner edge to avoid fraying the officer's uniform.

The Rifle and Foot Guards regiments carried a steel half-basket-hilted sword (1827 Pattern and 1854 Pattern) of similar design to the 1822 Pattern "Gothic" hilt but with the addition of their regimental badges within the

hilt. In 1857, the Royal Engineers were designated a pierced gilt-brass, half-basket-hilted sword which they carried until 1892, when they reverted to the standard 1897 Pattern Sword for all infantry officers.

French infantry swords

The French Model 1821 and 1845 Infantry Officer's Sword was a radical departure from previous infantry swords, and its elegant design inspired many other countries, particularly the United States. It comprised a decorated brass, half-basket hilt with a single knuckle bow guard and a slightly curved, single-edged, quill point blade. Grips were of ribbed horn and brass twistwire. The later Model 1845 continued the knuckle bow into a pierced shell guard with floral decoration. The blade was also a little straighter and produced in both pipe-back and quill-pointed form. Scabbards were leather and gilt-brass mounted. In 1855, the blade was changed to a single-fullered, spear-point type. This sword was carried until 1882, when the French Army introduced a nickel-plated steel, four-bar hilted sword with a much narrower, straight blade.

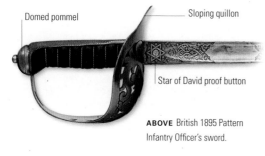

Domed pommel

Sloping quillon

Star of David proof button

ABOVE British 1895 Pattern Infantry Officer's sword.

French sword design

In 1822, a new light cavalry sword was issued to French cavalry troopers. It comprised a three-bar brass hilt, slightly curved blade, and heavy steel scabbard. It would be adopted by many other countries during the 19th century. This was also true of the French Model 1829 Mounted Artillery Sword that featured a single "D-guard," brass knuckle bow and unusual, slightly domed pommel. This style of sword was copied by the United States (Model

1840 Artillery Officer's Sword) and carried throughout the American Civil War by Union forces. Other European nations such as Spain, Germany, Belgium and even Russia were all heavily influenced by French three or four-bar hilt design and French-designed blades.

BELOW French Model 1822 Light Cavalry Officer's Sword. Unlike the trooper's version, the hilt has been decorated.

Slightly curved blade

French cavalry swords

The Model 1822 Light Cavalry Sword had a long service life, only being replaced in 1896 by a new universal cavalry sword, which served for both light and heavy cavalry. The officer's version of this 1896 Pattern Cavalry Officer's Sword is quite unique with an innovative hilt style. It is very much an example of contemporary Art Nouveau decorative art forms influencing the design of a weapon of war. The hilt ornamentation was designed by the French sculptor and painter Jean Alexandre Falguière (1831–1900), who was a professor at the École des Beaux-Arts in Paris.

Falguière designed the hilt around a pattern of flowing lines and botanical motifs that draped itself around the bowl guard. Symbolism was important to exponents of Art Nouveau (1890s–early 1900s), and we see this with the striking incorporation of the mythological figure of Medusa's head into the curving quillon. The sword has always had an important association in mythology. In this case the designer has focused on the myth of Perseus and Medusa. The sight of the gorgon Medusa would turn men to stone, but Perseus managed to kill her by only viewing her image reflected in his shield. He cut off her head with his sword and gave the head to Athena, who placed it in the middle of her shield to terrify her enemies.

In 1923, a universal model of sword for all officers of the French Army was issued. This was an attractive sword with a gilt-brass, shallow-bowl hilt, and single knuckle bow. The sides of the bowl guard were pierced and decorated with leaf patterns, and its overall appearance was still clearly influenced by the Art Nouveau movement.

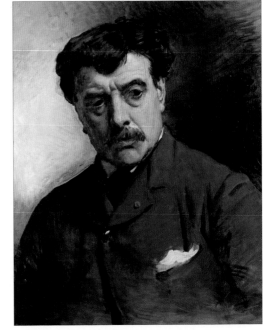

ABOVE A professor at the École des Beaux-Arts in Paris, Jean Alexandre Falguière (1831–1900), designed the hilt of the 1896 Pattern Cavalry Officer's Sword in the Art Nouveau style.

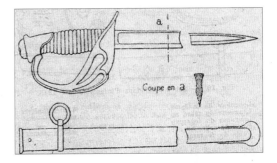

ABOVE An official diagram of the 1896 Pattern Cavalry Trooper's Sword, issued in 1937 by the French Ministry for War.

Naval swords and edged weapons

The truly naval sword probably originated in the 16th or 17th century. Before then, naval officers and sailors carried swords identical to those on land. During this time, navies began to evolve from legalized privateers serving under covert royal patronage into more organized enforcers of a state's military and commercial interests. Ship and crew underwent changes in their administration, equipment and appearance. The emergence of "fighting ships" in the 18th century meant that close hand-to-hand boarding engagements became common. Effective swords, axes and pikes were needed for chaotic, confined naval encounters.

The emergence of the British cutlass

Cutlasses were provided for seamen by the Board of Ordnance. This was a British government authority created in the 15th century with the responsibility for the design, testing and production of armaments for both the British Army and Navy. From the late 1500s, a short-bladed weapon described as a "curtleax", or coute-lace, was carried on British ships. Although this is now thought to have been more of an axe than a sword, the name was established and, by the 18th century, ships' captains began to refer to a specific sword for use on board ship as a "cuttlashe".

British cutlasses in the 18th and 19th centuries

The number of cutlasses carried on board a ship was actually small in relation to the numbers of sailors, and not every seaman was issued with a cutlass. Other weapons such as pikes and axes were employed to fill the gaps. The manufacturing quality of these early cutlasses was quite poor and most cutlass hilts were made from a single piece of thin sheet steel, which opened out into two discs for better hand protection. Blades were flat, single-edged, straight or slightly curved.

Cutlass manufacture for the Royal Navy was undertaken by a number of English sword makers, resulting in a marked variation in both quality and reliability. The official inspection and testing of sword blades was still in its infancy during this period. In 1804, a regulation pattern of seaman's cutlass was adopted.

This was the "figure-of-eight", or double disc-hilted, cutlass and is probably the one most commonly associated with British seamen during the Napoleonic Wars. It comprised a blackened cast-iron hilt with ribbed grip and a straight, flat, unfullered blade.

Subsequent patterns followed in 1814, 1845, 1858 and 1889 until 1900, when the last official pattern was introduced. Naval planners of the 1900s realized that boarding actions in the age of the ironclad battleship were unlikely and no more patterns were introduced after this date. In 1936, the cutlass was withdrawn from British naval use except for ceremonial purposes.

British naval officers' swords in the 17th and 18th centuries

Up until the beginning of the 19th century, a Royal Navy officer was given considerable leeway as to which edged weapons he carried. During the latter part of the 17th century, the rapier was abandoned by naval officers in favour of short-bladed, hunting-type hangers. These short swords were far more practical when officers were fighting amongst the rigging and confined spaces of a ship's deck. Many contemporary portraits show British naval officers carrying these swords. Naval officers might also have carried a smallsword, which was similar in design to those carried by civilians or army officers, although some rare examples displayed nautical motifs to the hilt and blade.

Flat-backed blade

Royal cypher

ABOVE This cutlass, introduced in 1804, became standard issue to the Royal Navy and was carried throughout the Napoleonic Wars.

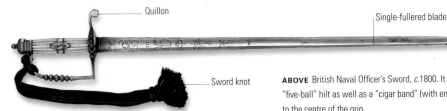

Quillon

Single-fullered blade

Sword knot

ABOVE British Naval Officer's Sword, *c.*1800. It has a beaded or "five-ball" hilt as well as a "cigar band" (with engraved fouled anchor) to the centre of the grip.

In 1786, the British Army formally adopted a new regulation pattern sword for all infantry officers, and naval officers soon copied this style. The cut-and-thrust blade was straight with a beaded or "five-ball" "D-guard" hilt and cushion pommel. An anchor was also engraved into a gilt-brass "cigar band" that was placed in the centre of a ribbed ivory or ebony grip. Some examples also had a small anchor placed in the centre of a side ring. Other sword types included "S-bar" hilts (which featured an anchor) and stirrup hilts engraved with anchors on each of the hilt langets. These swords imitated contemporary infantry and cavalry swords.

By the late 18th century, the hunting hanger was dropped in favour of a more traditional short infantry sword with "slotted" guard, lion's-head or ovoid pommel and slightly curved blade. To distinguish them from infantry swords, many had a small fouled anchor inserted into the slotted guard or engraved on the pommel.

BELOW A British naval officer's sword, *c.*1815. It has the standard lion's head pommel and the ivory grip indicates that its owner was a high-ranking officer. This is not a fighting sword and would have been carried as a dress weapon, reserved for social occasions.

British naval officers' swords in the 19th century

The 1805 Pattern Naval Officer's Sword was a more recognizably "naval" style of sword. It featured a gilt-brass lion's-head pommel and engraved fouled anchor to the langets (located in the centre of the cross guard). Blades were straight and single-fullered. Many had extensive blue and gilt decoration, including naval motifs such as flags, trophies, anchors and buoys. A Royal Navy midshipman (junior officer) of the early 1800s carried a sword similar in design to senior officers but with black rather that white fishskin or ivory grips. In 1827, officers adopted a solid, gilt-brass, half-basket hilt, a pattern that mirrors the 1822 Pattern Infantry Officer's Sword. The grip was composed of white fishskin (black for warrant officers), and blades were initially of pipeback and quill point profile, changing to a single-fullered "Wilkinson"-type blade in the mid-1850s. The 1827 Pattern is still carried by serving Royal Navy officers today.

Other British naval sword designs included a mameluke sword for flag officers; open rather than solid hilts; "dove-head" pommels (for warrant officers); and a Scottish Highland, or "claymore", blade, which became popular in the late 19th century.

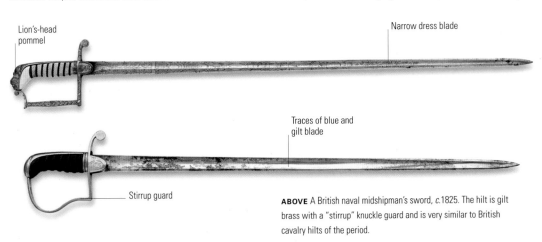

Lion's-head pommel

Narrow dress blade

Traces of blue and gilt blade

Stirrup guard

ABOVE A British naval midshipman's sword, *c.*1825. The hilt is gilt brass with a "stirrup" knuckle guard and is very similar to British cavalry hilts of the period.

Presentation swords

It was common practice during the Napoleonic period for British naval officers to receive presentation swords in honour of their gallant acts in the face of the enemy and bodies such as the Corporation of London regularly bestowed presentation or commemorative swords.

The Lloyds Patriotic Fund presentation swords have since become famous for their opulence, craftsmanship and breathtaking beauty. They were paid for and presented by members of the insurance house, Lloyds of London, between 1803 and 1810, and were given in recognition of the recipient's bravery under fire. They were also an acknowledgement of (and a vote of thanks for) the protection afforded by the Royal Navy to British commercial interests, both home and abroad, during the long wars with Napoleon.

The swords were awarded in four categories depending on the cost of manufacture and rose in magnificence as their value increased. They were presented as swords of £30, £50 and £100 value. There was also a special sword of truly epic grandeur awarded to the 29 captains and lieutenants who commanded ships during the Battle of Trafalgar, in 1805.

The Lloyds' swords had heavy, slightly curved blades with lavishly applied blue and gilt decoration, white ivory grips and opulent hilts of fire gilt. The hilt backpiece was decorated in imitation of a lion skin and the quillons displayed ancient Roman fasces (tied bundles of birch rods wrapped around an axe and symbolizing "strength through unity"). The knuckle guard took the form of a stylized interpretation of the

club of Hercules entwined by a serpent. Scabbards were even more elaborate, encased in either leather or blue velvet (depending on the value awarded) and decorated with numerous classical reliefs and panels. The production of these swords was a showcase for the artistry and imagination displayed by some of the finest artisans in Georgian London.

Lion's mane backstrap

Embossed decoration

ABOVE From the Patriotic Fund at Lloyds to Lieutenant James Bowen of HMS *La Loire*, who was commader of one of the boats that successfully attacked a French national brig in 1803.

French cutlasses in the 18th and 19th centuries

In the 18th century, cutlasses in the French Navy were formally standardized with the introduction of a Model 1771 Seaman's Cutlass (modified in 1782-83). The hilt was brass with a ribbed grip and prominent pommel cap. It was similar to contemporary infantry grenadier hilts, but differed in having a three-bar hilt rather than a single knuckle guard.

The Napoleonic Model Year XI (1801–02) Cutlass had a large, half-basket guard of blackened iron, with a smooth octagonal grip and a slightly curved and wide-fullered blade. A later model (1833) saw the addition of an engraved anchor to the blade. The Model 1872 was the last regulation pattern French cutlass and

comprised a hilt of plate steel, shaped grip and perforated guard.

French naval officers' swords in the 18th and 19th centuries

During the 18th century, French naval officers followed the British practice of carrying swords similar to those in the army. Later, a more uniform sword was introduced based on a French Light Cavalry Officer's sword differing only in having an engraved anchor within the lozenge-shaped hilt langets. In 1805, a new pattern saw the complete removal of langets and the placing of an anchor within the cross guard.

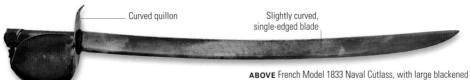

Curved quillon

Slightly curved,
single-edged blade

ABOVE French Model 1833 Naval Cutlass, with large blackened bowl guard. It evolved from the Year XI Model, 1801–02, Naval Cutlass, introduced during the Napoleonic period.

In 1837, a completely new sword design is noted. It comprised an elaborately decorated gilt-brass, half-basket hilt, incorporating an anchor, royal crown and display of martial trophies. There followed some slight changes to the hilt decoration in the years 1848 (removal of the royal crown), 1852 and 1870.

German cutlasses in the 19th and 20th centuries

During the mid-1800s, Prussian naval seamen carried a cutlass that was almost identical to the French Model 1833 Cutlass, differing only in having a distinctive falchion-type blade. It was the standard naval cutlass for the Prussian and, later, the Imperial German Navy throughout the 19th century. In 1911, a new model was introduced that comprised an open steel, three-bar hilt of cavalry type, with a blade similar to contemporary German "butcher"-type bayonets, featuring a gradually widening and double-edged blade.

German naval officers' swords in the 19th and 20th centuries

It is difficult to present an accurate picture of German naval officers' swords before the unification of the country in 1871, as there was no dedicated "German" Navy until the formation of the mainly Prussian Imperial Fleet (Reichsflotte) during the revolutionary period of 1848–52. No tangible attempts were made to standardize sword patterns, and, before 1871, German naval officers carried swords that were similar to contemporary British naval officers' swords, including solid half-basket hilts and lion's-head pommels.

With the establishment of the Kaiserliche Marine, or Imperial Navy, after reunification in 1871, naval officers' swords took on a more specifically "German"

BELOW Portrait of Louis-Jean-Marie de Bourbon (1725–1793), Admiral of the French fleet. He is carrying a smallsword favoured by officers.

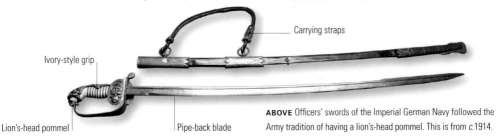

Carrying straps

Ivory-style grip

Lion's-head pommel

Pipe-back blade

ABOVE Officers' swords of the Imperial German Navy followed the Army tradition of having a lion's-head pommel. This is from *c.*1914.

The boarding pike

For many centuries the simple spear or javelin was a weapon that had been carried on land and at sea. It was only when European nations began to formalize their navies in the 17th and 18th centuries that a designated polearm for boarding ships begin to emerge.

The polearm had many other names, including half pike, strong pike or short pike, and comprised a drastically reduced traditional infantryman's pike. The boarding pike was particularly effective at thrusting and fending off enemies in the confined and restricted spaces of a ship's deck. Pikes were normally kept in racks on board ship.

Early 17th century examples had a pick-style point, square or triangular in cross-section, with long langets, and were designed to deliver a thrusting blow. Later pike heads of the 18th century were more streamlined in profile and so avoided snagging in the rigging of the crowded upper decks of sailing ships. An account by an American, Jacob Nagle, serving on

a British sloop of war off the coast of Spain in 1800, gives a dramatic illustration of the primitive effectiveness of a pike when used in trained hands.

In the smoke I perceiv'd the French capt. drawing a pistol from his belt to fire at our capt. that was giving command. I drew a pistol at the same time and let him have the contents. At the same time a stout Frenchman made a blow at me with a large hangar, from the netting, but the man behind me saw the blow and covered my head with his boarding pike, which was cut that it fell and the bare point struck me in the head and I fell, but the man ketch'd up he pike and run it into his body and he fell between two vessels…

from the *Nagle Journal*, 1775–1841, (Weidenfeld & Nicolson, New York, 1988).

BELOW A boarding pike with tomahawk head.

BELOW A boarding pike with spiked point.

style. The solid, gilt-brass hilt and lion's-head pommel remained but became flatter in profile, with the addition of a fold-down guard and Imperial Crown cartouche (a tablet within the hilt). Grips were bone or ivory. This style remained until Germany's defeat in 1918 when the Imperial Crown was removed. During the Nazi period (1933–45), naval officers' dirks, but not swords, bore an eagle and swastika.

Imperial Russia in the 19th and 20th centuries

Like most European navies, Russia did not attempt to formally regulate its naval swords until the 1800s. Russian naval officers of the early 1800s would have carried swords similar to the British 1796 Pattern Infantry Officer's Sword. The 1811 Pattern Naval Officer's Sword set the trend for future Russian naval officers' swords, comprising a brass three-bar hilted sword with a distinctive canted or curved backpiece

and pommel. This is a style also found on many French and German military swords of the period. The pattern was updated in 1855 and 1914.

Naval swords remained unchanged until the Russian Revolution of 1917. Thereafter, all Imperial designations to both blade and hilt were erased, and the sword became plainer in design, although some naval officers were known to place Soviet hammer-and-sickle or red-star devices on the blade pommel.

Russian cutlasses

A formal pattern of naval cutlass for Russian seamen was not issued until 1810. Before then, naval ratings carried a short hanger of French "briquet" form. The 1810 Pattern was worn on a shoulder belt and issued to naval bombardiers and gunners. The blade was of Turkish yataghan (forward-curved) style with a brass-hilt cross guard, wooden grip and swollen pommel.

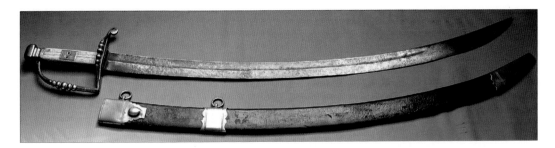

ABOVE An American officer's naval sword from *c.*1790. The blade is slightly curved and the grip is made from bone.

It was more of a hanger than a cutlass, and did not have the protective bowl guard or disc hilt more commonly associated with European naval cutlasses of this time. The Russian 1856 Pattern Boarding Cutlass was traditionally "western" in style and imitated British and French cutlasses. It had a blackened iron hilt with ribbed grip and matching blackened steel scabbard mounts. Cutlass design remained unchanged until 1940, when a new pattern was introduced for naval cadets. It had a double-edged, slightly curving blade and steel hilt with a pronounced guard and ribbed wooden grip. The need for a cutlass in the 1940s seems rather tenuous, although the Soviet Navy insisted on it being carried when outside the naval school. After 1958, it was only worn on ceremonial occasions.

Russian gallantry swords

Imperial Russian naval presentation swords were very popular in the 19th and early 20th centuries. They differed from standard naval patterns in having solid gilt, ribbed metal grips rather than the usual leather and brass twistwire wrapping. They were known as "Gold Swords" and featured engraved Cyrillic (Russian) lettering (normally with wording such as "For Gallantry") on the hilt bars. A number of grades, or orders, were also presented. An enamelled cross representing either the Order of St George or that of St Anne (before 1869) was also attached to the hilt pommel. Bullion sword knots were worn and their design differed according to the level of order attained.

American naval swords to the 20th century

Both during and after the American Revolutionary War (1775–83), American naval officers carried swords of traditional British or French style. Most were manufactured and exported from these countries to the United States during periods of peace between the two countries. In 1841, an eagle-headed naval officer's sword was introduced and its design closely followed sword styles already prevalent in the army. The Model 1852 Naval Officer's Sword was inspired by European (particularly French) solid, half-basket-hilted naval swords and it is still carried today. Cutlasses of English style were issued in 1797 and 1808.

The Model 1841 and Model 1860 USN cutlasses were both designed by the N.P. Ames sword company of Springfield, Massachusetts. The Model 1841 was derived from contemporary French "gladius" short swords, and the Model 1860 was an interpretation of the French Model AIX (1801–02), albeit with brass hilt and scabbard mounts, rather than the blackened sheet iron used in the French version.

Unusually, there was also an officer's model, differing from the ordinary seaman's cutlass in having the letters "USN" or "US" cut out of the hilt. This cutlass had a long service life and was only replaced in 1917 by a new model based on the Dutch army klewang (machete-style) cutlass. There are two versions: the early model has a solid iron bowl guard while the 1941 variation has a guard with separate branches.

BELOW The Model 1917 cutlass was carried on US Navy ships until the beginning of World War II. It was declared obsolete in 1949.

Bowl guard

Swords of the two World Wars

Despite significant advances in warfare technology during the latter half of the 19th century, including the development of ever-more destructive firearms and artillery, many military commanders entered the first years of the new century still believing that the use of massed cavalry and the flash of steel would easily overcome the new machine guns and rapid-firing rifles. They would be sadly mistaken.

World War I swords

Paradoxically, the very first recorded casualty inflicted by a serving British soldier in Europe during World War I occurred when Captain Charles Hornby of the 4th Royal Irish Dragoon Guards killed a German Uhlan with his sword on 22 August 1914. He was leading a charge against four troopers of the 2nd Kurassier Regiment near the village of Casteau, north of Mons, in Belgium.

Both British and German officers continued to wear swords in the early stages of World War I but it soon became apparent that this was an anachronism totally unsuited to the practicalities of trench warfare. Officers also realized that the carrying of a sword

ABOVE The retreat from Mons during World War I in August to September 1914. Notice that the British cavalry are carrying lances.

The final British cavalry sword of 1908

Probably one of the most radical of all known sword designs is the 1908 Pattern Cavalry Trooper's Sword. It comprised a thin, rapier-like blade, large enclosed bowl-hilt and unique pistol grip. It was as far removed from traditional sword design as could be possible. Its very uniqueness finally resolved the argument within the British military establishment of whether to use a thrusting or cutting blade. The pattern was unashamedly thrusting and designed for the shock of a cavalry charge. The grip was also manufactured in a new composite material, dermatine (the 1912 Pattern Officer's version retained a fishskin covering), and included a thumb depression on the backpiece to enable the carrier to grip the sword in a fashion similar to the gripping of a lance.

Despite the fact that King Edward VII (r.1901–10) described this new design as "hideous", the 1908 Pattern went into full production and was soon standard issue in British cavalry regiments. The advent of World War I (1914–18) was regarded by the military as the ideal testing ground for this new pattern of sword, but the conflict actually sounded its death knell. Confronted with grinding trench warfare and an immovable battlefield typified by the Western Front, the opportunity for massed mobile cavalry action had simply disappeared.

BELOW 1908 Pattern Cavalry Trooper's Sword. Note the solid steel bowl guard and the pistol grip. The blade is rapier-like and designed for thrusting rather than cutting.

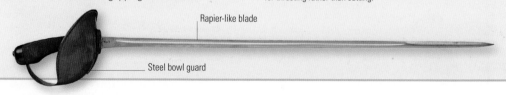

Rapier-like blade

Steel bowl guard

Russian cavalry swords

The active use of the sword within cavalry regiments in eastern Europe, and particularly Russia, was still commonplace throughout World War I and well into the 1930s. The vast, open terrain of the Russian landscape was well suited to the use of massed cavalry, and the Russian Cossack troops of both the Czarist and post-Revolutionary Soviet period wielded their favourite shasqua swords (a slightly curved sabre with a single-edged blade) against both German and Bolshevik enemies. The Soviets of the 1920s and 1930s continued issuing swords to Cossack troops (now "integrated" into the Soviet Republic), and these weapons were last called upon during the German invasion of Russia in 1941, when they were recorded as being used by troops undertaking brave but ultimately futile massed attacks against advancing German tanks.

ABOVE Cossack troops charge against German forces in 1942.

made them an obvious and prized target for machine gunners and snipers from both sides. Swords were still purchased but only for dress occasions.

The last massed British cavalry charge was at the Battle of Mughar, near Jerusalem, on 13 November 1917, when a combined force of the Buckinghamshire Hussars, supported by the Dorset and Berkshire Yeomanry Regiments, overran a significant Turkish position, capturing hundreds of prisoners.

British Air Force swords in the 20th century

The 1920s witnessed the emergence of a unique sword for a new branch of the British Army. This was the British 1920 Pattern Royal Air Force Officer's Sword, the last official regulation pattern sword of the British Army. Designed by the Wilkinson Sword Company of London, the hilt was based on the 1897 Pattern Infantry Officer's

Sword. This was an acknowledgement of the crucial role played by the Royal Engineers' Balloonist Unit (raised in 1878) in establishing the future Royal Flying Corps (RFC) in 1912 and the Royal Naval Air Service (RNAS) in 1914. They were later merged in 1918 to form the Royal Air Force (RAF). British airmen from the RFC or the RNAS would have originally been posted from different army or naval units, and consequently they would have carried a dress sword appropriate to their original branch of service or regiment. The need for a standardized pattern was therefore obvious. The 1920 Pattern had a gilt-brass, half-basket hilt with eagle-head pommel and crowned winged albatross inset into the hilt cartouche. The grip was white sharkskin. This pattern of ceremonial sword is still carried by serving officers of the RAF.

Italian/German Air Force swords in the 20th century

Both Italy and Germany produced their own air force swords, with both nations drawing heavily on the contemporary Art Deco influences of the 1920s and 1930s. The Italian Air Force officer's sword of the 1930s had a sweeping, gilt brass eagle-head hilt, and the German Model 1934 Air Force Officer's Sword exhibited a very modernistic hilt design, with dramatically downswept quillons and exaggerated pommel.

Nazi swords before World War II

The catastrophic defeat of Germany and its allies in World War I brought a temporary halt to the widespread promotion and wearing of swords in these countries. The size of the German Army during the Weimar Republic (1919–33) was also reduced significantly and the famous German sword-making town of Solingen experienced a drastic reduction in military orders for its edged weapons. Only when the Nazis came to power in 1933 were the fortunes of Solingen reversed. A delegation of officials from the town met the new German Chancellor, Adolf Hitler, and persuaded him that the production of swords and daggers for the Nazi Party (and the armed forces) would create new employment in a town badly hit by the worldwide economic slump of 1929 and the early 1930s (the Great Depression). Soon numerous government and quasi-military organizations within the new Nazi state had adopted edged weapons. The German Army (Heer), Air Force (Luftwaffe) and Navy (Kriegsmarine) all started to carry new sword designs created in the workshops of Solingen.

Japanese swords and polearms

The traditional Japanese Samurai sword is both a devastating weapon of armed combat and an object of great aesthetic beauty. This makes it rather unusual when compared with most military swords, which are primarily functional tools of war. The manufacture of Samurai swords was, for the master swordsmith, part religious ceremony and part spiritual journey. The Samurai warrior, clad in exotic lacquered armour and fearsome horned kabuko helmet, would always ensure that he went into battle armed with a range of swords and daggers, most notably the katana and wakizashi.

Mythical beginnings

The history of the Japanese sword begins with the traditional mythology of Shinto (the native religion of Japan). The Sun Goddess, Amaterasu Omikami, is said to have given her grandson, Ninigi-no Mikoto, a special sword when he was sent down to reign on Earth. The Shinto religion and the worship of the Japanese sword have always been closely linked.

Japanese swords were thought to have miraculous spiritual powers and even a personal identity of their own. Japanese soldiers who were defeated in battle would pray at the shrines of the war god Hachiman, asking why their swords had lost their martial spirit.

This extreme personalization of a Japanese warrior's sword resulted in the application of a strict code of etiquette for the handling and maintenance of swords.

Influence of China and Korea

In historical terms, the origin of the Japanese sword has a timeline of nearly 2,000 years. Japanese sword design mirrored very much the designs in China and Korea during the first two millennia. Swords that have been found in Japanese burial mounds and dated to *c.* AD300 have blades that were long and single-edged, very much like the Chinese jian, with a simple tsuba mount (a disc-shaped swordguard at the end of the handle).

Japanese clansmen warriors from this early period were predominantly horsemen who needed a long-bladed sword that could be used against infantry. Many Japanese swords were actually imported from China and Korea. A truly Japanese home-based sword-making industry only developed later.

The Heian period (AD794–1192)

During the early medieval period, the classic Japanese Samurai sword style started to become more recognizable. This process evolved through the gradual change of the blade shape from straight to slightly curved. During the Heian period, Japanese swordsmiths also began to mark their own work on the blade "tang" (the plate of metal that secures the blade to the sword handle), so enabling future generations to identify both the date of manufacture and the name and province in which the swordsmith lived. The appearance of a more distinctive "hamon", or pattern to the blade, is also evident during this period.

LEFT A 15th-century depiction of a Japanese Samurai warrior carrying sword and polearm. He lived by a code of honour, bravery and loyalty.

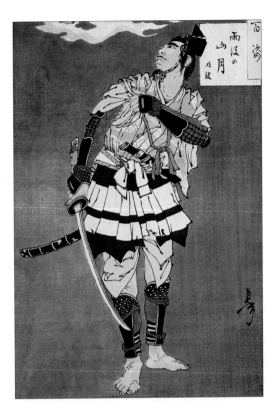

RIGHT 19th-century print of a Samurai holding his sword. Note the wakizashi (short sword or side arm) in his belt.

The Heian period, under the direction of Emperor Kammu (AD781–806), produced blades that are regarded as some of the most perfect ever manufactured and they have now acquired an almost mythical status. During this period the Fujiwara class of military nobility began to emerge and adopt this distinctive style of sword.

Other important periods of sword manufacture include the Kamakura period (1192–1333), Shoshino or Namboku Cho period (1333–93), Muromachi period (1338–1573), Edo period (1603–1867) and Showa period (1926–89). These periods relate to dynasties or clans that were based in separate areas of Japan, some at the same time.

The "way of the warrior"

Any history of the Samurai and his association with the sword must first begin with an explanation of bushido, or "the way of the warrior". This was a strict code of behaviour that had to be followed with honour, bravery and utmost loyalty. The Samurai was also taught to live with "freedom without fear". Allied with this moral philosophy was a strong reliance on training in the art of combat (bujutsu).

Early Samurai used a combination of bows and arrows, and swords. Later Samurai used swords, spears and naginata (halberds). Samurai often named their swords as a mark of personal devotion, and believed that their own warrior spirit was actually contained within these swords.

The Kamakura Period (1192–1333)

Samurai warrior culture developed from a series of territorial wars during the Kamakura period amongst the Minamoto, Fujiwara and Taira clans. These feudal groups were constantly at war with each other, and the Samurai (literally meaning "to serve") were drawn from these battle-hardened warriors.

BELOW An 18th-century Samurai sword. Training in its use was complex and required great skill. It was traditionally worn by the Samurai with the blade edge-up.

This period of Japanese history is viewed as the highpoint of the Samurai warrior, with many stories chronicling their honour, bravery and stoicism in battle. Ironically, this period also allowed the Samurai, as privileged members of society, to kill any unfortunate peasants who offended them. It is also no surprise that some of the best Japanese swords were manufactured during this period.

The Muromachi period (1338–1573)

An interesting period in Samurai history is the Muromachi period, as it witnessed the emergence of the Samurai as an artist-warrior. The culture of the Samurai had now developed to such a degree that it was considered necessary for training to include the ritualized tea ceremony and flower arranging. These rituals were considered to add refinement and balance to the usually warrior-like persona of a Samurai.

Kabuto-gane (pommel)

ABOVE The naginata polearm was commonly used by the Samurai warriors.

Lacquered wood shaft

Blade sharply curved towards point

The decline of the Samurai (1603–1867)

During the Edo period (1603–1867) the gradual decline of the Samurai began. The unusual absence of any wars in Japan during a period of about 250 years meant that the Samurai were unable to play a warlike role in Japanese society. Although they were allowed to wear their traditional swords in public, they now had to accept civilian jobs to survive. The last Shogun, or Governor of Japan, resigned during the Meiji Restoration (1868–1912), and dissatisfied Samurai then led a revolt against a progressive and pro-Western government, which promptly abolished feudalism and in 1871, finally stripped the Samurai of all their special privileges. The carrying of Samurai swords in public had already been outlawed in 1867, resulting in a rapid decline in the number of working swordsmiths.

Changes in sword design in the 19th century

After the demise of the Samurai class in the late 19th century, Japan entered into an unprecedented period of contact with the West. This was reflected by dramatic changes in sword design for regular army forces. Although the traditional Samurai sword was still being made during this period (albeit in very small numbers), military swords from the 1870s to the 1900s were heavily influenced by European designs, most notably the French military. Some Japanese officers' swords were virtual copies of contemporary French military swords.

The Showa period (1926–89)

With the revival of Japanese nationalism during the Showa period, a parallel revival in sword making also occurred. One of the most common Japanese sword styles of the Showa period is the kyu-gunto pattern. It retained the long grip associated with traditional Samurai swords, but had a knuckle bow and pommel of European design. There were many variations of this pattern, including a version for both officers and non-commissioned officers. From the 1920s, when a rebirth of Japanese nationalism brought with it a new-found interest in their Samurai past, many officers reverted back to the classic Samurai sword form. This was the new shin-gunto pattern. Blades were either machine-made or hand-forged, or earlier family or ancestral blades were attached to new hilts. These swords were carried by all branches of the Imperial Japanese Army. Large numbers were destroyed at the end of World War II, but significant quantities were also brought home as souvenirs by the victorious Allied forces.

Indigenous Japanese sword making came to an abrupt end with the defeat of Japan in 1945, but the craft revived again from the 1970s, with great demand for particular swordsmiths.

The naginata polearm

This was a common polearm used by Samurai warriors and is most commonly associated with the Kamakura and Muromachi Periods (1338–1573). The naginata comprised a lacquered (sometimes inlaid with mother-of-pearl) wooden pole approximately 2m (6.5ft) in length. Onto this was forged a curved blade in very much the same way as traditional katana blades – and, indeed, many naginatas were actually mounted with recycled katana blades. The blade, or nakago, of a naginata was secured onto the pole by a single peg, or mekugi.

The yari

A short lance or spear, the Japanese yari was not intended to be thrown in the traditional Western military fashion. It was used by both the Samurai and the common Japanese foot-soldier, or ashigaru. There are many different styles of yari. The two main types are the su yari (straight-bladed) and the kama yari (with horizontal crossbars on the blade).

Lacquered decoration

ABOVE The yari, or short lance or spear, was used by Japanese infantry soldiers and the Samurai.

Types of Japanese edged weapons

There are four main types of Samurai edged weapon.

Tachi (longsword)

This is the original historic sword of the Samurai and had a typical blade length ranging from 60–70cm (23.6–27.5in). It was worn with the blade edge downwards and suspended from a belt with two straps. It was later replaced by the daisho (a combination of the katana and wakizashi worn together) but continued to be worn at ceremonial events and when attending the Imperial Japanese Court. Many tachi were considered important family heirlooms and stored with great care.

Katana (standard sword)

This sword type had an average blade length of over 60cm (23.6in), and was generally used for outdoor combat. The single-edged blade was slightly curved. The sword was developed in the 10th century to accommodate the growing use of Japanese cavalry and was worn hung from the belt, with the cutting edge facing upwards.

Wakizashi (side arm or short sword)

With a blade length of around 30–40cm (11.8–15.7in), this sword was also worn indoors as it provided more ease of movement than the longer katana. Its shorter blade functioned as a side arm, and was well suited for stabbing at close quarters. It was also used to decapitate beaten opponents and take their heads from the battlefield. The traditional Samurai form of ritual suicide (*seppuku*, sometimes known as *hara-kari*, or "cutting the belly") was normally conducted with this type of short sword.

Tanto (short knife)

This is a small knife used in much the same manner as a wakizashi. The average length is 15–30cm (5.9–11.8in). Unlike other traditional Japanese swords that feature a sharpened edge, the tanto was used primarily as a stabbing weapon and was also designed to pierce armour.

Accessories are:

Saya (scabbard)

A Japanese sword is sheathed in a scabbard called a saya, usually made of magnolia wood and lacquered for weatherproofing. A sageo, or length of strong braid, attaches the scabbard to the owner's belt.

Tsuba (guard)

The tsuba is a rounded (sometimes squared) guard placed at the end of the grip of a traditional Japanese sword. The swordsman would place his right index finger on the tsuba to aid his balance and so control the blade more easily.

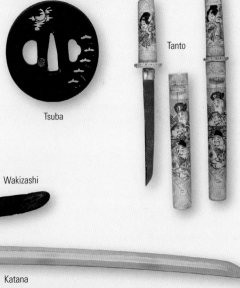

Tsuba

Tanto

Wakizashi

Katana

Tachi

Chinese and Central Asian swords

The origins of the Chinese sword are rooted in ancient legend. Solid-gold dao swords were reputedly made for the mythical San Huang emperors Fu-Xi-Shi, Shen-Nong-Shi and Sui-Ren-Shi (c.3000–2700BC). These swords were said to have extraordinary powers: they could glow in the dark, utter sounds, frighten evil spirits and even change into dragons. Their spiritual powers were embodied in the personal (or perhaps supernatural) strength of their owners. Like Viking swords, these weapons were sometimes accorded individual names.

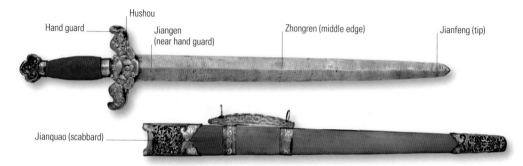

Hushou

Hand guard

Jiangen (near hand guard)

Zhongren (middle edge)

Jianfeng (tip)

Jianquao (scabbard)

The jian
With a history dating back well over 2,500 years, the oldest type of Chinese sword is the jian. The earliest jian had short, double-edged and straight blades about 35cm (13.8in) in length and were made of bronze. Iron and steel had replaced bronze by the time of the Tang Dynasty (AD618–906), and during the Northern Song Dynasty (AD960–1127) notable jian of high quality were being produced in the Longquan area of Zhejiang province (on China's north-east coast). Raw materials such as iron ore and good access to water helped these swordsmiths to produce very fine blades.

The hilt
A jian hilt comprised a grip of either bound cord, carved wood, horn or wood covered in ray skin (sometimes stained green), with a wide ring or ferrule at each end of the grip. A large, stepped pommel was added for balance. The use of fish skin (normally the rough, dried-out skin of a ray or shark) provided an excellent non-slip surface on which to place a hand. The use of a tassel (a tuft of dyed cotton threads) placed through a hole in the pommel was popular during the Ming Dynasty (1368–1644), and during the Qing Dynasty (1644–1912) a tassel hole was driven through the grip itself.

ABOVE The jian is a straight, double-edged sword used for over 2,500 years in China. The blade itself is normally divided into three sections for use in different techniques of attack and defence.

Hilt fittings were usually made of brass, bronze or silver, and, on rare occasions, gold. Either the hilt was cast as a whole or both the hand guard and pommel were cast separately and then forged together. Decorated sheet metal was also applied to the hilt, and traditional motifs such as dragons and interlaced designs were punched or incised onto the metal.

The blade
A jian blade was divided into three distinct areas. Each had a specific function. The tip of the blade, or jianfeng, had a spear point designed for stabbing and rapid cuts. The middle section was known as the zhongren, and was effective at long cleaving cuts and deflection of the opponent's bade. The last section of blade (closest to the hand guard) was called the jiangen and would have been used for defensive blocking.

The dao – "Marshal of all Weapons"
In China, the dao was regarded as one of the four major Chinese weapons of combat, alongside the qiang (spear), jian (straight sword) and gun (staff

Sabres of the Mongols

When the Mongols invaded China in the early 13th century, they brought with them a curved, one-handed and single-edged cavalry sabre that had been used by Turkic peoples (from central Eurasia) since the 8th century. The curved design of the sabre influenced the shape of the Chinese dao, superseding the straight-bladed jian. During the Ming Dynasty, (1368–1644) sabres of increased curvature appeared, primarily for mounted troops.

RIGHT A 19th-century illustration of the Mongols in China. They are carrying long spears and sabres. Their horsemanship skills and ferocious fighting spirit were greatly feared by the Chinese forces of the Ming Dynasty.

or pole). Described as the "Marshal of all Weapons", it was an effective wide-bladed sword with excellent slashing or chopping capabilities. The word "dao" simply means "knife", and is also used to describe a whole range of single-edged and broad-bladed knives and tools.

Early history

Swords of dao form first emerged during the Shang Dynasty (c.1700–1100BC) and were initially manufactured in bronze, but by the time of the late Warring States (c.221– 5BC) iron and steel would have been utilized by Chinese swordsmiths to produce stronger and more durable blades.

During the Tang Dynasty (AD618–906) of southern China, dao were exported to both Korea and Japan, and became an important influence on the future development of the traditional Japanese Samurai sword, particularly the tachi (long sword) and the katana (standard sword).

BELOW Dao blades have varied greatly over the centuries but most are moderately curved and single-edged. Guards are typically disc-shaped with grips bound in cord.

Characteristics of the dao

Dao blades were broad, slightly curved and single-edged, with canted (angled) hilts, usually bound in cord, leather, wood or ray skin (fish skin). If a dao was to be used in battle, grips would be wrapped in silk, and the colours chosen were specified by strict military regulation. In Chinese culture, the use of particular colours and types of knots was considered to bring their owner luck and bravery.

Most dao had one or more fullers, or "blood grooves", deeply cut into the blade. This would have given the blade extra strength and flexibility. The sword bearer's hand was also protected by a disc-shaped and cupped guard. When the blade entered the scabbard, the "cup" acted as a barrier against rainwater penetrating it, or blood dripping down to the grip and so making the sword difficult to handle. Blade lengths averaged around 65–75cm (25.5–29.5in).

Dao scabbards were usually made of wood, covered with thick lacquer or fish skin, although sometimes they were made from lacquered leather, and many had heavily embossed and gilded panels. The scabbard was mounted with two rings that were attached to a belt.

Disc-shaped and
cupped guard

Broad, slightly
curved blade

Two-handed swords

Introduced into China around 2,000 years ago, two-handed swords have a long history in Chinese swordsmanship. Although not common, there was a two-handed jian of up to 1.6m (5.2ft) in length. It was known as a shuangshou jian (literally meaning two hands placed together). The dao sword also had a two-handed equivalent, the dadao, or "great sword". This comprised a massive falchion-type blade and simple cord-bound metal hilt with ring pommel. The dadao was used well into the 20th century and there are many photographs showing Chinese Nationalist forces carrying this weapon during the Second Sino-Japanese War (1937–45). Chinese troops boasted that it could sever the head of a Japanese soldier with one blow.

BELOW Emperor Chu Yuan-Chang (1328–98), founder of the Ming Dynasty. During this period the military began to use polearms in favour of the dao sword.

Ring-pommelled sword

The eastern Chinese Han Dynasty (AD23–220) adopted a unique type of sword – the single-edged huanshou dao, or "ring-pommelled sword". The blade was quite narrow, with a length of around 90cm (35.4in). The tang was very broad and forged with an integral and distinctive ring pommel. A peg was used to hold both tang and grip together. These ring-pommelled swords were still being used right up until the end of the 19th century. During the Boxer Rising of 1900, these swords were particularly popular amongst the rebel forces who besieged the European contingent in Beijing (Peking).

Polearms and percussive weapons

With the overthrow of the Mongols (or the Yuan Dynasty, 1279–1368) and the establishment of the Ming Dynasty, the Chinese Army began to rely more heavily on the use of long polearms and percussive weapons for their infantry soldiers. In purely economic terms, these weapons were much cheaper to produce and the training required to use them was minimal, unlike the prolonged training necessary to develop a proficient swordsman.

These polearms were still regarded as forms of the dao sword, but in this case the dao blade was attached to a wooden staff or pole. Their names highlight the close relationship they bore to the dao family of swords and included halberds (pointed axes) such as the jidao, and long-bladed glaives (axes) such as the yanyue dao, meijian dao and quadao. In keeping with European military staff weapons of this period, the long reach of the polearm was considered more effective when used by massed infantry formations in battle.

Double or paired swords

In 1644, the last Ming emperor Chung-Chen committed suicide after Beijing (Peking) was captured by the Manchus (from Manchuria, on

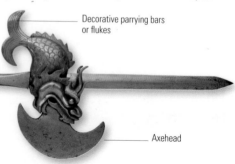

Decorative parrying bars or flukes

Axehead

ABOVE This Chinese halberd has a number of defensive bars and a crescent blade. The halberd was used from as early as the Shang Dynasty (c.1700–1100BC) until the end of the Qing Dynasty (1644–1911).

China's eastern seabord). The new emperor Qing Shunzhi, of the Qing (Manchu) Dynasty, did not alter the design of Chinese swords in any radical way, and Ming-style swords, including the traditional jian and dao, continued to be worn until the end of the Qing Dynasty.

However, the Qing Dynasty (1644–1912) did witness the appearance of shuang jian, or paired swords. They are also known as "butterfly knives". These innovative swords were designed in such a way that they fitted back-to-back in the same scabbard and had half hilts that fitted on top of each other. The swordsman could quickly draw these short, double-edged swords out of their scabbard, wielding one in each hand. Hilt and blade design remained similar to the traditional jian.

ABOVE Chinese "Big Sword" troops wield their dao swords during a battle to defend the old Chinese province of Jehol (west of Manchuria) from the attacking Japanese army in March 1933.

BELOW A pair of butterfly swords. The butterfly sword was usually wielded in pairs. They were held side by side within the same scabbard, to give the impression of a single weapon.

Half hilt

Half hilt

Swords of Tibet

The Tibetan longsword was called the ke tri (pronounced "kay dreh") or patang. These single-edged blades had a short-angled tip with an average blade length of up to 65cm (25.6in). They were usually worn with their edge facing upwards and diagonally across the front of the body, with the hilt located so that the right hand could rest upon it. The sword and scabbard were tucked into a long woollen-fabric waist belt worn with traditional costume. Belt attachments

are seldom seen on scabbards. Decoration is quite ornamental, with extensive use of carved turquoise and inlaid coral to the hilt and scabbard. Incised silver work, including filigree (silver wire), is a common decorative feature.

BELOW 19th-century Tibetan longsword. Similar to the Chinese jian, it has a hilt embellished with turquoise and coral and includes an embossed silver scabbard.

Rings for sword belt

Jewelled decoration

African swords

In some African cultures the sword was regarded not merely as a weapon of war but also as an important element in ritual ceremonies. In the hands of a monarch it symbolized divine kingship and power over his subjects. There are great differences in sword design between North Africa, with its distinctively Arabic-inspired swords, and the eastern and Central African empires of the Yoruba, Benin and Asante, where strong beliefs in local spirits encouraged extravagant swords that were symbolic rather than weapons of war.

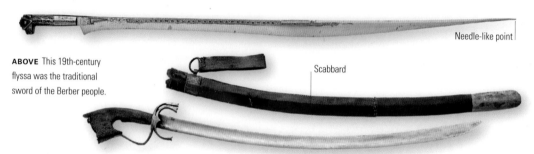

Needle-like point

ABOVE This 19th-century flyssa was the traditional sword of the Berber people.

Scabbard

ABOVE The Moroccan nimcha sword (and scabbard) was often fitted with a European blade.

Swords of North Africa

The influence of the Islamic Arabic world had a profound effect on the indigenous peoples of North Africa. Arab armies began a series of invasions of North Africa after AD600, and with them they brought Islam and new weapons. They introduced both curved and straight-bladed swords over time, some directly influenced by earlier medieval designs, while new hilt and blade forms were developed that became emblematic of distinct regions, peoples and cultures.

The flyssa

This is the traditional sword of the Berber peoples of north-eastern Algeria and parts of Morocco. Swords of this type have single-edged, swelling blades of great length, up to 95cm (37.4in). They feature deeply incised and inlaid brass decoration and pommels of animal heads. The blade point is extremely long and needle-like. This sharp point was effective for piercing chain mail, which was still worn in North Africa well into the 19th century. The flyssa sword grip is without a conventional guard and normally manufactured in iron.

The nimcha

From the 15th century, a unique type of single-handed sword hilt was developed in north-western Africa, especially Morocco. The hilt displayed downward pointing quillons and a wooden or inlaid metal handle with squared-off or "hooked" pommels. From the cross guard, a thin knuckle guard began beneath the quillons and ran to the bottom of the pommel, although not actually joined to it.

Nimcha blades were usually sourced from older, European broadsword blades and many nimcha have Solingen (German), Venetian and Genoese blades from as early as the 17th century. The use of European rather than locally manufactured blades highlights the unique geographical position of this part of North Africa, as it had been an important area of both trade and conflict with the West for many centuries.

The takouba

This sword was used by the nomadic Tuareg tribes of the middle and western Sahara from the 16th century, and is still carried to this day. Up to 1m (3.3ft) in length, the takouba blade is wide and double-edged with three or more hand-ground fullers, or grooves, and a rounded point. The hilt is of simple, cruciform shape. The sword and scabbard are normally worn with a long tasselled baldric (shoulder belt) slung over the right shoulder.

Unfullered blade

Swollen end to scabbard

Tassel

The takouba sword is still made for the Tuareg by a special sword-making caste, known as the Ineden, who are reputed to have come originally from the Sudan. The Ineden speak their own language, Ténet. They are not allowed to intermarry and are regarded as having magical powers.

Swords of Sudanic West and Central Africa

The ancient empires of the western Sudan and Central Africa (also known as the Sahel) rose to prominence during the medieval period because of the success of their mounted horsemen. Using these horsemen for both raiding and trading parties, they procured large numbers of slaves, gold and ivory from Central Africa, and in return received weapons, most notably swords, spears and lances, from both indigenous peoples and European traders.

ABOVE African takouba short sword and scabbard from the nomadic Tuareg tribes of the middle and western Sahara.

The "Crusader" sword

A most distinctive African sword was carried by the Hausa peoples of southern Sudan and northern Nigeria. It comprised a straight, double-edged blade with a cruciform cross guard and disc-shaped pommel. There have been many theories over the years concerning these cruciform-hilted swords, based mainly on the misguided belief that their overtly European and medieval style was introduced into this region by Crusaders of the 12th and 13th centuries.

The kaskara

This sword is readily identified with the Sudan. Blades are double-edged, with a spatulate, or spoon-shaped, tip and a blade length of around 95cm (37.4in). A broad central fuller, or "blood groove", is found on some examples, with others exhibiting multiple fullers. Interestingly, many blades are heavily stamped with spurious European swordsmith marks. Imported European blades were attached to kaskara blades from the 17th and 18th centuries, but most examples still surviving date from the 19th century and these marks were actually added by local sword makers to increase the perceived value and quality of a blade.

The cross guard is usually composed of forged iron although brass examples are also known. It also exhibits a long and thin langet (an extension of the guard). Pommels are of flat, disc form, and the grip is round and normally bound in leather. The 19th-century kaskara sword of the Sultan Ali Diner of Darfur has a hilt of solid gold and the blade is decorated with incised Koranic invocations or prayers.

BELOW A Sudanese kaskara, c.1898, with an Italian blade. This sword was owned by Sultan Ali Dinar of Darfur. It has a highly decorated blade and a gold hilt.

Round pommel

Cruciform cross guard

Multi-fullered blade

The African blacksmith

In traditional African societies, the blacksmith is still widely regarded as a figure of mystery and magic, possessed of supernatural powers. As such, he is considered ethnically distinct.

His mythology and status can be traced back to the acquisition by sub-Saharan blacksmiths of the knowledge to work iron. This probably derived from ancient Egypt and moved steadily southwards, so that by the 3rd and 4th centuries BC, iron was being worked in north-western Tanzania, northern Nigeria and the Sudan.

There was no Bronze Age in Africa; therefore, the blacksmiths' leap from producing stone and wood tools and weapons to iron must have seemed revolutionary (even supernatural).

A blacksmith's appearance in a village would initiate great excitement. A forge was set up and he would use a stone or iron anvil, iron tongs, bellows of

stitched animal skins and clay tubes to funnel air to stimulate the fire. He produced a range of weapons, most notably daggers, swords and spearheads. The scarcity of reliable, durable weapons to subjugate rival tribes made him a revered figure. He would also manufacture agricultural tools to help sustain the village in more peaceful periods.

RIGHT These 18th–19th-century iron-bladed swords with wooden handles were characteristic of the weapons made by local blacksmiths.

Swords of eastern Africa

Originating in Abyssinia (ancient Ethiopia), the shotel is an extremely curved sword that is very reminiscent of a large sickle. The blade is diamond-sectioned and usually flat-backed or with a central ridge. The blade length is about 80cm (31.5in) and the wooden hilt is simple, smooth and undecorated. There is no guard. This sword would have been carried in a close-fitting leather scabbard.

Shotel swords were not very practical for slashing an opponent, but the extremely curved blade was used primarily to hook the enemy by reaching around his shield and then stabbing him in vital areas, such as the kidneys, heart or lungs.

Swords of West Africa

By AD900 the Yoruba people, originally located in central Nigeria, had slowly begun to move southwest. This was a reaction to northern Hausa expansion southwards into

their lands, combined with long periods of devastating drought. The Yoruba finally settled in an area now comprising south-west Nigeria, Benin and Togo. They were noted swordsmiths and were involved in the mining and smelting of iron ore before AD800.

Yoruba and Edo swords

Between 1100 and 1700, the Yoruba kingdom of Ife flourished in conjunction with the neighbouring Edo kingdom of Benin, and part of this cultural cross-fertilization saw the introduction of the ada sword. This was an all-iron longsword (used either one-handed or double-handed), with a narrow and then greatly widening leaf-shaped and double-edged blade, designed for hacking and cutting. The oral tradition of the Edo people says that the ada sword was used primarily for ceremonial purposes and it would have been presented to the early rulers of Benin. They were known as the Ogiso, or "rulers of the sky".

RIGHT The shotel – the traditional curved sword of Ethiopia. This particular weapon was presented to Benito Mussolini following Italy's conquest of Abyssinia (Ethiopia) in 1936.

RIGHT An Asante oath-taking sword or mponponsuo from Ghana, with a gold and leopard skin handle.

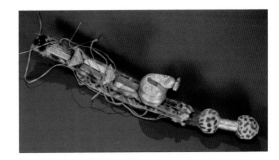

In the 15th and 16th centuries, when Yoruba kings, or Obas, had taken over the rule of Benin, the ordinary soldier began to carry a short sword called an opia. This was a double-edged and smaller version of the ada. Benin tribal chiefs carried a specific sword called an eben. It was seen as a symbol of authority and comprised a broad blade with looped handles, elaborately decorated with openwork and brass inlays. If a neighbouring kingdom was at war with Benin and captured a Benin blacksmith, he would not automatically be executed (which was the usual fate for ordinary warriors). His metalworking skills were highly prized and he would quickly be put to use producing tools and weapons for his captors.

Asante state swords

The empire of the Asante (a federation of Akan-speaking and neighbouring tribes) was located in present-day Ghana. During the mid-18th century its influence began to replace that of the Benin empire. The Asante's divine king, or Ansantehene, was given a state sword, or afena. This was recognized as the

ABOVE Dating probably from the 17th century, this bronze plaque from Benin depicts the Oba of Benin with attendants.

supreme symbol of kingly power. The iron blade was curved, with a broad point gradually tapering towards the tang where a hilt of wood was covered in gold. The rounded grip expanded into a sphere at both ends. On both the hilt and the sheath there were a number of elaborate gold castings called abosodee. They had great symbolic importance and represented complex stories within the culture of the Asante kingdom. The decoration included grotesque human heads, knots, shells, fighting warriors and fantastical creatures.

There were also a number of derivations of the afena sword. These included the asomfofena. This would be carried by representatives of the Asantehene (king), whose primary role would be to disseminate the king's will throughout the land. If an Asante was in the presence of this sword, he would know that the royal bearer deserved great respect and that the judgement of the king imparted through this instrument of the state could have both benign and fearful consequences.

The "keteanofena" was a term used to describe a group of important Asante state swords. The akrafena sword was associated with the religious and spiritual well-being of the community and was always carried on the right side during official processions. The bosomfena represented political and secular authority and would be carried on the left during official processions. The mponponsuo was the largest of the state swords and it was used to swear allegiance to the king. The bosommuru was used to swear allegiance to the Asante nation.

The afenatene was a most unusual ceremonial sword that comprised three widening blades that splayed outwards. The blade had a cut-out of fretwork decoration with animal motifs. The long iron shaft sometimes represented the body of a snake, links of a chain, or a series of complex, entwined knots. This sword would have been placed behind the king as he sat in state in his palace at Kumase, in present-day Ghana.

Indian swords

Distinguished by the sheer variety and uniqueness of their design, Indian swords are totally unlike Western swords. They reveal a strong visual extravagance that perfectly mirrors the huge size of the Indian subcontinent and its diffuse melting pot of cultural influences. From the Arabic-inspired north Indian talwar, sword of the Mughal princes, to the European-bladed south Indian firangi, or "foreign" sword, Indian sword makers were constantly producing weapons to amaze and instil terror in their enemies.

Downward-curving cross guard

Double-edged yelman

Jade hilt

The Indian dynasties

From around 180BC, ancient Hindu India experienced a number of invasions from Central Asia. The Indo-Parthians (from the area now known as Afghanistan), the Kushans (from what is now Tajikstan, Afghanistan and Pakistan), the Scythians (from Central Asia) and

ABOVE An Indian sword of the Mughal era, 1526–1857, when most of the Indian subcontinent was ruled by a dynasty founded by the Mongol conqueror, Babur. The jade hilt is decorated with rubies.

even the Greeks (under Alexander the Great) all established either kingdoms or strong cultural influences, particularly in northern India.

The Maurya Empire (184BC–*c.* AD320) drove out these foreign invaders, and their pan-religious empire stretched from the Himalayas in the far north to the extreme southern Indian provinces of what are now Karnataka and Kerala. By the early 4th century AD, India had experienced a series of devastating internal wars, and, despite another period of internal unity (under the Gupta Dynasty, AD320–*c.*550), dynastic wars continued for the next few hundred years.

Militarily, however, the Indian subcontinent appears to have lagged somewhat behind the West and it is interesting to note that iron weapons did not appear in India until *c.*500BC. The sword was not even regarded as an important weapon and infantry were largely composed of bowmen. India's greatest military treatise, the *Siva-Dhanur-Veda* (*c.*500BC), concentrated on describing the important role of archers and their bows and arrows, to the detriment of any other bladed weapons.

To explain this anomaly, we must first consider the benign influence of Hindu religious culture in the conduct of war. Hand-to-hand conflict was usually avoided, as was mass slaughter. Nevertheless, despite

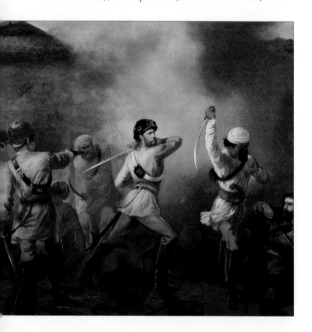

ABOVE Indian troops depicted using curved talwars against the English at Khurkowhah, 15 August 1857, during the Indian Mutiny.

the constraints imposed by religious beliefs, some astonishing edged weapons would be produced in the following centuries.

During the 11th and 12th centuries, India witnessed continuous and devastating invasions from Muslim Turks, Arabs and Afghans. In 1206 the Mamluk Dynasty (the first Muslim dynasty) was established, and there followed three centuries of Muslim rule throughout northern India. The south of the continent was not affected by this Muslim invasion and remained independent under the Hindu Vijayanagara Dynasty (1336–1646). In 1526, Babur Timurid, a Central Asian emperor and descendant of Genghis Khan, established the highly influential Mughal Empire (1526–1857), which reigned successfully over most of India and Afghanistan until its dissolution under British rule in the 19th century following the Indian Mutiny of 1857–58.

The British Raj

During the late 18th and early 19th centuries, the British East India Company had extended its control over most of India, paving the way for the establishment of the British Raj. These political changes had a limited impact on Indian swordsmiths, who continued to produce swords in a great diversity of forms. These included not only mainstream swords in the Muslim and Hindu traditions, such as the talwar and the khanda made for the princely states that survived under British rule, but also many regional or tribal variants.

The talwar

One of the most common of Indian swords, the origins of the talwar (*war*, or *vaar*, means "strike", as in "strike a blow") can be traced back to Central Asian invaders (the Saka-Jushans, ancestors of the Turks) who established their kingdoms in north-western

India during the 13th century. They brought with them a curved sword of scimitar shape which was soon adopted by the indigenous Indian warrior clans, ancestors of the future Rajputs (a Hindu warrior dynasty, c. AD700–1947, originally from Rajasthan, a north Indian region bordering present-day Pakistan).

The all-metal talwar includes a disc pommel and a curved knuckle bow of inverted S-shape that is a continuation of the cross guard but does not actually attach itself to the pommel. Hilt quillons are usually globulous (rounded) and the middle part of the knuckle bow splays outwards towards the blade, forming pointed langets (the central area of the cross guard).

Scabbards are normally made of wood with leather or bright velvet covering.

BELOW This Indian talwar sword from the late 18th or early 19th century is all steel. Typically, it has a curved blade of up to 76cm (30in) and a disc-shaped pommel. It was used for slashing and thrusting.

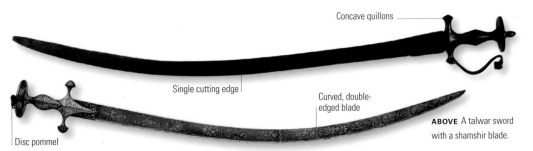

Concave quillons

Single cutting edge

Curved, double-edged blade

Disc pommel

ABOVE A talwar sword with a shamshir blade.

Although plain hilts were common, especially for the ordinary infantry soldier, many talwar hilts were decorated with ornate designs, including intricate chiselling or exquisite gilding. This gilding was done by a process called kofgari (meaning "goldbeating") or damascening (the complex inlaying of steel and gold). Hilts made for local rulers and people of rank are found with superb enamelling and inset jewels. Decoration was not just limited to the hilt. Blades were also decorated with fine incising (metal carving) or damascening.

BELOW An Indian presentation sword dated 1847, made for Henry Hardinge, Governor General of India, 1844–48. It was most likely produced by Indian craftsmen in Lahore.

of the complex process of blade pattern welding. This involved the continuous hammering, twisting and folding of the blade to produce not only a very hard and durable weapon but also one that exhibited a finely textured and patterned surface.

Persian talwar blades
In the medieval period, blades made in Persia (modern-day Iran) were highly prized in India. Persian swordsmiths were recognized as being masters

The "forty steps"
One specific pattern that was held to be superior to all others was known as the Ladder of the Prophet, or kirk nardaban (forty steps). It was a highly skilled effect and exhibited an application of a number of decorative chevrons, or stripes, down the blade. The bidr or qum (gravel) effect was another type of patterning applied to the blades of talwar swords.

Indian-made talwar blades
By the 16th century, the supply of blades from Persia and Damascus (Syria) had virtually dried up, and so Indian swordsmiths had to start producing their own work rather than rely solely on imported blades. They did this by introducing their own unique patterned steel, known as wootz (meaning "steel" in some south Indian languages). Importantly, the production of wootz blades replaced the time-consuming method of folding and hammering the steel. This was because the local iron ore naturally produced crystallized structures in the steel that local craftsmen were able to enhance by simple polishing.

Talwar blade marking
Blades of high quality were invariably marked by their makers in the form of a cartouche or tablet in the area just below the hilt (the forte). A gilded bedouh, or

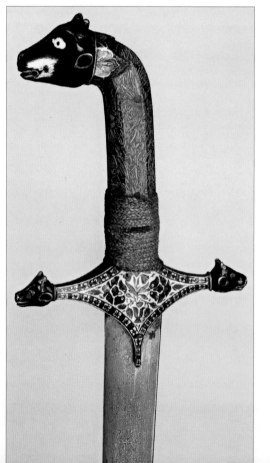

LEFT An 18th-century Indian shamshir from Jaipur. The ends of the quillons and the pommel are modelled as animals' heads, which have been coated with blue enamel.

square, was also applied to this part of the blade and then divided into four quarters, each quarter displaying one of the Arabic numerals for the numbers 2, 4, 6 and 8. These numbers were thought to bring good fortune to the sword's owner.

Rounded cartouches inlaid in gold and carrying invocations or prayers from the Koran were also added. Another decoration that is common to many Indian swords is bidri, a combination of black-stained pewter and silver. This produced a dramatic contrasting effect. Bidri decoration originated in the city of Bider, northwest of Hyderabad (now capital of the present-day southern Indian state of Andhura Pradesh).

The talwar in battle

Being a curved sword, the talwar was useful when striking against bone or armour because it would not easily become embedded, as in the case of straight blades. The Rajput horsemen had a fearsome reputation for wildly attacking infantry formations, and, at close quarters, the short, spiked end on some talwars was efficient at stabbing an opponent in his face if unprotected.

The talwar in Indian culture

An extremely important symbol of Rajput traditions and customs, the talwar sword also became an inseparable part of their culture. It was used to bestow honours and titles to tribal chiefs and it symbolized prestige and honour. In the case of a groom being unable to attend his own wedding due to illness, his personal talwar sword could be sent along to take his place and so enable the wedding rituals to continue without him.

An oath of allegiance to a tribal clan was also sworn on a talwar sword by Rajput warriors. It comprised the words *dhal talwar ki aan* ("by the honour of my sword and shield").

BELOW By the 16th century, the supply of superior blades from Persia and Damascus had virtually ceased. In response, Indian swordsmiths produced their own patterned blades. This Persian sword would have been made with Damascus steel.

ABOVE A mid-17th-century Indian miniature from Bijapur showing a warrior with talwar and pata, or gauntlet sword.

Afghan pulwar or talwar

Due to the talwar's growing popularity within the Mughal Empire, its influence spread northwards, and its design was interpreted by Afghan warriors who produced their own version, the Afghani talwar, or pulwar. Despite this acceptance of an "enemy's" sword, the Afghan and Rajput regions were constantly at war with each other, and contemporary Rajput texts frequently state how "…the Afghan army's sword broke under the Rajput talwar."

Unsharpened edge   Inlaid gold decoration

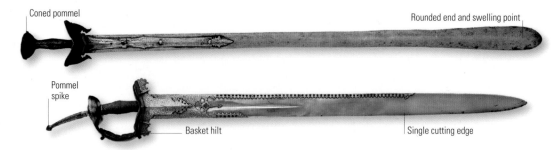

Coned pommel

Rounded end and swelling point

Pommel spike

Basket hilt

Single cutting edge

The khanda

It is thought that the origins of the khanda can be traced back to the Gupta Dynasty (AD320–550), as khanda-type swords have been recognized on period sculptures. During the medieval period, Rajput kings are depicted in wall paintings wielding this type of sword. The name "khanda" is thought to originate in the Sanskrit word for sword, *khanda*.

The khanda has a distinctive, wide and straight, watered steel (pattern-welded) blade that widens towards a spear-pointed tip. A light, flexible blade is characteristic of the khanda, as are two stiffened, ribbed reinforcements that run alongside the blade edge on either side; one is almost the length of the blade and the other is much shorter, to allow a cutting edge. This reinforcement produced a much lighter sword, having greater manoeuvrability than a thick, heavy blade.

TOP A khanda sword from around 1800 with a light and flexible spatulate blade, from Malabar in south-west India. It has a reinforcement bar that runs part of the way down the blade.

ABOVE Late 18th-century khanda sword with a typical Hindu basket hilt. It has a pronounced spiked pommel which was used if the swordsman needed a two-handed grip.

The khanda's hilt and pommel are similar to firangi swords, but with the addition of a wide, disc-like cross guard and knuckle bow. The hilt is also more basket-like in form than other open-hilted Indian swords. The long, spiked and canted (slightly curved) pommel that is found on khandas is thought to have a double use, both producing a double-handed option and acting as a handy walking stick (when unsheathed) or hand rest (when sheathed).

The pata (gauntlet sword)

One of the most unusual of Indian edged weapons, the pata comprises a long, straight-bladed and doubled-edged sword attached to an armoured, half-gauntlet hilt. The overall length could be up to 110cm (44in). In order to wield the sword effectively, the wearer gripped a concealed cross bar inside the gauntlet. Pata swords were favourite weapons of the southern and central Indian Maharatta Empire. The extended grip provided by the encasing

of the forearm also allowed the user a very powerful, sweeping blow. Some warriors chose to carry a pata on each hand and would adopt the stance of a whirling windmill as they attacked swathes of infantry or even armoured cavalry.

Shivaji Bhosle (1627–80), founder of the Maharatta Empire, was known to be a practised exponent of this sword. It is said that one of his famous generals, Tanaji Malusare, wielded a pata in each hand during the Battle of Sinhagad (1670), a now legendary encounter between the Maharattas and Mughal forces besieged in a hilltop fort, near Pune (the present-day western Indian state of Maharashtra).

BELOW Indian pata, 18th century. It was considered a highly effective weapon for the infantry and also used against armoured cavalry.

Gauntlet

Straight, double-edged blade

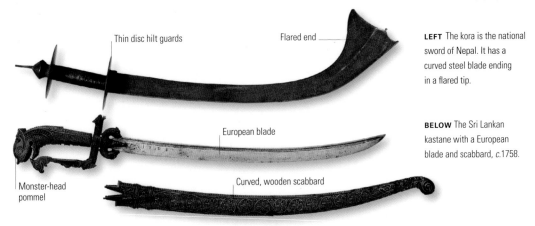

Thin disc hilt guards

Flared end

LEFT The kora is the national sword of Nepal. It has a curved steel blade ending in a flared tip.

European blade

BELOW The Sri Lankan kastane with a European blade and scabbard, *c*.1758.

Monster-head pommel

Curved, wooden scabbard

Weapon of last resort

To a Rajput horseman, the khanda was very much a lethal weapon of last resort. If unhorsed and surrounded by the enemy, he would quickly draw the large blade and begin swinging it around his head, taking full advantage of its estimable hacking and slashing functions. Because of the great width of the khanda blade, it was never perceived as an efficient thrusting sword.

The khanda was effective against the leather and chain-mail armour of the Mughal invaders, as its great strength (especially when wielded with two hands) could cut through these materials with considerable ease. When carried by infantrymen, this sword gave them a chance against horse-mounted soldiers.

The firangi

This was a typical sword of the Hindu southern and central Indian Maharatta Empire (1674–1818). The firangi had a narrow, straight blade, commonly made from imported European blades (the word "firangi" literally means "foreigner") and sometimes decorated with kofgari-worked inlaid gold or silver. When it was fitted with a home-made blade, it was called a sukhela, and in the Deccan (comprising the south Indian plateau), a dhup.

Like the khanda, the firangi blade is also reinforced along the blade edge, combined with a disc-shaped pommel terminating in a long spike used for a two-handed blow. Kofgari or inlaid gold ornamentation frequently decorated the hilt. The large, basket-type hilt is also padded and embroidered with silk or coloured velvet. In the 17th and 18th centuries, the Maharattas of the Western Deccan relied heavily on imported European trade goods and especially sword blades. The Maharattas' preference was for German and Italian blades, since they regarded English blades as very inferior.

The shamshir

Translated literally as "curved like a lion's tail", the shamshir was a distinctively curved sword introduced into India during the 16th century. Persian (Iranian) in origin, its fine pattern-welded or watered blades are some of the finest blades ever to have been produced.

The kora

Nepalese edged weapons were strongly influenced by the medieval Indian Rajputs, who brought Indian weapon styles into the region. Alongside the legendary kukri knife (a heavily curved tool and weapon), the kora is the traditional weapon of the Gurkhas (from Nepal and northern India). Its simple all-metal design comprises a wide and heavy blade with a massive flared tip. The grip was tubular, including a thin, disc-shaped pommel and cross guard. Decoration of koras includes chiselling and mounting of precious metals to the hilt.

The kastane

Sri Lanka's national sword, this distinctive weapon has a short, flat-backed or unfullered blade. The hilt is usually highly ornamented and includes fantastical creatures located at the end of multiple quillons. Gold and silver decoration is richly applied throughout, including the blade, where gilt damascening is worked for most of its length. European blades were frequently mounted on kastane hilts of the 17th and 18th centuries, highlighting the strong commercial ties with the West, particularly Portugal, which established successful trading bases in the country.

Swords and daggers come in an incredible variety of forms, depending on their historical period and place of origin.

A directory of swords and sabres

In this substantial catalogue, you will find details of some of the most important weapons from around the world and throughout history, along with information about their manufacture and use. Arranged chronologically as well as by geographical area, each of the weapons has a description and a specification that lists its country of origin, date and length.

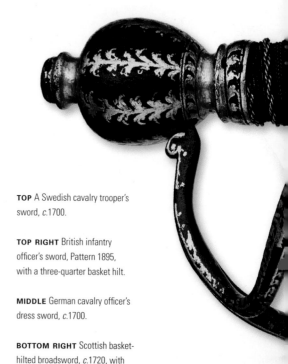

TOP A Swedish cavalry trooper's sword, *c.*1700.

TOP RIGHT British infantry officer's sword, Pattern 1895, with a three-quarter basket hilt.

MIDDLE German cavalry officer's dress sword, *c.*1700.

BOTTOM RIGHT Scottish basket-hilted broadsword, *c.*1720, with exquisite brass inlay to the hilt.

Design of the sword

Over the centuries, the sword has evolved into many different forms and styles, but there is general agreement concerning how its parts should be named. From the hilt pommel that provides balance, to the blade fullers that give both strength and flexibility, sword makers have defined both types and parts of the sword in a way that makes it easier for us to understand this most universal of weapons.

Types of swords

Light cavalry officer's sword

Fishskin grip
Ricasso
Back-edge

The curved blade of this cavalry sword was designed to provide the mounted horseman with an effective slashing and cutting weapon.

Rapier

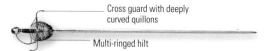

Cross guard with deeply curved quillons
Multi-ringed hilt

Rapiers are defined by their long, needle-like blades and complex, multi-bar hilts. They were purely thrusting swords and most effective when used in the duel.

Basket-hilted broadsword

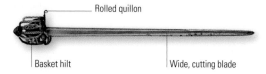

Rolled quillon
Basket hilt
Wide, cutting blade

The large, enclosed basket hilt protected the swordsman's hand, and the wide, double-edged, slashing blade was devastating at close quarters.

Smallsword

Grip
Pas-d'âne

The smallsword developed from the earlier rapier and usually took the form of a trefoil or three-sided blade. This blade shape provided exceptional strength.

Parts of a sword

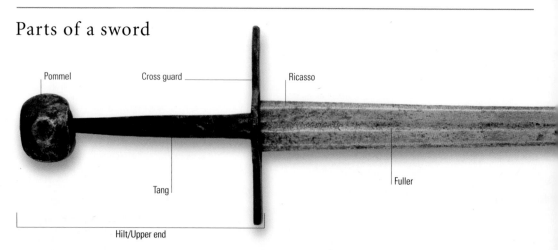

Pommel
Cross guard
Ricasso
Tang
Fuller
Hilt/Upper end

Types of blades

The sheer range of blade types that have been produced throughout history and across vast geographical areas is testament to the variety of functions that a sword could perform. Within any army or cultural group, different blades performed specific tasks. For example, cavalry swords were required to be of considerable length to enable the trooper to reach down and attack foot-soldiers. Blades were either curved or straight, depending on whether a thrusting or slashing motion was desired.

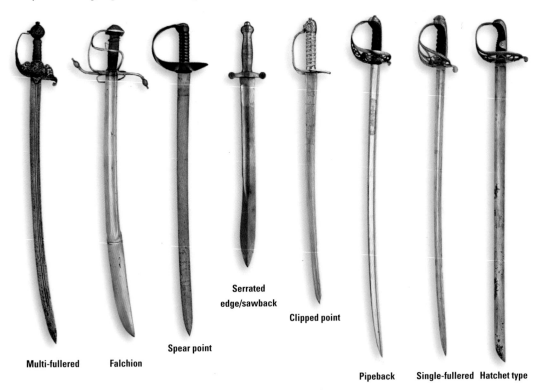

Serrated edge/sawback

Clipped point

Spear point

Multi-fullered   **Falchion**

Pipeback   **Single-fullered**   **Hatchet type**

A sword is a bladed hand weapon comprising a blade and a handle. The blade is usually manufactured in metal, with at least one sharp edge and a pointed tip for thrusting. The handle, called the hilt, can be made of many materials, but the material most commonly used is wood covered by leather, fishskin or metal wiring. A cross guard prevents the user's hand from slipping onto the blade.

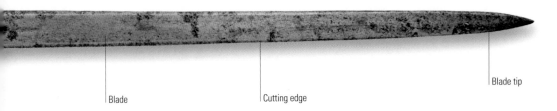

Blade   Cutting edge   Blade tip

Early stone weapons

Flint axes and points were the practical day-to-day tools of the Stone Age and not designed to be weapons of war. They were for hunting, dissection of carcasses and manufacture of basic domestic tools. Only when a tribe was threatened by outsiders would these tools be transformed into weapons of defence.

Acheulean flint hand axes, 1.4 million BC

Over one million years ago, early humans (*Homo erectus*) moved from Africa to Eurasia and created these distinctive oval and pear-shaped flint hand axes. Some of the first examples were found in St Acheul (northern France) during the late 19th century.

Cutting edge   Oval shape   Gripped out bottom

DATE	1.4 MILLION BC
ORIGIN	EURASIAN
LENGTH	UNKNOWN

Solutrean laurel-leaf flint spear point, 28,000BC

Slim profile

Symmetrical knapping

The Solutrean culture (named after Solutré, in central France) produced distinctive chipped flint points that are symmetrical and very finely crafted. Most examples date from around 17,000 years ago and were produced by pressure flaking. Slim, leaf-shaped projectile heads are characteristic of this type of flint point.

DATE	28,000BC
ORIGIN	FRENCH
LENGTH	UNKNOWN

Atlatl, 23,000BC

Banner stone

The atlatl was an effective hunting tool that used the leverage of the human arm to project a flint dart or spear at great speed against a moving target. The flint was placed on a hollowed shaft and the power of the upper arm and wrist was engaged to instantaneously propel the flint. A banner stone could be added as a weight to increase resistance. A range of up to 100m (328ft) could be achieved.

DATE	23,000BC
ORIGIN	EUROPEAN/AMERICAN
LENGTH	UNKNOWN

Clovis spear point, 11,500BC

Symmetrical point —————

————— Shaped groove for attaching to wooden shaft

DATE	11,500BC
ORIGIN	NORTH AMERICAN
LENGTH	19.6cm (7.7in)

First discovered in Clovis, New Mexico, in 1931, these small flint points have been dated to about 13,500 years ago, during the time of the Paleo-Indians. Created by pressure flaking, they were very thin and fluted in shape, and would have been effective at piercing animal (or human) flesh.

Full grooved axe, 8,000–1,000BC

DATE	8,000–1,000BC
ORIGIN	NORTH AMERICAN
LENGTH	13.9cm (5.5in)

Groove for —————
attaching shaft

Early stone axes had grooves chiselled into them so the axe could be attached with twine to a wooden handle. The Archaic peoples (7,000–1,000BC) were also responsible for the development of the atlatl (hand-held weapon that fired darts) and the net sinker (notched pebbles used to sink fishing nets).

Yadkin point, 8,000–1,000BC

————— Knapped groove

Serrated edge —————
for sawing

DATE	8,000–1,000BC
ORIGIN	NORTH AMERICAN
LENGTH	5cm (2in)

American archaeologists unearthed these flint arrowhead points from the Yadkin River, in Stanly County, North Carolina. This example has a serrated edge that has been finely knapped (chipped or broken with sharp blows), to produce a sawing tool.

Oakville arrowheads, 1,000BC–AD1,000

Narrowed point

These projectile points were used in the south-eastern part of the United States (Alabama). Like their Archaic predecessors, Woodland Indians hunted small game and foraged in the forests. With the adoption of the bow and arrow came the need for smaller projectile points.

Cutting edge —————

DATE	1,000BC–AD1,000
ORIGIN	NORTH AMERICAN
LENGTH	4.4–5cm (1.7–2in)

Bronze Age weapons

Leaf-shaped sword blades and riveted hilts are the defining features of many swords of the Bronze Age. The anthropomorphic and free-flowing style of these weapons, typical of European Celts, was also found in Eurasia, particularly Persia (Iran), where swords of great originality and elegance were made.

Turkish bronze sword, 3,350–3,000BC

Hilt and blade cast as one piece

Flattened central ridge

This sword is one of the earliest identified sword types in Europe. It was excavated in Turkey and is of one-piece construction, with the hilt and the blade cast together. The domed hilt has been hammered, ground and polished, and is also inlaid with silver roundels and pyramids. The blade has a slightly flattened central ridge that would have added extra strength.

DATE	3,350–3,000BC
ORIGIN	TURKISH
LENGTH	39.5cm (15.5in)

European bronze sword, 1,500BC

False rivets

Central ridge to a point

Of a type that was carried throughout western Europe, this sword has a series of false rivets worked into the hilt cross guard, indicating that it was cast in one piece. Many swords of this period do have separate hilts and blades that were attached to each other by means of large rivets.

DATE	1,500BC
ORIGIN	WESTERN EUROPEAN
LENGTH	60.5cm (23.8in)

German bronze sword, 1,100BC

Broad, leaf-shaped blade

Flat pommel

Before the introduction of iron into the sword-making process, bronze dominated sword manufacture. This sword has a typical leaf-shaped and double-edged blade. Flattened, disc-shaped pommels were also extremely common. An incised pattern has also been worked around the blade point.

DATE	1,100BC
ORIGIN	GERMAN
LENGTH	85cm (33.5in)

Persian bronze sword, 1,000BC

Rectangular tang

Lenticular blade

DATE	1,000BC
ORIGIN	PERSIAN
LENGTH	85cm (33.5in)

This bronze sword features an unusually long blade of lenticular (outwardly bulging) shape. The tang is rectangular, engraved with geometric patterns. The pommel has distinctive ear-shaped or antennae-like projections. The shoulders of the cross guard are squared and the whole sword has been cast as one piece.

Persian bronze sword, 1,000BC

Pommel ears

Bronze grip

Flattened midrib to blade

DATE	1,000BC
ORIGIN	PERSIAN
LENGTH	94.5cm (37.2in)

The bronze grip on this sword has been covered in decorative nubs that would have provided its owner with a rudimentary grip and more adhesion for the hand. There is a flattened midrib to the centre of the blade, a hollow, ear-shaped pommel and traces of a geometric design to the cross guard.

Italian large bronze spearhead, 500BC

Pronounced median ridge

Socket

DATE	500BC
ORIGIN	ITALIAN
LENGTH	47.5cm (18.7in)

The pronounced median, or central, strengthening ridge on this socketed spearhead would have provided its user with considerable thrusting power and strength. It is likely that its large size meant it would have been particularly effective against armour or mounted troops.

Chinese bronze sword, 500BC

Rounded grip

Diamond-sectioned blade

DATE	500BC
ORIGIN	N.W. CHINESE
LENGTH	56cm (22in)

The earliest Chinese swords come from north-western China and this example is typical of a bronze jian (straight-bladed sword). The wide blade is diamond-sectioned, with a solid tang reinforced by a central ring in the centre of the grip. The cross guard has inlaid decoration and the pommel is flat and rounded.

Weapons of early civilizations

The ancient Greek and Egyptian armies fought in massed ranks and did not regard the sword as their primary weapon of war. The spear or javelin, bow and arrow and axe were all regarded as superior and were proven in battle. The sword was still carried but used more as a weapon of last resort. Conversely, the Roman and Celtic soldier held the sword in high regard and understood its supreme effectiveness in battle.

Egyptian sickle sword or khepesh, 1,400–1,200BC

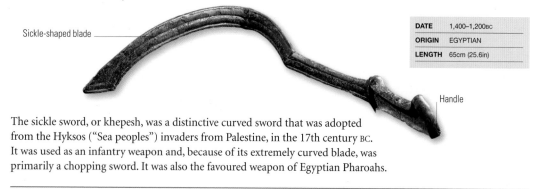

Sickle-shaped blade

Handle

DATE	1,400–1,200BC
ORIGIN	EGYPTIAN
LENGTH	65cm (25.6in)

The sickle sword, or khepesh, was a distinctive curved sword that was adopted from the Hyksos ("Sea peoples") invaders from Palestine, in the 17th century BC. It was used as an infantry weapon and, because of its extremely curved blade, was primarily a chopping sword. It was also the favoured weapon of Egyptian Pharoahs.

Egyptian khepesh, 1,250BC

Inside edge

Ivory handle

The handle of this khepesh was originally inlaid with ivory. Its sickle-shaped blade was sharpened on either the inside or the outside edge of the blade. The outside edge was extremely effective at producing deep, slashing wounds, while the inside edge was utilized for hacking at an opponent.

DATE	1,250BC
ORIGIN	EGYPTIAN
LENGTH	Unknown

Ancient Greek spear

The Greek hoplite was a part-time soldier who normally carried a long spear (doru) and rounded shield (aspis). One battle tactic was to hold the spear overarm and lock the shield over the left forearm. The hoplites then pushed forward with their shields, confronting the enemy with a seemingly impenetrable wall.

RIGHT Greek hoplites, c.500BC.

Celtic sword, *c.*400–350BC

Chape

Blade tang

Decorated scabbard

DATE	c.400–350BC
ORIGIN	CELTIC
LENGTH	69cm (27.2in)

This is a Celtic sword from the early La Tène period, which has been cleaned following excavation. It has an iron blade with short, tapered tang (the area near the hilt) that has become fused into the scabbard. There are three strengthening ridges to the scabbard and a decorated chape (tip).

Celtic sword, 300–100BC

Cross guard

Ridged scabbard

DATE	300–100BC
ORIGIN	CELTIC
LENGTH	89cm (35in)

The absence of any remains to the grip of this sword probably indicates that it was made with a wood-based material and has simply decomposed over time. The blade is stuck in the scabbard but is recognizable as a broad-bladed weapon with a typically downward-curved, iron cross guard. The scabbard has a number of narrow rings that would have provided extra strength for the sheath.

Roman sword, AD14–37

Corroded steel blade

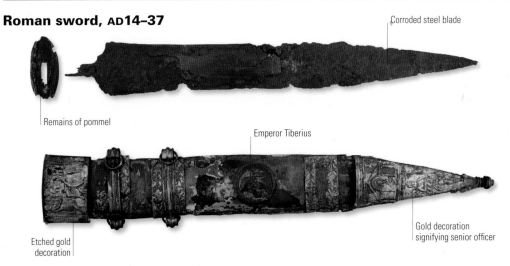

Remains of pommel

Emperor Tiberius

Gold decoration
signifying senior officer

Etched gold
decoration

DATE	AD14–37
ORIGIN	ROMAN
LENGTH	57.5cm (22.6in)

This Roman gladius sword was worn by a senior military officer during the reign of Emperor Tiberius (AD14–37). The scabbard mounts are decorated in fine gold and silver engraving, including depictions of Tiberius. The gladius was employed in a stabbing, thrusting motion and Roman soldiers were repeatedly trained to use the sword in a close, fighting formation.

Frankish, Viking and Saxon weapons

Both the Vikings and the Saxons had a deep reverence for the sword. Death in battle was seen as a great honour and a dead warrior's sword would be passed down the generations. Warriors also carried the spear and the great bearded war axe. In the right hands, these were devastating weapons of war and conquest.

Francisca throwing axe, *c.*600

Short handle for easier throwing

Angled, socketed axehead

This type of axe was originally carried by the Frankish tribes of western Germany. It was a short-handled weapon thrown with great force and in close proximity to the enemy.

DATE	c.600
ORIGIN	GERMAN
LENGTH	37.5cm (14.8in)

Viking bearded battle-axe, *c.*900

Iron axehead with hardened convex blade

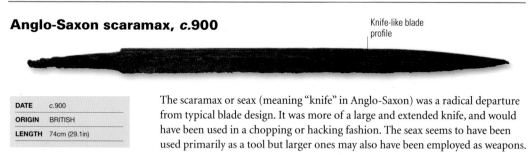

This war axe is based on the traditional wood-splitting axe, and its very long handle would have given its owner the potential to create considerable momentum, especially when swinging the axe over his head. The weapon would have been brought down with devastating force.

DATE	c.900
ORIGIN	SCANDINAVIAN
LENGTH	180cm (70.9in)

Anglo-Saxon scaramax, *c.*900

Knife-like blade profile

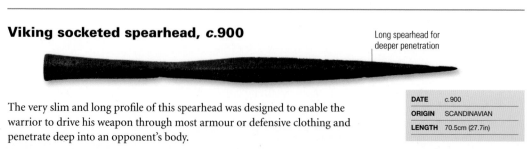

DATE	c.900
ORIGIN	BRITISH
LENGTH	74cm (29.1in)

The scaramax or seax (meaning "knife" in Anglo-Saxon) was a radical departure from typical blade design. It was more of a large and extended knife, and would have been used in a chopping or hacking fashion. The seax seems to have been used primarily as a tool but larger ones may also have been employed as weapons.

Viking socketed spearhead, *c.*900

Long spearhead for deeper penetration

The very slim and long profile of this spearhead was designed to enable the warrior to drive his weapon through most armour or defensive clothing and penetrate deep into an opponent's body.

DATE	c.900
ORIGIN	SCANDINAVIAN
LENGTH	70.5cm (27.7in)

Viking winged spearhead, *c.*900

Thrusting leaf-shaped spearhead

Winged or lugged spearheads were used for both war and hunting. The leaf-shaped blade included double wings at the bottom of the socket that would have been effective at parrying sword blows or stopping an opponent's blade travelling down the spear and injuring the user's hands.

DATE	*c.*900
ORIGIN	SCANDINAVIAN
LENGTH	44.8cm (17.6in)

Viking sword, *c.*900

Straight cross guard

Double-edged blade

Wide fuller

DATE	*c.*900
ORIGIN	SCANDINAVIAN
LENGTH	95.5cm (37.6in)

The deep, single fuller (the rounded or bevelled groove on the flat side of a blade) of this double-edged blade was not designed to allow an opponent's blood to channel down the blade, but was carefully crafted by the sword maker to give the blade less overall weight and consequently, more flexibility.

Viking sword, *c.*900

Pattern-welded blade

This sword has a wide, double-edged, pattern-welded blade that would have given it superb strength and durability. The pommel, which forms an ornament on the end of the hilt, is rounded in shape and very typical of late Viking sword hilts. The pommel needed to be heavy to counterbalance the heavy blade.

DATE	*c.*900
ORIGIN	SCANDINAVIAN
LENGTH	89cm (35in)

Late Viking sword, *c.*900–1150

Later Viking tapered blade

DATE	*c.*900–1150
ORIGIN	SCANDINAVIAN
LENGTH	90.1cm (35.5in)

The large, rounded iron pommel of this sword acted as the perfect counterweight to its long and wide blade. At this late stage of Viking sword development, the blade has now become tapered towards the end and is in contrast to earlier Viking swords that had blades of equal width and more rounded points.

Medieval swords

The wide-bladed and double-edged knightly sword had developed into a highly effective weapon of war and important signifier of social rank. It could slice through chain mail with ease. Only at the end of the medieval period were swords developed with especially hardened points to penetrate plate armour.

Scandinavian late Viking/early medieval sword, *c.*1050

Fuller extends to almost full length of blade

Straight, squared cross guard

This sword has a distinctive "brazil nut" pommel that was common in the early medieval period. Unlike earlier Viking swords of the 900s, the cross guard has now increased considerably in width. The blade is also more finely tapered. This sword is very much a transitional piece.

DATE	*c.*1050
ORIGIN	SCANDINAVIAN
LENGTH	82cm (32.3in)

English late Viking/early medieval sword, *c.*1100–50

Curved cross guard

Although this sword was excavated from a river in southern England, it is in a remarkable state of preservation. The distinctive late Viking, lobated style of the pommel is clearly evident, but the sharply downswept cross guard has resulted in many authorities wrongly dating this sword to the later medieval period.

DATE	*c.*1100–50
ORIGIN	ENGLISH
LENGTH	92cm (36.2in)

European knightly sword, *c.*1150

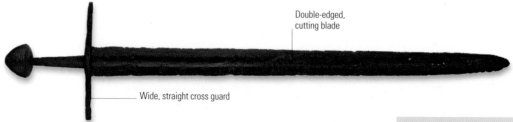

Double-edged, cutting blade

Wide, straight cross guard

This is representative of the type of broadsword that would have been carried by a mounted knight during the Crusades (1095–1291). Pommel design was evolving from earlier triangular shapes to more rounded or "wheel" forms.

DATE	*c.*1150
ORIGIN	EUROPEAN
LENGTH	96.5cm (38in)

German knightly sword, *c.*1250–1300

Large, rounded pommel with flattened sides

Blade graduating to spear point

Cruciform-shaped cross guard

DATE	c.1250–1300
ORIGIN	GERMAN
LENGTH	112cm (44in)

This sword has a spear-point blade with impressive cutting and thrusting capabilities. Its narrow blade and the consequent reduction in weight are likely to have provided its knight with considerable flexibility and agility, particularly when fighting on foot.

European knightly sword, *c.*1250–1300

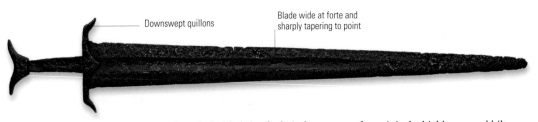

Downswept quillons

Blade wide at forte and sharply tapering to point

DATE	c.1250–1300
ORIGIN	EUROPEAN
LENGTH	91.4cm (36in)

Although the blade is of relatively common form, it is the highly unusual hilt design that sets this sword apart from all other contemporary examples. Where most medieval swords display a wheel pommel, this sword features a two-pronged pommel and sharply angled quillons. This hilt design is rarely seen in contemporary medieval illustrations of knights, and the only two recorded visual references are represented in the royal seals of King Edward I of England (1239–1307) and Charles of Anjou, King of Sicily (1227–85).

The Crusades

When the Christian and Muslim forces clashed in battle during the Crusades (1095–1291), their sword types were quite varied in style and manufacture. The European knight carried a sword with a wide, single-fullered and double-edged blade, with rounded pommel and straight cross guard. When King Richard I of England (1157–1199) battled against the forces of Saladin, or Salah al-Din Yusuf ibn Ayyub (1137–1193), many Muslim troops carried the scimitar, a curved, single-edged sword with a much wider blade than the European weapon. Scimitar blades of very high quality were made from Damascus steel.

ABOVE A battle between Crusaders and Muslims. The Crusaders fought with double-edged blades against the curved scimitars.

English knightly sword, c.1300–1400

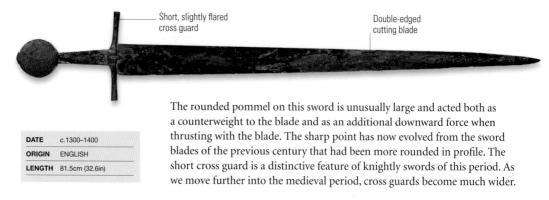

Short, slightly flared cross guard

Double-edged cutting blade

DATE	c.1300–1400
ORIGIN	ENGLISH
LENGTH	81.5cm (32.6in)

The rounded pommel on this sword is unusually large and acted both as a counterweight to the blade and as an additional downward force when thrusting with the blade. The sharp point has now evolved from the sword blades of the previous century that had been more rounded in profile. The short cross guard is a distinctive feature of knightly swords of this period. As we move further into the medieval period, cross guards become much wider.

European knightly sword, c.1300–25

DATE	c.1300–25
ORIGIN	EUROPEAN
LENGTH	96.5cm (38in)

This knightly sword has a wide, single-fullered and doubled-edged blade. The grip appears to be a modern, wooden replacement. The original grip would have had a wooden core overlaid with leather. Very few of these have survived the centuries.

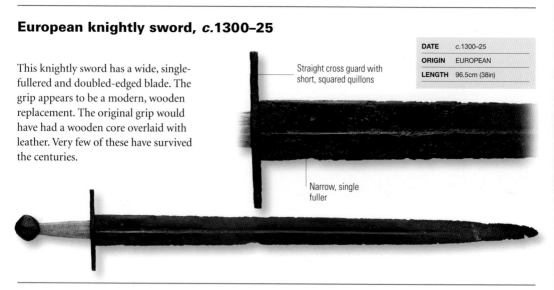

Straight cross guard with short, squared quillons

Narrow, single fuller

European knightly sword, c.1300–50

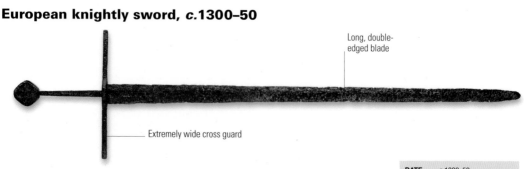

Long, double-edged blade

Extremely wide cross guard

This sword has an unusually wide cross guard and a long, double-edged blade. Considerable hand and arm strength would have been required to wield the sword effectively. The owner might have used two hands to control this weapon.

DATE	c.1300–50
ORIGIN	EUROPEAN
LENGTH	121.5cm (47.8in)

English knightly sword, *c.*1325

Blade in excavated condition

Tapering quillons

DATE	*c.*1325
ORIGIN	ENGLISH
LENGTH	80cm (31.5in)

The sword is heavily corroded and was found in the River Nene, in the east of England. The rounded pommel is covered in a copper alloy and the decoration includes a raised shield with incised coat of arms (unidentified). It is of "riding sword" proportions (swords with a lighter, more flexible blade), worn at court or on a hunt rather than in battle.

European knightly sword, *c.*1350

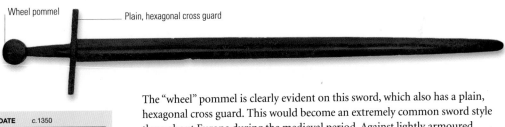

Wheel pommel

Plain, hexagonal cross guard

DATE	*c.*1350
ORIGIN	EUROPEAN
LENGTH	105.4cm (41.5in)

The "wheel" pommel is clearly evident on this sword, which also has a plain, hexagonal cross guard. This would become an extremely common sword style throughout Europe during the medieval period. Against lightly armoured opponents (such as those encountered in the Middle East), this heavy, double-edged sword could be quite devastating.

European knightly sword, *c.*1350–80

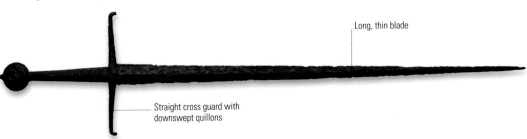

Long, thin blade

Straight cross guard with downswept quillons

DATE	*c.*1350–80
ORIGIN	EUROPEAN
LENGTH	112.4cm (44.2in)

This sword has a needle-like blade specifically designed to penetrate plate armour. Held aloft and brought down with considerable force against an opponent, this type of sword would expose any inherent weaknesses in the armour, particularly under the arms (where armour had to be jointed to allow the wearer freedom of movement). Its thin, strong blade could also be pushed through the slits in closed helmets.

European riding sword, *c.*1380

Globular pommel

Edge nicks caused by corrosion

Downward-curving cross guard

The downswept cross guard of this sword is a new departure and is a style that was particularly common in medieval France and Germany. The pommel is globular, with a pronounced tang "button" at the top. The blade is shorter than the regular knightly sword of the period. This type of sword is normally categorized as a "riding sword", and it was worn mostly for civilian occasions such as a hunt or while at court.

DATE	*c.*1380
ORIGIN	EUROPEAN
LENGTH	90cm (35.4in)

European knightly sword, *c.*1380

Downward-curving quillons

Blade with needlepoint for penetration

The extremely tapered blade of this sword is evidence of its transitional role from a purely hacking and slashing weapon to one that had both cutting and thrusting capabilities. In the late 14th century, improved plate armour was beginning to appear and a new kind of sword was now required to successfully penetrate this all-encompassing protection. This type of longsword would become important during the Renaissance period.

DATE	*c.*1380
ORIGIN	EUROPEAN
LENGTH	126cm (49.6in)

German knightly sword, *c.*1380

Cruciform-shaped cross guard

Thrusting, penetrative blade

The long, thin blade of this sword was designed solely for penetration of plate armour and it is likely that use of the blade edge in combat was minimal. The weapon is in a heavily corroded condition and is likely to have been excavated. It is very fortunate that such a fragile blade from this period survives.

DATE	*c.*1380
ORIGIN	GERMAN
LENGTH	128.5cm (50.6in)

English knightly sword, *c.*1400

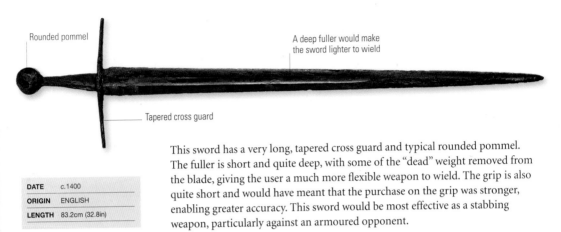

Rounded pommel

A deep fuller would make
the sword lighter to wield

Tapered cross guard

DATE	c.1400
ORIGIN	ENGLISH
LENGTH	83.2cm (32.8in)

This sword has a very long, tapered cross guard and typical rounded pommel.
The fuller is short and quite deep, with some of the "dead" weight removed from
the blade, giving the user a much more flexible weapon to wield. The grip is also
quite short and would have meant that the purchase on the grip was stronger,
enabling greater accuracy. This sword would be most effective as a stabbing
weapon, particularly against an armoured opponent.

German knightly sword, *c.*1450

Single fuller to add
flexibility and strength

Globular pommel

Flanged, cruciform
cross guard

DATE	c.1450
ORIGIN	GERMAN
LENGTH	107.9cm (42.5in)

The flanged and slightly cruciform-shaped cross guard of this sword is a popular
style found in many German swords of this period. The pommel is extremely
globular and exhibits a raised tang button at the top. This sword would probably
have been very flexible and lightweight to handle.

European knightly sword, *c.*1450

Wide cross guard, with
downward-curving quillons

Diamond-shaped cross-
section to blade

Sharp-pointed
blade

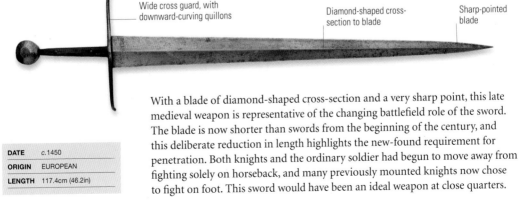

DATE	c.1450
ORIGIN	EUROPEAN
LENGTH	117.4cm (46.2in)

With a blade of diamond-shaped cross-section and a very sharp point, this late
medieval weapon is representative of the changing battlefield role of the sword.
The blade is now shorter than swords from the beginning of the century, and
this deliberate reduction in length highlights the new-found requirement for
penetration. Both knights and the ordinary soldier had begun to move away from
fighting solely on horseback, and many previously mounted knights now chose
to fight on foot. This sword would have been an ideal weapon at close quarters.

Late medieval and Renaissance swords

By the end of the 15th century, the nature of warfare had changed dramatically. The introduction of sophisticated plate armour had made the effective use of the traditional double-edged cutting broadsword more difficult. Consequently, sword makers now produced weapons with extremely hardened points for deep penetration into the armour. Great hand-and-a-half and two-handed broadswords also emerged and became important weapons against massed ranks of pikemen.

English cross-hilted sword, *c.*1450

Globular quillons or finials

DATE	c.1450
ORIGIN	ENGLISH
LENGTH	94.4cm (37.2in)

A group of 80 similar swords was found on the battlefield site of Castillon, near Bordeaux, France, where English and French forces met in 1453. The pommel is quite unusual, and is known as a "scent-stopper" type. The cross guard has globular finials, unlike the usual plain, squared cross guard which is found on swords of the period.

English two-handed sword, *c.*1450

Thin, two-handed grip

Straight cross guard with globular quillons

Long, thin blade for greater reach

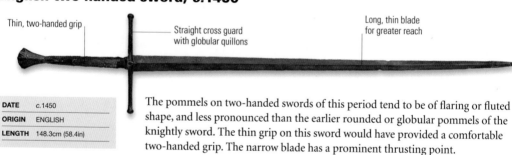

DATE	c.1450
ORIGIN	ENGLISH
LENGTH	148.3cm (58.4in)

The pommels on two-handed swords of this period tend to be of flaring or fluted shape, and less pronounced than the earlier rounded or globular pommels of the knightly sword. The thin grip on this sword would have provided a comfortable two-handed grip. The narrow blade has a prominent thrusting point.

European two-handed sword, *c.*1450

Long tang

Squared cross guard

Tapering blade

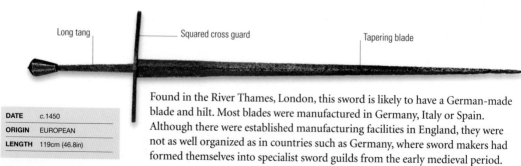

DATE	c.1450
ORIGIN	EUROPEAN
LENGTH	119cm (46.8in)

Found in the River Thames, London, this sword is likely to have a German-made blade and hilt. Most blades were manufactured in Germany, Italy or Spain. Although there were established manufacturing facilities in England, they were not as well organized as in countries such as Germany, where sword makers had formed themselves into specialist sword guilds from the early medieval period.

German broadsword, *c.*1450

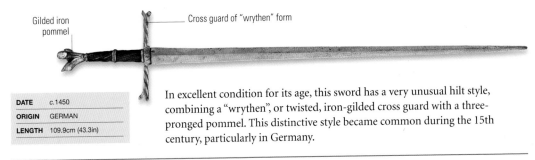

Gilded iron pommel

Cross guard of "wrythen" form

DATE	c.1450
ORIGIN	GERMAN
LENGTH	109.9cm (43.3in)

In excellent condition for its age, this sword has a very unusual hilt style, combining a "wrythen", or twisted, iron-gilded cross guard with a three-pronged pommel. This distinctive style became common during the 15th century, particularly in Germany.

German two-handed sword, *c.*1500

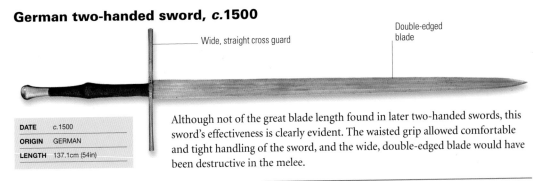

Wide, straight cross guard

Double-edged blade

DATE	c.1500
ORIGIN	GERMAN
LENGTH	137.1cm (54in)

Although not of the great blade length found in later two-handed swords, this sword's effectiveness is clearly evident. The waisted grip allowed comfortable and tight handling of the sword, and the wide, double-edged blade would have been destructive in the melee.

German Landsknecht-type sword, *c.*1500

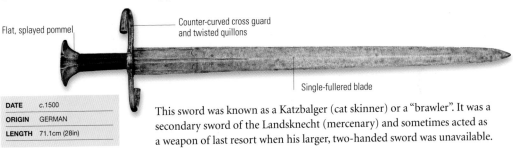

Flat, splayed pommel

Counter-curved cross guard and twisted quillons

Single-fullered blade

DATE	c.1500
ORIGIN	GERMAN
LENGTH	71.1cm (28in)

This sword was known as a Katzbalger (cat skinner) or a "brawler". It was a secondary sword of the Landsknecht (mercenary) and sometimes acted as a weapon of last resort when his larger, two-handed sword was unavailable.

Swiss ceremonial broadsword, *c.*1500

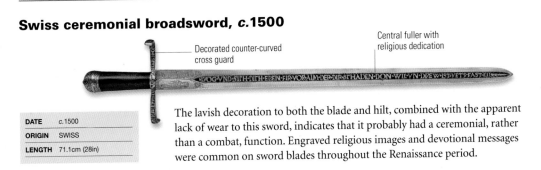

Decorated counter-curved cross guard

Central fuller with religious dedication

DATE	c.1500
ORIGIN	SWISS
LENGTH	71.1cm (28in)

The lavish decoration to both the blade and hilt, combined with the apparent lack of wear to this sword, indicates that it probably had a ceremonial, rather than a combat, function. Engraved religious images and devotional messages were common on sword blades throughout the Renaissance period.

363

German two-handed Landsknecht sword, *c.*1500

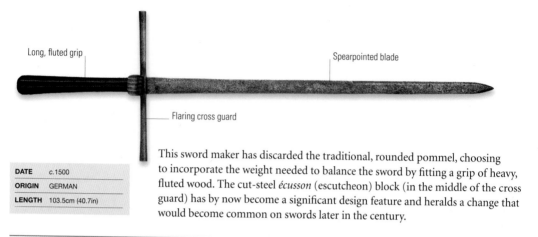

Long, fluted grip

Spearpointed blade

Flaring cross guard

DATE	*c.*1500
ORIGIN	GERMAN
LENGTH	103.5cm (40.7in)

This sword maker has discarded the traditional, rounded pommel, choosing to incorporate the weight needed to balance the sword by fitting a grip of heavy, fluted wood. The cut-steel *écusson* (escutcheon) block (in the middle of the cross guard) has by now become a significant design feature and heralds a change that would become common on swords later in the century.

Italian cinquedea, *c.*1500

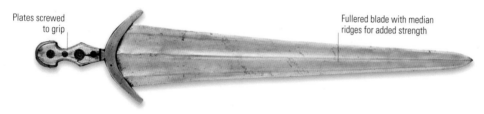

Plates screwed to grip

Fullered blade with median ridges for added strength

DATE	*c.*1500
ORIGIN	ITALIAN
LENGTH	71.1cm (28in)

The Italian cinquedea is an extremely handsome sword type of the early 16th century. It was carried extensively in Italy during the Renaissance but found little favour outside its borders. The name is derived from the five deep fullers, or "fingers", on the blade. Many fine examples have blades with elaborately engraved and gilded decoration. The opportunity for the Renaissance craftsmen to embellish such an unusually wide area on a sword blade was rarely ignored.

German hand-and-a-half sword, *c.*1520

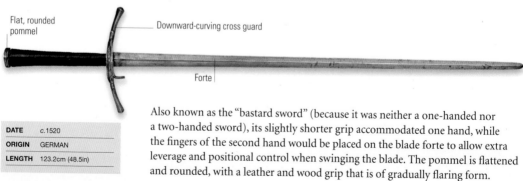

Flat, rounded pommel

Downward-curving cross guard

Forte

DATE	*c.*1520
ORIGIN	GERMAN
LENGTH	123.2cm (48.5in)

Also known as the "bastard sword" (because it was neither a one-handed nor a two-handed sword), its slightly shorter grip accommodated one hand, while the fingers of the second hand would be placed on the blade forte to allow extra leverage and positional control when swinging the blade. The pommel is flattened and rounded, with a leather and wood grip that is of gradually flaring form.

German Landsknecht broadsword, *c.*1550

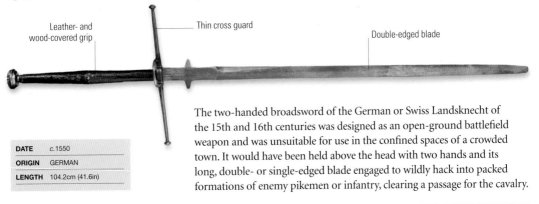

Leather- and wood-covered grip

Thin cross guard

Double-edged blade

DATE	*c.*1550
ORIGIN	GERMAN
LENGTH	104.2cm (41.6in)

The two-handed broadsword of the German or Swiss Landsknecht of the 15th and 16th centuries was designed as an open-ground battlefield weapon and was unsuitable for use in the confined spaces of a crowded town. It would have been held above the head with two hands and its long, double- or single-edged blade engaged to wildly hack into packed formations of enemy pikemen or infantry, clearing a passage for the cavalry.

German two-handed Landsknecht sword, *c.*1550

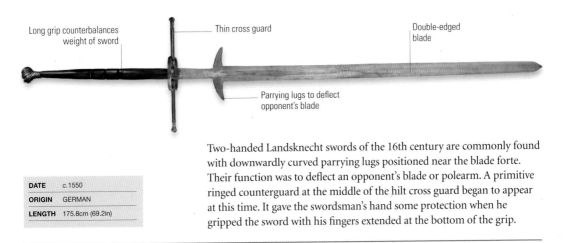

Long grip counterbalances weight of sword

Thin cross guard

Double-edged blade

Parrying lugs to deflect opponent's blade

DATE	*c.*1550
ORIGIN	GERMAN
LENGTH	175.8cm (69.2in)

Two-handed Landsknecht swords of the 16th century are commonly found with downwardly curved parrying lugs positioned near the blade forte. Their function was to deflect an opponent's blade or polearm. A primitive ringed counterguard at the middle of the hilt cross guard began to appear at this time. It gave the swordsman's hand some protection when he gripped the sword with his fingers extended at the bottom of the grip.

German sword of the State Guard of the Duke of Brunswick, 1573

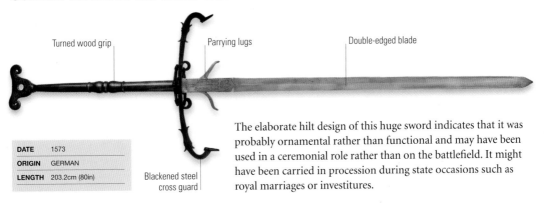

Turned wood grip

Parrying lugs

Double-edged blade

DATE	1573
ORIGIN	GERMAN
LENGTH	203.2cm (80in)

Blackened steel cross guard

The elaborate hilt design of this huge sword indicates that it was probably ornamental rather than functional and may have been used in a ceremonial role rather than on the battlefield. It might have been carried in procession during state occasions such as royal marriages or investitures.

Rapiers

The elegant profile of the rapier is a striking image often associated with the Renaissance gentleman. It was not just an effective weapon and the first choice for duels but it also signified a person's social rank and wealth. Its origins were in 15th-century Spain and Italy, and the name derives from the Spanish term *espada ropera* (sword of the robes), meaning it could be worn with civilian clothing.

Italian transitional rapier, *c.*1520

Straight, double-edged blade with short, single fuller

This sword is a transitional piece and not yet a fully formed rapier. The blade is similar to wide, pre-1500 broadsword blades, and the large, rounded pommel, although stylishly fluted (to reflect Renaissance tastes), still echoes earlier knightly swords. It is only when we view the "swept" and flowing hilt guards that a more traditional, albeit simple, rapier shape is becoming apparent.

DATE	c.1520
ORIGIN	ITALIAN
LENGTH	111.5cm (43.9in)

German rapier, *c.*1550

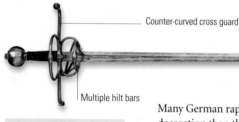

Counter-curved cross guard

Multiple hilt bars

DATE	c.1550
ORIGIN	GERMAN
LENGTH	96.3cm (37.9in)

Many German rapiers tend to have simpler and less elaborate hilt design and decoration than their Italian and Spanish counterparts. This example has a large, plain, rounded pommel that acted to counterbalance the weight of its long, double-edged blade. The hilt bars, although elaborately formed, are not unnecessary. They are designed to protect the wearer's hand.

Italian rapier, *c.*1590

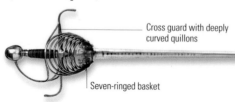

Cross guard with deeply curved quillons

Seven-ringed basket

Multi-ringed rapiers are quite common but most surviving examples have a maximum of three to four hilt rings. Seven-ringed rapiers like this piece are rare. Many of these rapiers feature a scalloped or ribbed bowl or plate which is located at the bottom of the hilt.

DATE	c.1590
ORIGIN	ITALIAN
LENGTH	136.9cm (53.9in)

Rapiers and parrying daggers in duels

The duelling era commenced in the fifteenth or sixteenth centuries and continued well into the nineteenth century. The rapier and left-handed parrying dagger were edged weapons used while opponents were engaged in a duel.

The dagger was held by placing four fingers around the grip, while the thumb was placed firmly behind the blade near the quillons. By using the dagger in this way, the duellist was able to parry the rapier for a crucial moment while his own rapier thrust could be made at his opponent's body.

ABOVE Two gentlemen engaged in a duel, c.1600. Both are using left-handed parrying daggers.

Italian swept-hilt rapier, *c.*1610

Pierced cross guard

Single fuller

DATE	c.1610
ORIGIN	ITALIAN
LENGTH	119.4cm (47in)

Here we see the rapier in its most advanced form and at the height of its development. The extensively pierced and chiselled hilt is of superb "swept-hilt" design, with the "sweep" beginning at the knuckle guard and moving downwards and around the guard, with three branches, or bars, detaching away and re-connecting at the shell guard just above the ricasso.

Italian swept-hilt rapier, *c.*1610

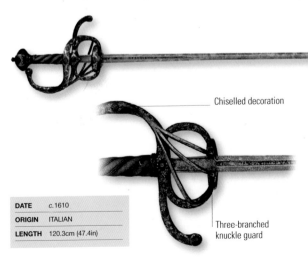

Chiselled decoration

DATE	c.1610
ORIGIN	ITALIAN
LENGTH	120.3cm (47.4in)

Three-branched knuckle guard

Of swept-hilt form, this Italian rapier highlights the superb artistry of the sword maker, particularly his phenomenal skills as a metalworker. The hilt is profusely decorated with deeply cut chiselled embellishments and the large pommel lends a perfect, symmetrical balance to the subject. The grip would have been manufactured from a wooden core, overlaid with a complex pattern of fluted silver twistwire and "Turk's-head" finials to each end of the grip.

German swept-hilt rapier, *c.*1610

Curved quillon

Long, slender, thrusting blade

Ringed knuckle guard

The hilt of this rapier features a flat, inwardly curving quillon. The open nature of the hilt and the large gaps between the bars probably afforded little protection to the sword hand. It was hoped that the great length of a rapier's blade would ensure a sufficiently safe and constant distance from any opponent, so reducing the threat of any injuries or even potentially fatal thrusts.

DATE	c.1610
ORIGIN	GERMAN
LENGTH	121.4cm (47.8in)

German swept-hilt rapier, *c.*1620

Blade inscriptions

Needlepoint blade

Three-ringed hilt

The plain, yet functional styling of this three-ringed swept-hilt rapier probably indicates a German origin. The blade has numerous armourer's marks and a religious inscription. Swordsmiths and armourers marked their swords in many different ways, with the cross motif being very common amongst European sword makers. They also stamped their names into the blade fuller. This blade has "Francesco" inscribed on it.

DATE	c.1620
ORIGIN	GERMAN
LENGTH	130.3cm (51.3in)

English Littlecote rapier, *c.*1630

Scalloped shell guard

Shallow, diamond-sectioned blade

This sword is from Littlecote House, in Wiltshire, southern England. This was the Elizabethan mansion of Sir John Popham (1531–1607), who was Speaker of the House of Commons and Lord Chief Justice of England. The scalloped shell guard would have afforded better protection for the hand, coupled with an extra two rows of open and linked hilt bars placed just above. There is a large ovoid pommel that would have been effective at providing the balance required to wield a sword with such a long blade.

DATE	c.1630
ORIGIN	ENGLISH
LENGTH	133.8cm (52.7in)

Flemish "Pappenheimer" rapier, *c.1630*

Diamond-sectioned blade

Shell guard

DATE	c.1630
ORIGIN	FLEMISH
LENGTH	127cm (50in)

This style of rapier is commonly referred to as a "Pappenheimer" type, named after the German Count Gottfried Heinrich, Graf von Pappenheim, an illustrious commander of cavalry forces during the Thirty Years' War (1618–48). His regiment of cuirassiers carried this type of military rapier, distinguished by its large, pierced shell guard.

English duelling rapier, *c.1640*

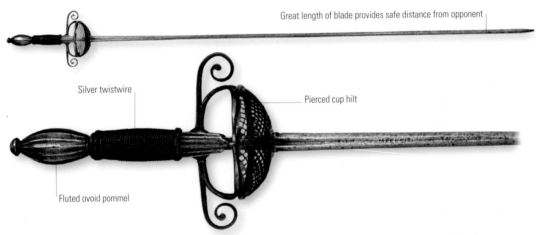

Great length of blade provides safe distance from opponent

Silver twistwire

Pierced cup hilt

Fluted ovoid pommel

DATE	c.1640
ORIGIN	ENGLISH
LENGTH	141.6cm (55.7in)

Rapiers of this type are normally referred to as "duelling rapiers", and are characterized by a "dish hilt" and an extremely long, diamond-sectioned blade. The shallow "dish", or guard, is located at the bottom of the hilt, and is of delicately pierced and cross-hatched form. The coiled quillons and the *pas d'âne* – the two curved bars that branch from the cross guard and rest on the dish – are a precursor to a hilt style found on later smallswords.

English rapier, *c.1640*

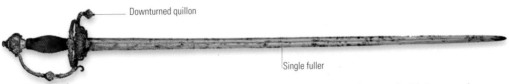

Downturned quillon

Single fuller

DATE	c.1640
ORIGIN	ENGLISH
LENGTH	97cm (38.2in)

Dating from the time of the English Civil War (1642–51), this is a very fine example of an English rapier. Many English sword makers of this period were noted for their ability to produce intricate, chiselled-steel decoration on the sword hilts.

English rapier, *c.*1650

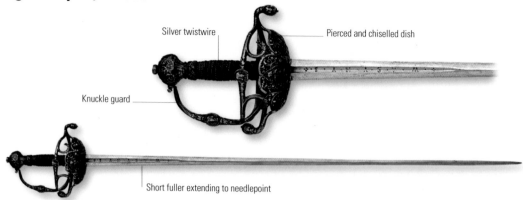

Silver twistwire

Pierced and chiselled dish

Knuckle guard

Short fuller extending to needlepoint

A superb example of an English Civil War period rapier, with a large, chiselled-steel ovoid pommel and pierced, scalloped shell guard. This style was influenced by "mortuary" broadswords of the period, and is particularly evident in the application of chiselled human faces to the hilt bars.

DATE	*c.*1650
ORIGIN	ENGLISH
LENGTH	108.2cm (42.6in)

Spanish cup-hilt rapier, *c.*1650

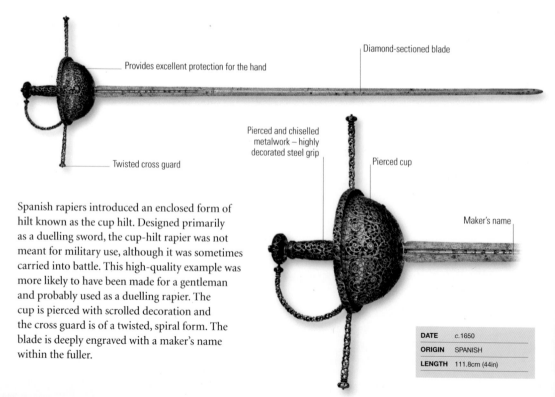

Diamond-sectioned blade

Provides excellent protection for the hand

Twisted cross guard

Pierced and chiselled metalwork – highly decorated steel grip

Pierced cup

Maker's name

Spanish rapiers introduced an enclosed form of hilt known as the cup hilt. Designed primarily as a duelling sword, the cup-hilt rapier was not meant for military use, although it was sometimes carried into battle. This high-quality example was more likely to have been made for a gentleman and probably used as a duelling rapier. The cup is pierced with scrolled decoration and the cross guard is of a twisted, spiral form. The blade is deeply engraved with a maker's name within the fuller.

DATE	*c.*1650
ORIGIN	SPANISH
LENGTH	111.8cm (44in)

Spanish swept-hilt rapier, *c.*1650

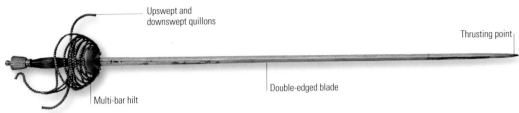

Upswept and
downswept quillons

Thrusting point

Double-edged blade

Multi-bar hilt

DATE	*c.*1650
ORIGIN	SPANISH
LENGTH	116.6cm (45.9in)

Spanish rapiers of the 17th century represent the height of the sword maker's art and are invariably of flamboyant and extravagantly fluid style. In this example, the many flowing hilt bars are present for both practical and aesthetic reasons.

Spanish swept-hilt rapier, *c.*1650

Short, strengthening fuller

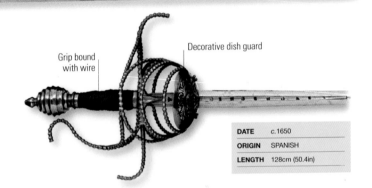

This is a rapier of very high quality, characterized by a distinctive cut-steel pattern to the hilt bars and an unusual faceted or layered ovoid pommel. The blade is deeply stamped with the sword maker's name and there is also a punched mark just below the ricasso.

Grip bound with wire

Decorative dish guard

DATE	*c.*1650
ORIGIN	SPANISH
LENGTH	128cm (50.4in)

Rapiers in action

The chaotic scenes depicted in so-called "swashbuckling" movies, in which the protagonists attack each other with rapiers in a violent and rapid series of lunging thrusts and desperate parrying, is not actually how an Elizabethan or Jacobean swordsman would have handled his rapier. Rather, the action of a fight with rapiers would have involved a series of premeditated and ferociously quick lunges from a standing position that would have been "voided", or dodged, by the opponent, and the process continued until an opening was found by one or other rapier.

ABOVE These two protagonists have chosen to use a cloak as a method of parrying each other's rapier. It was hoped that the rapier would be caught and dragged away in the cloak, providing an opportunity for a thrust.

Halberds

Developed primarily as an edged weapon that could vastly extend a soldier's reach, combined with the cutting capabilities of an axe and the thrusting, penetrative function of a spear point, the halberd reached its zenith during the massed battles of the medieval and Renaissance periods. The halberd gave the ordinary soldier an opportunity both to unhorse and to kill mounted troops.

Swiss/German halberd, *c.*1480

Parrying or grappling hook

Fluted spear point

This is an early form of halberd, comprising a large rectangular cutting blade with a short, fluted spearhead. The hook for dismounting or parrying an opponent's blade is still very crude and it would have taken great skill and practice to wield effectively.

DATE	c.1480
ORIGIN	SWISS/GERMAN
LENGTH	226.7cm (89.3in)

Halberd, *c.*1550

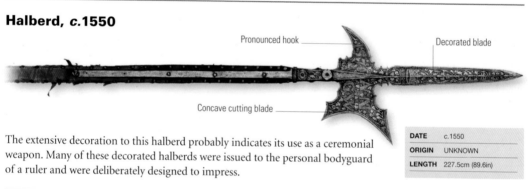

Pronounced hook

Decorated blade

Concave cutting blade

The extensive decoration to this halberd probably indicates its use as a ceremonial weapon. Many of these decorated halberds were issued to the personal bodyguard of a ruler and were deliberately designed to impress.

DATE	c.1550
ORIGIN	UNKNOWN
LENGTH	227.5cm (89.6in)

German halberd, *c.*1550

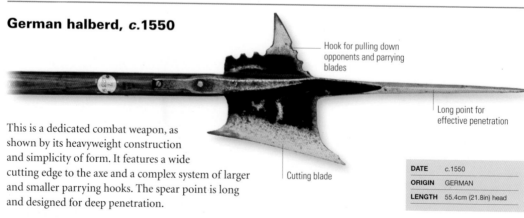

Hook for pulling down opponents and parrying blades

Long point for effective penetration

This is a dedicated combat weapon, as shown by its heavyweight construction and simplicity of form. It features a wide cutting edge to the axe and a complex system of larger and smaller parrying hooks. The spear point is long and designed for deep penetration.

Cutting blade

DATE	c.1550
ORIGIN	GERMAN
LENGTH	55.4cm (21.8in) head

Italian halberd, *c.*1570

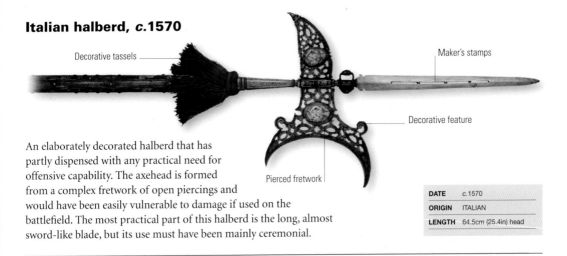

Decorative tassels

Maker's stamps

Decorative feature

Pierced fretwork

An elaborately decorated halberd that has partly dispensed with any practical need for offensive capability. The axehead is formed from a complex fretwork of open piercings and would have been easily vulnerable to damage if used on the battlefield. The most practical part of this halberd is the long, almost sword-like blade, but its use must have been mainly ceremonial.

DATE	c.1570
ORIGIN	ITALIAN
LENGTH	64.5cm (25.4in) head

German halberd, *c.*1580

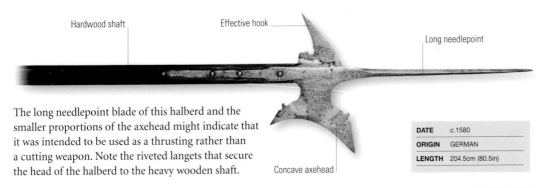

Hardwood shaft

Effective hook

Long needlepoint

Concave axehead

The long needlepoint blade of this halberd and the smaller proportions of the axehead might indicate that it was intended to be used as a thrusting rather than a cutting weapon. Note the riveted langets that secure the head of the halberd to the heavy wooden shaft.

DATE	c.1580
ORIGIN	GERMAN
LENGTH	204.5cm (80.5in)

English halberd/partizan, *c.*1700

Long langet to secure

Spear-shaped head

Decorative hooks

DATE	c.1700
ORIGIN	ENGLISH
LENGTH	239.7cm (94.4in)

The halberd had become militarily superfluous by the end of the 18th century, particularly with the advent of more close-range firearms and artillery. This example is very much a transitional piece and would still have been quite effective as a polearm, especially when employing the sharpened axehead and spear-shaped, double-edged head.

Partizans and glaives

Both the partizan and glaive were common staff weapons on the battlefields of Europe from the late medieval period (approximately the 13th to 14th centuries). However, the glaive had ceased to be used by the 18th century, by which time the partizan had become more of a symbolic weapon and signifier of military rank, being carried by officers and non-commissioned officers (NCOs).

Italian glaive, *c.*1550

Convex cutting edge

The glaive was a significant cutting polearm, consisting of a long convex blade with a small parrying hook. This glaive also had twin parrying hooks, or lugs, at the bottom of the blade, just above the socket. Many early glaives were simply sword or knife blades mounted onto long wooden shafts.

DATE	c.1550
ORIGIN	ITALIAN
LENGTH	75.5cm (29.7in) head

French glaive, 1564

Motto: DEUS PROVIDEBIT
(God will provide)

This particularly fine example was made for a soldier in the service of the Duke of Burgundy. The deeply etched blade features the ducal coat of arms and two intertwined letter "M"s representing Maximilian II (Holy Roman Emperor, 1564–1576) and Maria of Spain (1528–1603).

DATE	1564
ORIGIN	FRENCH
LENGTH	71cm (27.9in) head

Yeomen of the Guard

The Yeomen of the Guard are the oldest established military corps in the British Army. They were formed by Henry VII after the Battle of Bosworth in 1485, and they still wear uniforms based on those worn at the time of the Tudor monarchy (1485–1603). The tunic displays the Tudor crown, the Lancastrian rose, shamrock and thistle and the motto DIEU ET MON DROIT (God and my right). Originally, the Yeomen carried the pike of the the ordinary foot-soldier but later they carried a decorated (blue and gilt) partizan, which is still carried today while they perform their ceremonial duties.

RIGHT The Yeomen of the Guard searching the crypt of the Houses of Parliament, 1894. The uniform and the partizan remain unchanged to this day.

French partizan of the Burgundian Ducal Guard, 1618

Cutting edge

Deeply engraved decoration with ducal coat of arms

Blade ferrule

Intricate decoration

Decorative hooks

DATE	1618
ORIGIN	FRENCH
LENGTH	64.2cm (25.3in) head

This elaborately decorated partizan would have been carried by a member of the Burgundian Ducal Guard. It would have been an extremely expensive weapon to produce and therefore only issued to a very limited number of carefully selected troops.

French partizan, *c.*1680

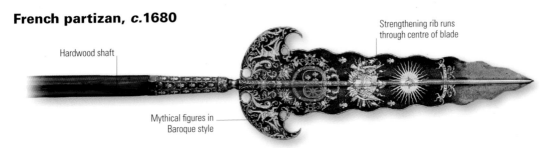

Strengthening rib runs through centre of blade

Hardwood shaft

Mythical figures in Baroque style

DATE	c.1680
ORIGIN	FRENCH
LENGTH	192.1cm (75.6in)

The increasing use of gilt decoration to both sword and polearm blades during the 17th and 18th centuries is clearly evident in this superb piece. It was produced for ceremonial and guard duties, and it features the French royal crown, coat of arms and classically inspired figures in the Rococo style. The sun motif on the blade is probably an allusion to Louis XIV (1638–1715), who was known as the "Sun King".

Pikes, bills and spontoons

The sight of massed ranks of opposing pike and billmen pushing against each other with their bills, pikes and spontoons was common during the battles of the 16th and 17th centuries. The average length of a pike during the English Civil War (1642–51) was around 4.9m (16.1ft) which was an obvious asset in keeping a safe distance, but the long, heavy, wooden shaft could also make it cumbersome and unwieldy.

Italian pike or lance, *c.*1550

Long, riveted langets

Leaf-shaped blade

The simple military spear has a history stretching back millennia and its use as an offensive military weapon was still undiminished in the 16th century. The only discernible change was to the length of the shaft, which had increased over the centuries in response to the prevalent use of massed ranks of infantrymen and the important need to keep a relatively safe distance from the enemy in front.

DATE	c.1550
ORIGIN	ITALIAN
LENGTH	182cm (71.6in)

Italian pike, *c.*1550

Flanged or fluted point

Even with the introduction of improved matchlock firearms during the 17th century, the only effective defence against a concerted cavalry charge was still a row of disciplined pikemen. Ironically, more time was needed to train a pikeman than a musketeer to fire his matchlock musket. This was due to the complex drilling manoeuvres required and the great physical strength needed.

DATE	c.1550
ORIGIN	ITALIAN
LENGTH	65.7cm (25.9in) head

English bill, *c.*1550

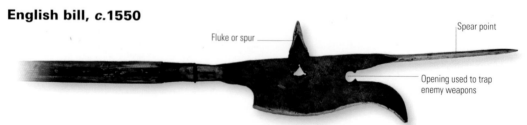

Fluke or spur

Spear point

Opening used to trap enemy weapons

English bills of the 16th century tend to be quite plain in form but robust in their manufacture. This bill has a number of projections that all serve different functions. The curved axehead would be a good cutting weapon, the long spear point had great penetrative capabilities and the pronounced parrying hook could deflect blows and bring down mounted soldiers and hamstring horses.

DATE	c.1550
ORIGIN	ENGLISH
LENGTH	195.5cm (77in)

Italian bill, *c.*1550

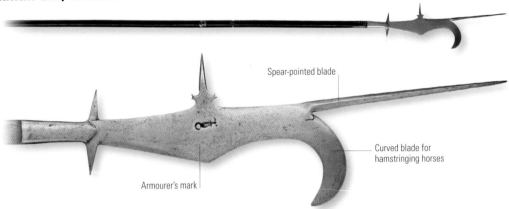

Spear-pointed blade

Curved blade for
hamstringing horses

Armourer's mark

DATE	c.1550
ORIGIN	ITALIAN
LENGTH	67.3cm (26.5in) head

The curved hook just below the spear point of this bill would have been used to hamstring the enemy's horses and consequently bring down their horsemen. The bill's needlepoint spear could then be employed to finish off the now vulnerable opponent on the ground.

Italian bill, *c.*1560

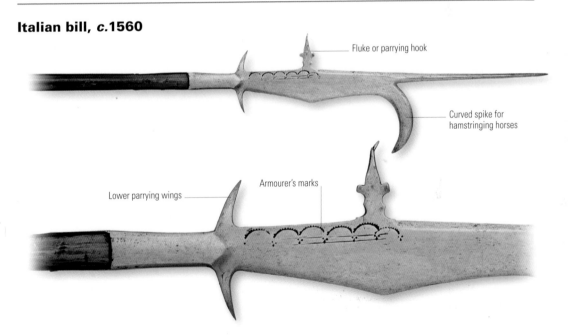

Fluke or parrying hook

Curved spike for
hamstringing horses

Armourer's marks

Lower parrying wings

DATE	c.1560
ORIGIN	ITALIAN
LENGTH	70.6cm (27.8in) head

Italian bills (roncone) were far more sophisticated in design than their English counterparts and tended to have longer heads with more piercing points. The blade on this bill has armourer's stamps of repeated crescent shape. Armourers used a wealth of different marks and many are quite obscure and bizarre in shape, making identification very difficult.

English bill, *c.*1580

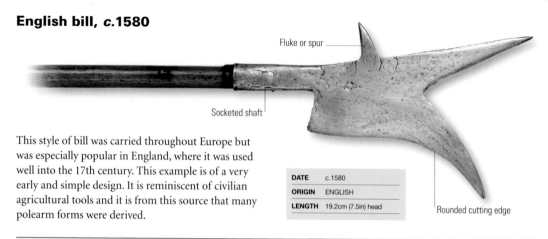

Fluke or spur

Socketed shaft

Rounded cutting edge

This style of bill was carried throughout Europe but was especially popular in England, where it was used well into the 17th century. This example is of a very early and simple design. It is reminiscent of civilian agricultural tools and it is from this source that many polearm forms were derived.

DATE	c.1580
ORIGIN	ENGLISH
LENGTH	19.2cm (7.5in) head

English bill, *c.*1580

Parrying hook

Decorated socket

The very long head of this bill is particularly unusual. It was probably used more as a thrusting than as a cutting weapon. Two winged parrying lugs are located near the bottom of the head and there is another effective parrying hook, or fluke, which is placed just above.

DATE	c.1580
ORIGIN	ENGLISH
LENGTH	217.2cm (85.5in)

English spontoon, *c.*1790

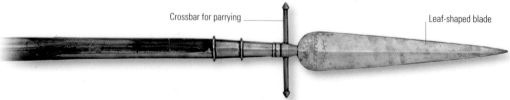

Crossbar for parrying

Leaf-shaped blade

By this time, the spontoon was purely a weapon signifying military rank and only carried by officers and NCOs. The curved parrying bars, or flukes, of earlier polearms have now disappeared, to be replaced by a simple crossbar with decorative finials or quillons.

DATE	c.1790
ORIGIN	ENGLISH
LENGTH	157.5cm (62in)

French officer's spontoon, *c.*1780

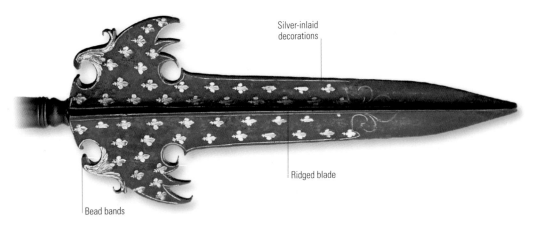

Silver-inlaid
decorations

Ridged blade

Bead bands

DATE	c.1780
ORIGIN	FRENCH
LENGTH	40.3cm (15.9in) head

This is a spontoon made of forged iron and used by the guards of French king Louis XVI (r. 1774–91). The blackened blade has a strong ridge on each side and approximately two thirds of its surface is decorated with silver-inlaid lilies and fine bead bands.

English spontoon, *c.*1800

Cut-out piercing

Counter-curved crossbar

Spade-shaped blade

DATE	c.1800
ORIGIN	ENGLISH
LENGTH	23.5cm (9.2in) head

The use of cut-out piercings and engraved decoration on the blade indicate that this spontoon was probably more of a ceremonial weapon, although its construction is still robust and durable enough for combat. The spontoon head is attached to the wooden shaft by long, riveted langets.

Spears, guisarmes and bardiches

The spear was used in battle long before recorded history and this longevity bears witness to its simple effectiveness. By the medieval and Renaissance periods, it was no longer thrown like a javelin but used more like a short, thrusting polearm.

The guisarme was a more sophisticated development of a peasant's agricultural tool. The bardiche was very much the weapon of the ordinary peasant soldier, with its long and heavy crescent-shaped blade that functioned as a devastating war axe.

German winged, or lugged, spear, c.1480

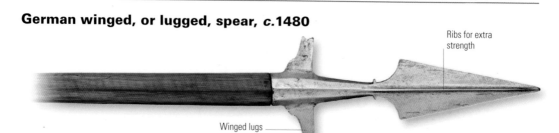

Ribs for extra strength

Winged lugs

The winged, or lugged, spear had a leaf-shaped blade with triangular side projections that acted as a barrier to stop the spearhead sinking too deeply into an opponent, thus becoming difficult to withdraw. This was to be avoided as it rendered the soldier vulnerable.

DATE	c.1480
ORIGIN	GERMAN
LENGTH	109.2cm (43in)

Italian military spear, c.1500

Long, median (or ribbed) ridge

The long, triangular blade of this military spear has a pronounced median or strengthening ridge down the centre of the blade to ensure that it can withstand the great force that would be generated by heavy penetration, particularly into armour or protective clothing.

DATE	c.1500
ORIGIN	ITALIAN
LENGTH	240cm (94.5in)

Italian military spear, c.1520

Of very simple form, this late Renaissance military spear would not have looked out of place at the Battle of Hastings (1066) some five hundred years earlier. Its function was still the same, except that it would not have been thrown but used instead as a short polearm.

DATE	c.1520
ORIGIN	ITALIAN
LENGTH	46.3cm (18.2in) head

English small spear, *c.*1550

Riveted langets

DATE	c.1550
ORIGIN	ENGLISH
LENGTH	33.2cm (13.1in) head

The riveted langets attached to the wooden staff of this spear are similar to those used on halberds and other polearms of the period, and they would certainly have added extra strength to the socket. It is likely that this is a smaller version of the military pike.

English guisarme, *c.*1580

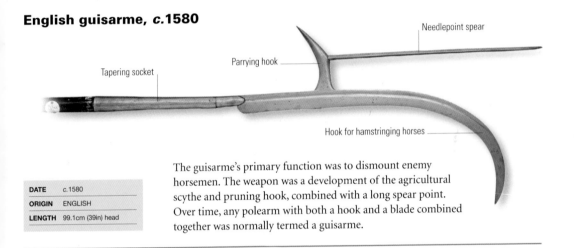

Needlepoint spear

Parrying hook

Tapering socket

Hook for hamstringing horses

DATE	c.1580
ORIGIN	ENGLISH
LENGTH	99.1cm (39in) head

The guisarme's primary function was to dismount enemy horsemen. The weapon was a development of the agricultural scythe and pruning hook, combined with a long spear point. Over time, any polearm with both a hook and a blade combined together was normally termed a guisarme.

North European bardiche, *c.*1480

Thrusting spike

Long, cutting edge

DATE	c.1480
ORIGIN	NORTH EUROPEAN
LENGTH	76.2cm (30in) head

A warrior would have required considerable strength to wield this weapon. The combined weight of the heavy axehead and thick wooden shaft would probably have created some manoeuvrability problems, unless used by an experienced soldier. The bottom of the axehead was secured to the shaft by strong rivets to ensure stability of the long blade. The bardiche was a standard infantry weapon in eastern Europe, particularly Russia and Poland, where 17th-century musketeers (an early form of infantryman armed with a musket) used the end of the pole at the back of the bardiche to rest their guns while firing. Presumably, a long spike would have been fitted into the bottom of the pole to secure it into the ground.

Poleaxes

The poleaxe's function was to smash and cut its way through armour and flesh. By the late 15th century, it had become the preferred battlefield weapon of the knight, who now fought primarily on foot, and had relegated the sword to a secondary role. The poleaxe usually comprised an axe, hammer and long spike. Effective training enabled a knight to dispatch any opponent with a series of well aimed, ruthless blows.

European poleaxe, *c.*1480

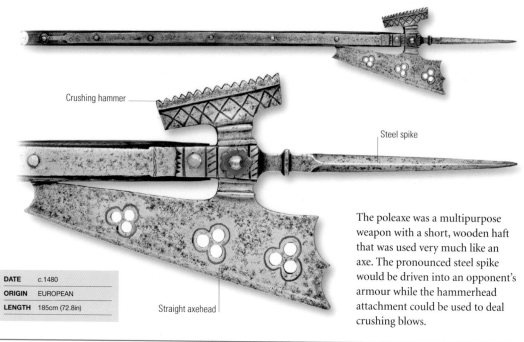

Crushing hammer

Steel spike

DATE	c.1480
ORIGIN	EUROPEAN
LENGTH	185cm (72.8in)

Straight axehead

The poleaxe was a multipurpose weapon with a short, wooden haft that was used very much like an axe. The pronounced steel spike would be driven into an opponent's armour while the hammerhead attachment could be used to deal crushing blows.

North European poleaxe, *c.*1480

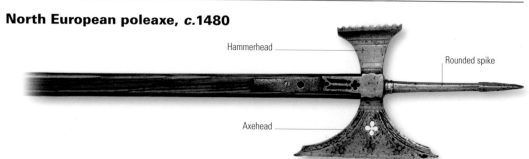

Hammerhead

Rounded spike

Axehead

Many poleaxes were decorated but this example is fairly plain. The spike has a rounded profile, unlike the usual triangular type that is normally encountered on a poleaxe. The name "poleaxe" is derived from the word "poll" which is the Old English name for head.

DATE	c.1480
ORIGIN	NORTH EUROPEAN
LENGTH	35cm (13.7in) head

Poleaxes on the battlefield

By the 15th century, English knights fought predominantly on foot and the poleaxe was their primary weapon of choice. A two-handed grip was essential when holding the poleaxe, and it was held at shoulder height with elbows tucked close to the body in order to protect the knight from blows to his vulnerable sides, particularly the underarm area where plate armour was normally absent.
While engaged in the melee of battle, the knight would dodge and parry enemy blades, and carefully wait for the right moment to strike with his poleaxe. Although any effective blow to the body that could maim or kill was the main priority of any attacker with a poleaxe, a shattering strike to the face was the most coveted. Incapacitated (or sometimes killed outright on the spot), the victim would be finished off by the poleaxe's hammerhead.

ABOVE 15th-century hand-to-hand fighting. Both knights are using poleaxe-type weapons.

North European poleaxe, *c.*1500

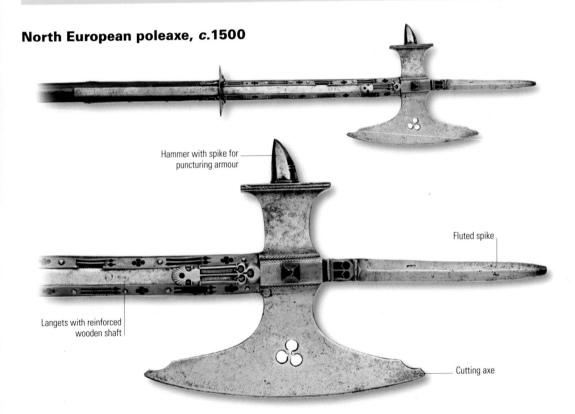

Hammer with spike for puncturing armour

Fluted spike

Langets with reinforced wooden shaft

Cutting axe

DATE	c.1500
ORIGIN	NORTH EUROPEAN
LENGTH	177.8cm (70in)

This poleaxe has a spike attached to the hammerhead. Made of solid steel, this tooth-shaped addition would have been highly effective at puncturing armour, providing the user with an opening in which to drive in the long spike at the end of the axehead.

Other polearms

As well as the halberd, pike and poleaxe, a number of lesser known polearms were used by the infantry soldier. They included the batwinged chauve souris (meaning "bat" in French) and the crudely effective war scythe, a development of the agricultural scythe and a tool familiar to the conscripted peasant soldier.

German war scythe, *c.*1480

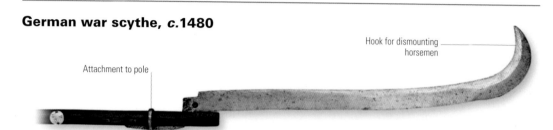

Hook for dismounting horsemen

Attachment to pole

The war scythe was little more than an adapted agricultural scythe used for harvesting wheat. The main difference was that the war scythe had a less pronounced curve than its agricultural counterpart. Swung with sufficient momentum, the war scythe could literally cut a swathe through opponents.

DATE	c.1480
ORIGIN	GERMAN
LENGTH	250.2cm (98.5in)

Italian corseque, *c.*1500

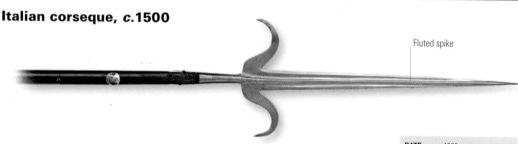

Fluted spike

The corseque had curved wings bending back towards the handle of the weapon. It was similar to the partizan but exhibited a fluted spike rather than the typical leaf-shaped blade more commonly associated with the partizan.

DATE	c.1500
ORIGIN	ITALIAN
LENGTH	74.9cm (29.5in) head

Italian chauve souris, *c.*1550

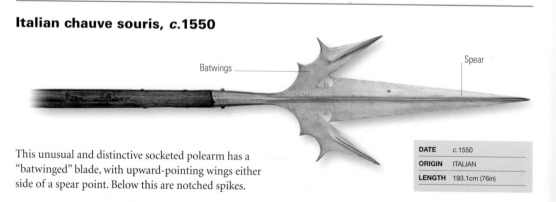

Batwings

Spear

This unusual and distinctive socketed polearm has a "batwinged" blade, with upward-pointing wings either side of a spear point. Below this are notched spikes.

DATE	c.1550
ORIGIN	ITALIAN
LENGTH	193.1cm (76in)

Italian chauve souris, *c.*1550

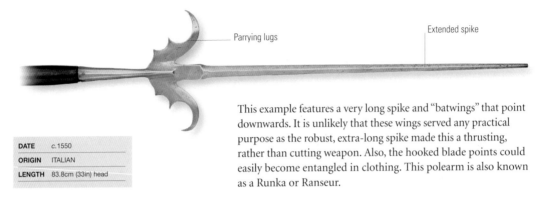

Parrying lugs

Extended spike

DATE	c.1550
ORIGIN	ITALIAN
LENGTH	83.8cm (33in) head

This example features a very long spike and "batwings" that point downwards. It is unlikely that these wings served any practical purpose as the robust, extra-long spike made this a thrusting, rather than cutting weapon. Also, the hooked blade points could easily become entangled in clothing. This polearm is also known as a Runka or Ranseur.

English war scythe, *c.*1600

Wide, cutting edge

DATE	c.1600
ORIGIN	ENGLISH
LENGTH	99.1cm (39in)

This is a very crude example of the type of peasant weapon that would have been carried from the early medieval period. Unlike the double-edged bill or halberd, the war scythe had a single-edged blade on the concave side. This weapon was very common in eastern Europe, particularly Russia and Poland, where the need to quickly raise peasant armies (in the face of the constant Ottoman threat) and therefore produce simply manufactured weapons meant that the war scythe would always be one of the first weapons to be called upon in a national crisis.

German military fork, *c.*1650

Double prongs

Metal stop to limit penetration

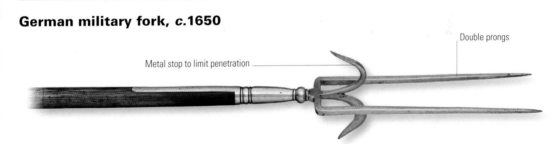

DATE	c.1650
ORIGIN	GERMAN
LENGTH	41.1cm (16.2in) head

An adaptation of the agricultural pitchfork, the military fork had a variety of uses on and off the battlefield. Its two long prongs, or tines, could easily dismount riders and enable their swift dispatch or capture. Many enemy knights were subsequently held to ransom following the application of the military fork to lever them unharmed off their horses. It could also be utilized as a practical tool during a siege when the prongs were used to raise up siege ladders or deliver supplies to ramparts.

Hunting swords and hangers

The use of a short-bladed sword for hunting has its origins in the late medieval period and reached its height of popularity during the 18th century, when this sword changed from being a handy tool to dispatch and carve up an animal to an overt excuse for displaying the wealth and status of its owner. The hanger was adopted by the military, particularly the foot-soldier, and was also a common weapon for naval officers.

English hanger, c.1640

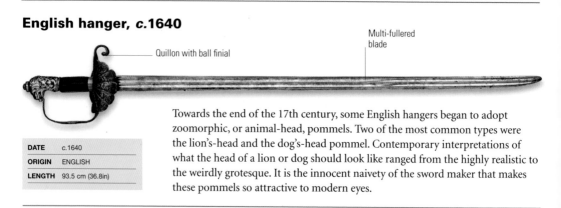

Quillon with ball finial

Multi-fullered blade

DATE	c.1640
ORIGIN	ENGLISH
LENGTH	93.5 cm (36.8in)

Towards the end of the 17th century, some English hangers began to adopt zoomorphic, or animal-head, pommels. Two of the most common types were the lion's-head and the dog's-head pommel. Contemporary interpretations of what the head of a lion or dog should look like ranged from the highly realistic to the weirdly grotesque. It is the innocent naivety of the sword maker that makes these pommels so attractive to modern eyes.

English hanger, c.1645

Coiled quillon

Fuller near blade edge

The hanger was a common infantry sword during the 17th century, particularly in England where it was combined with many hilt types. This example has a pierced, steel shell guard with a slightly curved and single-fullered blade. There is also a pronounced tang button at the top of the flattened pommel.

DATE	c.1645
ORIGIN	ENGLISH
LENGTH	81cm (31.9in)

English/German hanger, c.1650

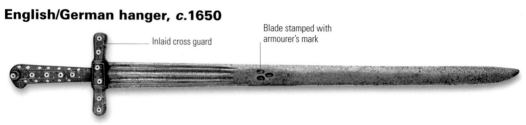

Inlaid cross guard

Blade stamped with armourer's mark

The cruciform hilt of this hanger is made from cow horn, with an inlay of metal studs in either silver or pewter, combined with stag-horn or ebony roundels. The blade was manufactured in Germany and imported into England, where it was mounted onto this hilt.

DATE	c.1650
ORIGIN	ENGLISH/GERMAN
LENGTH	78.8cm (31in)

English hanger, *c.*1650

Cut-steel pommel

Fuller extends to length of blade

Inlaid shell guard

DATE	*c.*1650
ORIGIN	ENGLISH
LENGTH	73.2cm (28.8in)

This is a very fine example of an English infantry hanger of the English Civil War (1642–51) period. The hilt is deliberately blackened to highlight the superb inlaid silver chequering. This would have been an expensive sword to purchase and was probably worn by a person of considerable means. It is likely that the leather scabbard would have had decorative mounts to match the hilt.

English hanger, *c.*1650

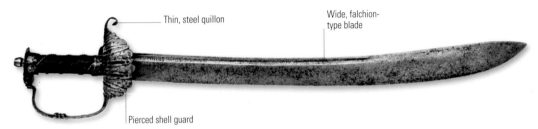

Thin, steel quillon

Wide, falchion-type blade

Pierced shell guard

DATE	*c.*1650
ORIGIN	ENGLISH
LENGTH	70cm (27.5in)

One of the most common blade types to be found on hangers of this period is the falchion. This is a curved blade that widens considerably near the point, sometimes ending with a false edge on the back of the blade. The shell guards are of pierced form and a thin knuckle guard is attached to the pommel by means of a flat-headed screw.

English hanger, *c.*1680

Rounded quillon

Single-fullered blade

DATE	*c.*1680
ORIGIN	ENGLISH
LENGTH	84.6cm (33.3in)

This hanger is typical of the type carried by huntsmen and naval officers of the 17th and 18th century. It was a practical choice for naval officers, as the short length of the blade meant that it was less likely to get caught up in the rigging and could be wielded within the limited space available on board a ship at war. The grip is made of stag-horn and the hilt is brass. Pommels tended to be slightly domed with the tang button prominent.

European hunting sword, *c.*1680

Double-edged point

Single-edged blade

This hunting sword has a fullered single-edged blade with a double-edged point. Each side of the upper third of the blade is etched with hunting scenes. It has a simple, iron, knucklebow hilt with clam shell and stag-horn plates, partially replaced. The grip ferrule is florally cut, and the grip panels are stag-horn with large, hemispherical rivets, one of which has been replaced.

DATE	1680
ORIGIN	EUROPEAN
LENGTH	84cm (33in)

English/German hanger, *c.*1690

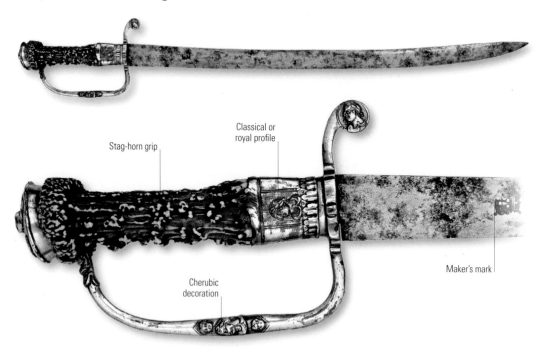

Stag-horn grip

Classical or royal profile

Maker's mark

Cherubic decoration

This fine hanger is marked on the hilt with the initials of Richard Fuller (*c.*1670–1731), a noted English sword cutler working in London. He was a skilled hilt maker and in this sword we can see the finely crafted detail he has applied to the pommel, knuckle guard, cross guard and ferrule (the metal band at the bottom of the grip). This stag-horn grip would have been specially chosen because of its gnarled properties and ability to keep the wearer's hand firmly in place. The grip's unusual shape is also aesthetically pleasing. The blade has the king's head-impressed stamp of the Wundes sword-making family of Solingen, Germany.

DATE	*c.*1690
ORIGIN	ENGLISH/GERMAN
LENGTH	63.5cm (25in)

English hanger, *c.*1700

Onyx handle

Bulbous quillon

Fuller extends to length of blade

DATE	c.1700
ORIGIN	ENGLISH
LENGTH	69.2cm (27.2in)

The grip of this silver-hilted hanger has been manufactured from natural stone agate and would have been highly distinctive when worn. The use of onyx for sword grips was very popular during the first half of the 18th century. The hilt mounts are solid silver and the long, straight blade has a fuller that extends for most of the blade length, giving the sword flexibility and strength.

English hanger, *c.*1730

Diamond-sectioned blade

DATE	c.1730
ORIGIN	ENGLISH
LENGTH	92.1cm (36.2in)

The shell guard of this silver-hilted hanger is decorated in the form of a bearded human face. It is probably an interpretation of the pagan Green Man (also known as "the wild man of the woods") and was a popular hunting motif in mid-18th century England.

Russian hanger, *c.*1750

Flat-backed blade

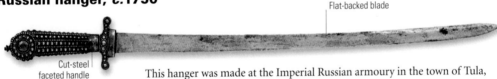

Cut-steel faceted handle

DATE	c.1750
ORIGIN	RUSSIAN
LENGTH	70.2cm (27.6in)

This hanger was made at the Imperial Russian armoury in the town of Tula, about 165km (102 miles) south of Moscow. The first factory was opened by Peter the Great (1672–1725) in 1712, and it soon became the centre of both sword and armaments making. This dress sword was probably made for a civilian gentleman, as indicated by the use of multiple cut-steel ornamentation to the hilt.

English hanger, *c.*1750

Counter-curved quillons

False edge to blade

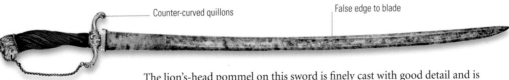

DATE	c.1750
ORIGIN	ENGLISH
LENGTH	80.3cm (31.6in)

The lion's-head pommel on this sword is finely cast with good detail and is combined with an ebony grip of spiral design. The shell guard is absent and has been replaced by a simple cross guard. From the mid-18th century, the normally solid knuckle guard was sometimes replaced by a linked metal chain guard. Chain guards were easily prone to damage and many have been lost over time.

English Civil War swords

Although the importance of firearms on the battlefield was beginning to be felt at the start of the English Civil War (1642–51), the sword was still the principal edged weapon of the mounted horseman. One of the most distinctive swords to emerge from this conflict was the so-called mortuary sword, a peculiarly English broadsword that featured a bowl or half-basket guard with extensive, decorative chiselling to the hilt. It would have been carried by Royalist (Cavalier) and Parliamentarian (Roundhead) troops.

English broadsword, *c.*1620

Rapier hilt

Spear-pointed blade

This sword is transitional in form and has a typical Renaissance "swept" rapier hilt and a long, broadsword blade. Protection for the hand is minimal and although this type of sword was still carried during the English Civil War (1642–51), the hilt was being superseded by mortuary-style basket hilts.

DATE	c.1620
ORIGIN	ENGLISH
LENGTH	94cm (37in)

English backsword, *c.*1640

Long, broadsword blade

This sword would probably have been carried by a mounted officer. The hilt design has echoes of contemporary rapiers but differs in that the blade is much broader and flatter, having a double-edged cutting function, in contrast to the thrusting capabilities of a rapier.

DATE	c.1640
ORIGIN	ENGLISH
LENGTH	90.6cm (35.7in)

English mortuary-type sword, *c.*1640

Chiselled hilt

Multi-fullered blade

Although the blade is longer than a hanger, its curved shape is similar to short-bladed English hangers or hunting swords of the period. The guard, knuckle guard and pommel have been heavily encrusted in silver.

DATE	c.1640
ORIGIN	ENGLISH
LENGTH	92.5cm (36.4in)

English cavalry broadsword, 1640

Deeply chiselled half basket

An early form of lion's-head pommel marks out this cavalry sword as being quite unusual. It is a very early example of an animal-headed pommel on an English broadsword. The hilt has a deeply chiselled half basket.

DATE	1640
ORIGIN	ENGLISH
LENGTH	112.7cm (44.4in)

English mortuary-hilted broadsword, c.1640

Broadsword blade

Multi-bar hilt

DATE	c.1640
ORIGIN	ENGLISH
LENGTH	102.9cm (40.5in)

The blade of this sword is engraved with the motto ME FECIT HOVNSLOE ("Hounslow made me") and is a reference to the west London borough that was a major sword-making town during the 17th century. Many diverse sword types, from hunting hangers to broadswords, were manufactured in Hounslow, and they are characterized by the use of chiselled and inlaid metalwork on the hilt.

English mortuary-hilted broadsword, c.1640

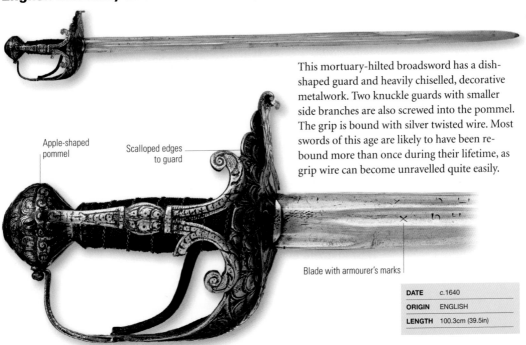

This mortuary-hilted broadsword has a dish-shaped guard and heavily chiselled, decorative metalwork. Two knuckle guards with smaller side branches are also screwed into the pommel. The grip is bound with silver twisted wire. Most swords of this age are likely to have been re-bound more than once during their lifetime, as grip wire can become unravelled quite easily.

Apple-shaped pommel

Scalloped edges to guard

Blade with armourer's marks

DATE	c.1640
ORIGIN	ENGLISH
LENGTH	100.3cm (39.5in)

English mortuary-hilted broadsword, *c.*1650

Long blade for use on horseback

Scrolled guard

The mortuary sword is so named because of the application of stylized, chiselled human heads to the decoration of many of these sword hilts. The title "mortuary" was erroneously given by Victorian sword collectors who believed that the likenesses of King Charles I (1600–49) and Queen Henrietta (1609–69) had been applied to the hilts by English sword makers as a form of silent memorial following his execution in 1649. The hilt of this sword is made from iron with a dish- or boat-shaped guard. Two side knuckle guards are linked to a central guard that screws into the pommel.

DATE	*c.*1650
ORIGIN	ENGLISH
LENGTH	109.7cm (43.2in)

English mortuary-hilted broadsword, *c.*1650

Enclosed bowl guard

Double-edged blade

A common feature of mortuary swords is the attachment of the hilt knuckle bow to the pommel by way of a securing screw. In this case, there is just one knuckle guard, but some mortuary hilts exhibit several knuckle guards screwed around a large apple-shaped pommel.

DATE	*c.*1650
ORIGIN	ENGLISH
LENGTH	104.4cm (41.1in)

English proto-mortuary sword, *c.*1650

Blackened steel hilt

Wide, double-edged blade

Short, narrow fuller

The term "proto-mortuary" normally refers to a group of English swords that was present in England just before the introduction of the fully developed mortuary sword in the mid-17th century. They are usually distinguished by their simple hilt design. In this case, the plain shell and knuckle guard indicate that this sword is of "munition" quality, meaning that it would have been produced for an ordinary soldier (to a prescribed pattern) rather than an officer.

DATE	*c.*1650
ORIGIN	ENGLISH
LENGTH	84.4cm (33.2in)

English mortuary-hilted sword, *c.*1650

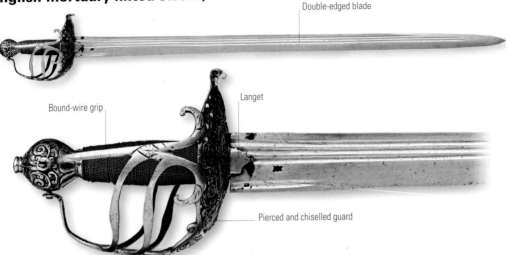

Double-edged blade

Langet

Bound-wire grip

Pierced and chiselled guard

DATE	c.1650
ORIGIN	ENGLISH
LENGTH	100.3cm (39.5in)

This sword has a wide, double-edged blade, probably German. One of the characteristic features of a mortuary hilt is the positioning of two shield-shaped langets on either side of the blade, where it enters the dish guard. It is thought that their function was to add extra strength and stability to the blade.

English mortuary sword, *c.*1650

Blade sharply graduated to needlepoint

DATE	c.1650
ORIGIN	ENGLISH
LENGTH	102.9cm (40.5n)

Although one of the main types of decoration found on mortuary-hilted swords is a chiselled human head, other forms of decoration are present. This can include family coats of arms, armed figures, floral motifs, geometric patterns and even nautical motifs such as stylized dolphins and sea creatures.

English mortuary sword, *c.*1650

Long fuller gives flexibility to the blade

Inlaid silver hilt

DATE	c.1650
ORIGIN	ENGLISH
LENGTH	99.8cm (39.3in)

The use of inlaid silver decoration was a common feature in mortuary-hilted swords. This example is covered with small pieces of solid silver that have been hammered into the blackened steel hilt. Two extra side branches on either side of the hilt are attached to the knuckle guard, giving the user extra protection.

393

Broadswords and sabres

Following the Renaissance, a number of distinctive sword types began to emerge. By the late 15th century, a diverse range of broadsword hilts and blades are noted. Swords with wide blades, both curved and straight, were used by cavalrymen as well as infantry soldiers. They had great slashing capabilities and were very robust. They largely replaced the medieval cruciform-hilted, double-edged knightly sword.

German broadsword, *c.*1550

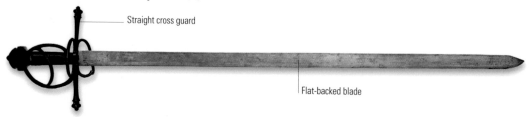

Straight cross guard

Flat-backed blade

These German fighting swords were extremely common during the 16th century and were carried throughout Europe. The sweeping hilt bars and straight cross guard are reminiscent of contemporary rapiers but differ in having a flattened pommel (as opposed to the traditionally ovoid rapier pommel) and a wide, broadsword blade.

DATE	c.1550
ORIGIN	GERMAN
LENGTH	108.5cm (42.7in)

German Dussäge or Sinclair sabre, *c.*1580

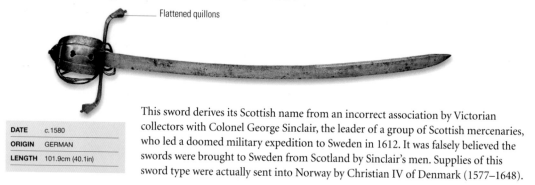

Flattened quillons

DATE	c.1580
ORIGIN	GERMAN
LENGTH	101.9cm (40.1in)

This sword derives its Scottish name from an incorrect association by Victorian collectors with Colonel George Sinclair, the leader of a group of Scottish mercenaries, who led a doomed military expedition to Sweden in 1612. It was falsely believed the swords were brought to Sweden from Scotland by Sinclair's men. Supplies of this sword type were actually sent into Norway by Christian IV of Denmark (1577–1648).

German clamshell sabre, *c.*1600

S-shaped cross guard

Of simple yet well-constructed manufacture, these robustly made broadswords have a large clamshell guard and S-shaped cross guard. Their weight would have made them an effective slashing sword, if wielded at speed and on horseback.

DATE	c.1600
ORIGIN	GERMAN
LENGTH	78.7cm (31in)

German sabre, c.1600

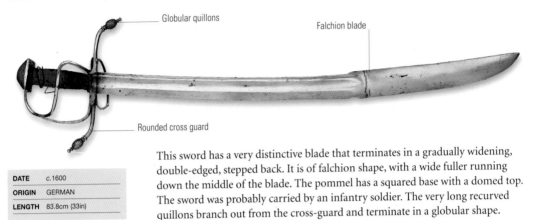

Globular quillons

Falchion blade

Rounded cross guard

DATE	c.1600
ORIGIN	GERMAN
LENGTH	83.8cm (33in)

This sword has a very distinctive blade that terminates in a gradually widening, double-edged, stepped back. It is of falchion shape, with a wide fuller running down the middle of the blade. The pommel has a squared base with a domed top. The sword was probably carried by an infantry soldier. The very long recurved quillons branch out from the cross-guard and terminate in a globular shape.

Italian/Spanish broadsword, c.1600

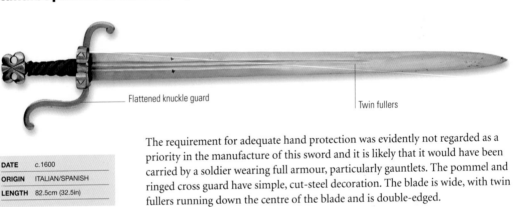

Flattened knuckle guard

Twin fullers

DATE	c.1600
ORIGIN	ITALIAN/SPANISH
LENGTH	82.5cm (32.5in)

The requirement for adequate hand protection was evidently not regarded as a priority in the manufacture of this sword and it is likely that it would have been carried by a soldier wearing full armour, particularly gauntlets. The pommel and ringed cross guard have simple, cut-steel decoration. The blade is wide, with twin fullers running down the centre of the blade and is double-edged.

German "crab claw" broadsword, c.1620

"Crab claws" for parrying blade

Thin, thrusting blade

DATE	c.1620
ORIGIN	GERMAN
LENGTH	94cm (37in)

The addition of extra "crab claws" to the hilt guard of this sword makes it an interesting piece. The purpose of these down-curving quillons was to parry or trap an opponent's blade. The long, thrusting blade indicates that it was probably carried by a mounted soldier.

Italian "crab claw" broadsword, *c.*1620

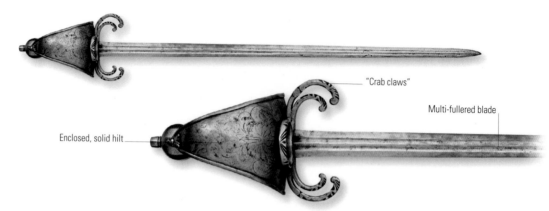

"Crab claws"

Multi-fullered blade

Enclosed, solid hilt

This sword is another variation of the "crab claw" hilted broadsword and features an enclosed, solid hilt. This is quite unusual as sword hilts of this period tended to be open, with an exposed knuckle guard and widely spaced hilt bars. The hilt would have given far more protection to the sword hand and is a precursor of much later sword types.

DATE	*c.*1620
ORIGIN	ITALIAN
LENGTH	92cm (36.2in)

English cavalry broadsword, *c.*1620

Coiled quillon

The emphasis of this sword is very much on the blade. Of considerable length and width, it would have been carried by a heavily armoured horseman or cuirassier. The user would need a strong arm to wield this sword. If used correctly, a weapon of these proportions could sever limbs with ease.

DATE	*c.*1620
ORIGIN	ENGLISH
LENGTH	101.8cm (40.1in)

Italian broadsword, *c.*1620

Decorative quillon

Double-edged blade

The hilt and blade style of this sword is reminiscent of medieval sword types. There are some subtle differences though, including the Renaissance-inspired classical styling to the cross guard and pommel. The small, clamshell guard is the only indicator that we are looking at a sword of the 17th century.

DATE	*c.*1620
ORIGIN	ITALIAN
LENGTH	102.1cm (40.2in)

Swiss cavalry broadsword, *c.*1620

Animal-head finial

DATE	*c.*1620
ORIGIN	SWISS
LENGTH	93.7cm (36.9in)

Brass dog's-head and lion's-head pommels were common on Swiss military swords of the 17th and 18th centuries. Embossed (or raised) panels were also inserted into the hilt guards. This example has a loose chain knuckle guard in place of the normally rigid bar, a rather impractical form of defence for this military sword.

German cavalry broadsword, *c.*1640

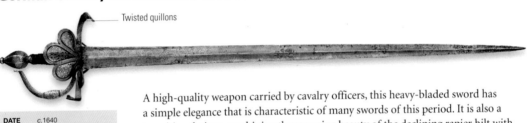

Twisted quillons

DATE	*c.*1640
ORIGIN	GERMAN
LENGTH	111.8cm (44in)

A high-quality weapon carried by cavalry officers, this heavy-bladed sword has a simple elegance that is characteristic of many swords of this period. It is also a transitional piece, combining the sweeping beauty of the declining rapier hilt with the new pierced and scalloped guard that had become a fashionable design feature on swords of the mid-17th century.

German broadsword, *c.*1640

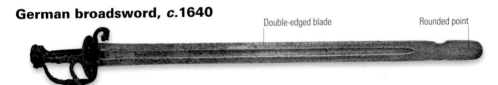

Double-edged blade   Rounded point

DATE	*c.*1640
ORIGIN	GERMAN
LENGTH	101.8cm (40.1in)

This is a sword of large proportions. The rounded point at the end of a huge, double-edged blade gives us a clue that it was possibly once used as an executioner's sword, although it might not have started out as one. Executioners' swords, particularly German examples, tend to have a simple cruciform hilt.

German cavalry officer's broadsword, *c.*1690

Wooden grip

DATE	*c.*1690
ORIGIN	GERMAN
LENGTH	98cm (38.6in)

This is a superb example of the sword maker's art. The name "Clemens" is found on the blade. He was a highly regarded German sword maker of the 17th century and his name was extensively copied on sword blades of the period. A blade of this quality is most definitely a Clemens original.

Cavalry lances

The cavalry lance was a popular weapon of the medieval mounted soldier and was used throughout Europe for many hundreds of years. It had fallen out of favour by the time of the Renaissance but was adopted again in the Napoleonic Wars (1799–1815), when the Imperial French Army established an elite regiment of Polish lancers. By the 1800s, most European nations had established regiments of lancers.

European lance head, *c.*1400

The war lance comprised a solid wooden shaft (usually made of ash, though cedar and poplar were also used), and the lance head was similar in shape to that of a spear.

Spear-pointed head

DATE	c.1400
ORIGIN	EUROPEAN
LENGTH	15cm (5.9in)

British cavalry lance, 1840 Pattern

Small pike point

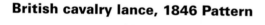

DATE	1840
ORIGIN	BRITISH
LENGTH	277cm (109in)

The long, riveted steel langets of this lance had a two-fold purpose. They secured the lance head to the shaft but were also effective at parrying sword blows. The lance head is larger than earlier patterns and more fluted.

British cavalry lance, 1846 Pattern

Long langets

Fluted head

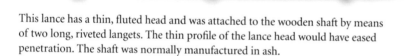

This lance has a thin, fluted head and was attached to the wooden shaft by means of two long, riveted langets. The thin profile of the lance head would have eased penetration. The shaft was normally manufactured in ash.

DATE	1846
ORIGIN	BRITISH
LENGTH	119.7cm (47.1in) head and langets only

British cavalry lance, 1846 Pattern

Spike point

Cavalry pennon

DATE	1846
ORIGIN	BRITISH
LENGTH	275cm (108.3in)

This is the type of lance that would have been carried by British lancers during the Crimean War (1853–56). It was a pattern used by the 17th Lancers, part of the ill-fated Light Brigade, who charged the Russian guns at the Battle of Balaklava in October 1854 (in present-day Ukraine). The pennon was attached to the shaft by means of studs that slotted into keyholes drilled into the shaft.

British cavalry lance, 1868 Pattern

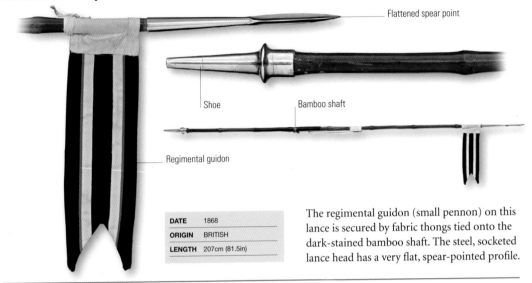

Flattened spear point

Shoe

Bamboo shaft

Regimental guidon

DATE	1868
ORIGIN	BRITISH
LENGTH	207cm (81.5in)

The regimental guidon (small pennon) on this lance is secured by fabric thongs tied onto the dark-stained bamboo shaft. The steel, socketed lance head has a very flat, spear-pointed profile.

British cavalry lance, 1885 Pattern

Lance head

The swallow-tail design of this lance pennon indicates that it is the last pattern of British cavalry lance. Pennon design changed between patterns and this particular design was carried through to the eventual withdrawal of lances from the British Army in the 1920s. Although it might be assumed that pennons were unfurled in battle, it was normal practice for them to be rolled up when on active service. The unravelled pennon was most commonly seen during parades.

Pennon attached to shaft by rivets

DATE	1885
ORIGIN	BRITISH
LENGTH	275cm (108.3in)

British practice cavalry lance, *c.*1890

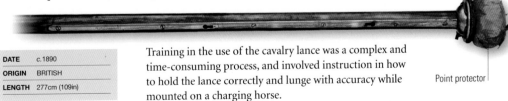

DATE	c.1890
ORIGIN	BRITISH
LENGTH	277cm (109in)

Training in the use of the cavalry lance was a complex and time-consuming process, and involved instruction in how to hold the lance correctly and lunge with accuracy while mounted on a charging horse.

Point protector

Military and tournament lances

The spectacle of a massed group of heavily armoured mounted knights, long lances couched under their arms, galloping towards a line of infantry, would have been an awe-inspiring sight. There would have been no defence against them if the opposing archers had failed to stop their advance. Outside of war, the jousting tournament was another opportunity to improve a knight's prowess with sword and lance.

English carousel lance, *c.*1600

By the 17th century, the lance as a weapon was restricted to the jousting field, with more emphasis on the exhibition of a knight's equestrian skills. This example is typical of a design carried for over 300 years. It is constructed from solid hardwood, although some lances were hollow to allow easier splintering.

DATE	c.1600
ORIGIN	ENGLISH
LENGTH	363.7cm (143.2in)

Italian lance head for jousting, *c.*1600

The aim of jousting was not to kill an opponent but to unhorse him or shatter his lance. To do this in relative safety, lances had to be fitted with a blunt end, or head. The weight and momentum of the charge could nevertheless still cause serious injury and occasionally death.

Head of lance

DATE	c.1600
ORIGIN	ITALIAN
LENGTH	12.7cm (5in)

Jousting knights

By the end of the 13th century, a Statute of Arms for Tournaments had been established to provide a series of rules and guidance for knights participating in jousts. Under the statute, knights were considered to be gentlemen and required to abide by the ideals of chivalry, including fair play and honour. Jousting tournaments became organized events and the introduction of blunted weapons massively reduced fatalities. If a knight was killed at the joust, it was not only deeply unfortunate but also considered to be dishonourable. Ironically, if a knight killed a horse, the public ire was even greater. The main object of a knight participating in the joust was to unhorse as many fellow knights as possible and, crucially, to break the highest

ABOVE Medieval jousting knights, *c.*1445. Note the limited vision available when wearing a closed helm (helmet).

number of lances. If he could do this without injury or death, the audience would regard him as displaying great skill with the lance and excellent horsemanship.

English jousting or carousel lance, c.1600

Painted shaft

Hand grip

DATE	c.1600
ORIGIN	ENGLISH
LENGTH	363.7cm (143.2in)

By the beginning of the 17th century, interest in the combative side of the joust had waned and an alternative form of equestrian entertainment was developed. This was the carousel (from the Italian *garosello* and the Spanish *carosella*, meaning "little war"). The lance was used in such games as "catching the ring", which involved lancing a swinging dummy or small rings suspended from a revolving apparatus. Later, brightly painted wooden horses and mounted figures were added as targets and this became the precursor to today's carousel rides.

European fluted cavalry lance, c.1620

Hand grip   Langets   Spear-shaped lance head

DATE	c.1620
ORIGIN	EUROPEAN
LENGTH	353.8cm (139.3in)

The military lance was not a common battlefield weapon in the 17th century. This example is similar to later lances, especially with regard to the long, riveted langets, but it still retains the earlier, medieval, rounded hand grip. The massed ranks of infantrymen armed with pikes and other polearms would have made it difficult to use this lance with any great effect.

English jousting lance, c.1850

Guard

Hand grip

Coronal helped unhorse the opponent

DATE	c.1850
ORIGIN	ENGLISH
LENGTH	353.8cm (139.3in)

A medieval revival in Britain during the early 1800s, boosted by the popular romantic novels of Sir Walter Scott (1771–1832), encouraged the restaging of many jousting tournaments. This lance has a two-pronged head (the coronal) and was designed to catch on an opponent's shield and then hold it fast, making it much easier to unhorse him. The wooden shaft is probably hollow, as this would make it shatter more easily.

17th- to 19th-century cavalry swords

The cavalry swords of the 17th to 19th centuries were designed to inflict maximum injury on their victims. They were wide-bladed, with either straight or curved double- and single-edged blades. Their great length would enable a galloping horseman to reach down and strike with devastating ease.

German cavalry officer's dress sword, 1697

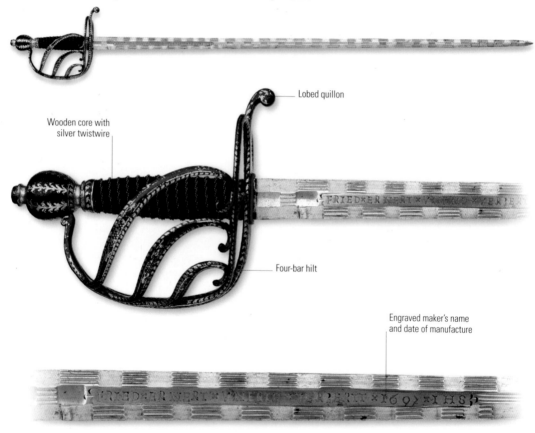

Lobed quillon

Wooden core with silver twistwire

Four-bar hilt

Engraved maker's name and date of manufacture

Although the blade of this fine-quality cavalry officer's sword is definitely German in manufacture, the hilt is possibly English. In many cases, sword blades were purchased directly from Germany and then attached to a hilt in a separate country. German blades were highly prized throughout Europe during this period. The four-bar hilt of this sword is finely decorated in silver inlay and the hilt has been deliberately blackened to highlight the silver. The blade is double-edged and comprises a series of cut-steel, chiselled niches that are purely decorative in nature. It is likely that it would have been carried in a leather scabbard with blackened steel or silver mounts.

DATE	1697
ORIGIN	GERMAN
LENGTH	96.5cm (38in)

French cavalry trooper's sword (Swedish style), *c.*1700

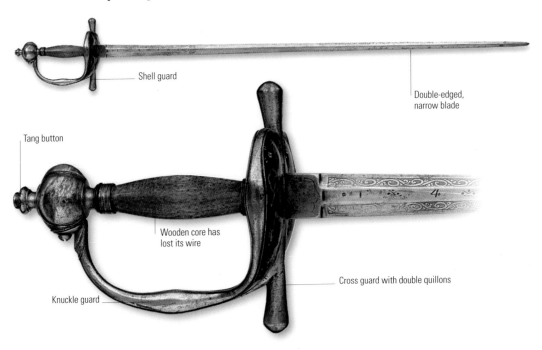

Shell guard

Double-edged, narrow blade

Tang button

Wooden core has lost its wire

Cross guard with double quillons

Knuckle guard

DATE	c.1700
ORIGIN	SWEDISH
LENGTH	111.5cm (43.9in)

This sword has an open hilt that would have left the swordsman's hand quite exposed. Sweden was one of the first nations in Europe to begin standardizing swords into specific patterns during the 17th century. The shell guards on this sword still have the distinctive piercings that are reminiscent of earlier, mid-17th century "Walloon" broadswords and indicate that this particular sword is a transitional piece. The hilt style is more in keeping with the new smallswords that were just beginning to become popular at this time.

British cavalry officer's sword, *c.*1740

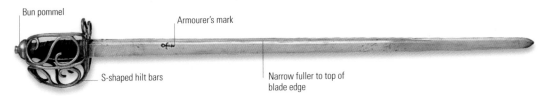

Bun pommel

Armourer's mark

S-shaped hilt bars

Narrow fuller to top of blade edge

DATE	c.1740
ORIGIN	BRITISH
LENGTH	87.6cm (34.5in)

This is a type of broadsword carried by British heavy dragoon officers during the Battle of Culloden in 1746. It has a substantial, single-edged backsword blade that would have been effective at hacking and slashing while on horseback. The guard has decorative, S-shaped hilt bars and a large bun-shaped pommel.

Austrian cavalry officer's sword, 1745

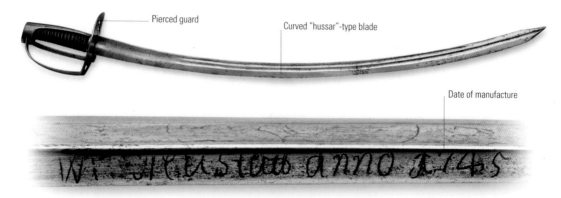

Pierced guard

Curved "hussar"-type blade

Date of manufacture

Many cavalry swords of this period tend to have long, straight blades, but this example features a curved, double-fullered blade that ends in a distinctive spear point. It has a folding attack hilt that pivots by means of a hinge underneath the hilt plate. Curved blades were popular with hussar regiments.

DATE	1745
ORIGIN	AUSTRIAN
LENGTH	90.2cm (35.5in)

French cavalry sword, c.1750

Double-edged, narrow blade

Basket hilt

This rather unique and unusual cavalry officer's sword has an intricate multi-bar hilt with a pierced dish guard. The extremely long, double-edged blade has a pronounced point that would have been used as a kind of short, thrusting lance.

DATE	c.1750
ORIGIN	FRENCH
LENGTH	118.1cm (46.5in)

Russian cavalry trooper's sword, c.1750

Bird's-head pommel

Double-edged, cutting blade

Brass hilt

Carried by Imperial Russian dragoons from the mid-18th century, this impressive sword has a brass hilt and bird's-head pommel. This hilt guard comprises a number of intersecting brass bars. Blades of this period are normally engraved with the monogram of the Empress Elizaveta Petrovna ("EPI"), also known as the Empress Elizabeth (1709–62).

DATE	c.1750
ORIGIN	RUSSIAN
LENGTH	104.9cm (41.3in)

French cavalry trooper's sword, "à la Suédoise", c.1770

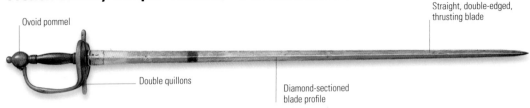

Ovoid pommel

Straight, double-edged, thrusting blade

Double quillons

Diamond-sectioned blade profile

DATE	c.1770
ORIGIN	FRENCH
LENGTH	109.2cm (43in)

Based on the hilt styles of contemporary Swedish cavalry swords, this French version has a brass hilt, with ovoid pommel, double quillons and a solid hilt plate. The blade is double-edged, with a slightly diamond-sectioned profile. The grip is wooden but would originally have had a twistwire binding. The open hilt would provide little protection to the sword hand and an opponent could easily disable his enemy by making a cut towards his hand.

Danish heavy cavalry trooper's sword, Model 1774

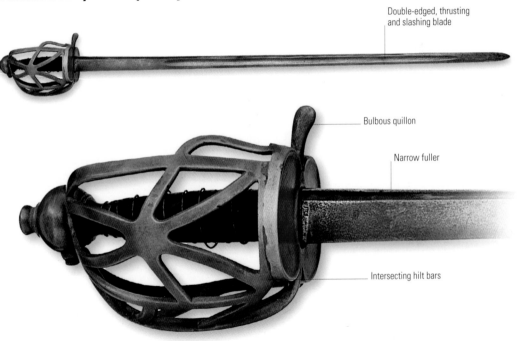

Double-edged, thrusting and slashing blade

Bulbous quillon

Narrow fuller

Intersecting hilt bars

DATE	1774
ORIGIN	DANISH
LENGTH	117.3cm (46.2in)

This large broadsword has a single-fullered, double-edged blade (towards the point) and would have been most effective as both a thrusting and a slashing weapon. The large brass basket hilt incorporates a series of intertwined bars with a thick and solid hilt plate at its base. During this period, a number of Scandinavian and North European armies adopted these heavy basket-hilted broadswords. They were popular within Cuirassier regiments.

French cavalry officer's sword, *c.*1780

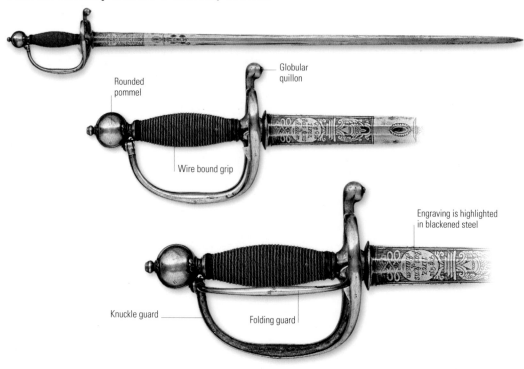

Rounded pommel

Globular quillon

Wire bound grip

Engraving is highlighted in blackened steel

Knuckle guard

Folding guard

This is an interesting early example of a so-called folding "attack hilt". Introduced during the 18th century, it comprises a traditional one- or two-bar hilt with an additional bar that could be opened out for use in combat and then retracted afterwards. The relative thinness of this folding guard would not have made an enormous difference to hand protection.

DATE	*c.*1780
ORIGIN	FRENCH
LENGTH	102.8cm (40.5in)

British light cavalry officer's sword, 1788 Pattern

Cross guard with double langets

Long fuller

Stirrup-shaped hilt

DATE	1788
ORIGIN	BRITISH
LENGTH	102.8cm (40.5in)

The British Army introduced this light cavalry sword at a time when there was great debate within the army as to whether a curved or straight-bladed sword was the most effective cutting weapon. It was decided that heavy cavalry regiments would continue to carry a straight-bladed sword but light cavalry regiments were issued with this new sword. Its design was based on Austrian and German "hussar" swords that had been carried since the early 18th century. It features a stirrup-shaped hilt with flattened pommel and distinctive double langets. The sword was very effective at close-quarter slashing and cutting.

French dragoon trooper's sword, *c.*1790

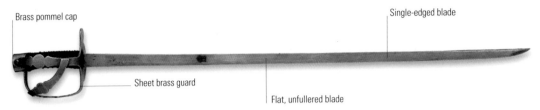

Brass pommel cap

Single-edged blade

Sheet brass guard

Flat, unfullered blade

DATE	*c.*1790
ORIGIN	FRENCH
LENGTH	108cm (42.5in)

This sword was carried by mounted *chasseurs* (meaning "hunters"), light cavalry soldiers who were engaged in various roles, primarily as skirmishers and shock troops. The blade is straight, single-edged and would have been most effective at thrusting. The hilt is brass and typical of swords carried by French cavalry at the time of the French Revolution (1789–99) and during the early years of the Napoleonic Wars (1799–1815).

British heavy cavalry officer's sword, 1796 Pattern (undress)

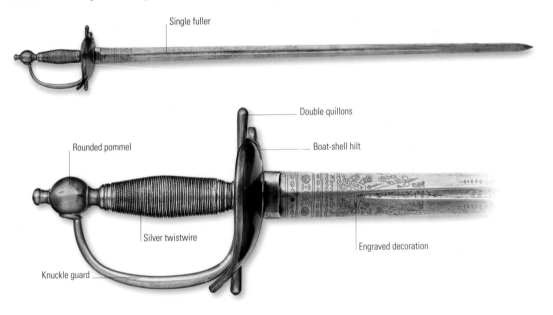

Single fuller

Double quillons

Rounded pommel

Boat-shell hilt

Silver twistwire

Engraved decoration

Knuckle guard

DATE	1796
ORIGIN	BRITISH
LENGTH	101.8cm (40.1in)

This elegant sword would have been worn for more formal dress occasions, including regimental parades and social functions. The hilt is of boat-shell type, with a solid, upwardly curving shell guard and double quillons. The knuckle guard is secured to the pommel by means of a screw. Many blades were left plain but in this case there is extensive engraving of military trophies and decorative foliage. While in the field, heavy cavalry officers would have carried a much more sturdy sword with a wide, cutting blade and basket-type hilt. This sword can be found with either a leather or a steel scabbard.

British Royal Horseguards trooper's sword, *c.*1796

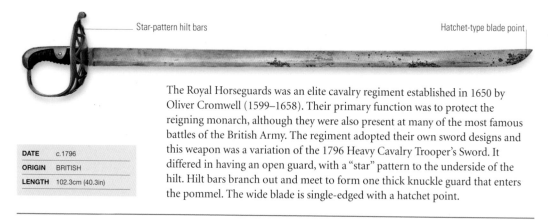

Star-pattern hilt bars

Hatchet-type blade point

DATE	c.1796
ORIGIN	BRITISH
LENGTH	102.3cm (40.3in)

The Royal Horseguards was an elite cavalry regiment established in 1650 by Oliver Cromwell (1599–1658). Their primary function was to protect the reigning monarch, although they were also present at many of the most famous battles of the British Army. The regiment adopted their own sword designs and this weapon was a variation of the 1796 Heavy Cavalry Trooper's Sword. It differed in having an open guard, with a "star" pattern to the underside of the hilt. Hilt bars branch out and meet to form one thick knuckle guard that enters the pommel. The wide blade is single-edged with a hatchet point.

Danish mounted infantryman's sword, Royal Guards Model 1799

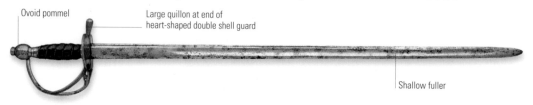

Ovoid pommel

Large quillon at end of heart-shaped double shell guard

Shallow fuller

The Danish Royal Guards regiment is one of the oldest guards regiments in Europe (established in 1658 by King Frederick III, 1609–70). Although ostensibly an infantry regiment, some infantry had mounted duties. The blade has a shallow fuller that begins around a third of the way down from the ricasso and is complemented by another narrow fuller that runs just below the top edge of the blade. The hilt is simple in design, with two side branches that emerge from the hilt plate and join the knuckle guard.

DATE	1799
ORIGIN	DANISH
LENGTH	107.3cm (42.2in)

Spanish cavalry trooper's sword, Model 1799

Bowl guard

Double-edged blade

Spanish cavalry forces carried the traditional and rather archaic cup-hilt rapier ("Bilbo") until the end of the 18th century and this model was quite a departure from previous Spanish sword types. The hilt and blade style is similar to other European swords of the period (particularly French). The hilt has a pronounced bowl guard, with three hilt bars leading to the domed pommel. The blade is unfullered and has a raised strengthening ridge that forms the ricasso. Grips were covered in leather and would not have been bound.

DATE	1799
ORIGIN	SPANISH
LENGTH	106.9cm (42.1in)

Spanish heavy cavalry officer's sword, *c.*1800

Blade engraved with the
name of King Carlos IV

Unfullered blade

Spear-pointed blade

Royal Spanish crown

DATE	c.1800
ORIGIN	SPANISH
LENGTH	98.2cm (38.7in)

This is a more elaborate version of the Model 1799 Cavalry Trooper's Sword and incorporates the Spanish royal crown and cypher inserted into the brass hilt. The flat-backed, double-edged blade is also engraved with the initials of King Carlos IV of Spain (1748–1819). The enclosed half-basket hilt would have provided a reasonable amount of protection for the hand.

Spanish cavalry trooper's sword, Model 1825

Double-fullered blade

Four-bar hilt

Long, thrusting blade for
effective penetration

DATE	1825
ORIGIN	SPANISH
LENGTH	109.2cm (43in)

This sword is very similar to French Napoleonic heavy cavalry swords and it is likely that the Spanish Army simply copied the design. It has a brass, four-bar hilt and a slightly canted, or angled, pommel. The blade is double-fullered and was carried in a heavy, iron scabbard. When used in the charge, the sword would have been held in an outstretched position and used as a type of short lance. The grip has a wooden core wrapped in leather and brass twistwire.

German cavalry trooper's sword, Model 1852

Single-edged blade
with narrow fuller

Cage-like hilt

DATE	1852
ORIGIN	GERMAN
LENGTH	64cm (25.2in)

A cage-like hilt is the distinctive feature of this sword and would have provided a certain amount of protection for the sword hand, although the gaps between the hilt bars could still allow the penetration of a well-directed sword point. There is also a leather thumb strap within the hilt that allowed the trooper to grip the sword more effectively, especially when at the charge. It would have been contained in a plated steel scabbard.

17th- to 19th-century infantry swords

During this time, the role of the infantry soldier changed and he became more reliant on the musket and socket bayonet as his primary weapons. Despite this, infantrymen still carried swords and popular styles included the short-bladed, brass-hilted hanger. Officers also chose short hangers and smallswords.

English infantry hanger, *c.*1700

Corroded blade

Hilt branches to
knuckle guard

The heavy pitting and corrosion on this sword indicate that it was probably excavated. This sword is of a general type that was carried by both infantry troops and even naval seamen (where it would have been used as a cutlass). The short, falchion-type blade was effective at close-quarter fighting, particularly amongst the close rigging of a ship's deck.

DATE	c.1700
ORIGIN	ENGLISH
LENGTH	85.7cm (33.7in)

Prussian hanger, *c.*1750

Single fuller

Cast-brass hilt

This style of short hanger was popular throughout Europe from the early 18th century. The hilt is cast brass and the blade is single-fullered and double-edged towards the point. Many of these Prussian swords are regimentally marked.

DATE	c.1750
ORIGIN	PRUSSIAN
LENGTH	79.3cm (31.2in)

British grenadier's hanger, *c.*1760

Enclosed basket hilt

Double-edged
towards end

There were many hanger types carried by British infantry regiments during the mid-18th century. This sword has a substantial iron hilt that is reminiscent of heavy cavalry (dragoon) swords of this period. The well-enclosed hilt would have provided a good level of protection to the hand.

DATE	c.1760
ORIGIN	BRITISH
LENGTH	110.3cm (43.4in)

British infantry private's hanger, *c.*1760

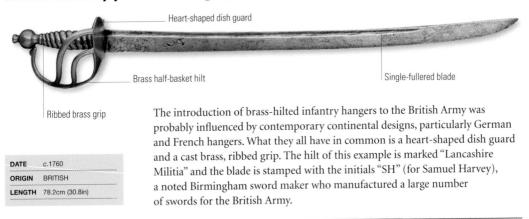

Heart-shaped dish guard

Brass half-basket hilt

Single-fullered blade

Ribbed brass grip

DATE	c.1760
ORIGIN	BRITISH
LENGTH	78.2cm (30.8in)

The introduction of brass-hilted infantry hangers to the British Army was probably influenced by contemporary continental designs, particularly German and French hangers. What they all have in common is a heart-shaped dish guard and a cast brass, ribbed grip. The hilt of this example is marked "Lancashire Militia" and the blade is stamped with the initials "SH" (for Samuel Harvey), a noted Birmingham sword maker who manufactured a large number of swords for the British Army.

British infantryman's sword with monster-head pommel, *c.*1760

Monster-head pommel

Bulbous quillon

Single-edged blade

DATE	c.1760
ORIGIN	BRITISH
LENGTH	Unknown

Monster-head or grotesque pommels were common on British military hangers for a brief period during the early to mid-18th century. They were superseded by the traditional lion's-head pommel before the end of the century. The slightly curved blade has a single sharpened edge, with a narrow fuller present at the top of the blade. The brass grip has an unusual simulated rope design. Swords of this hilt type are known to have been carried by grenadier companies.

British infantry officer's sword, *c.*1770

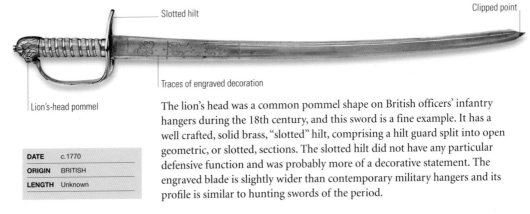

Slotted hilt

Clipped point

Traces of engraved decoration

Lion's-head pommel

DATE	c.1770
ORIGIN	BRITISH
LENGTH	Unknown

The lion's head was a common pommel shape on British officers' infantry hangers during the 18th century, and this sword is a fine example. It has a well crafted, solid brass, "slotted" hilt, comprising a hilt guard split into open geometric, or slotted, sections. The slotted hilt did not have any particular defensive function and was probably more of a decorative statement. The engraved blade is slightly wider than contemporary military hangers and its profile is similar to hunting swords of the period.

British infantry officer's hanger, *c.*1780

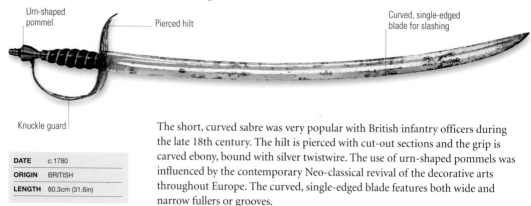

Urn-shaped pommel

Pierced hilt

Curved, single-edged blade for slashing

Knuckle guard

DATE	c.1780
ORIGIN	BRITISH
LENGTH	80.3cm (31.6in)

The short, curved sabre was very popular with British infantry officers during the late 18th century. The hilt is pierced with cut-out sections and the grip is carved ebony, bound with silver twistwire. The use of urn-shaped pommels was influenced by the contemporary Neo-classical revival of the decorative arts throughout Europe. The curved, single-edged blade features both wide and narrow fullers or grooves.

British Tower Hamlets volunteer infantry officer's sword, *c.*1803–14

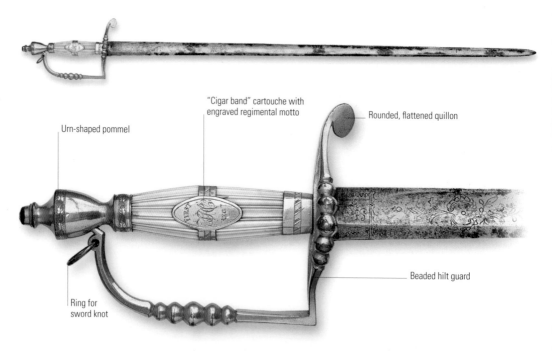

"Cigar band" cartouche with engraved regimental motto

Rounded, flattened quillon

Urn-shaped pommel

Beaded hilt guard

Ring for sword knot

DATE	c.1803–14
ORIGIN	BRITISH
LENGTH	97.8cm (38.5in)

The Tower Hamlets Volunteer Militia was one of many volunteer cavalry and infantry units that were raised during the Napoleonic Wars (1799–1815). The primary role of the militia was to protect Britain from an anticipated French invasion. Militia officers would have carried swords identical to those of the regular army. This rare example has a gilt-brass "five-ball" beaded hilt and a ribbed ivory grip with a "cigar band" cartouche wrapped around the centre. A regimental device is engraved onto the band.

British infantry officer, 1812

The British infantry officer did not carry a regulation infantry sword until 1786. Before this, a series of smallswords or hangers were carried into battle and some officers even chose to arm themselves with a short polearm or spontoon. Its fighting capabilities must surely have been dubious and it was used more as a symbol of rank or a signpost to gain attention when the officer was rallying his troops. The spontoon was also issued to senior NCOs.

The 1786 Pattern Infantry Officer's Sword brought in a measure of uniformity with regard to blade and hilt specifications, but it was not until 1796 that a universal design of infantry officer sword became standard within the British Army. And, even then, elite infantry regiments such as the Rifle Corps and some Scottish lowland regiments still chose to wear swords of a completely different design.

RIGHT Officer of the King's Own Scottish Borderers, *c.*1812. He is carrying a sword of mameluke design that became popular after the Egyptian campaigns of 1798–1801.

Batavian Republic infantry officer's sword, *c.*1810

Knight's-head pommel

Traces of original blueing

Straight cross guard

In 1795, William V (1748–1806), the Prince of Orange and the Netherlands, fled to England and a republic was subsequently declared in the Netherlands. Napoleon Bonaparte (1769–1821) invaded the new country and it became a vassal of France until 1806, when he installed his younger brother Louis Napoleon (1778–1846) as King of Holland (1806–10). The hilt style of this sword clearly shows the influence of French sword styling, particularly on the Neo-classical knight's-head pommel that is typically French Napoleonic.

DATE	c.1810
ORIGIN	DUTCH
LENGTH	89.7cm (35.3in)

French pioneer or sapper's sword, *c.*1810

Cockerel-headed pommel

Downward-curving quillons

Saw-back blade

Clipped point

DATE	c.1810
ORIGIN	FRENCH
LENGTH	81cm (31.9in)

The cast-brass hilt of this particular sword is surmounted by an impressive crowing French cockerel. The blade is slightly curved and serrated on one edge. It would have been used by pioneer or sapper troops to construct fascines. These are sticks or brushwood which are firmly bound together to be used for filling up trenches or ditches, and constructing batteries or creating other lines of defence.

Basket-hilted swords

The basket-hilted sword developed as a particular type of weapon that gave the swordsman much greater protection to his sword hand. From the 17th century onwards, this would be adopted by most European nations and it found its apogee in the superbly crafted basket hilts of the Scottish Highlander. In most examples, the basket hilt was attached to a wide, double-edged blade.

English basket-hilted sword, c.1590

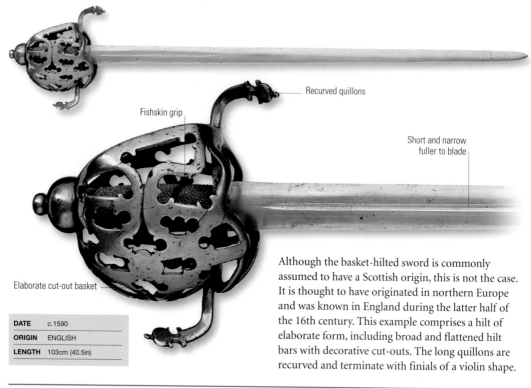

Recurved quillons

Fishskin grip

Short and narrow fuller to blade

Elaborate cut-out basket

DATE	c.1590
ORIGIN	ENGLISH
LENGTH	103cm (40.5in)

Although the basket-hilted sword is commonly assumed to have a Scottish origin, this is not the case. It is thought to have originated in northern Europe and was known in England during the latter half of the 16th century. This example comprises a hilt of elaborate form, including broad and flattened hilt bars with decorative cut-outs. The long quillons are recurved and terminate with finials of a violin shape.

Scottish basket-hilted broadsword, c.1680

Ribbon bars

This type of basket hilt is Scottish in origin and referred to as a "ribbon hilt". This description comes from the flat and ribbon-like appearance of the hilt bars. These weapons are also known as "beaknose" or "snoutnose" swords, because of the small counter-curved quillons that project from the bottom of the hilt.

DATE	c.1680
ORIGIN	SCOTTISH
LENGTH	92.9cm (36.6in)

English basket-hilted cavalry broadsword, *c.*1680

Apple-shaped pommel

Inlaid silver hilt

DATE	c.1680
ORIGIN	ENGLISH
LENGTH	104cm (40.9in)

This is a late 17th-century English basket-hilted sword of superb quality. With typical apple-shaped pommel and inlaid silver hilt, these swords are commonly mistaken for Scottish basket hilts; the pommel, hilt plate and bar shape are what differentiate the sword types.

English basket-hilted broadsword, *c.*1680

Wide, double-edged, broadsword blade

Intertwining basket hilt with bun pommel

DATE	c.1680
ORIGIN	ENGLISH
LENGTH	96.5cm (38in)

Basket hilts of this style had been common since the end of the 16th century and were carried by English cavalry troopers throughout the English Civil War (1642–51) and for some time afterwards. This example is of "munition" quality, meaning that it was produced relatively cheaply and lacks decoration.

Italian schiavona broadsword, *c.*1700

Complex basket hilt

DATE	c.1700
ORIGIN	ITALIAN
LENGTH	94.2cm (37.1in)

The schiavona (meaning "Slavonic") sword is a weapon that is closely associated with mercenaries from eastern Europe who served both Spain and the Republic of Venice from the 16th to the 18th century. The complex cage-like arrangement of the basket hilt is a consistent feature of these swords. There are great variations in both quality of manufacture and decoration, some being very plain and functional while others have superb chiselling and applied brasswork.

Scottish basket-hilted broadsword, *c.*1720

Complex basket hilt

Double-edged blade

Hilt retains original liner

This Scottish basket hilt still retains its original red-felt and buff-leather hilt liner. The liner would have protected the swordsman's hand from chafing against the hilt bars. The blade is double-edged with an incised bun-shaped pommel to the hilt and heart-shaped piercings to the hilt plates.

DATE	c.1720
ORIGIN	SCOTTISH
LENGTH	96.2cm (37.9in)

Scottish basket-hilted broadsword, *c.*1720

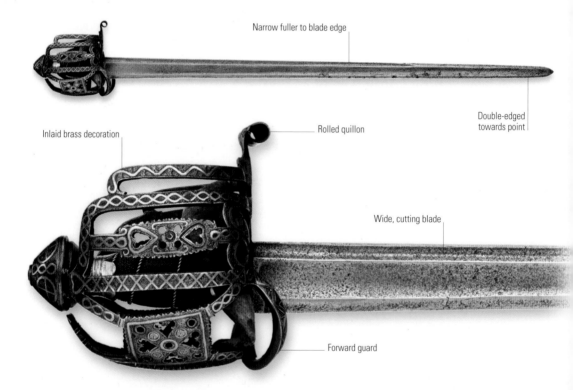

Narrow fuller to blade edge

Double-edged towards point

Inlaid brass decoration

Rolled quillon

Wide, cutting blade

Forward guard

The intricate and superb brass inlay to the hilt marks this out as a sword of historic importance. It would have been made in either Glasgow or Stirling (in the Scottish Lowlands), where a number of sword-making "schools" were successfully established in the 17th and 18th centuries. These sword-making families spanning a number of generations created hilts of rare artistry and quality. Most surviving examples are to be found in museums or prominent private collections.

DATE	c.1720
ORIGIN	SCOTTISH
LENGTH	104.1cm (41in)

Italian schiavona sword, *c.*1730

Double-edged blade

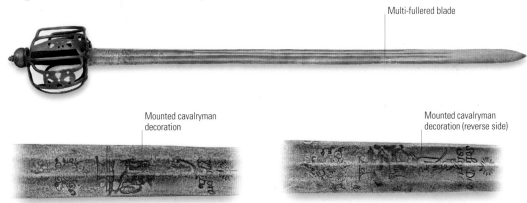

Brass "cat's-head" pommel

Steel hilt decorated
with studs

The schiavona has its origins as the sword type carried by Dalmatian (eastern European) mercenaries recruited to fight for Spain and the Republic of Venice during the 17th and 18th centuries. The complex arrangement of the hilt bars and the "cat's-head" pommel are characteristic features of this sword. These double-edged broadswords would have been relatively lightweight and easy to handle, thus making them very effective fighting weapons.

DATE	c.1730
ORIGIN	ITALIAN
LENGTH	99.3cm (39.1in)

English basket-hilted cavalry broadsword, *c.*1740

Multi-fullered blade

Mounted cavalryman
decoration

Mounted cavalryman
decoration (reverse side)

The long, double-edged blade of this broadsword would have made it an effective slashing and cutting weapon. English basket hilts tended to have more widely spaced hilt bars compared with Scottish basket hilts, which were manufactured with thicker bars and more solid and protective hilt plates. The use of engraved depictions of mounted cavalrymen became more common after this period.

DATE	c.1740
ORIGIN	ENGLISH
LENGTH	104.1cm (41in)

English basket-hilted broadsword, *c.*1750

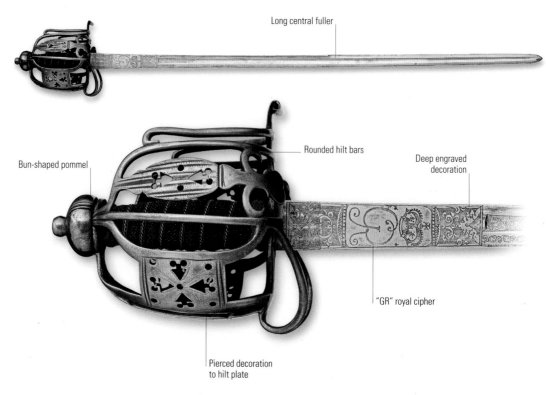

Long central fuller

Bun-shaped pommel

Rounded hilt bars

Deep engraved decoration

"GR" royal cipher

Pierced decoration to hilt plate

This is an interesting sword as the hilt has all the characteristics of a Scottish-made basket hilt, although it is not. This sword would have been manufactured in England for a heavy dragoon officer in a British cavalry regiment. The blade is etched with the "GR" royal cipher of King George II (*r.*1727–60).

DATE	*c.*1750
ORIGIN	ENGLISH
LENGTH	99cm (39in)

Scottish basket-hilted broadsword, *c.*1750

Forward-curving quillon

Wide, double-edged blade

Scottish Jacobite Highlanders (followers of the House of Stuart, 1371–1714) purchased their basket-hilted swords with blades that were invariably manufactured outside of Scotland. This example is likely to be fitted with a German blade, manufactured in Solingen, and then exported to Scotland where a local hilt maker would have attached it to the hilt.

DATE	*c.*1750
ORIGIN	SCOTTISH
LENGTH	101cm (39.8in)

English basket-hilted broadsword, *c.*1780

Thin, sheet-metal hilt

DATE	c.1780
ORIGIN	ENGLISH
LENGTH	97.5cm (38.4in)

Although easily mistaken for a Scottish Highland sword, this sword was actually issued to English troops serving in Highland regiments during the latter half of the 18th century. The blade is marked "Drury" and would have been made in Birmingham, England. The quality of these swords tended to be quite poor.

British regimental basket-hilted broadsword, *c.*1860

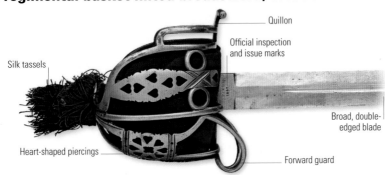

Quillon

Official inspection and issue marks

Silk tassels

Broad, double-edged blade

Heart-shaped piercings

Forward guard

DATE	c.1860
ORIGIN	BRITISH
LENGTH	98cm (38.6in)

This sword would have been carried by a sergeant (Non-Commissioned Officer) of one of the Scottish Highland regiments. Unlike officers who had to purchase both uniform and sword through private means, this sword would have been issued to the NCO by the British Army. Government-issue swords tended to be passed around the regiment over a long period of time and, consequently, very few now survive because of this heavy service wear.

Highland regiments

The Highland regiments of the British Army were established after the defeat of the Jacobite cause under Prince Charles Edward Stuart (1720–88), also known as the "Young Pretender" or Bonnie Prince Charlie, at the Battle of Culloden (1746). The British realized that some form of permanent and substantial garrisoning of Scotland would be required. Before this time, Scottish landed gentry loyal to the English Crown had raised independent companies to protect the government's interests and keep the peace amongst rival clans.

RIGHT An officer of the Gordon Highlanders, *c.*1854. He is carrying a regulation basket-hilted broadsword that is attached to his belt by white leather slings.

419

17th- and 18th-century smallswords

The smallsword was a natural evolution of the rapier into a more manageable weapon and an acknowledgement that a gentleman no longer required both armour and a large sword for everyday protection. Its smaller proportions meant that it could be worn comfortably with civilian clothes and it soon became a fashion accessory and signifier of rank and status. The development of the three-sided colichemarde blade in the 17th century also made the smallsword surprisingly strong, especially when fencing.

English smallsword, *c.*1660

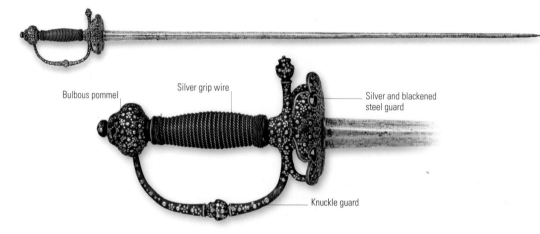

Bulbous pommel

Silver grip wire

Silver and blackened steel guard

Knuckle guard

English sword makers of the 17th and 18th centuries were noted for their particular skills at mounting precious metals into sword hilts. This sword is an excellent example of their artistry. All available surfaces have been inlaid with small pieces of silver individually hammered into the hilt. The blackened background of the metal brings out the silver in a superb fashion.

DATE	c.1660
ORIGIN	ENGLISH
LENGTH	98.7cm (38.8in)

English smallsword, *c.*1690

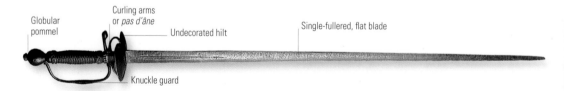

Globular pommel

Curling arms or *pas d'âne*

Undecorated hilt

Single-fullered, flat blade

Knuckle guard

This early smallsword is quite simple in design and very much of transitional form. The single-fullered, flat blade is reminiscent of earlier rapiers, although it does not have the extended length found in these earlier swords. The undecorated hilt is made from iron and displays a globular pommel, D-shaped knuckle guard and swollen quillon. Distinctive features include the two curling arms that reach down to the slim dish guard, which became a common stylistic addition to smallswords.

DATE	c.1690
ORIGIN	ENGLISH
LENGTH	UNKNOWN

Italian smallsword, *c.*1690

Short fuller

Narrow, double-edged blade

DATE	c.1690
ORIGIN	ITALIAN
LENGTH	99.2cm (39.1in)

The transitional nature of this sword is clearly evident as it shows design characteristics of both a rapier and a smallsword. The long, rapier blade is attached to a hilt that is of early smallsword form. The two downward-pointing arms that reach from under the cross guard are known as a *pas d'âne*.

English smallsword, *c.*1690

Wide blade

Pierced guard

DATE	c.1690
ORIGIN	ENGLISH
LENGTH	98cm (38.6in)

The unusually wide blade of this smallsword indicates that it was probably carried by a military officer, as it is more robust than the standard "civilian" examples found on smallswords of this period. The pierced guard and bulbous pommel are reminiscent of earlier rapier styles and highlight its transitional nature.

French smallsword, *c.*1720

Twistwire with "Turk's-head" binding at each end

Rococo decoration

Rounded pommel

Chiselled gilt decoration

DATE	c.1720
ORIGIN	FRENCH
LENGTH	100.2cm (39.4in)

This smallsword was produced at the height of the Rococo period in the early 18th century, when French decorative influence spread throughout Europe. The hilt is blued steel and encrusted with gold decoration, including helmets, stands of arms and delicate flowers. The top of the blade (the forte) shows traces of the original applied blue and gilt wash, and the remainder of the blade etching is highlighted in gilt. Sheathed in a stiff leather scabbard, the mounts would have repeated the style of decoration already present on the sword hilt.

English smallsword, *c.*1730

Multiple bands
of twisted wire

Small oval dish guard
offering limited protection

Pas d'âne ring

Slim knuckle guard

Etched representation
of the Apostles

From the end of the 17th century onwards, smallswords are found with the
addition of two *pas d'âne* rings or arms, which form from the cross guard and
terminate with an inward curl at the top of the dish guard. Their purpose was
mainly one of decoration, although they probably also added some strength
to the hilt. They became a common design feature in smallswords.

DATE	*c.*1730
ORIGIN	ENGLISH
LENGTH	92.3cm (36.3in)

English silver-hilted smallsword, *c.*1745

Wide forte for added strength

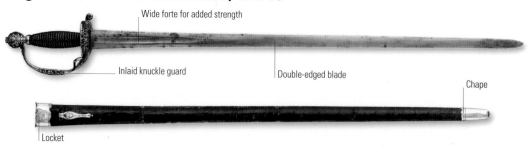

Inlaid knuckle guard

Double-edged blade

Chape

Locket

This is a typical example of a high-quality solid silver-hilted gentleman's
smallsword of the mid-18th century. It is assayed (silver marked) for London and
stamped with the initials "W.G.", probably for William Garrard. Unusually, the
leather and silver mounted scabbard has survived.

DATE	*c.*1745
ORIGIN	ENGLISH
LENGTH	75cm (29.5in)

English smallsword, 1756

Colichemarde blade

Strengthened forte

DATE	1756
ORIGIN	ENGLISH
LENGTH	99.6cm (39.2in)

The silver hilt is marked with the initials of the silversmith John Carman II (c.1721–64), who worked in London. On his trade card he describes himself as making and selling "all Sorts of Gold and Silver Work at ye lowest prices Likewise Choice Swords and Cuteaus…". The sword has a distinctive colichemarde blade that comprises a wide, triangular forte and needle point.

French smallsword, c.1770

Trefoil blade

Blued and gilded decoration

DATE	c.1770
ORIGIN	FRENCH
LENGTH	100.3cm (39.5in)

This is an elegant smallsword and very typical of the restrained Neo-classical style encountered in late 18th-century smallswords. The trefoil, or three-sided blade, has been blued and gilded near the forte, and the decoration includes fanciful embellishments. Pommels of this period tended to be spherical in shape.

English smallsword, c.1770

Needle point blade

Twistwire and silver banding

Pierced dish guard

Trefoil blade

DATE	c.1770
ORIGIN	ENGLISH
LENGTH	95cm (37.4in)

This is a fine silver-hilted smallsword that is marked "IR" on the hilt. These letters represent John Radborn (1737–80), who was a gifted sword cutler and silversmith of London. The delicate hilt piercings of this sword are executed with great craftsmanship. This is very much a dress sword and would have been worn on special occasions.

French smallsword, *c.*1780

Silver hilt

Locket

Leather covering

Engraved pattern

Slim blade

The slim, thrusting blade of this smallsword is engraved with the following motto: "*La Prudence se fait voir dans le vin.*" Roughly translated it means: "Prudence is shown in the wine," a cautionary warning for the owner to not use the sword unnecessarily when intoxicated.

DATE	c.1780
ORIGIN	FRENCH
LENGTH	92cm (36.2in)

English smallsword, *c.*1790

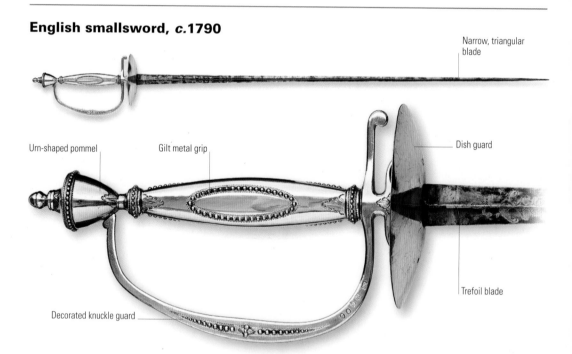

Narrow, triangular blade

Urn-shaped pommel

Gilt metal grip

Dish guard

Trefoil blade

Decorated knuckle guard

A vogue for urn-shaped pommels on English smallswords is evident during the last quarter of the 18th century. This was a reaction to the influence of such Neo-classical architects as Robert Adam (1728–92), who used the design of the classical Roman urn on many of his decorative features. The grip of this sword does not have a normal wooden core bound in twisted wire but is made of silver gilt. This sword was manufactured by Cornelius Bland of London (1748–94). The silver hallmarks, including the maker's initials, have been clearly punched into the bottom of the knuckle guard.

DATE	c.1790
ORIGIN	ENGLISH
LENGTH	95.2cm (37.4in)

English mourning smallsword, *c.*1800

Blackened hilt

Plain, trefoil blade

A loose, linked chain forms
the knuckle guard

DATE	*c.*1800
ORIGIN	ENGLISH
LENGTH	93cm (36.6in)

Towards the end of the 18th century, a specific type of smallsword was designed
to be worn by gentlemen while they were attending a funeral and then during an
appropriate period of mourning. The steel hilt was deliberately blackened and
many examples have cut-steel or faceted decoration. Scabbard mounts would also
have been blackened. Most examples of this type of sword feature a loose chain
in place of the normally rigid knuckle guard.

English smallsword, *c.*1800

Needle-like blade

A linked chain would have
formed the knuckle guard

DATE	*c.*1800
ORIGIN	ENGLISH
LENGTH	97.8cm (38.5in)

Although now absent, this dress sword would have had a thin, gilt metal chain
knuckle guard strung from the end of the cross guard quillon and terminating
at the bottom of the pommel. Because of the inherent fragility of these knuckle
guards, many have become detached and lost over the intervening years.

Late 18th-century gentleman

The carrying of a smallsword by a late 18th-century gentleman
was both a necessary evil and an opportunity to display his wealth
and status. In sword-making centres such as London, numerous
small workshops produced high-quality smallswords for discerning
gentlemen customers. London gained a reputation for manufacturing
silver hilts of exceptional quality. Most blades would have been
imported from such blade-making countries as Germany and
then mounted to the hilt. Accessories such as the scabbard and
sword belt would also have been made locally. Most English silver
smallswords were hallmarked with a number of impressed stamps
that indicated the city of manufacture, year of production and
the maker's initials.

LEFT Late 18th-century gentleman equipped with a smallsword.

North American swords

The influence of Europe on American sword design was quite profound. Most of the cavalry and infantry swords carried by the US Army after 1840 were interpretations or direct copies of European swords,

particularly French designs. At the beginning of the American Civil War (1861–65), both Confederate and Union forces had to import a large number of their swords from Europe.

US militia NCO's sword, *c.*1840

Knight's-head pommel

Cruciform cross guard

Double-edged blade

Many US states raised their own militias and each officer and NCO carried their own particular sword style. Swords with knight's-head pommels were popular throughout the US and heavily influenced by French sword designs of the period. The grip on this example is either ribbed ivory or bone and the sword would have been carried in a plain or engraved brass scabbard.

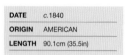

DATE	c.1840
ORIGIN	AMERICAN
LENGTH	90.1cm (35.5in)

US infantry NCO's sword, Model 1840

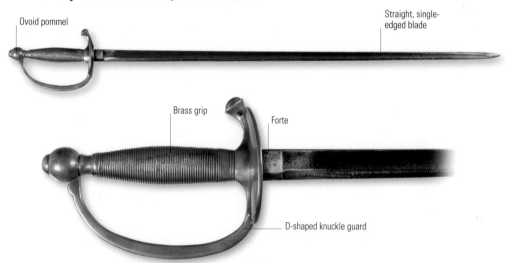

Ovoid pommel

Straight, single-edged blade

Brass grip

Forte

D-shaped knuckle guard

Of rather limited use in battle, this sword was very similar to French infantry swords of the mid-19th century. The hilt was cast brass, with an ovoid pommel, plain shell guard and D-shaped knuckle guard. Most examples were produced in the North for Union forces. This sword would have been sheathed in a brass and leather mounted scabbard.

DATE	1840
ORIGIN	AMERICAN
LENGTH	94cm (37in)

US cavalry trooper's sword, Model 1860

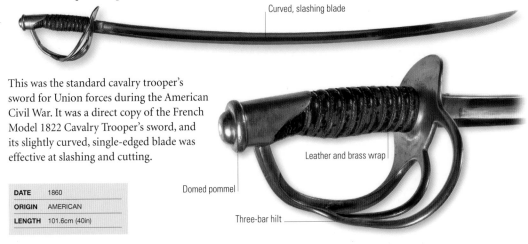

Curved, slashing blade

This was the standard cavalry trooper's sword for Union forces during the American Civil War. It was a direct copy of the French Model 1822 Cavalry Trooper's sword, and its slightly curved, single-edged blade was effective at slashing and cutting.

Leather and brass wrap

Domed pommel

Three-bar hilt

DATE	1860
ORIGIN	AMERICAN
LENGTH	101.6cm (40in)

US Confederate States field officer's sword, c.1864

Crudely cast hilt

Plain blade

DATE	c.1864
ORIGIN	AMERICAN
LENGTH	101.6cm (40in)

At the outbreak of civil war in 1861, most Confederate officers would have carried the same sword models as their Union adversaries. This sword is loosely based on a contemporary US infantry field officer's sword but it would have been manufactured in the South. Overall quality was generally poorer than examples in the North.

US Army infantry officer's sword, Model 1902

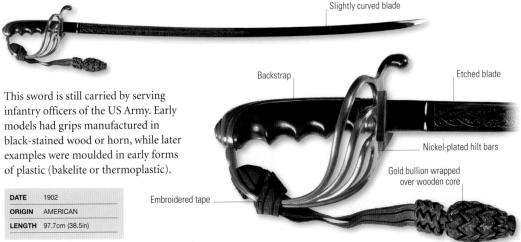

Slightly curved blade

This sword is still carried by serving infantry officers of the US Army. Early models had grips manufactured in black-stained wood or horn, while later examples were moulded in early forms of plastic (bakelite or thermoplastic).

Backstrap

Etched blade

Nickel-plated hilt bars

Gold bullion wrapped over wooden core

Embroidered tape

DATE	1902
ORIGIN	AMERICAN
LENGTH	97.7cm (38.5in)

Fencing swords

The art of fencing has its origins in the Spanish and Italian fencing schools of the 15th century. It was regarded as an important element in the training of a gentleman and an important signifier of social rank. During the 18th century, the blunted fencing foil was developed in France and fencing became extremely popular among university students, particularly in Germany, where the large-hilted Schlager fencing sword was used extensively. New schools of fencing emphasized finger control over arm strength.

French fencing foil, *c.*1890

Double-ringed guard

Rectangular blade

This is a typical late 19th-century French fencing foil and comprises a double-ringed hilt guard, with velvet protective liner. The grip is bound cord and terminates in a plain pommel. The blade is of rectangular section, unsharpened and with a blunted point.

DATE	*c.*1890
ORIGIN	FRENCH
LENGTH	107cm (42.1in)

German fencing Schlager, *c.*1890

Unsharpened blade

Multi-bar hilt

The Schlager (meaning "hit") fencing sword was a popular design in German academic fencing schools of the 19th century. This example has a large, multi-bar hilt with a canted, or angled, grip, which allowed better manoeuvrability while fencing. The blade is unfullered and blunted.

DATE	*c.*1890
ORIGIN	GERMAN
LENGTH	106cm (41.7in)

German fencing Schlager, *c.*1890

Unfullered blade

Protective liner

Complex hilt design is a regular feature of German Schlager swords, and this example exhibits an extravagant series of hilt bars that form near the base and expand into a large basket hilt. The hilt liner is multi-coloured and possibly represents the colours of a particular fencing school.

DATE	*c.*1890
ORIGIN	GERMAN
LENGTH	90cm (35.4in)

Italian fencing sabre, *c*.1900

Shallow bowl guard

Slightly curved blade

DATE	c.1900
ORIGIN	ITALIAN
LENGTH	106cm (41.7in)

This sword has a decorated, shallow bowl guard with a pronounced rolled steel quillon. It is likely to have been used in military schools to train cavalry officers. The blade is slightly curved and the hilt design mirrors full-size cavalry swords of the period. These military fencing swords would not have had a scabbard and were probably hung up in racks in the fencing hall.

British fencing épée, *c*.1980

Protective blunted point

Canted grip

Bell guard

DATE	c.1980
ORIGIN	BRITISH
LENGTH	111cm (43.7in)

The épée was introduced during the 19th century as a response to the more common, lighter foil that was regarded by some fencers as not providing a realistic enough experience of duelling with a proper rapier sword. It is slightly heavier than the fencing foil and features a larger bell guard. During a fencing bout, the combatants can aim for the whole body and double hits are allowed.

British fencing foil, *c*.1980

Electric "arm" for point scoring

Protective point

DATE	c.1980
ORIGIN	BRITISH
LENGTH	109cm (42.9in)

The foil was developed during the 17th century as a practice weapon for training in the use of the smallsword. The modern fencing foil is very similar to those carried by fencers of a hundred years earlier. This lightweight sword is used during fencing competitions. The torso is the only area of the body permitted to be struck and only single (rather than double) hits are allowed.

British electric fencing foil, 1994

Protective point

Shallow bell guard

Pistol grip

DATE	1994
ORIGIN	BRITISH
LENGTH	105.5cm (41.5in)

The electric fencing foil was a technological breakthrough that provided a reliable method of scoring while in competition. The fencer wears a metallic vest (lamé) with a flexible body cord that is attached to the foil, which has a button in the grip with electric wires that then run down the blade. When a touch is made, a buzzer goes off and a light illuminates on the side of the fencer who has been touched.

Naval weapons

A dedicated sword for naval use was not evident until the 17th and 18th centuries and its introduction coincided with the more efficient organization of European navies into proper fighting branches of the nation state. The cutlass, pike and axe were specialist naval weapons and ideally suited to fighting in the confused close-quarter conditions found on board a fighting ship from the age of sail.

Imperial Russian naval officer's hanger, *c.*1760

Clipped point

Turned, hardwood grip

Engraved anchor

This is a very rare Imperial Russian Naval Officer's hanger from the time of Empress Elizabeth Petrovna (1709–62). It has a turned wooden grip and gilt-brass hilt mounts. The blade is etched on one side with the royal cypher of Elizabeth Petrovna, coupled with the double-headed eagle symbol of Russia. A simple anchor is etched to the other side, which provides the only indication that it is naval in origin.

DATE	c.1760
ORIGIN	RUSSIAN
LENGTH	52cm (20.5in)

British boarding pike, *c.*1800

This is an early type of British boarding pike and has a distinctive, decorative brass band around the neck of the pikehead. There were no official patterns of British boarding pikes until well into the 19th century.

DATE	c.1800
ORIGIN	BRITISH
LENGTH	254cm (100in)

British boarding pike, *c.*1800

From the 1800s, British boarding pikes tended to adopt a wider, leaf-shaped head with a more squared profile. This example has dispensed with the long retaining langets of earlier pikes and relies on a sturdy brass socket. The regulation of British boarding pikes was quite haphazard and it was only after the Napoleonic Wars (1799–1815) that a form of standardization was introduced.

DATE	c.1800
ORIGIN	BRITISH
LENGTH	251.4cm (99in)

British "tomahawk" boarding axe, *c.*1800

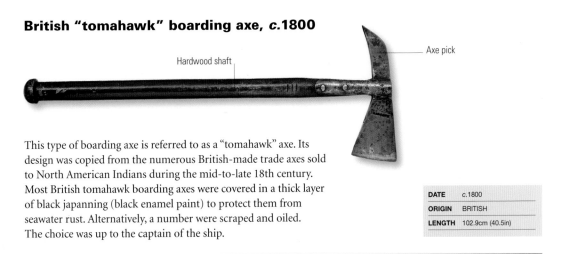

Hardwood shaft

Axe pick

This type of boarding axe is referred to as a "tomahawk" axe. Its design was copied from the numerous British-made trade axes sold to North American Indians during the mid-to-late 18th century. Most British tomahawk boarding axes were covered in a thick layer of black japanning (black enamel paint) to protect them from seawater rust. Alternatively, a number were scraped and oiled. The choice was up to the captain of the ship.

DATE	c.1800
ORIGIN	BRITISH
LENGTH	102.9cm (40.5in)

British naval officer's sword, *c.*1800

Quillon

Single-fullered blade

Sword knot

DATE	c.1800
ORIGIN	BRITISH
LENGTH	99cm (39in)

British naval officers began to carry this type of sword at the end of the 18th century. It has a "five-ball", beaded knuckle guard and a side ring with an inset brass anchor. The hilt is virtually identical to an infantry officer's sword and features a brass cushion pommel, ribbed ivory grip and sword knot. The scabbard was normally leather with gilt brass mounts.

British cutlass, *c.*1805

Acceptance mark

Flat-backed blade

Figure-of-eight guard

DATE	c.1805
ORIGIN	BRITISH
LENGTH	85cm (33.5in)

This iron-hilted cutlass is known as a "figure-of-eight" cutlass due to the shape of its hilt guard, which resembles a solid figure eight. It was introduced in 1804, became standard issue to sailors of the Royal Navy and was carried throughout the Napoleonic Wars. The hilt would have been blackened or "japanned" to protect it from the risk of saltwater corrosion. The straight, flat-backed blade is impressed with the "GR" (George III) acceptance mark, indicating that it had been approved for military service.

British naval officer's sword, *c.*1815

Narrow, dress blade

DATE	c.1815
ORIGIN	BRITISH
LENGTH	84.5cm (33.3in)

The white ivory grip of this sword would normally indicate that its owner was of commander rank. Its Neo-classical hilt design is very typical of army and navy swords of the Napoleonic period. This is not a fighting sword and would have been carried as a dress weapon, reserved for social occasions such as balls and formal dinners. By this time, the use of a pommel in the form of a lion's head had become standard on most swords in the Royal Navy. Blades were sometimes etched with nautical motifs and many had blue and gilt decoration. Scabbards were leather and gilt brass mounted.

British midshipman's sword, *c.*1825

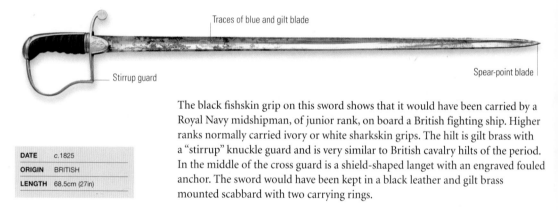

Traces of blue and gilt blade

Stirrup guard

Spear-point blade

DATE	c.1825
ORIGIN	BRITISH
LENGTH	68.5cm (27in)

The black fishskin grip on this sword shows that it would have been carried by a Royal Navy midshipman, of junior rank, on board a British fighting ship. Higher ranks normally carried ivory or white sharkskin grips. The hilt is gilt brass with a "stirrup" knuckle guard and is very similar to British cavalry hilts of the period. In the middle of the cross guard is a shield-shaped langet with an engraved fouled anchor. The sword would have been kept in a black leather and gilt brass mounted scabbard with two carrying rings.

French naval cutlass, *c.*1840

Curved quillon

Slightly curved, single-edged blade

Blackened, iron hilt

This is a French Model 1833 Naval Cutlass and is an evolution of the Model IX (1800–01) Naval Cutlass that was introduced during the Napoleonic period. The blade is slightly narrower than the original and normally included the engraved anchor. The large, blackened iron hilt would have afforded excellent protection for the hand.

DATE	c.1840
ORIGIN	FRENCH
LENGTH	80.5cm (31.7in)

British naval cutlass, *c.*1850

Spear point

Blackened, steel guard

Flat, unfullered blade

The British Napoleonic "figure-of-eight" cutlass was replaced in 1845 with a new pattern of British naval cutlass. It had a shallow bowl guard with a ribbed iron grip and was very similar to contemporary British cavalry troopers' guards. Originally, it would have had a straight, flat-backed blade, but in 1887, all cutlass blades were changed to a slightly curved and single-fullered profile. This was thought to provide the seaman with a better-cutting sword.

DATE	c.1850
ORIGIN	BRITISH
LENGTH	84.5cm (33.3in)

French naval cutlass, *c.*1880

Wide fuller

Knuckle guard

DATE	c.1880
ORIGIN	FRENCH
LENGTH	82.5cm (32.5n)

This is a Model 1833 French Naval Cutlass that has had the original iron bowl guard removed. This was done after the 1880s in order to reduce the space taken up by the cutlass while in storage on board ship, and was also deemed more practical when carried on land. The cutlass would have been sheathed in a leather and brass mounted scabbard. During the 1900s, quantities of these cutlasses were sold by the government to private companies.

US Navy cutlass, 1917

Bowl guard

DATE	1917
ORIGIN	AMERICAN
LENGTH	76.2cm (30in)

When the US Navy decided to adopt a new naval cutlass in the first half of the 20th century, they chose a sword design that was already available. The Model 1917 US Navy Cutlass is a copy of a Dutch Army "klewang", or double-edged machete, which had been developed following colonial experience in the Dutch East Indies. The grips are held in place by three recessed screw nuts. A later US model features an open hilt, with a two-branched guard. This cutlass was still carried on US Navy ships until the beginning of World War II.

French Napoleonic swords

The French Revolution (1789–99) and the subsequent accession of Napoleon Bonaparte (1769–1821) brought with it a renewed feeling of pride in the Imperial French Army. This resulted in the rapid development of a great variety of military swords, many designed for individual regiments and heavily influenced by the contemporary vogue for Neo-classical decoration.

French dragoon trooper's sword, *c.*1790

Straight, single-edged blade

S-shaped brass hilt bar

Flat, brass cap pommel

Most French cavalry swords of this period are found with hilts of either brass (for troopers) or gilt brass (for officers). This sword has a decorative S-shaped hilt bar that begins at the cross guard, forming a branch that joins the knuckle guard. Flat-topped pommels were common on French Napoleonic swords.

DATE	*c.*1790
ORIGIN	FRENCH
LENGTH	143.1cm (56.3in)

French cuirassier officer's sword, *c.*1790

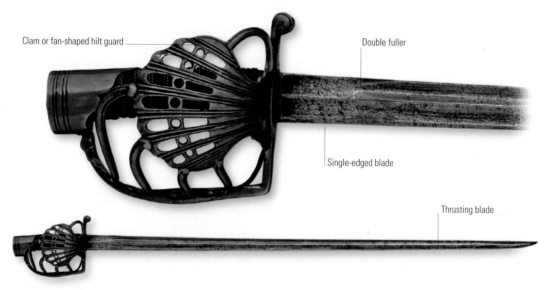

Clam or fan-shaped hilt guard

Double fuller

Single-edged blade

Thrusting blade

This sword has a distinctive fan-shaped and pierced hilt guard. The long, single-edged blade would have been used primarily as a thrusting weapon. French heavy cavalry troops inflicted more fatal wounds with this type of sword than their English counterparts, who carried a long, slashing sword.

DATE	*c.*1790
ORIGIN	FRENCH
LENGTH	103.7cm (40.8in)

French cadet's sword, École de Mars, *c.*1790

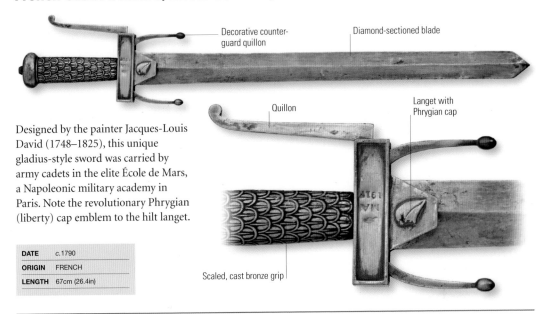

Decorative counter-
guard quillon

Diamond-sectioned blade

Quillon

Langet with
Phrygian cap

Designed by the painter Jacques-Louis
David (1748–1825), this unique
gladius-style sword was carried by
army cadets in the elite École de Mars,
a Napoleonic military academy in
Paris. Note the revolutionary Phrygian
(liberty) cap emblem to the hilt langet.

Scaled, cast bronze grip

DATE	*c.*1790
ORIGIN	FRENCH
LENGTH	67cm (26.4in)

French light cavalry officer's sword, *c.*1800

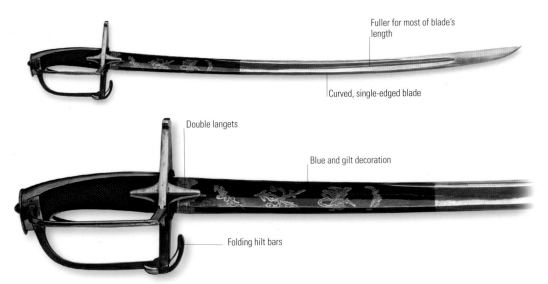

Fuller for most of blade's
length

Curved, single-edged blade

Double langets

Blue and gilt decoration

Folding hilt bars

DATE	*c.*1800
ORIGIN	FRENCH
LENGTH	88.5cm (34.8in)

Unlike their British counterparts, the French favoured the "attack hilt" sword.
This comprised a series of one or two sliding hilt bars that could be engaged
during battle and then folded away afterwards. This sword retains a considerable
amount of its original blue and gilt decoration to the blade, and would have been
sheathed in a gilt brass and leather mounted scabbard.

Napoleon Bonaparte

During his military career, Napoleon Bonaparte (1769–1821) carried a wide range of swords and we are able to document a number of them through their depiction in famous paintings. One of the most notable is a ceremonial sword designed and made by the goldsmith Martin-Guillaume Biennais (1764–1843). The gold hilt is elaborately decorated with classical and imperial themes, including a Napoleonic eagle with outstretched wings and a profile of Napoleon. Interestingly, the sword is of rather small proportions and reflects the French emperor's small stature. Jacques-Louis David (1748–1825), a French painter at the forefront of Neo-classicism, produced a series of paintings of Napoleon, including the study featured right. His most famous work is Napoleon at St Bernard (1800). In this painting, the young Napoleon is astride his horse and carries a sword of distinctly eastern or mameluke style, no doubt influenced by his recent campaigns in Egypt.

ABOVE Napoleon Bonaparte in his study. To his left can be seen a smallsword in its scabbard. It is likely that he would have carried this sword while on campaign.

Napoleon's smallsword, 1780

Decoration on shell guard and blade

Flattened diamond section

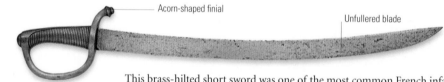

DATE	1780
ORIGIN	FRENCH
LENGTH	99.7cm (39.2in)

This officer's smallsword was presented to Napoleon Bonaparte by his contemporary, Alexandre Desmazis, with whom he attended the Ecole Militaire. They were later comrades at the Régiment de La Fère, where they both served as lieutenants at Valence in 1775. The engraved blade has a flattened, diamond-section profile with a narrow, central fuller. There is an engraved inscription to one of the hilt shell guards and also on the blade.

French infantry briquet (sword), c.1800

Acorn-shaped finial

Unfullered blade

DATE	c.1800
ORIGIN	FRENCH
LENGTH	47cm (18.5in)

This brass-hilted short sword was one of the most common French infantry swords of the Napoleonic Wars (1799–1815) and would have been carried by infantry privates. It had a heavy, ribbed brass grip, with a D-shaped knuckle guard and a slightly curved, flat-backed, single-edged blade. It was copied by most European nations, although rejected by Britain.

French hussar officer's sword, *c.*1800

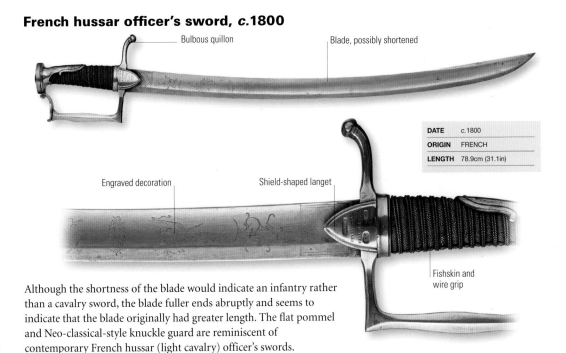

Bulbous quillon

Blade, possibly shortened

Engraved decoration

Shield-shaped langet

Fishskin and wire grip

DATE	*c.*1800
ORIGIN	FRENCH
LENGTH	78.9cm (31.1in)

Although the shortness of the blade would indicate an infantry rather than a cavalry sword, the blade fuller ends abruptly and seems to indicate that the blade originally had greater length. The flat pommel and Neo-classical-style knuckle guard are reminiscent of contemporary French hussar (light cavalry) officer's swords.

French heavy cuirassier trooper's sword, *c.*1810

Four-bar hilt

Double-fullered blade

DATE	*c.*1810
ORIGIN	FRENCH
LENGTH	113cm (44.5in)

This is a Model AN XIII Cuirassier Trooper's Sword and was issued to heavy cavalry regiments. The sword has a straight, single-edged and double-fullered blade. The large, brass, four-bar hilt has a domed pommel cap. These swords are normally engraved with the date and place of manufacture on the blade's edge.

French light cavalry officer's sword, *c.*1810

Double langets

Double-edged at end of blade

These swords were originally carried by officers of German hussar regiments and later adopted by French cavalry officers. The double langet is a design feature commonly encountered on Napoleonic swords. The end of the blade is double-edged, with a clipped point.

DATE	*c.*1810
ORIGIN	FRENCH
LENGTH	95.3cm (37.5in)

British Napoleonic swords

By the end of the 18th century, the British Army was embroiled in a global conflict with Napoleon Bonaparte of France (1769–1821) and his allies. The British Army began to re-arm on a massive scale.

The old haphazard and corrupt system of sword purchasing by regimental colonels was ended and a new range of officially approved "pattern" swords was introduced for all branches of the Army and Navy.

British heavy cavalry officer's sword, 1788 Pattern

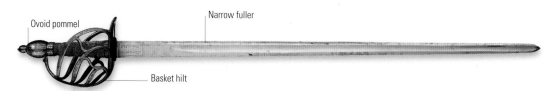

This basket-hilted sword has a large, enclosed iron hilt made up of a number of inter-linked bars. The long, double-edged blade would have been counter-balanced by the heavy, ovoid pommel.

DATE	1788
ORIGIN	BRITISH
LENGTH	102.8cm (40.5in)

British heavy cavalry officer's sword, 1788 Pattern

While a sword of this great size and weight would have been effective at the charge, contemporary accounts of British cavalry troopers constantly bemoan its cumbersome handling and the brittleness of the blades. This blade is engraved with the royal cypher ("GR") and crown.

DATE	1788
ORIGIN	BRITISH
LENGTH	120.6cm (47.5in)

British light cavalry officer's sword, 1788 Pattern

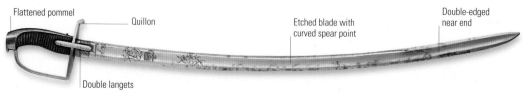

This sword has a straight knuckle guard, double langets and a slightly curved blade, double-edged for the last 15cm (6in). The grip consists of a wooden core, bound with either cord or string and then wrapped in wet fishskin or leather. While drying, the covering would shrink over the cord, producing a tight, ribbed grip.

DATE	1788
ORIGIN	BRITISH
LENGTH	63.5cm (25in)

The Duke of Wellington

As a general officer in the British Army, the Duke of Wellington (1769–1852) was normally obliged to carry a sword of regulation pattern. He certainly purchased or recieved a 1796 Pattern General Officer's Sword (see below) but it is unlikely that he carried this pattern sword while on campaign. He is actually more well known for carrying a mameluke-style sword and his decision to wear this eastern-inspired sword design was directly influenced by the campaign he fought in Egypt (1798–1801). Fellow British officers soon copied their commanding officer and the mameluke sabre became de rigueur within the British Army of the 1800s.

RIGHT Equestrian portrait of the Duke of Wellington with British hussars on a battlefield, 1814. He carries a sword of mameluke style.

General Officer's 1796 Pattern sword of the Duke of Wellington

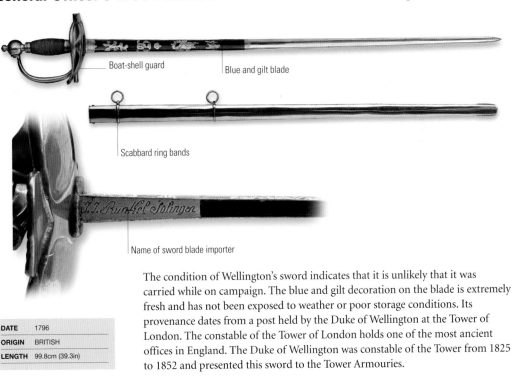

Boat-shell guard

Blue and gilt blade

Scabbard ring bands

Name of sword blade importer

DATE	1796
ORIGIN	BRITISH
LENGTH	99.8cm (39.3in)

The condition of Wellington's sword indicates that it is unlikely that it was carried while on campaign. The blue and gilt decoration on the blade is extremely fresh and has not been exposed to weather or poor storage conditions. Its provenance dates from a post held by the Duke of Wellington at the Tower of London. The constable of the Tower of London holds one of the most ancient offices in England. The Duke of Wellington was constable of the Tower from 1825 to 1852 and presented this sword to the Tower Armouries.

British heavy cavalry trooper's sword, 1796 Pattern

Wide, single fuller

Disc hilt

The 1796 Pattern Heavy Cavalry Trooper's Sword was based on an earlier Austrian design and featured a distinctive disc hilt. The blade was single-edged with a wide, single fuller. The hatchet point at the end of the blade was most effective as a slashing and cutting weapon.

DATE	1796
ORIGIN	BRITISH
LENGTH	101.5cm (40in)

British light cavalry trooper's sword, 1796 Pattern

Wide, single fuller

Stirrup hilt or knuckle guard

The light cavalry regiments of the British Army were issued with a sword that had a blade of "hussar" shape. This comprised a stirrup hilt, leather-bound grip and slightly curved, broad-fullered blade. It would have been carried in a heavy plain iron or steel scabbard with two carrying rings.

DATE	1796
ORIGIN	BRITISH
LENGTH	94cm (37in)

British light cavalry officer's sword, 1796 Pattern

Wide, single fuller

Shield-shaped langets

Fishskin grip

Blue and gold decoration to blade

DATE	1796
ORIGIN	BRITISH
LENGTH	94.7cm (37.3in)

The officer's version of the 1796 Pattern is almost identical in shape and form to that of the light cavalry trooper's sword, but was generally lighter in weight and better finished. Blue and gilt decorated blades were very popular at the end of the 18th century and invariably featured stands or arms, floral motifs and the "GR" royal cypher of King George III (1738–1820). The hilt has a "stirrup" knuckle guard and shield-shaped target.

British infantry officer's sword, 1796 Pattern

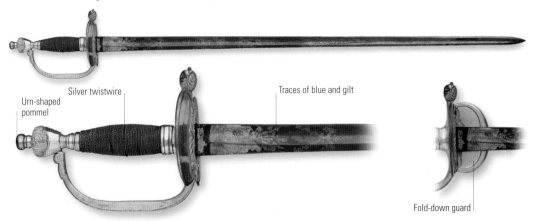

Urn-shaped pommel

Silver twistwire

Traces of blue and gilt

Fold-down guard

DATE	1796
ORIGIN	BRITISH
LENGTH	100cm (39.3in)

Inspired by the Neo-classical designs of Georgian architects, such as Robert Adam (1728–92), the urn-shaped pommel and acanthus-leafed decoration on this infantry officer's sword would appear very elegant alongside an officer's uniform. Unfortunately, it was far too flimsy to be an effective battlefield weapon.

British infantry officer's sword, 1803 Pattern

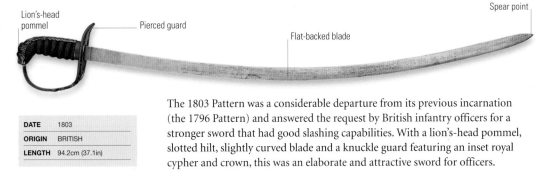

Lion's-head pommel

Pierced guard

Flat-backed blade

Spear point

DATE	1803
ORIGIN	BRITISH
LENGTH	94.2cm (37.1in)

The 1803 Pattern was a considerable departure from its previous incarnation (the 1796 Pattern) and answered the request by British infantry officers for a stronger sword that had good slashing capabilities. With a lion's-head pommel, slotted hilt, slightly curved blade and a knuckle guard featuring an inset royal cypher and crown, this was an elaborate and attractive sword for officers.

British rifle officer's sword, 52nd Regiment, *c.*1810

Strung bugle badge on grip

Quill-point to blade

The elite 52nd (Oxfordshire) Light Infantry Regiment served with Wellington during the Peninsular Campaigns (1808–13) and at the Battle of Waterloo (1815). The strung bugle motif of a rifle regiment is placed on the fishskin grip.

DATE	c.1810
ORIGIN	BRITISH
LENGTH	90.1cm (35.5in)

Swords of the British Empire

The British Army experimented with many new sword designs during the 19th century and army committees were regularly established to design the perfect sword: one with both cutting and thrusting capabilities. The designs were never wholly successful and often proved to be unsatisfactory in the field. Despite this, the sword was still used extensively in battle throughout the British Empire.

British Life Guards trooper's sword, 1820 Pattern

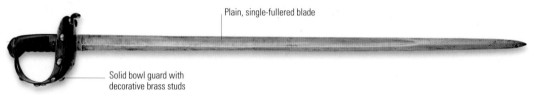

Plain, single-fullered blade

Solid bowl guard with decorative brass studs

The distinguishing feature of this sword is a solid bowl guard and 12 decorative brass studs placed around the outside edge. The single-edged blade was unusually long (about 95cm, or 37.4in) and could be quite effective (albeit a little unwieldy) if used correctly by a strong sword arm.

DATE	1820
ORIGIN	BRITISH
LENGTH	110.5cm (43.5in)

British Royal Horse Guards trooper's sword, 1820 Pattern

Strengthening "ears"

Pierced guard

Similar to heavy cavalry officers' swords of this period, the Royal Horse Guards Trooper's Sword has a "honeysuckle" hilt, with the hilt bars arranged to give the appearance of a stylized, trailing plant. Unlike an officer's sword, the backstrap has strengthening "ears" riveted through the tang.

DATE	1820
ORIGIN	BRITISH
LENGTH	111.3cm (43.8in)

British heavy cavalry officer's sword, 1821 Pattern

Etched panel

Pipe-back blade

"Honeysuckle" hilt

The introduction of this pattern coincided with the development of a new kind of service blade, known as the "pipe back". This blade has a tubular strengthening "pipe" that runs down the top edge of the blade, terminating in a quillpoint. The bowl guard was pierced and decorated with a "honeysuckle" pattern.

DATE	1821
ORIGIN	BRITISH
LENGTH	92.1cm (36.2in)

British light cavalry trooper's sword, 1821 Pattern

Backstrap
with "ear"

Quillon

Single-fullered blade

Double-edged near
end of the blade

DATE	1821
ORIGIN	BRITISH
LENGTH	103.6cm (40.8in)

The arrival of the 1821 Pattern was a deliberate attempt to produce a true cut-and-thrust sword. It had a slightly curved, spear pointed and single-fullered blade that was double-edged towards the end. The leather-covered grip had a strengthening "ear" that was formed from the backstrap and riveted into the grip.

British heavy cavalry trooper's sword, 1821 Pattern

Single fuller

Bowl guard

DATE	1821
ORIGIN	BRITISH
LENGTH	107cm (42.1in)

The 1821 Pattern Heavy Cavalry Trooper's Sword was part of a new generation of cut-and-thrust bladed swords that were introduced in the 1820s by the British Army to counter complaints that previous patterns were not effective in either requirement. Unfortunately, the solid bowl guard was too thin and the blades were prone to break in combat.

Light dragoons

The light dragoon regiments of the British Army were formed during the mid-18th century with the primary function of providing a reconnaissance and skirmishing role for the main army before a battle. They did not take part in the initial charge (normally reserved for the heavy cavalry), but by the time of the Napoleonic Wars (1799–1815) this strategy had changed and light dragoons now took an active part in any major battle. They gained particular experience and acclaim during the long campaigns of the Peninsular War (1808–14). Occasionally, they were also known to fight dismounted if the occasion required it. The 22nd Dragoons fought on foot during the Anglo-Dutch Java (Dutch East Indies) Campaign of 1811. The main sword pattern carried by British light dragoons during the Napoleonic period would have been the stirrup-hilted 1796 Pattern light cavalry trooper's sword.

ABOVE Light dragoons at the charge in the East Indies, c.1821.

British infantry officer's sword, 1822 Pattern

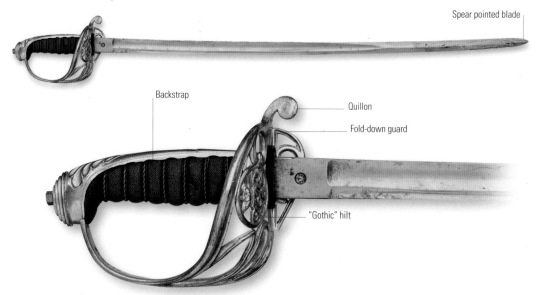

Spear pointed blade

Backstrap

Quillon

Fold-down guard

"Gothic" hilt

This sword was a radical departure from previous British infantry swords and displayed a pierced brass "Gothic" style, half-basket hilt. The term "Gothic" refers to the hilt design, which closely resembled the shape of church windows in the medieval Gothic style, a design motif popular in Britain during the first half of the 19th century. Within the hilt is an open-work cartouche with the royal cypher of the reigning monarch.

DATE	1822
ORIGIN	BRITISH
LENGTH	89.3cm (35.1in)

British 5th Dragoon Guards sword, *c*.1825

Decorative quillons

Blued blade

Double-edged towards point

The French invasion of Egypt (1798–1801) by Napoleon Bonaparte was an attempt to protect French trade interests and hinder Britain's access to India. The involvement of the British Army during this campaign meant that many officers came into contact with eastern swords and led to British cavalry officers adopting the mameluke sword. Many officers brought home curved eastern swords and they became extremely fashionable, especially within hussar regiments. This example is typical and comprises an ivory-slab grip, double quillons, langets and an *écusson* (cartouche) in the middle of the cross guard. Blades are always curved.

DATE	*c*.1825
ORIGIN	BRITISH
LENGTH	83.9cm (33in)

British rifle officer's sword, Madras Native Infantry, 1827 Pattern

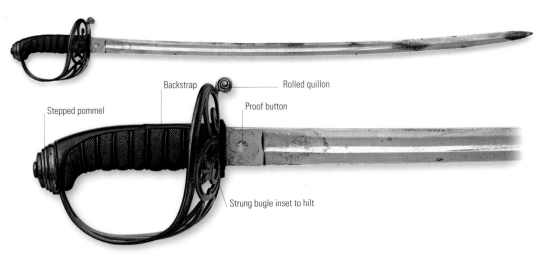

Backstrap

Rolled quillon

Stepped pommel

Proof button

Strung bugle inset to hilt

DATE	1827
ORIGIN	BRITISH
LENGTH	100cm (39.4in)

Formed in 1800, the Rifle Brigade (95th Regiment) carried this 1827 Pattern Rifle Officer's Sword throughout the 19th century. It has a steel Gothic hilt, with a strung bugle (symbolizing the use of a bugle to control troops) in the centre of the hilt. The strung bugle motif is usually repeated on the blade.

British Life Guards officer's dress sword, c.1840

Upturned quillon

Sharpened edge

DATE	c.1840
ORIGIN	BRITISH
LENGTH	104cm (41in)

This sword would have been worn for evening (levee) or parade use. It is based on the 1796 Pattern Heavy Cavalry Officer's Dress Sword and has a boat-shell hilt, straight, single-edged blade and a distinctive, flattened pommel. The scabbards have unusually long frog lockets (used to secure the scabbard to a sword belt).

British infantry officer's sword, c.1860

Single-fullered blade

DATE	c.1860
ORIGIN	BRITISH
LENGTH	96.5cm (38in)

This is a later variation of the 1822 Pattern Infantry Officer's Sword and comprises a Gothic pierced gilt-brass, half-basket hilt. By this time, the fold-down guard had been removed and the pipe-back blade had been substituted with a single-fullered and spear-pointed version.

British cavalry trooper's sword, 1853 Pattern

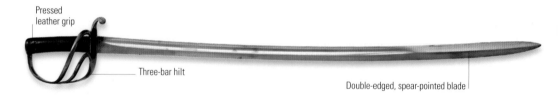

Pressed leather grip

Three-bar hilt

Double-edged, spear-pointed blade

This sword was an attempt by the British Army to combine the hilt and blade characteristics of both the light and the heavy trooper's sword into one universal pattern. The chequered leather grip was riveted into the tang, giving the sword much more strength. Troopers using the sword often complained that the three-bar hilt allowed an enemy to thrust his sword point through the gaps.

DATE	1853
ORIGIN	BRITISH
LENGTH	104.6cm (41.2in)

British cavalry trooper's sword, 1864 Pattern

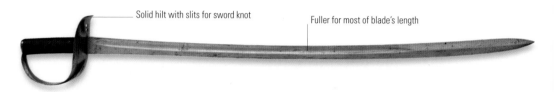

Solid hilt with slits for sword knot

Fuller for most of blade's length

This is quite a scarce sword as relatively few were manufactured. It uses the blade from an 1853 Pattern Cavalry Trooper's Sword but the open, three-bar hilt of the previous pattern has been replaced by a shallow, solid hilt, with a cut-out Maltese Cross design. Unusually, two small slits (for sword knots) were placed at the back of the hilt, in imitation of contemporary Austrian cavalry swords.

DATE	1864
ORIGIN	BRITISH
LENGTH	107.5cm (42.3in)

British cavalry trooper's sword, 1882 Pattern

Rolled edges to protect uniform

Single fuller

There were two blade lengths for this pattern, termed either "short" or "long". The reason for the different lengths is unclear, although it has been suggested that certain regiments recruited taller troopers and the longer pattern was needed for these soldiers. In any case, the pattern was changed three times due to constant blade and hilt failings. Despite these drawbacks, the pattern was widely issued to cavalry regiments and German sword companies had to make up the shortfall when British suppliers could not produce enough swords for the British Army.

DATE	1882
ORIGIN	BRITISH
LENGTH	101.6cm (41.3in)

British infantry officer's sword, 1895 Pattern

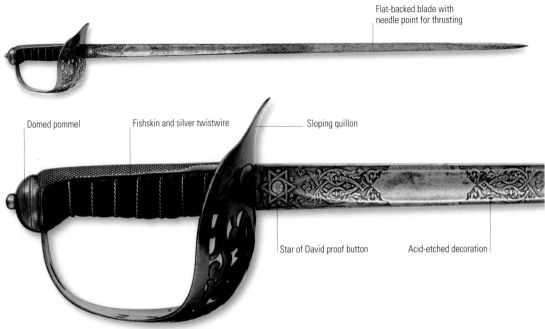

Flat-backed blade with
needle point for thrusting

Domed pommel

Fishskin and silver twistwire

Sloping quillon

Star of David proof button

Acid-etched decoration

DATE	1895
ORIGIN	BRITISH
LENGTH	97.3cm (38.3in)

This sword was a considerable improvement on previous patterns as the design afforded much better protection for the wearer's hand through the provision of a three-quarter basket hilt. Combined with a more robust blade introduced in 1892 and boasting a ruthless thrusting point, the sword proved quite effective on the battlefield. An alteration was made in 1897, with the addition of a small, turned-down, inner guard to prevent fraying of the uniform. Most swords of this pattern are found with either a fishskin or leather-wrapped grip.

British cavalry trooper's sword, 1899 Pattern

Strengthening
rivets

Spear point

Stamped, steel guard

DATE	1899
ORIGIN	BRITISH
LENGTH	101.8cm (40.1in)

A solid guard made from thin sheet metal distinguishes this pattern, coupled with an unusually long, stamped, leather grip. The serving soldier, however, soon complained that the long grip slipped out of his hand (particularly in the hotter climes of the British Empire) and the thin guard was prone to breaking once it had been struck by a sword blade. It was also issued with a thin, steel scabbard that tended to be easily damaged. This was a pattern loathed by cavalry troopers and it necessitated a radical re-evaluation of British military sword design.

Swords of the Russian Empire

Before the Napoleonic Wars (1799–1815), Russian swords were heavily influenced by eastern sword design. During the 19th century, European-inspired swords became more common in Russia. Swords from her one-time enemy, France, were also heavily copied and large stocks of captured French swords were reissued to Russian troops following Napoleon's disastrous march on Moscow, in 1812.

Russian cavalry trooper's sword, Model 1826

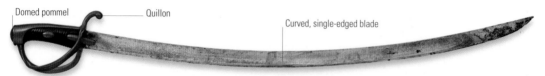

Domed pommel — Quillon

Curved, single-edged blade

This sword is a later copy of the French Model AN XI Light Cavalry Trooper's Sword. It has a wide, single-edged, slightly curved blade, brass three-bar hilt and double langets. Overall, it was quite a robust sword and would have been an effective close-quarter, hacking weapon.

DATE	1826
ORIGIN	RUSSIAN
LENGTH	101.8cm (40.1in)

Russian pioneer sword, Model 1827

Saw-back edge

Heavy, cast-brass grip

The enormous saw-back blade of this sword was used by pioneer troops to cut away undergrowth and construct defensive works. The cast brass hilt was extremely heavy and it must therefore have been a cumbersome weapon to carry for any great distance.

DATE	1827
ORIGIN	RUSSIAN
LENGTH	67.9cm (26.7in)

Russian artillery short sword, Model 1847

Rounded quillon

Serrated edge

This is the successor to the Model 1827 Pioneer Sword and has a "gladius" style identical to contemporary French designs. It still incorporated a saw-back blade, although it is doubtful whether these swords were actually used in combat. The end of the blade is double-edged and bulbous. The sword was carried in a leather and brass mounted scabbard. Most are in good condition, indicating little use.

DATE	1847
ORIGIN	RUSSIAN
LENGTH	63.5cm (25in)

Napoleon's invasion of Moscow

The French Army that invaded Russia in 1812 comprised many different European nationalities and, consequently, they would have carried a wide range of edged weapons. During this period Napoleon raised several regiments of lancers who would have frequently clashed with the Russian Cossack cavalry during the retreat from Moscow.

RIGHT The entry of French forces into Moscow on 14 September 1812. The troops are carrying a wide range of weapons.

Russian infantry/artillery officer's sword, Model 1865

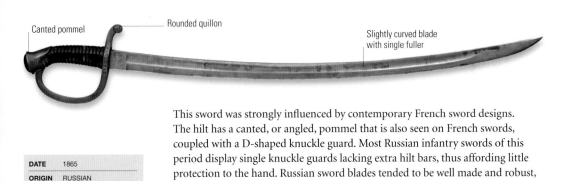

Canted pommel

Rounded quillon

Slightly curved blade with single fuller

DATE	1865
ORIGIN	RUSSIAN
LENGTH	89.7cm (35.3in)

This sword was strongly influenced by contemporary French sword designs. The hilt has a canted, or angled, pommel that is also seen on French swords, coupled with a D-shaped knuckle guard. Most Russian infantry swords of this period display single knuckle guards lacking extra hilt bars, thus affording little protection to the hand. Russian sword blades tended to be well made and robust, and they stood up well to battle conditions when compared with contemporary European (particularly British) sword blades.

Russian cavalry trooper's sword, Model 1881

Ribbed wooden grip

Hollow quillon

Single fuller

D-guard

DATE	1881
ORIGIN	RUSSIAN
LENGTH	101.6cm (40in)

These swords were produced in vast quantities for the Imperial Russian Army. Later models have an attachment on the scabbard for the provision of a socket bayonet (Model 1891 Moisin-Nagant). The hilt comprises a ribbed wooden grip and a D-shaped knuckle guard. The quillon is unusual in being hollow. Many swords are regimentally marked on the cross guard, although it is common for this designation to be defaced. The post-1917 revolutionary Bolsheviks regularly erased any traces they could find of the Imperial Russian monarchy on both swords and weapons.

Swords of the German Empire

Before the unification of Germany in 1871, independent German states carried their own distinctive sword styles and models, with most following the sword fashions of the day in Europe.

After unification, more standardized patterns were developed for use in all branches of the new Imperial German Army, although individual state emblems were still incorporated into the design of the sword.

Prussian infantry officer's dress sword, *c.*1870

Straight quillon

Single fuller

This style of sword was influenced by earlier Napoleonic smallswords and featured a double shell guard, D-shaped knuckle guard and ovoid pommel. The blade was straight and single-edged. It was not an effective combat weapon and would have been relegated for use as a dress sword.

DATE	c.1870
ORIGIN	PRUSSIAN
LENGTH	100.3cm (39.5in)

German officer's sword, *c.*1880

Quill-point blade

Stirrup knuckle guard

The dove-head pommel is a common feature on German swords of this period. In this case it is combined with a stirrup hilt and shield-shaped langets that display a silver badge of oak leaves and crossed swords. This indicates use by a cavalry officer.

DATE	c.1880
ORIGIN	GERMAN
LENGTH	92.2cm (36.3in)

Bavarian infantry officer's sword, Model 1889

Folding hilt

Sword knot or portopee

Quill-point blade

This is a very high-quality example of a late 19th-century Bavarian infantry officer's sword. It is etched with the Bavarian national motto *In Treue Fest* (Firm in Loyalty). The lion's-head hilt is gold plated and has a folding guard. It still retains its original green and silver bullion sword knot.

DATE	1889
ORIGIN	GERMAN
LENGTH	94cm (37in)

Prussian cavalry trooper's sword, Model 1889

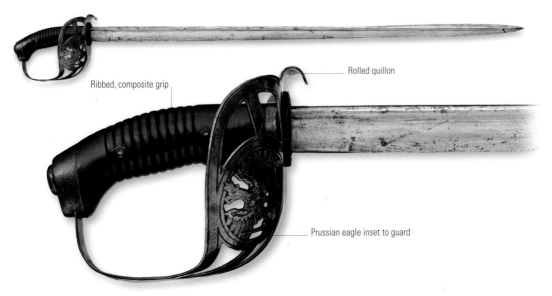

Rolled quillon

Ribbed, composite grip

Prussian eagle inset to guard

DATE	1889
ORIGIN	PRUSSIAN
LENGTH	96cm (37.8in)

This is a very common German cavalry sword and was widely issued to mounted regiments from the end of the 19th century and right through World War I. It incorporates an angled pistol grip (for better lunging) of composite material and has a steel guard inset with the Prussian eagle.

Bavarian regimental sword of Kaiser Wilhelm II, *c.*1900

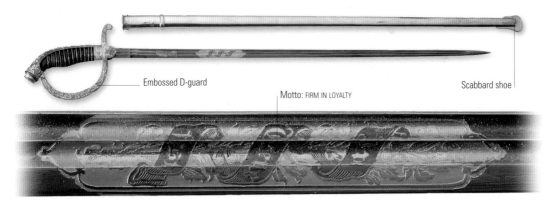

Embossed D-guard

Motto: FIRM IN LOYALTY

Scabbard shoe

DATE	c.1900
ORIGIN	GERMAN
LENGTH	92cm (36.2in)

This sword was carried by Kaiser Wilhelm II (1859–1941) and worn with his Bavarian regimental uniform. The engraved, double-fullered blade is of watered, or patterned, steel, with a gold-plated hilt. The Bavarian national coat of arms is embossed on the hilt back plate and the grip is covered in sharkskin, bound with gilt wire. The scabbard is nickel-plated iron. The screw pommel cap bears the engraved royal cipher "WII" beneath a crown.

Swords of the Austro-Hungarian Empire

The Austro-Hungarian Empire (1700–1915) stretched across a large area of central Europe and was second in size only to the Russian Empire. There were many different cultures within the empire and this melting pot also influenced sword design. One of the most striking sword designs was the curved, stirrup-hilted, light cavalry sword of the Hungarian hussar. Over time, it would be adopted by most European armies.

Austro-Hungarian hussar officer's sword, *c.1750*

Wide hatchet point

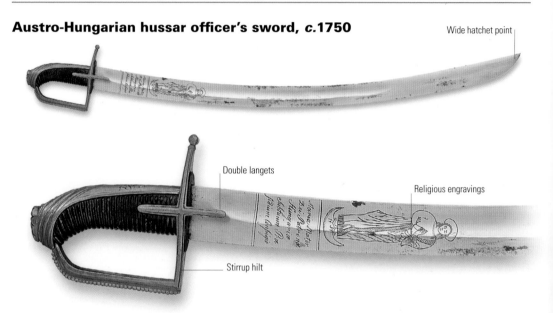

Double langets

Religious engravings

Stirrup hilt

Hussars were lightly equipped, mounted soldiers, known for their speed and mobility. The "stirrup" hilt is a design that was first recognized on hussar swords, combined with double langets positioned in the centre of the cross guard. The blade is of substantial width, and single-edged with a hatchet point. Religious themes, particularly representations of saints and invocatory prayers, were commonly engraved into blades.

DATE	c.1750
ORIGIN	AUSTRO-HUNGARIAN
LENGTH	93.4cm (36.8in)

Austrian infantry pioneer's sword, *c.1780*

Serrated edge

Hardwood grip

Saw-backed hatchet blade

This short hanger was carried by sappers or pioneers. The row of teeth on top of the blade would have been used for sawing through wood and constructing rudimentary defences. The brass and hardwood grip is reminiscent of eastern or Ottoman (Turkish) swords.

DATE	c.1780
ORIGIN	AUSTRIAN
LENGTH	85.7cm (33.7in)

Austrian infantry officer's sword, c.1800

Double-edged blade

Boat-shell hilt

Of smallsword style, this infantry officer's sword has a boat-shell hilt that mirrors contemporary European designs. The blade is double-edged and has a rapier-like profile. As a thrusting weapon, it would have been quite effective.

DATE	c.1800
ORIGIN	AUSTRIAN
LENGTH	91.7cm (36.1in)

Austrian infantry officer's sword, Model 1837

Curving cross guard

Single-edged blade

Exaggerated stirrup-shaped knuckle guard

DATE	1837
ORIGIN	AUSTRIAN
LENGTH	96.7cm (38.1in)

A bulging and exaggerated knuckle guard was fashionable on infantry swords of this period and is also seen on contemporary infantry swords from Prussia, Bavaria and Saxony. A spring catch was normally fitted to the top of the blade to prevent it slipping out of the scabbard.

Austrian cavalry officer's sword, Model 1850

Fishskin covering

Pierced, half-basket hilt

Single fuller

DATE	1850
ORIGIN	AUSTRIAN
LENGTH	97.8cm (38.5in)

This Austrian cavalry officer's sword of the mid-19th century has a slightly curved blade and a pierced, half-basket, or shallow, cup hilt. The grip is made of wood, wrapped in fishskin and twistwire. The sword would have been carried in a plain iron scabbard with two loose rings.

Austrian cavalry trooper's sword, Model 1861

"Ear"

Open guard

Double-edged towards end

DATE	1861
ORIGIN	AUSTRIAN
LENGTH	97.8cm (38.5in)

The iron hilt of this sword is ornamented with circular and triangular perforations, and there are two slits at the back for placing a sword knot. The backstrap has a side projection, or "ear", with a rivet driven into the tang to further strengthen the grip and blade.

Swords of the French Empire

French sword design had considerable influence over military swords throughout Europe and beyond. During the 19th century, French hilt and blade styles were adopted by the armies of many countries.

Brass, three-bar hilts and domed pommels were common features on French cavalry swords, with infantry officers' swords displaying quill-pointed or spear-pointed blades and ribbed horn grips.

French infantry officer's sword, Model 1821

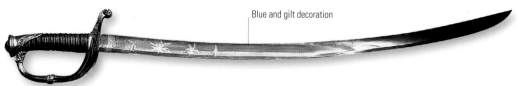

Blue and gilt decoration

This is an interesting example of an infantry officer's sword with a fine blade decorated with blue and gilt. By the time that this model was introduced, the use of blue and gilt was beginning to lose favour within the French Army and subsequent models of this sword had completely plain blades.

DATE	1821
ORIGIN	FRENCH
LENGTH	105.9cm (41.7in)

French light cavalry trooper's sword, Model 1822

Single-edged blade

Three-bar brass hilt

The Model 1822 was a lighter version of the sword carried by heavy cavalry troopers and featured a three-bar brass hilt, with leather and brass twistwire on the grip. The blade was slightly curved and single-edged. The sword was carried in a heavy, iron scabbard.

DATE	1822
ORIGIN	FRENCH
LENGTH	105.9cm (41.7in)

French artilleryman's short sword, Model 1831

Brass ribbed grip

Spear-pointed blade

Known as a "cabbage chopper", this short sword has its design origins in the ancient Roman "gladius" short sword. It had a solid brass, ribbed grip and a wide, spear-pointed blade. This sword is marked with an anchor and was probably carried by soldiers in the marine artillery. It is unlikely that it would have been used in a combat situation.

DATE	1831
ORIGIN	FRENCH
LENGTH	63.5cm (25in)

French infantry officer's sword, Model 1845

Ribbed horn grip

Quillon

Spear-pointed blade

DATE	1845
ORIGIN	FRENCH
LENGTH	89.3cm (35.1in)

French infantry swords of this period were normally fitted with slightly curved, spear-pointed blades. Invariably, the blades were plain and without engraved decoration. Grips were manufactured from either dark stained horn or from a wooden core wrapped in leather and bound with brass twistwire.

French dragoon officer's sword, Model 1854

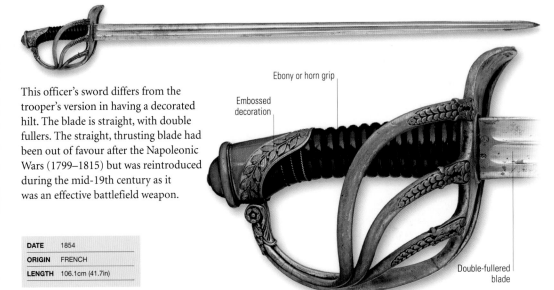

This officer's sword differs from the trooper's version in having a decorated hilt. The blade is straight, with double fullers. The straight, thrusting blade had been out of favour after the Napoleonic Wars (1799–1815) but was reintroduced during the mid-19th century as it was an effective battlefield weapon.

Ebony or horn grip

Embossed decoration

Double-fullered blade

DATE	1854
ORIGIN	FRENCH
LENGTH	106.1cm (41.7in)

French cavalry officer's sword, Model 1896

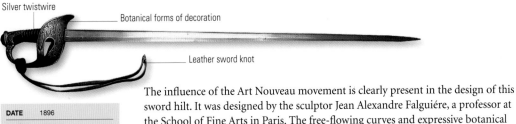

Silver twistwire

Botanical forms of decoration

Leather sword knot

DATE	1896
ORIGIN	FRENCH
LENGTH	91.7cm (36.1in)

The influence of the Art Nouveau movement is clearly present in the design of this sword hilt. It was designed by the sculptor Jean Alexandre Falguiére, a professor at the School of Fine Arts in Paris. The free-flowing curves and expressive botanical forms are evidence of the contemporary vogue for natural themes, even in military decoration. The grip is made of buffalo horn, wrapped in silver twistwire.

Swords of the Ottoman Empire

At one time, the Ottoman Empire covered a vast geographical area in eastern Europe and the Middle East and was at the height of its power from the 15th to the 17th centuries. One of the most recognizable sword types of these Turkic peoples was a curved sabre, the inspiration for the Mamluk or mameluke sword, later to be adopted by European armies during the Napoleonic Wars (1799–1815).

Turkish sword (kilij), *c.*1770

Yelman point

Horn grip

Hanging rings

Hilt langet slot

The kilij (meaning literally "sword") is a variation of the Turko-Mongolian wide-bladed and curved cavalry sabre that was carried throughout Eurasia from the 13th century. The end of the blade is flared and double-edged. This is known as the yelman. It added greater heft towards the front and substantial slashing power.

DATE	c.1770
ORIGIN	TURKISH
LENGTH	84cm (33.1in)

Persian sword (shamshir), *c.*1800

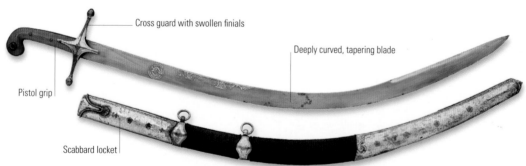

Cross guard with swollen finials

Deeply curved, tapering blade

Pistol grip

Scabbard locket

DATE	c.1800
ORIGIN	PERSIAN
LENGTH	90.9cm (35.8n)

Persian sword makers were long acknowledged as the undisputed masters of their craft and their blades exhibited superb tempering, sharpness and exquisite gold koftgari (inlaid gold on steel) decoration. This sword has a mameluke-style horn hilt with typical double langets and a cross guard that terminates in swollen finials. The blade flares into a double-edged yelman towards the point. The scabbard is brass and leather mounted, with an inset for the hilt langet.

Turkish sword (yataghan), *c.*1800

Bone or ivory grip

Embossed decoration

The yataghan is a distinctive sword with a forward-curving blade and very reminiscent of the kopis blade carried by the ancient Greeks. The yataghan was the standard weapon of the famous Turkish Janissaries (Turkish infantry), whereas the cavalry tended to carry the kilij. The handle of this sword is probably made from walrus ivory or bone, secured by a series of rivets. Scabbards were usually heavily decorated.

DATE	*c.*1800
ORIGIN	TURKISH
LENGTH	83cm (32.7in)

Turkish sword (yataghan), *c.*1800

Raised decoration

Forward-curving blade

The Turkish yataghan blade is similar in profile to the Indian sosun pattah (with a forward-curving, leaf-shaped blade) and the Nepalese kukri, and has a forward-curving blade that would have been used like a large chopper, hacking and slashing with devastating effect. The raised decoration that flows from the end of the handle and on to the blade ricasso is a common feature on these swords. The decoration was usually made from inlaid gold or silver and the pattern was often repeated on the scabbard mounts.

DATE	*c.*1800
ORIGIN	TURKISH
LENGTH	78.8cm (31in)

Turkish sword (yataghan), *c.*1800

Straight blade with upturned point

DATE	*c.*1800
ORIGIN	TURKISH
LENGTH	85cm (33.5in)

This sword is quite unusual in that the blade shape is not typical of most yataghans. Instead of the usual forward-curving blade, this version has a straight blade that ends with an upturned point. This blade is similar in shape to those used on Russian or Cossack swords.

Japanese swords

The production of a Japanese sword blade is the result of a complex and ritualized process, involving the creation of a blade that has a hard, cutting edge and a softer, more durable core and back. The sword maker undertakes a careful process of enfolding a number of steel layers and then selectively cooling different areas of the blade to produce a distinct range of qualities and a unique pattern (hamon). Japanese sword blades are considered to be amongst the finest ever created.

Japanese sword (nagamaki) by Unji, *c.*1300

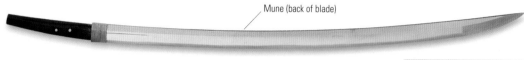

Mune (back of blade)

This sword blade was manufactured for use on a two-handed polearm, known as a nagamaki (translated as "long wrapping"). The weapon would have had a long metal or lacquered-wood handle, mounted with a katana-type blade.

DATE	c.1300
ORIGIN	JAPANESE
LENGTH	85.8cm (33.8in)

Japanese sword (katana) by Masamitsu, *c.*1370

Nakago (tang)

Kissaki (point)

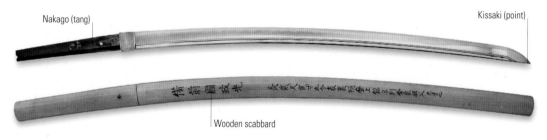

Wooden scabbard

This is a very early katana sword made by the swordsmith Masamitsu. He was from Takano, in Geishu (near present-day Hiroshima), and was a notable smith. His blades were known for their superb cutting qualities. This sword is housed in a protective wooden scabbard which is likely to be a later addition.

DATE	c.1370
ORIGIN	JAPANESE
LENGTH	76.4cm (30.1in)

Japanese sword (wakizashi) by Kanesada, *c.*1550

Hole for mekugi
(peg or pin)

Yakiba (hardened edge)

The swordsmith Kanesada was working in the town of Seki (between Tokyo and Osaka) during the 16th century. Known as the "City of Swords", Seki was a sword-making centre of excellence for well over 800 years. Kanesada gained a reputation for producing robust and practical blades. This is a wakizashi, or short sword, and would have been carried with a katana.

DATE	c.1550
ORIGIN	JAPANESE
LENGTH	59cm (23.2in)

Japanese sword (wakizashi) by Kaneyasu, *c.*1550

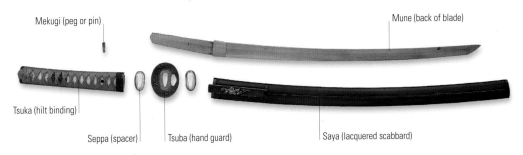

Mekugi (peg or pin)

Mune (back of blade)

Tsuka (hilt binding)

Seppa (spacer)

Tsuba (hand guard)

Saya (lacquered scabbard)

DATE	c.1550
ORIGIN	JAPANESE
LENGTH	62cm (24.4in)

Here we see the disassembled parts of a wakizashi sword. In order of importance, the blade – the heart of the sword – always came first. The blade's cutting qualities were the first consideration. Fittings such as the grip, hand guard and scabbard were always regarded as decorative (albeit important) extras, and were usually decorated with traditional Japanese motifs.

Japanese sword (katana) by Kunitsugu, *c.*1550

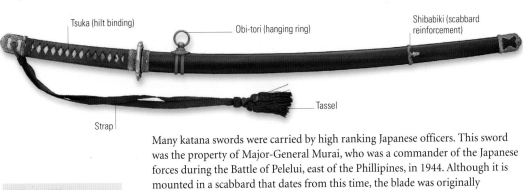

Tsuka (hilt binding)

Obi-tori (hanging ring)

Shibabiki (scabbard reinforcement)

Tassel

Strap

DATE	c.1550
ORIGIN	JAPANESE
LENGTH	97cm (38.2in)

Many katana swords were carried by high ranking Japanese officers. This sword was the property of Major-General Murai, who was a commander of the Japanese forces during the Battle of Pelelui, east of the Phillipines, in 1944. Although it is mounted in a scabbard that dates from this time, the blade was originally produced by Takeda Kunitsugu, a swordsmith working in Aizu, near Tokyo, during the 16th century. Many Japanese swords have hilts and scabbards that were made at a much later date than their blades.

Japanese sword (katana) by Sadayuki, *c.*1650

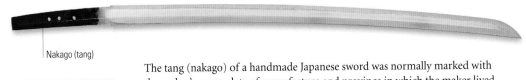

Nakago (tang)

DATE	c.1650
ORIGIN	JAPANESE
LENGTH	93.9cm (37in)

The tang (nakago) of a handmade Japanese sword was normally marked with the maker's name, date of manufacture and province in which the maker lived. Yamato Dairoku Sadayuki is on a list of 228 great katana swordsmiths published in a work of 1805 (the *Kaihokenshaku*) by the Samurai Yamada Asaemon, who worked as a tester of Japanese sword blades.

Japanese sword (wakizashi) by Kanemoto, *c.*1650

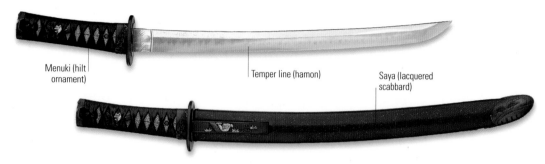

Menuki (hilt ornament)

Temper line (hamon)

Saya (lacquered scabbard)

The wakizashi was a short sword favoured by the Samurai and worn with civilian dress or in combination with his longer katana sword. The wakizashi was more comfortable to wear indoors than the katana, which the Samurai would place on a sword rack upon arrival. An owner's status and wealth were signified by how elaborately the hilt mountings were made. The hamon or temper line is clearly visible on this sword. This is a pattern created during the tempering process when the sword was made.

DATE	c.1650
ORIGIN	JAPANESE
LENGTH	57.6cm (22.7in)

Japanese sword (katana), *c.*1780

Tsuka (hilt binding)

Military leather scabbard cover

This sword is a good example of an early blade carried by a Japanese officer during World War II. This is evident in the military issue leather scabbard cover. Large numbers of these were either captured or surrendered by Japanese officers to Allied forces at the end of the war. Regrettably, a great number were destroyed.

DATE	c.1780
ORIGIN	JAPANESE
LENGTH	71.2cm (28in)

Japanese sword (katana) *c.*1850

Mune (back-edge)

This sword blade was manufactured not long before the demise of the Samurai warrior class. This resulted in the carrying of Samurai swords in public being made illegal in 1867. After this date, the Japanese military chose to adopt swords of a western design instead.

DATE	c.1850
ORIGIN	JAPANESE
LENGTH	74cm (29.1in)

Japanese weapon (tanto) and scabbard, *c.*1890

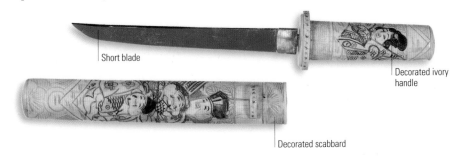

Short blade

Decorated ivory handle

Decorated scabbard

DATE	c.1890
ORIGIN	JAPANESE
LENGTH	30cm (11.8in)

The tanto (meaning "short sword") is a short-bladed weapon that was used for thrusting rather than cutting. Blades tend to be flat and unfullered, with some displaying considerable thickness near the hilt, enabling a blade to pierce through armour. This example has a decorated ivory hilt and scabbard. It was probably a souvenir for Western travellers to Japan.

Japanese sword (shin-gunto), *c.*1930

Kabuto-gane (pommel)

Machine-made blade

Kuchi-gane (throat)

DATE	c.1930
ORIGIN	JAPANESE
LENGTH	86.4cm (34in)

Japan experienced a period of rising nationalism during the 1930s and army officers adopted a sword very similar to the Samurai tachi, called the shin-gunto. Most of these swords were fitted with machine-made blades, although much older blades were also attached to military hilts. Scabbards were made from either leather or painted steel.

Japanese sword (tachi) by Kanesane, *c.*1940

Saya (lacquered scabbard)

Tsuba (hand guard)

DATE	c.1940
ORIGIN	JAPANESE
LENGTH	91.6cm (36in)

Asano Kanesane was a swordsmith during the Showa era (1926–89). Born in 1910 in Seki, known as the "City of Swords", he was apprenticed to master swordsmith Kojima Kanemichi in 1923 and worked in Seki all his life. The tachi shown here has a blade of great length. Earlier versions of this sword would have been worn slung over a Samurai's shoulder.

Japanese polearms

The Japanese Samurai warrior was not solely reliant on the sword as his primary battlefield weapon. Polearms, including spears and sword blades attached to shafts (naginata), were regularly carried by Japanese warrior clans. The effective use of such arms involved considerable training. The production of polearms became a specialist skill and some Japanese sword makers only produced naginata blades.

Japanese polearm (nagamaki), *c.*1450

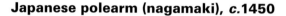

Cross guard   Curved, steel blade

The nagamaki is a polearm associated with the warring Samurai clans of the Kamakura (1192–1333) and Muromachi (1338–1573) eras. This example comprises a long sword blade (similar to a katana blade) attached to an all-metal shaft. Blades had lengths upwards of 75cm (29.5in), and the overall length varied from 1–1.5m (3.2–4.9ft).

DATE	c.1450
ORIGIN	JAPANESE
LENGTH	195cm (76.8in)

Japanese spear (yari), Edo period (1603–1867)

Lacquered wooden shaft

Yari (lance head)

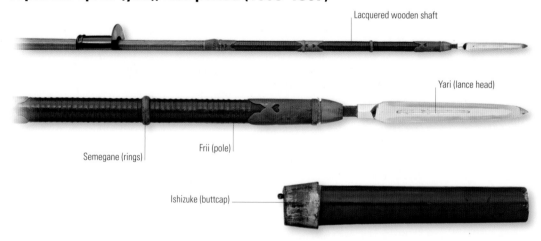

Frii (pole)

Semegane (rings)

Ishizuke (buttcap)

The Japanese yari is a spear or short lance that was not intended to be thrown but to be used as a thrusting weapon. It was carried by both Samurai warriors and the ordinary foot-soldier. This yari is known as a su yari, which is a reference to its straight blade, and is the most common type of Japanese spear. Some yari have horizontal crossbars on the blade (kama yari) and very long yari are known as omi no yari. The quality of yaris varies considerably. Yaris manufactured by swordsmiths exhibit fine, tempered blades with a hamon pattern across the blade and are of a two-piece construction, while others are one-piece and crudely wrought.

DATE	EDO (1603–1867)
ORIGIN	JAPANESE
LENGTH	368.5cm (145.1in)

Japanese staff weapon (naginata), *c.*1650

Curved steel blade

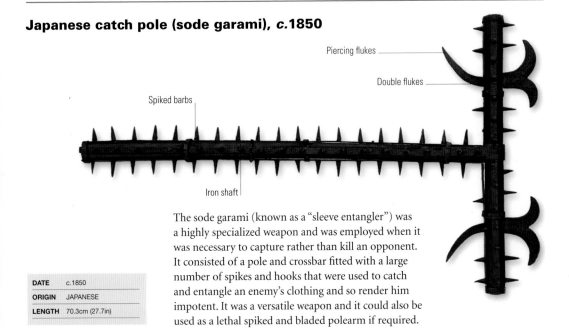

Holes for fixing tang to shaft

DATE	c.1650
ORIGIN	JAPANESE
LENGTH	105cm (41.3in)

This weapon is very reminiscent of the European glaive and consists of a curved blade with a very long metal tang attached to a wooden shaft by means of a series of wooden pegs driven through the handle. This example is of fine quality and would have been produced by a master swordsmith.

Japanese catch pole (sode garami), *c.*1850

Piercing flukes

Double flukes

Spiked barbs

Iron shaft

The sode garami (known as a "sleeve entangler") was a highly specialized weapon and was employed when it was necessary to capture rather than kill an opponent. It consisted of a pole and crossbar fitted with a large number of spikes and hooks that were used to catch and entangle an enemy's clothing and so render him impotent. It was a versatile weapon and it could also be used as a lethal spiked and bladed polearm if required.

DATE	c.1850
ORIGIN	JAPANESE
LENGTH	70.3cm (27.7in)

Japanese staff weapon (naginata), *c.*1850

Lacquered wooden shaft

Blade sharply curved towards point

DATE	c.1850
ORIGIN	JAPANESE
LENGTH	211.4cm (83.2in)

To use a naginata effectively, a series of swift, propeller-like moves were directed at all parts of the enemy's body. So successful was the naginata during the Muromachi period (1338–1573) that it hastened the introduction of protective armour for the legs and lower body parts. The wives of Samurai warriors were particularly skilled in the naginata's use and Japanese women still use the naginata in martial arts sports.

Chinese and Tibetan swords

The straight-bladed jian and the curved-bladed dao are some of the most recognizable Chinese sword types and were used for many centuries. The jian is regarded as the most venerable of Chinese swords and has its origins in antiquity. Unlike in western Europe, where sword design went through discernible changes in form and function, Chinese swords remained virtually unchanged over millennia.

Chinese/Tibetan sword, c.1420

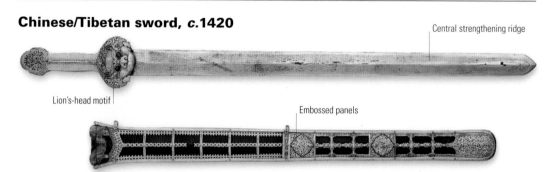

Central strengthening ridge

Lion's-head motif

Embossed panels

This sword is of exceptional quality and was presented by the Yongle Ming emperor (1326–1424) to the ruler of Tibet. The blade has a central strengthening ridge and is typically plain. The cross guard includes an impressive lion's-head motif and the scabbard displays a fretwork pattern, with embossed panels.

DATE	c.1420
ORIGIN	CHINESE/TIBETAN
LENGTH	90.3cm (35.5in)

Chinese sword (qibing dao), c.1800

Single-edged blade

This long-bladed dao was probably carried by a mounted soldier and has a single-edged blade that ends in an upturned point which was particularly effective at thrusting. The cutting edge was made of harder steel, while the back of the blade was forged in softer steel to avoid the blade becoming too brittle.

DATE	c.1800
ORIGIN	CHINESE
LENGTH	95.3cm (37.5in)

Chinese sword (fang), c.1850

Single-edged blade

Hook for capturing blades

Downward cross guard

The simple construction of this unusual sword indicates that it was a weapon of the ordinary soldier. A downturned crossguard served the function of blocking or trapping an opponent's blade. There is another projecting bar near the end of the blade. The blade itself is of rather crude manufacture.

DATE	c.1850
ORIGIN	CHINESE
LENGTH	73.1cm (28.8in)

Chinese double, or butterfly, swords, *c.*1850

Double-edged blade

Carrying rings

Half cross guard

Chape

Brass scabbard throat

DATE	c.1850
ORIGIN	CHINESE
LENGTH	67.3cm (26.5in)

The double sword is uniquely Chinese and was designed to provide the user with a two-handed combination of weapons housed in just one sheath. Hilt and blade design is based on the traditional straight-bladed jian. Blades are invariably plain and diamond-sectioned, although some examples are found with inlaid copper or brass roundels. This sword is of a higher quality than normally encountered and has a well-carved hilt and scabbard.

Chinese double, or butterfly, swords, *c.*1850

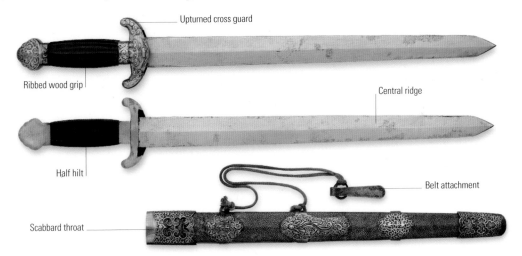

Upturned cross guard

Ribbed wood grip

Central ridge

Half hilt

Belt attachment

Scabbard throat

DATE	c.1850
ORIGIN	CHINESE
LENGTH	56.8cm (22.3in)

These double, or butterfly, swords are of above-average quality and feature a decorated, brass mounted hilt with ribbed wooden grips. The blade is double-edged with a central ridge. The scabbard still retains the original carrying cord and metal clip that would have been attached to a belt. Although these swords were effective as close-combat weapons, the shortness of the blades meant that against wider broadswords they were rather ineffective.

Chinese double, or butterfly, swords, *c.*1850

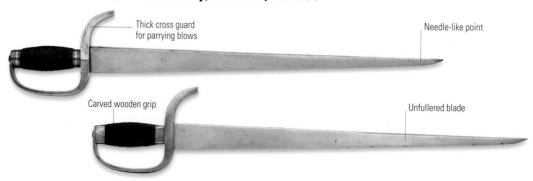

Thick cross guard
for parrying blows

Needle-like point

Carved wooden grip

Unfullered blade

The needle-like shape of these sword blades indicates that they were used more as long, thrusting knives, while the thick cross guard and knuckle guard could also be used as an effective knuckleduster. The blade was normally only sharpened from halfway down, so that the unhoned part could be used for blocking.

DATE	c.1850
ORIGIN	CHINESE
LENGTH	62.3cm (24.5in)

Chinese sword (jian), *c.*1850

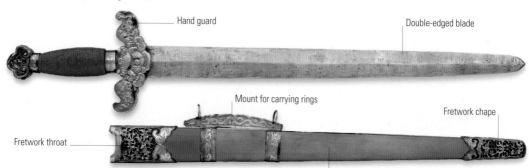

Hand guard

Double-edged blade

Mount for carrying rings

Fretwork chape

Fretwork throat

Scabbard

As the 19th century progressed, the Qing Empire (1644–1911) laid more emphasis on the use of fire-arms over edged weapons. This jian sword highlights how the need for elaborate decoration had overtaken the practical necessities of producing an effective combat weapon. The short, flimsy blade would have been useless against any kind of heavy, broad-bladed sword.

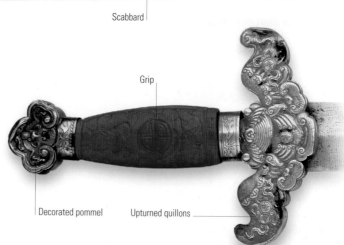

Grip

Decorated pommel

Upturned quillons

DATE	c.1850
ORIGIN	CHINESE
LENGTH	77.8cm (30.6in)

Tibetan/Chinese sword, *c.*1850

Rings for sword belts

Jewelled decoration

DATE	c.1850
ORIGIN	TIBETAN/CHINESE
LENGTH	71.2cm (28in)

Tibetan swords are usually highly decorated, particularly on hilts and scabbards, where the application of heavy gilding, silver wire, carved turquoise and inlaid coral is a common theme. Blades tend to be plain. Quality varies considerably, although this example is better than most. There is a possibility that this sword was actually manufactured in China, in the Tibetan style.

Chinese sword *c.*1850

Brass pommel

DATE	c.1850
ORIGIN	CHINESE
LENGTH	67.3cm (26.5in)

The blade of this broadsword is very much designed as a chopping weapon and could have been used with both hands as the grip is quite long. It would probably have been sheathed in a plain leather scabbard.

Chinese sword (jian), *c.*1870

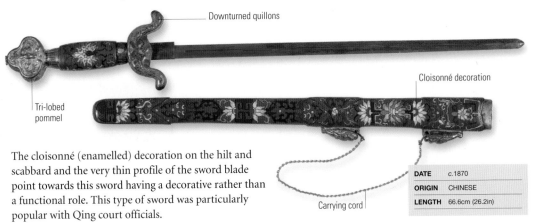

Downturned quillons

Cloisonné decoration

Tri-lobed pommel

The cloisonné (enamelled) decoration on the hilt and scabbard and the very thin profile of the sword blade point towards this sword having a decorative rather than a functional role. This type of sword was particularly popular with Qing court officials.

Carrying cord

DATE	c.1870
ORIGIN	CHINESE
LENGTH	66.6cm (26.2in)

Chinese polearms

The polearm was an important weapon of the Chinese infantry and the sheer range and variety of polearms that have survived are a testament to this. Most of them are similar in function to western European polearms such as the glaive and halberd, but their designs are radically different, incorporating motifs such as dragon-head sockets and features such as extremely curved blades.

Chinese polearm (yan yue dao), *c.*1840

Notch for catching opponent's blade

Cutting edge

Dragon-head socket

Also more commonly known as the guan dao, the yan yue dao (meaning "reclining moon blade") is similar to the European fauchard and comprises a heavy, single-edged blade that terminates with an exaggerated curve. Serrations and notches on the top edge of the blade were used to catch an opponent's blade. This weapon would have been effective at sweeping cuts to the lower body.

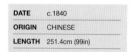

DATE	*c.*1840
ORIGIN	CHINESE
LENGTH	251.4cm (99in)

Chinese polearm (yan yue dao), *c.*1850

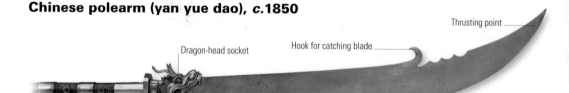

Thrusting point

Dragon-head socket

Hook for catching blade

DATE	*c.*1850
ORIGIN	CHINESE
LENGTH	252.5cm (99.4in)

This type of polearm was usually mounted on a wooden or metal pole, 1.5–2.5m (4.9–8.2ft) in length, with a heavy counterweight at the bottom that balanced the great weight of the blade and could also be used as a bludgeoning weapon. The dragon's head was a common motif on Chinese polearms.

Chinese halberd, *c.*1850

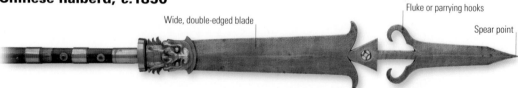

Wide, double-edged blade

Fluke or parrying hooks

Spear point

This is a complex weapon and would have served several functions. The blade has a needle-like spear point that could easily pierce armour. At the base of the point are two downward projections, or flukes, that would catch an opponent's blade. Another wide, double-edged blade is below this and used for parrying.

DATE	*c.*1850
ORIGIN	CHINESE
LENGTH	250.5cm (98.6in)

Chinese halberd, *c.*1850

Socket

Double-edged blade

Crescent-shaped blade

The very long socket and blade of this halberd were designed to keep an opponent at a safe distance. It has a "flamboyant", or snake-like, double-edged blade to the head as well as a crescent-shaped blade just below, which was employed as both a parrying and a cutting weapon.

DATE	*c.*1850
ORIGIN	CHINESE
LENGTH	256.8cm (101.1in)

Chinese halberd, *c.*1850

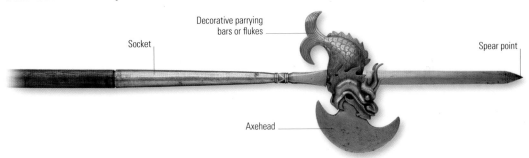

Decorative parrying bars or flukes

Socket

Spear point

Axehead

DATE	*c.*1850
ORIGIN	CHINESE
LENGTH	250cm (98.4in)

This unusual halberd has a distinctive brass axehead in the shape of a snake-fish. It is likely that the long, double-edged, spear-pointed blade was the most effective part of this halberd, with the axehead serving a more decorative rather than functional role. Many Chinese polearms had tassels hanging from where the pole and the blade were joined. They were coloured red as this is regarded as an auspicious colour in Chinese culture.

First Sino-Japanese war

The Chinese and Japanese forces that faced each other during the First Sino-Japanese War over the control of Korea (1894–95) carried a wide variety of edged weapons. The Chinese soldier still used a range of polearms, while Japanese troops adopted more western swords. The war demonstrated Japan's military and technical superiority over China and its new-found ability to compete with, rather than be dominated by, the Western powers.

RIGHT Detail from battle scene, Sino-Japanese War. Note the polearms being used by the Chinese forces.

African weapons

Swords from the African continent vary according to both geographical and cultural factors. North African sword design was heavily influenced by the Arabic Muslim invaders of the medieval period, while central and west African swords tended to be produced on a very small scale, with the local blacksmith forging swords and edged weapons primarily for his village.

North African sword (saif), *c*.1800

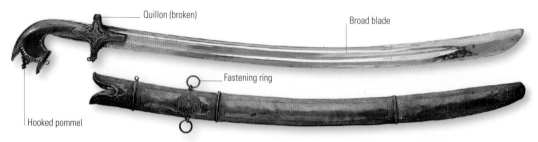

Quillon (broken)

Broad blade

Fastening ring

Hooked pommel

The saif is an Arab sword type that was brought into North Africa by Arabic invaders. It comprises a broad, curved blade and hooked pommel. It was carried in front of the body, slung from two rings fastened to a wide band around the scabbard. It may have had a chain knuckle guard (now missing).

DATE	c.1800
ORIGIN	NORTH AFRICAN
LENGTH	83.5cm (32.8in)

Sudanese spear, *c*.1850

Leaf-shaped blade

DATE	c.1850
ORIGIN	SUDANESE
LENGTH	113.2cm (44.6in)

The African spear was used primarily as a throwing weapon. It would be thrown at the beginning of a skirmish and was only used in close combat conditions when an opponent was badly injured and could be finished off easily. This Sudanese spear has a leaf-shaped blade and long, iron shaft, which is then mounted on a further wooden shaft.

Somalian sword, *c*.1850

Leather grip over wooden core

Iron blade

The long, slightly curved blade of this sword probably indicates that it could have been used while on horseback. The blade shape is similar to European Napoleonic cavalry swords, particularly the hatchet point. Weapons such as these had a dual function. They were obviously implements of war but could also be utilized as everyday tools of the home and the field.

DATE	c.1850
ORIGIN	SOMALIAN
LENGTH	84.6cm (33.3in)

Kenyan short sword, *c.*1850

Leather-bound grip

Carrying strap

Leather scabbard

DATE	c.1850
ORIGIN	KENYAN
LENGTH	53.3cm (21in)

This Masai short sword is of machete type and has a distinctive double-edged blade that widens towards the point. The weapon would have been used more for chopping rather than thrusting and no doubt would also have had an agricultural function if required. The sword's scabbard is made from heavy, stitched leather, as is the carrying strap.

Tunisian short sword, *c.*1850

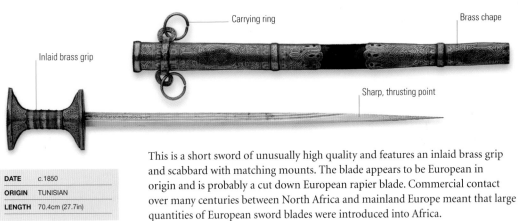

Carrying ring

Brass chape

Inlaid brass grip

Sharp, thrusting point

DATE	c.1850
ORIGIN	TUNISIAN
LENGTH	70.4cm (27.7in)

This is a short sword of unusually high quality and features an inlaid brass grip and scabbard with matching mounts. The blade appears to be European in origin and is probably a cut down European rapier blade. Commercial contact over many centuries between North Africa and mainland Europe meant that large quantities of European sword blades were introduced into Africa.

South African Zulu spear (umKhonto), *c.*1870

Tapering spearhead

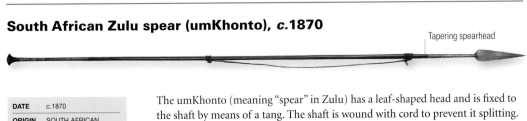

DATE	c.1870
ORIGIN	SOUTH AFRICAN
LENGTH	77cm (30.3in)

The umKhonto (meaning "spear" in Zulu) has a leaf-shaped head and is fixed to the shaft by means of a tang. The shaft is wound with cord to prevent it splitting. It is also known as the assegai and was designed for throwing, although there are shorter versions (made in iron), for stabbing.

Moroccan sword (flyssa), *c.*1880

Needle-like point

The flyssa is the national sword of the Kabyles tribe of North Africa, part of a confederation of tribes that form the Berber race. Blades are straight and very long, with a pronounced needle-like point. Many are engraved with inlaid brass decoration on the top of the blade edge. Animal-head pommels are common.

DATE	c.1880
ORIGIN	MOROCCAN
LENGTH	101.3cm (39.9in)

Sudanese sword (kaskara), *c.*1880

Flat, double-edged blade

Straight cross guard

The Sudanese kaskara sword is sometimes confused with medieval Crusader swords, as the cruciform hilt and wide, fullered blade is similar to European broadswords. Some blades were heavily etched for most of their length with Koranic verses. The rounded grip is wrapped in strips of leather.

DATE	c.1880
ORIGIN	SUDANESE
LENGTH	106.4cm (41.8in)

Nigerian sword (takouba type), *c.*1880

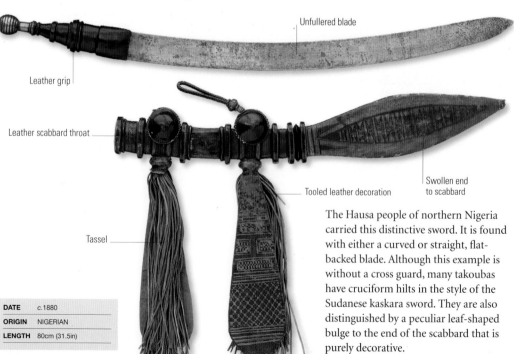

Unfullered blade

Leather grip

Leather scabbard throat

Tassel

Tooled leather decoration

Swollen end to scabbard

DATE	c.1880
ORIGIN	NIGERIAN
LENGTH	80cm (31.5in)

The Hausa people of northern Nigeria carried this distinctive sword. It is found with either a curved or straight, flat-backed blade. Although this example is without a cross guard, many takoubas have cruciform hilts in the style of the Sudanese kaskara sword. They are also distinguished by a peculiar leaf-shaped bulge to the end of the scabbard that is purely decorative.

Kenyan sword (seme), *c.*1880

The Masai people were traditionally armed with a spear, short sword (seme) and occasionally a shield. In a lion hunt, the seme was a weapon of last resort and also used as a side-arm if the spear was lost in combat.

Central median ridge

Leather sheath, dyed red

DATE	c.1880
ORIGIN	KENYAN
LENGTH	32.6cm (12.8in)

Zairean sword, *c.*1880

Iron blade

Moulded grip

Leather-and-wood-covered scabbard

DATE	c.1880
ORIGIN	ZAIREAN
LENGTH	57.1cm (22.5in)

The Salampasu people of southern Zaire used this iron-bladed sword. It has a carved black wood grip and a blade of waisted shape. The scabbard is wood, covered with raw hide and reinforced with rattan fibre at its mouth and tip. The double-edged blade has a pronounced thrusting point.

Sudanese sword (kaskara), *c.*1890

Round pommel

Cruciform cross guard

Double-fullered blade

DATE	c.1890
ORIGIN	SUDANESE
LENGTH	99.5cm (39.2in)

This kaskara sword was owned by the Sultan Ali Dinar of Darfur (Sudan), who was khalifah or "caliph" (the country's civil and religious leader) until he was killed by the British in 1916. The cruciform hilt is wrapped in sheet gold and the blade has false European armourer's marks. These were thought to add an element of quality.

South African pair of swords, *c.*1910

Human-head pommel

DATE	c.1910
ORIGIN	SOUTH AFRICAN
LENGTH	79.4cm (31.2in)

These swords are likely to be of southern African origin and have male and female matching hardwood pommels. The blades are double-edged and were probably made by a local blacksmith, with the pommel carving done separately.

Sri Lankan and Indian swords

Despite the enormous cultural influence of the British Raj (1858–1947), Indian sword makers continued to produce a wide variety of indigenous designs with little regard to their new Western rulers. Muslim, Hindu and Sikh traditions had become solidly entrenched following centuries of invasion and assimilation, and sword forms reflected these established cultures.

Sri Lankan sword (kastane), *c.*1750

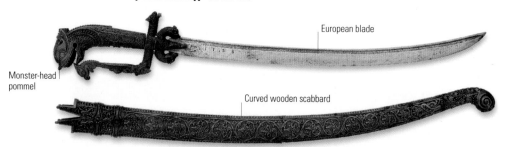

European blade

Monster-head
pommel

Curved wooden scabbard

This Sri Lankan kastane has a typical monster-head pommel and a short, slightly curved European blade. Many kastane blades bear the marks of the Dutch East India Company (1602–1800), a commercial trading company of the Netherlands.

DATE	c.1750
ORIGIN	SRI LANKAN
LENGTH	66.7cm (26.2in)

Indian ritual sword, *c.*1750

Hole for ceremonial bells

DATE	c.1750
ORIGIN	INDIAN
LENGTH	80cm (31.5in)

Double-edged blade

This is a ceremonial temple sword from southern India and dates from the early 18th century. The steel blade is double-edged and there are holes along the blade to allow the hanging of small bells that would jangle during ceremonies. The iron hilt is of talwar form.

Indian two-handed sword, *c.*1750

Steel handle for two hands

Indian warriors brought a wide range of swords and polearms on to the battlefield. This all-steel, two-handed sword has an unfullered, double-edged blade with spear point. It is likely that it would have been swung over the head in the same way as a battle-axe. The blade is similar in form to a khanda blade and is secured to the metal handle by means of a long, rivetted flange or hinge.

DATE	c.1750
ORIGIN	INDIAN
LENGTH	150.2cm (59.1in)

Indian sword (khanda), *c.*1790

Reinforcement bars

Rounded, swelling point

DATE	c.1790
ORIGIN	INDIAN
LENGTH	108cm (42.5in)

The khanda was a Hindu sword from the Maratha culture (originally a Hindu warrior class based in present-day Marahashtra, south-west India). This example has extensive brass reinforcement bars on both sides of the blade, to give support and strengthen the sword.

Indian sword (khanda), *c.*1790

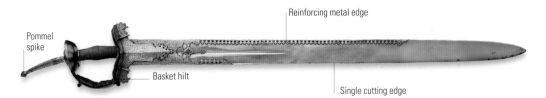

Reinforcing metal edge

Pommel spike

Basket hilt

Single cutting edge

DATE	c.1790
ORIGIN	INDIAN
LENGTH	105.3cm (41.4in)

Here we have a fine example of a khanda with typical Hindu basket hilt. The blade is straight with the back-edge strengthened by a metal rib. A curved spike projected from the centre of the pommel and could be used as an effective penetrative weapon. The hilt and strengthening rib are covered with gilt brass.

Indian sword (khanda), *c.*1800

Coned pommel

Rounded and swelling point

DATE	c.1800
ORIGIN	INDIAN
LENGTH	91.5cm (36in)

Khandas are normally encountered with a straight, watered (or patterned) blade that swells towards the tip. Blades are relatively thin and flexible and require reinforcement bars that run part-way down the blade. The spiked projection on the top of the pommel normally served as an extra grip for two-handed use but could also be engaged as a convenient hand rest when the sword was sheathed. The hilt shape of this khanda is unusual. Many khandas have a cushioned velvet liner to the basket hilt. The khanda was a heavy weapon designed to inflict damage through sheer force and was used for hacking rather than thrusting.

Indian sword (pata) *c.*1800

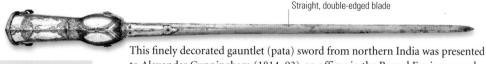

Straight, double-edged blade

DATE	c.1800
ORIGIN	INDIAN
LENGTH	133.5cm (52.5in)

This finely decorated gauntlet (pata) sword from northern India was presented to Alexander Cunningham (1814–93), an officer in the Bengal Engineers and founder of the Indian Archaeological Survey. The sword would have been held by grasping a bar inside the gauntlet. Some warriors carried one of these swords in each hand and attacked the enemy with a whirling, windmill-like action.

Indian sword (tegha), *c.*1800

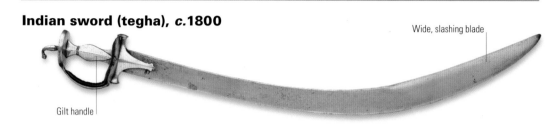

Wide, slashing blade

Gilt handle

DATE	c.1800
ORIGIN	INDIAN
LENGTH	88.3cm (34.8in)

This sword has a tulwar-style hilt and a very wide, double-edged blade. They were carried by the Mahrattas (south-west India) and the Rajputs, who ruled much of pre-Mughal India. Because of the great width and thickness of the blade, many are thought to have been used as executioner's swords.

Indian sword (talwar), *c.*1800

Globular quillons

Curved, double-edged blade

Disc pommel

DATE	c.1800
ORIGIN	INDIAN
LENGTH	95.5cm (37.6in)

Known as a talwar, talwaar or tulwar, this Indian sword type has its origins in 13th-century Persian (Iranian) swords such as the shamshir and the Turkish kilij. Blades tend to be wider than Persian swords and it has a distinctive, flat disc pommel. Hilts are all metal and many of them are decorated with exquisite koftgari (inlaid gold) designs.

Indian sword (talwar), *c.*1800

Concave quillons

Knuckle guard

Single cutting edge

DATE	c.1800
ORIGIN	INDIAN
LENGTH	95.3cm (37.5in)

This talwar dates from the late 18th and early 19th century and is of all-steel construction. It has a curved blade, disc-shape pommel and a knuckle guard that curves away from the pommel. It was both a slashing and thrusting weapon.

Indian sword (kora), *c.*1800

This is the national sword of Nepal and features a uniquely shaped, dramatically curved blade that terminates with a flared point. Koras of this great size are sometimes attributed to ceremonial use, although some were also employed as executioners' swords.

DATE	*c.*1800
ORIGIN	INDIAN
LENGTH	27.9cm (11in)

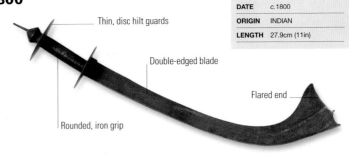

Thin, disc hilt guards

Double-edged blade

Flared end

Rounded, iron grip

Mughal sword, *c.*1800

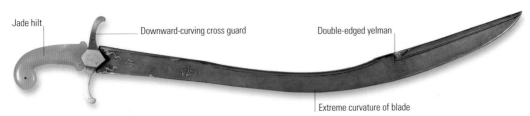

Jade hilt

Downward-curving cross guard

Double-edged yelman

Extreme curvature of blade

DATE	*c.*1800
ORIGIN	INDIAN
LENGTH	91cm (35.8in)

The Mughal Dynasty (1526–1857) ruled a great part of India (particularly the northern areas) for many centuries and the strong influence of earlier Mongol sword design is evident in this sword. The hilt is made from jade and decorated with rubies. The end of the blade has a typical yelman, or double-edged, swelling.

Indian sword (shamshir), *c.*1840

Cross guard with finials

Inlaid decoration

Ram's-head pommel

Blued steel

Scabbard shoe

DATE	*c.*1840
ORIGIN	INDIAN
LENGTH	97.7cm (38.5in)

The shamshir is Persian (Iranian) in origin and functions purely as a cutting weapon, due to the curved point being inadequate for thrusting. This sword is of extremely high quality, and comprises an enamelled, ram's-head pommel and heavily decorated scabbard. Blades tend not to be decorated except for the name of the maker and possibly the date of manufacture. Blades of this status are invariably made in watered (pattern-welded) steel, a process of repeated forging that produced a unique pattern on the surface of the blade that was highly prized.

Indian polearms

The use of the polearm in India continued long after it had become obsolete in Europe and it was still carried into battle during the 19th century. The long spear was a particular favourite and was used as a thrusting, rather than throwing, weapon in massed infantry formations. Tridents, great battle-axes and spiked maces were all brought into play during Indian battles of the 18th and 19th centuries.

Indian lance, *c.*1750

Spiked point

Heavy wooden shaft

Despite the pre-eminence of infantry formations over cavalry in Indian armies, mounted soldiers, particularly Mughal cavalry, used the lance or spear with notable success. The heavy weight of the wooden shaft world have added considerable power and striking impetus.

DATE	c.1750
ORIGIN	INDIAN
LENGTH	38.8cm (15.3in) head

Indian spear, *c.*1800

Ball to stop spike running in too far

Wooden shaft

This Indian spear is more reminiscent of a European pike and would have served the same purpose, being used as a thrusting weapon in massed infantry formations. The large ball at the end of the spearhead would have stopped the spear travelling too far into an opponent and becoming difficult to extract.

DATE	c.1800
ORIGIN	INDIAN
LENGTH	31.1cm (12.2in) head

Indian spear, *c.*1800

Decorative balls

Double-edged, triangular head

The wickedly sharp, triangular point of this spear would have been driven through the light armour of Indian warriors with relative ease. The spearhead is secured to the shaft by means of a flange. The mounts are in silver and probably indicate that it had a possible ceremonial role, perhaps as the weapon of a royal guard. Indian cavalry also carried spears of this great length, and they were used primarily as lances.

DATE	c.1800
ORIGIN	INDIAN
LENGTH	233.2cm (91.8in)

Indian spear, *c.*1800

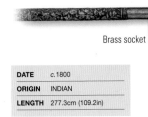

Brass socket

Long spike

DATE	c.1800
ORIGIN	INDIAN
LENGTH	277.3cm (109.2in)

Indian infantry of the early 19th century would have faced British and European forces with this simple weapon. Against disciplined musket and artillery fire, it would have been quite useless, although if a warrior could get within close enough range of his opponent the extremely long spike would have been driven through an unarmoured Western military uniform with ease.

Indian javelin, *c.*1800

DATE	c.1800
ORIGIN	INDIAN
LENGTH	228cm (89.8in)

This javelin has a very long, iron shaft with a needle-like spiked end. It was probably carried by a horseman and used very much like a traditional cavalry lance. Although Indian armies tended to be composed mainly of infantry, the use of cavalry was not uncommon and these long polearms would have been very effective at charging massed ranks of foot-soldiers.

Indian trident, *c.*1800

Trident spikes

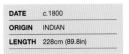

DATE	c.1800
ORIGIN	INDIAN
LENGTH	92.5cm (36.4in)

The trident has great religious significance in the Hindu faith and is depicted as the favoured weapon of Lord Shiva, "the Destroyer". It was probably most effective at pulling down a horseman and the two spikes were used to finish off an opponent. It could also be employed to trap an enemy's blade.

Indian battle-axe, *c.*1800

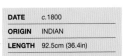

Head for deflecting blows

Tubular iron shaft

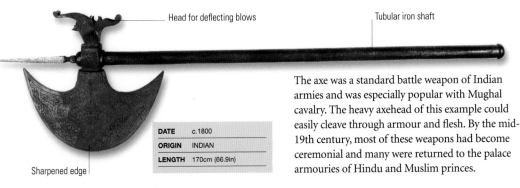

Sharpened edge

DATE	c.1800
ORIGIN	INDIAN
LENGTH	170cm (66.9in)

The axe was a standard battle weapon of Indian armies and was especially popular with Mughal cavalry. The heavy axehead of this example could easily cleave through armour and flesh. By the mid-19th century, most of these weapons had become ceremonial and many were returned to the palace armouries of Hindu and Muslim princes.

Weapons of South-east Asia

The variety of hilted weapons in South-east Asia is surprisingly large; and many are peculiar to certain distinct areas and cultures. One sword that is common throughout this region is the kris or keris, a sword design that appears to have no imitators and comprises an unusual, hand-forged blade. The Burmese dha and the Naga dao also bear a passing resemblance to the traditional Japanese sword.

Malayan spear, *c.*1800

Silver ferrule

Steel head

Traditionally, Malayan spears had wooden or steel heads – the wooden heads were used for throwing and the steel heads for thrusting. The best examples are beautifully made and inlaid. This spear has a shaft carved to imitate bamboo.

DATE	c.1800
ORIGIN	MALAYAN
LENGTH	216.9cm (85.4in)

Philippine sword (kris), *c.*1850

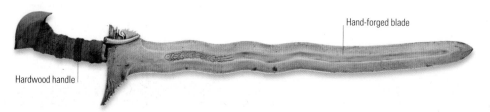

Hand-forged blade

Hardwood handle

Kris blades are straight and wavy in profile with a surface that is rough and coarse to the touch. This is the result of a complex and laborious process of manufacture that sees many different types of iron forged, re-forged and then folded on to each other. A distinctive and unique pattern is then produced for each sword. The surface is left unpolished.

DATE	c.1850
ORIGIN	PHILIPPINE
LENGTH	60cm (23.6in)

Burmese sword (dha), *c.*1850

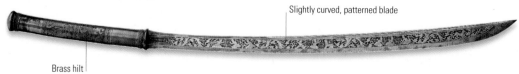

Slightly curved, patterned blade

Brass hilt

This is the national weapon of Burma and similar to a Japanese katana sword, although there is no comparison in terms of the quality. The blade is slightly curved, single-edged and terminates in a narrow point. The rounded brass handle is without a guard. Most dhas are carried in wooden sheaths, with some of them decorated in sheet silver.

DATE	c.1850
ORIGIN	BURMESE
LENGTH	85.5cm (33.7in)

Malayan sword (mandau), *c.*1850

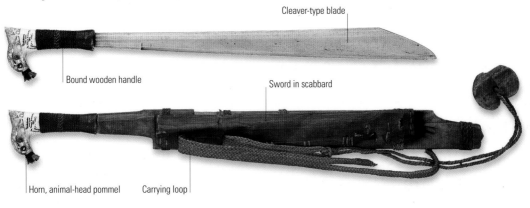

Cleaver-type blade

Bound wooden handle

Sword in scabbard

Horn, animal-head pommel

Carrying loop

DATE	*c.*1850
ORIGIN	MALAYAN
LENGTH	67cm (26.4in)

This Dayak head-hunter's sword has a finely carved, horn, animal-head pommel (they usually depict either demons or dragons), wooden grip and heavy, double-edged blade. The scabbard is made from two shaped, wooden boards (normally teak) and bound with cane and rattan. Pommels are frequently found with tufts of human hair, purportedly from slain opponents. A large number of these swords were brought back to Europe during the colonial period.

Malayan sword (mandau), *c.*1880

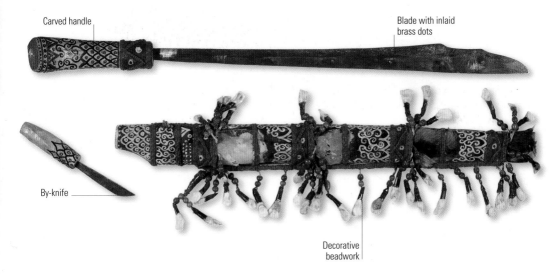

Carved handle

Blade with inlaid brass dots

By-knife

Decorative beadwork

DATE	*c.*1880
ORIGIN	MALAYAN
LENGTH	27cm (10.6in)

The mandau was a sword used by the Dayak peoples of Borneo (now modern-day Malaysia). The blade has an unusual profile, with one face slightly convex and the other slightly concave. The Dayaks were known as prolific head-hunters and the small knife that accompanies this sword was said to have been used to clean heads taken from the enemy. It is likely that the blade would have been used in a chopping motion in the manner of a machete.

Presentation swords

The presentation of a sword to an individual for either gallantry in the field of battle or loyal service to a monarch or state has a long history going back to the medieval period. Usually the sword is extensively decorated and in a number of cases, a presentation inscription is also added. During the Napoleonic Wars (1799–1815), the presentation sword became very popular, particularly in Britain, where the grateful nation regularly presented highly decorated and valuable swords to officers who had shown exceptional courage and leadership in the face of the enemy.

Royal Persian scimitar presented to Catherine the Great, *c.*1600

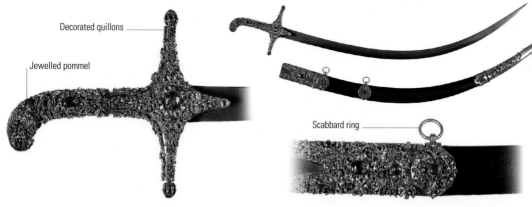

Decorated quillons

Jewelled pommel

Scabbard ring

This opulent scimitar was originally a Persian court sword commissioned by Abbas the Great, Shah of Persia (1571–1629). It is decorated with 1,295 diamonds and 50 karats of rubies, finished with an 11-karat emerald set into the hilt. The Ottoman Turkish government presented this sword to Empress Catherine the Great of Russia (1729–96).

DATE	c.1600
ORIGIN	PERSIAN, IRAN
LENGTH	100cm (39.4in)

British Patriotic Fund sword presented to James Bowen, *c.*1803

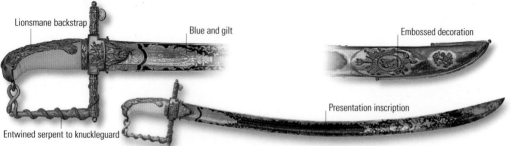

Lionsmane backstrap

Blue and gilt

Embossed decoration

Presentation inscription

Entwined serpent to knuckleguard

The Lloyds Patriotic Fund, comprising a group of London bankers, presented this sword to Lieutenant James Bowen of HMS *La Loire*, after a successful engagement with the French brig (a ship with two, square-rigged masts), Venteux. The hilt and scabbard mounts are richly covered in fire-gilt and the blade has extensive use of blue and gilt decoration.

DATE	c. 1803
ORIGIN	BRITISH
LENGTH	89cm (35in)

Corporation of the City sword presented to VA Lord Collingwood, *c.*1805

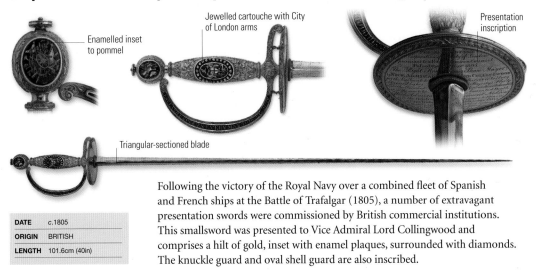

Enamelled inset to pommel

Jewelled cartouche with City of London arms

Presentation inscription

Triangular-sectioned blade

DATE	*c.*1805
ORIGIN	BRITISH
LENGTH	101.6cm (40in)

Following the victory of the Royal Navy over a combined fleet of Spanish and French ships at the Battle of Trafalgar (1805), a number of extravagant presentation swords were commissioned by British commercial institutions. This smallsword was presented to Vice Admiral Lord Collingwood and comprises a hilt of gold, inset with enamel plaques, surrounded with diamonds. The knuckle guard and oval shell guard are also inscribed.

King of Sweden, Charles XIV sword presented to Lord Bloomfield, *c.*1822

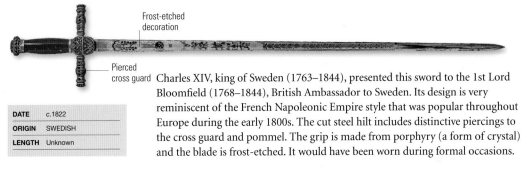

Frost-etched decoration

Pierced cross guard

DATE	*c.*1822
ORIGIN	SWEDISH
LENGTH	Unknown

Charles XIV, king of Sweden (1763–1844), presented this sword to the 1st Lord Bloomfield (1768–1844), British Ambassador to Sweden. Its design is very reminiscent of the French Napoleonic Empire style that was popular throughout Europe during the early 1800s. The cut steel hilt includes distinctive piercings to the cross guard and pommel. The grip is made from porphyry (a form of crystal) and the blade is frost-etched. It would have been worn during formal occasions.

Legislature of Nova Scotia sword presented to Sir Fenwick Williams, 1856

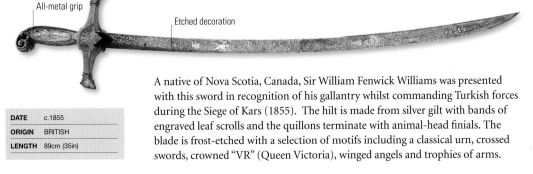

All-metal grip

Etched decoration

DATE	*c.*1855
ORIGIN	BRITISH
LENGTH	89cm (35in)

A native of Nova Scotia, Canada, Sir William Fenwick Williams was presented with this sword in recognition of his gallantry whilst commanding Turkish forces during the Siege of Kars (1855). The hilt is made from silver gilt with bands of engraved leaf scrolls and the quillons terminate with animal-head finials. The blade is frost-etched with a selection of motifs including a classical urn, crossed swords, crowned "VR" (Queen Victoria), winged angels and trophies of arms.

Civilian and regimental swords

One of the main driving forces behind the production of a civilian or regimental sword is the desire to produce a distinctive and memorable sword that can encompass either the history or the ethos of an organization or regiment. Regimental swords usually incorporate the regiment's badge or battle honours on both the hilt and the blade. Civilian swords are not designed to be used in battle, so they are normally of a lightweight form and are produced mainly for dress purposes.

Knights of Malta sword and scabbard, *c.*1800

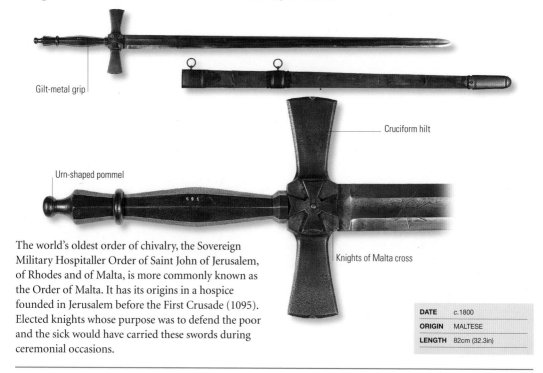

Gilt-metal grip

Cruciform hilt

Urn-shaped pommel

Knights of Malta cross

The world's oldest order of chivalry, the Sovereign Military Hospitaller Order of Saint John of Jerusalem, of Rhodes and of Malta, is more commonly known as the Order of Malta. It has its origins in a hospice founded in Jerusalem before the First Crusade (1095). Elected knights whose purpose was to defend the poor and the sick would have carried these swords during ceremonial occasions.

DATE	c.1800
ORIGIN	MALTESE
LENGTH	82cm (32.3in)

British Coldstream Guards officer's sword, 1854 Pattern

Regimental badge

The Coldstream Guards is the oldest serving regiment in the British Army and was founded by Oliver Cromwell (1599–1658) in 1650. A specific regimental sword was issued in 1854 and includes a regimental badge in the middle of the hilt cartouche.

DATE	1854
ORIGIN	BRITISH
LENGTH	109cm (42.9in)

British officer's sword, the Border Regiment, *c.*1870

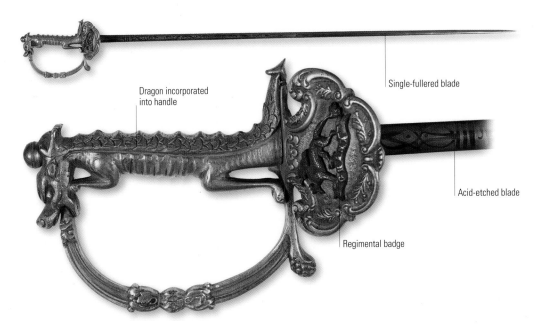

Dragon incorporated into handle

Single-fullered blade

Acid-etched blade

Regimental badge

DATE	c.1870
ORIGIN	BRITISH
LENGTH	85cm (33.5in)

This extraordinary sword was carried by British infantry officers of the Border Regiment during the 19th century. Their regimental badge featured a dragon and this has been incorporated into the hilt. This sword was for dress purposes rather than being used in battle.

Scottish Royal Company of Archers short sword, 1910

Cast brass handle

Spear point

Scabbard shoe or drag

Scabbard locket

DATE	1910
ORIGIN	SCOTTISH
LENGTH	56cm (22in)

The Royal Company of Archers was founded in 1676 and acted as a personal bodyguard to the monarch while in Scotland. This sword would have been carried by a bodyguard of below officer rank. The hilt is heavy cast brass with an acid-etched blade. This sword design was developed during the late 19th century: the influence of Gothic Victorian style is evident in the handle and cross guard.

Dress swords

The wearing of dress swords became popular after the demise of the rapier in the late 17th century, and was also hastened by the introduction of the smallsword soon after. These lightweight swords were not meant for battle conditions and their role was primarily one of dress and ornamentation. Military officers, diplomats and government officials all had the right to wear one and the range of designs is simply enormous.

English dress sword, *c.*1790

Dish guard

Trefoil blade

The rather distinctive hilt styling of this sword is very similar to designs manufactured by Matthew Boulton (1728–1809), a sword maker and engineer from Birmingham, England, who is famous for his collaboration with the steam-engine engineer, James Watt. In his earlier career, Boulton established a factory making cut steel and marcasite (imitation diamond) buttons and sword hilts.

DATE	c.1790
ORIGIN	ENGLISH
LENGTH	97cm (38.2in)

French dress sword, *c.*1800

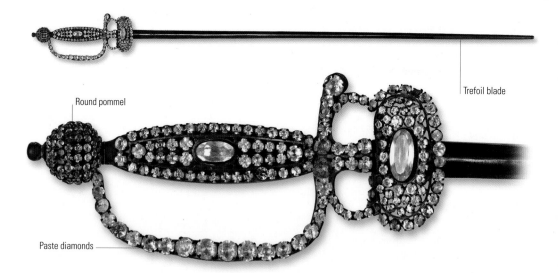

Trefoil blade

Round pommel

Paste diamonds

This dress sword represents the height of late 18th-century smallsword ornamentation. The hilt, guard and pommel are all encrusted with paste (artificial) diamonds. The sword would have been carried by a person of very high social rank and worn at only the most formal of occasions.

DATE	c.1800
ORIGIN	FRENCH
LENGTH	73.5cm (28.9in)

French infantry officer's dress sword, *c.*1800

Egyptian
motifs

Gilt-brass D-guard

Trefoil, or triangular, blade

DATE	c.1800
ORIGIN	FRENCH
LENGTH	92.5cm (36.4in)

The hilt styling of this dress sword is typically Napoleonic. The inlaid brass Egyptian motifs on the grip were clearly inspired by Napoleon's Egyptian campaigns (1798–1801). French Napoleonic smallswords had a wide range of pommel styles, including knight's-helmet, tri-lobed, urn-shaped, globular and lion's head.

French infantry officer's dress sword, *c.*1815

Slender blade with traces
of blue and gilt decoration

Mother-of-pearl

Neo-classical decoration to shell guard

DATE	c.1815
ORIGIN	FRENCH
LENGTH	95.5cm (37.6in)

This French dress sword of the First Empire (1804–14) has a mother-of-pearl grip and extensive Neo-classical decoration to the hilt, including stands of arms, a combed helmet and scrolling foliage. The canted, or angled, pommel was a popular style during the early 19th century. Although of dress appearance, this sword was probably also carried in the field.

French dress sword, *c.*1820

Plain, triangular blade

Decorated hilt

DATE	c.1820
ORIGIN	FRENCH
LENGTH	96cm (37.5in)

The opulence of post-Napoleonic France under King Louis XVIII (1755–1824) is evident in this dress sword, particularly the fantastical and classically inspired decoration to the gilt-brass hilt. The sword would have been carried by a senior military officer or official. The shell guard features mythical sea monsters and this might allude to a naval origin.

English court sword, *c.*1890

Flat-backed blade

Beaded brass decoration

DATE	c.1890
ORIGIN	ENGLISH
LENGTH	92.5cm (36.4in)

When attending the Court of Queen Victoria, both civilian and military officers carried a smallsword. This example is likely to have been carried by a civilian official and comprises a cast brass hilt with "beaded" decoration. Blades were normally flat-backed and plain, although some were etched with the royal crown and floral decoration.

Swords of the two World Wars

During the 19th century, the sword was a crucial part of any soldier's list of equipment. As the century progressed and the rapid firing rifle and pistol became the predominant first weapons of choice within the major armies of Europe and beyond, the use of the sword in battle became rather anachronistic. At the commencement of World War I in 1914, the sword had been relegated to a very marginal role and by 1939, it had become a purely decorative or dress item in officers' wardrobes.

German naval officer's sword, *c.*1914

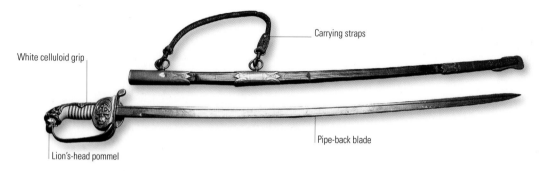

Carrying straps

White celluloid grip

Pipe-back blade

Lion's-head pommel

Officers' swords of the Imperial German Navy followed the Army's tradition of having a lion's-head pommel but differed in the design of the hilt guard. This took the form of a hinged, folding guard. Grips were normally made from ivory, bone or simulated ivory. Blades were often etched with nautical scenes, including crowned anchors and battleships.

DATE	*c.*1914
ORIGIN	GERMAN
LENGTH	90cm (35.5in)

Turkish infantry NCO's sword, *c.*1915

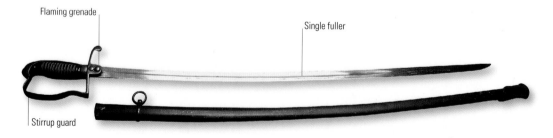

Flaming grenade

Single fuller

Stirrup guard

The Turkish military tended to emulate the sword designs of its Axis partners (Germany, Austria-Hungary, the Ottoman Empire and Bulgaria), with many Ottoman swords actually manufactured in Germany. This sword would have been carried by an NCO of sergeant rank and features a flaming grenade, probably signifying a grenadier or artillery regiment. The scabbard is black painted steel and has one carrying ring.

DATE	*c.*1915
ORIGIN	TURKISH
LENGTH	92.5cm (36.5in)

German Army officer's sword, *c.*1940

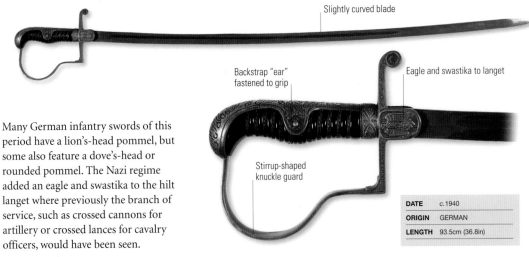

Slightly curved blade

Backstrap "ear" fastened to grip

Eagle and swastika to langet

Stirrup-shaped knuckle guard

Many German infantry swords of this period have a lion's-head pommel, but some also feature a dove's-head or rounded pommel. The Nazi regime added an eagle and swastika to the hilt langet where previously the branch of service, such as crossed cannons for artillery or crossed lances for cavalry officers, would have been seen.

DATE	c.1940
ORIGIN	GERMAN
LENGTH	93.5cm (36.8in)

German Luftwaffe sword, *c.* 1941

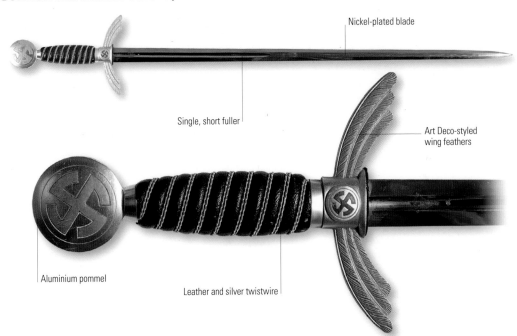

Nickel-plated blade

Single, short fuller

Art Deco-styled wing feathers

Aluminium pommel

Leather and silver twistwire

DATE	c.1941
ORIGIN	GERMAN
LENGTH	93.5cm (36.8in)

The styling of this sword was directly influenced by the Art Deco movement of the 1930s, and especially its obsession with speed and air flight. The downswept cross guard is typical Art Deco inspired design. The hilt and scabbard mounts are manufactured in aluminium. The Nazi swastika is depicted in an unusual form on the rounded pommel.

Marks and decorations

Swords and edged weapons have been marked and decorated since ancient times. From the crude engraving of a sword maker's name on a Roman gladius, to the bold lettering found on a Viking pattern-welded broadsword, and through to the fanciful blue and gilt styling of a Napoleonic sword blade, the need for recognition and decoration has always been paramount. Swords were also marked to ensure continuity of quality, and many are found with official stamps of approval. Identifying the marks of sword makers who practised their trade many centuries ago has become a difficult process, and many are now completely lost in the mists of time.

German knightly sword, *c.*1050

Slightly curved quillons

Wide fuller

Inscription

This is a typical broad-bladed knightly sword with a single, wide fuller. On one side of the blade there are remnants of an inscription "VERUSFVERUSF". Its meaning is unknown but could relate to the maker. The quillons are of square section, curved slightly downwards and ending in conical finials. The tang terminates with a large, mushroom-shaped pommel.

DATE	*c.*1050
ORIGIN	GERMAN
LENGTH	102.5cm (40.3in)

German knightly sword, *c.*1250–1300

Double-edged blade

Spear-point blade

Flared cross guard

This sword has a pronounced spear-point blade that would have had impressive cutting and thrusting capabilities. The blade is narrow and the consequent reduction in weight enabled the knight to wield the sword with flexibility and agility. The blade has a crude running wolf mark on both sides. This indicates manufacture in Passau, Germany, and was a common mark used by many sword makers in that region.

Wolf mark

DATE	*c.*1250–1300
ORIGIN	GERMAN
LENGTH	112cm (44.1in)

German knightly sword, *c.*1300

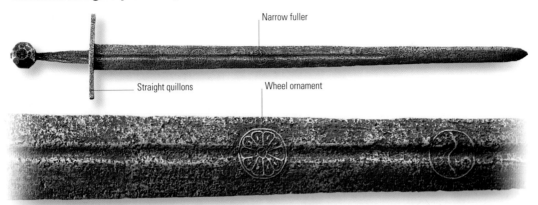

Narrow fuller

Straight quillons

Wheel ornament

DATE	c.1300
ORIGIN	GERMAN
LENGTH	112cm (44.1in)

The heavy double-edged, cutting blade of this sword would have been quite devastating when wielded on horseback. The blade has two inlaid silver wheel ornaments. Their meaning is unknown, although they might be armourer's marks or armourial symbols.

French/German knightly sword, *c.*1450

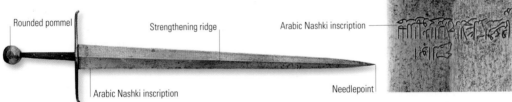

Rounded pommel

Strengthening ridge

Arabic Nashki inscription

Arabic Nashki inscription

Needlepoint

DATE	c.1450
ORIGIN	FRENCH/GERMAN
LENGTH	117.2cm (46.1in)

This European sword was captured by Ottoman (Turkish) forces and stored in a government armoury in Alexandria, Egypt. There is an Arabic Nashki inscription on the blade forte detailing its origins and new owner.

N. European Halberd, *c.*1450

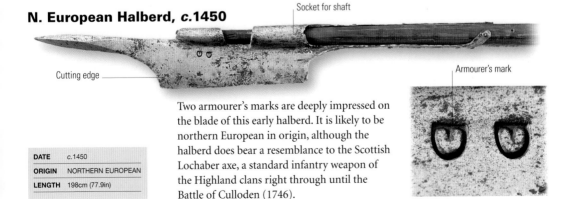

Socket for shaft

Cutting edge

Armourer's mark

DATE	c.1450
ORIGIN	NORTHERN EUROPEAN
LENGTH	198cm (77.9in)

Two armourer's marks are deeply impressed on the blade of this early halberd. It is likely to be northern European in origin, although the halberd does bear a resemblance to the Scottish Lochaber axe, a standard infantry weapon of the Highland clans right through until the Battle of Culloden (1746).

German hand-and-a-half sword, *c.*1520

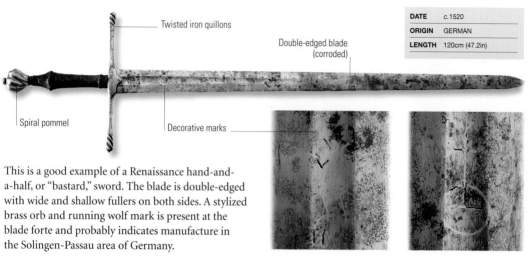

Twisted iron quillons

Double-edged blade
(corroded)

Spiral pommel

Decorative marks

DATE	c.1520
ORIGIN	GERMAN
LENGTH	120cm (47.2in)

This is a good example of a Renaissance hand-and-a-half, or "bastard," sword. The blade is double-edged with wide and shallow fullers on both sides. A stylized brass orb and running wolf mark is present at the blade forte and probably indicates manufacture in the Solingen-Passau area of Germany.

German halberd, *c.*1570

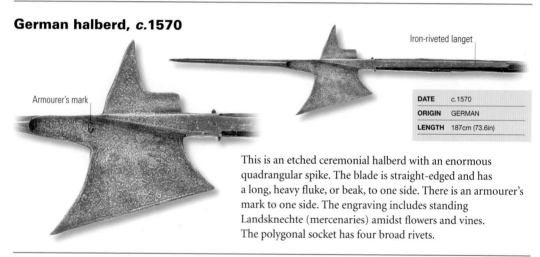

Iron-riveted langet

Armourer's mark

DATE	c.1570
ORIGIN	GERMAN
LENGTH	187cm (73.6in)

This is an etched ceremonial halberd with an enormous quadrangular spike. The blade is straight-edged and has a long, heavy fluke, or beak, to one side. There is an armourer's mark to one side. The engraving includes standing Landsknechte (mercenaries) amidst flowers and vines. The polygonal socket has four broad rivets.

German rapier, *c.*1600

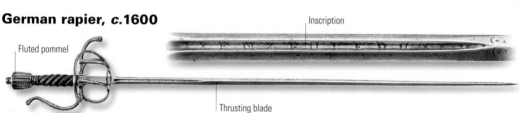

Inscription

Fluted pommel

Thrusting blade

The simple yet functional hilt design of this rapier indicates a probable German origin. Although the hilt is German, the blade is Spanish in origin and inscribed with the words "In Toledo" within the central fuller. Toledo, in central Spain, was an important manufacturing centre for sword blades, and noted for their exceptional quality and were exported throughout Europe.

DATE	c.1600
ORIGIN	GERMAN
LENGTH	106.5cm (41.9in)

Dutch "Walloon" broadsword, *c.1660*

Pierced dish guard

Double-edged blade with short fuller

Running wolf mark of Passau

DATE	c.1660
ORIGIN	DUTCH
LENGTH	109cm (42.9in)

This style of north European broadsword is commonly known as a "Walloon" type and has its origins in the Netherlands. The blade displays the running wolf mark of Passau, Germany, and a crowned "P". There are also impressed inspection marks for the city of Amsterdam on the blade forte. The hilt is constructed in iron, with a heart-shaped and pierced, double-shell guard. It retains the original iron twistwire to the grip.

German broadsword, *c.1695*

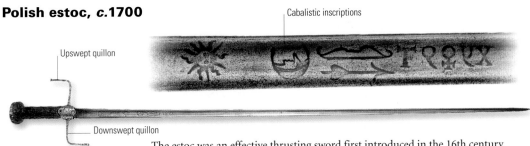

Widely spaced hilt bars

Engraved decoration

Double-shell guard

DATE	c.1695
ORIGIN	GERMAN
LENGTH	87cm (34.2in)

The curved blade of this broadsword has an unusual and rare depiction of a 17th-century horse race. There are 15 numbered riders, each designated by their individual names. The blade features crescent marks on both sides, a common symbol used by sword makers of this period. The open hilt has widely spaced bars, enabling the user to hold the grip with a large, leather, military riding gauntlet.

Polish estoc, *c.1700*

Cabalistic inscriptions

Upswept quillon

Downswept quillon

DATE	c.1700
ORIGIN	POLISH
LENGTH	158cm (62.2in)

The estoc was an effective thrusting sword first introduced in the 16th century. During the 16th and 17th centuries, it was adopted by Austrian and Polish hussars. This example has a long, narrow blade etched with depictions of the sun, moon, crossed sabres, bow and arrow, and cabalistic (mystical) inscriptions that were thought to bring luck to the owner of the sword.

German sword, *c.*1700

Multi-fullered

Horn grip | Engraved motto

The blade of this sword is engraved with the motto NO ME SAQUES SIN RAZON–NO ME ENTRAINES SEN HONOR. Literally translated, it means: "Do not draw me without reason. Do not sheath me without honour". This is a common motto found on many European swords of the 18th and 19th centuries.

DATE	*c.*1700
ORIGIN	GERMAN
LENGTH	80.5cm (31.7in)

Venetian schiavona, *c.*1700

Armourer's mark

Cage-like basket hilt

This is a very fine Venetian schiavona sword with typical complex basket hilt and cat's-head pommel. There is only one small armourer's mark on the blade that cannot be identified. This is the case with many marks of this period, where armourers or sword makers used a number of sometimes obscure symbols to mark their work. Unfortunately, time has erased all knowledge of who these people were.

Impressed mark

DATE	*c.*1700
ORIGIN	VENETIAN
LENGTH	107.5cm (42.3in)

Spanish cup-hilt rapier, *c.*1700

The blade of this Spanish cup-hilt rapier is clearly engraved with the signature of Abraham Stamm, a member of a noted Solingen (German) family of sword makers. They were established in the late 16th century and continued production until the 1920s.

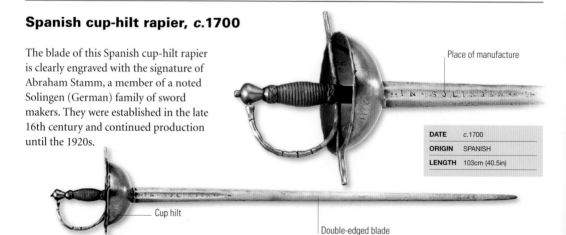

Place of manufacture

DATE	*c.*1700
ORIGIN	SPANISH
LENGTH	103cm (40.5in)

Cup hilt

Double-edged blade

German hunting sword, *c.*1740

The quality of this hunting sword is quite exceptional. The slightly curved, double-fullered blade is etched on both sides with flowers and tendrils. The whale ivory grip is thought to be an earlier piece (*c.*1660) and comprises sculptured figures of hunting dogs fighting a bear and a male goat. The pommel and open shell guard are gilt brass. The ivory carving is attributed to the Maucher family of ivory sculptors, who worked in Germany during the late 17th century.

Carved ivory grip

Open work shell guard

DATE	c.1740
ORIGIN	GERMAN
LENGTH	78cm (30.7in)

Spanish cup-hilt rapier, 1769

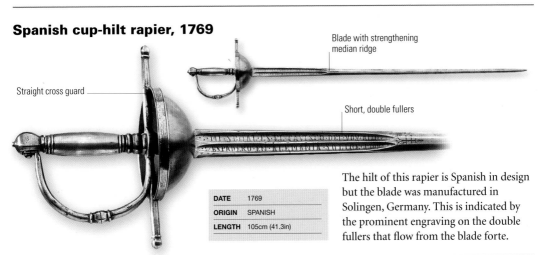

Blade with strengthening median ridge

Straight cross guard

Short, double fullers

The hilt of this rapier is Spanish in design but the blade was manufactured in Solingen, Germany. This is indicated by the prominent engraving on the double fullers that flow from the blade forte.

DATE	1769
ORIGIN	SPANISH
LENGTH	105cm (41.3in)

Spanish broadsword, 1774

Wide, broadsword blade

Large, plain shell guard

Tightly bound twistwire

DATE	1774
ORIGIN	SPANISH
LENGTH	106cm (41.7in)

The Spanish military began issuing officially approved pattern swords from the late 18th century. This cavalry trooper's sword has been engraved with the date of manufacture or issue and *"Por El Rey Carlos III"*. This refers to King Carlos III of Spain (1716–1788).

Glossary

Aikuchi Type of Japanese dagger with a handle but no guard.

Antennae dagger Dagger with a pommel that is shaped into a pair of curved arms.

Atlatl Hunting tool that uses the leverage of the human arm to project a flint dart or spear at great speed against a moving target.

Back-edge The unsharpened edge on a single-edged weapon.

Backpiece Metal plate at the back of the grip that meets the pommel.

Backsword Straight or curved, single-edged broadsword.

Bagh nakh The Indian "tiger claw". A crossbar pierced for the fingers fits over the knuckles; curved blades are attached and hidden inside the palm.

Baldric Belt (leather or cloth) worn across the shoulder as a carrier for a sword.

Ballock (kidney) dagger A medieval form of dagger with a hilt shaped like the male genitalia.

Baluster-turning Method of decorating metalwork, commonly used in the 17th century to decorate stiletto hilts and ricassos.

Bardiche Long poleaxe used in medieval or Renaissance Europe.

Baselard Type of dagger or short sword with a hilt shaped like a capital "I".

Basket hilt Large sword guard that was designed to enclose the hand through a series of interconnecting hilt bars.

Bastard sword Also known as the "hand-and-a-half" sword. It was a long, straight-bladed sword first introduced in the 15th century. Used with one hand and fingers of free hand for extra grip.

Bayonet Dagger or fighting knife designed to be fitted onto the end of a firearm to convert it to a stabbing weapon for close-combat.

Bearing swords Large, two-handed broadswords carried during public ceremonies to signify the authority of the individual, state or institution.

Belt frog A leather or cloth sleeve in which a sword scabbard is held.

Bhuj Indian weapon comprised of a stout, single-edged cutting blade attached to an axe haft. Also called a "gandasa".

Bichwa Short Indian dagger with a long, narrow looped grip to which is attached a narrow undulating blade.

Bidr (qum) A form of Arabic blade patterning that results in a gravel effect – mainly applied to the blades of talwars.

Bill A polearm with various projecting spikes or flukes at the end of a shaft. It was especially popular in England during the 16th century.

Blarka ngirdi Style of southeast Asian pattern-welding, producing a blade with the distinctive "palm-leaf" design.

Boar sword Introduced during the 14th century. A double-edged sword with stiffened blade and spear point. Designed to withstand the power of a charging boar or large animal.

Bowie knife Large fighting knife said to have been invented *c.*1827.

Broadsword Straight, wide and single-edged sword. Popular from the 17th–18th centuries. Often attached to a basket hilt.

Buckler Small, rounded defensive shield worn on the wrist and used in conjunction with a sword. Common in Europe from the 13th–17th centuries.

Butt The end of the handle of an edged weapon, having no pommel.

Byknife Small utility knife made as a matching companion to a sword or dagger, held in a small sleeve built into the scabbard of the larger weapon.

Cartouche Oblong or oval space, surrounded by scrollwork, often with a dedication or image in the centre. It usually appears on the pommel, hilt or blade of a sword.

Chape Top of the scabbard shoe or drag.

Chilanum Indian dagger with a slightly curved blade and a hilt incorporating a pommel section with broad narrow arms.

Choil Unsharpened, rounded cut-out section of the blade on some knives, separating the sharp edge from the ricasso, or cut into the ricasso itself.

Cinquedea Wide-bladed Italian short sword popular in Italy during the late 15th and 16th centuries. The name derived from the "five fingers" width of the blade.

Claymore Two-handed Scottish "great sword" of the 15th–17th centuries.

ABOVE Italian cinqueda, *c.*1500

Clipped point Blade type with short, upturned point.

Colichemarde blade Sword blade of the 17th and 18th centuries. It is noted for its triangular profile. Designed with wide and long forte for added strength.

Coronal Crown-shaped metal cap (of three or more metal prongs) at the end of a lance. It was used during a joust to catch on to an opponent's shield.

Coutiaus a pointe "Stabbing knife" – a medieval term used to describe a narrow, stiff-bladed dagger designed specifically for stabbing with the point.

Coutiaus a tailler "Cutting knife" – a medieval term used to describe a wider bladed dagger, often single-edged.

Cross guard An extended bar across the bottom of the hilt to prevent slippage of the hand. It also protects the hand from sword blows.

Cross-hilt Hilt incorporating a simple cross guard. Also called "cruciform" hilt.

Cuirassier Mounted cavalry soldiers of the 17th–19th centuries who wore a cuirass breastplate and a helmet. They were armed with firearms as well as a sword.

Cultellus Medieval Latin for "dagger".

Cup hilt Round hilt cup protecting the sword hand on a rapier.

Cutlass Short sword with straight or slightly curved, single-edged blade. It normally refers to a sword used on board a ship.

Cutler Sword or edged-weapon maker.

Dadao Chinese heavy sword. Its name means "big knife". It has a large, machete-like blade, based on the style of agricultural knives.

Daisho Pair of Japanese swords including the katana and wakizashi.

Dao Straight-bladed sword of the Naga peoples of Assam, north-east India. The blade is squared off at the point.

Damascening The process of inlaying soft metal into a hard metal to produce intricate patterns.

Dirk A small, typically Scottish dagger. Used as a backup to the broadsword, and carried on a waistbelt.

Doru Traditional spear of the hoplites, with a large, leaf-shaped spearhead.

Dudgeon dagger Late Anglo-Scottish ballock knife of the 17th century, the handle of which was carved from a single piece of box-tree root or "dudgeon".

Ear Securing strap leading from the hilt backstrap that is riveted into the grip.

Ear dagger Form of dagger that probably originated in Spain in the 14th century. Characterized by the two large disks that make up the pommel section.

Épée Duelling sword used by fencers.

Ersatz bayonet Emergency bayonet, often rudimentary, made to fit a rifle for which it was not originally intended.

Escutcheon Small shield-shaped plate mounted on an object, usually to display the coat of arms or device of the owner.

Estoc A forerunner to the rapier, and designed to puncture plate armour or cut the links of chain mail. It featured a long, triangular and heavily pointed blade.

Falcata Sword of the ancient Celts, with a kukri-type, single-edged blade.

Falchion Short sword with a broad, slightly curved blade. It was popular during the medieval and Renaissance periods and used mainly by archers and infantry soldiers.

False edge Usually seen on longer, single-edged swords. The final section of the blade was sharpened to make penetration and withdrawal easier.

Ferrule Metal protective band or short tube at the bottom of sword hilt, fitted just above the cross guard.

ABOVE Saudi Arabian janbiyya/khanjar, early 20th century.

497

BELOW North European poleaxe, *c.*1500

Fire-gilding A decorative technique for covering iron, steel, copper, silver or bronze with a thin layer of gold.

Fluke Pointed projections at end of a polearm blade.

Flyssa A heavy-bladed sword. It was the traditional sword of the Kabyles tribe of Algeria. The sword was in use until the 19th century.

Foible The upper, weaker half of a sword blade.

Foil Modern fencing sword with a quadrangular blade and blunted tip.

Forte The lower, stronger half of a sword blade.

Francisca axe Short, throwing axe used by Germanic tribes from around AD300.

Frog stud A small metal button or knob mounted onto a scabbard for fastening it securely into the "frog", a tab of leather mounted to a belt.

Fuller Straight and shallow ridges on a sword blade that provide flexibility and strength.

Ganja The narrow guard of the Southeast Asian kris.

Garniture (trousse) Set of carving tools, including knife and fork, found with hunting sword. Sheathed in a pocket within the scabbard alongside the main sword blade.

Gladius Ancient Roman double-edged, straight-bladed short sword, with a hilt of carved wood and a stout double-edged blade.

Glaive Polearm with single-edged blade. Sometimes fitted with small hook to dismount riders. Used from the 13th to the 16th centuries.

Granulation A form of decoration wherein a surface is ornamented with tiny closely-set beads or spheres.

Grip Part of the sword hilt grasped by the hand. Usually covered in either leather or metal, or a combination of both.

Guard Protective metal plate at the bottom of handle that protects the wearer's hand.

Haft Wooden pole/handle attached to both axes and polearms.

Halberd Polearm with cleaver-like blade and extended spike. It was used from the 16th to the 17th centuries.

Hamon Blade patterning on Japanese sword blades created by tempering.

Hanger Short infantry or hunting sword with a single-edged, curved or straight blade.

Hatchet point Cleaver-type end to blade point.

Hilt The area of a dagger, knife or sword that is held in the hand, usually comprising a pommel, a handle and some kind of guard for the hand.

Holbein dagger Type of dagger popular in Germany and Switzerland in the mid-16th century, having a wide double-edged blade and a wooden hilt shaped like a capital letter "I".

Hoplites Greek heavy infantry, formed from a citizen militia. They were armed with spears for use in the phalanx formation and they also carried a short sword.

Hunting sword Short sword with either curved or straight blade (some

with saw-back edges). Popular from the 17th century, they were used during the hunt to carve up the kill.

Hussar Lightly armoured horseman, who normally carried curved sabres. They were considered the elite soldiers of their time and usually wore ornate and decorative uniforms.

Jambiya Arabic for "dagger".

Javelin A lightweight throwing spear.

Jian Chinese sword with straight, double-edged blade.

Kard Persian for "knife".

Kastane National sword of Sri Lanka, with a short, curved blade and monster-head pommel. Blades are normally of European origin.

Katana Japanese longsword, larger than the wakizashi (short sword) but smaller than the tachi (two-handed sword). With a very slightly curved, single-edged blade. Used with either one or two hands.

Katar Form of push dagger common in India. Also called a "jamdhar".

Katzbalger Short sword of the 16th to the 17th centuries, with a figure-of-eight guard. It was popular with Landsknechte (mercenaries).

Khanda Indian sword of the Marathas. It has a distinctive broad blade that widens towards the tip. The hilt is of basket form with a long, spiked pommel.

Khanjar Arabic for "dagger".

Khanjarli Type of Indian dagger with a strongly recurved blade and a wide half-moon-shaped pommel.

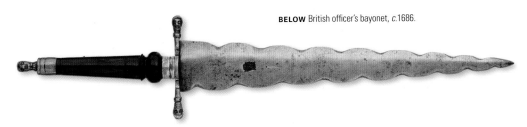

BELOW British officer's bayonet, *c.*1686.

Khepesh Extremely curved, single-edged sword of the ancient Egyptians and the favoured weapon of the Pharaohs.

Kilij Persian scimitar sword with pronounced flared point, or yelman.

Klewang Traditional, single-edged, machete-type sword from Indonesia.

Knuckle bow This is also known as the knuckle guard. Normally a thin, curved bar that extends from the hilt, designed to protect the hand from sword cuts.

Knurling Method of decoration involving a series of small beads, knobs, ridges or hatch-marks.

Koftgari Indo-Persian term for false or counterfeit damascening.

Kogai The Japanese byknife.

Kopis An ancient Greek short sword with a heavy, forward-curving blade for chopping or cleaving blows.

Kora National sword of Nepal and also used in northern India. It has a heavy blade that flares towards the tip.

Koshi-gatana "Waist-sword", a long Japanese dagger or shortsword with no guard, worn with the *tachi* (two-handed sword).

Kris Short sword or long dagger from Southeast Asia. It has a distinctive wavy blade that is forged from many different types of metal, giving a watered appearance.

Kukri Wide-bladed axe-like knife, the signature weapon of the Gurkha people of Nepal.

Lance A long cavalry spear used by mounted horsemen both in battle and during jousts or tournaments.

Landsknecht dagger A modern term referring to three distinct types of 16th-century European dagger: the "katzbalger" shortsword; a rondel dagger variation with a drooping guard; or an early type of ring-hilted dagger.

Langets A downward extension of the cross guard that fits into the scabbard and protects the sword. It also refers to a long metal strip attached to the shaft of a polearm.

Lochaber axe Scottish infantry polearm used from the 17th century. It has a wooden shaft with heavy axe blade similar to a bardiche.

Locket Metal fitting where the blade enters the scabbard.

Longsword A late medieval and early Renaissance broadsword which had a cruciform hilt and two-handed grip.

Lowland sword Scottish two-handed broadsword of the 16th century, similar to the claymore.

Main gauche Left-handed dagger used in conjunction with a rapier. It was a popular weapon in the 16th-century duel.

Mameluke Sword with curved scimitar-shaped blade.

Mandau National short sword/knife of the Dayak peoples of Borneo.

Mokume-gane "Wood-grain metal", a Japanese form of pattern-welding.

Mortuary sword English basket-hilted broadsword of the mid-17th century. The hilt is commonly decorated with human heads.

Mouthpiece Protective metal lip at the top of a scabbard.

Nagamaki Japanese two-handed polearm with a blade similar to that of a katana sword.

Navaja Type of folding fighting knife that originated on the Iberian peninsula in the 18th century.

Nimcha Single-handed sword used primarily in Morocco from the late 18th century onwards. It usually has forward-pointing quillons, and squared-off, "hooked" pommels.

Pappenheimer Military rapier of the 17th century. It was named after a German Field Marshal of the Thirty Years' War (1618–48).

Parry A defensive movement and the primary function of the parrying dagger.

Partizan Polearm with a broad, triangular blade and projections at its base. It was used from the 16th century.

Pas-d'âne Two curling arms that reach down to a dish guard – a common stylistic addition to smallswords.

ABOVE British light cavalry sword, *c.* 1788

Pata Indian sword, with the handle encased by a gauntlet-like cover. Traditionally used by specialized infantrymen against armoured cavalry.

Pattern welding Forging of several different types of metal that are twisted to form a pattern on a sword blade.

Peshkabz Type of Indo-Persian dagger with a straight or recurved blade of T-section.

Pike Long infantry spear with a small head mounted on a wooden shaft. It was popular from the medieval period to the 17th century.

Pilum Ancient Roman heavy javelin, normally with a triangular head.

Pipe-back blade Type of blade found on 18th- and 19th-century military bayonets and swords, where the unsharpened back of the blade is given a rounded or tubular cross-section.

Plug bayonet The earliest form of bayonet – a dagger, usually with a double-edged blade, fitted with a handle that tapers down to a very narrow end.

Polearm Close-combat infantry weapon comprising a wooden shaft upon which is placed a bladed head.

Poleaxe Short infantry polearm with combination of axe, hammer or spiked head. It was common during the medieval period.

Pommel A metal weight at the top of the hilt. Acts as a counter-balance for the sword and, when screwed into the tang, ensures that the sword is solid, without any looseness or wobble.

Pugio Short wide leaf-bladed dagger of the ancient Romans.

Pulwar Single-handed Afghan sword. Heavily inspired by Indian tulwar designs, the hilt features two short quillons turned to face the direction of the blade.

BELOW Indian Mughal dagger with knucklebow, c.1625

Push dagger Dagger having a grip set at a right angle to the blade, so that the weapon is held in the fist with the blade projecting along the line of the arm.

Quillon Post-medieval term referring to one of the arms of the cross guard of a sword or dagger.

Rapier Thrusting sword of the mid-16th and 17th centuries. It is noted for its long, narrow blade.

Ricasso Squared-off and flattened part of the sword blade near the hand guard. It was originally designed to allow a finger to hook around it to improve the user's grip.

Rondel A medieval term denoting any circular plate used to protect a part of the body.

Sabre Cavalry or infantry sword with a curved blade.

Sageo Cord for tying a Japanese Samurai sword scabbard into belt.

Saif Arabic word loosely translated to mean "sword". It is usually attributed to curved sabres.

Saw-back blade A blade, the back of which is toothed like a saw though otherwise unsharpened.

Saya Japanese sword scabbard.

Scabbard Sheath in which a sword blade is placed.

Scramasax (seax, sax) One of the primary edged weapons used by most north and west Europeans during the Early Medieval Period. Made in a wide range of sizes, from extremely long sword types (langseax) to very short ones (handseax).

Schiavona Renaissance, double-edged broadsword with a complex cage-like hilt. It was associated with Dalmatian mercenaries of the 16th to the 18th centuries.

Scimitar Middle Eastern sabre with curved blade.

Scutum The large, rectangular shield carried by Roman legionaries. It was made of wood and calfskin, with a heavy, iron rim and centrepiece.

Seax Anglo-Saxon knife.

Seme Short sword used by the Maasai peoples of East Africa. Traditionally used to hunt lions, it features a wooden handle, with a scabbard covered with red rawhide and tipped with a coin.

Seppa Copper spaces fitted on each side of a Japanese Samurai sword guard.

Shamshir A Persian sabre with a curved blade.

Shell guard A small rounded plate of metal incorporated into the guard of some types of sword and dagger to give additional protection to the hand.

Shin-gunto Japanese sword based on the Samurai tachi. Introduced during the 1930s and normally manufactured with machine-made blades.

Shoe Protective metal extension at the end of the scabbard.

ABOVE British L1A3 bayonet for L1A1 SLR, c.1957.

Shotel Large, sickle-like sword from Abyssinia. It features a simple, wooden hilt with no guard and a curved blade.

Shoulder This is the unsharpened cutting edge of a blade near the hand guard and is designed to protect the user's hand if it slips over the guard.

Side-ring A small ring of metal mounted on the outside of the cross guard of most 16th- and early 17th-century parrying daggers.

Sgian dubh (skean dhu) Small knife worn with formal Scottish Highland dress from the 19th-century onwards.

Smallsword Light, one-handed sword developed from the rapier. It was common from the late 17th century and often worn for dress purposes. Designed primarily for thrusting.

Socket bayonet A bayonet generally with no hilt, just a narrow tube or socket of metal, onto which is attached the narrow, often triangular section blade by means of a short curved arm.

Sosun Pattah Traditional form of Indian sword with forward-curving blade.

Spadroon Light infantry sword designed for cutting and thrusting. Introduced in Europe and carried from the mid-18th century.

Spatha Ancient Roman, straight, double-edged sword with a long blade.

Spear point Sharpened point of a sword that resembles a spearhead.

Spiculum Ancient Roman throwing spear or javelin.

Spontoon European polearm of the 17th and 18th centuries, with a spear-shaped head. Used primarily by officers and NCOs as a symbolic or rallying weapon on the battlefield.

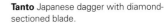

BELOW English mortuary hilted sword, c.1650

Stiletto (stylet) Small stabbing dagger dating from the end of the 16th century.

Stirrup-hilted Knuckle guard of sword hilt that resembles a horse's stirrup. Popular on cavalry swords (particularly British) from the late 18th century.

Swept hilt Type of rapier hilt guard formed by a number of intertwining bars that "swept" around the hand. Introduced during the late 16th century.

Sword bayonet Very long type of bayonet having a sword hilt and wide cutting blade.

Tachi Long Japanese Samurai sword which is worn slung over the shoulder.

Takouba Traditional sword of the Saharan Tuareg tribe. Typically, it has a brass grip due to their owners' traditional aversion to touching iron. It usually features three or more fullers and a rounded point.

Talwar Wide-bladed Indian sword with distinctive dish pommel and one-piece grip of lozenge-shaped cross-section.

Tang Unsharpened end of the blade, over which fits the hilt or handle.

Tang button The end of the tang that is hammered (peened) over the top of the pommel. It adds stability and strength. Some tang buttons are screwed into the pommel and attached to the tang.

Tanto Japanese dagger with diamond-sectioned blade.

Targe Old English word for a concave shield. It was traditionally carried by Scottish Highlanders alongside their broadsword. Highlanders carried targe shields throughout the 17th century.

Telek The northwest African arm dagger. Also called a "gosma".

Trefoil Three-sided or triangular blade most commonly seen on smallswords.

Trumbash The sickle-knife of the Mangbetu people of the Congo.

Tsuba The guard, usually round or oval and beautifully decorated, of most Japanese daggers and swords.

Tuck (estoc in French) Late medieval variation of the longsword with strengthened point to penetrate plate armour.

Ukiran The carved handle of the kris.

Volute A spiral or circular motif often found in 16th-century weapons.

Wakizashi Japanese Samurai short sword. It is normally carried in combination with a katana.

Wootz Indian method of patterning a sword blade with iron ore, charcoal and glass.

Yataghan Ottoman (Turkish) sword with a forward-curving blade.

Yelman The flared end of a Persian sword blade which gave the blade greater heft or weight when cutting. It is found on Persian kilij swords.

Yoroi doshi Specially-thickened armour-piercing Japanese dagger or tanto.

Xiphon The short sword carried by the Greek hoplites. It had a large, leaf-shaped blade and was only used after the spear had been discarded.

ABOVE Coorg Tamil knife (pichangatti), mid-19th century.

Further information

BELOW Austrian infantry officer's sword, *c.* 1837

BIBLIOGRAPHY

Anglo, Sydney, *The Martial Arts of Renaissance Europe* (Yale, London, 2000).

Annis, P.G.W., *Naval Swords. British and American Naval Edged Weapons 1660–1815* (Arms and Armour Press, London, 1970).

Aylward, J.D., *The Smallsword in England* (Hutchinson, London, 1960).

Blair, Claude, *European and American Arms* (Batsford, London, 1962).

Bosanquet, H.T., *The Naval Officer's Sword* (H.M.S.O., London, 1955).

Burton, Richard, *The Book of the Sword* (Dover Publications Inc., New York, 1987).

Castle, Egerton, *Schools and Masters of Fence, from the Middle Ages to the End of the Eighteenth Century* (G. Bell, London, 1910).

Coe, Michael D.; Connolly, Peter; Harding, Anthony; Harris and others, *Swords and Hilt Weapons* (Multimedia Books Ltd., London, 1989).

Dolinek, Vladimir and Durdik, Jan, *The Encyclopedia of European Historical Weapons* (Hamlyn, London, 1993).

Elgood, Robert, *Hindu Weapons and Ritual: Arms and Armour from India 1400–1865* (Eburon, Delft, 2005).

Elgood, Robert ed., *Islamic Arms and Armour* (Scolar, London, 1979).

Evangelista, Nick, *The Encyclopedia of the Sword* (Greenwood Press, London, 1995).

Foulkes, Charles and Hopkinson, E. C., *Sword, Lance and Bayonet* (Arms and Armour Press, London, 1967).

Frey, Edward, *The Kris: Mystical Weapon of the Malay World* (Images of Asia) (Oxford University Press, New York, Dec 1989).

Gardner, G.B., *Keris and Other Malay Weapons* (Progressive Publishing, Singapore, 1936).

Gilkerson, William, *Boarders Away: With Steel-Edged Weapons and Polearms 1626–1826* (Andrew Mowbray Publishers, Lincoln RI, 1991).

Gyngell, D.S.H., *Armourer's Marks* (Cambridge University Press, New York, 1963).

Hayward, J.F., *Swords and Daggers* (H.M.S.O., London, 1964).

Holmes, Richard ed., *Weapon: A Visual History of Arms and Armour* (Dorling Kindersley, London, 2008).

Hutton, Capt. Alfred, *The Sword and the Centuries* (Grant Richards, London, 1901).

Johnson, Thomas M., and Bradach, Wilfrid, *Third Reich Edged Weapons Accouterments* (Johnson Reference Book, Fredericksburg, 1978).

Kulinsky, A.N., *European Edged Weapons* (Atlant, St Petersburg, 2003).

May, W.E. and Annis, P.G., *Swords for Sea Service* (H.M.S.O., London, 1970).

May, W.E. and Kennard, A.N., *Naval Swords and Firearms* (H.M.S.O., London, 1962).

National Trust for Scotland, Culloden, *The Swords and the Sorrows* (NTS Trading Company, Edinburgh, 1996).

Neumann, George C., *Swords and Blades of the American Revolution* (Rebel Publishing Co., Inc., Texarkana TX, 1991).

Norman, A.V.B., *The Rapier and Smallsword, 1460–1820* (Arms and Armour Press, London, 1980).

Oakeshott, R. Ewart, *European Weapons and Armour* (Lutterworth, London, 1980).

Oakshott, Ewart, *Records of the Medieval Sword* (The Boydell Press, New York, 1991).

Peterson, Harold, *The American Sword 1775–1945* (Riling Arms Books, Philadelphia, PA, 1996).

BELOW Burmese dha sword, *c.*1850

502

ABOVE French smallsword, *c.*1720

Peterson, Harold L., *American Knives: The First History and Collector's Guide* (Charles Scribner, New York, 1958).

Peterson, Harold Leslie, *Daggers and Fighting Knives of the Western World* (Dover, Mineola, 1968).

Reid, William, *Arms Through the Ages* (Harper & Row, London, 1976).

Robinson, H. Russell, *Japanese Arms and Armour* (Crown, New York, 1969).

Robson, Brian, *Swords of the British Army. The Regulation Patterns, 1788 to 1914* (National Army Museum, London, 1996).

Southwick, Leslie, *London Silver-Hilted Swords* (Royal Armouries, Leeds, 2001).

Stone, George Cameron, *A Glossary of the Construction, Decoration and Use of Arms and Armor in all Countries and in all Times* (Southworth Press, Portland, 1961).

Thompson, Leroy, *Commando Dagger: The Complete Illustrated History of the Fairbairn-Sykes Fighting Knife* (Paladin Press, Boulder, 1985).

Thompson, Logan, *Daggers and Bayonets* (Paladin Press, Boulder, 1999).

Tirri, Anthony C., *Islamic Weapons, Maghrib to Moghul* (Indigo, USA, 2003).

Turnbull, Stephen, *Samurai – The World of the Warrior* (Osprey, London, 2006).

Valentine, Eric, *Rapiers* (Stackpole Books, Harrisburg, PA, 1970).

Van Zonneveld, Albert G., *Traditional Weapons of the Indonesian Archipelago* (C. Zwartenkot, Amsterdam, 2002).

Various authors, *Swords and Hilt Weapons* (Weidenfield and Nicolson, London, 1989).

Veleanu, Mircea, *Antique Swords and Daggers* (Schiffer Publishing, 2007).

Wagner, Eduard, *Cut and Thrust Weapons* (Spring Books, London, 1967).

Wallace, John, *Scottish Swords and Dirks, An Illustrated Reference Guide to Scottish Edged Weapons* (Arms and Armour Press, London, 1970).

Wilkinson, Frederick, *Swords and Daggers, An Illustrated Reference Guide for Collectors* (Arms and Armour Press, London, 1985).

Wilkinson, Frederick, *Swords and Daggers* (Ward Lock and Co., Ltd, London, 1967).

Wilkinson-Latham, John, *British Cut and Thrust Weapons* (David and Charles Publishers, Newton Abbott, 1971).

Wilkinson-Latham, John, *British Cut and Thrust Weapons* (David and Charles Publishers, Newton Abbott, 1971).

Wilkinson-Latham, John, *British Military Swords from 1800 to the present day* (Crown Publishers, Inc, New York, 1967).

Wilkinson-Latham, R.J., *Pictorial History of Swords and Bayonets* (Ian Allan, London, 1973).

Withers, Harvey, *British Military Swords 1786–1912. The Regulation Patterns. An Illustrated Price Guide for Collectors* (Studio Jupiter Military Publishing, Sutton Coldfield, 2003).

Withers, Harvey, *World Swords 1400–1945. An Illustrated Price Guide for Collectors* (Studio Jupiter Military Publishing, Sutton Coldfield, 2006).

ABOVE Landsknecht-type sword, *c.*1500

MUSEUMS OF INTEREST

UNITED KINGDOM
The British Museum
Great Russell Street
London, WC1B 3DG
www.britishmuseum.co.uk

The Fitzwilliam Museum
Trumpington Street
Cambridge , CB2 1RB
www.fitzmuseum.cam.ac.uk

National Army Museum
Royal Hospital Road
Chelsea, London
SW3 4HT
www.national-army-
museum.ac.uk

National Museum of Scotland
Chambers Street
Edinburgh
EH1 1JF
www.nms.ac.uk

National War Museum
Edinburgh Castle
EH1 2NG
www.nms.ac.uk

The Royal Armouries, Leeds
Armouries Drive,
Leeds
LS10 1LT
www.royalarmouries.org

V & A South Kensington
Cromwell Road
London
SW7 2RL
www.vam.ac.uk

The Wallace Collection
Hertford House
Manchester Square
London
W1U 3BN
www.wallacecollection.org

Windsor Castle
Windsor
SL4 1NJ
www.royalcollection.org.uk

AUSTRIA
**Historisches Museum der
Stadt, Vienna**
A-1040 Wien
Karlsplatz
www.wienmuseum.at

Landeszenghaus, Graz
Abteilung Landeszeughaus
Herrengassse16
A-8010, Graz, Austria
www.zeughaus.at

Kunsthistorisches Museum
1010 Vienna
Maria Theresien-Platz
www.khm.at

BELGIUM
**Les Musée aux d'Art et
d'Histoire**
Parck du Cinquantenaire, 10
1000 Brussels
www.kmkg-mrah.be

DENMARK
Tojhusmet, Copenhagen
Tøjhusgade 3
DK-1214, Copenhagen K
www.thm.dk

FINLAND
National Museum of Finland
Mannerheimintie 34
Helsinki
www.nba.fi/en/nmf

FRANCE
Musée de l'Armée, Paris
Hôtel National des Invalides
129 Rue de Grenelle
75007 , Paris
www.invalides.org

Musée du Louvre, Paris
34, Rue du Louvre
75001, Paris
www.louvre.fr

GERMANY
**Historisches Museum,
Dresden**
Zwinger
Semperbau
D-01067
Dresden
www.skd-dresden.de

**Museum für Deutsche
Geschicte, Berlin**
Unter den Linden 2
10117, Berlin
www.dhm.de

**Württembergisches
Landesmuseum**
Altes Schloss
Schillerplatz 6
70173, Stuttgart
www.landesmuseum-
stuttgart.de

ITALY
Museo Nazionale, Florence
Piazzale degli Uffizi,
50122
Firenze
www.polomuseale.firenze.it

Stibbert Collection, Florence
Via Frederick Stibbert 26
50134 , Firenze
www.museostibbert.it

NETHERLANDS
Dutch Army Museum
Korte Geer 1, Delft
www.legermuseum.nl

NORWAY
Universitetets Oldsaksamling
Fredriks Gate 2
Oslo 0164
www.ukm.uio.no

POLAND
Wawel Armoury, Cracow
31-001 Kraków, Wawel 5
www.wawel.krakow.pl

SPAIN
**Armoury, Palacio Réal de
Madrid, Madrid**
Calle Bailén , 28071 Madrid
www.patrimonionacional.es

SWEDEN
Historiska Museet
Narvavägen 13–17
114 84
Stockholm
www.historiska.se

ABOVE South Italian main-gauche dagger, c.1650.

SWITZERLAND
Historischemuseum, Basel
Steinenberg 4, CH–4051
Basel
www.hmb.ch

**Schweizerisches
Landesmuseum**
Museumstrasse 2,
8021, Zurich
www.musee-suisse.ch

UNITED STATES
Metropolitan Museum of Art
1000 Fifth Avenue
New York, NY
10028–0198
www.metmuseum.org

Smithsonian Institution
Several locations at
PO Box 37012
SI Building
Room 153
MRC 010
Washington, D.C.
20013–7012
www.si.edu

Allentown Art Museum
31 N. 5th Street
Allentown, Pennsylvania
PA 18101
www.allentownartmuseum.org

Brooklyn Museum
200 Eastern Parkway
Brooklyn
New York, NY
11238–6052
www.brooklynmuseum.org

Cleveland Museum of Art
11150 East Boulevard
Cleveland, OH
44106
www.clevelandart.org

Higgins Armory Museum,
100 Barber Avenue
Worcester, Massachusetts
01606–2444
www.higgins.org

RUSSIA
**Hermitage Museum,
St Petersberg**
34 Dvortsovaya Naberezhnaya
St Petersburg
190000
www.hermitagemuseum.org

Index

ABOVE 17th-century Indian khanjar with decorated blade and Mughal hilt.

ABOVE British Raj personalized hunting knife, late 19th century

E

BELOW Japanese tanto, Meiji, *c.*1870

F

G

ABOVE Spanish swept-hilt rapier, *c.* 1650

BELOW Balkan Ottoman bichaq, mid-19th century

ABOVE Chinese halberd, *c.*1850

BELOW Italian cross-hilt dagger, late 16th century

ABOVE Persian khanjar, c.1800

BELOW European knightly sword, *c.*1300–50

ABOVE Japanese sword (shin-gunto), *c.*1930

BELOW Chinese sword (jian), *c*.1850

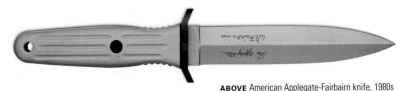

ABOVE American Applegate-Fairbairn knife, 1980s

Picture credits

ABOVE Japanese aikuchi dagger. The blade is dated 1625, the rest was made later.

The publisher would like to thank the following for kindly supplying photos for this book:

AKG: 11t, 16l, r, 19t, 21t, 22t, 23t, 24t, 25bl, 26tl, 27t, b, 28bl, 35tr, 36r, l, 37tr, 40b, 42r, 43br, 44t, 57bl, t, 58bl, 59tl, 61t, 64t, 66tr, 67t, 68b, 77t, 83br, 85tr, 94bl, br, 97t, b, , 100tl, 101b, 120b, m, 121t, 150b, 177b.

Alamy: 15br, 34b, 43, 18t, 73t, 84tl, 89tr, 301br, 310bl, 331tr; AKG: 263br, 264bl, 266bl, 270tl, 274bl, 276tr, 279br, 283t, 284br, 285tr, 291br, 308tl, 341tr, 352b, 449tr.

Ancient Art & Architecture: 23b, 265tr, 336tr.

Art Archive, The: 264tr, 268br, 269t, 271b, 296b, 307tl.

Barrett, Jonathan: 117ml, mr.

Berman Museum of World History, Alabama: 9b, br, 81b, 12mt, 61b, 63t, 69b, 73b, 106br, 107tr, 109bmr, 123t, 154m, 156b, 162b, 166mb, mt, 166b, t, 169b, t, 170bb, bt, 171m, t, 174m, 192t, 199t, 200m, t, 205m, 206b, 217t, 229t, 238m, 248b, 249br, 257tr, 258br, 259b, 260t, 305b, 312t, b, 313m, 327b, 329br, 333b, 336br, 338t, 339b, 341b, 342b, 348bl, 349tr, m, mr, br, 426t, b, b, 427t, m, b, b, 433b, 454b, 460m, m, 461b, b, 464b, 465t, 467t, t, m, m, b, 471b, 473t, b, 476b, 477t, m, 479b, 482t, 484t, 486t, 489t, b, 490t, 491m,b, 492t, m, b, 493t, m, b.

Bridgeman Art Library: 9tl, tr, 10b, 17tr, b, 18b, 19b, 20t, 22b, 25t, 26tr, 30b, 33bl, 34mt, 38b, 39tr, 42l, 46b, 47t, 51t, 55ml, 63b, 65br, 71bl, 78tl, 84br, 91tr,

109tm, 119t, 120t, 121b, m, 122t, 124t, m, b, 125t, 128b, 131b, 147b, 159b, 221b, 261m, 262bm, 269b, 272b, 275tr, 276br, 277tr, bl, 280tl, 288tl, 291tl, 292bl, 294tl, 298t, bl, 299tr, 305br, 306bl, 317mr, 321mr, 332bl, 337tr, 338bl, 353b, 371b, 436t, 443br, 469br.

Brink, Jean: 317tl, b.

Bruun-rasmussen: 15tl.

Corbis: 10, 62tl, tr, 69t, 75t, 83tr, 123b, 171b, 204b, 254; Ernest, PJ: 212b; Furrer, Richard 102b, 258t, 304mr, 326b, 357b, 425bl.

Getty Images: 72b, 74b, 191b, 325ml, 327tr, 333tr.

Hermann Historica Auctioneers, Munich: 11b, 14t, 25br, 26b, 29b, 37bb, 39b, 46mr, 47b, 50t, 54b, 55r, 60t, 85tl, 87t, mt, 89b, 90b, 91m, tb, bb, 93tr, bl, 95tl, tm, 96tm, 98t, 99br, 100bm, 109mlt, mrt, tl, 110b, m, 111b, 113m, t, 115bb, bt, tl, tr, 119b, m, 122m, 125m, 126t, 135m, 136b, b, 138b, 139b, m, 140t, 143mt, tt, 152m, 153m, 161b, m, 166b, t, 167m, t, 169m, 186b, m, 187m, 194m, 197m, 215b, 218b, m, 219b, m, t, 220b, 221t, m, 222b, 223b,

224b, 225tl, tr, 226b, t, 227b, t, 229b, mb, 230b, t, 231mb, t, 232b, m, 233b, mt, t, 234m, t, 235mt, t, 236t, 240b, t, 241m, t, 242b, t, 243b, m, 245b, 249t, 250b, 251b, 252b, t, 253t, 267tl, 267tm, tr, br, bl, 286t, b, 289t, mr, b, 328b, 334tm, 350t, m, 351t, t, b, 353t, m.

Holford, Michael: 263tr, 348tl, m, 352m379b, 388t, 421t, 424t, 450b, 451b, b, 490t, t, 491t, t, 492t, t, t, m, m, b, b, 493t, t, m, m, b, b, 494t, t, m, m, b, b, 495t, t, t, m, m, b, b.

iStock: 419br.

Jupiter Images Corporation: 263tl, 265br, 273tr, 278tl, 300tl, 303tl, 313tr.

Kenney, DX: 125b; photos.com: 49tr.

Picture Desk: 79tl, Stephens, Frederick: 205t, b.

Royal Athena Galleries: 115mb, mt, 118b, m, t, 122b; Topfoto: 14bb, tb, 19mr, 20b, 24b, 28t, 31r, 41b, 52b, 53bl, 70t, 77br, 80b, 81t, 82tt, mt, 86tr, 99t.

TopFoto: 271ml, 293br, 295t, b, 315mr, 324tr, 336tr, 337bl, 339f, 340tr, bl, 374br.

Wallis and Wallis Auction Gallery: 78br, 79tr, 107tl, 116tb, tt, 155m, t, 156m, 157b, m, t, 158b, m, t, 159t, 186tt, 187b, t, 189bb, 214b, m, t, 215t, 246b, t, 247b, t, 248m, t, 249bl;

Werner Forman Picture Library: 50b.

Withers, Harvey: 308b, 311b, 321b, 323t, 413t, 420b, 430t, 454t, 455b, 484b, 486t, 487m, b, 488t, b

Xavier Kenney, David, South Beach FL (www.RomanOfficer.com): 270bl, 271tr.

All other images from the Royal Armouries, Leeds in England. All artwork by Peters & Zabransky Ltd.

Every effort has been made to obtain permission to reproduce copyright material, but there may be cases where we have been unable to trace a copyright holder. The publisher will be happy to correct any omissions in future printings.

ABOVE Italian schiavona sword, *c.*1730

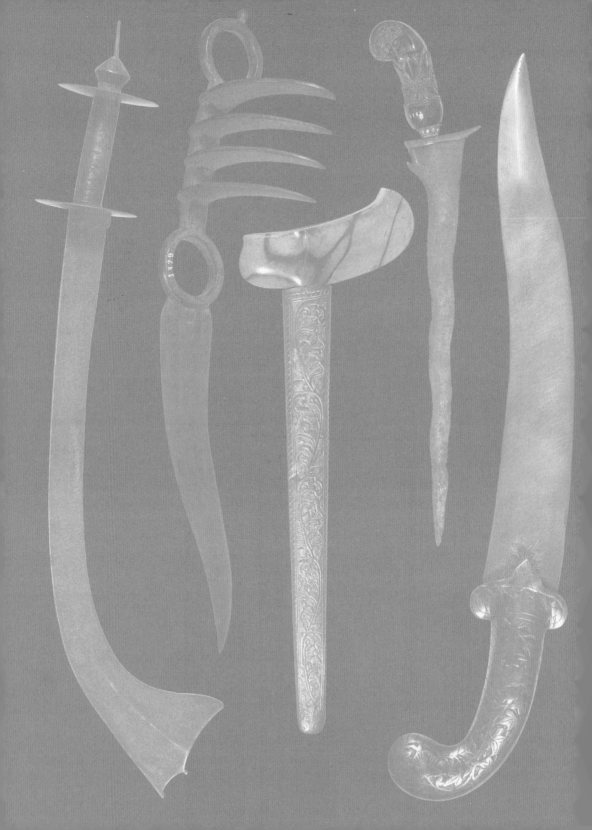